APPROACHES TO
BEGINNING READING

APPROACHES TO BEGINNING READING

ROBERT C. AUKERMAN
University of Rhode Island

JOHN WILEY & SONS, INC., NEW YORK • LONDON • SYDNEY • TORONTO

Library of Congress Catalogue Card Number: 70–144330

ISBN   0–471–03690–0 (cloth)
ISBN   0–471–03691–9 (paper)

Printed in the United States of America

10   9   8   7   6   5   4   3   2

To my precious wife, Louise

PREFACE

The recent proliferation of materials, methods, systems, devices, programs, gimmicks, and gadgets in the field of beginning reading generated the urge to write this book. The time spent in this effort has been rewarding for two reasons: (1) I have been able to clarify about 100 approaches to beginning reading, which are now available; and (2) I hope this book contributes to the entire reading profession, which has been caught in the confusion resulting from so many approaches to beginning reading.

Additional satisfaction has been received almost daily from scores of writers, authors, editors, and publishers who have so generously contributed their materials, unpublished research studies, and comments. Without their help, this book would most certainly have been severely limited in scope and accuracy, and, consequently, in usefulness.

The format of the book is arranged so that it may be used in the traditional college course in Methods of Teaching Reading. As such, it provides the student with materials which will take much of the mystery out of beginning reading.

Approaches to Beginning Reading also should prove useful as a handbook of essential information to be used by every supervisor of reading, primary teacher, elementary principal, and reading coordinator. As a handbook, it provides practitioners in the field with information and quick-reference materials nowhere else available in one volume.

This compendium of approaches to beginning reading is organized to be encyclopedic, presenting the origins of each approach; the backgrounds of the authors and originators of the various materials and methods; complete descriptions of the methods and materials, together with illustrations of the essential features of each; a capsulated summary of the significant contribution each approach to beginning reading provides; and, wherever possible, a summarization of some of the definitive research studies.

The author would hardly run true to form as a university professor if he did not respond to the opportunity of professing an objective evaluation here and there. It is hoped that such evaluations are as objective as humanly possible and that personal and subjective likes and dislikes do not show through too strongly.

The purpose of this volume is to present as honestly as possible the significant features of the many approaches to beginning reading, emphasizing their strengths and weaknesses, so that the reader may be better informed and, thus, better able to arrive at his own evaluation and decision.

One hundred or more approaches to beginning reading have arbitrarily been classified under ten categories. Criteria for each category have been stated in the introduction to each chapter. Such arbitrary classification has the inherent probability that some readers may disagree. In some cases, admittedly, the materials and/or the method could and, perhaps, should be classified in more than one place. As the book has evolved, some have been shifted here and there until this final date of publication finds each approach in a spot which seems most logical.

The author welcomes and encourages any and all constructive criticism so that, collectively, the strength of such opinions may be reflected in subsequent revisions of this book.

CONTENTS

APPROACHES TO
BEGINNING READING

APPROACHES TO
BEGINNING READING

Generations of Americans have lived and have learned to read by drill on ABCs on their *Horn Books* in bleak colonial schoolhouses; by memorizing the alphabet couplets of the *New England Primers*; by purposeful recitation of moral verse from McGuffey's *Eclectic Readers*; and now by memorizing the sight vocabulary of one of the fifteen major basal reader series.

The incredible fact seems to be that each of these methods has worked. Children have learned to read. Our nation has grown and prospered until we now consume far more pounds of printed material than the rest of the world combined. Equally strange is the fact that methods which have produced literacy in young citizens were eventually supplanted with methods which garnered enthusiastic supporters in hope that they would produce even better reading proficiency. In many cases, little or no research supported such hopes, yet changes took place with ever-increasing speed, until now the English-speaking world is literally inundated with a flood of materials, methods, and proposals. Some of the new approaches modestly claim partial answers to our problems of teaching reading to all children of school age; others boldly claim full-scale success; and a few appropriately ask to be heard and tried.

Most of them deserve consideration, and some of them probably have inherent qualities that will make them significant forces in the field of reading for a good long time. All seem to have a substantial number of advocates, among whom are many who are willing to give certain materials and methods a tryout under actual classroom conditions. This is as it should be, for any proposal should stand the test of scientifically-designed, carefully-planned, and honestly-reported research.

Change in the Educational World

The education profession expects to be experimenting with proposals in reading that involve change. Indeed, in some instances, change for the sake of change seems to have merit in itself. In some cases, it appears that administrators and laymen may equate the number of experimental projects taking place in a school system with progressive administration and scientific search for a better way of teaching. Moreover, it is not difficult to find teachers who express an urgency to be "doing something", and who approach each faculty meeting with uneasiness, lest some new project in reading be launched into orbit with them in the capsule.

Indeed, many such reading experiments have had the effect of producing a weightlessness and a lack of relativity, resulting in an unguided rocketing into the educational stratosphere, only to burn out upon re-entry from outer space. Few such hastily-devised projects are salvaged and relaunched. Unfortunately, many could not even be replicated, due to lack of adequate processing and control data. Few can serve as pilot projects, for few contain enough general and universal factors which might have application under varying conditions.

Change in the materials and teaching of reading has been taking place in more than just a casual manner in the past fifty years.[1] The twentieth century began with a carry-over of the whole-word-pronunciation method which had been so popular the last quarter of the last century. Children learned whole words much as oriental scholars learned whole gestalts symbolizing a combination of sounds. In both cases the whole symbol could be broken down into the components. In the early twentieth-century American school, there were no teachers' manuals and little thought given to word-attack skills, word analysis, or linguistics. Criticisms of early whole-word methods have been, perhaps, too severe; for, upon reasonable investigation, it is clear that the objectives of reading were not merely the pronunciation of each successive word, but the comprehension and enjoyment of the story. Inasmuch as the latter was the objective, it was found efficient to have all children working together on the same story, "following along" as one child after another was called upon in sequence (or at random to catch the "sleepers") to read "aloud."

Reading "aloud" had its advantages and its disadvantages. It provided the poor reader with a good portion of the story which he otherwise

---

1. Smith, Nila Banton, *American Reading Instruction*. Newark, Delaware: International Reading Association, 1965.

may not have been able to get. On the other hand, it provided him with a good case of jitters in anticipation of being called upon to exhibit his failure in front of his peers. Oral reading gave the teacher a check on "which pupils are good readers and which pupils are poor readers"; but did not provide the teacher with a structure for handling the children in small groups for the correction of common difficulties. It assured everyone—teacher, pupil, parent, and administrator—that the reading text which was commonly called the "Reader" would be covered; but it did not provide for standardized testing with results compared with norms. It neatly kept all children "together" even though some "lost their places" at times; and, at the same time, it ignored individual differences by keeping potentially-rapid readers from going ahead at their own rates. It also provided a day-to-day public relations contact with the homes, as children brought their "Readers" home and performed proudly for any one who would listen to them read. Even the non-reader could "mouth the words" in the story and turn the pages at appropriate times if he had maintained reasonable attentiveness and had plodded through the story with his classmates earlier in the day at school.

It was not until some perceptive parents began to realize that their offspring were not actually reading and, furthermore, that they were totally unable to be self-sufficient in books other than their "Readers" that protests began to call for an evaluation of the whole-word-pronunciation method. In spite of protests, research,[2] and some changes, the whole-word-pronunciation method still is used as the exclusive method of teaching reading in many American classrooms even today.

The scientific movement which hit the educational world in the form of testing and research studies in the 1920s had its fallout on the children in the classroom . . . and on the teacher, too. It was then not just enough to "cover the material in the Reader", but children's performance on "standardized" tests threatened to be a reflection of the quality of instruction in the classroom, and to become a part of the child's cumulative record. Obviously change was called for. Children had to learn to read "silently." Children had to learn to take reading tests, answering questions designed as comprehension checks.

Another contributing factor to the "silent reading" movement was the growing accumulation of evidence from research studies showing superiority of silent reading over oral reading. Thus an enigma arose for the teacher. How could the teacher know how well children were reading if they just read silently? Moreover, how could poor readers get

---

2. University of Chicago, Conference on Reading, *Reading: Seventy-Five Years of Progress.* Chicago: University of Chicago Press, 1967.

anything out of the story without the help of hearing the entire group read in sequence? Finally, wouldn't silent reading unloose the unity of the class, allowing some to rush ahead while others fell farther behind; creating the problem of promotion to the next grade of a heterogeneous group of readers, the arrival of which would catapult the teacher into direct flight to the principal's office?

In spite of these problems, silent reading was "in", and evangelists arose to preach its virtue and to warn teachers of the sins of other "false" methods. By that time the National Society for the Study of Education had achieved top leadership in educational circles, comprising the vanguard of educational researchers. It is significant to note that Part II of its *Twentieth Yearbook*,[3] published in 1920, carried the title "Report of the Society's Committee on Silent Reading."

So dynamic was this proposal for silent reading, that it almost completely replaced "reading aloud" in most schools except those located in the educational hinterland.

As could be expected, there were peacemakers who emerged, advocating a middle-of-the-road approach utilizing the best features of both extremes. It took the educational scientists only a short time to tool up for research to prove that this not only could be done successfully, but better. By 1925 the NSSE *Yearbook*[4] was promoting the use of both oral *and* silent reading.

Dynamic proposals for handling the individual differences that were being revealed by "standardized" tests were being made, and by the 1930s, "grouping for individual differences" had become the slogan of the progressive reading teacher. Like the "Blind Men Who Came to See the Elephant," however, there was much argument as to what was the nature of grouping.

With the renewal of publishing that followed the shortages of the war years, golden opportunity lured many from their classrooms and from research to undertake around-the-clock crash programs of writing and getting some new aspect of reading onto the market to meet the competition in an industry that was experiencing mergers which were creating giant publishing complexes, each planning strategy for capturing the expanding textbook market which had resulted from the population ex-

---

3. National Society for the Study of Education, *Report of the Society's Committee on Silent Reading*, Twentieth Yearbook, Part II. Chicago: National Society for the Study of Education, 1921.

4. National Society for the Study of Education, *Report of the National Committee on Reading*, Twenty-fourth Yearbook, Part I. Chicago: National Society for the Study of Education, 1925.

plosion. It is not surprising, therefore, to discover that scores of new proposals in reading emerged during the past twenty years. To be sure, a handful were revivals of systems previously suggested to an unreceptive audience; thus, for all intent and purpose, they may be considered as new. Those approaches have had varying degrees of dynamic impact upon the professional community of reading specialists, teachers, and children. Indeed, the effect has not stopped there but has served as impetus for many a PTA meeting, TV program, and lively after-dinner discussion.

It was predestined that controversy and confusion would follow. "Which system is best?" was sure to be raised as a question in any conference of teachers and reading specialists considering two or more proposals.

In many instances the approaches are not mutually comparable, some being built upon phonemics or linguistics, while others are pre-packaged do-it-yourself type kits and even individual teaching machines. Some are designed to employ simple inexpensive materials, whereas others involve the use of elaborately programmed machines costing thousands of dollars. Some are planned for the training of masses of students at a time; others depend upon the undivided attention of a teacher or tutor in a one-to-one ratio. Several approaches are aimed at the education of beginning readers at what are ordinarily considered pre-school ages, while an equal number are designed for the improvement in high school reading or college, or in adult life, by those who have already mastered the basic reading skills. Workbooks are a significant part of a number of approaches, while other make use of a number of supplementary audio and/or visual and/or kinesthetic aids.

It is quite obvious, therefore, that it is not possible to conclude "which one is best." Moreover, when an evaluation is made of the research that has been reported on the success and failure—of the advantages and disadvantages—of each system, it is evident that the multiplicity of variable factors that are uncontrolled in most research almost certainly makes comparisons on the basis of research a most unrewarding operation. Any study that would attempt an answer to "which is best" would certainly explode into a major undertaking. It would, first, have to be limited to approaches that are comparable in the aspects of reading with which each is dealing. Second, the approaches being compared would have to apply to the same grade and age levels, with I.Q. measured in non-verbal terms. Other factors such as socio-economic-cultural background, experiential background, health and physical fitness, motivation for reading, emotional adjustment, psychoneurological conditions, atti-

tude toward self and significant others, teacher preparation, availability
of time, amount and type of reinforcement and reward, knowledge of
success, previous experience with reading, and/or reading skills, as well
as many other variables should be controlled within reasonable limits
to provide a sound basis for factoral analysis. Furthermore, comparisons
of "results" can only be valid in longitudinal studies which allow for study
of long-term results rather than what may be merely temporary improvement due to a short-term shot-in-the-arm type of experiment in which
measured improvement tends to fade at the conclusion of the experiment.

It is probable that, with modern IBM equipment, federal grant
money, an abundance of graduate students, and plenty of administrative
support, longitudinal studies of such suggested magnitude could be—and,
probably, should be made. Such studies have their precedent in "Project
Talent,"[5] the magnificent longitudinal study undertaken in 1957 with
over one-half million students who will be followed into adult life with
"results" reported near the close of this century.

It is with a full knowledge of the limitations of research available
on some of the approaches that they are, nonetheless, presented. Every
effort has been made to unearth reports of classroom experience with
each system. In the absence of definitive research findings, testimonials
have been scanned to assess the opinions of classroom teachers who have
had direct experience with materials and methods.

It is felt that professional integrity dictates an unbiased, objective
discussion of each approach. This has been done with the full cooperation of the originators and/or proponents of each approach to beginning
reading. Indeed, without their personal help, the following chapters
would not have been possible.

In a sense, therefore, the originators of the various materials and
methods are saying to the reader, as many have personally said to the
author, "I have found a good way to teach beginning reading. I think
I can prove that it is a better way. In fact, others who have tried my
materials and methods have also found that my way is better. All I ask,
therefore, is that my approach to beginning reading be given a fair and
an unbiased chance to prove itself."

Shortsighted, indeed, would be the teaching profession if it turned
its back on such offers; for, by so doing, it may be rejecting the very
messiah for whom we have so long been watching and waiting.

---

5. Flanagan, John C., *Project Talent News*, Palo Alto: American Institutes for Research, published periodically, 1961 through 1983.

BIBLIOGRAPHY

CORDTS, ANNA D., *Phonics for the Reading Teacher.* New York: Holt, Rinehart & Winston, Inc., 1965. Ch. 12.

DODDS, W. J., "Highlights From the History of Reading Instruction," *The Reading Teacher,* 21: (December, 1967), 211–226.

MATHEWS, MITFORD M., *Teaching to Read: Historically Considered.* Chicago: University of Chicago Press, 1966.

National Society for the Study of Education "Report of the Society's Committee on Silent Reading," National Society for the Study of Education *Yearbook,* Part II, 1920. See also Part II, *Yearbook,* 1925.

SMITH, NILA B., *American Reading Instruction.* Newark, Del.: International Reading Association, 1965.

University of Chicago Conference on Reading, *Reading: Seventy-Five Years of Progress.* Chicago: University of Chicago Press, 1967.

BASIC PHONEMIC
APPROACHES

2

Basic phonemic approaches is the category selected for classification of what many reading specialists call "phonics". "Breaking the code", "code emphasis", "synthetic phonics", and "phonetic" are terms loosely and interchangeably used to identify systems in which letter-sound relationships are taught as first steps to beginning reading. Inasmuch as concentration is on the individual sounds of our language, we prefer the term *phonemics,* with the full knowledge that it may seem strange to some readers.

Phonemics is used throughout as the broad term referring to systems of reading that pay special initial attention to presenting the sounds of the language matched with the graphemes, with subsequent efforts to synthesize those sounds into whole words.

A *basic phonemic* system is a method of teaching reading in which major and almost exclusive attention is directed toward learning the sounds of vowels and consonants; followed by blending, and the construction of phonemic families or phonograms.

Originators of such approaches to teaching reading are convinced that our American English is regular enough in spelling to lend itself to a phonemic approach. Consequently, most of the basic phonemic systems start with the sounds of the letters, followed with work in which the student assembles those letter sounds into words.

The theory behind basic phonemic systems is twofold: 1. that our language is phonemically regular; and, 2. that, once a child has learned the phonemic elements, he can obtain the pronunciation of the printed word by assembling the sounds together in blended sequence. If our

9

language were 100% phonemic, this would be true; and learning to read for most children would be quite a simple process. Likewise, remedial reading would be no problem except in cases of severe mental, emotional, or physical anomalies.

Psychological Foundations

Inasmuch as learning to relate sounds to letters depends upon rote learning, all basic phonemic systems use memorization as the method of learning. Psychologically, rote memorization of this sort involves both auditory memory and visual memory. Furthermore, it is often independent of meaning; and, consequently, learning to read by a basic phonemic approach calls upon the child to undertake the most difficult type of learning.

Children with high intelligence normally have high visual and auditory retention and, therefore, can learn through the phonemic approach without much, if any, difficulty. Rote memorization, however, calls for repetition and overlearning, both of which are subject to a wide range of individual differences. Indeed, many children with low intelligence find it almost impossible to remember phonemes from one day to the next. Teachers often find such children merely "going through the motions" of repeating sounds with the entire class or group.

Learning by a basic phonemic system also involves the psychology of "part learning". By "part learning", the psychologist means the learning of individual elements—usually through memorization—and necessitates the final assembling of those elements into wholes. Promoters and users of basic phonemic systems believe that this is the most valid and most efficient system for learning to read. They argue that, once the sounds of the twenty-six letters are learned, the child merely has to use those learned sounds to unlock the sounds of the tens-of-thousands of words which appear in print. Their contention is supported by research[1] that indicates that a child who has lived in a normal American home for five or six years has acquired an oral vocabulary of thousands of words. It is claimed that, once the individual has learned the sounds of the letters, he can "sound-out" the words. Once he has pronounced the word, he can "read", because the words have prior meaning through use and through past experience. Consequently, it is assumed that compre-

---

1. Kolson, Clifford J., "The Vocabulary of Kindergarten Children," unpublished doctoral dissertation, School of Education, University of Pittsburgh, 1960.

hension will automatically result from pronunciation. Thus, past experience is a factor in learning that is utilized indirectly, and only after a lengthy period of rote memorization of what psychologists would term "nonsense" learning of isolated sounds tied to isolated symbols.

Method

Some basic phonemic systems attempt to have a child learn to read with pure isolated drill using the letter symbols exclusive of any supplementary cues. The idea behind such an approach is that the child will not have pictures of apples, and elephants, and balls and other little "helpers" sprinkled along the printed page as he reads ordinary print. Thus, it is argued, why should we introduce crutches for him to lean upon and then expect him to read later without those crutches? Such logic has considerable psychological support, for learning is considered best when it is in the setting in which it is to be used. Furthermore, learning that the printed symbol "b" should be sounded as in "baseball" or "bat" merely introduces an additional learning element which must later be unlearned and dropped out of the reading process in the interest of efficiency.

However, when sounds and symbols are to be matched and learned without any relationship to prior learning or to meaningful elements, higher-order learning is involved, and the learner is called upon to operate at the abstract level.

Recognizing the advantages of utilizing sounds which the child has heard and knows, most basic phonemic systems are less stark in their learning requirements; making use of the names of things which have the same initial printed letters and sounds as those being learned.

To prevent undue confusion, the most common practice is to introduce one phonemic element at a time. A few systems introduce two or more in groups, contending that the child can learn the elements in pairs by utilizing the similarities and contrasts as aids.

Most basic phonemic systems introduce the short vowel sounds first, most often associating them with a graphic representation of "apple" for the short sound of "a"; "elephant" for "e"; "indian" for "i"; "ostrich" for "o"; and "umbrella" for "u". Others introduce the long vowel sounds first, contending that those are most easily learned because the child is learning to "say" the letter names. Furthermore, it is pointed out that the long vowel sound, corresponding to the letter name, is always regular. It is the one vowel sound that can be depended upon.

A few basic phonemic systems tend to confuse the child by intro-ducing the two elements simultaneously; namely, the letter name (which is a long vowel sound) with the short vowel phoneme. The resultant method is something like this:

"A" (pronounced *ay*) says *aah* as in *a*pple
"E" (pronounced *eey*) says *eah* as in *e*lephant
"I" (pronounced *eye*) says *ihh* as in *i*ndian
"O" (pronounced *oh*) says *aw* as in *o*strich
"U" (pronounced *you*) says *uuh* as in *u*mbrella

It should be noted that basic phonemic systems which *do not allow* the student to use the letter names recognize this problem and are careful to insist that the child associate the letter sounds directly with the grapheme (printed letter symbol).

As they are dealing with letters—and their sounds—in isolation, some of the systems require a memorization of the alphabet as a prerequisite to learning any pronunciation of any single letter. Although there appears to be no logic to this procedure, promoters of such an idea could muster support from certain research studies[2] which indicate that children who knew the alphabet first were superior in beginning reading to others who did not know the alphabet. The naive might easily accept this as proof of a cause-and-effect relationship, whereas it more probably indicates a com-mon factor which accounts for both achievements.

Those basic phonemic systems which introduce the alphabet first usually present capital (upper case) letters, and then for no accountable reason, present all phonemic instruction in lower-case letters. A few systems present both upper- and lower-case letters in pairs, simultaneously, followed by instruction in lower case. The argument for the latter pro-cedure is that it is just as easy for the child to learn both forms when learning the alphabet. This may be true, but we still lack substantive proof that this is so.

Regardless of whether or not the individual has learned the alphabet first, it still remains for him to acquaint himself individually with each letter-sound separately. In a logical attempt at regularity, a few basic phonemic systems begin with the initial consonant sounds. Promoters of such an approach point out the fact that there are no variations in initial consonant sounds. Their regularity is said to provide a feeling of success and security for the beginner which is not possible when dealing with the five vowels and their many variations. Such arguments have

---

2. Durrell, Donald, and Murphy, Helen A., "Boston University Research in Elementary School Reading: 1933–1963," Boston University *Journal of Education*, 145 (Decem-ber, 1963) 1–53.

considerable validity as long as one is working with phonemics in isolation.

In the argument concerning "Which comes first: vowels or consonants?" a good case can be worked up on either side. However, when an individual takes the next step, namely, the assembling of phonemes into words, there can be no argument, for it takes both consonants and vowels to make a word.

It should be quite evident that it is extremely difficult to isolate sounds and to maintain such isolation beyond the initial steps in learning pronunciation of letters in isolation and almost impossible in the reading of total words. Promoters of basic phonemic systems have allowed for some variations and adjustments in order to provide transfer from the initial phonemic learning effected by their systems.

The concept of *readiness* is discounted by most basic phonemic systems. It is argued that a child can just as easily learn to differentiate the characteristics and shapes of letters as he can trucks and cats and dogs. Furthermore, most basic phonemic systems begin with a limited number of letters (five at most) and suggest that time spent in direct learning of those letters produces far better results than an equal amount of time spent on so-called "readiness" exercises. Moreover, there is no proof of positive transfer from the learning in most readiness programs to the learning of letters of the alphabet. Indeed, it is difficult to find common elements that could possibly transfer.

Consequently, basic phonemic systems recommend that the teacher start directly on visual and auditory pairing of letter graphemes and letter phonemes. One system goes to the extreme of suggesting that the teacher start right in "on the first day of school" in September. The manual[3] for that system of phonemics promises that, by the end of the *first* week of school, first graders will have mastered the short sounds of the five vowels! Few first grade teachers could accept such a statement, nevertheless it does indicate the enthusiasm with which that particular system is promoted.

Regardless of timing, most basic phonemic systems do depend upon a rather intense dedication to the business of memorizing. This demands strict concentration and undivided attention to the teacher. Recent studies of the problems of culturally-disadvantaged children indicate that they need long periods of training in listening and participating in normal conversation. This being so, it would appear logical that training in listening to such abstractions as phonemes, graphemes, and morphemes

3. Hay, Julie, and Wingo, Charles E., *Reading With Phonics, Teacher's Manual.* Philadelphia: J. B. Lippincott Co., 1967, Ch. 1, "Getting Results with Phonics."

in isolation would need to be postponed for such children until a later period of auditory readiness. Such a possibility needs to be researched.

The use of "key words" is common to many basic phonemic systems. "Key words" are used to reinforce the learning of each basic letter sound. For example: the long vowel sound of "ay" for the letter "A" is found in the "key word" "cake." The child then learns to refer to the key word in order to obtain the sound of the letter. Most basic phonemic systems rely upon key words rather than on the less-reliable[4] "rules."

The use of "key words" demands that the child equip himself with all the key words related to each vowel sound. He then must try out his stock of key words in order to get the correct sounds of the vowel in the word. The child's mental processes might go like this, with a word like *Baltimore*.

1. The initial consonant sound is *buh* as in *boy*
2. The vowel *aye* as in *cake*—or *aah* as in *cat* or *aw* as in *ball*; hold these in mind
3. The consonant *ull*
4. First syllable is either *buhl* or *bayle*, or *bahl*; hold those in mind
5. The *tee* says *tuh* as in *top* [actually it is sounded *tih* because of the following short vowel, but the child is not taught that, for his key word for *t* is *top*]
6. The *i* could be *eye* as in *bike* or *iah* as in *fish*
7. The next consonant is *m* sounded *mmm* as in *money*
8. The second syllable, therefore could be *tyme* or *tim*—or it could be *tye* or *tiah*; keep those possibilities in mind
9. The next vowel is *o* which could be *oh* as in *bone* or it could be *aah* as in *top* or *ouw* as in *cow* or *oah* as in *boy*
10. *R* is usually *ur* as in *rabbit*
11. *E* says *eee* as in *tree* or *eah* as in *bed*
12. The last syllable could be *or*; or it could *ahr*; it could be *ouwr*; or perhaps it could be *oree*, or even *oreah*—and if the *m* is added, there could be more possibilities.

At this point, the teacher usually suggests, "Now, children, let's see if we can find any little words that we know in our big word". The class will usually be depended upon to provide "or", "Tim", "ore", and "more". This helps salvage an otherwise-impossible guessing game.

At this point it should be obvious that even the "purest" of basic

---

4. Clymer, Theodore, "The Utility of Phonic Generalizations in the Primary Grades," *The Reading Teacher*, 16 (January, 1963), 252–258.

phonemic systems must rely upon some whole-word learning in order to aid in reassembling the parts into a whole. The phonemics enthusiast would point out that the "little words in the big word" actually were first learned by means of phonemics.

Inasmuch as any phonemic system depends upon auditory perception and discrimination, much attention is given to "ear training". Teachers spend many hours with "listening games" in which the teacher pronounces words to which the children have been instructed to respond in a particular way.

Listening to initial consonants is, probably, the most common "listening game". The usual procedure is as follows: The teacher informs the children that she is going to pronounce some words—most of which will begin with a particular consonant sound ("buh" as in 'ball', for example), but there will be some words which will be pronounced that will not begin with the "buh" sound. The children are instructed to raise their hands when they hear a word which does not begin with the "buh" sound. They are usually challenged with "Let's see who gets caught!"

The same general method is used for rhyming words; words with a particular final consonant; words with a particular vowel sound as the medial vowel; and other variations.

Although listening and responding *en masse* involves the risk of the slow child hiding behind the mass achievement of the whole group, it does offer some distinct advantages. First, he can "save face" and pretend to be accomplishing. Thus he is not a total failure. Second, there is considerable "fall-out" from the rest of the group, and some of this is bound to affect him by contributing to his learning. Third, it gives the teacher an opportunity to scan the group and to single out those who apparently need help. This is, admittedly, a much more efficient procedure than testing each person individually—and less painful to the child. It does have the inherent risk, however, of lulling the self-satisfied teacher into a stupor of complacency in which the sound of the multitude chanting its phonemes and morphemes is prima facie evidence that "all" are learning.

Sooner or later, most basic phonemic systems provide extensive practice in "word families"; sometimes called "phonograms." Phonograms are built upon a base sound—phoneme or morpheme. The base may be a beginning sound, a medial sound, or an ending sound. Later on, it may be an entire root word. Specifically, it would be done thus:

Using the short vowel sound of *a* (as in apple), the children are encouraged to "see how many combinations can be made using that 'aaah' sound." Using final consonants, the result is as follows:

a = "aaah"	ab	al
at	add	ap or apt
am	agg	as or ask
an	ack or ak	ax or axe

Most basic phonemic systems encourage nonsense syllables as well as meaningful words on the theory that those nonsense syllables actually are parts of meaningful words and will, thus, be encountered later.

When initial consonants are to be added to the "aaah" sound, the list that results is likely to be similar to this:

baah (or just ba) more	ha or hat	ma or mat
likely "bam!"	ra or rat	na or nap
ca (or more likely "cat")	ta or tap	pa or pat
da or dad	ja or jab	sa or sat
fa or fat	ka	va or vat
ga or gad	la or lad or last	wham!

From the simple two-letter or three-letter syllable, the child is then led to the next step, namely, the building of four- and five-letter words which more accurately may be called "word-building" or "word families." Some systems accept four-letter nonsense words, and in such cases, the phonograms based upon the "en" sound could be as follows:

ben	beng	bens
bend	benk	bent
		benx
		benz

By changing the initial consonants, any number of four-letter morphemes can be constructed; some with meaning, others not.

Making use of the principle of learning by similarities and differences, some phonemic systems then introduce pairs of four-letter words in contrast, such as:

bump	lump	mend	bend	pant	rant
kill	till	sell	self	sill	silk

On the other hand, some systems hold to more regularity and provide practice in which the child deals with a base which changes only in terms of the five short vowel sounds, and to which he is to add an initial consonant. The resultant exercise would, of necessity, be similar to the following:

b-ell	j-ell	r-ell
d-ell	m-ell	s-ell
f-ell	n-ell	t-ell
h-ell	p-ell	w-ell

followed by

| b-ill | f-ill | h-ill | k-ill | n-ill | r-ill | t-ill |
| d-ill | g-ill | j-ill | m-ill | p-ill | s-ill | w-ill |

Word-building or "phonograms" could go on indefinitely. It is limited in basic phonemic systems only by the restrictions imposed by the particular system and/or the energy and commitment of the teacher and students. The experience of teachers using such systems indicates that phonograms is one of the most popular exercises with the children. Great competition is generated when it is done orally. It can form the basis for competitive team games . . . with teams matched against each other for speed and accuracy within the limits of the rules.

It can readily be seen that there is little, if anything, new or novel about the methods used by basic phonemic approaches to beginning reading. Indeed, it is their time-proven use that is relied upon to validate their continued usage today. It is also their time-proven use, moreover, which makes it difficult for anyone to be "against phonics". Indeed, few in the field of reading research or reading instruction are actually "against phonics."

On the other hand, many teachers are such strong phonics advocates that they overlook the fact that phonemic instruction alone does not constitute reading nor does it guarantee that it will produce effective readers.

It is no longer a question as to whether or not we are to have "phonics" in reading instruction. No one will deny the necessity for it. There are, however, three questions:

First, whether or not we wish to subscribe to one of the several basic phonemics approaches, or

Second, do we wish to utilize one of the basic phonemic approaches as a prelude to a basal reader series or as preliminary to some other approach to reading, or

Third, do we wish to rely upon the phonemic exercises suggested in the Teachers' Manuals of the basal reader series, and purchase some of the good materials from one or more of the good basic phonemic systems to be used as supplementary aids?

With these possibilities in mind and with an understanding of the general elements of a basic phonemic approach, we can now examine in detail the various materials and methods available for use in our schools, giving attention to their strengths and weaknesses—to their similarities and differences.

THE PHONOVISUAL METHOD

Origins

The *Phonovisual Method* results from the synthesis of the lifetime experiences of three teachers: Miss Lucille D. Schoolfield, a speech correction teacher; Miss Josephine B. Timberlake, a teacher of the hard-of-hearing; and Mrs. Marie Buckley, a primary teacher.

Experience with children who relied on careful pronunciation and enunciation for communication in our language convinced Miss School-field and Miss Timberlake that learning the sounds of the language is the key to both reading and spelling as well as to listening and to speaking.

Utilizing their methods and knowledge of speech sounds, they teamed up with Mrs. Buckley for several years to develop and test a system which, originally, was conceived as a method for preventing reading failures. Indeed, it was the outgrowth of concern for what seemed to be an alarming number of reading failures in the schools.

Their backgrounds and experiences had centered around the relationships between sounds comprising spoken words and the letters which represent those sounds. Miss Schoolfield was convinced that reading disability could be corrected by a modification of the methods she had found successful in her speech correction work. Similarly, Miss Timberlake had proved that deaf and hard-of-hearing children who have to acquire speech through careful, laborious, and patient work with phonemics had no difficulty when they later were taught the mechanics of reading by her phonemic method.

When these two teachers of special education came together and compared their work, they discovered a striking similarity. Subsequent discussion led them to the decision to make the system available to others.

Method and Materials

The *Phonovisual Method* is a basic phonemic system, highly organized into a sequential plan for training in auditory and visual discrimination, together with careful reproduction of correct speech sounds. It is intended to be an initial teaching system of basic phonemics which will prepare the child for handling the task of reading either in basic readers or in supplementary and enrichment materials. Consequently, it is neither a system of readers nor workbooks designed to supplement the basal reader series. On the contrary, it is a system by which the child may obtain a skill in phonemics which will enable him to apply phonemic analysis and structural analysis in his reading from the very beginning.

There are four main steps in the method:

1. Learning to recognize initial consonant sounds. This is done through the use of the key pictures on the *Phonovisual* Consonant Chart. Children make a transition from the practice with the beginning sounds associated with the key pictures on the consonant chart to the beginning sounds of words in their pre-primers and primers of the basal series.

2. Learning to recognize initial and final consonant sounds. This skill requires listening and the children are taught to "listen through the word"; identifying and writing both the initial and final consonant sounds.

3. Learning the vowel sounds is the third step and is accomplished through the use of the *Phonovisual* Vowel Chart. This requires rote memorization of vowel sounds, vowel diphthongs, and digraphs.

4. Advanced use of consonants and vowels. This fourth step involves the learning of the secondary spellings on the *Phonovisual* charts, and extensive structural analysis drill and practice on compound words, polysyllabic words, roots, prefixes, and suffixes.

The backbone of the method is its consonant chart and its vowel chart. These are absolutely basic pieces of equipment.

THE CONSONANTS. The consonant chart consists of the graphemes for the 26 consonant sounds matched to 26 corresponding key-word pictures. The printed symbols are arranged in a sequence which is thought to be scientifically determined. The first sounds taught are "p", "wh", "f", "th", and "t". The large colorful consonant chart is always on display in the front of the room and serves as a constant point of reference for both teacher and children.

For the first week or two, children are taught to listen to the slow, careful enunciation of the teacher. Directions warn teacher against distorting sounds in isolation. Teacher must be careful *never* to sound "p" in "pig" as "puh"; "k" in "key" should never be "kuh"; nor is the voiced sound "g" in "goat" formed as "guh". To avoid such errors requires practice on the part of teacher as well as children.

Utilizing the experience of the founders in working with speech correction and lip reading, *Phonovisual* provides many effective suggestions for encouraging children to reproduce speech sounds correctly.

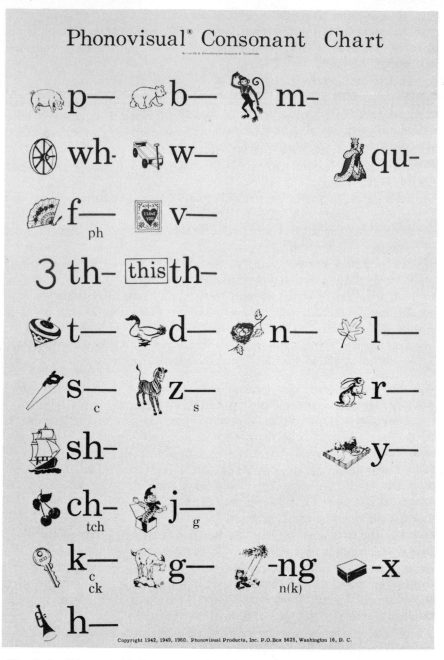

Fig. 2–1   *Phonovisual Consonant Chart reproduced with the permission of Phonovisual Products, Inc., 4708 Wisconsin Avenue, N.W., Washington, D.C., 20016.*

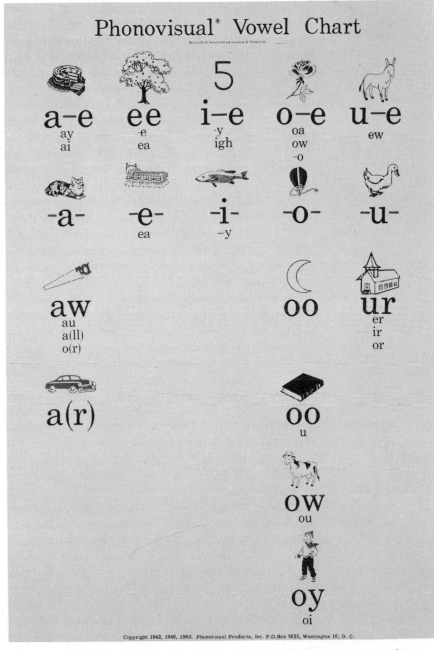

Fig. 2–2   *Phonovisual Vowel Chart reproduced with the permission of Phonovisual Products, Inc., 4708 Wisconsin Avenue, N.W., Washington, D.C., 20016.*

Special attention is concentrated on the movement of the teacher's lips. By so doing, the child can see as well as hear the sounds being spoken. He is then asked to imitate the teacher. This is followed by practice in which the teacher makes the lip movements but not the sound. This game of lip reading is quite popular with children.

The entire first column on the consonant chart is called the "breath" sounds, and the children are encouraged to exaggerate the breath when working with the first five graphemes: "phhh" in "pig"; "whhh" in "wheel"; "fhhh" in "fan"; "thhh" in "three"; and "tuh" in "top". (Note that letter names are never used with the chart work.)

Slow, careful repetition by the teacher, using games with lip reading, hand puppets which open their mouths wide when it is called for in the formation of the sound, and other clever devices provide group and individual practice and result in rote memorization of the first five consonant sounds—which Phonovisual designates as "breath" sounds. The *Phonovisual Method Book* recommends that the first half hour daily should be on phonemic instruction using the charts and method, followed by a sight reading period of one half hour.

When the first five "breath" consonants have been memorized, the teacher introduces planned mistakes in the listening games. Each mistake is exaggerated so that the children can easily recognize it. It is the objective of *Phonovisual* never to have a child learn an error. Thus it is better for the teacher to produce the errors and to alert the children to distinguish and reject them.

The next step in this highly-structured program is a review of the first five initial consonant breath sounds, followed by the addition of one new sound each day, or slower, depending upon the speed of the class. Inasmuch as the method makes use of whole-group participation in learning, little provision can be made in adjusting to individual differences without establishing several sub-groups, each operating at a different speed.

Once the children have mastered the "breath" sounds in the first column, the "voiced" sounds in the second column are learned more quickly. The third column presents the related consonants which have "nasal" sounds, and the fourth column presents related sounds. After all consonants are learned in initial position, there is practice in final sounds, and consonants in isolation, together with auditory discrimination of them at the beginning and ending of words. At that stage of accomplishment, the child is ready to learn the vowel sounds.

THE VOWELS. The vowel chart at the front of the classroom now becomes the center of attention for at least half an hour daily.

Inasmuch as the children have learned all the consonants, it now is a relatively simple task for them to learn the five vowels and to "tuck them in" between the consonants. Actually, this "tucking in the vowels" is one of the clever aspects of the *Phonovisual Method.*

The first vowel taught is "E". It was selected because, when doubled, it is regularly the long sound. Thus, the key-word, "tree" becomes the symbol for the long sound of either single or double "E". The double "E" gestalt is easily recognized visually, and a phonogram pattern such as "see", "seed", "keep", "peep", "jeep", "feel", "sheep", etc., is easily constructed by "tucking in the vowel" between previously-learned consonants.

Although *Phonovisual* usually deals with whole words and the structural analysis necessary for syllabication, it becomes necessary to deal with each phoneme in small three-letter and four-letter words. Consequently, the child is asked to "sound out" the "k", followed by the "ee", and the "p" at the end. Although the enunciation of the letter sounds is exaggerated by the children, every effort is made to prevent gross abnormalities in the pronunciation of whole words. This may be more easily done with short three-letter words than with longer and more irregular words.

In the *Phonovisual* system, after the long vowel "ee", the short vowels are introduced in the following order: "a", "i", "u", "o", and "e". In presenting the long sound of "ee", the key-word is "tree". The sound is also indicated as belonging to the graphemes "e" and "ea" which are found on the chart in smaller print.

The other long vowel sounds also have their accompanying key-words. For example: the long sound of "i" is presented as "i-e", with the other spellings of the sound following in smaller print, as "y" and "igh". The "key word" for the long "i" sound is the numeral "5". The long sound of "o" is presented as "o-e", followed by the alternative spellings of "oa", "ow", and "o". "Rose" is the key-word. Finally, the "u" is presented as "u-e", with "ew" as an alternate spelling for the sound. The letter "u" is not included, possibly because it does not appear frequently enough in our language as representing its long sound. The key-word for the long "u" sound is "mule".

The key-word "saw" is used for one of the sounds represented by the letter "a". The spellings are "aw"; "a(r)" (as in the key-word "car"); "au"; "a(ll)"; and "o(r)".

Two sounds of double-o are represented by the key-words "moon" and "book". The vowel chart is completed by three other digraphs: the "ow", as in "cow", with the alternate form "ou"; the "oy", as in "boy", with the alternate "oi"; and the four forms of the "ur" as in "fur" or "church", followed by "er", "ir", and "or".

Materials. It has been pointed out that the large consonant charts and vowel charts are the backbone of the *Phonovisual Method*. The "Method Book" is the teacher's manual, and provides the structured step-by-step procedures, with photographs which help the teacher visualize those steps.

A book of almost fifty phonics games is available to add variety to the drill in the early stages of learning the method. Also, for Kindergarten or Grade One there is a "Transition" book which provides "seat work" with action verbs.

Like most basic phonemic systems, *Phonovisual* rejects the need for the usual type of Kindergarten readiness activities. In their place, a "Readiness Book" has been produced which concentrates its work on tasks that zero in on particular initial consonants. In some ways this workbook is a misnomer for, rather than "readiness", it is really a post-learning workbook and check-up upon the mastery of each consonant.

For First, Second, and Third grades there also is a consonant workbook and a vowel workbook, as well. It is obvious that such books would not be repeated in cases where the individual child has already mastered the consonants and/or vowels.

The large *Phonovisual* consonant and vowel charts have been reproduced in individual form in a size reduced to 8½ × 11 sheets. These are very useful for work with the individual child or with pairs or very small groups. Individual "incomplete" consonant charts and vowel charts are also available in practice-sheet size, making the *Phonovisual Method* adaptable to both whole-class instruction and individual tutoring.

Research Findings

The *Ontario Journal of Educational Research* (Spring, 1965) reported an experimental study[5] of the *Phonovisual Method* of teaching phonemics. The study investigated the problem of the effectiveness of the method compared with the usual basal reader approach in Grade Two, with the usual three groupings according to reading ability. The results reported show superiority in spelling and in word-attack skills for those pupils who learned the *Phonovisual Method*. As a result of the study and the further experimentation with the method during the 1963–64

---

5. Sweeney, John R., "An Experimental Study of the Phonovisual Method of Teaching Phonics," *Ontario Journal of Educational Research*. Spring, 1965, 263–272.

school year, all Kitchener, Ontario, teachers were advised to use the method.

A much more extensive study[6] was undertaken in Pasadena (California) in 1964–1965. This was done in Grade One, Grade Two, and Grade Three. Experimental and control groups were set up with carefully selected pairs: 60 in the first grade, 68 pairs in the second grade, and 54 matched pairs in the third grade.

Those children who received *Phonovisual* training in the First Grade were compared with those who did not receive such training. It was found that, of those matched pairs of First Graders who were in the "superior" readiness group in September, 85% of those who had received *Phonovisual* training had reached their achievement potential or beyond by the end of First Grade, contrasted with only 29% of the control group. At high normal and average levels of readiness, those receiving *Phonovisual* train-ing were also significantly better than their paired counterparts in the control groups.

In the Second Grade, performance on vocabulary, comprehension, and spelling on the *California Achievement Tests* at the end of the year indicated significant differences at the .01 level in favor of the *Phonovisual* group.

At the end of the Third Grade, there was also a significant difference at the .01 level in favor of the *Phonovisual* group on the vocabulary and comprehension sections of the *California Achievement Tests*, with a difference in spelling at the .05 level.

The study was done during the 1964–65 school year and was published as the "Pasadena City Schools Evaluation Report Number Seven". It is available from the Department of Research of which Dr. Joseph T. Hanson is the Administrative Director.

There appear to be a good number of strong features which have been incorporated into *Phonovisual* by its originators. They have drawn upon their years of experience with speech sounds, and upon their training in dealing with children who need careful enunciation of speech sounds to facilitate their learning. Moreover, the method incorporates a number of sound principles of learning. An excellent color film is available for showing to teachers' groups.

Because of the positive features of the *Phonovisual Method*, it is likely that it will continue to enjoy continued acceptance by a growing number of teachers.

---

6. Hanson, Joseph T., "Final Evaluation of the Phonovisual Method, Grades 1–3," *Pasadena City Schools Evaluation Report Number Seven*. Pasadena, Calif.: Pasadena City Schools, September, 1965.

READING WITH PHONICS

Origins

For twenty years Miss Julie Hay carried on a study of the unabridged dictionary in an attempt to determine a set of basic, generalized phonemic principles. In 1942 Miss Hay's school principal, Charles E. Wingo, teamed up with her on a five-year study aimed at transferring those phonemic principles into practice.

The schools chosen for the study were in the Argo-Summit-Bedford Park (Illinois) school system. In 1948 the study resulted in what has become known as the "Hay-Wingo" basic phonemic method, printed under the name, *Reading With Phonics*.

Unfortunately, Miss Hay passed away the same year as the new method came from the press. Miss Mary Hletko then was invited to join Professor Wingo in the work, but it was many years before the system became known as the Wingo-Hletko method. Indeed, it is still most generally referred to as the "Hay-Wingo" system. Mr. Wingo, now Professor of Education at Monmouth College in Illinois, conducts numerous workshops in which the *Reading With Phonics* method is demonstrated.

In her research, the late Miss Hay found justification for her claim that our language is "87% phonemic and only 13% partially non-phonemic." Consequently, the concept of a phonemically-regular American language provides the cornerstone for *Reading With Phonics*. Accordingly, the claim is reiterated by Professor Wingo to the effect that systematic, sequential training in the 19 vowel sounds and 25 consonant sounds will result in a tool which the child can use to unlock the pronunciation of 87% of our words. At the same time it is claimed that the 13% "partially-phonemic" words also may be partially unlocked by this intense mastery of phonemics. It has been unequivocally stated that "systematic, sequential training [in phonemics] . . . provides correct pronunciation of any strange words falling within the aforementioned 87% in any reading situation."[7] Such a broad statement serves to emphasize the fact that *Reading With Phonics* is a highly-structured basic phonemic system.

The objective of the approach is for a child to have an independent command of 62% of all phonemic syllables in our language by the time he recognizes short vowel sounds; 20% more by the time he has learned the blends and the "final-*e*" rule and the five long vowel sounds. Another 10% increment is said to be added when the child learns the rule of

---

7. Hay and Wingo, *Reading With Phonics, Teacher's Manual. op. cit.*

"vowels modified by *r*". The manual summarizes this rapid accumulation of phonemic power during the First Grade by stating that the child is left with only 8% of the phonemic syllables to be learned by means of memorization of orderly phonemic rules.

Although there were others such as Paul McKee[8] and E. W. Dolch[9] who in the 1940's were recommending an increased attention to phonemic elements in beginning reading, Professor Wingo states that his own research alone convinced him that the schools should "return to a teaching of phonics". It is noteworthy that he reached that conclusion fully a decade prior to the pronouncements of Rudolph Flesch who capitalized on the "phonics controversy" with his best seller, *Why Johnny Can't Read.*[10] Flesch is mentioned here, not because he contributed anything other than fuel for the fire, but because his suggestions for correcting the reasons "why Johnny can't read" are so very similar to the materials delineated in the Hay-Wingo *Reading With Phonics*.

Viewed in the historical perspective of the "phonics controversy", it is certainly fair to credit Hay-Wingo with the development of a system of phonemics based on years of painstaking work. Of equal historical and professional importance is the fact that their method was not an opportunistic "crash program" to get something on the market to cash in on the new demand for a book that offered a solution to the "phonics controversy".

Method and Materials

The *Reading With Phonics* system has been termed by Mr. Wingo as a "synthetic" method as opposed to the "analytic" method most often used in the basal reader series. The distinction is more clear if one thinks of the "synthetic" method as "synthesizing" or blending together the separate sounds of the letters to form wholly-pronounced words. The "analytic" method, on the other hand, is one in which the child sees the whole word and attempts to use "word analysis" skills by breaking it down structurally or phonemically into its parts. Psychologically, the "synthetic" phonemic method is part learning—later to be assembled into a whole.

---

8. McKee, Paul, *The Teaching of Reading in the Elementary School*. Boston: Houghton, Mifflin Co., 1948. Ch. 8–11.
9. Dolch, Edward W., and Bloomster, Maurine, "Phonics Readiness," *Elementary School Journal*, XXXVIII (Nov. 1937) 201–205.
   Dolch, Edward W., "How a Child Sounds Out a Word," *Elementary English Review*, XXII (Nov. 1945) 275–280.
10. Flesch, Rudolph, *Why Johnny Can't Read—and What You Can Do About It*. New York: Harper and Bros., 1955.

Like most basic phonemic systems, *Reading With Phonics* by-passes reading readiness activities. It is assumed that at the time children reach school age, most of them are ready to learn to read. It states:

If a teacher will begin THE FIRST DAY OF SCHOOL (in the First Grade) to teach youngsters that the symbol *a* represents the first sound in *apple,* she will have put in motion the most effective "readiness" program ever devised for a first grade reading program.

Some concession is made in the teacher's manual, for it recognizes the need for a basic sight vocabulary before being thrown into rote memorization. It is suggested that a few one-syllable sight words be learned—perhaps through experience charts in Kindergarten. The child should learn to read and write those words before starting his phonemic training so that he may construct short sentences with their aid.

The basic (and only) text in the Hay-Wingo system is the hard-cover book, *Reading With Phonics,* which is used daily throughout the First Grade.

The teacher's manual instructs the teacher to proceed immediately in Grade One (or in second semester of Kindergarten) with the five short vowel sounds. It is implied that this can be accomplished by Friday of the first week of the First Grade in September, but it is probable that experienced teachers would provide a more realistic time schedule.

Reading With Phonics provides some very vivid and colorful pictures for teaching the five short vowel sounds. The sound of "a" is represented by a full-page picture of a big red apple. A circus elephant is used to represent the initial consonant sound of short "e". A full-page rendering of an Indian is associated with the short "i" sound. The short "o" sound is graphically related to a picture of an ostrich. And the short sound of "u" is learned through the picture of an umbrella.

A set of 25 very colorful phonemic picture cards, which are reproductions of the colorful pictures in the text, is available for use as flash cards and/or for display around the room. They constitute one of the best sets of phonemic picture cards available.

One important difference in the Hay-Wingo system is the manner in which the short sounds of the five vowels are presented. Actually, all five are supposed to be learned simultaneously through rote memorization of the sequence: "ahh", "eah", "iah", "awh", "uah". The class works on those short vowel sounds constantly. After the children as a group have mastered those sounds—always in sequence—they then learn them in association with the "key-words," thus:

ă   as in apple
ĕ   as in elephant
ĭ   as in indian

ŏ   as in ostrich
ŭ   as in umbrella.

It should be pointed out that the pages in the text and the larger phonics picture cards have both the small and capital vowel letters on them. Thus, it is hoped that the children will learn both parts of the alphabet simultaneously.

The class starts with the picture of the big red apple on page 5 and continues through page 20 of the text almost without interruption. This is to be accomplished in from three to five weeks, at the end of which it is expected that the five vowel sounds and the ten consonant sounds, together with their key-words, will have been mastered.

In the listening games, the children are asked to close their eyes and to listen to the teacher pronounce a list of words that begin with "ăhh" as in "apple". They are instructed that when a word is pronounced that does not begin with "ăhh", the right hand is to be raised.

The word-drill exercises contain many words which are not in the usual vocabulary of children. For example, one of the drills includes such words as "album", "avalanche", and "atlas". An additional word list suggests that the teacher dictate words of from three to five syllables, such as "admiral", "alibi", "antelope", "antenna", "Amazon", "absurd", "accelerator", "agony", and many others.

The justification for including such words is vocabulary improvement. It is claimed that such words are "not too difficult for bright first graders to read, spell, and understand before the end of the year".

As drill progresses with the "ăhh" sound of "a", the teacher is supposed to insert words with initial vowel sounds of "eah" and "iah"—not to confuse the child—but so that the class "may learn to make the nice discriminations between these closely related sounds". It is also promised that "these basic auditory drills tend to increase attention span and encourage concentration".

Drill on the ten most-frequently-used consonant sounds proceeds thus:

sss . . . as in squirrel	guh . . . as in goat
mmm . . . as in monkey	buh . . . as in bear
fff . . . as in fox	th . . . as in tiger
rrr . . . as in rabbit	pph . . . as in pig
nnn . . . as in nest	duh . . . as in dog

When working with the ten most-commonly-used initial consonants, a distinction is made between the first five (s, m, f, r, and n) and the five "stopped" consonants (g, b, t, p, and d). Inasmuch as the letter names are never pronounced, it is incumbent upon the teacher to have the class pronounce as purely as possible the first five sounds and the "stopped" consonant sounds which need a vowel as a helper. Thus, in making the "gu" sound, or the "bu", "tu", "pu", and "du" sounds, the sound of the "u" should be minimized as much as possible.

The acquisition of the five short vowel sounds and the ten most-frequently-used consonants constitutes what is called the "Phonic Readiness" stage, from which the class advances to the next "plateau". On "Plateau Two", the class is taught to blend—by assembling each of the ten consonant sounds with each of the five short vowel sounds. This is to be accomplished in each instance all in one breath—thus producing a morpheme which is a word fragment or a pronunciation unit.

Reading With Phonics calls this process "short vowel blends." Actually, this is the "synthesizing" of a consonant sound with a vowel sound—or more specifically, an initial consonant sound synthesized with a short vowel sound, with another consonant sound added at the end —thus creating a three- or four-letter word or syllable.

The special feature used in *Reading With Phonics* for accomplishing this synthesis is, "Who can slide from 's' to 'a'?" As the children "slide" from the initial consonant "s" to short vowel "a", the teacher writes that blend on the board. These blends are called "helpers" because they are used to help make words. This is followed with work on "sliding" from "s" to short vowel "e"; from "s" to short vowel "i"; from "s" to short vowel "o"; and from "s" to short vowel "u". This accomplished, the next step is to construct words by sliding in this manner:

> "sa", and add "d"
> "se", and add "t"
> "si", and add "t"
> "so", and add "b"
> "sa", and add "m"

Using the "sliding helpers", the class constructs what the Hay-Wingo system calls "ladders", not only starting with "sa", but with the other nine previously learned "commonly-used" consonants.

The phonics ladders in the Hay-Wingo system always begin with the short "aah" at the bottom and proceed up the ladder to the short vowel "u", as illustrated in the following ladder using short vowel "helper" blends:

su		sun
so		sob
si		sit
se		set
sa		sat

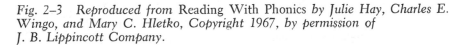

ten

t

tent

a	e	i	o	u
ten	mill	hum	tin	
tent	milk	hump	tint	
bum	till	den	bell	
bump	tilt	dent	belt	
sell	pan	sill	pen	
self	pant	silk	pent	
hill	men	fill	ten	
hilt	mend	film	tend	

38

Fig. 2–3   Reproduced from Reading With Phonics *by Julie Hay, Charles E. Wingo, and Mary C. Hletko, Copyright 1967, by permission of J. B. Lippincott Company.*

The use of such "ladders" is one of the features of *Reading With Phonics.* They are printed in two colors, thereby emphasizing the specific phonemic element being stressed in the lesson. The use of color as a visual reinforcement is one of the strengths of the phonics text.

Another, but somewhat less successful, scheme is used to indicate the three spellings of the "k" sound, and its application in use. The "c" as in "cat" is indicated with a "c_1". The "k" as in "kid" is "k_2" and the "ck" as in "sock" is "ck_3". The usage of the "k" sound is indicated thus:

c_1 to be used before the vowels a, o, and u.
k_2 to be used before the vowels e and i.
ck_3 to be used *after* vowels.

The accompanying "ladder" to illustrate the use of the "k" sound is:

cu	cut	(c_1)
co	cob	(c_1)
ki	kiss	(k_2)
ke	keg	(k_2)
ca	cat	(c_1)

Examples of "ck_3" are:

sack, sick, tuck, and back

The students are then encouraged to use the three types of "k" sounds in constructing phonograms, first in single-syllable words, and later in poly-syllabic words.

Work with short vowel sounds is complete with an elaborate set of exercises for drill on some of the more troublesome short vowel "blends". In each instance the initial consonant "slides" into a vowel as follows:

"l" as in lion   "v" as in valentine
"h" as in horse   "qu" as in queen
"j" as in jug   "y" as in yarn
"w" as in wagon   "z" as in zebra

Upon completion of work on those short vowel "blends", the structure of the method then shifts to consonant digraphs. Inasmuch as the "di-graph" consists of two letters pronounced as one, it occasionally presents a difficult problem to a young child who, up to this point, has been taught that each letter has a separate sound. Generally, the consonant digraphs represent but one sound. In the Hay-Wingo system, the child learns it thus:

"sh" as in sheep   "nk" as in bank
"ch_1" as in chicken   "th_1" as in thimble
"tch_2" as in witch   "th_2" as in that
"ng" as in king   "wh" as in whip

and finally the "x" sound is added, as in box.

Recognizing the fact that systems of phonics cannot rely completely upon rote memorization, the Hay-Wingo system has devised some phonics rules which apply to digraphs:

1. "ch₁" is used at beginning of words "chop" and after letter "n" as in "bench".
2. "tch₂" is used after all short vowels and on the end of a one-syllable word.
3. "ng" changes to "nk" in "thank" or "think".
4. "th" is "voiced" when used in "then" and "unvoiced" when used in "thing". The two sounds of "th" are counted as part of the 44 sounds of our language.
5. The consonant digraph "wh" is actually pronounced in reverse.

Ladders, using the five short vowel sounds, have been devised for practice with two consonants blending with a vowel that follows. The ladder using the "bl" digraph follows the pattern with "a" at the bottom

blush

block

blink

bless

black

Other consonant digraphs are: cl, fl, sl, pl, gl, sc, sm, sn, sp, st, sw, br, cr, dr, fr, gr, tr. In each instance, the consonants slide into the following short vowel sounds of: a, e, i, o, and u. These and the others previously cited are called "GIANT" helpers.

Reading With Phonics states that, when all the consonant sounds and all their blends with the five short vowel sounds have been taught, "a child will have at his command the skill to unlock 62% of all the phonetic syllables in our language."

The major work with basic phonemics is completed with practice on the five long vowel sounds. This is extended to include the "final-e" rule which is stated:

If a word has two vowels, and the second one is a final *e*, then the first vowel is usually long and the final *e* is silent.

Practice is given in changing short vowels to long with the addition of a final "*e*":

can	pet	rip	hop	tub
cane	Pete	ripe	hope	tube

Once the sequence of phonemic drills has reached this stage—much of it having been accomplished by means of rote drill by the whole group in unison—the individual child is considered to be ready to read and

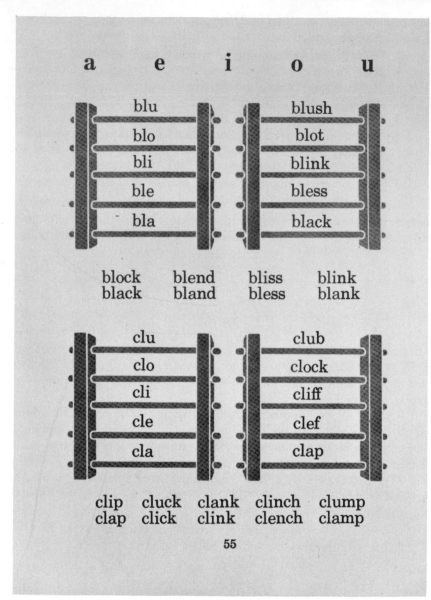

Fig. 2–4 *Reproduced from* Reading With Phonics *by Julie Hay, Charles E. Wingo, and Mary C. Hletko, Copyright 1967, by permission of J. B. Lippincott Company.*

write and tell stories, using all of the words he has learned to make in word-family exercises and "synthesizing".

The child then progresses to word construction by forming two-syllable words through the addition of endings such as "ing" to verbs, and the making of compound words. The remainder of Grade One is utilized in drill on the 13% "partially phonetic" and on the irregular elements of our language. This includes work on the following phonemic elements:

The fact that double-o represents two sounds as illustrated in the words "cool" and "cook".

The three spellings of hard-j, designated as j_1 in "jam"; ge_2 as in the ending of "change"; and dge_3 as in the ending of "judge".

The double-e sound is learned as associated with "tree" as ee_1 and with "seat" as ea_2.

The sound represented by ew in the word "blew" is designated with two spellings: ew_1 and ue_2 as in "due".

The aw_1 in "saw" is compared with the au_2 as in "haul".

The al_1 in "salt" is learned as a different spelling from all_2 as in "ball".

Three spellings are learned to indicate the oa sound. They are: oa_1 as in "boat"; oe_2 as in "toe"; and ow_3 as in "slow".

"House" and "now" are used as key words for spelling ou_1 and ow_2.

oi_1 as in "oil" and oy_2 as in "boy" represent that sound.

ai_1 as in "rain" is paired with ay_2 as in play.

The *Reading With Phonics* system also introduces what are called "modified" vowels, in which the five short vowels are modified by the letter "r", thus: ar as in "farm"; er_1 as in "her"; ir_2 as in "girl"; or as in "for"; and ur_3 as in "burn".

It should be noted that the three spellings of the er sound are designated by the three sub-exponents but are kept in the "a, e, i, o, u" sequence.

Finally, Hay-Wingo introduces an interesting innovation by designating the following *equivalents*:

ce = se   as in "cent"
ci = si   as in "cider"
cy = si   as in "cyclone"
tion = sion   as in "nation"
or = er   as in "actor"
ph = f   as in "phone"
se = z   as in "chose"
gh = *no sound*   as in "sigh" and "night"

Reading With Phonics is designed to be used as a basic phonemics text in Grade One. It is never claimed that it is a total reading program. Inherent in its emphasis on a basic phonemic approach to beginning reading is the necessity for continuous rote memorization accomplished through drill. In order to make such drill somewhat more concrete, three workbooks have been made available. *Sounds, Letters, and Words* is designed to be used with work on "plateau one". *More Letters and Words* is for "seat work" chiefly on consonant digraphs, giant helpers, and long vowel sounds.

Skills With Sounds and Words is a review workbook dealing with the more difficult phonemic factors. It is probable that the more gifted children could handle this workbook as they work from page 74 through page 119 of *Reading With Phonics*. It is also suggested that this, as well as the two easier workbooks, be used with remedial cases.

Furthermore, inasmuch as Dr. Wingo recommends that a complete phonemic review and reinforcement be carried on throughout grades two and three, the supplementary workbooks are available for such review independently of the first-grade text.

Research Findings

Dr. Wingo has been helpful in providing the extant research studies involving his method. One of the significant studies was done as a doctoral dissertation at Southern Illinois University by David E. Baer.[11] He compared the Hay-Wingo basic phonics method with an analytic or whole-word method. During the 1956–57 academic school year in Alton, Illinois, Baer worked with fourteen classes—divided into those seven working with Hay-Wingo "synthetic" phonics and the other seven groups (control) working with "analytic" phonics.

Both groups used the basal reader. The control group used the phonics presented through the basal reader series. The experimental group used a basal reader plus thirty minutes of daily phonemics work in the Hay-Wingo *Reading With Phonics* plus the three supplementary workbooks and the picture cards.

The work was done in eleven elementary schools. Only students who completed the academic year in the program were included. The median was 27 students per classroom. An attempt was made to equate the groups on hearing-test results, vision test results, previous kindergarten experience and teacher preparation, experience, age, and rating. Both groups were given 150 minutes of reading instruction per day . . . the only difference being in the additional phonemic materials.

---

11. Baer, David E., "Phonics for First Grade: A Comparison of Two Methods," *Elementary School Journal*, 59 (April, 1959) 394–402; "Two Methods of Teaching Phonics: A Longitudinal Study," *Elementary School Journal*, 64 (Feb., 1964) 273–279.

The *Gates Primary Reading Test* was administered to both groups in January and again in May. There was little difference between the achievement of the groups on the January testing. The test in May, however, produced the following results:

	experimental	control
word recognition	31.90	27.95
sentence meaning	31.55	28.35
paragraph meaning	18.13	16.30

Also in May, the *Metropolitan Achievement Test* yielded the following means:

	experimental	control
word pictures	32.25	29.40
word recognition	21.25	20.29
word meaning	19.18	17.92

In three cases cited above, the differences were considered to be beyond the possibilities of chance. The report further states that the groups of average intelligence benefited most from the use of "synthetic" phonics, whereas that was not the case with children with higher IQs nor with those of lower IQs. In each of the latter groups there was little or no difference between the two methods.

Baer later extended his original experiment into a longitudinal study of some of the same children until they had reached Sixth Grade. In Grade Two the Hay-Wingo phonemic instruction was discontinued, and children in both experimental and control groups received only basal reader instruction. This was done until Grade Six. In May of their sixth year they attained mean scores on Form 2, *Gates Reading Survey*, as follows:

	experimental	control
vocabulary	7.27	6.67
comprehension	7.42	7.01
speed	8.50	8.33
spelling (real words)	12.84	11.1
spelling (nonsense words)	16.7	14.9

In assessing the results, the middle 50% on IQ retained the greatest benefits from the "synthetic phonics" . . . with a slight difference for the low IQ children. It would be a mistake to believe that the results reported on the follow-up phase of the study are of great significance, for there is no mention of controls such as quality of teaching, continuance of children in matched groups, nor even a test of the significance (if any) of the differences.

Reading With Phonics represents what Dr. Wingo calls "56 years of research and rewarding practice". He is, of course, referring to the twenty years which Julie Hay spent in research and classroom use, together with his own work with children and teachers during the 16 years which he has directed the reading laboratory in the Argo-Summit-Bedford Park Schools in Illinois. In addition, he has worked with hundreds of teachers during the many years in which he has directed the workshop and classes in reading at Monmouth College.

Reading With Phonics provides what is aptly referred to by its authors as a "synthetic phonics" approach to the whole complicated task of reading and comprehending. As such, it has enjoyed wide acceptance by teachers who feel the need for a compact package of phonemic exercises and a teacher's manual keyed to them.

YOUR CHILD CAN LEARN TO READ

Origins

Your Child Can Learn to Read is, actually, a collection of several books and flash cards which have evolved over the years from the experiences of their originator, Mrs. Margaret McEathron, one of the pioneers in the phonics revival in the United States.

Beginning in 1937, she began research in reading with special emphasis on a phonemic approach. In 1938 Mrs. McEathron established the "Reading House" in Southwest Los Angeles (now located at Costa Mesa, California), as a center for training teachers and mothers in a phonemic approach to beginning reading. There, for more than 30 years, she has concentrated her efforts in remedial reading, and it was out of her early experiences with phonemics that she developed manuals for parents and teachers and the materials known as *Your Child Can Learn to Read*. The McEathron materials are published by the Kenworthy Educational Service, Inc. of Buffalo, N.Y. *Your Child Can Learn to Read* has been a best seller for over 20 years, with a total sale reported to be nearly a million copies.

Method and Materials

The materials which Mrs. Margaret McEathron has developed consist primarily of a paperback 8½ × 11 manual for parents and teachers and two workbooks for children, plus boxed kits of cards and phonemic games.

The parents-teachers manual carries the sub-title, "A Simplified Course in Phonics," and undertakes the task of providing a series of steps, lesson-by-lesson, to "develop the sounding-out skill in reading." It is stated that "Any person—child or adult—must take these steps. . . . (and). . . .It can be learned by anyone who follows the rules or lessons in this book."[12]

The book is also available in a hard-cover edition, printed by Grosset and Dunlap, New York.

The student's workbook, *I Learn to Read*, is also a paperback which correlates lesson-by-lesson with the pages in the teacher's manual. Book 1 is designed for phonemic drill in Grades 1, 2, and 3. Book 2 is for Grade 4 and beyond.

A small box of flash cards is available to correlate with the program. It is called, "5 First Steps and Pop Words." The box contains 150 sight words printed on cards. Also there are 15 "easy consonants" and 4 less-used consonants—including the three sounds of *y*, the two sounds of *g*, the two sounds of *c*, the short sounds of the five vowels, and consonant digraphs *ch*, *wh*, *th*, and *sh*, constituting about 75% of the words ordinarily found in the first-grade program of the basal readers.

The "Doghouse Game" consists of twelve game cards on which are printed 35 phonograms. At the bottom of the cards are printed rules of pronunciation. For each card, there are 84 consonants and consonant blends with which a child or a group can build words. Actually, the phonograms on the card are roots of word families such as *-ap*, *-ell*, *-ack*, *-ang*, *-ung*, etc. There are several variations for playing the "Doghouse Game", all of which are thought to serve as reinforcing drill in phonemics.

Package deals are available, first under the title "First Steps in Learning to Read" (which consists of the manual *"Your Child Can Learn to Read* and the "5 First Steps" drill cards) or the larger box which contains the manual, the drill cards, the "Doghouse Game" and two other sets of drill cards which Kenworthy publishes. This kit is marketed under the title *Reading Made Easy*.

The essentials of Mrs. McEathron's method are found in the teacher's manual and contain some unique features. Although her method concentrates on "sounding-out" through phonemics, she recognizes the fact that most basal series books start with sight words. The 200 sight words in the Dolch list are the foundation of the "Pop" words which are on the flash cards. The total list of "Pop" words is given on page 59 of the teacher's manual, *Your Child Can Learn to Read*. The Dolch

12. McEathron, Margaret, *Your Child Can Learn to Read—Manual*. Buffalo: Kenworthy Educational Service, Inc., 1963.

list is reproduced on page 60. The manual recommends that the children practice on the flash cards until they become so familiar with them that recognition should be instantaneous. Skill in recognizing the "Pop" words should be developed by daily practice. The words have been divided into four categories: colors, numbers, nouns, and "service" words, which actually are verbs, pronouns, adjectives, prepositions, etc.

It is pointed out in the manual that some children cannot learn by a whole-word approach and that all children will benefit from a phonemic approach not only to reading but to spelling, as well.

Apparently it is assumed that a child will have learned the large and small letters of the printed and cursive alphabet before undertaking the course. Lesson 1 is, therefore, essentially a review of such learning. Where the child has not learned these elements of the alphabet, he will have to stay with lesson 1 until he has a satisfactory recall of the alphabet.

The fifteen "easy" consonants comprise the bulk of lesson 2. They are called "easy" because they are phonemically regular—having only one grapheme-phoneme relationship each. *Your Child Can Learn to Read* presents a page of those consonants in both capital and small print in the pattern:

baby
Bb as in   Bobby
boy

see
Ss as in   six
stop

Practice on those "easy" consonants is in isolation by seeing and listening to them and writing them. They are treated primarily as initial consonant sounds.

An interesting feature of the method in dealing with the two sounds represented by the letter *c* is the rule that "The next letter *after c* makes the difference and tells you whether the *c* says *s* or *k*." The little poem helps the learner remember the rule:

C coughs like K
Except when he
Is followed by
I, Y, or E.
Then, my dears,
No need to guess
He starts to hiss
Just like an S.

A similar rule and poem have been made for the two sounds of *g*. Chapter II provides practice on the vowel sounds. Once they have

Lesson 12

FUN WITH "3 SIGNAL" WORDS

1. Take a card with **a** on it.

   Now select cards with: **m, t, s, p, f, n.**

   Use the **a** card EACH TIME, but choose two of the other letters and try to make a word out of each combination of "3 signals." You will get words like: sat, fan, tap, etc. Each combination that makes a REAL WORD, "capture" it by writing it down.

   See how many you can capture with just these 7 letters.

2. Take a card with **i** on it.

   Now select cards with: **b, w, h, f, s.**

   Do the same with these letters as you did in No. 1.

3. Use the **o** vowel card.

   Do the same, using with: **p, t, r, d, l.**

4. Use a **u** vowel card.

   Do the same, using with: **b, t, n, m, s.**

5. Use a card with **e.**

   Do the same, combining with: **p, b, r, d, t.**

Can you read every word you captured?

Fig. 2–5   Reproduced from Your Child Can Learn to Read *by permission of Kenworthy Educational Service, Inc.*

been learned, the child can then "make-up" words, using the clever scheme of "3 Signal" words. The game is to "capture" three letters and tie them together to make a word. Using the consonants b, w, f and s, and the vowels, the child tries to capture as many "3 signal" words as possible. Additional practice is given in finding vowels in words and in lists of letters.

Chapter III provides practice in word building, using the "families" on the short vowel phonogram chart on page 32. They are essentially the same family roots as found printed on the flash cards in the "Doghouse Game."

The "ER Sisters and the OY Boys" is an interesting approach to the three spellings, *er, ir,* and *ur,* and the two spellings, *oy* and *oi.* The page from lesson 19 on page 46 illustrates this feature of the workbook.

The "two vowel" rule is given in two or three forms in lesson 22. A poem suggests that a vowel is "polite" (short sound) when with consonants, but becomes noisy and shouts his name when another vowel comes along.

Lesson 25 provides practice with the long vowel "families" of roots.

Chapter V deals with such phonemic elements as *y* as a vowel, *-ite* ending, *-ight* ending, syllabication, the double $\overline{oo}$ sound, *aw* and *au,* *ow* and *ou,* and words that have irregular phonemic elements, designated as "Words With Tricks".

The entire program is illustrated to appeal to the amusement of the learner, with clowns as the actors. The 64-page parents-teachers manual contains the essentials of the program. The workbook provides coordinated activity, and the flashcards and game provide additional practice for reinforcement.

In 1970 the materials of *Your Child Can Learn to Read* were expanded into audiovisual form with slides, tapes, and filmstrips. Another variation of Mrs. McEathron's phonics program has been developed with the aid of Walter Tipton, founder of the Psynetics Foundation of Orange, California. It is a workbook and card game, marketed by R. V. Weatherford Co. of Glendale, California, under the title, *20 Key Words.*

A beginning phonics primer and student workbook for teenagers and adults who have not learned to read was introduced by Mrs. McEathron in 1971. It is done in a much-illustrated, large print and breezy style and is published by Lawrence Publishing Co. of Los Angeles.

Research Findings

The parents-teachers manual has had wide distribution over the past twenty years, especially since it is a very inexpensive paperback and

Lesson 19

THE ER SISTERS AND THE OI BOYS
These are Triplets

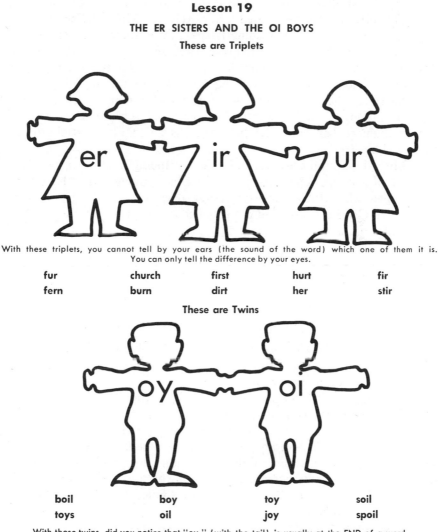

With these triplets, you cannot tell by your ears (the sound of the word) which one of them it is.
You can only tell the difference by your eyes.

fur	church	first	hurt	fir
fern	burn	dirt	her	stir

These are Twins

boil	boy	toy	soil
toys	oil	joy	spoil

With these twins, did you notice that "oy," (with the tail) is usually at the END of a word,
and "oi" is in the middle?
In our language, we don't like to end a word in an I, so we write it: **boy,** not **boi.**

36

Fig. 2–6 *Reproduced from* Your Child Can Learn to Read *by permission of Kenworthy Educational Service, Inc.*

has been merchandised through variety stores as well as by educational supply booths at teachers' meetings. The teacher's manual contains a number of testimonials from individuals who have used the method.

The method has been used extensively by Mrs. McEathron, the author, at her school, "The Reading House". As a result of her experience there, she states that "Phonic helps are not offered as a cure-all for all reading difficulties, nor is it offered as a substitute for the accepted progressive methods of teaching reading approach to reading." Mrs. McEathron states that "In every case of remedial reading to come under my observation, a simple, clear understanding of the phonetic elements in our language has been greatly needed as a logical approach to the reading difficulty."

Mrs. McEathron states that "I have not found, in all my experience, one case of a normal child being a non-reader, although some have been so classified when their case was turned over to me." The author of *Your Child Can Learn to Read* presents her own success with the program as evidence of its effectiveness.

SPEECH-TO-PRINT PHONICS

Origins

Speech-To-Print Phonics is intended to be a self-sufficient program which provides an entire class of 30 or more children with materials for phonemic practice on-their-own.

The *Speech-To-Print* materials are the culmination of more than thirty years of work with non-readers by its originator, Dr. Donald D. Durrell, Professor Emeritus at Boston University. He was aided in the work by Dr. Helen A. Murphy, now Professor Emerita of Boston University. More than 200 masters and doctoral studies done under Dr. Durrell's direction concerned readiness for reading and the problems of First Grade readers. They showed that the children who failed to learn to read had the following difficulties:

1. inability to identify separate sounds in spoken words:
2. incomplete mastery of phoneme-grapheme relationships;
3. inability to apply whatever phonemic training they may have received.

Dr. Durrell states that "The experience of patching the results of inadequate learning in phonics programs led us to design a program to overcome the observed weaknesses."

Speech-To-Print Phonics is an improved version of *Building Word Power* which was published originally in 1942. It carries a copyright date of 1964.

It is claimed by the authors of the program that the key to success in beginning reading is "ear training". This establishes the ability to notice phonemic patterns in spoken words. Thus, the child is able to tie the phonemes to their printed forms and to combine the sounds in sequence into words. Without the ability to do this, the child cannot acquire a sight vocabulary, nor can he "sound-out" words. Speech, therefore, is the primary step, with the learner moving from speech which he already knows to the printed words which he is learning as symbols for his speech. Hence, *Speech-To-Print Phonics* was selected as the name for the program, and reveals the philosophy behind it.

The extensive research studies carried on at Boston University by the authors and their graduate students indicated that a program should be developed that would contain the following elements:

a. Start with phoneme perception in spoken words, in order of ease of learning and frequency of use.

b. Call attention to the speech mechanisms in producing the phonemes.

c. Attach the phonemes to the words in print, using whole words but isolating the element to be learned.

d. Provide immediate use of each element taught through using it in connection with common phonograms.

e. Teach the vowels in common phonograms, since the phonogram gives stability to the vowel sound. This avoids teaching confusing rules and exceptions. It also minimizes the difficulty with varied spellings of sounds.

f. Maintain meaning-imagery behind all words, adding context clues and utilizing the "discovery" technique in phonics use.

g. Use words of highest frequency in children's speech and reading; also use phonograms which produce the greatest number of words.

h. Use every-pupil-response techniques to avoid waiting turns and to provide an easy check on individual learning in the class.

i. Provide for differences in levels and learning rates through whole-word meaningful presentation. Rapid learners acquire a sight vocabulary while slow learners master particular phonic elements.

j. Be easy for the teacher to use, enjoyable to the pupils, effective.

Dr. Durrell and Dr. Murphy used those criteria as their frame-of-reference in developing the *Speech-To-Print Phonics* program, published by Harcourt, Brace, and World, Inc.

Materials and Method

All of the materials in *Speech-To-Print Phonics* are contained in a large, sturdy box, which serves as a classroom storage center.

The basic materials are printed on 250 3″ × 14″ cards which may be used by the teacher as flash cards in whole-class learning. They are, essentially, designed for teacher use, inasmuch as the backs of the cards are printed with very specific directions, including questions to ask, comments to make, and other aids.

Pupil materials consist of 34 sets (enough for an entire class) of "pupil-response" cards, size 2″ × 3″. Each set consists of the 26 letters of the alphabet, printed in capital letters on one side and lower-case letters on the reverse side. Cards containing 21 separate consonant blends complete the phonemics cards set. In addition there are response cards printed with *yes, no, 1, 2,* and *3*.

The authors of the program recommend that all children learn the letter names of the alphabet in a ten-day period preceding work with phonemics. They point out the fact that, "since each letter (except h, w, and y) contains its sound, the child who knows letter names has the beginnings of phonics and finds it easier to attach sounds to letters."

Once the children have learned the letter names of the alphabet, the class is ready for a series of 55 "ear-training" lessons, in which they learn to identify graphemes and the phonemes which constitute parts of words. Initial consonant sounds and some initial vowel sounds are introduced in the first lessons. Each lesson concentrates on a beginning sound, and a number of words that begin with that sound are printed on the chalkboard by the teacher.

Each child is asked to select from his pack of pupil-response cards that card which represents the sound being practiced that particular day. For example, if the beginning consonant *f* is the sound for the day, each child will select the *f* card. The teacher has placed such words as *fun, fall, fix, find, fight, fish* and *forget* on the board. Each child also gets out his "1", "2", and "3" pupil-response cards, and the teacher selects from the box the set of 3″ × 14″ flash cards which are designated for use with the *f* lesson on initial word sounds.

As the teacher points to each of the words on the chalkboard, she and the class say the words and talk about their common beginning consonant sound. The teacher emphasizes the use of the speech mechanism —tongue, lip muscles, breath control, teeth—in producing each speech sound.

The "fringe benefits" of such instruction are practice in careful enunciation and learning of a whole-word sight vocabulary in addition to concentration on phonemics.

The speech sounds are always used immediately in words which are part of the normal child's vocabulary. Practice in listening is given while the teacher pronounces words beginning with the *f* sound as well as some which do not. Each child holds up the *f* card if he identifies the *f* sound at the beginning of each word spoken by the teacher. Thus, as the lessons proceed, it is easy for the teacher to identify any child who consistently is unable to identify the different sounds.

Additional practice in whole-word identification is given as the teacher says a sentence, leaving it incomplete at the end. This calls for a response in selecting from the words on the board that word which "makes sense" in the sentence. For example, the teacher says, "When the baseball is lost in the high grass, it is hard to _____." The children easily identify the word *find*.

Following initial work with the words on the chalkboard, the teacher then uses the "Applied Phonics Practice Cards". Card A, for example, contains three words: *far*   *car*   *tar*
         Card B: *six*   *fix*   *mix*
         Card C: *bun*   *fun*   *sun*
Note that each of the three words is built upon a word-family root such as *ar*, *ix*, and *un*. This feature is discussed as each card is used with the class. Since the children have learned the phoneme *f*, they can pronounce the words that begin with *f* after the word-family base has been discussed. As the lesson develops, the children hold up the "1", "2", or "3" card which indicates which of the three words on the teacher's flash card begins with the *f*. As each child applies his new knowledge to discover other words beginning with *f*, the learning of the phonemes is reinforced. A picture dictionary is a good source of additional practice within the *Speech-To-Print Phonics* pattern of learning.

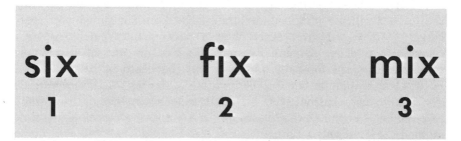

Fig. 2–7 *Reproduced from* Speech to Print Phonics *by permission of Donald D. Durrell and Harcourt Brace Jovanovich, Inc.*

The sequence of lessons is based upon the order of ease of learning:
a. Initial consonants in order of frequency.
b. Initial digraphs and blends.
c. Final consonant sounds.
d. Short vowel sounds in phonograms.
e. Long vowel sounds in phonograms.
f. Homophones.

Through the use of teacher flash-cards, between 600 and 700 printed words are read and discussed as separate words and in sentence context. The word-family roots are discussed, and the initial sounds are learned. It is inevitable that a good number of those words in isolation will be learned by many children as whole-word sight vocabulary.

The emphasis in the Durrell-Murphy system is always on sounds within words—never on phonemics in isolation. No phonemic rules are taught, but the authors claim that children who use the system learn to make the generalizations in a natural way, within their own speech patterns. The authors point out that "The movement from print to speech is a backward one that emphasizes 'what letters say.' In English this movement is undesirable because what letters 'say' varies greatly." The authors also indicate that they have found that children accept varied spellings without difficulty. "In matching phonemes with their various spellings, as in *Speech-To-Print Phonics*, the child acquires phonemics principles inductively and learns to accept varied spellings."

Speech-To-Print Phonics is not intended as a complete reading program. It is designed to do one job only—that is, to provide materials and a method by which children may practice as a whole class on meaningful phonemic elements. It is claimed by the authors that "this program is sufficiently comprehensive to replace entirely the word-analysis service of a basal reader." In fact, the *Speech-To-Print Phonics* materials are intended for use with any basal series "to supplement word study without conflicting with different phonemic approaches."

The "every-pupil response cards" have the advantage of providing the teacher with an instant and constant check on the progress of every child. Moreover, it gives every child a positive involvement in every phase of the daily phonemics lesson. This is in contrast with those systems which call for one child to go to the board or to the flannel board and to point or circle something while the rest of the entire class sits and watches passively. Dr. Durrell calls his system of every-pupil involvement "high-intensity" learning, and dubs the one-child-at-a-time method "low-intensity" work.

There are no pictures and no color work of any kind on the *Speech-To-Print Phonics* cards. All of the cards are of light grey cardboard stock, selected in that shade to minimize the smudge from little fingers. Although the cards are eventually expendable, they are of sufficient thickness and quality to withstand several years of work. Indeed, their life-expectancy is longer than one might suppose at first thought for, actually, the phonemic-drill which they provide lasts only through the first half of the first grade, usually only through January. The 55 lessons may be covered with "fast learners" before Christmas. "Slow learning" groups may take through the Spring months to cover the program.

Research Findings

Since more than 200 graduate studies are relevant to the development of the *Speech-To-Print* materials, a complete resume of that research would require too much space in this publication. In the field of auditory discrimination alone, there were 48 group and individual Ed.M. studies and 12 doctoral studies done under the direction of Dr. Durrell. Those research studies established the nature of phoneme perception, studied its relationship to the reading process, determined the order of ease of learning of various elements, and evaluated different types of programs for teaching it.

Similar studies provided the originators of the *Speech-To-Print Phonics* program with information on letter and phoneme perception, and a number of other related approaches to learning the phonemic elements of our language.

A complete listing of relevant studies appears in "Boston University Research in Elementary School Reading: 1933–1963," by Donald D. Durrell and Helen A. Murphy. Boston University *Journal of Education*, Vol. 145: 1–53, December, 1963.

With this comprehensive body of research data at their command, Dr. Durrell and Dr. Murphy developed the program and then had it researched in a pre-publication tryout in 100 First Grade classrooms to discover ease of administration, clarity of the manual, suitability of lessons for differing segments of the school population, and acceptability of the lessons to pupils and to teachers.

A complete and detailed inventory of growth in each element taught in the lessons was conducted among 450 First Grade students in a low economic community. The average IQ of the children was 92. Those inventories were spaced after the fifteenth lesson, the thirty-fifth lesson and the final lesson. They included:

—Ability to identify letters named; upper and lower case;
—Ability to identify letters by sound;
—Ability to identify phonemes in spoken and printed words;

—Growth in phonogram recognition;

—Ability in word recognition through oral reading, sampling 400 of the 1,200 words of the phonemics program;

—Ability to use phonemics in solving words—final lesson.

The results of that study revealed that four-fifths of the First Graders mastered more than 75% of the phonemics elements taught. The one-fifth with lower mastery were those whose pre-tests showed a knowledge of fewer than ten lower-case letters and no ability in phoneme recognition or perception.

The word-recognition study showed the potential of incidental learning of words in this type of phonemics program. In the study, all First Graders acquired three to five times as many sight words from the *Speech-To-Print Phonics* program as from the sight-vocabulary lessons in the accompanying basal reader. (The results of the study are detailed in Susan B. Arkin's Ed.M. thesis, Boston University, 1963.)[13]

Five of the centers in the National Study of First-Grade Reading[14] used *Speech-To-Print Phonics* in one or more of their comparative approaches. Although the results cannot be attributed to the phonemics program alone, it is significant to note that the programs in which *Speech-To-Print Phonics* was used were superior to the programs against which they were being compared.[15]

As a result of research with the Durrell-Murphy *Speech-To-Print Phonics* programs, it was clear that children who were in the bottom one-fifth of their class in First-Grade performance needed supplementary practice. Consequently, the authors developed additional lessons based upon research in sequence of learning phonemic elements. Those were first available from Harcourt, Brace and World in 1967 under the following titles: *Letter-Name Lessons*, and a *Phonics Practice Program*. Both are self-directing and self-correcting, and should prove to be very useful, not only for the slower First Grade learners, but for those who have arrived in the upper grades without having acquired adequate phonemic skills.

The *Speech-To-Print Phonics* program is not designed to be glamorous, but it certainly may be considered as being the result of the pooling of many ideas and experiences, refined through years of carefully-planned research and experimentation. It is accompanied with an excellent 163-

---

13. Arkin, Susan B., and others, "Growth Patterns in First-Grade Reading," unpublished Ed. M. Thesis, Boston University, 1964.
14. Spencer, Doris U., and Moquin, Doris, "Individualized Reading vs. a Basal Reading Program at First Grade Level in Rural Communities," *Cooperative Research Project* No. 50484. Washington: U.S. Office of Education, 1965.
15. *Ibid.*

page teacher's manual which provides a teaching plan, utilizing whole-class participation, uniquely individualized through the use of the individual "pupil-response" cards.

THE SOUND WAY TO EASY READING

Origins

Bremner-Davis Phonics—which is advertised under the descriptive title: "The Sound Way to Easy Reading"—was developed as a self-teaching system of phonics by A. J. Bremner and Mrs. Josephine Davis, an elementary teacher in the Chicago Public Schools for some twenty years. In 1953, Mrs. Davis and Mr. Bremner first produced for sale their do-it-yourself kit for children. The directions to the child were given on the four small phonograph records. The directions were very simple and designed so that a child could play the record by himself and, by following directions, he could work with the individual phonemics cards which are also part of the system.

The kit of records and phonemics cards was advertised to parents and, according to reports, more than 80,000 have been sold to parents. The home-tutoring course eventually came to the attention of teachers who also ordered it for classroom use. As a consequence, Bremner-Davis designed a classroom-size set of wall charts and revised the four phonograph records for classroom use. They also produced a Teacher's Guide which contains suggestions and a sequence for using the charts and recordings.

Method and Materials

The Bremner-Davis system is a pure phonemic approach to reading. It utilizes four phonograph records which provide classroom drill in what is claimed are 123 basic phonemics. To reinforce this auditory drill there are fifteen wall charts containing letter symbols and key words, plus a black-and-white illustration of the object designated by the key word. For example, apple is the key word for the first letter "a", and a drawing of an apple appears on the same line as the letter and the key word.

The first two charts and the first record provide the materials for drill on the basic single sounds of the 26 letters of the alphabet, plus

CHART 1

1	a		apple
2	b		boat
3	c		cake
4	d		doll
5	e		elephant
6	f		fox
7	g		gate
8	h		hand
9	il		Indian
10	j		jam
11	k		kite
12	l		ladder
13	m		milk
14	n		nut
15	o		octopus
16	p		pail

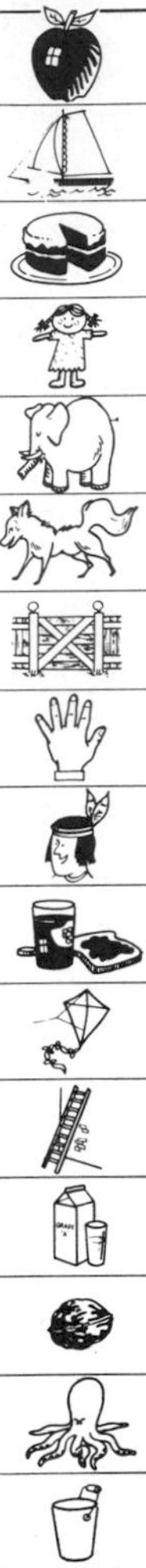

Fig. 2–8   Chart 1 reproduced by permission of Bremner Davis Phonics, Inc.

two additional sounds of "y", and the digraphs: "wh"; "sh"; "ch"; and "th". These constitute what is called the "Sound Dictionary".

    The method is as follows: The teacher sets up chart 1 and starts the record on Band 2. (Band 1 is an introduction). The voice on the recording pronounces a letter and its key word. The teacher simultaneously points to the letter symbol and word on the large wall chart.

The children are admonished to "listen-look-repeat" as the routine for learning, thus utilizing the sense of seeing and hearing for input and the repeating of the sound as output or response. Throughout the program there is concern for the exact reproduction of the recorded sounds. Specifically, the children must not pronounce "duh" for the letter "d", nor "buh" for the letter "b".

After the class has gained some familarity with the drill using the phonograph record, the teacher will use home-made flashcards of the same letters on the wall charts. On the opposite sides of the cards, the teacher will have printed the letter symbol and the key word. Children also are required to make their own set of flashcards for home drill with their parents.

This flashcard drill continues through the 123 phonemics of the course. To ensure transfer, the program provides what are called "Transfer Word Lists" that illustrate the wide usage of each of the 123 phonemes. Each list is identified by the same number as the letter or blend on the 15 phonics charts. The "Transfer Lists" are provided for the teacher in the Teacher's Guide. The list for the short "u" sound (as in "umbrella," for example) is: up, nut, must, just, shut, ugly, upset, club, skunk, truck. The teacher is directed to copy this list onto the chalkboard for whole-class practice. The process of "analyzing" each word in the list requires that the child respond as follows: Let us suppose that the word is "cash", one of the words in list #1. In analyzing the word, the class is supposed to respond that the word "cash" contains "a, apple", "c, cake", and "sh, shoe". Since the "a, apple" sound is the sound which is being "transferred" in Transfer List #1, the "a, apple" sound is selected as the first response to each word in the list.

The Teacher's Guide states that "You will find your children participating eagerly." It goes on to explain that they (the class responding in unison) will have a feeling of achievement. In some cases the class will have been divided into reading groups, and instruction will be at the smaller group level rather than whole-class directed.

Record #2 and the charts which accompany it introduce the vowel sounds and consonants. Chart #3 shows the entire alphabet with the vowels circled. As the record is played, the teacher points to the circled vowels on the chart and the children respond in unison with the sounds of either the long vowels or the short vowels as the recording presents them. At the end of that segment of learning, it is suggested that the class recite in unison the short and long vowels, then the entire alphabet, and then the alphabet, using letter sounds. Chart #4 and Band #3, Side 1 of the second record provide an interesting diversion called the "Scrambled Vowel Game."

A "Vowel Sound Dictionary" (long and short sounds) is presented through Charts 5 and 6 and the second side of record #2. Also on the same recording are vowel rules and consonant rules to accompany and direct work with Charts 7 and 8.

Charts #9 through #14 present a total of 90 so-called "blends", ranging from such digraphs as "er", "ir", "ur", "ee", "ew", "ank", "chr", "ould", "gh" (with the "f" sound), "squ", only to mention a few.

The Bremner-Davis method ends with Chart #15 and directions from Record #4 on a method of "unlocking words". The word selected as an illustration is "astronaut". To unlock the word, the class must learn some principles of syllabication. They are taught (1) that each syllable has only one sound in it; (2) that we usually separate syllables between consonants; (3) that we usually separate syllables between double consonants; (4) that, in words which end in "le", the letter "l" substitutes for a vowel sound; and (5) that *ble, cle, dle, fle, gle, kle, ple, sle, tle,* and *zle* are always final syllables and are pronounced with the "l" sound substituting for a vowel sound.

After practice in syllabication, the class is supposed to be ready to "unlock" the word "astronaut". The vowels are first identified. The first syllable is sounded out by the response: "a, apple; s, sun". The second syllable is "tr, train; o, overcoat". The third syllable is "n, nut; au, saucer; t, top". Assuming that the learners have adequate visual and auditory memory, it is assumed that the child and/or class can put the sounds together and produce the word "astronaut".

Recently, Bremner-Davis has started to market a fifteen piece transparency kit for use with overhead projectors. The transparencies are reproductions of the 15 wall charts and are to be used instead of them.

Research Findings

Inasmuch as the Bremner-Davis method and materials were originally designed for home use as a tutorial aid, very little classroom-oriented research has been done on the system. The one research study[16] known to this author was done in the Chicago Public and Parochial schools during the 1956 schoolyear.

The study was done in the Third and Fourth grades and involved 214 children from low socio-economic and culturally-disadvantaged homes. Pre-tests and post-tests were given. Children in the experimental groups

---

16. Luser, Carolyn; Stanton, Eileen; and Doyle, Charles I., "Effect of an Audio-visual Phonics Aid in the Intermediate Grades," *Journal of Educational Psychology*, 49:1 (September, 1958) 28–30.

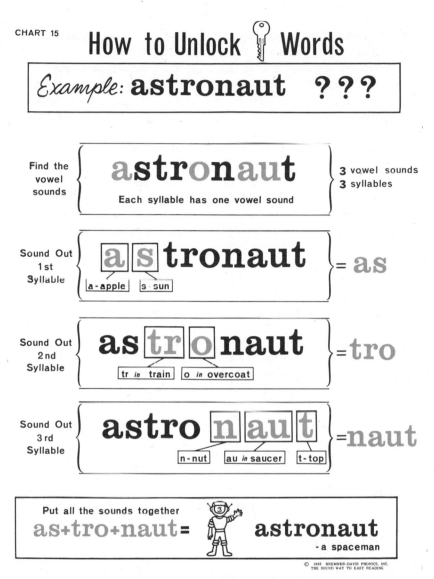

Fig. 2–9   Chart 15 reproduced by permission of Bremner Davis Phonics, Inc.

were given three phonics-drill sessions with Bremner-Davis home kits for a total of fifteen weeks. The drill sessions were twenty minutes in duration.

At the end of the fifteen-week period, gains in oral reading ability, paragraph meaning and spelling were significantly higher for the experimental group over the control group. It is interesting to note that, during the fifteen weeks, a group intelligence test also registered significant gains in intelligence. This, probably, is due to gains in ability to handle vocabulary and other components of a word-oriented intelligence test.

In conclusion, it should be stated that the Bremner-Davis "Sound Way to Easy Reading" is a purely phonemic approach to sounding out parts of words. It is in itself not a complete reading system. It was designed for home help and originally consisted of do-it-yourself recordings and flashcards for small children. More recently it has been revised to provide whole-class instruction in 123 phonemes.

The value of the method and materials appears to lie in the fact that *any* teacher can use them to provide structured phonemic drill, even though she may have had no previous training in that aspect of learning. The directions are simple and easy to follow. The whole-class response is structured so that all may participate regardless of individual differences.

The method, structured as it is, and the materials may be useful for untrained teachers and parents. However, they do contain features that would annoy reading specialists. For example, the "listen-look-repeat" routine is not only antiquated but violates a principle of learning by presenting sounds in isolation instead of in context. The "unlocking" of words is a devious method of synthetic phonics. The use of homemade flashcards is not justified in today's school. The system confuses phonemes, blends, and several other linguistic elements. Finally, the system requires that the sound being studied must be pronounced *first*, even though it may not be the initial phoneme in the word.

FUNCTIONAL PHONETICS

Origins

Functional Phonetics is the name given to a series of books by Dr. Anna D. Cordts, Professor of Education for thirty years at Rutgers University.

The program is one of the older, yet still used, programs of basic phonemics as an approach to beginning reading. Dr. Cordts, once a rural school teacher and a grade school teacher in Iowa, is well-known for her work in teacher education, and for her writings[17] in speech and

---

17. Cordts, Anna D., *Phonics for the Reading Teacher*. New York: Holt, Rinehart and Winston, Inc., 1965.
——— "The Phonetics of Phonics," *Reading Teacher*, 9 (Dec. 1955), 81–84.

language arts. Her chief interest has been in the field of phonemics as an approach to beginning reading.

The original books were published in hardback editions in 1953 under the titles *I Can Read, Hear Me Read,* and *Reading's Easy.* A paperback teacher's manual, *Readiness for Power in Reading,* was also published in 1953 and still is the manual which describes a readiness program which leads into reading.

Materials and Method

The present edition of *Functional Phonetics* includes the readiness manual for teachers and a *Phonics Readiness Book.* In place of the original hardbacks are three workbooks now appearing under the titles: *Phonics Book I* (the former *I Can Read,* revised); *Phonics Book II* (the former *Hear Me Read,* revised); and *Phonics Book III* (the former *Reading's Easy,* revised).

Readiness for Power in Reading, the paperback teacher's manual provides the method for the readiness phase of *Functional Phonetics.* Dr. Cordts explains that "These readiness exercises serve a double purpose. They prepare pupils for power in reading and offer opportunities for speech improvement." "Faulty speech habits are corrected," she claims, "as the background for independent reading is established."

The basic format of the readiness activities is: blending parts of words into whole words; learning what is meant by the beginning of a word; matching beginnings of words; matching endings of words, and learning to differentiate the sounds of the beginnings of words spoken orally.

The "beginning" of words means not just the initial consonant but a combination of letters constituting what the author considers the part which the child of six can hear best. The consonant is pronounced with the vowel. As examples, the book suggests that *"hop* begins with *ho* and ends with *p; hack* begins with *ba* and ends with *ck; spot* begins with *spo* and ends with *t; . . .* and *scratch* begins with *scra* and ends with *tch . . ."* It is explained that "the vowel is included in the beginning of a syllable because it is pronounced with the beginning consonant, and not with the ending consonant."

The first work in the readiness book gives directions for "experiences in blending." Each of the words given is to be pronounced in two parts; some with a single consonant ending and some with a consonant digraph. Directions are given for tongue and breath control so that the teacher does not manufacture grossly exaggerated or incorrect sounds.

Much of the readiness work is done in the form of listening-and-repeating types of "games".

After the class has had work in blending the beginnings and endings of words, they try to identify the beginnings of words by themselves, and attempt to say what they think is the entire beginning of words which the teacher hints at and gives clues to in an "I am thinking about. . . ." type of game. For example, "I am thinking about something on the wall of this classroom that begins with *clo*. . . ." The game is played with the names of animals, parts of the body, things to wear, things to eat, things to do, and countless other categories.

In addition to responding orally to the teacher, the children take turns going to the chalkboard and circling the "beginnings" of words in lists that the teacher has printed on the chalkboard. The whole class watches while one child performs.

The next step in the readiness program of *Functional Phonetics* is practice in matching the beginnings of words that sound alike. This is done by "framing" the beginnings by cupping the hands or by using two pointers. In this exercise, two children can operate as pairs. The manual suggests a number of lists of words for the teacher to place on the chalkboard.

The same routines are suggested in the last half of the readiness book for the matching of the "endings" of words.

A somewhat more sophisticated level is reached at the end of the readiness period when the class is given practice in recognizing the beginnings and endings when the whole words are pronounced by the teacher without stress on syllabication.

It was predicted by Dr. Cordts that First Grade children of average ability would be able to complete the readiness work in "listening" to beginning and ending sounds in words by the middle of the First Grade. When this has been accomplished, the class is then "ready" to go into the formal phonemic workbooks in the *Functional Phonetics* program.

Phonics Book I is designed for First Grade. It provides 36 lessons in "framing" beginnings and endings of words, all of which are words containing short vowel sounds tied to the initial consonant or consonant-digraph, with only two exceptions: *sheep* and *chief*. Keywords are used as "cues", and little "stick-men" are used to indicate the parts of the word to be "framed." There is a minimum of "reading" as such in the first book. Most of the work is with words in isolation. In addition to the 36 "cue" words, the book ends with a list of 85 "sight" words which the author assumes the children will have learned by the end of Grade One.

Fig. 2–10 *Reproduced from* Functional Phonetics *by permission of Benefic Press, Westchester, Illinois.*

Phonics Book II is a continuation of the practice routines established in the readiness period and in Book I. It continues the work with "cues" from number 37 on to 63. A review of the short vowel sounds is followed with work on double vowels, final-*e* and a number of beginning consonant digraphs (followed by vowels): *th, st, cl, pl, sl, bl, fl, sp, cr, dr, tr, gr, br, fr,* and *sw*. In each case, the "cues" are to be found in the keywords.

An increased amount of reading material is included in Book II, even though it is to be used in conjunction with the Readers of the basal series.

Book III completes the *Functional Phonetics* materials and provides the child with practice in the irregular phonemic elements which are most common elements of the language.

It is anticipated that the three workbooks of the series will be used over the first three grades, or will be covered in faster time by better-than-average classes. To this extent, the program is flexible. In fact, it

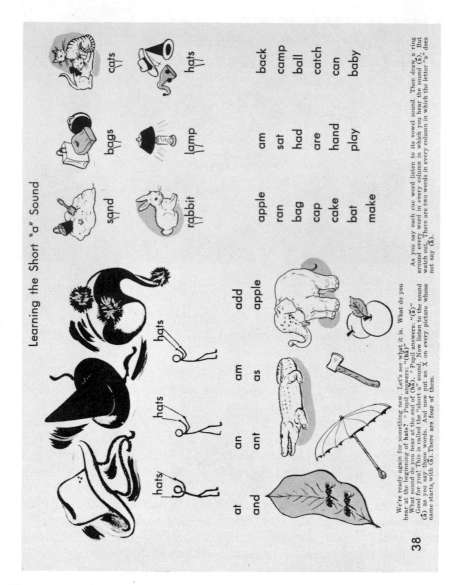

Fig. 2–11   *Reproduced from* Functional Phonetics *by permission of Benefic Press, Westchester, Illinois.*

is suggested that at each level, the class be divided into groups with which the teacher works, according to the ability of the group.

All through the program, there is some writing done by the children, but not as much is provided in *Functional Phonetics* as in some of the more recent phonemic approaches to beginning reading.

Research Findings

Although *Functional Phonetics* has been on the market for fifteen years, little or no definitive research has been carried out on it. This may be due to the fact that the books have sold so well and acceptance has been so widespread in hundreds of schools when the program first was introduced that the author and publishers have relied upon empirical evidence that the program is good.

Consequently, as long as Benefic Press continues to be satisfied with the sales which they total up yearly for the Cordts' program, that seems to be the only proof they need to assure them that *Functional Phonetics* is doing a notable job as an approach to beginning reading.

It seems presumptuous to evaluate a program that represents the accumulated know-how of a lifetime of work with children in the primary grades. Dr. Anna D. Cordts has for years held an enviable place in the field of the phonemic approach to beginning reading. It has stood the test of time.

It may be, of course, that some of the new "slants" in reading will attract the attention of the newer generation of teachers and they will be more interested in recordings, programming, linguistics, and visual tracking to the extent that *Functional Phonetics* will soon be labeled "tiresome" and "old-fashioned."

One thing is certain, however, and it is that, after the new gimmicks and gadgets have had their day, we will still need a system of teaching phonemic elements and will still find some of the solid work of Anna Cordts adaptable to whatever new look is then in vogue.

THE LANDON PHONICS PROGRAM

Origins

The *Landon Phonics Program* is a relatively new addition to the numerous phonemic approaches to beginning reading, yet it has at least two features that distinguish it from many of the others.

The program was developed by Mrs. Alline Landon, while she was acting as a supervisor in language arts in the Fremont, California public schools. Mrs. Landon originally developed the program to help teachers who were having trouble teaching phonemic elements. Dr. Larry Carrillo of San Francisco State College edited the program as the consulting editor in Language Arts for the Chandler Publishing Company.

Mrs. Landon states:

> This program developed gradually, first in my mind, and then in actuality as I worked, trying it out with groups of school children—using taped lessons I recorded myself and worksheets patched together from old workbooks and my own drawings and then mimeographed.
>
> I wanted to build a logical and sequential program combining both auditory and visual training, one that would involve children in listening, looking, thinking, and writing. I felt it should be a program that, despite the 'drill' inherent in the teaching of phonics, would be enjoyable as well as meaningful to beginning readers.[18]

Thus, like many good teachers, Mrs. Landon set about to develop materials and a method which would improve her own teaching and soon found that others had the same needs.

Materials and Method

The *Landon Phonics Program* is contained in a kit of materials packaged in a box for total classroom use. The box houses sets of worksheets presenting the most common sounds of English. The basic kit provides 3,800 worksheets, consisting of 50 copies each of 76 different sheets. They are organized, of course, by dividers in the kit.

Initial consonants are presented through 21 worksheets, and final consonants by 9 different worksheets. There are 16 sheets for initial consonant blends, and 10 worksheets for consonant digraphs.

The long and short vowels are presented through 12 worksheets and digraphs such as *ee, ea, ai,* and *oa,* and the *oi, oy, ou,* and *ow* diphthongs are shown on 8 more worksheets.

The initial consonant worksheets provide only picture clues, but the subsequent worksheets provide keywords as well as picture clues.

Instructions for guiding the students through the worksheets are

---

18. Landon, Alline, *Landon Phonics Program—Teacher's Manual.* San Francisco: Chandler Publishing Co., 1967, preface, p. 3.

provided on 20 twelve-inch 33⅓ rpm recordings. The instructions for two worksheets are contained on each side of the record. The duration for the instructions for one worksheet averages about ten minutes. They are also available on tape.

A well-written teacher's manual provides the philosophy of the program, the objectives, the basic procedure, and many suggestions for variations and follow-up.

Each lesson is designed to provide six elements of beginning reading instruction:

1. a meaningful presentation of sounds of letters and letter combinations;
2. standard American English pronunciation (the recordings were done by Professor Joseph A. Milsak of San Francisco State College);
3. practice in association of grapheme-phoneme relationships;
4. auditory and visual discrimination of likenesses and differences;
5. left-to-right progression;
6. individualized learning, as well as the versatility that permits the same materials to be used with small groups or with an entire class.

The program may be given to one child, to a small group of children, or to an entire class. The method is for each child to have a crayon or pencil and the worksheet which is correlated with the recording. The worksheets are consumable and are replaceable at a nominal cost. They are, in fact, the only cost of maintaining the program once the original kit has been purchased.

When the children are ready, the record or tape is started. It may be run through earphones plugged into a distributor center, or the children may listen to the recording without the aid of earphones. The earphone set-up and the phonograph or tape recorder are not part of the kit. It is expected that they will be part of the normal equipment of modern classrooms.

The students each have a worksheet and a crayon for marking. The narrator directs the children to note the first line of pictures and the first picture in that line. When studying the worksheet for the initial consonant *m*, for example, the narrator indicates that the first picture is "money". He periodically refers to the beginning sound of the words as "the sound of the letter *m*". He never refers to it as the "mmmm" sound.

Subsequent worksheets and recordings provide directed practice on the following initial consonants: b, s, f, c (k-sound), h, l, p, n, d, t, hard-g, r, k, soft-c, w, j, g (j-sound), v, z, and y.

Mm

Initial m

Fig. 2–12 Reproduced from the Landon Phonics Program *by permission of Chandler Publishing Co.*

Fig. 2–13 Reproduced from the Landon Phonics Program by permission of Chandler Publishing Co.

The narrator directs the children to listen carefully and to try to differentiate sounds when they are not the same. The child then uses his crayon to mark out the picture in which the beginning sound is different from that being studied.

The children do not receive direct practice in writing the graphemes in the *Landon Phonics Program.* Essentially, the program is a listening and auditory discrimination program, linked to a number of keywords and hundreds of black ink drawings of objects in the environment. The main feature of the program is that it provides the child with a standard American English model of pronunciation on a recording. The recording also instructs the child to repeat the words during the pauses on the record.

An additional advantage claimed for the *Landon Phonics Program* is its time-saving factor. Once a group of children are plugged into the recording, the teacher may be able to move on to other groups, assuming, of course, that the children will be able to operate on their own as the recording directs. The directions on the recording are direct, simple, easy to follow, and slow enough for all but the very slowest children. In fact, they may be too slow for the brighter children who will be impatient to move ahead. There are places in the recordings, too, where children should be cautioned *not* to mark anything *until* they hear the complete directions. Such a caution must be repeated daily by the teacher as each new group is started on the program for the day. It might be noted that one of the fringe benefits of the Landon program is that it teaches children to listen to directions.

Another advantage of the program is that it permits the teacher to repeat a phonemic lesson as many times as necessary with no additional effort or class time. Children who have been absent may "catch up" with an additional ten-minute recorded lesson while others are doing some other whole-class activity.

Inasmuch as the program is available on recordings that are correlated with worksheets, the *Landon Phonics Program* is flexible enough to be used with any basal reading series. Indeed, the Landon program is not designed to be a complete approach in itself, but a supplement to the total reading program.

Research Findings

There has been no attempt to undertake a systematic research on the *Landon Phonics Program* as an approach to beginning reading. In fact, it would be difficult to delineate the objectives of such a research or its design, for the Landon program is specifically organized as a supplement and not a complete program.

A number of teachers who used the program experimentally in California have indicated its value through testimonials. They include Kindergarten, First-Grade, Multi-Grade, and Remedial teachers.

At this writing, it appears that the best evaluation of the success of the *Landon Phonics Program* is for the interested individual to try it in actual classroom work. It is probable that it would be a most beneficial program where the teacher and/or the children need a structured and standard American English phonemics program.

TIME FOR PHONICS

Origins

Time for Phonics is a four-book series of 11″ × 8½″ paperbacks written by Dr. Louise Binder Scott, presently Associate Professor of Speech Education at Los Angeles State College.

The series, developed both from Professor Scott's[19] knowledge of phonemic elements of our language and from language materials she had previously written and which had been successfully used, supplied an answer to the urgent needs expressed by numerous participants in graduate workshops and classes which she conducted. Indeed, teams of assistants and classroom teachers contributed many of the word lists which are used in the series.

Words were selected from the pre-primers, primers, and other primary readers of twelve basal series. Added to those were sensory words of Professor Scott's own choosing. Other phonemically-regular words which could be "sounded" by means of a simple phonemic generalization were added where needed. Those structured words were included to strengthen the pupil's ability to attack more challenging words. Sensory words were added to provide style and flavor to the content.

A large team of assistants, supervisors, and classroom teachers worked over a period of several years in selecting "key words". Moreover, as experimentation with the materials under actual classroom conditions produced information on pupil and teacher reaction, the keywords were analyzed and frequently changed so that they would contain vowel

---

19. Scott, Louise Binder, and Thompson, J. J., *Phonics*. Manchester, Missouri: Webster Publishing Co., 1962.

phonemes usually presented first to young children (long and short vowels) and would lend themselves to development of interesting story and poetry content.

Materials and Method

Book R of the *Time for Phonics* series is the "readiness" book, and is intended for use with Kindergarten and First Grade children. It introduces a child to first experiences with writing in a creative way through the mnemonic device of a picture representing the initial vowel and consonant letter sounds. The keywords are one of the essential features of the entire series.

Book A is the First Grade book of the series (and could be used for lower Second Grade). It is arranged in 30 lessons—each dealing with a special phonemic element of our language—and each utilizing approximately two days of teaching time and two pages of the workbook. This means that the First Grade program could be completed in twenty weeks. With slower children, it might be continued throughout the entire year. Teachers are urged to time the work with ample consideration for the total language aspects of the program and to proceed slowly without pressure.

Time for Phonics is conceived as a strong balanced program which will be used to complement any basal series or any language program leading to beginning reading. Book A deals with basic phonemes essentially through listening and pronouncing, reinforced by visualizing and writing letter-forms, thus amalgamating all four communication skills at the onset of teaching them.

The following types of activities are part of the daily skills work in First Grade: tracing capital and lower-case letters; broken-letter forms; writing letters independently without the aid of the broken letter forms; naming and recognizing keywords; underlining pictures whose names begin with a given letter sound; matching pictures with other pictures; matching pictures with letters according to beginning sounds; and finding words that begin with the specific beginning sound being studied on a particular day.

Initially, a teacher reads aloud a rhyme that contains the keyword repetitively used as an introduction to the page. She encourages the group to read it with her, thus engaging the child's oral participation. Oral reading on the part of the child is encouraged so that he can get feed-back of what he is perceiving and doing.

Starting on page 44, there are a number of stories with simple sentence structure, again using the keyword and other words beginning

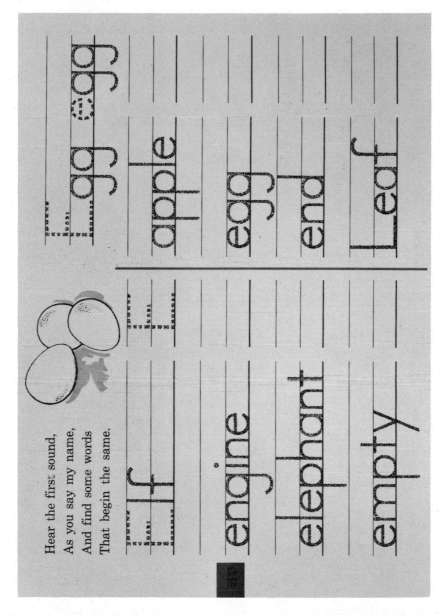

Hear the first sound,
As you say my name,
And find some words
That begin the same.

Egg gg gg

apple

engine

egg

elephant

end

empty

Leaf

Elf

Fig. 2–14 *Reprinted by permission of the publisher from* Time for Phonics, Book A, *by Louise Binder Scott, Copyright © 1962 by McGraw-Hill, Inc.*

like it. Because the child has been highly motivated with the "Soundie Stories" and visual-writing-conversation experiences, he will desire to read the content of the page even though he may not actually be able to do so at this point.

The keywords are presented at the top of the page for each new lesson, together with the key pictures. In traditional order, the consonants are presented first, followed by the short vowels, and then six consonant digraphs (*sh, ch, wh, th*—voiceless and voiced—and *ng*). Finally, four suffixes (*s, d, ed,* and *ing*) are taught.

The author states that, "Thus the child's attention is extended beyond the initial consonant and vowel sound of a word, and he consciously and thoughtfully visualizes and pronounces the whole word." It is interesting to note that final *d* is emphasized before *ed*; final *s* as in "bus", before plural *ss*; and *ng* before *ing*, to aid in visual and auditory discrimination.

Before each letter-form and phoneme is introduced to the class in their books, the teacher reads one of the 29 "Soundie" stories provided in the *Teacher's Edition*. "Soundie" is an elf who places the sounds he collects into his little leather treasure bag. Each "Soundie" story is pitched to the imagination of five- and six-year-olds, and is structured so that the children actively participate in producing the sounds several times as the story progresses.

A few examples may help the reader to visualize the method: In the first story, "Soundie" explores (a natural tendency of the young child) and hears the wind singing and subsequently "collects" the "singing-wind" sound for his bag. The teacher is instructed to "Place the tongue tip high, touching the ridge behind the upper teeth, so that the children see the placement as she produces the sound".

The children are then asked to make the "lll" sound several times. The teacher is careful not to "analyze" the production of the sound but to "have fun" with it.

Similarly, when "Soundie" finds a baby fieldmouse, he imagines that it says "i" (short i). Many children whose perception has been dulled now begin to experiment with sounds for themselves as they follow "Soundie's" adventures. Experimentation with sounds is a keynote in growth and development in early childhood.

As the program progresses, each "Soundie" story incorporates some of the previously-learned sounds which the children repeat and, thus, retain and reinforce previous learnings. More important, perhaps, is the practice such repetition gives them in auditory and kinesthetic comparison of similarities and contrasts of sounds within words.

The heavy emphasis on sound reflects Professor Scott's specialization in phonemics and speech. She states: "Now the child is ready to visualize the symbol which stands for the new letter-sound that he has learned to recognize aurally and produce vocally." Listening, therefore, is the first step in *Time for Phonics*.

A detailed sequence of steps are delineated for presenting the letter forms. First the teacher writes (prints) the capital and small letters on the chalkboard. The children trace the letter form in the air with the teacher as leader. They say the rhyme that describes their pantomimic movements. They then go to the chalkboard and trace the many letter forms that the teacher has printed along the lower portion of the chalkboard. This large-muscle, kinesthetic and tactile practice is, of course, not new, but is much in vogue at present with the sudden increased emphasis on directionality, patterning, gestalts, and dyslexia. Professor Scott believes that, inasmuch as some children are aided by one or another of the sensory stimulators, all sensory avenues should be brought into play. Following this whole-class practice, each child copies the letter-form many times on lined newsprint or primary paper with widely spaced lines. The pages of *Book A* provide guidelines for correct letter-forms.

The *Teacher's Edition of Book A* of the *Time for Phonics* series is, actually, a complete, stereotyped teacher's manual. In traditional manner, it includes every bit of the teacher's "patter": the questions to ask; the responses to expect; the words to write; where to write them; directions to children; motions to make; and everything else that a "new" teacher might need in carrying out the *Time for Phonics* program.

Unfortunately *Time for Phonics* is partially a misnomer, for the program and approach to beginning reading utilizes more than the usual phonemic approach. Indeed, phonemics is only one of the several devices used in helping the child toward achieving word recognition and word independence. Listening, sounding, speaking, and writing are all part of the multi-sensory factors involved in this approach to beginning reading.

Research Findings

As with most phonemic systems which are designed for use with basal readers, *Time for Phonics* has not been "researched" independently of the effect it has had on reading.

The teacher who has been "brought up" with the basal series' teacher's manual in one hand should be delighted with the *Teacher's Edition* of *Time for Phonics*. It provides complete and detailed instructions for assuring the success of the method. Many teachers need the security of such a manual, and fear the teaching of "phonics" because they feel insecure in this area. Louise Binder Scott's work, then, is a blessing to them. They can teach "phonics" without fear if they will follow the manual.

I like the "Soundie" stories. They are childlike enough, and are motivational, yet they involve each child in active identification and response, rather than just "listening". They utilize several basic principles of learning, making them effective motivators in an otherwise abstract and uninteresting phase of learning to read. With the "Soundie" stories at the beginning of each new lesson in a phonemic element, the chore of learning letter-forms and letter sounds is turned into fun rather than a dead period of rote memorization.

PHONICS WE USE

Origins

For almost one-fourth of a century, *Phonics We Use* has been one of the most widely used workbook programs for phonemic practice. Lyons & Carnahan, originally of Wilkes-Barre, Pennsylvania (now Chicago) publish the series with an original copyright of 1946 and a 1966 revision.

The original materials were done by Mary Meighen, then of Seattle, Marjorie Pratt, who was director of Elementary Education in Spokane for fifteen years, and by Mabel Halvorsen, who was a primary teacher in Shorewood, Wisconsin, where Miss Pratt formerly served as curriculum director. The materials were assembled in the 1940's from the classroom experiences of these teachers.

The materials have remained much the same through several revisions. The 1966 revision was sufficient to warrant an independent copyright.

Materials and Method

Although there are now seven workbooks in the *Phonics We Use* series, only Book A and Book B are related to beginning reading. Book A is designed to be used with readiness, pre-primer, and primer materials of any basal series. Book B correlates with First Grade materials. All of the work in *Phonics We Use* is intended as supplementary, and provides ample practice materials for phonemic learning.

Typical workbook methods are used: "Place an X in the box on the picture whose name has the same beginning sound as the name of the

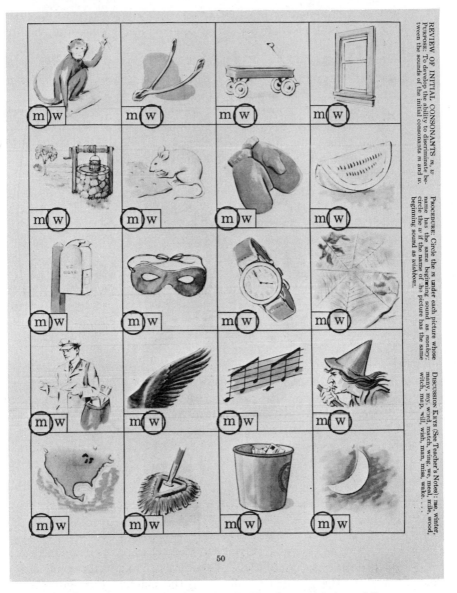

Fig. 2–15 *Reproduced from* Phonics We Use *by permission of Lyons and Carnahan, Educational Division, Meredith Corporation,*

key picture," etc. In this manner, auditory perception exercises are used to direct attention to beginning sounds and to ending sounds. Similarly, rhyming sounds are identified.

Visual discrimination practice starts with objects that are alike, geometric configurations that are alike, alphabetical letters, and, finally, words that are alike.

Auditory and visual discrimination skills are then combined in practice recognizing initial consonants *f*, *t*, hard *c*, *b*, *h*, *m*, *w*, *s*, hard *g*, *d*, *n*, *l*, *r*, and *p* in that order.

Book B in the 1966 copyright is almost entirely new. It contains much practice material related to word recognition skills. Practice in substitution of initial consonants, blends, and digraphs is specially good. Similarly, the new material for helping the child recognize final consonants calls for the application of thinking skills rather than rote memorization.

The new 1966 edition of *Phonics We Use* comes dressed in attractive rainbow-colored slick covers. Like its predecessors, it is a relatively inexpensive phonemics program.

In 1968 Lyons & Carnahan augmented their *Phonics We Use* program with the addition of a "Learning Games Kit." It consists of ten board games to be played with a spinner. It appears to be one of the good phonemics games, with considerable motivation inherent in its colorful format.

Research Findings

There are no specific research studies *per se* on *Phonics We Use*. It should be noted, however, that some of the First Grade Studies indicated results favoring the use of supplementary phonemic practice of the sort provided in the Lyons & Carnahan workbooks. There is no doubt that teachers find the materials useful, for the *Phonics We Use* has continued to maintain a position of leadership in phonemics workbook sales for more than two decades.

OTHER PHONEMIC SYSTEMS

Space does not permit a complete description of the genesis and nature of all of the phonemic systems on the market. Furthermore, the many elements already described are common to most phonemic systems. Mere reference to them and annotation should prove useful and sufficient.

Phonics Is Fun is a workbook program originated in 1963 by Louis Krane, and published by Modern Curriculum Press of Berea, Ohio. The system consists of two 160-page pupil workbooks with teachers' manuals accompanying them. In addition, three pre-primers have been completed and it is planned that a complete series of small readers will accompany the entire First-Grade program.

The first pre-primer is A *Big, Big Man*, introducing the short *a, i, u* sounds. *In the Tent* is the second pre-primer, introducing the short *o* and *e* sounds. Long vowel sounds are introduced in A *Mule on a Kite*. These new pre-primers claim to be linguistically controlled.

The workbook program centers around the short-vowel rule, the long-vowel rule, the y-at-the-beginning-of-a-word rule, and the final-y rule. In addition, the program provides the teacher and the child with suggestions that several other "rules" should be learned: w as a consonant; w as a vowel; soft-c; and soft-g.

The workbooks provide practice with capital letter and lower-case letter recognition, letter matching and discrimination of letters found in words, initial and final consonant sounds, to be matched with pictures, v-c-v (vowel-consonant-vowel) words, blends, digraphs, murmuring diphthongs (see *Breaking the Sound Barrier* discussed in Chapter 3), prefixes, suffixes, double vowels, and diphthongs.

The publishers also market alphabet cards, flash cards, picture cards, and charts to accompany the workbook program.

Modern Curriculum Press also publishes another phonemics workbook program under the title, *Phonics Workbook*, with authors listed as Elwell, Murray, and Kucia. It is advertised as "A Modern Linguistic Approach to Reading," but a close inspection of the sequence of lessons in the three workbooks fails to reveal any elements that would warrant classifying the program as a linguistics-phonemics approach. In fact, the irregularities which are a part of the program from its very beginning violate the very essence of a linguistics approach, namely, that all differences in phonemic sequences be kept at a minimum. The *Phonics Workbook* series is designed for Grade One, Grade Two, and Grade Three.

The Modern Curriculum Press is a subsidiary of the Cleveland publishing house; Reardon, Baer and Co. which has specialized in publishing materials for Catholic parochial schools. Reardon, Baer and Co. also produces phonemics workbook materials with the titles *First Fun in Phonics, More Fun in Phonics,* and *Phonics Worksheets.* They are to accompany the *Christian Child Reading Series.* Extensive lesson plans are provided in the spiral-bound manuals which accompany the phonemic program designed for the first two grades in parochial schools.

American Education Publications, publishers of the widely-used *My Weekly Reader,* has a set of three phonemics practice workbooks for each of three "programs". "Program 1" is designed for Grade One; "Program 2" is designed for "second grade level"; and "Program 3" is for "third grade level". The nine booklets in the program all carry the title *Phonics and Word Power.* Like the *My Weekly Reader,* they are printed in two colors on newsprint stock.

The program provides practice in initial consonants, rhyming, vowels, word building, and an array of various activities of a workbook type, but involves considerable reading skill from the very beginning. For that reason the practice books may be considered as supplementary, rather than as a basic phonemics program that would precede reading.

The authors of the program are listed as Eleanor M. Johnson, Carleton M. Singleton, and Elaine Wonsavage. The copyright is 1964.

McCormick-Mathers Publishing Co. of Wichita, Kansas, has had its *Building Reading Skills* phonemics workbooks on the market for almost a score of years. The authors were Rowena Hargrave and Leila Armstrong. The six workbooks are 96 pages each. Their titles are: *Speedboat Book, Streamliner Book, Jet Plane Book, Rocket Book, Atomic Submarine Book,* and *Space Ship Book.*

Bound into the center of each of the first three workbooks are "Phonics Skill Builders" cards printed on heavy oaktag. The workbooks provide practice in the usual exercises of filling in letters, identifying pictures of things that begin with the same consonant sounds, rhyming, filling in words which are selected from a list.

One element in which this program is strong is the extensive practice provided in visual discrimination of look-alike words such as made-make, lift-left, trial-trail, sacred-scared, etc.

Like most phonemics workbook programs, the McCormick-Mathers workbooks are designed to be consumable items.

Mrs. June Lyday Orton has formalized the phonemic approach to beginning reading developed by her late husband, Dr. Samuel T. Orton (see Chapter 10). The 100-page plastic-bound teacher's manual is titled *A Guide to Teaching Phonics.* It contains directions through 24 lessons, describing the Orton method.

Several quotes from the manual will indicate the nature of the program:

> It is a *direct* approach to the study of phonics, presenting the sounds of the phonograms orally as separate units and teaching the process of blending them into syllables and words for recognition in reading and recall in reading.
>
> It is an integrated, total language approach. Each unit and sequence is established through hearing, speaking, seeing and writing it. Auditory, visual, and kinesthetic patterns reinforce each other, and this also provides for individual differences among the students. It is a circular, multi-sensory process.
>
> It is a systematic, step-by-step approach, proceeding from

the simple to the more complex in orderly progression in an upward spiral of language development.

The program starts with children hearing the teacher produce
sounds in isolation and seeing the symbols written on the chalkboard.
After several consonants and a short-vowel sound have been learned,
words are built, using the grapheme cards. As the teacher points to each
letter and slowly blends the sounds together, the children hear the blending and then repeat the process, slowly at first and then more rapidly.

The Orton program is set up in sequential steps:

1. short a; b; s; f; m; t.
2. h; j; n; p; l.
3. r; hard-g; d; prefix ab- .
4. short-i and doubles, short-o; short-u; short-e.
5. prefixes
6. digraphs, consonant blends
7. long vowels and regular "long-vowel teams" such as *oa, ow, ou, ui*
8. irregular "long-vowel teams"
9. vowels plus r, diphthongs
10. word structure.

The reader may be interested in comparing the method described
by Mrs. Orton with the Spalding Method described in the *Writing Road
to Reading* and discussed in Chapter 6.

One quite recent addition to the many phonemics materials is the
series of little booklets by Mrs. Esther Broudy Levy entitled *Phonics in
Rhyme.* The series is designed to keep sight words to a minimum of six:
I, is, on, the, to.

Each booklet introduces one new phonemic element, for example,
one is the "short-o" booklet, another is the "short-a" booklet, one is the
"ai—ay" booklet, and one is the "magic-e" booklet, etc.

Teaching Technology Corporation of North Hollywood, California
is the publisher.

Another recent addition to the many phonemic workbooks on the
market is the series known as "i-Med", and written by Dr. Selma E. Herr.
The name "i-Med" is derived from the full name of the publisher:
Instructional Materials and Equipment Distributors. The booklets in the
series carry only the title: *Phonics.* To distinguish them from others, it
is probably appropriate that this system should be known as "The Selma
Herr Phonics Workbooks."

The Reading Readiness booklet of about 64 pages contains rows
of pictures and a key picture at the top of the page. The child is directed to place an "X" under the picture if its name begins with the

same sound as in the key picture. Also the child is sometimes asked to draw a line connecting pictures whose names begin with the same sound.

The usual type of phonemic workbook activities is found in the pages of Book 1, Book 2, Book 3, and Book 4. These booklets run in size from 100 pages up to 140 pages. Book 5 is for students in the upper grades who have failed to obtain an adequate foundation in phoneme-grapheme relationships and are, consequently, having difficulty with reading. Book 5 is the most recent addition to the series, with a 1964 copyright.

The *Bourn Sound Method* is a promising, but unpublished, phonemic approach developed by Mr. Kenneth Bourn, a teacher in the Joppa, Maryland, Public Schools. The essence of the method is the concentration on phonemes rather than on letter names, and the materials used are essentially a picture book of 65 mimeographed pages. The pages are arranged in pairs facing each other. One page is a felt-pen drawing of an object, and the facing page contains the upper and lower case letters in cursive writing and the keyword, also in cursive.

In addition to the 26 alphabet letters, the *Bourn Sound Method* provides practice through key pictures, keywords, and cursive writing for a few additional common sounds such as *ch* (church), *er* (perfume), *oo* (book), *oo* (broom), *ou* (ouch), *sh* (shoe), and *th* (theater).

The use of the *Bourn Sound Method* has been primarily as a remedial reading instrument. In 1966 and 1967 an experiment with the method was conducted in the Baltimore (Maryland) County schools. Two Eighth Grade classes and one Ninth Grade class were the experimental students and the control group consisted of students who had had only the usual sequential developmental reading techniques.

Performance in reading was tested by the *Gates Reading Survey*. Inasmuch as students in need of remedial help were the population of both control and experimental groups, only six months' growth in the school year was to be expected as average.

The statistics provided by the Director of Educational Research for the Baltimore County schools show an average growth of seven months for the students in the control group after an entire academic year of instruction in traditional developmental reading methods. The experimental groups showed considerable disparity, due partly to dropouts. The Seventh Grade class gained six months in three months instruction in the *Bourn Sound Method*. Although the Eighth Grade class made no gains at all during the three-month instructional period, at the end of the academic year they showed two years' growth.

It is possible that with refinement in method, more professional artwork, and commercial distribution by a publishing house, the *Bourn Sound Method* may become attractive as an approach to beginning reading. This is the claim and expectation of its enthusiastic originator.

Several companies who are concentrating on tape recorders and other electronic aids to learning are marketing what might be called "phonemic audio-visual flash cards." They are, essentially, cards approximately 4" × 8" on which have been printed an alphabet letter, a word, and/or a key picture. The added feature is a strip of audio tape across the bottom of the card. When the end of the card is placed in the specially-designed tape recorder, the card is drawn across the sensing head and the recorder reproduces a pronunciation of the phoneme or the word.

In some programs it is possible for the child to respond by placing his own pronunciation on a second track of the tape and then to re-run the card and hear both the "master" voice and his own for comparison.

One such approach being widely promoted is *Patterns in Phonics*, marketed by Electronic Futures, Incorporated of North Haven, Connecticut, and appearing as the *efi Patterns in Phonics* program.

The *efi* program was developed by Dr. Carlton M. Singleton and Dr. Sandra M. Brown, publishers of the national newsmagazine in reading, *The Reading Newsreport*. Together with a team of teachers, they developed a sequentially-programmed set of audio-visual flashcards which provide practice in alphabet letter names, phonemes, and blends of consonant-short vowel sounds.

The *efi Patterns in Phonics* program is typical of the several electronic audio-visual flashcard approaches on the market. A similar program, the Language Master, produced by Bell and Howell of Chicago, has been purchased widely by schools fortunate enough to have obtained federal monies, inasmuch as it was brought onto the market at about the same time as Title I money became available.

The Teaching Technology Corporation of North Hollywood, California, also produces magnetic phonics cards and an electronic card-reader.

All of the electronic card-reader programs are designed for individual use and, consequently, permit wide variations in the speed with which beginners complete the programs. It is estimated that the average beginning reader can complete the *efi Patterns in Phonics* program in sixty-two twenty-minute lessons.

Individually-paced phonemics programs are becoming more popular and eventually may replace the whole-class phonemics drill of former years.

Dr. Donald D. Durrell and Dr. Helen A. Murphy, authors of *Speech-to-Print Phonics* described earlier in this chapter, have devised a follow-up program of phonemics practice. It consists of 259 re-usable coated cards.

On each card there are picture clues and whole words. The child writes the words in the cutout "windows" and then checks the correctness of his response on the back of the card. Dr. Durrell enjoys referring to this as "self-directing, self-correcting learning" that is highly individualized.

Another unique self-correcting phonemics program has been devised with the title, *Write and See Phonics,* marketed by Appleton-Century-Crofts of New York. It is a set of three phonemics workbooks. The child uses a special pen which activates the invisible ink which is used in printing part of the material in the workbooks. As the child writes his answer, he immediately sees whether he is correct or wrong. If correct, a bold striped line appears in the answer box. If he is wrong, a solid gray line appears.

A recently-devised set of materials which is being intensively promoted is the *Sullivan Decoding Kit,* published by Behavioral Research Laboratories of Palo Alto, the same organization that promotes the programmed materials also originated by Dr. M. W. Sullivan. The kit contains 22 flash cards, 26 teacher letter cards, almost 800 student letter cards, an alphabet chart and a teacher's manual. In addition, the first four books of Sullivan's Reading Readiness materials are included. It is claimed that the kit of phonemics drill materials is directly correlated with the Sullivan Reading Readiness booklets.

The vocabulary cards in the *Decoding Kit* are carefully done, with remarkably fine illustrations of the objects which the nouns represent. On one side of the card is the illustration, and on the reverse side is the printed word.

The *Sullivan Decoding Kit* provides practice and drill in what reading specialists commonly refer to as "phonetic word analysis," which, of course, is one phase of beginning reading instruction.

The *Sight and Sound Phonics Program,* introduced in 1968 by Weber, Costello Company of Chicago, is a collection of recordings and classroom charts. Three 10″ recordings provide phonemic practice, interspersed with music. Six illustrated charts provide vowels (short and long in parallel columns), digraphs, diphthongs, consonants, and consonant blends. The charts are to be used for classroom whole-class drill.

Another new and even more elaborate program is entitled *Alpha One: Breaking the Code.* This approach is unique in that it is entirely in rhyme. The alphabet characters are personified through hand puppets and in three-dimensional pictures, on filmstrips, and on recordings. Wall charts and games provide whole-class drill in decoding, and workbooks are available for individual practice. The objective of this new approach is to add some excitement and motivation to what otherwise is often uninteresting rote drill.

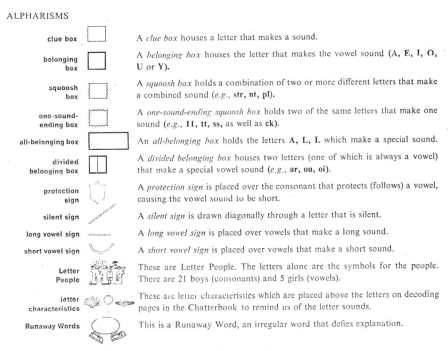

A junky jewel
 or junky toy
Makes Mr. J
 jump for joy.
Anything that's
 thrown away
Is a joy
 for Jumbled J.

Fig. 2–16 Reproduced from Alpha One: Breaking the Code *by permission of New Dimensions In Education.*

ALPHARISMS

clue box — A *clue box* houses a letter that makes a sound.

belonging box — A *belonging box* houses the letter that makes the vowel sound (**A, E, I, O, U** or **Y**).

squoosh box — A *squoosh box* holds a combination of two or more different letters that make a combined sound (*e.g.,* **str, nt, pl**).

one-sound-ending box — A *one-sound-ending squoosh box* holds two of the same letters that make one sound (*e.g.,* **ll, tt, ss**, as well as **ck**).

all-belonging box — An *all-belonging box* holds the letters **A, L, L** which make a special sound.

divided belonging box — A *divided belonging box* houses two letters (one of which is always a vowel) that make a special vowel sound (*e.g.,* **ar, ou, oi**).

protection sign — A *protection sign* is placed over the consonant that protects (follows) a vowel, causing the vowel sound to be short.

silent sign — A *silent sign* is drawn diagonally through a letter that is silent.

long vowel sign — A *long vowel sign* is placed over vowels that make a long sound.

short vowel sign — A *short vowel sign* is placed over vowels that make a short sound.

Letter People — These are Letter People. The letters alone are the symbols for the people. There are 21 boys (consonants) and 5 girls (vowels).

letter characteristics — These are letter characteristics which are placed above the letters on decoding pages in the Chatterbook to remind us of the letter sounds.

Runaway Words — This is a Runaway Word, an irregular word that defies explanation.

Fig. 2–17 Reproduced from Alpha One: Breaking the Code *by permission of New Dimensions In Education.*

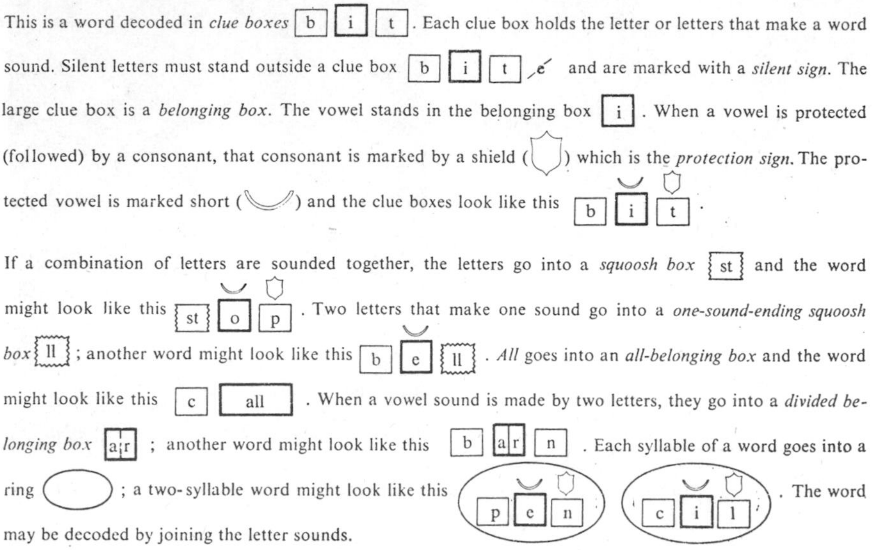

This is a word decoded in *clue boxes* b i t . Each clue box holds the letter or letters that make a word sound. Silent letters must stand outside a clue box b i t e̷ and are marked with a *silent sign*. The large clue box is a *belonging box*. The vowel stands in the belonging box i . When a vowel is protected (followed) by a consonant, that consonant is marked by a shield ( ) which is the *protection sign*. The protected vowel is marked short ( ) and the clue boxes look like this b i t .

If a combination of letters are sounded together, the letters go into a *squoosh box* st and the word might look like this st o p . Two letters that make one sound go into a *one-sound-ending squoosh box* ll ; another word might look like this b e ll . *All* goes into an *all-belonging box* and the word might look like this c all . When a vowel sound is made by two letters, they go into a *divided belonging box* a r ; another word might look like this b a r n . Each syllable of a word goes into a ring ( ) ; a two-syllable word might look like this (p e n) (c i l) . The word may be decoded by joining the letter sounds.

Fig. 2–18 *Reproduced from* Alpha One: Breaking the Code *by permission of New Dimensions In Education.*

It would not be right to conclude this chapter on phonemic approaches to beginning reading without some word concerning the many little supplementary aids which are available through school supply catalogs and at the display tables at annual teachers' conventions. Boxed flash cards of the type made famous by Dr. Edward W. Dolch are published by many companies, but cannot be considered as complete phonemic systems. Therefore, they have not been included here under the phonemic approaches category.

Each year finds a number of newcomers to the family of approaches through basic phonemics. The recent trend is toward more and more electronically-oriented systems, but new boxed materials also continue to appear. Among some of the recent additions are the following:

The "Read to Learn" is a collection of head sets, tapes, pictures on a television-type screen, picture dictionary, the use of the rebus in stories, and flash cards. This collection is marketed by Hoffman Information Systems of Arcadia, California.

A somewhat less extensive program is marketed by the Instructo Corporation of Paoli, Pennsylvania. It is called "First Experiences With Vowels and Consonants" and has the recordings, storybook, spirit masters, and phonics picture-cards packaged in a box. Its special claim to distinction is the up-to-date and clear reproduction of the key pictures on the phonics cards.

The "Road to Reading" (not to be confused with the *Royal Road Readers* or with Romalda Spalding's *Writing Road to Reading*) is also a box of materials. It contains 33 tapes of long and short vowel sounds and stories with accompanying music and sound effects. Ditto masters are provided for "seat work." It is offered by Spoken Arts, Inc. of New Rochelle, N.Y.

Another box of filmstrips, records, and spirit masters is provided by Filmstrip House, New York City. It concentrates on word games in phonogram style.

Imperial International Learning of Kankakee, Illinois has launched an extensive promotion of what its advertising suggests is a "self-contained supplemental program of readiness, study skills, comprehension skills, and word-attack skills. The primary reading program is on 40 tapes.

"Decoding Games" is the name that Multimedia Education, Inc. (publishers of *Reading Newsreport*) uses for its three boxes of cards. Boxes I and II are phonogram cards, and box III contains sentence cards. The chief feature of these materials is the cartoon illustrations on the cards.

International Education and Training of Farmingdale, N.Y. has produced an overhead projector transparency program. The first set of transparencies is a readiness program. Set II consists of word wheels providing a phonogram program on short vowel sounds, and Set III concentrates on long vowel sounds.

Another collection of materials, entitled *Individualized Phonics*, was introduced in 1970 by Teachers Publishing Corporation. It was originated by Mrs. Marie Jonke, a teacher-coordinator in Hartford, Connecticut for use in individualized instruction situations. Dr. Richard E. Wylie of the University of Connecticut produced the teacher's guide, which contains a model lesson and scope and sequence of the program. The components of the program consist of 54 up-to-date picture wall-charts, which illustrate specific letter sounds (beautifully done); flash cards carrying the same illustrations as the wall charts; and an enormous number of spirit masters for studying phonemes.

The package of *Individualized Phonics* is marketed through Collier-Macmillan Services.

Dr. Donald Durrell and Dr. Helen Murphy, well-known leaders in the field of reading, distilled some of the features of their research at Boston University on the relationship of letter names to beginning reading success and packaged a kit entitled *Letters in Words*. It contains a test of reading readiness, based on knowledge of letter names and phonemes, and on lesson sheets designed to help children learn to identify letters by writing them, saying their letter names and sounds they represent.

Letters in Words is distributed by a new Wellesley, Massachusetts company: Curriculum Associates.

There is no end in sight to the proliferation of basic phonemics materials. Each individual promoter may be motivated by the belief that he, indeed, has devised something better than anyone else has dreamed up in the past. The chance for profit from something "new" cannot be ignored as a factor. It is evident that thousands of dollars are being spent in promoting the new as well as the old materials. The question that should concern those contemplating the launching of another new basic phonemics approach is: Can the market stand *another* new box of tapes or cards or filmstrips? And the question that educators should ask is: "Are we adequately using the many materials that are already available?"

It is safe to predict that the future will bring additional phonemics approaches, but that the approaches which survive will utilize some entirely new medium of learning.

CONCLUSIONS

Written language results from the encoding of language phonemes into printed graphemes. One aspect of reading, therefore, is the decoding from the graphemes back into the phonemic elements. The score or so of systems for doing this have been classified here as *basic phonemic approaches.* Their common purpose is to provide materials and a method for helping the individual learn how to "break the code."

This *code-emphasis* approach is dependent on a knowledge of the 44 or more phonemes in American speech, and on the manner in which they are represented by graphemes individually and in combination. Learning the phonemic-graphemic code is a basic skill in beginning reading. The originators of each of the approaches described in this chapter had reasons to believe that theirs was superior to the others.

There are differences, to be sure. Some, for instance, *Phonovisual, The Sound Way to Easy Reading,* and *Sight-to-Sound Phonics* rely heavily on classroom charts, whereas the traditional action has been in individual workbooks of the type used in the majority of the programs. A few have recordings on discs or tape to supplement charts or worksheets. The Durrell and Dolch materials are on flashcards, and the *efi* and *Language Master* systems employ electronic and audiovisual cards to be run through audio machines.

The common element in all of the programs categorized as *basic phonemics approaches* is that they are systems for teaching letter-sound relationships. They all are designed as preliminary and/or supplementary to a larger comprehensive reading program and are structured independent of any basal reader series.

The chief contribution made by the *basic phonemic approaches* is the separate structured packaging of a synthetic phonics program apart from the effort of basal reader phonics instruction. The programs cannot be correlated with a basal reader approach. Any phonemic approach described in this chapter must be run independently—either prior to, or concurrent with the basal reader program or some other broad approach beginning reading.

A *basic phonemic approach* is structured from *a* to *z* and, consequently, provides assurance to the teacher, the administrator, the parent, and the school board that the school is "teaching children phonics."

BIBLIOGRAPHY

ARKIN, SUSAN B., and others, "Growth Patterns in First Grade Reading," Unpublished Ed. M. Thesis, Boston University, 1964.

BAER, DAVID E., "Phonics for First Grade: A Comparison of Two Methods," *Elementary School Journal*, 59 (April, 1959) 394–402; and "Two Methods of Teaching Phonics: A Longitudinal Study," *Elementary School Journal*, 64 (Feb., 1964) 273–279.

BAGFORD, JACK, *Phonics: Its Role in Teaching Reading*. Iowa City: Sernol, Inc., 1967.
    A very useful 80-page paperback.

BLIESMER, EMERY P., and YARBOROUGH, BETTY H., "A Comparison of Ten Different Beginning Reading Programs in First Grade," *Phi Delta Kappan* (June, 1965).

BURROWS, ALVINA T., *What About Phonics?* Bulletin No. 75, Washington: Association for Childhood Education, 1951.

CHALL, JEANNE, *Learning to Read: The Great Debate*, New York: McGraw-Hill Book Co., 1967.
    This book is the result of a Carnegie Corporation grant. Inasmuch as the study centered upon the relative merits of various approaches to reading, it was destined to rekindle the debate on phonemics and whole-word instruction. Special attention is directed to Dr. Chall's recommendations, pp. 307–310.

CLYMER, THEODORE, "The Utility of Phonic Generalizations in the Primary Grades," *The Reading Teacher*, 16 (January, 1953) 252–258.
    A noteworthy study of the percentage of times each rule applies in our language.

CORDTS, ANNA D., *Phonics for the Reading Teacher*. New York: Holt, Rinehart and Winston, Inc., 1965.

——, "The Phonetics of Phonics," *Reading Teacher*, 9 (Dec. 1955).

DOLCH, EDWARD W., and BLOOMSTER, MAURINE, "Phonics Readiness," *Elementary School Journal*, XXXVIII (Nov. 1937) 201–205.

——, "How a Child Sounds Out a Word," *Elementary English Review,* XXII (Nov. 1945) 275–280.

Dolch, William E., *The Teaching of Sounding.* Champaign: Garrard Publishing Co., 1951.

Durkin, Dolores, *Phonics and the Teaching of Reading.* New York: Bureau of Publications, Teachers College, Columbia University, 1962.

Durrell, Donald, and Murphy, Helen A., "Boston University Research in Elementary School Reading: 1933–1963," Boston University *Journal of Education,* 145 (December, 1963) 1–53

Flesch, Rudolph, *Why Johnny Can't Read—and What You Can Do About It.* New York: Harper and Bros., 1955.

Gans, Roma, *Fact and Fiction About Phonics.* Indianapolis: Bobbs-Merrill, 1964.
    Especially see Chapter 4 and Chapter 5.

Hanna, Paul R., and Research Associates, *Phoneme-Grapheme Correspondences as Cues to Spelling Improvement,* Washington, D.C., USOE Publication 32008, 1966.
    This is a monumental project in which more than 17,000 most commonly-used words were analyzed by means of computer in an effort to determine the percentage of regularity of the phoneme-grapheme relationships.

Hanson, Joseph T., "Final Evaluation of the Phonovisual Method, Grades 1–3," *Pasadena City Schools Evaluation Report Number Seven.* Pasadena, Calif.: Pasadena City Schools, September, 1965.

Hay, Julie, and Wingo, Charles E., *Reading With Phonics, Teacher's Manual.* Philadelphia: J. B. Lippincott Co., 1967. Ch. 1 "Getting Results with Phonics."

Heilman, Arthur W., *Phonics in Proper Perspective.* Columbus: Charles E. Merrill Books, Inc., 1964.
    A concise 98-page paperback.

——, "Research Findings Concerning Phonics in Beginning Reading," in *A Decade of Innovations: Approaches to Beginning Reading,* Elaine C. Vilscek, Editor. Vol 12, Part 3, Procedings of the Twelfth Annual Convention, IRA. Newark, Delaware: International Reading Association, 1968, 100–107.

Herr, Selma E., *Phonics Handbook for Teachers.* Los Angeles: E. R. A. Publishers, Inc., 1961.

Hillerich, Robert L. "Vowel Generalizations and First-Grade Reading Achievement," *Elementary School Journal,* 67: (February, 1967) 246–250.
    Reports the results of a study of children who were taught vowel generalizations in First Grade and who scored significantly higher on tests of nonsense syllables than those who had no instruction. On the other hand, they scored lower in comprehension. The writer questions the need for teaching vowel generalizations and suggests that consonants are more important than vowels in beginning reading.

Kolson, Clifford J., "The Vocabulary of Kindergarten Children," Unpublished doctoral dissertation, School of Education, University of Pittsburgh, 1960.
    Kolson's study reports that the Kindergarten child has an average of 3,728 words.

Landon, Alline, *Landon Phonics Program—Teacher's Manual.* San Francisco: Chandler Publishing Co., 1967.

McEathron, Margaret, "Teaching Phonics in the Home and in the Classroom," *Parents Magazine*, (Nov., 1946).

——, *Your Child Can Learn to Read—Manual*. Buffalo: Kenworthy Educational Service, Inc., 1963.

McKee, Paul, *The Teaching of Reading in the Elementary School*. Boston: Houghton, Mifflin Co., 1948. Ch. 8–11.

Murphy, Helen A., "Reading Achievements in Relation to Growth in Perception of Word Elements in Three Types of Beginning Reading Instruction," *Cooperative Research Project* No. 2675. Washington: U.S. Office of Education, 1965.

Scott, Louise Binder, and Thompson, J. J., *Phonics*. Manchester, Missouri: Webster Publishing Co., 1962.

Smith, Edna Burrows, "The Phonovisual Approach," *Reading and the Curriculum*. Bethlehem: Lehigh University, 1963. Proceedings of the Eleventh Annual Reading Conference.

Spache, George D., "Book Review of *Breaking the Sound Barrier*," *Reading Teacher*, 16 (Nov. 1962) 125.

Spencer, Doris U., and Moquin, Doris, "Individualized Reading vs. a Basal Reading Program at First Grade Level in Rural Communities," *Cooperative Research Project* No. 50484. Washington: U.S. Office of Education, 1965.

Sweeney, John R., "An Experimental Study of the Phonovisual Method of Teaching Phonics," *Ontario Journal of Educational Research*, 7, 3 (Spring, 1965), 263–272.

Experimental and control groups were matched. The results show some differences, but there is no statistical treatment to indicate significance of differences.

QUESTIONS AND ACTIVITIES FOR DISCUSSION AND GROWTH

1. Develop a chart on which the 44 phonemes are related to the graphemes. Compare the chart you have devised with the *Phonovisual* charts and the Bremner-Davis charts.

2. Using the chart you produced in question one above, write a planned sequence of steps for teaching the phoneme-grapheme relationships.

3. Prepare at least one tape on which you provide instructions to the child and the exemplary pronunciation of phonemes, using any of the approaches described in this chapter.

4. You are a supervisor of reading, and your superintendent has asked you to prepare a brief in which you present the strengths and weaknesses of "all available phonics programs." With what would you provide him?

5. You are asked to speak at a regional meeting of teachers and reading specialists on the "code emphasis" approach to reading. What points would you make?

6. You are a teacher and your principal asks you to select a "phonics workbook" for next year. Which one would you choose? Why?

7. The salesman for a particular phonics system described in this chapter is claiming that his approach is a "complete reading program". What reasons signify that this cannot be true?

8. It has been said that children can learn the phonemics phase of reading better by working on a programmed electronics machine instead of from a teacher. What is to be said to support and/or to contradict that statement?

9. Scan the advertisements in recent issues of *Grade Teacher, Instructor, Reading Newsreport,* and *The Reading Teacher* to find notices of new phonemics approaches that were not available for review in this book. Do they differ from the ones described? If so, how?

10. What must be done to our language to make a phonemics approach "foolproof" for learning the code?

3

PHONEMIC-PRONUNCIATION APPROACHES

A phonemic-pronunciation approach to beginning reading is one in which principles of phonemics and rules of pronunciation are presented as aids in helping a child in pronouncing new words. Any such approach would be useful to the extent to which the child encounters new words which are reasonably regular phonemically. Moreover, as the child becomes involved in the actual practice of reading wherein he encounters irregular spellings and non-regular phonemic elements, his need for exceptions to the rules becomes greater.

Inasmuch as our American English utilizes only 26 symbols to handle the 44 or more sounds, it would be helpful if rules could be devised which would aid the beginner in his encounters with the phonemic deviants of our language. Furthermore, the spelling of our language is one of the slowest aspects of our culture to respond to the need for change and modernization. This may remain so for many more decades. It is probable that the use of computers for sensing pages and use of mechanical reading and typesetting devices to speed the process of modern communication will hasten the cleaning up of our language and the elimination of obsolete and cumbersome spellings.

Until that time comes, the child is faced with one of the most difficult phonemic tasks of any child on earth. He is faced with two printed consonants which represent the "hard-k" sound, one of which also represents the "soft-k" sound—as in the word "come", and which, in other settings, duplicates the "s" sound, which, in turn, could just as easily be represented by "s" as in "cent" and in "sent", both of which are pronounced the same, yet are different in meaning. If this last complicated sentence describes just one phonemic puzzle which a small six-year-old has, is it any wonder that many are confused and in need of phonemic-pronunciation rules?

There are other problems. Our language has a number of "silent" letters that should be thrown out of words where they do not belong. My favorite example is to be found in the word "through". It contains three silent letters. All across America the word is spelled "THRU" on road signs indicating "THRU STREET", and "THRUWAY". Never is it spelled in its obsolete form. Yet, it may never appear on paper in an American classroom without an uprising from the purists. Those same purists tend to forget that their British forebears were not so hot on spelling in the olden days, either. Just look at the mistakes perpetrated even down into the XIX Century (or was it the 19th Senchuree?). According to American purists, the British are still spelling some words incorrectly.

It is useless to attempt to fight the battle for phonemic spelling. If we can wait a few years, electronic devices may settle the problem for us. Until then, our less able readers in school need help. Phonemic-pronunciation systems make claims to providing such help.

In general, a phonemic-pronunciation system would provide "rules" for those aspects of the language which are reasonably regular and consistent. Rules for the short vowel sounds might be part of such an approach. Attempts should be made to devise rules for the long vowel sounds, and for instances where two vowel graphemes are used in a word, but only one of the vowels is sounded.

Rules have been devised to indicate the effect syllabication and stress and accent have upon pronunciation. In other cases, the variation of usage for consonants in various contexts has been set in "rules". The so-called "final-e" rule appears in all phonemic-pronunciation rule systems in one form or another. Diphthongs and the effect of "r" on the vowels which it follows are also necessary components of "rule" systems. Attempts have also been made to construct reliable rules for the pronunciation of the suffix "ed"; hard and soft c; hard and soft g; the three sounds of ch; the five spellings of the sh sound; and many more irregularities which contribute to the inefficiency of our printed language.

Two strictly phonemic-pronunciation approaches to beginning reading are described here. They are Sister Mary Caroline's *Breaking the Sound Barrier* and Sister Monica Foltzer's *Professor Phonics Gives Sound Advice.*

A third system of phonemic-pronunciation is part of the larger and more extensive total language-arts approach devised by Mrs. Romalda Spalding in her *Writing Road to Reading,* described fully in Chapter 6 and, therefore, not included here.

BREAKING THE SOUND BARRIER

Origins

Breaking the Sound Barrier is a little handbook of pronunciation rules to help the child through the maze of phonemic regularities and irregularities in our language.

The system of phonemic pronunciation presented in the book was developed by Sister Mary Caroline, I.H.M. In her lecture to teacher groups Sister Caroline tells of the frustration that she experienced as a high school teacher. She felt that, every year, there seemed to be more and more students who were unable to read well enough to master the work in geography, history, and English. She decided that this could be corrected at the lower grades—perhaps in the junior high school. As she made attempts to pinpoint the level in school where correction of the difficulty could be achieved, Sister Caroline decided that it must be at the very beginning of the reading process.

After six years in the first grade with basal readers and whole-word techniques, Sister Caroline was convinced that children would succeed in reading if only they had some additional training in phonemic analysis.

With that aim in mind, she set about the task of devising some basic rules that were simple enough for young children. In addition to that, the rules were not to be merely something that would be recited by rote, but must elicit thinking and understanding even on the part of First Graders.

The aim of the system is to provide the child with a systematic, yet easy-to-learn method of phonemic analysis which has an adequate set of rules to which the child can refer when he encounters a new word on a page.

Sister Caroline recognized that the research on the amount of vocabulary a child knows orally far exceeds his visual vocabulary. Using this fact as a basis, *Breaking the Sound Barrier* is devised to force the child to refer constantly to the words he already knows as double-checks. Thus, the system is in effect one of checks and balances, providing the child with rules for phonemic analysis, yet forcing the child to check his decisions in the light of contextual analysis.

In the few short years since *Breaking the Sound Barrier* was introduced, it has become one of the best-known proposals in beginning reading. This has been accomplished almost entirely through the seemingly boundless energy of its originator, Sister Mary Caroline, who with evangelistic zeal, guarantees sure success for teachers who will give her method a try.

Materials and Method

It should be remembered that *Breaking the Sound Barrier* is not an isolated and self-contained system of teaching reading. It is specifically a handbook of rules to assist in pronunciation. Since it is so generally referred to as a method of teaching reading, it is classified as a "phonemic-pronunciation" method. It is designed for use with any good basal reader series. It is a cleverly illustrated handbook which appeals to children. Its illustrations are not only amusing but are meaningful; and, as such, provide a double reinforcement for the rules which they illustrate.

The system is divided into three parts, and starts with the sounds of consonants and consonant "clusters" or combinations and blends such as "th", "sh", "kn", "sl", "st", and the rest. Each consonant is introduced with a simple key word. Each consonant blend is, similarly, tied to a key word. The key words, moreover, are illustrated with interesting artist's sketches.

The consonants are introduced first in initial position in the words. This is one of the essential elements of the method; that is, that the child is always admonished to discover how the word begins.

If the word begins with:	It begins like:	If the word begins with:	It begins like:
b	bed	m	man
c (hard k)	cat	n	nest
c (soft s)	cent	p	pen
d	dog	q (always with *u*)	queen
f	fish		
g	gun	r	ring
g (soft j)	gem	s	sun
h	hat	t	top
j	jar	v	vest
k	kite	w	web
l	leaf	y	yarn
		z	zebra

When dealing with double and triple consonants, the blends are distinguished from those digraphs in which one consonant is silent. The term "consonant digraph" is not used in the handbook, but "consonant blend" becomes an everyday word for the child and is cleverly illustrated with two spoons in a mixing bowl. Each spoon represents a separate consonant sound. The bowl represents the mixture or blend. Children remember this graphic method of presenting the consonant blends.

When consonant digraphs such as "th", "sh", and "ch" produce a brand-new sound—as they do—these are learned as such. Similarly, the

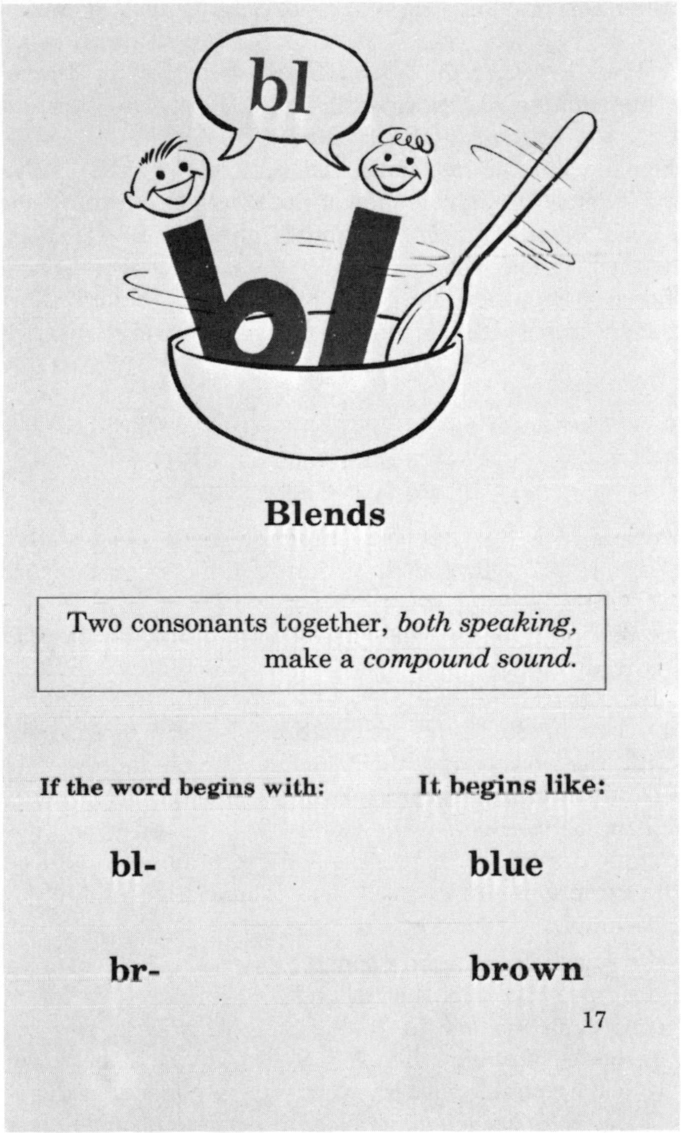

Blends

Two consonants together, *both speaking,* make a *compound sound.*

If the word begins with:	It begins like:
bl-	**blue**
br-	**brown**

17

Fig. 3–1 Reproduced from Breaking the Sound Barrier *by permission of the author, Sister Mary Caroline and the publishers the MacMillan Company. Copyright, 1960.*

digraphs in which one consonant is silent are also studied separately. They include such pairs as "pin", "ps", "kn". Since they are relatively rare in beginning reading, they are not emphasized at that stage of learning.

Part II of *Breaking the Sound Barrier* provides the learner with a complete presentation of the vowels. The five long vowels are first, and require only the learning of their names.

When the short sounds are presented, the slogan is "What do the vowels say?" Since the short sounds of the vowels occur much more often than the long sounds, much attention is given in *Breaking the Sound Barrier* to their various short sounds.

Children using the handbook, *Breaking the Sound Barrier* must learn the key words which contain the five short vowel sounds. They are:

ă as in "at"
ĕ as in "end"
ĭ as in "it"
ŏ as in "on"
ŭ as in "up"

Classes where drill is the common means for learning the method chant: "at, end, it, on, up"; "at, end, it, on, up". Others memorize the entire short vowel chart.

Once the short vowel sounds have been learned, the beginning reading class is ready for Part III, which is the presentation of the rules and the exceptions to the rules.

Part III is, in effect, the presentation of a structured procedure for dealing with the vowels and their sounds in new words. Sister Mary Caroline considers it the "heart" of the method.

The basic premise is that the vowel "says its short sound unless. . . ." There are four basic parts to the possible exceptions . . . and one exception to the exceptions. In essence, the pronunciation of the vowels in a word are as follows:

1. the vowel "says its short sound" unless. . . .
2. the vowel "says its short sound" . . . unless it is followed by a consonant and a final "e". This is what is known by teachers as the "final *e* rule". Thus, in the word "hat", the vowel changes to a long vowel when the final "e" is added, making the word "hate." In *Breaking the Sound Barrier* the child learns it by rule and not by comparison as shown above.
3. the vowel "says its short sound" . . . unless it is a part of a vowel *digraph* or is part of a *diphthong*.

The beginning learner actually learns the terms "digraph" and "diphthong". In fact, children who have been reared on "BTSB" know digraphs and diphthongs better than most of our elementary teachers.

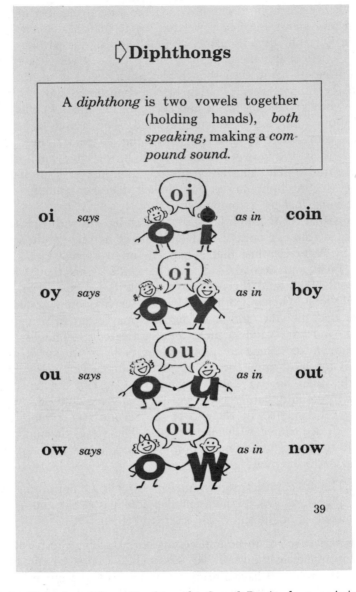

Fig. 3-2 *Reproduced from* Breaking the Sound Barrier *by permission of the author, Sister Mary Caroline and the publishers the MacMillan Company, 1960.*

This amazing skill is acquired by means of very amusing illustrations, and by the clever designation of "Polite Digraphs" and "Impolite Digraphs".

A "Polite Digraph" is one in which the second member of the pair bows out and allows the first vowel to "say its name." Conversely, the "Impolite Digraph" says its name without allowing his partner to make a sound. There is also the digraph in which the first vowel says a sound different from its name even though the other vowel is silent.

Another impressive illustration of the diphthongs shows a girl and boy (the vowels) holding hands and speaking together. In this manner the "oi", "oy", "ou", and "ow" are presented. The *oi* says "oi", as in the keyword, "coin". The *oy* says "oi", as in the keyword, "boy". The *ou* says "ou", as in the keyword, "out". And the *ow* says "ou", as in the keyword, "now". The illustration makes this rule easy to remember. The rule is: "A diphthong is two vowels together (holding hands), both speaking, making a compound sound".

The signal for the diphthong is a vowel digraph with the letter "o" as the first of the two vowels. Although this is not always the case, it is claimed by Sister Caroline that it happens often enough to be a useful clue for First- and Second-Graders. The child learns that, when two vowels hold hands, and the first vowel is the letter "O", it is likely to be a diphthong, wherein both vowels make a compound sound. Later he learns that the "ou" and "ow" digraphs may occur in such words as "through" and "sow" and in such cases be treated as digraphs.

Although key words are provided for each of the vowel digraphs, the rule is the most important thing. It is claimed that, if the child can master the rule, he can handle digraphs. Constant reference to his *Breaking the Sound Barrier* book will gradually acquaint him with the various vowel digraphs. By the end of the Second Grade, most children will be well acquainted with all of them. The vowel digraph principle will be learned and used almost from the very beginning; certainly by Christmas of First Grade.

  4. The vowel says its short sound unless it is a "murmuring" vowel.
  5. The vowel says its short sound unless it is at the end of a short word, or at the end of an accented syllable.

This rule almost seems to be unnecessary for attacking short words. For example, it applies to the word "be". Any child who is far enough along to master the rule will have already been able to figure out most, if not all, short words in our language which end with vowels. The number is quite limited.

The application of the rule to accented syllables introduces another quite different element not heretofore dealt with in the system. The matter of accent is one of usage. The child who has had such limited experience with the language is not at all aware of accented syllables.

Yet, the rule has some valid application for vowels at the end of accented syllables. In the word, "nation", for example, the first syllable is accented, therefore, the vowel does not say its short sound.

> 6. The vowel says its short sound unless . . . unless it is an exception to any of the exceptions previously stated.

This last of the basic vowel rules has been the object of a considerable number of good-natured jibes in the discussion of *Breaking the Sound Barrier*. Some have felt that it is a "catch-all" for anything not covered by the rules. And, indeed, it may be that.

We must admit, however, that a number of oddities have crept into our language over the years, especially during the centuries when the language was chiefly an oral means of communication. In addition, in pioneer America, spellings of the language differed according to the education of the scribes, and the peculiarities of local pronunciation. Even today, two spellings of many words are acceptable. It is not surprising, therefore, that our American language has a number of pronunciations that cannot be covered with a set of pronunciation rules simple enough to be handled by six-year-olds.

Such a simple word as "do" is an exception not covered by any of the rules. It is, therefore, an exception to the exceptions. The common word, "many" is similarly an exception to the exceptions. Such words, as well as a number of others, are just unexplainable in any logical way. It is doubtful if any set of rules *could* be devised to cover them.

The test of any system of word analysis is whether its user can arrive at a word pronunciation which he recognizes as a word; and, if so, does the word make sense in the context in which it is used.

In *Breaking the Sound Barrier*, this is the final test of whether or not the child is following the two basic fundamental principles:

> "Use the rule.
> Then use your head."

Inasmuch as the method is based both on rules and on a thinking process, the child must follow a set of guidelines in his thinking as he selects and applies the rules. The structure of the thinking is as follows:

> 1. How does the word begin?
>   If it begins with such and such a vowel or consonant, then which rule may apply?
> 2. What are the vowels in the word?
>   Is there one vowel? Two vowels? Are the vowels alone or together? Is any vowel followed by a consonant and a final "e"?
>   Check the vowels and apply the appropriate rules for their pronunciation.

3. What do the vowels say?

This is arrived at by an application of the vowel rules that apply according to the position of the vowels in relationship to the consonants and their position in the whole word.

4. What is the word?

The pronunciation is arrived at by assembling the sounds which the child has decided upon by means of the rules.

5. Does this sound like a word you already know?

The child often can make slight adjustments in pronunciation or in accent to produce the correct word. Assembling phonemic elements alone does not assure American pronunciation.

6. Does the word make sense in the sentence?

This is the final check. Up to this point, the child has been engaged in phonemic analysis. The essence of *Breaking the Sound Barrier* is the fact that it is a thinking process going beyond phonemics-pronunciation. It requires application through contextual usage.

The six steps outlined above are "musts" in attacking new words. This structured way of thinking becomes a way of life wherever *Breaking the Sound Barrier* is used. Children are never allowed to deviate from it. Even when they make a correct guess at a new word, they must go through the steps to prove that they are correct.

A few examples will illustrate the procedure of applying the above principle. Let us take, for example, the analysis of the word, "met".

1. It begins like "man"
2. The vowel is "e"
3. "e" says the short sound, e
4. The word is "met" . . . try it in the sentence.

For a second example, let us try the word, "forgot".

1. It begins like "fish"
2. The vowels are "o" and "o"
3. The first "o" is a murmuring vowel because it is followed by the "r" sound. It says "or"; the second vowel says its short sound o
4. The word is for—got.

A third example presents a somewhat more difficult word for analysis. The word is "father".

1. It begins like "fish"
2. The vowels are "a" and "e"
3. What do the vowels say?

First try the short sound. It will work unless the vowel is followed by a consonant; is modified by "r"; is at the end of an accented syllable; or is an exception. In this case, it must be an exception. In the case of the second vowel, the "e" is modified by the "r" and, therefore, is a murmuring vowel.

4. The word is "father"—a word which the child has encountered with regularity in the primer and even in the pre-primer of many basal series. Certainly the adjustment can be made so that the child arrives at the word which he already knows as a spoken word.

It is intended that Part II and Part III of *Breaking the Sound Barrier* be covered in about six weeks following whatever period is necessary for the children in First Grade to have acquired a sight vocabulary of from 80 to 100 words.

The little handbook, *Breaking the Sound Barrier*, is intriguing to the child from cover to cover. Its rules are stated in very simple principles; the key words are very simple and well-known; and the illustrations are in clever cartoon style.

The use of illustrations and clever statements of rules makes *Breaking the Sound Barrier* entertaining and easy learning, rather than the drudgery a rule system might otherwise become. There are many school systems which find this method just the sort of phonemics rule drill that is desired. The highly-structured school may be more likely to find Sister Caroline's method easier to introduce than schools which pride themselves on their "democratic" environment. Like all skills, the learning of phonemic-pronunciation rules requires drill and application in real situations. The latter is accomplished in Part IV of the method.

The story provided in Part IV is about "Chappie", Sister Caroline's pet parakeet and classroom mascot. The story is devised to provide words which illustrate all of the vowel and consonant problems which a child might encounter. Thus, it provides actual pre-planned practice in the application of *all* of the rules.

Application by the child in his own basal reader is, however, the test of the method. In fact, the basal reader is the home-base of operations, and it is the specific intent of *Breaking the Sound Barrier* to aid the child in his basal reader work.

The teacher's manual which Sister Caroline has written is specific in showing exactly how BTSB work fits in with the phonemic analysis work in the basal reader teacher's manuals. It is pointed out that, in the beginning basal reader work, the child learns a sight vocabulary. This is usually accomplished by means of teacher help. In other words, it is general practice for the teacher to tell the child each word. The child repeats the word many times in context as he "reads" the pages in the pre-primer. By being told and by repetition of the word in context, the child develops a collection of ten, twenty, or thirty words which are his "sight vocabulary".

Acquiring a sight vocabulary gives the child immediate success in his attempts at reading, and satisfies one of the important psychological principles of learning. That is, that immediate success reinforces learning, and immediate correction of errors helps prevent their recurrence.

There is, however, a limit to the amount of sight words that a six-year-old can be expected to memorize as whole configurations. All of the tens of thousands of words in our language are constructed with just twenty-six letters. Attention to the sounds of those letters not in isolation, but in relationship to their position in the whole syllable is the key to pronunciation of our language. *Breaking the Sound Barrier* provides the child with enough (some people fear that it is *more than enough*) simple rules so that, after he progresses beyond the initial sight vocabulary stage, he can be on his own in pronunciation.

This seems to be a reasonable objective, for certainly no Second- or Third-Grade teacher could possibly with stand the onslaught of thirty children seeking pronunciations for every new word on the page. It is true that the basal reader teacher's manuals do provide suggestions for phonemic and structural analysis work. Through such work, most children do receive instruction in phonemic analysis. It is, however, usually done as a whole class project and whatever retention there may be is an individual matter.

When *Breaking the Sound Barrier* is used as the phonemic analysis "Bible", it is always within arm's reach of the child, and is his reference companion. Only in cases of totally unfamiliar words will the child need to go either to the teacher to check his pronunciation or to a dictionary. In the latter case, of course, he will have to learn the additional skills of deciphering the diacritical marks in the dictionary—or else use a dictionary which provides some simple phonemic spelling. Teachers who use the method prefer to have the child check with them until he is in at least the Third Grade. They feel that personal encouragement and praise is more valuable in the first two years.

Research Findings

Since *Breaking the Sound Barrier* is designed as a supplementary aid to the basal reader program, it should be a relatively simple matter to devise a research in which groups of children working in basal readers alone were matched with others working in the same basal readers but with the aid of Sister Caroline's handbook. A longitudinal study of such groups over three or four years should yield some significant results.

Unfortunately, such a study is not yet available. A study[1] done with 323 children in Grades One, Two, and Three in Warwick (R.I.) schools attempted to make comparisons somewhat like suggested above. It was, however, not a longitudinal study following the same groups through the three years. That study reported few statistically-significant differences between the groups.

Search for other reliable studies on the comparative value of *Breaking the Sound Barrier* has been fruitless. Reports from teachers who have used the system and/or are still using the system are conflicting. Some teachers have had and are still having almost unbelievable success with the method. Other teachers have adapted parts of it and have discarded the parts they believe are cumbersome. Some teachers have tried it and have discarded the entire system, claiming that it is far too complicated for young children.

No attempt was made to provide rules for all of the freak spellings in our language. Even linguists, as will be seen in Chapter V, had to admit that some phonemically-irregular words were necessary in order to construct stories that made sense. In such cases the words just have to be used and children just have to memorize them as sight vocabulary, and attempt to remember their spellings. In spelling, such words are referred to as "spelling demons".

Before scholars condemn *Breaking the Sound Barrier* as a futile attempt to bring order out of chaos, a well-designed study needs to be made of the 5000 most common words in the Rinsland list to discover the extent to which Sister Caroline's "rules" take care of the more-than-fifty-percent of the exceptions. This has not been done. It may well be that *Breaking the Sound Barrier* is all its originator modestly claims it to be.

PROFESSOR PHONICS GIVES SOUND ADVICE

Origins

The interesting 112-page handbook of word-lists and phonemic-pronunciation rules was developed by Sister Monica Foltzer, principal of St. Ursula Junior High School in Cincinnati.

---

1. Padula, Hilda Blake, "A Study of Two Procedures in Phonetic Instruction as Reflected in Reading Progress," Unpublished M.A. Thesis, University of Rhode Island, Kingston, 1963.

Professor Phonics Gives Sound Advice, although carrying a copy-right date of 1965, is the distilled work of almost thirty years' experience and experimentation with word lists and phonemic rules, starting back in 1929 when Sister Monica first became frustrated with the "look-say" readers she was using in her Second Grade. She explains her long search for a better way to teach beginning reading, tapping every source she could find. She readily admits adopting good ideas wherever she found them. "During the search," she says, "one paragraph in one book stated that the best foundation for word attack was to teach the short vowels, the consonants, and then make up small words to apply this knowledge, and later to add the long vowels." With that sequence as a guide, Sister Monica set about the task of developing word lists which form the main core of her book.

All through the early 1930's, Sister Monica developed and reworked lesson sheets of word lists, phonics charts, and later she adopted the idea of key words which she phased into her materials and method.

After teaching Second Grade for six years, she was transferred to the junior high, then to senior high, and then back to the elementary school as principal for eleven years. She states that "In all this varied activity, I still worked on and off with phonics . . . when I became principal, I inaugurated and guided a program of phonics . . ." She explains further: "We had two difficulties with this program. The first was the securing of good phonic material . . . the second was the in-service training necessary."

After several years of experimentation with phonemics materials in the elementary school and with foreign students as well, the book soon became a reality, even though at first she had no intention of putting the material in a form for publication and distribution. The demand for her materials became so great, however, that in 1965 it was decided that it would be wise to·copyright them and to print them in a form which could be sold. In addition to the student book, a Manual of Instructions was completed and published in 1967, and, more recently, a set of Key Word Pictures has come from the press as an important part of the total program.

Materials and Method

At first inspection, *Professor Phonics Gives Sound Advice* gives the appearance of being a take-off on Sister Mary Caroline's *Breaking the Sound Barrier.* The art work of the two approaches to beginning reading through phonemic rules is somewhat similar—both employing colorful and strong illustrations of a cartoon type. The two books are similar in that they both have a rule for operation. In BTSB, it is "Use the Rule, then use your head!" In *Professor Phonics*, the admonition is:

"Think the key word;
start the sound."

The key words for the 16 basic vowel sounds are based upon 13 single vowel sounds and 3 double vowel sounds, called "diphthongs." The author divides them into four groups. The five short vowel sounds and the five long vowel sounds make up groups one and two in the usual manner. The third group consists of the three single vowels that generally have a third sound. The last group of basic vowel sounds includes the diphthongs, *oi* and *ou*, and the "murmur" diphthong, *ur*. (Here, again, it may be noted that there is a similarity in use of the "murmuring" diphthong concept by Sister Caroline and by Sister Monica.

The short vowel key words are: *apple, Eskimo, igloo, ostrich*, and *umbrella*. The long vowel key words are: *ate, eat, ice, old*, and *use*. The vowels, *a, o,* and *u* are designated as having a third sound and are shown with sub numberings: a_3, o_3, u_3 and are cued with *all, to,* and *put* as the key words.

Key words for the diphthongs are:

$$\text{owl} = \frac{\text{ou}}{\text{ow}} \qquad \text{oil} = \frac{\text{oi}}{\text{oy}} \qquad \text{urn} = \frac{\begin{array}{c}\text{er}\\\text{ir}\end{array}}{\text{ur}}$$

Sister Monica has stated that she believes page 5, on which those key words and basic vowel sounds are listed, is the most important part of her book.

The key words and designated sounds for the consonants are presented on pages 6 and 7. Key words for the 26 basic consonant sounds are: *bed, cap* and *cent* (for the two sounds represented by *c*), *duck, fish, gun* and *gem* (for the two sounds represented by *g*), *hat, jet, kid, lamp, mop, nest, pup, quack, rug, sun* and *bells* (for the two sounds represented by *s*), *tent, van, web, box, exit* and *Xavier* (for the three sounds represented by *x*), *yak*, and *zipper*.

Since the vast majority of all vowel sounds are the short sounds, the book deals with them first. The teacher is directed to present *all* of the sounds of one particular vowel at the same time. For example, the short, the long, and the third sound of *a* are all to be memorized in that order and together. The short sound is then to be worked upon. It should be noted that the learning of the short and long vowel sounds (plus any third sound) is exactly the same as the method used by Romalda Spalding in the *Writing Road to Reading*.

When the class knows the three sounds of *a* through their keywords, they can attempt any word containing an *a* without knowing any of the rules. They are told to try the three sounds to see if they can sound out a word they know.

This is followed with the two sounds of *i* and the three sounds of *u*. These, also, are taught through the medium of keywords. After that, the three sounds of *o* and the two sounds of *e* are introduced. These comprise the thirteen important single vowel sounds. Lastly, the three diphthong sounds are taught.

The sequence of teaching throughout the first part of the book is one of synthesizing the initial consonant sound with the short vowel and then finally blending it into a three-letter monosyllable which may be a real word or a nonsense word. A few examples will illustrate:

m	w	g	l	k	ck
ma	wa	ga	la	ka	ack
ma t	wa g	ga s	la d	Ka t	la ck
mat	wag	gas	lad	Kat	lack

The rules which *Professor Phonics* gives are to be memorized by the children. Moreover they are to remember them by *number* so they may refer to them and recite them for review. There are nine vowel rules. Practice on the words which are regular phonemic spellings illustrating those nine rules takes more than half of the book.

1. "When there is only one vowel in a word or syllable and the vowel comes between two consonants, the vowel is usually short."

This is illustrated by a large number of three-letter monosyllables such as *bad, did, yak, rot.*

2. "When there is only one vowel in a word or syllable and the vowel comes at the beginning of the word, the vowel is usually short."

Examples are *up, egg, and at.*

Two of the vowel rules are cited to illustrate the manner in which they are stated.

The rules are often surrounded by interesting illustrations of "Professor Phonics."

The "final-*e*" rule is illustrated by words which are called "Magic *e* words."

Other vowel rules deal with the vowel at the end of a single-syllable word being long; the *a* followed by *u, w, r,* double-*l* and the digraph *lt* is the third sound, *ä*; the *y* is sounded as long *ē* at the end of an unaccented syllable, and as a long *ī* at the end of an accented syllable; words which have a vowel, followed by two consonants, and ending with suffixes

Fig. 3–3 Reproduced from Professor Phonics Gives Sound Advice *by permission of the author, Sister Monica Foltzer.*

ing, ed, and *er* are pronounced with the short vowel sound and similar words in which there is only one consonant have the vowel pronounced with the long vowel sound.

Professor Phonics states the rules in a different manner, but they are cited above only to indicate the extent of the nine vowel rules. Consonant rules are similar in nature, and attempt to cover the more generally-used consonant pronunciations. A number of regular and irregular digraphs are illustrated and rules given where possible.

Part II of the phonemic pronunciation handbook presents a number of minor rules and exceptions. There is also a very helpful list of common words which are not phonemically regular. The various spellings for a number of common sounds are given with columns of words which illustrate each. Those comparisons of regularity and irregularity are helpful aids to phonemic drill.

At the end of the book, *Professor Phonics* brings the consonant rules all together on one page in summary fashion. Similarly, the nine vowel rules are summarized in clear style on two pages. Three pages of rules for syllabication are interspersed with pages of words for practice.

In addition to the rules, the book contains from 4500 to 5000 different examples of words which can be learned by practice in the context of the rules which they illustrate. Such a comprehensive and extensive list, arranged so conveniently, may be the most useful feature of the book when used with the rules.

The "Preface" to the handbook suggests "Four indispensable procedures that will help teachers":

First, the use of memorized key words and rules. This gives students a "home-base".

Second. "Written dictation is the only way a teacher can be sure a learner is hearing correctly."

Third, "What is taught must be applied the rest of the day in other classes. No word should be told if the student can sound it."

Fourth, "It is very important not to continue to the next page unless the previous pages have been well grasped, or phonetic indigestion will occur."

The publication in the late summer of 1967 of Sister Monica's "Manual of Instructions" for *Professor Phonics Gives Sound Advice* makes available to the classroom teacher the simple and easy manner in which the program is intended to be used. A few excerpts from the manual of instructions will illustrate its simplicity:

"It is very wise not to go on until written dictation proves that the five short sounds can be distinguished. Take all the time necessary for sufficient ear training. Don't rush, since about 62% of all vowel sounds are short sounds. When these are known, the most important hurdle has been crossed." Other places in the Manual provide opportunities for the reader to feel the years of experience of its author stated in such a natural manner. It is like an older experienced teacher giving a few tips to a new teacher.

As the name implies, *Professor Phonics Gives Sound Advice* both to the learner and to the teacher.

Research Findings

Inasmuch as this is a handbook of phonemic rules, together with thousands of practice words, it is unlikely that definitive statistical findings will ever be available to "prove" or "disprove" the system. For generations, teachers and students have wished for fool-proof rules with which to unlock the irregularities of our language. Research may eventually seek to find the answer. Until that time, aids such as *Professor Phonics Gives Sound Advice* can be helpful with the assurance they convey that "rules are rules," and that the child who practices the rules and the hundreds of sample words that are given as samples of each will, indeed, have an extensive exposure to a vocabulary which he can use as an approach to beginning reading.

It is likely that *Professor Phonics Gives Sound Advice* was intended to be an accompaniment to a basal reading program, and not a preliminary year-long drill involving rote memorization of words in isolation.

Professor Phonics Gives Sound Advice contains many excellent materials which represent months of work in compiling them. It is unlikely that such an exhaustive list of words is available anywhere else to the teacher who wishes to give students concentrated practice on the application of rules of phonemic pronunciation. Elsewhere one can find rules. Here in this little book one finds lists and lists and lists of words— all related to the rules and illustrating them in an orderly sequence.

The cover of the book contains the sub-title: "A Comprehensive Phonics Practice Book." That is exactly what it is.

CONCLUSIONS

This chapter has presented two approaches to reading which are based on pronunciation rules. Both *Breaking the Sound Barrier* and *Professor Phonics Gives Sound Advice* are handbooks that provide guidelines in the form of phonics generalizations. Neither one claims to be a complete reading system. Each contains useful materials that help in establishing an understanding of the regularities of our language.

Some scholars have questioned the reliability of any phonemic rules when one attempts to apply them to our highly unreliable and inconsistent language. Indeed, the campaign for spelling reform to correct the irrational aspects of our language has been going on in America for over two hundred years, or more. Noah Webster was enthusiastic for spelling reform, as were Horace Mann, Brigham Young, Nicholas Murray Butler, Theodore Roosevelt, and many others.

The phonemic inconsistency of our language so impressed Dr. Frank Laubach, the world's greatest missionary of literacy, that he stated that "our English language is the most horrible language in existence today.[2]'

---

2. Laubach, Frank, Statement at 9th Annual Conference on Reading, University o Rhode Island, July, 1963.

His outburst against the inconsistencies of our spelling is based upon a lifetime of actual on-the-spot experience in teaching reading to one hundred million primitive peoples all over the world, and in teaching reading to American illiterates.

Several thorough studies and scholarly reports in the past few years seem to be in agreement on the relative difficulty of devising rules that apply to our phonemically-irregular language. Ruth Oaks studied a number of basal readers that were used from 1932 through 1939 with the intent of discovering whether or not the words used in them would lend themselves to the consistency required in the application of a set of phonics rules. She found that more words defy the vowel rules than obey them.[3]

Dr. Alvina Burrows of New York University enlisted the help of a co-worker, Mrs. Zyra Lourie, in an attempt[4] to settle, once and for all, the question of how reliable the vowel rules are in actual practice. She started with Henry Rinsland's list of the five thousand words that constitute the vocabulary of highest frequency in basal readers and other elementary school reading materials (1945).

Dr. Burrows reported in 1963 that, out of 5000 basic words, 1,728 contained two vowels "holding hands together"; and, of those, only 668 followed the rule. Words in which ea were together comprised the largest group. There were 268 ea words, of which 157 "followed the rule". There were 139 ai words, of which 103 followed the rule. There were 151 ie words, of which only 29 followed the rule.

In the same year, Dr. Theodore Clymer reported his now-famous study[5] of "The Utility of Phonic Generalizations in the Primary Grades". He found few which held in more than 50% of the cases.

The studies cited lead one to question the practical uses that any system of rules would have in dealing with our language, and rightly so.

The monumental study by Hanna,[6] however, convinces us that our language, indeed, may be analyzed according to phonics generalizations. The practical problem is to simplify the rules adequately for use by six-year-olds. It should be noted that Hanna's study was carried out by computer. The study concludes that more than 80% of the 17,000 common words in the study were spelled correctly by the computer when adequate phonics generalization rules had been established for the computer pro-

3. Oaks, Ruth E., "A Study of Vowel Situations in Primary Vocabulary," unpublished masters thesis, Philadelphia: Temple University, 1950.
4. Burrows, Alvina T., and Lourie, Zyra, "Two Vowels Go Walking," *Reading Teacher*, 17 (Nov. 1963), 72.
5. Clymer, Theodore, "The Utility of Phonic Generalizations in the Primary Grades," *Reading Teacher*, 16 (Jan. 1963) 252–258.
6. Hanna, Paul R., and others, *Phoneme-Grapheme Correspondences as Cues to Spelling Improvement*, Washington, D.C., USOE Publication 32008, 1966.

gram. The phonemically-spelled words were fed into the computer. The computer analyzed the words according to the phonics rules under which the program was operating. The resultant spell-out was more than 80% correct.

Assuming that the converse could be done, the implication is that more than 80% of our language can be pronounced when adequate phonics generalization rules are established.

There is no reasonable excuse, therefore, not to utilize some of the more reliable phonics generalizations as one aspect of the total approach to beginning reading.

BIBLIOGRAPHY

BAILEY, MILDRED HART, "The Utility of Phonic Generalizations In Grades One Through Six," *The Reading Teacher,* 20 (February, 1967) 413–418.

——, "Utility of Vowel Digraph Generalizations in Grades One Through Six," *Reading and Realism,* Proceedings of the Thirteenth Annual Convention, International Reading Association, Newark, Delaware. Vol. 13, Part 1, 654–658.

BURMEISTER, LOU E., "Usefulness of Phonic Generalizations," *The Reading Teacher,* 21 (January, 1968) 349–356.

——, "Vowel Pairs," *The Reading Teacher,* 21 (February, 1968) 445–452.
This is a follow-up of the Hanna study of phoneme-grapheme relationships. The writer illustrates the reverse process and applies it to the generalization: "When two vowels go walking . . ."

BURROWS, ALVINA T., and LOURIE, ZYRA, "Two Vowels Go Walking," *Reading Teacher,* 17 (Nov. 1963) 72.
The authors concluded that *Breaking the Sound Barrier* complicates learning with too many rules to be applied.

CLYMER, THEODORE, "The Utility of Phonic Generalizations in the Primary Grades," *Reading Teacher,* 16 (Jan. 1963) 252–258.

DOWNING, JOHN, "The Implications of Research on Children's Thinking for Early Stages of Learning to Read," *Proceedings of the 35th Annual Claremont Reading Conference,* Claremont, California: Claremont Graduate School, 1968 (In Press).
In this presentation, Dr. Downing reviews research that he believes indicates that verbalized rules are ineffective in the development of concepts.

EMANS, ROBERT, "The Usefulness of Phonic Generalizations Above the Primary Grades," *The Reading Teacher,* 20 (February, 1967) 419–425.

——, "When Two Vowels Go Walking and Other Such Things," *The Reading Teacher,* 21 (December, 1967) 262–269.

FRY, EDWARD, "A Frequency Approach to Phonics," *Elementary English,* XXXXI (Nov. 1964) 759–765.

HANNA, PAUL R., and others, *Phoneme-Grapheme Correspondences as Cues to Spelling Improvement*. Washington, D.C.: USOE Publication 32008, 1966.

The first 130 pages of this 1700+ page research report describe the most significant project in determining the extent to which the individual phonemes of 17,000 common words can be spelled, provided adequate rules are established. The implications of this study in considering a phonemic-pronunciation approach to reading are tremendous.

HILLERICH, ROBERT L., "Vowel Generalizations and First-Grade Reading Achievement," *Elementary School Journal*, 67 (February, 1967) 246–250.

Reports the results of a study of children who were taught vowel generalizations in First Grade and who scored significantly higher on tests of nonsense syllables than those who had no instruction. On the other hand, they scored lower in comprehension. The writer questions the need for teaching vowel generalizations and suggests that consonants are more important than vowels in beginning reading.

OAKS, RUTH E., "A Study of Vowel Situations in Primary Vocabulary," unpublished master's thesis, Philadelphia: Temple University, 1950.

PADULA, HILDA BLAKE, "A Study of Two Procedures in Phonetic Instruction as Reflected in Reading Progress," Unpublished M.A. Thesis, University of Rhode Island, Kingston, 1963.

WALCUTT, CHARLES C., *Tomorrow's Illiterates*. Boston: Little, Brown and Co., 1961.

Ch. VII contains favorable comments on *Breaking the Sound Barrier*.

WEINTRAUB, SAMUEL, "A Critique of a Review of Phonics Studies," *Elementary School Journal*, 67 (Oct. 1966) 34–41.

QUESTIONS AND ACTIVITIES FOR DISCUSSION AND GROWTH

1. Obtain the Dolch list of 220 "basic words" and mark the ones that do not conform to regular phonetic generalizations. How do you conclude that these irregular words must be taught and/or learned?

2. Use a copy of *Breaking the Sound Barrier* with one child who is just beginning to learn to read. Observe his reactions to the cartoon illustrations.

3. Use multiple copies of *Breaking the Sound Barrier*: first, with superior children and, second, with children of low ability. What significant differences, if any, do you notice?

4. Borrow a copy of Hanna's huge research report on *Phoneme-Grapheme Correspondences*. This can be obtained from a university library or from the United States Office of Education. Reword the most reliable phonics rules into language that First-Graders can understand. How many of these rules can be obtained in this manner?

5. Obtain a copy of *Professor Phonics Gives Sound Advice*. Make lesson plans that utilize one of the phonics rules and the accompanying practice words. Is it possible to phase the words into meaningful context instead of using them as a drill in isolation?

6. Devise some simple "adjustments" or "extensions" of the graphemes of our language that can be used to make pronunciation more reliable.

7. Compare the "rules" in *Breaking the Sound Barrier* with the "rules" found in a phonics book in use 50 or 75 years ago. During the intervening years, what improvements have been made in phonics rules?

8. How can one of the phonemic-pronunciation approaches be used concurrently with a basal reader?

9. Develop a lesson plan that uses Sister Mary Caroline's "polite digraph" rule. Try it on a class.

10. Write a story that includes words which give extensive practice in the application of at least five pronunciation rules. Try it on a class.

PHONEMICS-READING
APPROACHES

4

A phonemics-reading approach is herein considered as being one in which practice is given first in auditory discrimination of the sounds of the letters separately and in combination, followed by practice in associating individual letter sounds with the printed graphemes, and finally in reading materials that are structured to contain the sounds being studied.

In previous chapters we have been considering beginning reading approaches that are concerned chiefly with practice in auditory discrimination of letter sounds and/or visual discrimination of graphemes and the sounds they represent. Such basic phonemic approaches seldom emphasize words in *meaningful* context. Moreover, basic phonemic systems generally reject the use of contextual clues, configuration clues, and graphic aids. Pictures are considered by some to be detriments to pure phonemic learning, in that picture clues are said to encourage guessing.

The phonemics-reading approach to beginning reading goes beyond the basic phonemics approach in its use of meaningful context as the medium of application for the phonemic generalizations learned. In this sense, then, the phonemics-reading approach employs the best techniques for following a phonemics sequence, plus direct practice in controlled materials into which each new phonemic element has been phased.

The difference between the two approaches is more apparent when one recognizes that most, if not all, basic phonemics approaches are designed to be supplementary to basal readers or to some other more complete approach to beginning reading, whereas the phonemics-reading approach tends to provide a unity which may constitute a total approach, independent of any basal reader series. Consequently, for a system to be classified as a phonemics-reading approach, it has to have two elements: structured phonemics materials and method, plus structured meaningful reading materials into which have been phased the phonemic elements in the sequence in which they appear in the program.

The first step entails auditory readiness through which a child achieves some proficiency in "hearing" differences in vowels and consonants. This is followed by practice in linking vowel and consonant phonemes to the printed symbols which represent the sounds. Finally, planned structured meaningful reading materials provide on-the-spot practice in the actual phonemic elements being stressed.

Phonemics-reading systems rely upon contextual meaning as an aid and guide to beginners in pronunciation. Although this may contribute to guessing, it must be classified as an "educated guess". Indeed, the child is encouraged to use his newly-acquired phonemics knowledge to help him verify his choice of a word, even when his choice is influenced by picture, configuration, and meaning clues, as well as context clues.

Thus, phonemics-reading approaches to beginning reading provide a synthesis of phonemic analysis and contextual analysis, plus structured reading materials for reading practice.

PHONETIC KEYS TO READING

Origins

Phonetic Keys to Reading is a system which attempts to provide the young beginner with "keys" for learning phonemics, word attack, and comprehension skills simultaneously. It is for this reason that it is classified as a "phonemics reading" system.

Phonetic Keys to Reading actually had its origin through twenty years of work by the late Mrs. Cornelia Brown Sloop who worked as a primary grade teacher and later as supervisor in the Consolidated School of Texas A & M College at College Station, Texas.

After the system became somewhat structured, she was joined by Dr. Harrell E. Garrison, a reading specialist, and by Mildred Creekmore, a former Texas teacher and reading consultant.

As a team, they modified some of Mrs. Sloop's materials and adapted them to a form which could be printed in text-activity book format by The Economy Company of Oklahoma City.

In one sense, the system is a reaction against the whole-word method which omits phonemics; yet, on the other hand, it proposes that it be used in conjunction with a basal reader series. It certainly does differ from most basal reader series which generally start out with the repetition and mastery of a store of sight words before any phonemic instruction is introduced.

Materials and Method

Unlike most basic phonemic systems, *Phonetic Keys to Reading* starts with a text-activity book, "Tag," which is part of a reading readiness program providing children with practice in auditory discrimination. At the same time the child marks the text-activity book and receives the visual reinforcement which comes from seeing the printed symbol for the sound being emphasized.

The readiness program is designed as a three-week daily lesson sequence in which long and short vowel sounds are taught. This is followed by a five week set of exercises which introduce consonant sounds.

The long vowels are taught first, because it is most easy for them to be accompanied with text-activity exercises in which the printed symbol's name is the same as the long vowel sound. Therefore, the long sound of "o" is presented as a listening exercise.

The teacher tells and reads stories using a few words which contain the long "o" sound. The child listens and learns to identify the sound when he hears it, and he marks the text-activity book when he finds the "o" in print. He is aided in his comprehension and identification of the word sounds by two factors: namely, his prior knowledge of words such as *home, road, boat*, and *coat*; and by the pictures which accompany the words on the workbook pages.

To enrich the learning of long vowel sounds, the teacher devises experience charts which are so structured that the long vowel sound is repeated in a number of settings.

Although the first fifteen lessons on long and short vowel sounds are intended to be given during the first three weeks of Grade One, it is possible that a more lengthened time sequence would be necessary for slow groups.

The second part of the readiness program consists of exercises in auditory discrimination of consonant sounds. Once that is started, the child is encouraged to analyze words by using his knowledge of the consonant sounds and the vowel sounds.

Experience charts are a significant part of the readiness program. In fact, they are introduced during the first three weeks. For example, children provide the stories of their own experiences, and the teacher

Fig. 4–1 Reproduced from Phonetic Keys to Reading, *copyright 1967, by permission of the Economy Company, publishers.*

makes an effort to get the child to accept words which can be used as examples of long vowel sounds. In their story telling the children are encouraged to express themselves by using full sentences that contain complete thoughts. As with all good Kindergarten work in readiness, the First Grade teacher using the *Phonetic Keys to Reading* readiness program emphasizes left-to-right eye movement by moving the hand from left to right under the words as they are spoken. The *Phonetic Keys to Reading* readiness program differs from the usual Kindergarten readiness program in two ways: First, it is being used with children who are one year older and consequently with 20% more maturation on the average; second, it is a structured program whose purpose is not just enjoyment of the story and the development of the child's own sight vocabulary, but whose aim is inserting as many usable teacher-chosen long and short vowel words as possible. The readiness program is completed with the introduction of some "Reading Charts" containing phrases and sentences. These are printed on cardboard strips to be matched with duplicate phrases and sentences on the big charts. They are part of a larger package of First-Grade phonemic cards.

THE PRE-PRIMER. The pre-primer work is contained in the second part of the "Tag" book, and it is claimed that "at this point the distinctive *Phonetic Keys to Reading* approach takes on full meaning for the children, for they begin to make use, in a reading situation, of their word-recognition skills and their ability to sound out words."

Actually, the pre-primer stories differ very little from the pre-primer stories of the usual basal reader. The text of page 90 in the "Tag" book reads as follows:

DOT AND JIM

Look, Dot, look.
I will make a boat.
I will make a big boat.
Can you make a boat?
The boat will not go.
The big boat will not sail.
I can not sail my boat.
I can not make it go.

The experienced primary teacher will recognize, however, that there is considerable diversity in vocabulary in this "pre-primer" section.

It is claimed that, by reviewing the phonemic principles learned in the first eight or so weeks of the First Grade, the child can then apply those principles to the words. A colored overlay strip at the bottom of the workbook page provides any new words that occur in the story. The new words are to be taught first.

An analysis of the readiness and pre-primer work shows that it is dependent to a large degree on phonemic analysis both visually as well as through listening. It seems that one inescapable principle of learning applies here, as it does in any method of learning to read, and that is that one will learn what he practices. The corollary to that is that one should practice materials or skills in the setting and in the matter in which they are to be used. Auditory practice in listening may have its place as readiness for reading, but it can never take the place of actual work with words on the printed page. The teacher's manual provides suggestions for both.

After the reading of each story, the teacher conducts the usual type of discussion lesson to develop comprehension or to check on its adequacy. The teacher's manual provides many suggestions for questions for the discussion.

Once "Tag" has been completed, it is recommended that the children then go into the pre-primers of whatever basal series is available in their school. By so doing, the children will get additional practice and reinforcement in using the phonemic analysis skills which they have learned in the *Phonetic Keys* program.

Whether or not this is necessary is questionable. It hinges upon the amount of "overlearning" that is necessary for purposes of recall. When dealing with a skill, however, the principle of overlearning does not apply as directly as with meaningful materials. The question remains unanswered: "Once a child has learned the principle that states that he pronounces the long sound of the first vowel when two vowels are found together, how much additional practice is needed to obtain retention of this principle"? This should not be considered as a weakness in the *Phonetic Keys to Reading* program, but just an admission on the part of reading specialists that the answer is not known.

THE PRIMER. "Dot and Jim" is the title of the primer in which there is considerable repetition of the basic phonemics learned in the earlier weeks of Grade One.

Ordinarily, the primer program would start in December and continue through January—a total of about six weeks. New sounds of vowels and some blends would be introduced together with the rules that have been devised to cover them.

The procedures of instruction for the primer include: (1) completing workbook pages which provide practice in structural analysis, prefixes, suffixes, roots, compound words, comparisons of similar-appearing words with different vowel sounds, etc.; (2) teaching new words by applying phonemic principles where they apply; (3) teaching any new words that are not regular (the child must learn these as sight words, but there are relatively few of these); (4) reading the story; (5) answering the comprehension questions at the end of the story, an exercise that often involves identifying main ideas.

By the end of January in Grade One, the plan calls for the child to go into the primer of his basal reader series. It is claimed that "any basal series may be used, because the child will not be held to a controlled vocabulary." This implies, of course, that enough phonemic skills have been learned by the child to enable him to unlock the pronunciation of most basal reader primers.

It is suggested that six weeks be spent on the primer of the basal reader series. This would take the class into mid-March, at least.

The method to be used in the basal readers is optional with the teacher, but it is expected that children will constantly be using phonemic rules and former phonemic learnings to arrive at the pronunciation of words in the basal reader primer. Furthermore, it should be noted that all through the *Phonetic Keys* method the comprehension as it grows out of the contextual setting is emphasized. Some may call this "guessing," but when the teacher has the child check his "guess" against his phonemic knowledge, it then becomes a real learning process.

THE FIRST READER. By the middle of March the first reader, "All Around with Dot and Jim," is introduced; and the same general procedure is followed. New words are introduced using phonemic principles and previous learnings. Irregular words are learned as sight words. All vocabulary is studied before the selection is read. There is much review of materials from the pre-primer and the primer, as well as some of the basics from the readiness workbook. After about five weeks on the first reader, the students are put into the first readers of other basal series and spend the remainder of the year in them.

SUPPLEMENTARY FIRST-GRADE MATERIALS. As mentioned previously, the reading readiness charts are a part of a larger package containing phonemic cards. This entire set contains 700 flash cards and word cards and 80 cards with phrases. There are also 13 large story charts, with accompanying strips of phrases and sentences for practice in matching.

The First Grade program is completed with the use of 200 picture cards which present pictures of objects whose names are representative of phonemes.

Research Findings

Although *Phonetic Keys to Reading* evolved and was first used in the 1940's and since then has been used rather extensively in schools throughout many regions of the country, research on the system is rather limited.

Apparently the most extensive research[1] was conducted by the Champaign, Illinois public schools in an attempt to evaluate the effectiveness of the method. That research was done by Miss Margaret Henderson who was Director of Elementary Education in Champaign. The study involved 30 teachers, and more than 700 students from a cross section of the socio-economic groups of the city and was initiated in the fall of 1952.

"Before" and "after" tests were given, but the findings were based primarily on a comparison of the performance of the children who had gone through the *Phonetic Keys* program with those who were in the control group. *Gates Reading Tests* and *California Primary Reading Tests* were used. It is reported that "there was a much smaller percentage of children scoring below the national norms on those tests in the experimental group than in the control group."

1. Henderson, Margaret G., *Progress Report of Reading Study, 1952–1955*. Champaign County, Ill.: Board of Education, Community Unit School District No. 4, 1955.

In 1955, a more detailed study[2] was done in Champaign by university research people. At that time, four additional tests were given. Conclusions were reported by Mrs. Margaret Henderson Greenman[3] at the Annual Meeting of the American Educational Research Association in February, 1959. Most of the conclusions, however, were opinions: (1) that parents and teachers thought that the *Phonetic Keys* experimental group were more independent not only in reading but in other subjects, as well; (2) experimental group youngsters could spell better; (3) after six years, the experimental children maintained their reading proficiency.

Unfortunately, the Champaign study reports the findings only on an arithmetical difference between the two groups and compares those figures with national norms. It does not provide any statistical evidence of the significance of the differences, or whether the differences are statistically due to chance.[4]

A somewhat less extensive research[5] was done in the Murphysboro Public Schools. One hundred pairs of Second Grade children were equated on the basis of I.Q. scores. The reading achievement scores showed a significant difference in favor of the *Phonetic Keys* group compared with those who had been taught by means of one of the basal reader series. The mean of the *Phonetic Keys* group was 8.46 months higher than the basal reader group.

Louisville, Kentucky was also the scene of research[6] from 1952 to 1955 in an effort to determine whether or not *Phonetic Keys* produced better results than the basal reader series. Two matched schools were used. Although neither method seemed to be superior to the other, some suggestions were made: (1) that a reading readiness program is not necessary for most First Grade children. (2) that most children can profit by a phonemics program before M.A. of 7, (3) there is no apparent need for a child to drill on a sight vocabulary of from 50 to 75 words before beginning word analysis; (4) that the *Phonetic Keys* learners were better spellers.

2. An Evaluation done by Dr. J. T. Hastings (University of Illinois) and Dr. Theodore Harris (University of Wisconsin).
3. Greenman, Margaret Henderson, "A Six-Year Experimental Study of Two Methods of Teaching Reading in the Elementary School," Paper delivered to the Annual Meeting of AERA, February 17, 1959.
4. See also a critique by Dr. A. Sterl Artley, "Progress Report on the Champaign Reading Study, 1952–55," *Elementary English*, 34:2 (February, 1957) 102–108.
5. Ketcham, Mrs. Herbert E., "Phonetic Keys to Reading: The Research Point of View," *Explorations in Reading*. Bethlehem: Lehigh University, June, 1962. Proceedings of the Tenth Annual Reading Conference.
6. Sparks, Paul, and Fay, Leo, "An Evaluation of Two Methods of Teaching Reading," *Elementary School Journal*, 57 (April, 1957) 386–390.

Although the Louisville study may not have been overwhelmingly conclusive as to which method was "best", it did show that children who learned by means of the *Phonetic Keys* method were equally as good as those who had the structured basal program.

On the other hand, this may not be at all a valid finding *if* the *Phonetic Keys* program included the practice in the basal readers that is recommended in the teacher's manual. Assuming that were done, it might be equally valid—or even more accurate—to conclude that it doesn't matter whether phonemics training is done before a child reads in the basal reader (as is the case with *Phonetic Keys*) or whether he gets phonemics training as he goes along in the basal reader series.

Research[7] from the Fort Apache Indian Reservation on two groups —one of which received an extra period of one half hour per day of *Phonetic Keys*—showed that the experimental group gained 1.3 grades in only six months and were speaking less pidgin English than the non-experimental group.

A more recent study[8] done in the Washington School District of Phoenix, Arizona appears to provide rather reliable results. It was reported that

1. Children in the Washington School District were far above the national norms.
2. First Grade scores far exceeded expectations on the basis of readiness tests.
3. First Grade pupils write independently much earlier after having had the *Phonetic Keys* program.
4. After *Phonetic Keys*, children read more on their own.

These observations were made after the system had adopted *Phonetic Keys to Reading* as a supplement to the regular basal program. Comparisons were made by experienced teachers who had expectations based upon years of experience with the basal readers alone.

Similar favorable opinion was expressed by Dr. Jack Monderer in a report[9] on the experiences of teachers in the Ridgefield, Connecticut schools. He reported that the *Phonetic Keys* program in Ridgefield produced above average scores for First Graders in 1961-62, and superior scores

7. Fort Apache Indian Reservation. Phonetic Keys to Reading reported by Mrs. Ketcham. (See 5 above)
8. Olson, Gerald, "Primary Reading Program Report for 1960–61 School Year," Phoenix, Arizona: Washington District No. 6, 1961.
9. Monderer, Jack H., "Analysis of the New First Grade Reading Program, 1962–63." Report submitted to the Ridgefield, Connecticut Board of Education, May 27, 1963.

for First Graders in 1962-63. He concludes by stating, "We made a good reading program better."

It is probable that a number of school systems view *Phonetic Keys* in this manner and use it as the fundamental phonemics foundation for independent reading, still retaining the rest of the basal series program. In fact, most of the research studies follow the teacher's manual, which provides timing in which *Phonetic Keys* training is followed by extensive practice in the basal readers.

The relatively inexpensive workbooks in the program call for a far less initial dollar outlay for reading materials than a basal series program would cost. It should be remembered, however, that they are consumable, and that the outlay needs to be repeated yearly.

Aside from cost, *Phonetic Keys to Reading* has the advantage of constant repetition of basics. This makes it possible to catch all newcomers into the Second- or Third Grade who have not had the phonemics training previously. This is a great advantage for a school system located in a service-impacted area where children of the military are in a constant state of migration. It has the advantage of attempting to provide a system that phases into the basal reader, yet provides some definite sequential applied training in phonemics. It provides a system that ties into the work with which the teacher is most familiar. It is not foreign to what the teacher ordinarily would be doing. In addition, it gives the assurance to teacher and parents that a systematic approach to phonemics is being used. It makes it possible for a superintendent to say, "We are using a basic phonemics system and the basal reader approach." This satisfies both the basic phonemics proponents as well as the let's-read-for-fun advocates.

By the same token, a school system which would adopt *Phonetic Keys to Reading* as its only method for teaching beginning reading without applying it to the basal series as suggested would be perverting the intent and purpose of the system and, predictably, would find itself with less than satisfactory results.

THE ROYAL ROAD READERS

Origins

The *Royal Road Readers* are the outgrowth of investigations into the psychology of the reading process conducted for a number of years by Hunter Diack and J. C. Daniels at the Institute of Education, University of Nottingham, England. From 1951 onward they worked as colleagues with what the British call "backward" (retarded) readers and reached conclusions about the psychological nature of the reading act, including some decisions on the process of perception in reading. As a result, they evolved certain basic considerations on the kinds of material that should be devised to be consistent with their findings on perception and the reading process.

Professor Diack observes that "It was, therefore, with a certain wry interest that we witnessed official blessing [from the report of the British Government Committee on reading (ed.)] still being bestowed upon theories that, as far as we could find out, had never been *proved* to be successful, and that we were in the process of showing to be inefficient."[10]

In 1953 and 1954 a discussion arose in England following the publication of a statement by Daniels and Diack spelling out their theories and an outline of the type of reading program they envisioned. The controversy intensified as supporters of the whole-word method of teaching reading began to attack the new method.

The new method gained widespread publicity when in 1954 the *News Chronicle* published 15,000 copies of Daniels and Diack's little pamphlet,[11] *Learning to Read* and distributed it free to participants in the annual conference of the National Union of Teachers.

Although the authors originally had no notion of developing a set of books, nor even a new method of teaching reading, it soon became apparent that, if their theories were to be fairly tested in classroom situations, materials that were then available would not suffice.

The problems that they faced in promoting their ideas were varied, for, on the one hand, they were obligated to deal with the pure phonemics advocates, with the whole-word "look-and-say" enthusiasts, and even with some who were advocating whole-sentence reading. What Americans would call an "eclectic" approach was most common in Britain and was referred to as "mixed methods", which the authors also had to face.

As their research and writing progressed, they concluded that there were two ways in which reading problems could be solved: (1) "to simplify our spelling; but the chances of this coming about are so slight as to be negligible." (2) "to reduce chaos into some kind of order by a careful choice of early reading material."

---

10. Diack, Hunter, *The Teaching of Reading in Spite of the Alphabet*. London: Chatto and Windus, 1965. 107. (See especially Chapter 6, "The Phonic Revolt," pp. 104–136).
11. Diack, Hunter, and Daniels, J. C., *Learning to Read: An Outline of a New Teaching Method*. London: *The News Chronicle*, 1954. A 28-page pamphlet published in Britain, now out of print.

The authors utilized their studies of perception and concluded that "visual analysis should be into letters; not such features as the dots on *i*'s and the tails on *y*'s." Consequently, they began to design what they call the "phonic word method" and which now appears in the form of the *Royal Road Readers.*

The "phonic word method" was designed to incorporate the basic vocabulary of the child, but to limit the words which he encounters on the printed page to those words which are spelled with letters which he has already learned. The words, thus, utilize those phonemic elements which the child knows, and only one new phonemic element should be added each day.

After our recent exposure to some of the amazing sentences in the new so-called "linguistics" primers, the first pages in the *Royal Road Readers* appear quite acceptable. But this, apparently, was not the case in "pre-linguistics" days in Nottingham. For, Mr. Diack writes, "The opposition to these ideas continued to show itself in a number of ways . . . . When the Institute of Education at Nottingham advertised a lecture by Daniels and myself, 900 teachers applied for tickets instead of the normal and expected forty to sixty. The discussions that followed the lectures often gave the impression that the meeting had been 'packed' by the 'opposition.' There were no brawls, but arguments frequently spread out into the street and continued long after the meeting had broken up."

The *Royal Road Readers* are concrete evidence of what the Nottingham University researchers have theorized reading to be, namely, the reconstruction of ideas by means of utilizing alphabetical symbols which are arranged in a time sequence in the order in which the sounds are made. Moreover, sounds or combinations of them in the form of words are *not* language, and, therefore, reading must be more than just pronouncing letters or words—it must be meaningful in context. The materials and method, consequently, emerge from such a logic.

Materials and Method

Daniels and Diack, authors of the *Royal Road Readers*, subscribe to the approach that the phonemic complexities of beginning reading should be limited; but, at the same time, the child should be given as large a vocabulary as possible within certain prescribed limits.

In Book I, therefore, the *Royal Road* authors have introduced almost 400 different words, at the same time attempting to limit the phonemic complexities and pitfalls to a minimum. They claim that the words in their first reader "present far fewer difficulties to the child than most look-and-say primers with a quarter of this vocabulary."

This simplicity is accomplished by limiting the vocabulary in the first two books to those words alone which contain *no silent letters,* and which have letters that are phonemically regular or which have the *most common letter-sound values.* For example, any words in the first two books that contain the letter *g* and/or *c* are words in which those consonants are pronounced with the "hard" sound, as in *pig* or in *cat.*

The short vowel sounds are adhered to religiously at first, and no words are used in which the long vowel sounds occur.

In order to attain some degree of interest and sensible continuity, the authors have found that it is necessary to utilize approximately 40 phonemically-irregular words. Their research indicated to them that children had no difficulty in using such words as "whole-word" learnings because such words were "natural" in the child's speech patterns and, therefore, were natural in the reading context.

It will be noted immediately that the first steps in the *Royal Road Readers* are, actually, a whole-word approach. This, however, does not conflict with the phonemics theories which are basic to the series. The difference is found in the regularity of the three-letter words which are used as "sight words". Indeed, they are quite similar to the word families which the linguistics scientists have "discovered".

The procedure in introducing the pictures and words is:

> This is a picture of a cat. You can tell it's a cat because it *looks* like one. The marks under it, however, do not look like a cat at all. They stand for the sound we make when we say, "cat". The picture *looks* like a cat: the printed word *says* "cat".

It is conceded that different teachers will devise different methods for presenting the concept of words as meaningful symbols. The authors warn that, at this beginning stage, the teacher should not pronounce the individual phonemes in the three-letter words. The emphasis at the beginning should be on whole words as standing for whole names of things.

With the booklet, *Book One, Part 1,* there is a cardboard sheet which the teacher is to cut up into segments, making small individual flash cards or matching cards for the child to use on the pages where the same nine pictures appear *without* the words printed underneath each picture. Thus, there are only four pages at the very beginning, the first one having the nine pictures *with* words; and, when the child turns the page, he finds the same nine pictures (arranged in a different order) with no words printed underneath. He then takes his small "matching" cards

Fig. 4–2 *Reproduced from the* Royal Road Readers, *by permission of the authors, Hunter Diack and John C. Daniels and the publishers, Chatto & Windus, Ltd.*

which contain the nine words and matches them up with the nine pictures. As the students match the words with the pictures they should "say the word to themselves." The authors give two reasons for this:

      1. it is part of the process of making them aware that alphabetic writing is a writing down of sound; and

2. when they are speaking, they are learning more actively and, therefore, more fully.

No estimate is given of the length of time a group of First Grade children should spend on practice with the eighteen matching cards, but the authors do suggest that there be adjustments for individual differences. When the majority of the class has had sufficient practice to be able to match the word cards with the pictures and to name the words at the same time, it is assumed that:

1. They are able to distinguish eighteen different words and have not been helped in that by differing word lengths, so they must have begun some analysis of the words.

2. They have begun to get hold of the idea that writing and printing have a connection with what we say as well as with what we see.

3. Some children will probably in the course of their initial steps in analysis have begun to distinguish some of the letters.

At that point in the initial learning process, the authors suggest that the teacher make wall charts, or use the "stiff card apparatus" (which is available) or make plasticine models of the nine objects. It could also be suggested that some of the McKee-Harrison small plastic "objects" could be used, plus small objects from the dime store. The difference between the *Royal Road* and the McKee-Harrison systems, however, is quite great. The former is interested in the objects as stimuli for whole-word identification, whereas the latter utilizes the small objects of hat, dog, bat, man, cat, pig, etc. as stimuli for identification and classification of initial sounds.

Pages 7 through 10 in *Book One* provide phrase reading, such as "the man stands"; "the dog runs". The purpose, according to the authors is to "show the pupil that words are printed with spaces between them and that they are read from left to right".

The authors of the *Royal Road Readers* then provide practice in initial consonant discrimination, starting with *t*, in such words as *tap* (water faucet) *top, tin,* (can), *tub.* The teacher exaggerates the *t* sound as she pronounces the words. This is followed with the same type of practice on initial consonant *p*. The children then write *t* and *p* until they can distinguish them. Using *Book One* as a workbook, they place a strip of paper on the margin and then insert the proper *t* or *p* in front of two-letter bases of *-in, -et, -un, -us, -ed,* etc. Also they affix consonant endings to bases such as *to-, ca-, ha-,* etc.

This stage is considered to be a most crucial step in the reading process, for it is here that the learner is not only learning to identify initial and final consonant sounds, but is unconsciously analyzing the words for the medial vowels.

In the first book of the series, the child is taught to write the word *the*, and at the same time is taught the sound of *th* and the principle that often two letters may stand for one sound.

The second half of the small 32-page workbook is devoted to sentence reading. Most of the beginning sentences are six words in length, such as "The hen stands on the tub." Each page has eight such sentences. Most of the words are three-letter nouns with enough directional prepositions (at, in, on, up) and some simple verbs such as run(s), stand(s), is, sit(s), etc.

The task of the child is to read the sentence and determine if it is the correct sentence to describe the action in the picture. This requires discrimination and selection, for there are eight sentences and only three pictures. This is followed by exercises in which the child writes down the number of the picture (1, 2, or 3) and writes the appropriate sentences after it. This writing apparently is accomplished without any special instruction in letter formation. To American educators, this would be an amazing feat.

It is also suggested that the pupils draw copies of the pictures and write the sentences after their pictures. Here the difference in American and British ideas of frugality and conservation are quite apparent. American workbooks are larger, with four-color pictures, cost much more and, hopefully, are completely expendible each year.

Another difference is apparent. The American workbook contains pages and pages of practice materials, whereas the *Royal Road* workbook moves from one page to the next with something new on each page, leaving the practice materials to be devised by the teacher and/or pupils.

From page 25 on to the end, *Book One* provides initial examples of the rest of the letters of the alphabet (except *q*, *z*, and *y*), together with vowel digraphs and double vowels; *ed* endings; and *ing* endings.

This first book, obviously, covers *much more* in the short space of time than does any other "system" for teaching beginning reading. It is not expected, however, that at this point the child will have learned all of the letter discrimination skills. In fact, it is somehow hoped that by the process of exposure he will have begun to distinguish those characteristics of the limited number of words with which he has been dealing. This is supposed to occur without direct teaching by the teacher, so that, by the time the child reaches the end of the book, he will have developed his own schemata for differentiating initial and final consonants in print as well as in sound, and he will also have devised some sort of method of differentiating medial vowels. How this happens is not clear, as no reference is given nor is any prior teaching to that end indicated. Only through repetition and practice in various ways is the child supposed to abstract those common elements of sight and sound which serve as his guideposts in identifying printed consonant symbols and oral consonant sounds.

By the time the children near the end of *Book One, Part 1,* they are given one of eight *First Companion Books.* These little books are actually pre-primers in which are small stories developed from the vocabulary of the workbook which the child has been using for several months. The children attempt to read these silently, and then are expected to read the book orally for the teacher. The supplementary *Companion Books* are only 16 pages in length, and can be undertaken in any sequence after the child has finished his *Book One* workbook.

There are also four small *Royal Road Question Time Books* which are used as "busy work" to fill in time for those students who might otherwise be idle while the teacher is working with a small group or individually with others.

The authors claim that "In completing Book I, Part 1, the child will have gained a good deal of insight into what reading is and will also have acquired a fair degree of skill and accuracy in reading with understanding phonically simple words and sentences."

Part II of Book I introduces a number of "special" words which come under the category of the most common irregularly-spelled words.

Whereas *Book One, Part 1* depended upon unstructured word analysis as the means to learning, Part II provides the means for word-building, which is just the opposite. Bases of words are written on the chalkboard and/or provided on mimeographed sheets. The letters which are left as blanks are to be filled in by the children. Using such bases as any number of two-letter short-vowel syllables, the child can actually build word families.

The "special" words are:

for, or, to, said, I, with, of, who, was, there, me, we, out, this, that, he, over, see, go, be, she, are, under, where, saw, they, by, down, too, were, after, all, so, you, then, now, have, been, them, why, what, my, do, does, one, two, which.

On page six, for example, the new "special" words are *for, or, to, said.* Those are printed along the top of the page. The teacher asks the children to point to the first word, *for,* and to listen to its pronunciation and then to repeat it. The children are asked to pick out the letters in *for* that they already know and can pronounce.

The last story in the Part II workbook is *At Sandrock* and contains a challenge to the child by not reproducing sentences which he may previously have memorized. The authors predict that, when he has successfully completed that story, "His confidence in his own abilities

a dog   a hen   a man   a tub   Tom

1.

The dog runs at the man.

The hen stands on the tub.

Tom stands on the tub.

2.

The man sits on the log.

The hen sits on the eggs.

The dog stands on the log.

3.

The dog runs at the hen.

The hen stands on the log.

23

Fig. 4–3 Reproduced from the Royal Road Readers, *by permission of the authors, Hunter Diack and John C. Daniels and the publishers, Chatto & Windus, Ltd.*

and his sense of achievement make him keen, rather than merely willing, to begin Book 2A or 2."

Book 2 is for those children who at this point are still considerably behind their classmates, and Book 2A is for the child who confidently can proceed into more independent reading for pleasure.

In Book 2A there are stories which are preceded by motivational exercises and vocabulary study. There are no questions following any of the stories, for the objective is to get the child to want to read the story for pleasure rather than with the objective of answering questions at the end.

It is not until children get into Books 3A or 3 that phonemic pronunciation principles are *taught,* and then only as associated learning and not as rote memorization of rules. In the third books, for example, there are nine grapheme-phoneme relationships that the child must learn and, hopefully, be able to differentiate:

oo	as in *pool*		*sh*	as in *wish*
oo	as in *book*		*ch*	as in *chin*
ee	as in *feel*		*th*	as in *thin*
qu	as in *quill*		*th*	as in *then*

and *y* as in *silly*

There are three *Companion Books* which are primers to go along with the Book 3 and Book 3A workbooks.

Additional *Question Time* books are available as supplements at each level.

Books 4 through 9 of the *Royal Road Readers* extend the phonemics complexity with which the child must deal, and, at the same time, provide a gradual but limited amount of vocabulary building. In those books, there are a number of exercises in which the child is required to go beyond the simple task of copying a sentence. He must, in fact, answer questions which require that he develop his own responses, and is expected to write them down.

The new edition of the *Royal Road Readers* was completed in 1969 with some revised copy and up-dated art work.

Research Findings

The authors of the *Royal Road Readers* make no claims that they have found the solution to all reading problems. Neither do they claim that their system is the *only* way to learn to read.

What they do say is that their modest workbooks and readers have grown out of a need to provide materials to demonstrate what they believe to be theoretically sound principles of learning applied to the area of reading. Furthermore, they do offer their own research at the University of Nottingham as proof of the effectiveness of certain of their materials with certain retarded readers with whom they worked.

Their investigation was reported in *Progress in Reading*[12] (Daniels and Diack) published by the Institute of Education at Nottington University in 1956. They compared beginning readers who had been taught with their own materials (the *Royal Road Readers*) with those who had been taught with look-and-say "mixed" methods. They called their own method, the "phonic word method".

Six tests were given to each group. Four tests were single-word tests (words in isolation). The child was asked to read each word aloud. A tape recording was made from which errors were analyzed.

The results of the investigation are shown in the following chart:

PERCENTAGES OF CORRECT AND WRONG ANSWERS AND
"NO-RESPONSES" ON FOUR VOCABULARY TESTS

Responses by Pupils Taught by the Phonics Word Method

	Correct	Wrong	No Response
Test 1	85.5	7.8	6.7
Test 2	60.5	13.1	26.4
Test 3	79.9	6.4	13.7
Test 4	73.5	8.0	18.5

Responses by Pupils Taught by "Mixed" Methods

	Correct	Wrong	No Response
Test 1	43.1	11.6	45.3
Test 2	35.2	11.5	53.3
Test 3	47.7	11.8	40.5
Test 4	44.9	10.4	44.7

In addition to the word-recognition tests, two sentence-reading tests were given. One was composed of words that were selected from the *Royal Road Readers* and, consequently, were considered to be regularly-spelled words. The second test was composed of mixed material, including irregularly-spelled words.

The differences between the groups were statistically significant, favoring the children who had learned by means of the regularly spelled phonemic elements of the *Royal Road Readers*. On the test which consisted of sentences of regularly spelled words, the *Royal Road* youngsters obtained a percentage of 87, whereas the other group scored only 62%.

12. Daniels, J. C., and Diack, Hunter, *Progress in Reading*. Nottingham: Institute of Education, Nottingham University, 1956.

On the mixed and irregularly-spelled word sentences, the *Royal Road* children were similarly ahead with a score of 82% against a score of 61% for the others.

In summary, it would be well to repeat that the authors of the *Royal Road Readers,* J. C. Daniels and Hunter Diack, call their method the "Phonic word method" primarily because it employs phonemically regular words as sight vocabulary for the first few months of reading instruction. During those first experiences with the words of our language, the child is supposed to develop an awareness to three facts: first, that letters in words "have meaning". The authors mean by "meaning" that a letter means a sound, and that at first, at least, the sounds will be kept phonemically consistent. Second, that the letters are arranged in sequence to represent the sounds that are heard in a time sequence. Third, that words can be differentiated by the letters (consonants at first) which stand for the sounds that are different.

The American teacher who is used to the accoutrements of our elaborate reading systems, and the insistence of linguistics experts and/or phonemics enthusiasts, that the child must learn ABCs; or correct delineation of letters; or expression, enunciation, emphasis; or that he must say his phonemes and tongue-twisters, may find the *Royal Road Readers* inadequate if for no other reason than the fact that they are incredibly simple. Indeed there is so little to them that it makes one suspect that anyone using them must rely upon some unseen magic for the development of efficient readers.

There are many elements of reading that do not appear either in the readers or in the teacher's manual. There is no readiness program either in visual discrimination or in auditory discrimination. There are no directions to the teacher to assure correct pronunciation. (This may be assumed.) There are only the most rudimentary developmental step-by-step lessons. There is only the slight suggestion of the need for training in visual discrimination between look-alikes in individual letters and in whole words.

When one finishes examining the books and the method, he is still left with the question of *how* does a child learn to distinguish between different individual graphemes except by repetition of whole words and by subsequent repetition of word families and phonograms.

For the American teacher who is so dependent upon elaborate step-by-step teacher's manuals,[13] the *Royal Road* system would leave much to

---

13. The originators of *The Royal Road Readers* do provide a small hardback "Teachers Book" (published by Chatto and Windus, London, 1960). The last 25 pages provide the essence of the "method."

be desired. It does have one or two elements in its favor. It does start with regular-spelled words and limits its vocabulary to eighteen words from which the bright child can abstract common elements in arriving at a schemata for attacking new words with the same regularized phonemic elements. Second, it is very inexpensive and, if used as the authors suggest, even the pupil workbooks will not be expendable.

The program has serious limitations. It is composed along the frugal lines and published for a population which is used to austerity. To those used to a more elaborate publishing environment, it appears very dull and inadequate.

Its greatest asset is the honesty and straightforward manner in which Hunter Diack presents the *raison d'etre*. It will take a considerable amount of comparative and definitive research to convince the members of the reading profession that the *Royal Road Readers* provide a method of reading that is significantly better than appears on the surface. Reports of any such research would certainly be appreciated by this author.

STRUCTURAL READING SERIES

Origins

The *Structural Reading Series*, published by the L. W. Singer Co., and copyright in 1963, was developed by Dr. Catherine Stern, Margaret B. Stern, and Toni S. Gould between the years 1944 and 1951 while they were operating an experimental school for five-year-olds in New York City. The structural reading approach at the Castle School, as it was called, now appears as a series of phonemics-reading workbooks. Marion Gartler is also listed as one of the authors.

The objective of Dr. Stern and her coworkers in developing another set of workbooks was to provide the child with some of the advantages of sound phonemic training plus direct application in a meaningful reading situation.

In 1965, Dr. Stern and Toni Gould coauthored a book, *Children Discover Reading*, published by Random House. It is, essentially, a description of the *Structural Reading* program. In addition to a description of the method, the authors refer to experiments in which *Structural Reading* has been tried in public school classrooms in Seattle, New York City and a number of other places. The book also reports testimonials of the effectiveness of the method and elaborates with four case studies. The main contribution of the book, however, is its full description of the method of "structural reading" developed at the Castle School.

Materials and Method

The first part of the program is readiness in which children learn to recognize the initial sounds that they hear in familiar words. At the same time, they learn to recognize the graphemes which are used to represent those sounds. *We Learn to Listen* is the readiness workbook. It is designed for either Kindergarten or First Grade.

The First Grade program that follows the readiness training consists of two workbooks: *We Discover Reading* and *We Read and Write*. Throughout the program, the first emphasis is upon listening to the spoken sounds and analyzing them in the spoken words. The first word in the short *a* family is *man*. The workbook provides practice materials and space for the child to see the words and accompanying pictures and to write the words. As an aid in writing the words, the letters appear on the lines in "ghost" type. Throughout the entire First Grade program this structuring for writing is an important feature. Another aid to learning is obtained by printing the consonants in blue and the vowels in red. All type throughout the entire two-year program is manuscript.

The program has eliminated all sounds in isolation. In contrast to the pure sight method so often found in basal readers, the *Structural Reading Series* provides the child with some phonemic generalities which he may use in aiding him to recognize words. As the child progresses through the structure of the program, he is not only building a firm basis for a sight vocabulary, but has the opportunity of using that vocabulary immediately in a self-contained reading sequence.

Without confining the program to the strict limitations of a linguistics-phonemics approach, the authors have obtained many of the advantages of a closely-structured phonemics sequence, and still provided some sensible reading materials. The addition of colorful pictures and the color-coding of consonants and vowels combine to make the workbooks interesting and pleasant.

The word families are also more interesting, yet hold to the short vowel pattern. The child immediately learns to recognize phonemically-related words such as *man, pan, cat, mat, map, bag,* and *sad*. Similarly, after a child has mastered the pattern of the word *flower*, he deals with related words such as *power, tower, shower*, etc. The ability to generalize through such phonemically-related drill is one feature of the system.

Set the _____.
        title   table

Put a _____ on it and
     cradle   candle

get some red leaves from the _____ tree.
                             maple   stable

A horse lives in a _____.
           cradle   stable   saddle

On New Year's Eve, you can hear horns toot
and bells _____.
     sprinkle   jingle   single

When the baby cries, give her the pink _____.
                        battle   rattle   candle

When you pat a rabbit, you must be very _____.
                      bundle   jumpy   gentle

You must pick up your things at night or someone
may _____ over them in the dark.
     bumble   stumble   giggle

21

Fig. 4–4 *Reprinted by permission of the publisher from* We Discover Reading *by Catherine Stern in the* Structural Reading Series. *Copyright* © *1966, 1963 by the publishers, Random House/Singer School Division.*

Another feature is the transfer into reading materials contained within the workbook. Throughout the First Grade program in the two workbooks, the child is expected to utilize his structural analysis skills in all his reading. Context clues are also utilized, but not as word attack skills. On the other hand, they are used to provide training in correcting incongruous words that have purposely been placed in the reading material.

When the "final-*e*" rule is introduced as the "magic *e*", the long vowel is printed in gold color. Green is used to indicate prefixes and suffixes.

The sequence is:

1. word is spoken by the teacher; children listen
2. word is analyzed aurally and orally
3. the printed symbols are presented.

The teacher is cautioned against reversing the order as was done in older "phonics" systems . . . that is, presenting the word *man* and asking the child to "sound out" *m-a-n*.

The First Grade program in the *Structural Reading Series* provides the child with phonemics practice on over 800 phonemically-related words, plus interesting reading materials phased into the program, so that the program becomes an entity in itself. Thus the program goes far beyond the Dolch Basic Word List of 220 words which the child should know at the end of the Second Grade. In fact, by the end of the Second Grade when the *Structural Reading Series* ends, the child will have added another 700 words. Altogether, more than 1,000 structurally-related words will have been covered. The two Second Grade books are *We Read More and More* and *Now We Read Everything*.

Research Findings

Very little published material is available to verify the claims of the authors that the *Structural Reading Series* is effective. Apparently the materials and methods that the authors used at the Castle School back in the 1940s convinced them that other educators could use this approach successfully.

Chall[14] compared the research on some of the approaches to beginning reading and included *Structural Reading* in her analysis.

---

14. Chall, Jeanne, *Learning to Read: The Great Debate*, New York: McGraw-Hill, 1968.

The *Structural Reading Series* has several features in its favor: color-cued vowels, consonants, and root words, plus *"magic e"*; interesting up-to-date key pictures in color; manuscript type; sensible story lines; ghost type as guidelines for writing letters and words; grouping of words that are phonemically and structurally related; excellent page layout; unusually good paper for workbooks; good Teacher's Guides for each of the five workbooks in the series.

CONCLUSIONS

The main feature of a phonemics-reading approach is the correlation of the reading material with the phonetic drill that it accompanies. This is an extension of the pure phonemic approach in which grapheme-phoneme relationships are learned independent of the reading materials in which they are to be applied.

The development of reading materials that are matched with phonemic practice requires a considerable expenditure of effort on the part of the authors. The three approaches described in this chapter are all outgrowths of years of practical classroom usage. None are new, yet there is little, if any, definitive research that indicates their effectiveness, compared with that of a basal reader series and an equal time spent on an independent phonics program.

There is another unanswered question that faces users and researchers alike: "Do children who have had initial reading instruction in a phonemics-reading approach remain significantly better readers when they transfer into other nonstructured narrative materials?"

One principle of learning is that skills should be practiced in the manner in which they are to be used. Another principle is that reinforcement through successful use is a positive factor in learning. Phonemics-reading approaches conform to the latter principle but violate the former. They provide reinforcement through immediate use in the manner in which they are learned. On the other hand, phonemics skills must be used in nonstructured context more often than in the structured-type reading that is provided in the controlled materials of the *Phonetic Keys to Reading*, the *Royal Road Readers*, and the *Structural Reading Series*.

It seems logical that children should practice using the skills that they have learned. If they have learned a phonemic skill, they should practice it immediately in a phonemically-controlled reading selection. This is what the phonemics-reading approaches provide.

The limitation of these approaches is related directly to the limitations of the structured reading materials that are available for applied practice.

BIBLIOGRAPHY

ARTLEY, T. STERL, "Progress Report on the Champaign Reading Study, 1952–55," *Elementary English*, 34:2, (February, 1957). 102–108.

DANIELS, J. C., and DIACK, HUNTER, *Progress in Reading*. Nottingham: Institute of Education, Nottingham University, 1956.

The originators of *The Royal Road Readers* do provide a small hardback "Teachers Book" (published by Chatto and Windus, London, 1960). The last 25 pages provide the essence of the "method."

——, *Learning to Read: An Outline of a New Teaching Method*. London: The *News Chronicle*, 1954.

A 28-page pamphlet published in Britain, now out of print.

DIACK, HUNTER, *The Teaching of Reading in Spite of the Alphabet*. London: Chatto and Windus, 1965. 107.

(See especially Chapter 6, "The Phonic Revolt," pp. 104–136.)

DUNCAN, ROGER L., "What's the Best Way to Teach Reading?" *School Management*, Vol. 8 (December, 1964) 46–47.

A report of the progress in the Tulsa Schools of 1355 First Grade children using Phonetic Keys to Reading compared with 1450 in traditional basal texts.

HENDERSON, MARGARET G., *Progress Report of Reading Study, 1952–1955*. Champaign County, Ill.: Board of Education, Community Unit School District No. 4, 1955.

This is a complete 57-page objective report from Mrs. Henderson to the Superintendent of Schools and the Board of Education.

——, "A Six-Year Experimental Study of Two Methods of Teaching Reading in the Elementary School."

Paper delivered to the Annual Meeting of AERA, February 17, 1959.

KETCHAM, MRS. HERBERT E., "Phonetic Keys to Reading: The Research Point of View," *Explorations in Reading*. Bethlehem: Lehigh University, June, 1962. Proceedings of the Tenth Annual Reading Conference.

MONDERER, JACK H., "Analysis of the New First Grade Reading Program, 1962–63."

Report submitted to the Ridgefield, Connecticut Board of Education, May 27, 1963.

OLSON, GERALD, "Primary Reading Program Report for 1960–61 School Year," Phoenix, Arizona: Washington District No. 6, 1961.

SPARKS, PAUL E., and FAY, LEO C., "An Evaluation of Two Methods of Teaching Reading," *Elementary School Journal*, 57 (April, 1957) 386–390.

An interesting report of a study involving more than 800 students divided into two groups, one of which was taught by means of *Phonetic*

Keys to Reading and one by a basal reader. Initial superiority for those students in the *Phonetic Keys* group was not viable beyond the second grade.

QUESTIONS AND ACTIVITIES FOR DISCUSSION AND GROWTH

1. Compare the practice reading material in the *Phonetic Keys to Reading* workbooks with the reading material in the *Structural Reading Series.* What elements do they have in common?

2. Develop a series of four lesson plans in which you will use the *Phonetic Keys to Reading* with material in a First Grade basal reader. What aspects do you find most difficult to correlate?

3. Write a story in which you provide phonemic practice on three phonemic elements. What limitations must you impose on yourself for structuring a story of this kind?

4. Locate the Economy Company representative in your region and ask him to direct you to a school system that uses *Phonetic Keys to Reading.* Make arrangements with the administration of the school to visit a classroom to observe and to talk with the teacher. Is the teacher actually doing what she thinks she is doing? On what do you base your opinion?

5. Demonstrate by means of specific examples how the *Phonetic Keys to Reading* preprimer program is comparable to or dissimilar to the basal reader preprimer approach.

6. Rewrite the *Royal Road to Reading* materials to conform to American usage. If this were done, would it be used extensively by American teachers? Give reasons for your answer.

7. In what important ways is the *Structural Reading Series* different from the *Royal Road Readers?* What do they have in common that qualifies them to be classified as phonemics-reading approaches?

8. Investigate the programs in reading at several private schools in an attempt to locate a school where you can observe the *Royal Road Readers* being used.

9. In what way does the use of experience charts in the *Phonetic Keys to Reading* readiness program differ from their use in a language-experience approach?

10. If you were a supervisor of reading and your superintendent asked you to provide an evaluation of the three approaches presented in this chapter, what evaluation would you prepare for him?

LINGUISTICS-PHONEMICS APPROACHES

5

For the last thirty years or more, linguistics scholars have been toying with the idea of applying the knowledge they have acquired on the development and characteristics of our spoken language to the problems of reading that language. In general, their dreams have remained at the theoretical level. One or two linguistics scholars have tried to assemble some of the regular characteristics of the spoken language into printed form which might serve as practice materials for children starting to read the language.

Linguistics scholars (and I use that term to distinguish them from *linguists* who are actually users and speakers of languages) who attempt to apply their knowledge of speech sounds to the printed language are faced with exactly the same problems that have been troubling reading specialists for over a century.

Neither linguists nor reading specialists would have much problem if we had 44 printed symbols to represent the 44 basic sounds of our American language. Linguistics scholars claim, however, that their knowledge of speech sounds can be of significant help to the reading profession which is hard pressed on one hand by the basic phonics people, and on the other hand by those who advocate a good beginning sight vocabulary.

Few, if any, true linguistics scholars claim to be reading specialists, yet a number of methods by so-called "linguists" have appeared in the last few years, and have caused a more-than-ordinary stir among teachers, reading specialists, and publishers. So great has been the excitement over the so-called "linguistics approach to reading," that some basal readers and supplementary materials now boldly claim to be "linguistically-oriented" without as much as a revision in their texts.

The origin of the present deluge of linguistics in reading may be traced to the publication in 1961 by Wayne State University Press of a large book, *Let's Read*.[1] The book was a compilation of the unpublished materials of the late Leonard Bloomfield, a renowned linguistics scientist, who had worked with an attempt to apply some principles of linguistics to beginning reading.

The materials for *Let's Read* were left to Clarence Barnhart, a friend of Bloomfield, who felt a personal obligation to see that they received a hearing by the reading profession.

At about the same time, several other linguistics scientists began to explore the possibilities of moving into the reading market. Dr. Charles C. Fries published his book, *Linguistics and Reading*[2] in 1963; and, in the same year, the first of a series of so-called "linguistics science readers" for children was published. The senior author was Dr. Henry Lee Smith, Jr., an anthropologist and linguistics scientist.

It was the invasion of the field of reading by the linguistics scientists that really generated interest. The reading professionals had been hearing about a linguistics approach to reading for several years prior to the publication of the Bloomfield-Barnhart book, but there appeared to be no more than a reading convention interest, with no follow-through with materials. In fact, Dr. Carl Lefevre[3] of Chicago Teachers College had achieved reputation among fellow reading specialists as a promoter of the theme of linguistics in reading. His paper on "Reading Instruction Related to Primary Language Learnings—a Linguistic View" was presented at the annual convention of the National Council of Teachers of English in 1960. The following spring, Dr. Lefevre presented a similar paper on linguistics and reading at the annual convention of the International Reading Association. Again in 1962, he was a featured speaker on linguistics in reading at the IRA convention. And his book *Linguistics and the*

1. Bloomfield, Leonard, and Barnhart, Clarence, *Let's Read, A Linguistic Approach*. Detroit: Wayne State University Press, 1961.
2. Fries, Charles C., *Linguistics and Reading*. New York: Holt, Rinehart and Winston, 1963.
3. Lefevre, Carl A., "Reading Instruction Related to Primary Language Learning—A Linguistic View," paper read at the annual convention of the National Council of Teachers of English, 1960.
———. "Language Patterns and Their Graphic Counterparts: a Linguistic View of Reading," *Changing Concepts of Reading Instruction*, International Reading Association Conference Proceedings. New York: Scholastic Magazines, 1961. VI, 245–49.
———. *Linguistics and the Teaching of Reading*. New York: McGraw-Hill Book Co., Inc., 1964.

Teaching of Reading, published later in 1962, was the first professional book in the field.

By 1963, the reading specialists were talking about linguistics and secretly were trying to determine what it was that they were actually talking about. While they were talking, the linguistics scientists were publishing reading materials without much concern for what the reading process actually is. By 1965, the linguistics scientists had captured the "linguistics in reading" corner of the market.

There seems to be some agreement that our language is technically an alphabetic language, even though it is incomplete with only 26 letters to represent the 44 sounds. Ideally, each letter (grapheme) should represent one sound (phoneme). However, in our American English, there are cases where two letters represent the same phoneme, and there are many cases where a single vowel letter represents several phonemes. Moreover, it takes several graphemes or letters to represent one phoneme, as in the case of *augh* in "laugh".

Some linguistics scientists talk in terms of the word: "graphonic". They analyze the language as consisting of letters or groups of letters representing sounds. The "graphonic base", according to them, is that group of letters which represent what reading specialists have called the root or base upon which phonograms are built. In essence, the two are the same.

The linguistics scientist illustrates his "graphonic base" as being *and* to which are affixed the consonant *h* to produce *hand*, *st* to produce *stand*, *b* to produce *band*, etc. The reading specialist years ago talked of building phonograms using the *and* "family."

In producing a basic beginning vocabulary restricted to phonemically-regular words, the linguistics scientist is restricted either to the utilization of the five long vowel sounds or the five short vowel sounds. These are the only "regular" vowel sounds in the language.

Let us assume that the five short vowel sounds are selected. A chart can be constructed using the short vowel *ă* sound, surrounding that sound with consonants. Such a chart would be as follows:

Phonemically-Regular Words Using the Short ă

	b	c	d	f	g	h	j	k	l	m	n	p	r	s	t	v	w	y
b			bad		bag						ban				bat			
c	cab		cad							cam	can	cap			cat			
d	dab		dad							dam	Dan							
f	Fab		fad								fan				fat			
g	gab				gag				gal			gap		gas				
h			had		hag				Hal	ham				has	hat			
j	jab				jag					jam		Jap						
k																		
l			lad		lag							lap						
m		Mac	mad		Mag					Mam	man	map			mat			
n	nab				nag						Nan	nap			nat			
p			pad						pal	Pam	pan				pat			
r					rag					ram	ran	rap			rat			
s			sad		sag				Sal	Sam		sap			sat			
t	tab		Tad		tag					Tam	tan	tap						
v											van				vat			
w					wag													
y																		

In addition to the above, there are the two-letter words utilizing the short ă sound:

> add (double consonants that are pronounced as one consonant are
>   acceptable)
> am, an, as, at

The word *and* also is necessary.

A linguistically-based reading lesson would utilize the words from the chart above, emphasizing the regularity of the short ă sound. It might read something like this:

> Pam ran to Sam and Dan.
> Sam had Pam's tan fan.
> Dan had Pam's fat cat.
> Sam and Dan ran with Pam's tan fan and fat cat.
> Pam is sad and mad.
> Sam and Dan are bad.

Several irregular words must be learned as "sight words" in order to produce sentences that are sensible.

Phonemically-Regular Words Using the Short ĕ

	b	c	d	f	g	h	j	k	l	m	n	p	r	s	t	v	w	y
b			bed		beg						Ben			Bess	bet			
c					ceg													
d											den							
f			fed						fell									
g															get			
h											hen							
j			Jed	Jeff					jell						jet			
k																		
l			led		log										let			
m											men				met			
n			Ned												net			
p					peg						pen				pet			
r			red															
s									sell						set			
t			Ted						tell		ten							
v															vet			
w			wed						well						wet			
y									yell		yen			yes	yet			

Phonemically-Regular Words Using the Short ĭ

	b	c	d	f	g	h	j	k	l	m	n	p	r	s	t	v	w	x	y
b	bib		bid		big				Bill		bin				bit				
c																			
d			did		dig					dim	din	dip							
f	fib				fig				fill		fin				fit			fix	
g																			
h			hid						hill			hip		his	hit				
i																			
k			kid						kill		kin			kiss	kit				
l			lid						Lil			lip			lit				
m									mill					miss	mitt			mix	
n	nib											nip							
p					pig				pill		pin				pit				
r	rib				rig					rim		rip							
s									sill		sin	sip			sit			six	
t									till		tin	tip							
v																			
w					wig				will		win				wit				
y																			

Phonemically-Regular Words Using the Short ŏ

	b	c	d	f	g	h	j	k	l	m	n	p	r	s	t	v	w	x	y
b	Bob				bog									boss				box	
c	cob		cod		cog							cop			cot				
d					dog				doll		Don				dot				
f	fob				fog													fox	
g	gob		God												got				
h	hob				hog							hop			hot				
j	job				jog										jot				
k																			
l					log									loss	lot				
m	mob		Mod							Mom		mop							
n	nob		nod												not				
p			pod							pom					pot				
r	rob		rod												rot				
s	sob		sod															sox	
t			Tod		tog					Tom		top		toss	tot				
v																			
w																			
y											yon								

Phonemically-Regular Words Using the Short ŭ

	b	c	d	f	g	h	j	k	l	m	n	p	r	s	t	w	y
b			bud		bug					bum	bun			bus	but		
c			cud									cup			cut		
d	dub		dud		dug				dull								
f											fun			fuss			
g									gull		gun				gut		
h	hub			huff	hug				hull	hum					hut		
j					jug										jut		
k																	
l					lug				lull								
m			mud		mug					mum				muss	mutt		
n	nub														nut		
p	pub			Puff	pug						pun	pup			putt		
r	rub				rug					rum	run				rut		
s	sub									sum	sun						
t	tub				tug												
v																	
w																	
y																	

It is obvious that a beginner must know the basic consonant sounds before attempting to differentiate the various sounds which are inherent in such an exercise. In fact, this is not far removed from the "tongue-twisters" which were so popular as phonemic exercises more than a century ago.

The method which is used is just the opposite of the phonemic-pronunciation rule system. In the latter, the child is given the rule and then he must apply it in deducing the sound of a word. It is a deductive method. In the "linguistics in reading" method, the procedure is an inductive one, in which the child is presented with pages and pages of reading material which concentrates on one basic sound with its accompanying regular spelling—the "root" or *graphone* referred to above. In the sample reading material, the *am* or *an* sounds are repeated until the child "gets it". He does not need a "rule".

Many "linguistics-in-reading" programs reflect the linguistics scientists' concept of reading as a decoding process. They base this concept on the idea that our language is alphabetic, and that the letters of the alphabet represent sounds. Obviously, the spoken language precedes the written language by many centuries of time, just as speaking precedes reading and writing in the experience of the child.

The encoding of speech sounds into graphic symbols produces our written language. Reading, according to the linguistics scientist, is the process of decoding—putting the sounds which the printed symbols represent back into spoken form. This involves more than just reproducing the individual letter sounds in sequence. It requires the grouping of letters into the correct spoken sound which they collectively represent. Moreover, it requires both inflection, intonation, and accent—none of which are represented on our printed page, except in the case of the "?" or "!" marks.

Although reading specialists do not view reading as such a simple process as envisioned by the linguistics scientist, there is much that can be said for the "linguistics" point of view. Psychologists would say that a set of abstract rules to be memorized before the child experiences success in reading violates one of the principles of learning, namely that concrete and meaningful material is learned and recalled more easily than abstract material. Some linguistics scientists have made attempts to provide such meaningful material. Others have not been so successful in producing meaningful products even though they may be "linguistically consistent and regular."

A quotation from one of the teacher's manuals which accompanies one of the new "linguistics-in-reading" systems will illustrate how the linguistics scientist envisions the system working:

Word attack, then, is developed by linguistic groupings. If the child can recognize the spelling pattern in a word that he has never seen before, and if he can group it with words that have the same pattern of sound *and* spelling relationships, then he can read the never-before-encountered word.[4]

The *spelling patterns* are the clue to every "linguistics-in-reading" system. They are always the three-letter words which utilize the short vowel sounds. Some series try to develop stories using only the short *a* sound. Others utilize all five of the short vowel sounds simultaneously, thereby appearing to violate the very cornerstone of their faith. At least one "linguistics-in-reading" system just provides page after page of grapheme-phonemes out of context, and includes nonsense syllables which appear later as parts of meaningful words.

Although linguistics scholars are not in agreement in their diagnosis of what is wrong with current reading instruction in our schools, they seem to be in agreement that a "linguistics" approach would solve the problems of reading.

LET'S READ

Origins

The late Leonard Bloomfield, probably more than any other one person, deserves credit for a structured approach to reading through a regularized introduction of speech sounds.

Throughout the professional career of that brilliant linguistics scientist, he advocated attention to the implications which research in the field of linguistics had for the reading field. Unfortunately, he did not enlist the aid of the reading specialists of his day, and died before his system had undergone the test of classroom application. His purpose was to provide educators with what he earnestly believed was an improvement on what he termed "unscientific and ineffective methods" of reading instruction.

In an attempt to present his theories to the education profession, he published in 1942 two articles[5] in the *Elementary English Review* on "Linguistics and Reading". In those articles, he begged for experimenta-

---

4. Rasmussen, Donald, and Goldberg, Lynn, *Teachers Handbook* for the SRA Reading Series. Chicago: Science Research Associates, 1965. p. 5.
5. Bloomfield, Leonard, "Linguistics and Reading," *Elementary English Review*, 19 (April, 1942) 125–130 and (May, 1942) 183–186.

tion with his method, recognizing its purely theoretical aspects. It was during the ten years prior to his death in 1949 that he and his protégé, Clarence Barnhart, sought in vain to have the work tried in schools and to be accepted for publication. It was a continual disappointment to the two men that the work received no hearing in educational circles.

Upon the death of Bloomfield, Clarence Barnhart became not only the sole missionary for the system, but became obsessed with a feeling of urgency and obligation to have the method published. He succeeded in this through Wayne State University Press, which in 1961 produced the large volume, *Let's Read*. Being a university press, dedicated only to providing scholarly works to the educational world, the work which now became known as the *Bloomfield-Barnhart Let's Read*, found very limited distribution. Again Barnhart was frustrated in his attempt to get the materials into the hands of classroom teachers.

As a result, he formed his own company, Clarence L. Barnhart, Inc., to publicize the method. Soon it was found that the master text should be divided into smaller, more-easily-managed books. Teacher's manuals were also needed, and this presented a real problem. Although Clarence Barnhart had once been a classroom teacher and also had pleaded with teachers to try the system, he was left with few practical applications as guides. Consequently, when faced with the task of preparing a teacher's manual, he had to draw upon his personal knowledge of how Bloomfield the originator of the system, conceived it to be.

Bloomfield's essay on "Linguistics in Reading" is reproduced in the master text, *Let's Read*. That volume also contains two pages which describe Bloomfield's conception of how the materials would be implemented in the classroom.

Materials and Method

Clarence Barnhart provides three generalizations which undergird the Bloomfield-Barnhart system:

1. Language is primarily speech. Instruction in reading should be based upon the oral language acquired by the child in the first five years of his life.
2. English has an alphabetic writing system whose code is easily broken. The child's immediate task when he starts to read is to master . . . (that code).
3. Language is systematic. It employs contrasting patterns that consistently represent differences in meaning . . . take advantage of the patterns and contrasts.

Generalization #3 is the key to the Bloomfield-Barnhart system. The regular patterns are presented and then are repeated with the contrasting elements in the pattern. The patterns are memorized by rote in isolation.

READINESS—THE ALPHABET. First the ABCs are learned by rote. Capital letters and lower case letters are both included, but initial emphasis in on the capitals. During the drills, the class sings the "alphabet song" to the tune of "Twinkle, Twinkle, Little Star."

While the "alphabet song" is being sung in unison by the class, the teacher is pointing to the cards above the chalkboard, or is flipping the flash cards. This is done as warm-up for each lesson twice a day for the first week of instruction. The class is told that every word in a book or in a newspaper is made from these letters which they are learning.

As soon as the second lesson, the children as a class are asked to respond to such questions as, "Tell me what the first letter is." "Tell me what the second letter is." "The third letter." "Now, class, tell me the names of the first three letters," and so on.

The naming of letters, singing of the alphabet song, and discussing speaking and writing continues through two weeks. During that time, discussion of the way symbols are formed with curved and straight lines includes other language symbols as well as English. Emphasis is placed first on the straight lines that form our capital letters: A, F, I, H, K, L, T, V, X.

The first words that the class spells are constructed from the "straight-line" letters: A, F, H, I, N and T. They are: HAT, HIT, FAT, and NAT. Lesson #9 is illustrative of the class procedure led by the teacher:

After singing the alphabet song, the teacher tells the class, "You know these letters: A, B, C, D, E, F, G, H, I, J, K, L, M, N, O, P, Q, R. What are the next four letters?" The class answers, "S, T, U, V." Then the teacher asks, "What are the last four letters?" The class answers, "W, X, Y, Z."

The teacher then says, "Now you know all the letters of the alphabet."

"Which letter is made with a small half-circle and a long line?" The teacher expects them to say "P." (This is possible because they are dealing only with capital letters.)

"Which letter is made with a small half-circle, a long line, and a small line added to it?" (R)

"Which letter is made with a long line and two small half-circles?" (B)

"Which letter is made with two very small half-circles reversed?" (S).

(It may be an erroneous assumption that First Graders in September will know the meaning of "reversed.")

"Which letter is made of a straight line and a little half-circle?" (J) (This may be confused with the first question.)

"Which letter is made of two straight lines and a little half circle joining them?" (U)

(This is a difficult visual discrimination for 6-year-olds to make—involving, as it does, a visual abstraction.)

"Here are two words made of letters: C A T, R A T."

In the above lesson, the children spell C A T and R A T and add them to the four previously spelled. In subsequent lessons, they will all be reviewed together to note similarities and differences.

Also, in subsequent lessons, the line-and-half-circle analysis of capital letters continues.

In the first week there are ten full lessons such as described above covering the twice-a-day sessions with Bloomfield-Barnhart's *Let's Read*. The assumpton is that "the class" will have learned all of the capital letters during that first week, and will be ready to start the small letters of the alphabet on Monday of the second week.

In the work with small letters, the regularities are learned first. Those letters which appear exactly as the capitals are introduced first, as follows:

c	k	o	p	s	v	w	x	y	z
C	K	O	P	S	V	W	X	Y	Z

By the middle of lesson 12, it is assumed that the class will be ready to see the similarities in spelling:

C A T	H A T	H I T	A T
c a t	h a t	h i t	a t

Other pairs are added as the second week progresses. At the end of the second week, the children are expected to know all capital and all small letters in alphabetical sequence and at random.

It is recognized that this may take longer than the recommended two weeks; but, when the teacher feels that the alphabet has been mastered by the class as described, they proceed on into work with the phonemically-regular spelling patterns which constitute the bulk of the work for the ensuing school year.

THE *ăt, ăn, ăd* AND *ăp* WORDS. *Let's Read* #1, the beginning small book for classroom use, provides a vocabulary printed in large type and totaling 86 monosyllables developed on the graphone (base) ă as in căt. Throughout the 74 lessons in which there is drill on the short ă sound, the consistently-regular spellings are arranged in nine different patterns. These are for purposes of comparison for similarity and contrast.

All of the monosyllables in the 74 lessons are in isolation. No reading takes place. It is a process of S—R, in which the "S" is the printed two- and/or three-letter word and the "R" is the oral response of the class by pronouncing that word. The class also orally spells each of the 86 words as they appear in various arrangements in the nine patterns in the 74 lessons.

Thus, by Christmas vacation, the class will have learned all of the monosyllables using short ă, with the ăt, ăn, and ăd bases. The work during that time also includes 30 lessons with nonsense monosyllables which are optional but strongly recommended. It is reasoned that, although they may be nonsense in isolation, they do constitute parts of meaningful words when encountered later. They should, therefore, be learned, and at the same time that the class is memorizing the ăt, ăn, and ăd spelling patterns.

Pairing or contrasting two monosyllables with only one difference as the variable in both spelling and its related sound is the chief distinction of the Bloomfield-Barnhart system. It is on that foundation that all new words are added. In that manner, the system closely adheres to the psychological learning principle of "step-by-step" increments in learning.

MONOSYLLABLES BASED UPON SHORT ĭ AND SHORT ŭ. *Let's Read* #2 provides a new vocabulary of 118 monosyllables with the short ĭ and *short ŭ* sounds as the base. The key words are ĭ as in bĭg, and ŭ as in fŭn.

The method of presenting Part #2 is an extension and, in many ways, a duplication of the method used in Part #1. Consequently, it is expected that a class which has thoroughly mastered the work and procedure of Part #1, will be able to pick up some speed in responding to the visual stimuli in part #2.

Although part #2 contains 67 full lessons, the authors hopefully suggest that it may be covered in about 7 weeks, or much less by more gifted students. Part #2 contains nonsense syllables which may be learned during that time, or may be postponed to be used in the end-of-the-year review and testing.

MONOSYLLABLES BASED UPON SHORT ĕ AND SHORT ŏ. *Let's Read* #3 provides 98 new words in 17 different comparison patterns based upon the short ĕ sound as in bĕt, and upon the short ŏ sound as in hŏt. If the methodology follows that of parts 1 and 2, it is expected that the 88 lessons in Part #3 will be covered by the class in March and April.

Let's Read, Part 4 is available for work with better classes during First Grade. And, if a teacher has a homogeneously-grouped top class, it is suggested that she and the class cover Let's Read, Part 5.

For average and slow classes, however, the months of May and June should be spent in review drill on the 46 patterns of 302 words and as many of the 14 patterns of nonsense syllables as possible. There are workbook tests which the children in the class should take in June.

Monosyllables with Consonant Digraphs. Let's Read, Part 4, provides class practice on 293 four-letter monosyllables in which the consonant digraphs appear either at the beginning or at the ending of the word, as in spot, split, or in band, and tempt. It is interesting to note that the consonant digraphs have been added to exactly the same bases as those used in Parts 1, 2, and 3; and, of course, the phonemic values of all letters in Part 4 remain constant with those presented in the first three parts. The four-letter monosyllables in Part 4 are presented in 41 spelling patterns.

Consonant Suffixes. Let's Read, Part 5 completes work on regularly-spelled monosyllables having consonant digraphs and suffixes. Part 5 provides 591 words in 37 spelling patterns covering such variables as plurals (cat+s), and possessives (cat's).

Although combinations such as the digraph, ng in "long" and ch in "such" have phonemic values that are not consistent with the individual sounds of each of the consonants, those combinations are taught in Part 5 as though they are "regular" spellings with regular sounds associated therewith.

Part 5 is concluded with the regular values of qu, which most reading specialists now accept as the only possible way to represent the sound of q, and the x sound as in box.

Although many classes probably will not cover Part 4 and/or Part 5 until Grade Two, it is almost a certainty that Part 6 will not be dealt with until the second year.

Long Vowel Sounds. Let's Read, Part 6 takes up the long vowel sounds as they appear in 597 words, including those double vowels which are regularly long. It is in Part 6 that reading specialists would find disagreement with some of the phonemic approach. There are 21 spelling patterns with such comparisons as the ee sound in see, and the ea sound in eat. Also the combinations of vowels with the consonants, y or w are presented to represent the ay sound as in day and the ow sound as in cow.

Inasmuch as all of the materials on the Bloomfield-Barnhart system are being printed and distributed solely through Clarence Barnhart's private company, the amount of supplementary materials has been limited. There are minimal workbooks for each Part, and mimeographed teacher's manuals to help the teacher get started.

The lack of pictures and art work is, however, not due to limited resources, but by design. It is explained that

> "We are emphasizing the breaking of the alphabetic code. We want the child to concentrate on the message the letters give without getting a clue and without distraction from a picture."[6]

Barnhart added, "It is worth noting, too, that we have not had a single complaint from a teacher that children object to the lack of pictures".

Research Findings

Little, if any, longitudinal research is available on *Let's Read*. This may be partly due to the fact that it is new to most classrooms. Second, it may be due to the fact that it is, in essence, a pronunciation system which concentrates on "breaking the pronunciation code", and is not really a system of reading, *per se*.

It appears that it would be extremely difficult to set up an acceptable design for definitive research in which results with *Let's Read* would be compared with results in which another system was used. This could be done only if one were sure that the *Let's Read* system were kept absolutely "pure" and uncontaminated with reading practice *in any and all other materials*. This is almost an impossibility in schools today where children eagerly rush to school with the expectation that they will be *reading*—and that right soon! It would be a monumental task to try to get the equally-eager parents to stand still while their children go through 35 to 40 weeks of nothing but pronunciation of phonemically-regular words and nonsense syllables. Such a comparative research, therefore, would have to eliminate any and all reading practice in children's literature, mathematics, science, weekly news magazines, and even spelling. In addition, it would have to placate the parents.

In spite of the probable impossibility of adequate control of variables making research on the system impossible, there have been a number of favorable reports of success with the system.

One of the authors of the system had first-hand experience in teaching his own son by means of the method. A number of years ago, a rather large number of parochial school classes in Chicago tried the

---

6. Barnhart, Clarence L., Speech presented to 9th Annual Conference on Reading, University of Rhode Island, July, 1963.

system with favorable results reported by Sister Mary Fidelia. From time to time others tried the method and reported satisfaction with it.[7]

More recently, the office staff of Clarence L. Barnhart, Inc. has been receiving reports such as the following[8] of success with the system. For example, P.S. 18, in Yonkers, N.Y. started using the *Let's Read* materials in 1964 and continued their use in 1965 with the children as they moved into the Second Grade. One boy was reported as reading at a 5.5 level by January of the Second Grade. In the fall of 1966, P.S. 18, Yonkers reported that "all First and Second Grades are using the *Let's Read* readers and workbooks this year." It was also reported that the pilot group which started in the Bloomfield-Barnhart approach in 1964 was in Third Grade and was completing the final readers of the series during the 1966–67 school year.

An experimental project in Arlington (Virginia) Public Schools has set up the Bloomfield-Barnhart system in the Kindergarten and First Grade of the Oakridge Elementary School. Both the First Grade teacher and the Kindergarten teacher expressed personal opinions to the effect that they and the children enjoyed working with the *Let's Read* materials.

End-of-the-year reports from the Oakridge School were based upon the First-Graders' performance on a battery of three tests. The classes had been set up in two groups: Group 1 being the fast learners and Group 2, the slower children.

On the *California Achievement Test*, Group 1 showed an average in total reading of Grade 3.6, and total language scores equivalent to an average of Grade 3.9. The lower group had an average in total language of 2.4 on the same test.

On the *Gates Primary Reading Test*, Group 1 had an average of 3.6 in sentence reading and 3.7 in paragraph meaning. Group 2 had an average of 2.8 in sentence reading and 2.6 in paragraph meaning.

On the *Metropolitan Achievement Test*, Group 1 had an average of 2.9 in word knowledge, 3.2 in word discrimination, and 3.4 in reading. Group 2 averaged 2.2 in word knowledge, 2.2 in word discrimination, and 2.1 in reading.

The experiment was continued at the Oakridge School through the 1967–68 school year.

Many who have not used the materials have been quite vocal in

---

7. *Ibid.*
8. A 4-page newsletter, "Let's Read," is published occasionally and carries reports from school systems and individuals who are using the Bloomfield-Barnhart linguistics-reading materials. Available free from Clarence L. Barnhart, Inc., Box 359, Bronxville, New York 10708.

condemnation of them. Objections have been raised to a number of facets of reading which are not touched in the "system". For example, there is no provision for contextual clues. In fact, every effort is made to exclude contextual clues. The same is true of picture clues.

There is no provision for work in structural analysis, or in any word recognition skills beyond the "regular" spelling patterns. Consequently, the child gets no training in work with the irregularities of our language which, really, are the stumbling-blocks to reading. Teachers and reading specialists are quick to point out that, if the language were all regular, "breaking the alphabetic code" would be no problem, and probably could be done in a lot less time than that required in the *Let's Read* program.

The similarity of the Bloomfield-Barnhart materials to those in use over a century ago is also cited,[9] yet it should be remembered that any linguistically-based system is severely limited when it places restrictions upon itself to keep within the realm of phonemically-regular words. Perhaps conditions today are different, but it should be noted that the logic of regularity claimed for linguistics-phonemics such as found in *Let's Read* was not great enough to overcome the inherent weaknesses of extended drill, unimaginative story content, lack of attention to reading as a thinking process, and whole-class recitation without concern for individual differences.

It is possible that materials such as *Let's Read* may be very useful with mentally-retarded or aphasic-type learners. The daily—or twice-a-day repetition of simple materials containing phonemically regular elements provides a daily base of operations for the child with little or no visual memory. Like all work with such children, however, it would have to be done largely on an individual basis. This is an excellent area for a good piece of research.

In support of the Bloomfield-Barnhart system, *Let's Read*, it should be said that it "keeps faith" with the basic tenets of linguistics science. It presents a "pure" and non-corrupted approach to pronunciation of those aspects of our language which are phonemically consistent. It presents those in terms of one or two good principles of learning theory. First, through "step-by-step" learning in which new materials are built upon previous learning with small daily increments; second, through repetition of likenesses and differences in every possible combination, thus providing the recurring patterns from which the learner can abstract generalizations for "breaking the alphabetic code".

---

9. Spache, George D., *Reading in the Elementary School*. Boston: Allyn and Bacon, Inc., 1964. Ch. 5: 116–129.

BASIC READING

Origins

Basic Reading, a linguistics-phonemic series of basal readers published by J. B. Lippincott Co. is the work of Dr. Glenn McCracken, who achieved considerable notice as the originator of the "New Castle Experiment",[10] and Dr. Charles C. Walcutt, a noted literary critic.

The "New Castle Experiment" ran during the decade of the 1950's and was conducted by Glenn McCracken, then director of Audio-Visual Services for the New Castle Public Schools. It began in the Thaddeus Stevens School and was later transferred to the McGill School.

The success which the armed forces had during World War II in using films to teach illiterates to read was the motivation for introducing the same medium of instruction as the nucleus for the "New Castle Experiment." The reasons given for using films for projecting an image on the screen or chalkboard as a means for beginning reading instruction are several: "Projected images tend to fix learning in the child's mind"; "much less repetition is needed"; "a picture is worth ten-thousand words."

From its inception in 1949, the "New Castle Experiment" worked in conjunction with a basal reading series. Filmstrips were designed to accompany every lesson in the basal reader pre-primers and primers. The details of the film lessons were slightly rearranged, and, as the experiment progressed, much of the textual practice material was replaced by work by the entire class, using the projected filmstrips.

Reports of the results obtained in the beginning reading class at the Stevens School indicated that, after eight months of work with McCracken's method and filmstrips, every student scored at the Second-Grade achievement level or higher on the *Gates Primary Reading Test,* and those figures included one child with 97 I.Q. who scored 2.61 and one with only 74 I.Q. who scored at 2.24!

When the experiment was transferred to the McGill School (which is in an even higher socio-economic neighborhood), even more astounding results were reported. Surprisingly, however, the classes at Stevens School were changed back to the traditional reading program in spite of the fact that comparisons of reading achievement scores obtained by students in the two experimental classes at that school were consistently higher than scores on the same tests given to children in all of the other

---

10. The "New Castle Experiment" is described by Dr. McCracken in the second half of his book, *The Right to Learn.* Chicago: Henry Regnery Co., 1959.

26 classes in the New Castle System. Moreover, it is reported that, when the McCracken procedure was dropped at the Stevens School, their ratings dropped from first and second places to 25th and 26th in a total of 28 classes of beginning reading.

Consequently, it is not surprising to find that, when the experiment was transferred to McGill School, its ranking jumped to first place. It was reported that, by the spring testing period of Grade One, the McGill School median was 3.18 (for First Graders) with a range from 2.08 to 3.51.[11]

As Glenn McCracken went about the country claiming "no reading failures" with his method, his almost unbelievable figures met considerable incredulity on the part of teachers and reading specialists.[12] He did, however, attract the attention of Dr. Charles C. Walcutt, Professor of English at Queens College, who for several years had been a leader of the "let's-return-to-teaching-phonics" group of reading critics. Dr. Walcutt had previously co-authored with a Mrs. Terman a blistering attack on basal reader instruction in *Reading: Chaos and Cure*,[13] and later edited a collection of speeches and writings under the title of *Tomorrow's Illiterates*.[14] In addition to those, Dr. Walcutt is author of a number of scholarly publications in literary criticism and has served as chairman of a national committee that makes annual awards for the best volume of literary criticism on English and American subjects. In 1957–58 he was director of the American Institute at the University of Oslo and in 1965–66 he was Visiting Professor at the University of Lyon, France, and has received numerous distinctive awards.

Dr. Walcutt and Dr. McCracken teamed up in 1960 to conduct a year-long national study of reading in American schools, after which they decided to write a new approach to beginning reading. The result is the development of *Basic Reading* which, when introduced by the publishers in 1963, was claimed to be the "first program ever published which integrates phonics and whole-word meanings". No mention at that time was made of "linguistics". But, in 1965, a flyer printed by Lippincott adds the statement that *"Basic Reading* is a fully developmental linguistic reading program, for Grades 1 through 8 . . ."

11. McCracken, Glenn, Speeches and discussion at the 4th and 9th Annual Conferences on Reading, University of Rhode Island, Kingston, 1958 and 1963.
12. Cleland, Donald D., "The McCracken Procedure in Teaching Reading," *Controversial Issues in Reading*, I (April, 1961) Proceedings of the Annual Reading Conference, Lehigh University. Reprinted in *New Perspectives in Reading Instruction*. Albert J. Mazurkiewicz, editor. New York: Pitman Publishing Corp. 1964. 491–505.
13. Terman, Sybil, and Walcutt, Charles C., *Reading: Chaos and Cure*. New York: McGraw-Hill, 1958.
14. Walcutt, Charles C., *Tomorrow's Illiterates*. Boston: Little, Brown and Co., 1961.

For these reasons, it seems appropriate that *Basic Reading* be included as one of the important, new linguistics-phonemics approaches to beginning reading, and that the beginning reading program for First Grade be described.

Materials and Methods

FIRST GRADE PROGRAM. The Grade One program of *Basic Reading* follows the pattern of most, if not all, basal readers. It includes the pre-primer, primer, 1¹, and 1². There is no "readiness" workbook as such, for it is claimed that the readiness work is phased into the pre-primer materials, and the workbook materials that accompany the pre-primer. There are also workbooks with each of the other three texts in the Grade One program.

The contribution of the "New Castle Experiment" is evident in the eight filmstrips that accompany the basal reader program. There also is a set of word-recognition flash cards which provides practice on the vocabulary of the pre-primer and primer.

Dr. McCracken explains how *Basic Reading* deals with "readiness":

> Studies over the past 15 years have convinced us that far less emphasis upon readiness is needed where the beginning reading method is interesting and clarifying to the learner. Therefore, this program has no readiness books as such. The new approach to readiness, unique with BASIC READING, is described as "functional" or "accompanying" readiness. It is there for teachers who wish and need to use it, but it occupies no extra pages in the program. To explain: there are readiness materials on the first nine pages of the Pre-Primer. But these nine pages also contain actual reading lessons. Thus, in those classes where the readiness features are employed, the child learns readiness, not before, but while he also learns to read. For an example, see Illustration 1. This is the first lesson in the program. It occurs on page 1 of the Pre-Primer. On this page the pupils learn the short sound of the letter *a*, and they learn how to write in manuscript the letter in both upper and lower cases. If the teacher wishes to use the readiness feature, the three apples in the illustration provide vivid means for working with sizes, shapes, colors, the left-to-right reading process, etc.[15]

The approach used in *Basic Reading* for presenting the vowel sounds is not truly in keeping with the linguistics scientists' demands for step-by-step regularity. Whereas Hay-Wingo presents all five vowels simul-

---

15. McCracken, Glenn, Correspondence with the author.

taneously, McCracken-Walcutt start by presenting only one at a time. Soon, however, the pre-primer is using them all, with the variables being the initial consonants. For example, the first word is *am*, followed by *man*, and then *Ann*. The next lesson presents *man, men, in, on*. Then *ran, ram, rim, run*. The first sentence is "Ann ran." The next sentence is "A man ran." The third sentence is "A ram ran."

Those are followed by work on more consonants and more vowel practice. The first full page of sensible nonsense is as follows:

> Run, rat, run.
> Run, run run.
> Run to a red sun.
> Run to a red sun.
> Run, run run.

The main features found in *Basic Reading* are both visually and linguistically oriented. For example, through colorful and very clever illustrations in the text, materials are provided for such readiness activities as visual discrimination, likenesses and differences, left-to-right progression, and basic sounds. An example may be cited. Page 8 in the pre-primer illustrates the consonant *r*. Both lower and upper case *r* and *R* are shown, followed with *ran, ram, rim, run*. The illustrations are of rabbits, which, hopefully, the child will not call "bunnies". Relative size —which is a usual readiness activity—is illustrated with large, medium, and small rabbits. "Finding the rabbit's missing ears" seems to be a favorite visual-discrimination readiness exercise. Sad-looking rabbits with missing ears are also provided on the same page.

Words which are not phonemically regular and/or are not in linguistics sequence are listed at the bottom of the pages with a tinted overlay. This indicates that they must be learned as sight vocabulary and that they will be used in sentences in order that such sentences be meaningful. Examples are the articles, *a* and *the*.

Sounds are never taught in isolation after they are first introduced as short vowel sounds or as regular consonant sounds. They are always used in phonemically-regular monosyllable words at first. Nonsense monosyllables are never used in *Basic Reading*.

The pre-primer introduces 194 monosyllable words using the five short vowel sounds, ten consonants and seven consonant digraphs. The 194 words constructed from those fifteen letters and seven digraphs are used in simple stories and poems—all in linguistically-controlled sequence.

The sequence of new phonemic elements introduced through the First Grade books and filmstrips is:

> short vowels in upper and lower case
> sight words *a, to,* and *the*

ar sound
er sound
ed ending
w, l, b, k, e, ow, ll, le, ck, nk, ee.
ea, ai, ie, ir, ore, or, oo, j, v.
sh, th, wh, qu, x, y, z.
y, ay, and *ey* endings, *ce, ci, cy, ge, gi, gy, dy, dge.*
two sounds of *oo,* and *ow, ou, oy, oi*
u, ue, ui, ew, eau, aw, au, ph, ch, uer, kn.
g, h, gh, f, ear, ei and *ie, eigh, ey, ough.*

As with most linguistics-phonemics systems, *Basic Reading* builds word families or phonograms on such bases as *am, at,* and others readily seen in the "phonemically-regular word charts" previously discussed on pages 144–146.

An illustration from the Primer will illustrate the manner in which an interesting story has been written to utilize the regular sound of the *oa* vowel digraph. The sound of *oa* is found frequently in the words, *goat, road, coat, coal,* and *toad.*

Page 65 of the Primer starts the story of "The Sad Goat" in which the above words are utilized. Note that the sentences start anywhere on the line—not just at the beginnings of lines, as in most Primers. There are quotation marks, representing conversation. The story starts with the "Once upon a time" theme which provides a point for discussion of fantasy in stories.

It is suggested that the teacher read the story aloud to the children first, emphasizing such literary techniques as conversation, inflection, emphasis, and repetition.

It is claimed that more than 2100 words are used in the First-Grade materials in *Basic Reading.* At the same time, it is stated that "Since word memorization and repetition are not a part of the *Basic Reading* method, the vocabulary growth rate obtained with the program is outstandingly rapid." This is possible, it is claimed, by the fact that "Children learn to make their own phonic generalizations on meeting new words."

Any phonemics generalization must be based upon the regularity of the phonemic elements. An example of how this possibly may be accomplished is found in the practice on the schwa sound—which some systems call the *er-ir-ur* trio. In the poem, "Can You Tell?" on page 55 of the Reader 1[1] the short vowel, modified by the consonant *r,* is found in the following words: *first, chirp, winter, summer, turn, flower, hotter, longer, skaters, hunters,* and possibly, *deer.* These are cleverly woven into a poem about the seasons.

The children are asked to find these *er, ir, ur* words in the poem. They then drill on the list of words until they can pronounce them as

The Sad Goat

Once upon a time a goat sat near the side of a road. He was an old, fat goat. His coat was black as coal.

The goat saw a green toad go down the road. "I want to hop like a toad," said the fat old goat. "I want to hop, hop, hop down the road."

once

65

Fig. 5–1   *Reproduced from* Basic Reading *by Glenn McCracken and Charles E. Walcutt, copyright, 1963, by permission of J. B. Lippincott Company.*

sight vocabulary. They then drill on the rhyming words. After this warmup, they read the poem several times. This is all done as a whole-class activity, followed by class discussion of science and the seasons.

"Goldilocks and the Three Bears" is one of the many fables and stories included in the First Grade Reader 1². The teacher's guide reads like the usual teacher's guide for a basal series. It suggests that the class be encouraged to look for main ideas, details, sequence, and cause-and-effect relationships; comprehension techniques which all good systems of reading must employ. The technique of dramatizing parts or all of some of the stories is also recommended to develop "expression and emphasis both in oral reading and in silent reading."

In summary, it should be noted that the significant characteristic of *Basic Reading* which distinguishes it from the usual basal reader and, indeed, from some other systems which also claim to be "linguistically oriented" is the manner in which regular phonemic elements are phased into interesting stories almost from the very first.

Dr. McCracken states that, "With the employment of just four basic books in Grade One, the pupils learn all of the sounds of the English language as well as most of the 250 spellings."

After beginning work in the pre-primer, children read their first story on page 8. By the time they have had 19 lessons, they learn 32 words in their 20th lesson, alone. Beyond this point, children learn as many as 70 new words in a single day. This contrasts significantly with the repetition of "controlled vocabulary" found in most basal reader series.

Because so many new words are taught in the Pre-Primer and Primer, story quality improves rapidly. However, stories and verse are presented using only the spellings and sounds that have already been taught. In the poem, "A Song of Spring," for example, the *ing* appears 20 times without overpowering the literary quality. Pupils read this poem readily because the *ing* sound is the only phonemic element which is new to them.

The *Teacher's Manual* that is bound into each teacher's edition contains a valuable Bibliography of poems, "read-aloud" books and stories, enrichment materials, recordings, music and songs, films, and filmstrips, all of which may be used to enrich this approach to beginning reading.

Research Findings

In 1964, the First Grade materials developed by Dr. McCracken and Dr. Walcutt were tried out under classroom conditions in about 500 schools.

Results from those tryouts reported that the children in First Grades averaged 3.5 in reading achievement after eight months of formal reading training using *Basic Reading*. It is claimed that this superiority is maintained throughout the primary grades.

A summary of comparisons of test scores of children using the *Basic Reading* materials with scores obtained by children using basal reader materials is reported as part of the U.S. Office of Education First Grade Reading Studies.[16]

It does not take structured "research" to indicate that *Basic Reading* provides an intelligent and restrained use of linguistics elements in its approach to beginning reading. Its emphasis on good story content will hardly elicit criticism, and the fact that it has included many of the best features of basal readers in its method would seem to predict that it would rate at least equally well when compared with traditional basal reader approaches.

Whether or not *Basic Reading* is, really "A Major Breakthrough in Reading Instruction"—as Lippincott advertises it to be—remains to be answered through carefully-designed research.

Obviously, McCracken and Walcutt are faced eventually with the same phonemic problems which puzzle all who deal with our language, namely, the fact that phonemically-irregular words must be used from the very beginning, and in increasing amounts as stories having any literary substance are utilized. The publishers of *Basic Reading* take pride in the "biography, humor, science, adventure, mystery, poetry, imaginative tales, history, and stories of contemporary cultures" which are included. They assure us that "Many of our greatest writers are represented". Obviously, "our greatest writers" have not been bound by the mechanical restrictions of linguistics-phonemics regularity.

How does *Basic Reading* handle this problem? It is simple. It provides a strong background of basic phonemic instruction, kept as regular as possible within a partial linguistics framework. This is the beginning program in Grade One. Soon, however, many whole-word basal reader techniques are phased in. In this manner, it provides material that is interesting to children, yet is written to emphasize over and over again the regular phonemic elements. Moreover, the language is equated to the normal language of First Graders. This is a long step forward, and away from the linguistics ruts built into a number of other linguistics approaches.

---

16. Bond, Guy L., and Dykstra, Robert, *Coordinating Center for First Grade Reading Instruction Programs, Final Report*, Project No. X–001, Contract No. OE 5–10–264. Minneapolis: University of Minnesota, 1967.

Is this properly called a "linguistic approach to reading", or is it a hybrid? Linguistics scientists would support parts of it, and reading specialists would recognize that many of their best techniques have been utilized. It is linguistically-oriented up to a point, and it is probable that such a point is as far as any so-called linguistics approach should go.

The First-Grade program of materials and method of *Basic Reading* is a careful fusion of a number of the best features of teaching of phonemic elements, plus a sensible utilization of linguistic control, plus the unavoidable, but carefully-chosen, sight words necessary to provide intelligent stories and poems. By means of such restraint, the authors have been able to satisfy a number of warring opponents: those who have been calling for "phonics"; those who have been criticizing the basal readers as "educational wastelands"; and even those who like the basal reader approach. It is real magic when three such apparently-opposing camps are brought together under one roof.

In addition to this, the authors have structured the sequence enough to allow it to be called a "linguistics" approach.

All of these features, plus the fact that the type, layout and illustrations are attractive, should make *Basic Reading* one of the most widely-accepted new approaches to beginning reading.

SRA BASIC READING SERIES

Origins

The SRA *Basic Reading Series* is a linguistics-phonemics approach to beginning reading which was programmed by Dr. Donald E. Rasmussen and Mrs. Lenina Goldberg. Rasmussen received a doctor's degree in sociology from the University of Illinois; and, in 1955 when he became principal of the Miquon (private) School in that Philadelphia suburb, he became interested in applying some of his academic training to the area of reading. He theorized that some of the linguistics principles which he had studied as part of his training in cultural and anthropological sociology might apply to American children who were attempting to learn their own language.[17] He also had acquired some practical experience in observing the methods used by the military in training thousands of servicemen in foreign languages.

---

17. Goldberg, Lenina, and Rasmussen, Donald, "Linguistics and Reading," *Elementary English Review*, 40 (March, 1963) 242–247.

Dr. Rasmussen began to promote the idea of applying a linguistics approach to beginning reading. In 1960, one of his teachers, Mrs. Goldberg, agreed to examine the possibilities of a linguistics-phonemic approach in her classroom. She and Dr. Rasmussen examined the new materials which were appearing under the category of "linguistics-reading". They tried some of the materials but, for one reason and another, all were discarded. Consequently they set about the task of devising their own materials and method; and, during the ensuing 1961–62 school year, tried them with children at their Miquon School.

After a year of revision, controlled classroom testing of the materials was done in schools in other parts of Pennsylvania, in Delaware, Massachusetts, New Jersey, Minnesota, and Illinois. It is claimed that, as a result of continuous tryouts and feedback, "almost a dozen revisions" were made before the program was ready for publication by Science Research Associates of Chicago in 1965.

Materials and Methods

The authors of the *SRA Basic Reading Series* have become convinced that reading is "at least in part a process of decoding". They arrived at that conclusion through the assumption that "reading is the opposite of writing." It is the skill of putting back quickly into oral form or into speech sounds what has been recorded by writing." Such a mechanistic definition of reading led to the linguistics-phonemics approach to beginning reading, and to its inevitable dependence upon the alphabet and letter names followed by the phonemically-regular patterns as the basis for spoken language and, therefore, for reading.

It is not surprising, therefore, to find the first item of equipment in the *SRA Basic Reading Series* to be the "Alphabet Book". That workbook was developed for the program by Edith Klausner of the Miquon (Pennsylvania) School. No Kindergarten reading readiness is involved in the SRA program. The "Alphabet Book" is intended for First Graders and draws upon the additional maturation which one year provides.

Although the teacher's handbook assures us that the *SRA Basic Reading Series* can be an individualized program, it goes on to state that "group or class-as-a-whole organization usually provides more opportunities for oral language experiences than do individualized programs." The work in the materials is generally tied to whole-class or group work, watching the teacher either at the chalkboard or with the workbooks, themselves.

There are six workbooks in the series in addition to the "Alphabet Book". The workbooks are essentially compilations of multiple-choice selections in which the child may underline or check his choice of answer.

Each workbook in the SRA *Basic Reading Series* is called a *Level*, with each level introducing new sound-spelling patterns. Although the SRA series is called a reading series, some emphasis is placed on *spelling*. Actually, it would be more acurate to say that the emphasis is on phoneme-grapheme patterns, if one were to accept the series at face value inasmuch as it claims to be a linguistic approach to reading.

The first two levels, Level A (*A Pig Can Jig*) and Level B (*A Hen in a Fox's Den*), present words that represent simple sound-spelling patterns in whole words, all of which are monosyllables such as *can, Dan, fan, bad, sad,* etc. They are phonemically regular and, according to the teacher's manual which accompanies the series, there is "a one-to-one relation between each letter and each sound (linguistically between each grapheme and each phoneme)."

The Level A reader, *A Pig Can Jig*, is arranged for teaching in fourteen lessons, each emphasizing a three-letter monosyllable pattern. There are few nonsense syllables in the series. Each new consonant-vowel-consonant word is different from the preceding one by only one initial consonant. Periodically, words are regrouped so that each consonant-vowel-consonant word differs from a preceding word by the final consonant sound-spelling relationship.

When the children are ready to "read" in their Level A, pre-primer, they do so in unison or individually, pronouncing the words in the sentences which they actually have learned both as sight words and as pattern words. It is suggested that unison reading will help carry the timid child along. The teacher keeps the pace of reading lively by reading along with the class. When a child reads alone, the teacher immediately supplies the correct word when an error or hesitation takes place. After much oral reading, children are asked to read the same materials silently.

Part two of Level A continues phonemically-regular sequence in vocabulary building with the addition of such words as *Nan, Dan, van,* etc., plus the article *a.* The third part of Level A introduces the base *ad* upon which a word family is built including *Dad, pad, had, sad,* and *mad.* The *ag* base with its word family members, *rag, bag, tag,* W*ag*—plus the word *and* are added in part four of Level A.

In the same manner, the fifth, sixth, seventh, and eighth parts of Level A introduce the word families built on *at, ap, am,* and short *a.* A few additional phonics elements such as plurals, possessives, the con-

Ten Pigs and a Hen

Ten pigs sat in a pigpen.

A fat hen ran by.

"The pigpen is big," said the fat hen.

"I cannot run in my pen."

"Why?" said the pigs.

"My pen is not big," said the hen.

The hen ran into the pigpen.

The hen said, "Pigs! Pigs! Can I run in the pen?"

A big pig said, "My pen is a pigpen. It is not a hen pen!"

23

Fig. 5–2 *Reproduced from* A Hen in a Fox's Den *by Donald E. Rasmussen and Lenina Goldberg,* © *1964, 1965. Reprinted by permission of Science Research Associates Inc. All rights reserved.*

sonants *k* and *z*, and a few phonics "exceptions" such as *said, of, into, began* and a few others are included in Level A.

The regular consonants are completed in the work in the Level B book, *A Hen in a Fox's Den* and its accompanying workbook. The short vowel sounds of *e* as in *pet*, *o* as in *pot*, and *u* as in *cut* are also introduced in Level B. A very few words which are phonemic exceptions are used, and a large number of compound words are introduced, utilizing three-letter monosyllable components such as *pigpen, suntan*, etc.

Each of the six sections in Level B starts with a phonemic word-chart similar to (but much more simple) that shown on p. 144 of this book under the discussion of linguistics-phonemics reading systems. Continual emphasis is placed in Level B on the five key words for the five short vowel sounds. They are *Pat* (a boy's name), *pit, pet, pot,* and *nut*. The teacher's manual encourages the teacher to recognize regional differences in vowel pronunciations and to accept the dialectical differences which may exist regionally.

Level C of the *SRA Basic Reading Series* is primarily concerned with four-letter words and words having double consonants, and digraphs representing consonant blends, such as *nd, sl, nt, st, sk, kt, pt, lf, lp, ld, tr, dr,* and many others. There are nine new patterns of sound-spelling relationships introduced in Level C.

A relatively large number of phonemically-irregular words are also used in the Level C book, *Six Ducks in a Pond* and the accompanying workbook. This indicates that the linguistics-phonemics base begins to give way to whole-word learning, rather than attempt to devise some phonemic rules that would cover the exceptions.

Level C presents words in charts and story form in which two consonants together represent but one speech sound. Such words are *bill* and *back*. Sections 3 and 4 and 5 present four-letter words in which two consonants represent two separate sounds, for example, *mend* and *jump*. The phonemic-exceptions *would, could* and *should* are introduced together as sight vocabulary with no attempt at ascribing a linguistics explanation for them.

Sections 6, 7, and 8 of Level C introduce initial consonant clusters such as found in *clam, flag, slip, clip, fled,* etc. These are relatively easy blends by the time children have reached this level.

Finally, on page 116 of *Six Ducks in a Pond* the child is introduced to five-letter words with four sounds such as *smack, press*, etc. all of which begin with consonant clusters. The contractions *don't* and *won't* are also included on the final page of Level C.

The stories and poems of Level D reflect the oral language patterns of children, rather than the "bookish" language of authors. Several contractions are used as children would use them in ordinary speech. They are such words as *I've, you're, don't, weren't* and *shouldn't*.

Endings such as *ng* in *sing, sang, sung; ing* as in *swimming, going;* and *nk* as in *sink, sank, sunk, rink* are all a part of the work of Level D. Beginning and ending consonant digraphs *sh, th,* and *ch* are introduced through such words as *think, this, that, path, rich, shin, chin, ship,* etc. The introduction of the trigraph *tch* naturally follows with such words as *match, itch, crutch,* as examples.

Kittens and Children is the Level E booklet in the *SRA Basic Reading Series.* It, and the workbook which accompanies it, expands the phonemic elements to include those vowel digraphs which cause the greatest trouble with learning to read. Examples are found in *moon, maid, meat, boat, cloud,* etc. Others of another type are what most teachers refer to as the "final *e*" rule, apparent in *made, mile, mole,* and *mule.*

Level E of the *SRA Basic Phonics Program* is its greatest challenge and, perhaps, the place where it surpasses many other so-called linguistics reading programs. The reason should be obvious, in that the SRA program is attempting to do something that others feel is virtually impossible. The SRA system stakes its success in doing the impossible on the hope that children will continue to generalize the sound-spelling patterns, even to applying inductive thinking where research shows generalizations to be less than 50% reliable. We will look forward to studies which may determine how children using this SRA approach compare with those using the phonics rules approach.

The Purple Turtle is the interesting little book which provides the content for Level F in the series. It is the objective of the SRA system to provide a systematic exposure to the most frequent sound-spelling patterns in our language. Obviously it would not be feasible to attempt to include all possible exceptions. Level F, however, does provide practice in a good number of less-frequently encountered exceptional words and irregular phonics elements. For example, the three spellings: *air, bear,* and *bare* are illustrated, along with *their* and *there.* These have always been among the "spelling demons". Those words that have phonemic similarity such as *pour, door, dwarf, more, corn* and *board* appear for children to tackle in context, as well as in chart form. Similarly a group consisting of *word, burn, clerk, bird, were,* etc. is introduced.

One of the most difficult irregularities is found in the group consisting of *all, cost, broad, cause,* and *wash* with *bought* and *caught* added considerably later. Other groupings are: *lose, move, shoe, loose,* and *fruit; among, above, double,* and *blood; ahead, else, again, friend* and *bury; book; bush;* and *woman; diamond, buy, goodbye,* and *eye.*

Squirrel is one of the most difficult to isolate and consequently has six possible pronunciations indicated by means of the IPA.

The fact that Level F deals with more than 100 of our most notorious sound-spelling irregularities is an indication of the level of difficulty which is concentrated in *The Purple Turtle* and the workbook for Level F.

Throughout the entire six Levels of the SRA Basic Reading Series the following "rules" apply:

1. The teacher should pronounce words in a way that is normal for her.
2. The teacher should not attempt to change a child's dialect or speech impediment at the same time she is teaching him to read.
3. The teacher should make certain that children know the meaning of all words in a section before they encounter them in a lesson.
4. The teacher should never teach an isolated sound for a letter, such as *buh* for *b*.
5. The teacher should not direct the child to use the context of meaning, configuration, or picture clues as a means of figuring out a word.
6. The teacher should spell out the letters of a pattern word which the child cannot read or which he misreads.
7. The teacher should never spell out exceptional words.

Reading specialists will not be able to restrain themselves from sharp criticism of rule #5, for it strikes at the very heart of word analysis techniques which are essential parts of most reading instruction today. The authors of the SRA approach, after admonishing the teacher several times *never* "to use the context of meaning, configuration, or picture clues as a means of figuring out a word," the last page in the teacher's manual gives this parting advice:

> How does the reader know that *fear* does not sound like *fare* by analogy with *bear*? The answer, of course, is that he uses, on his own and without being taught, the context of meaning to figure the word out. . . . If he does not do it automatically, however, the teacher should point this technique out to him.

Teachers, well-versed in good techniques of reading instruction, of course, will use any and all clues that may be utilized by readers in the process of developing effective, efficient reading skills.

In summary, it may be stated that the *SRA Basic Reading Series* reaches beyond the usual "safe" confines of several other so-called "linguistic" reading series; yet, at the same time, it develops along a carefully-planned linguistics-phonics path. The expendable workbooks which accompany the six readers provide relatively inexpensive practice materials for each child. The series in its initial printing lacks some of the refinements such as letter cards, key-word cards, and other aids which are characteristics of some of the other approaches to beginning reading.

Research Findings

The authors of the SRA approach present their own experience with the materials as evidence of its worth. Certainly the experimental tryouts with hundreds of children in several states, and the resultant revisions prior to publication are indicative of an honest attempt to provide teachers with what the authors hoped was a new, "better", and workable programmed approach through a linguistics-phonemics structure.

The SRA *Basic Reading Series* conforms to the best requirements for a linguistics-phonemics approach to reading. The little paperback pre-primers, primers and readers look much like those of an ordinary basal reader series. Their colorful and imaginative full-color illustrations are in the contemporary tradition. The type is much smaller and lighter-face than that usually recommended for six- and seven-year-olds. Without serifs, however, the print is clear but still appears to be smaller than optimum.

THE LINGUISTIC READERS

Origins

The Linguistic Readers, formerly published by Harper & Row, were purchased in 1970 by Benziger, Inc., subsidiary of CCM. They were formerly called "*The Linguistic Science Readers*" to indicate their true nature and origin, namely that of the science of linguistics. Dr. Henry Lee Smith, Jr., noted linguistics scientist at the State University of New York at Buffalo is the senior author, with Dr. Clara Stratemeyer of Trenton, New Jersey, State College as the author of the first three books in the series.

Some teachers and administrators misinterpreted the title of the series, thinking it to be some new approach to general science. Consequently, the title was changed to the form now in use.

During the preparation of the First- and Second-Grade materials of the *Linguistic Readers* series, several members of the Harper & Row editorial staff were involved. The primer and first reader were principally the work of Jack E. Richardson, Jr., a former schoolteacher and poet, while Eugene P. Williams produced some of the workbooks and teacher's manuals. The name of Bernard Weiss, at that time an editor for the old Row, Peterson division and now with the Detroit Public Schools, appears on the series. The continuity of linguistic-phonemic regularity and the contents of the series, which extends only over the first three years, has been the responsibility of Dr. Henry Lee Smith, Jr.

The authors of the *Linguistic Readers* accept the premise that the English writing system "is technically called alphabetic and is based, in theory, on what is referred to as the 'phonemic principle'" (one letter = one sound). Dr. Smith, however, is the *only* author of a linguistics-phonemics system who is careful to qualify this phonemic principle by recognizing from the outset that "But we know that such an ideal is far from realized in English spelling.

It is further stated that "Careful selection is critical because writing systems based on the phonemic principle are both incomplete and inconsistent." Also, reflecting his interest in cultural and regional differences in dialects, Dr. Smith states that one of the purposes of his *Linguistic Readers* is to "minimize the problems presented by the dialectical features of spoken English." It is significant to note that he also unequivocally states that "Any reading series based on purely phonemic-alphabetic considerations would be imperfect and incomplete." This latter statement of fact certainly can be accepted by all reading specialists.

Dr. Smith states: "From the very beginning we have endeavored to present material which could have the widest possible appeal and present the fewest number of situations designed to discourage the 'culturally deprived'."[18]

Materials and Method

The first pre-primer is *Frog Fun*. The teacher's guidebooks are small, uncluttered, and simple. It is suggested that the children become oriented to the pre-primer through a short discussion of the means for identifying the two frogs: one has spots and the other hasn't. The frogs also have names: *Pud* and *Zip*.

The teacher demonstrates through careful articulation that the sounds in *Pud* and *Zip* are different. Differentiation of those visual and aural differences help identification of the words. The main idea is that hearing and seeing symbols help in the identification of the words.

At first look, there appears to be no difference between the story

---

18. Correspondence with author.

line of the *Linguistic Readers* and that of the usual basal reader which has been so soundly ridiculed for its repetitious nonsense, such as:

> Look.
> Look, look Tom.
> Look look, Jerry.
> Oh, Oh.
> Oh, Look.
> Oh, Look Tom.
> Oh, Look Jerry.

The *Linguistic Reader* preprimer appears to be little improvement with:

> Hop, Zip.
> Hop, Pud.
> Hop, Zip, hop.
> Hop and jump.
> Jump and hop.
> Jump, Tad.
> Hop, Tad.
> Tad jumps.
> Tad hops.

Yet there *is* a significant difference. It is to be found in the consistency with which the new words are introduced. Like all attempts to approach reading through a linguistic-phonemic means, the short vowel sounds are consistently used first. Consequently, the first step in every lesson is both vocabulary review and the presentation of new vocabulary.

To be sure, these are learned as sight words in exactly the same way that sight words are learned in any basal reader series, with a new increment, plus review, each day. Yet the *Linguistic Readers* differ in that they attempt to keep the vocabulary within a regularly evolving linguistics sequence. Consequently, the short vowel sounds may be introduced in different sorts of words. However, unlike most other linguistics-phonemics series, they are not restricted to three-letter monosyllables using only the basic consonants.

The *s* form of verbs is introduced in the words *hops* and *jumps* within the second week, and the word *little* is used as a comparative word at the same time that *big* is introduced.

As vocabulary is developed, each child has either word cards, or words, printed by the teacher, which he keeps for review and for use in constructing his own sentences.

Another activity which is used in vocabulary development is the use of phonograms or word families, built on the bases of: *ump, ip, and, ig, et,* and *ad,* with initial consonants added to form monosyllable words.

Tuggy runs to the bug.

It jumps on Tuggy.

The bug has fun.

Tuggy runs to the pond.

Tuggy gets wet in the mud.

Fig. 5–3 Reproduced from Tuggy *by Clara G. Stratemeyer and Henry Lee Smith Jr., copyright 1965, by permission of Benziger, Inc.*

All vocabulary-building lessons are whole-class activities during which the teacher and children talk and share experiences, thoughts and words together.

Step II in all levels of the *Linguistic Readers* series is "Directed

Reading". This, also, starts with a whole-class discussion of the story to be read; its title, and any other elements of format which could be ascertained from a visual survey of the page. As the series progresses, children are urged to develop the habit of anticipating cause-and-effect relationships, with predicted outcomes based upon the child's identification of his own experience with the situations illustrated in the artwork that accompanies the story.

Art work is, thus, an important contributing factor in this series, and differentiates it from those linguistics-phonemics systems that fear contamination from visuals. The artwork in the series is very simple, almost childlike, and is done in only one color in addition to black. It was planned that way so that it will be merely a suggestion, but so it will not carry the story for the reader.

Following a whole-class preview, each individual reads silently in terms of the framework of ideas developed in the pre-reading discussion. He has a purpose, which usually is to find out what happened and to check the predicted outcomes which the class discussed. The teacher, of course, follows through with a summary discussion.

Silent reading and class discussion are followed with a rereading of the story orally. The purpose of that activity is to help the children develop intonation, pitch, accent, and flow of language as it ordinarily is spoken. As the children progress through the series, additional attention is directed to the use of question marks, conversation punctuation, exclamation marks, etc. as typographical adjuncts which serve as aids to correct inflection and more meaningful reading.

It is also claimed that, by reading orally after they have read the selection silently, they will be alert to correct themselves on their own reading errors. Unfortunately, of course, oral reading provides practice for a limited few; but it is hoped that the remainder of the class will be doing "oral" reading vicariously.

Step III provides "activities for developing abilities in comprehension, auditory and visual discrimination, manipulation of words and letters, and recognition of recurring spoken-written patterns." This Step III is said to be the most important aspect of the *Linguistic Readers*. It is based primarily upon the students' abilities in auditory and visual discrimination. The objective is to aid the child in making an association between specific letters and the sounds they symbolize. This is to be followed by helping him develop the ability to classify auditory-visual patterns. For example, a number of words are placed on the chalkboard, and the children as a whole-class activity are to take turns "framing with their hands" all words which end in the digraph *ck*. The *ck* ending is

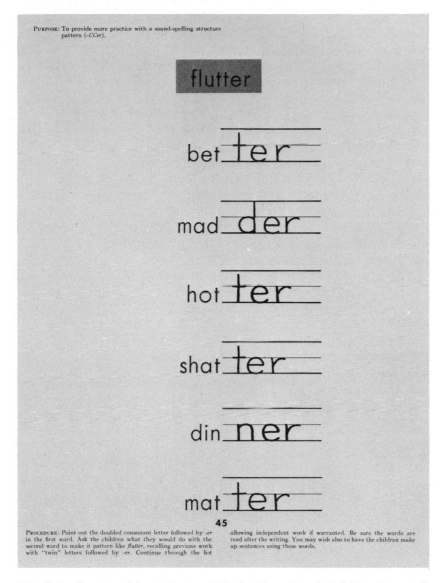

Fig. 5–4 Reprinted from Six in a Mix *by Henry Lee Smith, Jr., Eugene P. Williams, Jack E. Richardson, Jr., and Bernard J. Weiss, copyright 1965, by permission of Benziger, Inc.*

used both for oral drill and for written visual drill in which the children attach various beginnings such as *si, bri, ta, lo,* etc.

Within the first year's work, children are introduced to grammatically-modified words, in which the base word is enlarged with such suffixes as *er, est, y, ing* (the latter often calling for dropping the final *e*, or doubling the consonant), *ed*, and *ly*. Possessives, and contractions such as *didn't, mustn't, we'd, they'll*, and many others are part of the first year's work. A large number of compounds are also used, including words that are modified by prefixes, such as *unselfish, unstuck*, etc.

Fourteen lessons are detailed in the teacher's manual for presenting the sequence of linguistics-phonemics learning in *Frog Fun*. In that booklet 22 monosyllables plus the word, "little" and some *s* forms such as *jumps*, are presented as regular phonemic elements. Twenty-two new words are added through the thirteen lessons in *Tuggy*. The *s* forms of six verbs and the plurals of three nouns and at least one contraction are also added. *Pepper*, the third pre-primer, has eleven lessons plus some review work. In its pages, the children are introduced to 24 new words, plus a review of all learned previously.

The Teacher's Plan Book (teacher's manual) contains useful lists of words, showing their derived endings; possessives; contractions; compounds; words modified by prefixes; and a schematic diagram for word wheels which a teacher might construct. Those teaching aids are mentioned for the use of any teacher who is specially interested in following a systematic linguistics-phonemics sequence such as found in the *Linguistic Readers*.

Research Findings

The *Linguistic Readers* are not entirely without some basis in research, although no formally researched studies have been reported on their use. The materials and ideas for part of the series were developed even before 1955 by Dr. Stratemeyer as an outgrowth of many years of experience as a teacher and trainer of teachers is in their favor. Indeed, the *Linguistic Readers* is one of the very few so-called "linguistics" approaches to beginning reading in which a co-author is an actual specialist in elementary education.

Consequently, teachers are asked to use any and all of the good educational techniques which they already know as a result of their basal reader work. "Experienced teachers will have a large fund of techniques to employ . . ." Unlike most other linguistics-phonemics systems which not only ignore, but reject basal reader techniques, the *Linguistic Readers* make use of the very techniques which have been effective with the basal readers.

It is difficult enough to try to produce a meaningful story with the ordinary language of beginning reading, but, when one tries to limit oneself to the structure of linguistics sequence, it is almost impossible. Nevertheless, the *Linguistic Readers* under those limitations have done a creditable job. But this is not their particular strength. Their novel feature is the presentation of story form in the guise of animals, rather than people, and the limitation of artwork to simple two-color drawings.

Utilizing the media of animals and simple drawings, the *Linguistic Readers* bridge the chasms created so often by culture-centered situations involving children, families, and situations with which Spanish-speaking children, American Indian children, and culturally disadvantaged children of all sorts do not identify. This feature of the *Linguistic Readers* was achieved through a team effort of an elementary education specialist and a cultural-linguistics scientist. We need more such team efforts by people who know something about what they are trying to do in the field of reading!

THE MERRILL LINGUISTIC READERS

Origins

Charles C. Fries, Professor Emeritus of the University of Michigan has for many years been interested—as was Leonard Bloomfield—in the application of the knowledge of linguistics science to the field of decoding our American English language. Like many linguistics scientists, Dr. Fries views the process of reading as essentially that of decoding the symbols which are used to represent the sounds of our language. His interest in reading became widely known through the publication in 1962 by Holt, Rinehart, and Winston Inc. of his book, *Linguistics and Reading*.[19] In it, Dr. Fries outlined his philosophy and a frame of operation which he theorized would be an effective approach to beginning reading.

With the aid of Dr. Rosemary Wilson,[20] then supervisor in the Philadelphia Public Schools, an experimental edition of the series of linguistic readers was written. The readers were used experimentally in the Allentown schools during the 1965–66 school year and in the Philadelphia

---

19. Fries, Charles C., *Linguistics and Reading. op. cit.*
20. Wilson, Rosemary G., "A Linguistic Approach to Beginning Reading Based on Fries' Principle," *Improvement of Reading Through Classroom Practice*. 9th Annual International Reading Association Conference Proceedings, 1964. 225–227.

schools for a longer period. A second co-author, Miss Mildred K. Rudolph is also on the administrative staff of the Philadelphia schools.

Dr. Wilson's interest in linguistics is also reflected in her consultative position with the U.S. Office of Education's linguistics project with First-Grade children.

Consequently, the *Merrill Linguistic Readers* have had a team of authors representing the most respected people in the linguistics field, public school curriculum development, and reading. Additionally, the experimental editions as they now appear represent revisions and refinements based upon experiences with them in the hands of more than 9,000 children. This background of authorship and pre-publication tryout is unequalled by any of the other linguistics-phonemics systems.

With such background, one would expect that the *Merrill Linguistic Readers* would surpass all others in the field. A look at their materials and methods may indicate whether or not such expectations have been reached.

Materials and Method

The series presently consists of six readers (three paperbacked and three hard covered), accompanied with six workbooks for skill development. In addition there is *My Alphabet Book*, designed for Kindergartners or for the first weeks of First Grade. Teacher's editions at each level are extremely well annotated.

The series of six readers is intended for use with the three primary grades, although it is anticipated that rapid learners will finish the basic program in two years and, thus, be prepared to move into reading materials of Fourth-Grade difficulty or higher.

The following objectives are stated for the program:

1. The development of the child's ability to respond rapidly and accurately to the written presentation of language symbols already firmly established in his auditory experience.

2. The development of the child's ability to understand cumulative meanings of printed language signals and to supply intonations, stresses, and pauses essential to comprehension.

In simple language these two major objectives mean that (1) the child already has a vocabulary which he understands aurally and it is the task of this Merrill system to teach him how to react rapidly to a set of printed words which represent the words he already knows when he speaks or hears them. (2) The Merrill series is designed to teach the child to read with sense, using punctuation marks as aids in proper inflection and accent in a normal speaking voice—not mechanical word-by-word pronunciation.

Most linguistics-phonemics systems base their *raison d'etre* on their claim that the child can learn to "break the alphabet code". The Merrill system conforms to that definition of reading, and, consequently, provides an alphabet book and practice in learning the letter names as the first step prior to any reading instruction.

My Alphabet Book attempts to teach children to recognize letters by means of contrasts and similarities. They call this process of emphasizing the special features of letters "minimum contrasts". For example, there is a very minimal difference between the letters *o*, *c*, and *a*. Similarly, there is a minimal contrast in *l* and *t*.

When the children work in *My Alphabet Book* they are taught letter names; not letter sounds. Soon they are supposed to be able to differentiate both capital and small letters, and to name them from left-to-right. There is no other readiness activity provided in the Merrill system, except some listening exercises which are quite different from any provided in other linguistics-phonemics series. Indeed, it should be noted that those listening exercises have little specific relationship to linguistics-phonemics, but could be used as a part of any method of pre-reading practice.

Someone a few years ago reported the "discovery" by a First-Grader that "reading is just talk, written down." Since this anecdote was first reported, individuals have accepted this as fact, without further or deeper analysis of what reading actually is. It appears that this naïve concept of reading is the basis for the supplementary so-called "readiness" activities that the Merrill series recommends. The teacher's manual reveals this point of view by stating:

> . . . readiness activity is often necessary to establish that the children "know" what a word is. Many nonreaders are not aware that "talk" is made up of separable units called "words." A bit of special practice is often necessary with the five- and six-year-old to develop this awareness.

It is questionable whether or not such an assumption is true. Nevertheless, the "readiness" activities may have some value in that they direct the learner's attention to each word in a sentence. On the other hand, this later may be a handicap to meaning which flows from entire phrases, rather than words as isolated components of the phrase.

Once the class has had practice in learning the alphabet and attending to the number of words in orally-spoken sentences, the formal reading work begins. The first step is work by the teacher at the chalkboard. All work in this linguistics-phonemics system is developed through what the author call "matrices". These are actually spelling patterns of words with regular grapheme-phoneme bases. In the first reader, for example, the short *a* vowel sound is developed into the *at, am, an, ap, ad* and *ag* bases. As with the other linguistics-phonemics systems, word families are developed by using those phonograms and prefixing a limited number of phonemically-regular consonants for beginning sounds.

The "difference" that is claimed as an advantage for the Merrill system is that it is held to a sequence of learnings based upon "minimum contrasts" in words. Obviously, with the *at* base, the addition of *b, h, c,* and *m* as the initial consonants provides minimal differences. With the *an* base, the addition of the beginning consonants *m, r,* and *p* are minimal. Some linguistics-scientists would object to the use of the grapheme *c* in the early stages of the pattern, inasmuch as it is phonemically irregular—sometimes the "hard k" sound and sometimes the "sss" sound.

The three-letter words derived from the bases and the initial consonants are said to be "sub-patterns" of spelling in the first major spelling pattern.

After work at the chalkboard, the children then start to use their first reader in which the same words are found. It is assumed that, if the child knows the alphabet names, he somehow will be able to reproduce the "sounds of the letters." This seems to be taking a great deal for granted, or else there are some steps in phonemic drill that somehow get done without being included in the recommended teaching procedure.

In the teaching procedure that is delineated in the series, the child goes directly from naming alphabet letters "in any order" to the process of pronouncing *short* vowel sound of *a,* to pronouncing consonants that *do not* "say their names". Specifically, the child without any phonemics instruction starts to pronounce *h* with a breath sound when he has previously learned it only as a letter name "H". Similarly, the letter name for "D" requires the vowel "ee" for pronunciation; yet, when used with the base *an,* a different phoneme is necessary. The most irregular of the "minimum contrasts" used is the consonant "C" which the child has learned to pronounce "See", and in the reading work must now pronounce as a "hard 'K' " in *cat* and *can.*

In contrast with some of the other linguistics-phonemics systems, the Merrill system provides silent reading first, which is then followed by oral reading. The method usually followed is to provide some questions from the teacher's annotated edition. The story material, printed in black, has teacher's questions in the wide left-hand margin for classes of normal ability. In the right-hand margin are more questions of a more simple nature for the slow groups. In a sense, the questions which are designed for the slower pupils provide a "second track" within the body of the series, itself. The purpose of giving the questions before the children read the sentence or line is to serve as "directed reading", and not as a means for checking comprehension, although, of course, the suggested questions or similar teacher-made questions could be used for that purpose.

One of the objectives of the Merrill linguistics-phonemics system is to develop a habit of reading with normal "expression." This is developed and checked by means of oral reading sessions. It is hoped that, through practice, the child will develop patterns of reading that will include tonal differences, pitch, inflection, stress, exclamation, disgust, surprise, sorrow, and other feelings as one would use in normal speech. It is contended that the child who uses such oral expression when reading reveals his understanding and comprehension of the reading materials. Practice in "expressive" oral reading is done with children individually and as a whole-group activity.

It is recognized that "a problem arises because, at the beginning of learning to read, pupils in their struggle to recognize the words develop habits of pronouncing words as separate items." It is the breaking of that habit that oral reading with "expression" is attempting to accomplish.

The *Merrill Linguistic Readers* are not glamorized by clever book titles. They are labelled only as *Reader 1*, *Reader 2*, etc. They do not include pictures; being printed only with the story text in black and white. "Pictures constitute a distracting element in the process of learning to read, and they furnish only superficial clues to word recognition." The authors also state that "pictures lead pupils to *guess* at words rather than to read them."

Book 1 of the *Merrill Linguistic Readers* starts with Nat, the fat cat and his mat and hat. Other monosyllables based upon the short-$\breve{a}$ sound are developed. Skills Book 1 is a workbook-type supplement which provides writing and spelling practice within the linguistic pattern of Reader 1. It also serves as an evaluative instrument whereby the teacher may check on the child's comprehension and achievement.

Book 2 repeats all words learned in Reader 1, with words in fourteen family bases: *-it, -in, -ix, -id, -ip, -ig, -un, -ut, -up, -ug, -us, -ud, -um,* and *-ub.* By attaching single consonants at the beginnings of those bases, the authors devised sentences like:

> A bit of ham is in the tin can.
> It's for Dan.

Several sight words must be utilized to provide normal speech patterns. When they are introduced they appear in circles at the bottom of the page. Examples found in the first two Readers are: *took, said, she, got, me, have, your, with,* and *little.* They are learned as whole words with no attention to spelling or to the pronunciation of the separate phonemes that constitute them.

The "three major spelling patterns in English" seems to be the *one* feature of the *Merrill Linguistic Readers* which distinguishes them from all others in the linguistics-phonemics category. The six books of the series make a systematic oral presentation—followed by reading practice—in those three patterns. The words in the spelling pattern are first presented in a list, then are used in story form. Students are taught to look for the minimum differences that distinguish one word from another in each family of words. The authors claim that children will develop the habit of paying close attention to the parts of words which show those minimum differences. "As each pattern is mastered, it is applied to the 'solving' of any number of words throughout the series representing or incorporating that pattern."

Fries identifies the first and most basic spelling pattern as the one-syllable words built with consonant-vowel-consonant sequence, in which the medial vowel is a short phoneme. Using the principle of minimum contrast, the task is to substitute initial consonants onto the *at, it, et, ot,* and *ut* bases. The next step is to substitute final consonants onto such bases as *ba, bi, be, bo,* and *bu.* In these two illustrations, it may be seen that the same consonants may be substituted as initial or final, and that the medial vowels may be changed, retaining the same initial and final consonants. In any case, the principle of "minimum" contrast is observed.

There are some words in which a consonant digraph may be used instead of a single consonant. This, for example, is true with the *th* which may be used in substitution as an initial consonant sound or as a final consonant sound. Similarly, a consonant trigraph may also be used (*str* and *tch* are examples).

Fries' second spelling pattern consists of words patterned with a consonant+vowel+consonant+final, silent *e.* Consequently, these words are the one-syllable words in which the medial vowel is long.

Minimum contrast is achieved by introducing pairs such as (*mad–made*), (*slid–slide*), (*hat–hate*). Other more-complicated changes are also minimum in contrast, as evidenced in such a pair as (*tall–tale*) and (*tack–take*).

The third spelling pattern consists of several sub-patterns in which the *ea* vowel digraph is substituted for the short vowel *e* or the double *e* is substituted for the short *e.* Such word pairs as (*met–meat*) and (*red–reed*) are examples. Another sub-pattern substitutes *ai* for short *a* (*ran–rain*); *oa* for short *o* (*cot–coat*); and *ou* for short *o* (*spot–spout*).

The Fries-Wilson materials, thus, utilize one of the basic principles

A Pin for Dan

A man had a tin pin.

It's a pin for a cap.

Can Dad win it for Dan?

Dad wins the pin.

The pin is in a bag.

On the bag is a tag,

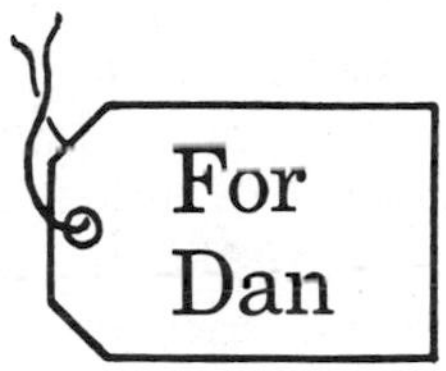

The pin fits on Dan's cap.

Dad pins it on the cap.

The pin is Dan's pin.

14

Fig. 5–5   Reproduced from the Merrill Linguistic Readers by permission of Charles E. Merrill Publishing Company, A Bell & Howell Company, Columbus, Ohio.

of learning, namely, that learning is aided through practice in the perception of likenesses and differences—similar elements and contrasting elements. In a sense, this may be an extension of some of the readiness exercises which also call for visual discrimination of likenesses and differences.

The philosophy of the authors of the Merrill approach suggests that the second step be called the "productive" stage. This is described as being the point at which "the responses to the visual patterns become habits so automatic that . . . the significant identifying features of the graphic shapes themselves sink below the threshold of conscious attention."[21]

Fries is referring to the letter shapes and parts of letters. In the third stage, he visions the reading process as a whole being automatic, so that attention is upon meaning and its relationship to the past experience of the reader.

An attempt is made to make the *Merrill Linguistic Readers* a self-contained approach to beginning reading. The little Readers contain stories constructed entirely from the vocabulary of the controlled linguistic pattern, yet having some story content, as well.

The small teacher's guides and the over-printed teacher's editions of the little Readers provide the teacher with very concise, yet adequate, instructions for teaching reading by means of this approach, even without specific training in linguistics. The over-printing in the teacher's editions provides the usual basal-reader-type questions concerning "how?" "why?" "where?" "what?" etc., plus the usual "what do you think?" questions.

Research Findings

It is possible that the *Merrill Linguistic Readers* have had more in-class testing prior to publication than any other linguistics-phonemics approach to beginning reading.

Some 9,000 children were engaged in the program in the city schools of Philadelphia. They used the experimental edition developed by Dr. and Mrs. Fries, who had moved to Philadelphia to work with Mrs. Wilson and Mrs. Rudolph. Other Pennsylvania schools also tried out the experimental materials and reported favorable results to the authors.

The program is designed to be covered in one year by high-achieving children and in two years by average children. In several schools in the Allentown, Pennsylvania system, First Grade children were able to cover

---

21. Fries, *op. cit.* 205.

the materials in one year, and in the Second Grade it was estimated that they were able to handle work normally given to Third Graders. In fact, by the time Christmas vacation arrived, the Second Graders were working in materials said to be at the 3^2 level.[22]

In Lansdowne, another Pennsylvania system, four First Grade classes consisting of 86 children started in the Fries-Wilson materials in September, 1965. By the spring of 1966, 64% of the children were in the 90–99th percentiles in reading on the *Metropolitan Achievement Tests*, and 73% were in the same decile range on word discrimination. It is also reported that 47% of the children were also in the top decile in word knowledge.

The Fries-Wilson approach was the subject of one of the studies in the USOE First Grade Reading Study. In the investigation[23] conducted by J. Wesley Schneyer of the University of Pennsylvania, the major objective was to compare the reading achievement of First Grade children taught by the *Merrill Linguistic Readers* with that of First Grade children taught by a basal reader approach. In the latter case, the Scott, Foresman 1962–63 edition was used.

Groups of children of high IQ, average IQ, and low IQ were set up, with end-of-the-year data available on 347 children in twelve linguistic-approach classes and 327 children in twelve basal-reader-approach classes. There was a wide range of ages of the teachers, but this was not significant for comparisons, inasmuch as younger teachers tended to have the children with lower abilities and older teachers had children with the higher abilities. The principal's ratings of the teachers' abilities favored the teachers who had the basal-reader children.

Pre-tests and post-tests were given. Perhaps the most significant finding is that children in the linguistics group scored higher on a linguistic reading test, while the basal-reader group obtained higher scores on ordinary reading materials, especially paragraph meanings. The results seem to indicate that the children in that experiment tested out better on materials with which they were most familiar. The experiment, however, did not provide conclusive evidence of the superiority of either approach. Neither did it indicate that the teachers who were rated "superior" by their principals did a better job of teaching.

The *Merrill Linguistic Readers* may lack definitive research support at this writing, but they do contain the elements of linguistic science which Dr. Fries has distilled from the hundreds of research studies which

---

22. Storch, Phil H. "Linguistics Reading Helps Fast and Slow Readers," Allentown, Pa.: *The Morning Call*, Thursday, March 17, 1966, 56.
23. Schneyer, J. Wesley, "Reading Achievement of First Grade Children Taught by a Linguistic Approach and a Basal Reader Approach," *The Reading Teacher*, 19: (May, 1966) 647–652.

have been familiar to him in his lifetime as a linguistics scientist. In addition, the professional know-how of Dr. Wilson and Mrs. Rudolph have been added to make the materials realistic for classroom use.

What the Readers lack in color and brilliance may be balanced with their regularity of sequential treatment of linguistics-phonemics elements.

There is little else that can be said about the *Merrill Linguistic Readers* as an approach to beginning reading. Feedback from classroom use and from good research studies should begin to appear in professional journals to substantiate or refute the claims of the publishers that this is "A major breakthrough in teaching reading in the primary grades."

PROGRAMMED READING

Origins

Programmed Reading is a linguistics-phonemics approach which grew out of the work of two individuals who had become especially interested in the possibilities of programmed instruction. In fact the major author, Cynthia Dee Buchanan, had been associated with some of the programming which had taken place at Harvard in the 1950's when she was working on her master's degree there. Her undergraduate work was done at Hollins College where she met the other author, Dr. M. W. Sullivan, who was then head of the Modern Language Department.

Interest in reading as a possible area in which programming techniques might be applied dates back to 1957 when the authors tried some linguistically-oriented materials arranged for teaching machines. The program was presented to children in Kindergarten, First Grade and Second Grade. It was reported that the children did not respond to either the program or to the machines. Consequently, there was some question as to whether the programmed format, the linguistic materials, or the machines were at fault. As a result of this problem, materials from regular basal readers were programmed into frames and placed on teaching machines. Again the children did not appear to be motivated.

The linguistics program was then rewritten in a programmed sequence for printing in booklet form. For the next three years it was tested in the Whisman, Cupertino, and Portola Valley School Systems in California. During those years, suggestions resulted in revisions.

By 1961 it was decided that the materials had been refined adequately, inasmuch as Kindergartners and First Graders who used them were able to cover what were estimated to be two years' materials in one year.

During the next two years, the workbooks were tested with First Graders in regular classroom use with the help of their teachers. The authors report that First Graders "began achieving a high Third Grade reading level and many Second Graders exceeded Fifth Grade level."

Having created such apparently effective materials and having devised a programming sequence, it was natural that the authors would enter into contract agreements to have their approach to beginning reading published. The Webster Division of McGraw-Hill Book Company first published Sullivan-Buchanan programmed linguistics-phonemics materials.

Materials and Method

Programmed Reading consists of a sequence of workbooks in which the child is required to write his responses rather than just to check choices as is the case with some other programmed materials. Thus, by writing letters and words as part of the process, the child reinforces "reading." Learning with this approach is, to a large extent, an encoding process and not what is usually thought of as "reading."

One of the advantages of programmed materials is that they permit the individual to proceed at his own rate of speed. Since that is so with the *Programmed Reading* sequence, it should be noted that the readiness program is not "programmed," but is a function of the entire class working closely with the teacher on letter symbols and their related letter sounds. The sounds are represented within the context of words which the child knows. These are what are commonly called the "key" words.

The sound-symbol flash cards used with the pre-reading program are unlike most introductions to reading. They include the vowels *a* and *i*, the consonants *m*, *p*, *f*, *n* and *t*, and the consonant digraph *th*. The foregoing letters are printed in lower-case type, with sketches of the key words: *ant, ink* (which few children in Kindergarten today have seen) *man, pan, fan, nest, tent,* and *thread*.

The teacher's manual suggests a sequence of teacher-class conversation something like the following: The teacher holds up letter-card with capital A. "This is the first letter of the alphabet. Who knows its name?" . . . . and the same sequence with letter Z, then fill in with B, C, D, and E. The purpose is to introduce the first five capital letters first in sequence, then at random, with Z thrown in as an extra at the end.

The second part of the alphabet drill is on capital letters F through

J, with Y added at the end. The third part consists of letters K through O, with X added. Fourth, P through T plus Y are learned. Finally, U through Z are learned.

Practice with the ABC's is supposed to last about three weeks, and this is followed with an introduction to the mechanics of using the novel programmed reading workbooks. It is assumed that the child has had experience with coloring books, and that he can, therefore, turn pages and keep track of his own progress. This may be a false assumption with children from disadvantaged communities. It is the task of the teacher to be constantly circulating throughout the class to check on children who may be having difficulties with the format of programmed materials.

Series I of *Programmed Reading* consists of 7 expendable workbooks in which the five short vowel sounds are presented in 14 different settings in a long series of frames. This work is followed with extensive work on consonants, presenting them in twenty-three different settings or positions. There are over 5000 "frames," each requiring a response, in the seven workbooks of Series I.

The prerequisites for starting the programmed materials in Book 1 of Series One are: knowledge of the alphabet and ability to print upper and lower case letters; ability to associate the phonemes with the graphemes *a, f, m, n, p, t, th,* and *i*; ability to discriminate the words *yes, no, ant, man,* and *mat*; and ability to read the sentence, *I am an ant.*

Those learnings are necessary, for the first frames call for a reading of such simple sentences as "I am an ant" and ability to answer "yes" or "no" after scanning the picture that accompanies the question. On an increasing level of difficulty, the child then begins to select the appropriate word from a choice in order to complete a sentence about a picture. After successive exposure to that word, he then begins to fill in the missing letter or letters in the word as his response task. Thus, the child learns to deal with individual letters in words which he encounters over and over again.

Series I provides practice on 13 vowel sounds and 26 consonant sounds, with two phonemic values for *s, th,* and *y*. By the end of Book 7, all the letters of the alphabet except *o, q,* and *z* have been encountered with at least one phonemic value for each.

The method is somewhat as follows:

At first the teacher asks the questions from her teacher's text, and the children respond as a group and make their individual responses in their workbooks. This is done through page 17, assuming that by then the children will have established the pattern of looking at each frame, sliding the cardboard "slider" strip down the margin to reveal the correct answer after they have entered their responses in the correct places, and have learned to work by themselves independently.

Inasmuch as *Programmed Reading* is planned as an individual approach to beginning reading, each child may move through the program at his own rate. He may work in his workbook at any time during the day, although it is recommended that the first thirty minutes each morning and afternoon be utilized in programmed workbook work.

The following sample pages from *Programmed Reading* indicate the type of responses that constitute the sequential steps. It may be noted that the program calls for discrimination of minimum differences and, consequently, the child responds at first with only one grapheme. Rather soon, however, children begin to use digraphs and, by the end of Series I, they are writing words. Series I covers all of the regular short vowel sounds and all of the phonemically-consistent consonant sounds, plus the double consonants.

In many ways the program follows that of the usual linguistics-phonemics reading program. However, use of two-syllable words in the First Grade goes beyond most other linguistics-phonemics approaches to reading. Of the approximately 400 words used in Series I, only 10 are sight words.

It is implied that average First Grade progress as described above will take the "average" First Grade achiever to the end of ordinary Second Grade materials by means of the *Programmed Reading* approach. The following is what the "Teacher's Guide" calls a "typical achievement schedule" . . . which "will give the first grade teacher . . . the approximate level of accomplishment which she may expect from her class."

Although *Programmed Reading* is essentially a series of 21 workbooks programmed in a linguistics-phonemics sequence, the program also includes an accompanying series of small hard-cover readers which narrate the adventures of Sam and Ann. Those "Storybooks," as they are called, are written so that one is appropriate for use at the end of each workbook. For example, at the end of Workbook 1, the Storybook 1 is *Pins and Pans.* Storybook 2 is *The Bag in the Sand.* They are the only applied reading practice which the child gets outside of whole-class practice with the teacher from time to time on word discrimination and word review exercises.

The Storybooks are by far the most fascinating materials so far produced within the format of linguistically-controlled vocabulary. The interesting stories are embellished by equally-interesting and extremely clever illustrations in color which tickle youngsters (and oldsters, as well). "Pure" linguistics scholars may well observe that the vivid illustrations

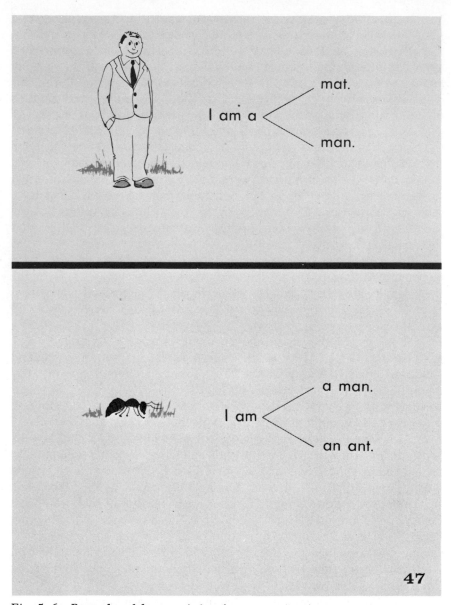

Fig. 5–6   *Reproduced by permission from page 47 of* Programmed Primer *by Sullivan Associates, copyright © 1963 by Sullivan Press, Published by Webster Division, McGraw-Hill Book Company.*

do, indeed, draw the child's attention away from concentration exclusively upon the linguistics-phonemics elements in print. It should also be

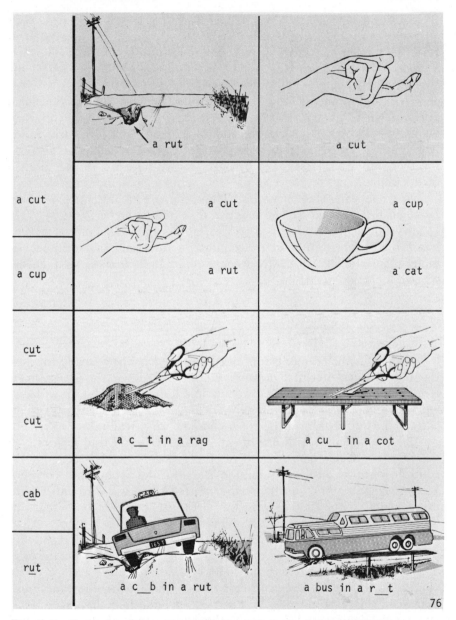

Fig. 5–7 Reproduced from page 76, Book 1, Series I, Reading *by M. W. Sullivan by permission of the publishers, Behavioral Research Laboratories.*

observed that the story lines provide fun for the reader to an extent not found in most other linguistics-phonemics approaches.

Testing within the *Programmed Reading* workbooks takes place after every fifty frames of learning materials. By means of these frequent tests, the teacher may easily keep a running record of each child's progress, as well as have a quick diagnosis of any immediate difficulty which the child is experiencing.

Testing is one of the strong features of the Sullivan-Buchanan program. In addition to the regular tests that are phased into the workbooks, 64-page test booklets are additionally available for each Series. Attractively printed in four colors, they contain a sequence of tests, together with a final test for each book. Lastly, there is a 15 page printed final examination for the end of each series. Accompanying the tests are charts showing student norms. These supposedly are national norms, although there are no data to indicate their source or reliability.

Although the tests may appear to be too long, it should be remembered that they are also in programmed format and, as such, require more than ordinary space to accommodate the "frames" and answer spaces.

Research Findings

Several rather carefully-controlled studies have been made to assess the performance of children who have studied under the *Programmed Reading* program. A First Grade study in California was set up with two equated groups of 21 children each. The groups were matched on the basis of mental maturity, IQ, socioeconomic, and readiness scores. The control group studied with one of the well-known basal reader series.

On the *Gates Diagnostic* Test, the average year-end score for the control group was 3.13 and for the experimental group the score was 4.22. Average reading growth for the control group was 2.13 and for the experimental group the growth was 3.22. It would appear that the difference is probably statistically significant.

In the 1963–64 school year, another California school reported a study in which larger groups of First Graders were equated on the basis of IQ. The control group, using a basal series, obtained average means on the *California Achievement Test* of 2.6, and the experimental group obtained average means of 3.3. There is no indication that there was a statistically significant difference in the performance of the two groups.

An Indiana First Grade experimental group obtained an average rating of 2.2 on the *Standard Achievement Test*, while the control group obtained 1.8. There is no indication of the significance of the difference.

In Detroit, a remedial class of children reading at Second-Grade level was divided into a control group and an experimental group. The control group, using other remedial materials made an average reading growth on the *Gilmore Oral Reading Tests* of .30 compared with an average growth of .58 obtained by the experimental group. (The growth was measured in months, based upon a 10-month school year.)

Reports such as those mentioned above have been printed periodically in the *Journal of Programmed Reading*,[24] published by Webster Division of McGraw-Hill and edited through the Sullivan Associates organization. The so-called "Journal" is quite similar to that published by those interested in disseminating information on the success of i/t/a as described in Chapter 8. One recent issue contains an extensive report[25] of First Grade experience with *Programmed Reading* in the Burlington (N.J.) Township Public Schools. Comparisons were made of the achievement of children in seven classes. The program was run during the 1966–67 school year. The report states that "Tests conducted in May revealed that 53% of all First Grade pupils were reading at 3.0 or higher level, 65% were reading at 2.5 or higher" and only 8% were below Second Grade level. Apparently, the scores referred to were on the *Gates Reading Tests*, although this is not entirely clear, for tabular reference is only made to "averages" for each child, without explaining what was meant.

The tabulated grade-equivalents are indicated for each child for January and May testing. Some groups, apparently, were homogeneously constituted, and some were "mixed."

In May of the first year, all members of the "high-average" group were listed as being at 2.8 or higher, with the median of the 23 students being at 3.7. In the "below-average" group, the median grade-equivalent for the 23 children was reported as being 2.3. Three children were below the equivalent for Grade Two, but two of those had no Kindergarten readiness.

Obviously, there is much to be desired statistically in this report, but it does provide some comparable data of several classes which have used *Programmed Reading* for one year.

The same issue of the *Journal* carried reports of success with *Programmed Reading* for remedial purposes. One study reported by Liddle[26] provides data that cannot be used, inasmuch as the materials

---

24. *Journal of Programmed Reading*, Arthur Welch, editor. Webster Division of McGraw-Hill Book Company.
25. Gentile, Charles A., "Burlington Township Reports on First Year of Program," *Journal of Programmed Reading*, No. 7:6–12.
26. Liddle, William, "Project Corrective Reteaching of Reading," *Journal of Programmed Reading*, No. 7:2–4.

used in the study included a rather large number of varied aids such as SRA Laboratories, phonics, charts, phonics skills games, etc.

The other study, reported by Sampson,[27] dealt with eight educable mentally-handicapped children who had been given training in the *Programmed Reading* workbooks. It is interesting to note that word recognition scores were significantly above comprehension scores in the fall, but that the differentials had been significantly reduced or eliminated entirely by the time of testing in the spring.

Satisfaction has been reported by others using the *Programmed Reading* materials with low and/or remedial groups. Indeed, it is possible that the materials will be most useful with such learners. The inherent advantages of having materials that are programmed with specific phonemic skills as a base and having self-tests and immediate knowledge of the results of each individual response should be of greatest value to low-achieving youngsters who need the constant and repetitious motivation that comes from immediate knowledge of success.

Moreover, programmed materials, such as found in the Sullivan-Buchanan sequence, provide the small increments of learning which slow learners can assimilate more easily. The fact that the programmed workbooks provide a means for individual speed of learning is also of prime importance in working with remedial cases.

Psychologically, programmed materials provide the distinct advantages resulting from conforming to certain principles of learning, namely, (1) step-by-step learning, (2) immediate knowledge of results, (3) regular and constant review and testing, (4) learning-by-doing, which, in the case of *Programmed Reading*, the child is responding by writing actual words and parts of words . . . not just pronouncing them, and (5) materials providing for individual differences of the learners.

THE MICHIGAN LANGUAGE PROGRAM

Origins

The *Michigan Language Program* is described as "a language arts curriculum for beginning reading instruction" by its originator, Dr. Donald E. P. Smith of the University of Michigan College of Education. In addition to being Professor of Educational Psychology and Chief of the

---

27. Sampson, William A., "Programmed Reading in a Level II EMH Class," *Journal of Programmed Reading*, No. 7:7–8.

Reading Improvement Service, Dr. Smith is also a member of the staff of the University's Center for Research on Language and Language Behavior and also the Center for Programmed Learning.

Early work on the program grew out of a team effort in which Dr. Smith was associated with Dr. Patrick Carrigan. Their book, *The Nature of Reading Disability*, is well known to reading specialists, for it proposed theories of learning dependent upon synaptic chemical-electrical impulses. Such theories had been extensively researched by some of the world's distinguished neuropsychologists. Smith and Carrigan were among the first to suggest a relationship between neuropsychological changes and reading.

Such intense interest in learning theory and its relationship to reading naturally led Dr. Smith to postulate on the conditions which would produce behaviors which would be the components of the reading process. This, in turn, led to a formulation of a theoretical model of visual and auditory stimuli and motor responses that would provide a sequence of learnings culminating in what is known as the ability to read.

In March, 1963, a group of Michigan researchers joined to work on a total language arts curriculum in programmed form. The programmed materials were to have the essentials which matched Smith's criteria in his theoretical model. Working with Dr. Smith on the program were a group of programmers including Judith M. Kelingos of Eastern Michigan University, Bernice J. Mayhew of the Oakland County Reading Clinic, Carl Semmelroth of the University of Michigan, Brunhilde W. Sommer of Northern Michigan University, and Frank P. Greene of Syracuse University.

The program they developed was known in its earlier stages as the "Michigan Successive Discrimination Language Program". It was, essentially, an extensively and intensively programmed sequence of steps involving discriminative responses by the learner. As the materials for the program were built and tested on children, day-to-day and week-by-week revisions took place whenever more than 5% errors appeared. The program is now available in workbook format, published by Learning Research Associates, Inc.

Methods and Materials

Although the teacher's manual which accompanies the *Michigan Language Program* describes the highly-structured nature of teacher behavior which is basic to the program, an understanding of the psychological principles underlying the program is necessary in order to relate the procedures to the theoretical model.

Indeed, without an understanding of the philosophy of operant behavior which permeates the method, the teacher might appear to be little more than an automaton in this unusual program which claims that its objective is "To teach reading, writing, and listening to all English speaking children and adults."

The originator of the program defines reading as "the production of verbal behavior under the control of visual symbols, usually words and word groups." He continues that, in its simplest form, reading consists of "naming" letters and words. Other definitions of writing, listening, and speaking all are couched in terms of responses to symbols, leading to the conclusion that there are "interwoven relationships among the language skills." Indeed, it is concluded by Dr. Smith that "the interdependence of the skills requires that they be taught concurrently."

With reference to his partiality for neuropsychological explanations of learning phenomena, Dr. Smith conjectures that "The relationship among the part learnings may be said to be across sensory channels or *modalities.*" By this, he means that learning to read involves a multisensory response in which seeing, hearing, speaking and writing are associated with at least three sensory channels.

Another kind of relationship is said to take place *within* modalities and, therefore, it may be termed a "developmental sequence" for it depends upon the temporal development of responses to increasingly-complex stimuli. The task of discriminating differences in a hierarchical fashion results from stimuli such as (1) similar appearing letters (such as *b* and *d* or *p* and *q*); (2) the order of letters in words wherein reversals are common (such as *on* and *no* or *was* and *saw*); and (3) similar appearing whole words (such as *though* and *through*).

The objective of programming stimuli and responses through the *Michigan* (Successive Discrimination) *Language Program,* thus, becomes more understandable. The task which the psychologists and programmers set for themselves was to identify the skills and the order in which they emerged, and then to arrange the stimuli in that order. At the same time, they set about to test the materials to assure each learner of at least 95% probability of success.

It should be clear from the aforementioned set of criteria that the stimuli should be programmed in an orderly sequence, and that the learner will respond and will receive knowledge of the correctness of his response. What role, then, does the teacher play? In a programmed-environment classroom, as Smith and his colleagues envision it, the teacher is a monitor, or manager; not a dispenser of information or rewards and punishment.

The materials of the *Michigan Language Program* are, therefore, self-instructional. Smith states: "The teacher in this classroom is quite different from the cultural stereotypes, the substitute mother (an unconditional love-giver) or a strict disciplinarian (a conditional love-giver). The teacher is not a parent and is not in the business of love giving or love receiving."

Teacher behavior is an essential part of the program. The teacher establishes one or two rules for learners. For example, the rule may be "No talking during work periods" and "No disturbing others". Any infraction of other normal behavior is ignored unless the behavior becomes greatly annoying and disruptive. When the "no talking" rule is violated, all the teacher does is ask the child "What is the rule?" And the teacher expects that the rule will be repeated. There is no punishment. It has been shown that those behaviors to which the teacher does not respond will fade and extinguish themselves. The third function of the teacher is to check tests.

Inasmuch as the *Michigan Language Program* is a highly structured programmed sequence of stimulus-response "frames", concentrated attention to the learning task is essential. "The classroom must be free from all distractions." It is implied that pictures, bulletin boards, or any other extraneous and diverting stimuli should either be at the rear of the room or not in the room at all.

The teacher's manual states that, "Before beginning the program, the teacher has achieved this degree of control: When a teacher says, 'Sit quietly and fold your hands,' the children do so."

Once having mastered the "Sit quietly and fold your hands" routine, the teacher can then launch into the so-called programmed sequence with the assurance from its authors that "The majority of children will be immediately successful in the program, and will work happily, quietly, and efficiently."

The program for the first two weeks consists of a sequence in listening, writing and reading all to be carried on concurrently—that is, all three programmed lessons will be done each day.

Book I and Book II are designed to develop sensitivity to the sounds of English. The sounds are dictated by the teacher in the form of simple words, all in the same tonal pattern. The simple difference between *pin* and *tin* is the initial consonant. It is contended that, if the tonal pattern were different, children would respond to that difference rather than to the phonemic difference.

Monosyllable monotone dictation is followed with responding by marking either "yes" or "no" choices in the workbook. As one investigates the nature of the "successive discrimination" reading program, it becomes more apparent why the system does not allow for any distractions, for the entire mechanics of the system is a continuum of monotone pronunciation timed to the second by the teacher. "A steady pace for presenting words is essential."

The following example illustrates the point:

The teacher pronounces the following trio of words:

BED	HEAD	BED		
1 second	1 second	1 second	=	3 seconds
			+	3 second pause

The teacher then proceeds to the next group of three words. During the three-second pause, each child is supposed to mark his workbook on the "yes" or "no" choice according to whether or not the three words are alike.

The teacher is admonished never to deviate from this pace; never to stop to answer a question; never to look at any one particular child; always to move ahead as though the children do not exist. One wonders at this point why it might not be better for each child to be plugged into a tape recorder. Apparently, one surmises the answer in Rule #3 below. There are, in fact, four cardinal rules of method and procedure:

Rule #1. "Directions are to be followed exactly as they appear in the script."

Rule #2. "Say each word of a set with the same inflection. Avoid dropping the voice on the third word." Obviously this is necessary, for the child's task is to ascertain whether or not the three words are exactly alike, and linguistics scientists have been reminding us of the differences that intonation and inflection make for discrimination as well as in meaning.

Rule #3. "Avoid watching a child . . . You tend to pace yourself by him." It is recommended in the manual that a teacher watch a sweep second hand in order to pace the dictation accurately. Perhaps a metronome would be even more effective.

Rule #4. "Control activity level by slight changes in presentation rate." It is recommended that the teacher speed up dictation when the children have become accustomed to the routine. Otherwise the children may become restless and noisy, it is warned.

After almost 1,200 yes–no discriminations of dictated words with accompanying pictures covering 211 pages in the child's Workbook I, the program begins to deal with separate sounds in dictated words. This refinement in auditory discrimination calls for a yes–no response depending on whether or not a certain specific sound is heard in the word dictated by the teacher. The method is:

"Listen to this sound: ssss"
"I will say a word. If you hear 'ssss', circle 'yes'."
                    "If not, then circle 'no'."
"Listen for ssss. Dog.
"Did you hear ssss?" Circle 'no'."
"Listen for ssss. horse." Draw a circle. pause. . .
"Listen for ssss. sit." Draw a circle. pause. . .
"Listen for sss. man." Draw a circle. pause. . .

Actually, the objective is to teach the child to discriminate final consonant sounds as listening exercises, and the listening program proceeds with work with final consonant sounds *sss, mmm, fff, lll, sh, nnn, th* and *ch*.

Beginning consonant sounds are then introduced in the following sequence: *sss, mmm, sh, ch*, and then the sound *cha* is suddenly introduced with no preparation in the long *a* vowel sound. This is followed with *choo, le, li, lo, lu* (as in *lump*), *thi* (*think*), *tha* (*that*), *tho, ra, ro*, and *ru*.

Then there is some work with a mixture of short and long vowel sounds in the following unexplainable sequence: *can* as in *candy, ki* as in *kitten, cu* as in *cut, ki* as in *kite, cri* as in *crib*, and *cle* as in *clean*. Obviously these are designed to introduce the hard *k* sound found both in *k* and in *c*.

The materials in Book I are continued and concluded with dozens of responses on sounds of *at, ish, arm, ate, ake, own* (as in gown), *un, ing, er, ine*.

The child is required to make more than 300 yes–no responses to this sort of monosyllable stimuli in Book I. Time suggestions given in the teacher's manual for Book I suggest 15-minutes per day for nine days.

Book II, with its 133 pages and almost 800 responses, starts with pairs of compound words somewhat like the spondaic words used for auditory testing. Pairs like *Sailboat, Boatsail, Fur coat, Coat fur* are common.

The "Listening" discrimination program is only part of the language program, of which the so-called "reading" program is considered most important. Book I of the Reading Program also occupies the time of the First-Grade children during the first two weeks of school. It is designed for visual discrimination of lower case letters which at first are heavy 1½" bold face, becoming progressively smaller and more to the page as the weeks progress.

The procedure is much like that called for on the old edition of the *Metropolitan Readiness Tests*, wherein there is a letter in the middle of the space on the page, with three letters directly below it. The task of the

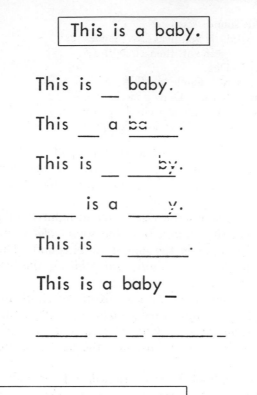

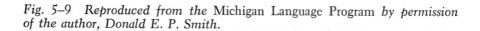

Fig. 5–9 Reproduced from the Michigan Language Program *by permission of the author, Donald E. P. Smith.*

child is to select that letter from among the three that is exactly like the sample above. An example from Smith's program will make this clear:

$$
\begin{array}{c}
\text{c} \\
\hline
\text{l \quad k \quad c}
\end{array}
$$

then
$$
\begin{array}{c}
\text{c} \\
\hline
\text{l \quad c \quad k}
\end{array}
$$

then
$$
\begin{array}{c}
\text{l} \\
\hline
\text{l \quad c \quad k}
\end{array}
$$

$$
\begin{array}{c}
\text{k} \\
\hline
\text{c \quad k \quad l} \quad \text{etc.}
\end{array}
$$

By the time the children arrive at page 82, they begin to have work as follows:

in which they must "mind their p's and q's". Book 2 also contains exercises in which children trace over split and dotted outlined letters. No justification is given for this, although it looks like an attempt to employ some of Grace Fernald's techniques, but, surprisingly, it is not followed through to any logical application. The author reports that some children carry out this procedure spontaneously, so it has been allowed to remain in the material to be used at the child's discretion.

The book ends with work with digraphs and trigraphs which become increasingly more difficult as the children attempt to match such as the following:

```
                     ae
lg      over     in       ae     ote     eod     but     ghid
                     vwx
xwv     vwx      wxv      vxw     wvx
```

The reading of whole words is the task that confronts the learner immediately in Book 3. A seemingly endless sequence of phrases are to be matched with other duplicate phrases. This is entirely a visual discrimination process. For example, the phrase is "This is Jack". Inasmuch as the child cannot read it, the teacher pronounces it in her monotone. The child looks on his workbook page and tries to find a sentence among the two or three that is exactly as the sample sentence.

As the program proceeds, the dictation and the material in the workbook is expanded to four-word phrases or sentences, and then five-word sentences. Some of the sentences from which the child may choose are sentences without proper spacing between the words. Thus the child is presented with inaccurate reading material. Hopefully he will discriminate and select the correctly-spaced words. Learning experiments, however, have reported studies in which children just as readily learned the incorrect responses and skills. There are 122 pages of dictated sentences in Book 3.

Book 4 begins to teach left-to-right progression which involves moving from the end of one line to the beginning of the next line in order to find the complete sentence that matches the sample to be matched. An arrow is drawn from the end of the line to the beginning of the next line to lead the child's attention. The work in Book 4 becomes progressively more difficult. The teacher reads a sentence, for example: "She saw a chair and some hair." That same sentence appears in the workbook for the child to match. His choices include sentences in which *chair* and *hair*

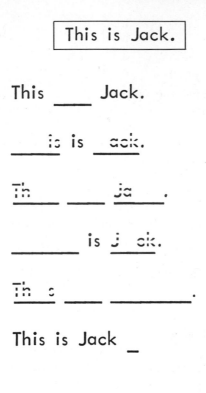

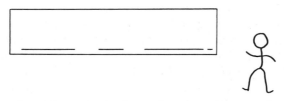

Fig. 5–8 Reproduced from the Michigan Language Program *by permission of the author, Donald E. P. Smith.*

appear as plurals and the word *some* is interchanged in several patterns of word order.

There are more than 100 pages of sentences and discrimination choices in Book 4.

Book 5 provides more of the same type of dictation and visual choices.

Book 6 calls for writing some words. It covers 124 pages of dictation and responding choices.

Book 7 is 193 pages of more of the same.

Book 8 is a huge production of 241 pages of much of the same, with some use of conversation and contractions *don't* and *I'll*.

The series is concluded with Book 9 which is a 163 page story about a "Walk in the Woods." It is, in effect, the first real sequential reading that the children encounter in the *Michigan Reading Program*.

The so-called "basal reading program" is supposed to be completed through Book 8 in 18 weeks plus the two weeks allotted to the first phases of the program.

The so-called "analytical reading" sequences found in Books 9, 10, and 11 will require an additional six weeks according to the author of the manual.

Research Findings

The originator of the *Michigan Language Program*, Dr. Donald E. P. Smith, has reported the steps which his team of researchers has taken in developing the programmed approach to reading. Some of the research has been supported by the U.S. Office of Education and the University of Michigan Center for Research on Language and Language Behavior. Various professional organizations have been kept informed by Dr. Smith, among them the College Reading Association, the American Speech and Hearing Association, the International Reading Association, and others. Talks which he has given at their annual meetings usually have been printed and are readily available in the professional journals.

The program is new, and it has been reported that it will be some time before wide scale testing of the program under ordinary public school condition will be completed. Large numbers of teachers in special classes and in clinical situations are experimenting with the program. They have reported uniformly favorable results.

The *Michigan Language Program* has within it some elements of "visual tracking" and progressive discrimination and choice which probably will be of special interest to those in the field of reading who are exploring the neurological and perceptual aspects of reading. Expanding interest in so-called "dyslexia" should lead to a thorough investigation of the effects such a program as Dr. Donald E. P. Smith suggests could have to contribute to the subject.

In summary, it may be stated that the *Michigan Language Program* is a system devised to utilize a number of basic laws of learning. It is a

OVERVIEW: The Process of Discrimination Learning

STEP 1

Phoneme Discrimination:

All 43 phonemes are discriminated from one another in all positions in which they normally occur.

Concept Development:

Oral language program elicits sentences similar to those in stories; stories are dramatized; a "picture discrimination" program in Book II develops those story concepts illustrated by picture-aids; group discussions of story concepts are held.

Letter Discrimination:

Includes single letters, two, three, four and five letter groups, order of letters, and word order of two and three nonsense word groups.

Word Discrimination:

Books 3 to 8 present 349 words representing Dolch basic words, most function words and common "phonemically regular" words from the Bloomfield list.

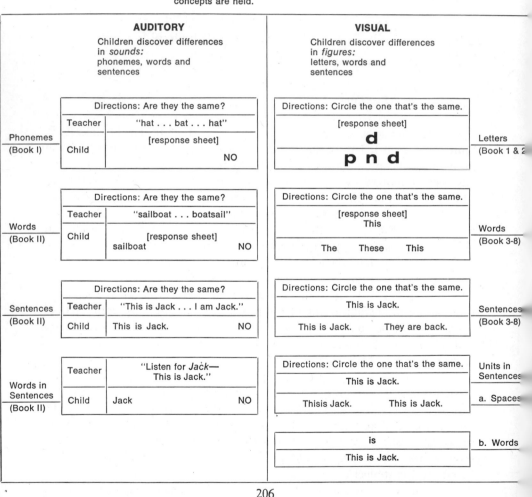

	AUDITORY		**VISUAL**	
	Children discover differences in *sounds:* phonemes, words and sentences		Children discover differences in *figures:* letters, words and sentences	

Phonemes (Book I) — Directions: Are they the same? Teacher: "hat . . . bat . . . hat" / Child: [response sheet] NO — Directions: Circle the one that's the same. [response sheet] **d** / **p n d** — **Letters (Book 1 & 2)**

Words (Book II) — Directions: Are they the same? Teacher: "sailboat . . . boatsail" / Child: [response sheet] sailboat NO — Directions: Circle the one that's the same. [response sheet] This / The These This — **Words (Book 3-8)**

Sentences (Book II) — Directions: Are they the same? Teacher: "This is Jack . . . I am Jack." / Child: This is Jack. NO — Directions: Circle the one that's the same. This is Jack. / This is Jack. They are back. — **Sentences (Book 3-8)**

Words in Sentences (Book II) — Teacher: "Listen for *Jack*— This is Jack." / Child: Jack NO — Directions: Circle the one that's the same. This is Jack. / Thisis Jack. This is Jack. — **Units in Sentences** / **a. Spaces**

is / This is Jack. — **b. Words**

STEP 2

Aural-Visual Discrimination:

Required in Books 3 and 4 only. Thereafter, discriminations are made spontaneously.

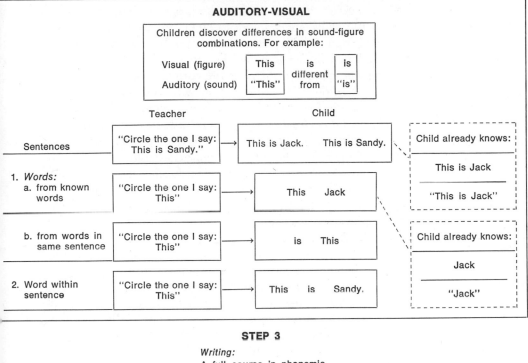

AUDITORY-VISUAL

Children discover differences in sound-figure combinations. For example:

Visual (figure)	This	is	is
Auditory (sound)	"This"	different from	"is"

Teacher / Child

Sentences — "Circle the one I say: This is Sandy." → This is Jack.   This is Sandy.

Child already knows:
This is Jack
"This is Jack"

1. *Words:*
   a. from known words — "Circle the one I say: This" → This   Jack

   b. from words in same sentence — "Circle the one I say: This" → is   This

Child already knows:
Jack
"Jack"

2. Word within sentence — "Circle the one I say: This" → This   is   Sandy.

STEP 3

Writing:
A full course in phonemic analysis is provided in the writing step. Terminal steps appear at end of Book 8.

[Letter formation learned in Books A & B] **WRITING** $\begin{bmatrix} \text{Th} \_\_ \text{ Ja} \_. \\ \_\_ \text{ is is } \_\_ \text{ ck.} \end{bmatrix}$

STEP 4

Oral Reading:
Each child demonstrates mastery of each unit by reading aloud to teacher (without pictures) before beginning next unit.

[Dramatization & oral composition precedes.] **ORAL READING** $\begin{bmatrix} \text{1. Sentences learned.} \\ \text{2. New sentences using words learned.} \end{bmatrix}$

psychologically-oriented approach to reading, and is structured in step-by-step frames, programmed to provide auditory, spatial, sequential, and visual discrimination responses.

All learning tasks are intrinsically self-rewarding. All of the skills which good readers develop are included in the program, according to its authors. Most of the skills are learned through imitation in which a "model" is provided, and the learner discriminates between the choices and selects the one which is the same as the model. Given a reasonable degree of attention, the child will discover the correct choice 95% of the time. This is assured through experimentation with the frames and the revision of each frame until consistently satisfactory results are obtained.

In the *Michigan Language Program*, careful attention is given to an environment for learning that does not allow distracting elements to be present. Neither the room nor the teacher-monitor are allowed to be distracting stimuli. The outcome is said to be increased attention to self-directed learning tasks, independent study habits, and the extinction of dependency behaviors and other self-defeating habits. In their place, it is reported that the learner meets with success, goes at his own rate, and competes only with himself.

There is no doubt that many children respond best to highly structured learning situations. Moreover they, and perhaps others, enjoy the success that is virtually assured through programmed learning. The *Michigan Language Program* has those essentials to offer. Further feedback from use in actual classroom situations will, undoubtedly, result in further refinements of the materials and, perhaps, the method.

At present, the *Michigan Reading Program* defies simple description. Moreover, it is so unique that it resists arbitrary classification under any of the headings in this book. It has been tentatively classified under "Linguistics-phonemic Approaches" because of its orientation toward a regular sequence of exercises dealing with phonemic elements. As the system evolves through experimentation and use, it may reveal other qualities which will dictate its classification elsewhere.

THE MIAMI LINGUISTIC READERS

Origins

The *Miami Linguistic Readers* were developed as an aspect of a Ford Foundation grant to the Dade County (Miami, Florida) Public Schools. The objective of the proposal was to provide a "breakthrough" on the problem of teaching reading and the language arts to children who were learning English as a second language.

The Miami (Dade County) schools had been suffering under the sudden impact of tens of thousands of such children who, with their families, had settled in the Miami area as refugees from Castro's Cuba.[28] Although many families had been rather substantial citizens of their homeland, when they reached Florida, they were obliged to live in camps and barracks. In fact, the problem became so acute that a massive attack on the problem was finally undertaken with the federal, state, and county governments all sharing in it.

The schools, of course, were far from prepared for such an influx of non-English-speaking children. There were neither teachers nor materials available for them, and one result of this lack was that the children often did not receive any reading instruction until the third grade. The idea for the project was conceived in the early 1960s, and took the shape of a project in reading in which a new series of readers would be developed for those children so that they could start sooner and get the reading instruction they needed to catch up with the English-speaking children. The rationale for the *Miami Linguistic Readers* was, consequently, twofold: (1) to develop books which were "culture-free," and which would have themes with which children of any background could relate; (2) to develop books which would provide an approach to American English with the least amount of phonemic irregularity—this being necessary, especially for children who already had some knowledge of a relatively-regular phonemic language: Cuban-Spanish.

As a result of these two stipulations, the committee in charge of the project concluded that no existing materials would suffice, most of them being quite culture-centered, and the majority of them involving a whole-word approach in which phonemic elements were not controlled, or, on the other hand, phonemics systems in which sounds were to be taught in isolation.

The *Miami Linguistic Readers* are, actually, a linguistics-oriented language arts program, and not just a reading program. The entire Miami program involves the learning of the sounds of our language, with special initial emphasis on speaking and listening, for it is recognized that the children using the program will have the dual task of acquiring a mastery of English as a new spoken language, as well as learning to read.

---

28. For a more detailed explanation of the origins of the program in the Dade County schools, see: Robinett, Ralph F., "A 'Linguistic' Approach to Beginning Reading For Bilingual Children," Chapter 9 in *First Grade Reading Programs*, Perspectives in Reading No. 5. Newark, Delaware: International Reading Association, 1965. 132–149.

The Ford Foundation Project director has been Pauline M. Rojas, assisted by Ralph Robinett and Paul W. Bell. Others who collaborated on the *Readers* were Hermenia Cantero, Rosa Inclan, Mildred Lash, June Granger, Hyacinth Stanton, Judy P. Reeder, and Mary Perdue. Richard O. White, Supervisor of Special Readings Services of the Dade County Schools provided suggestions. Thus, the *Miami Linguistic Readers* grew as a team effort.

A preliminary edition was published by D. C. Heath and Company of Boston in 1964, 1965, and 1966, to be tried out in schools in Texas, New Mexico, Arizona, California, Colorado, and Puerto Rico—all having similar problems to those found in the Dade County schools. The present edition is also published by Heath.

Materials and Method

The *Miami Linguistic Readers* complete two-year program consists of twenty-one small paperback booklets, and sixteen "seatwork" workbooks and teacher's manuals to match. The small booklet primers and readers have stories developed with extremely limited vocabulary which is phased in accordance with some selected linguistics-phonemics principles. There are also some rather large charts with pictures (referred to as "Big Books") which are to be used with the whole class and/or with small groups of children for oral practice on the language.

The pictures on the charts have the same quality as those black-and-white drawings in the small booklets, namely, a rather heavy inky contrast, but with considerable appeal to children. The illustrations are credited to Rose L. Nash. The only color used in the series is on the various colored paperback covers for the booklets and the workbooks and teacher's manuals which are "color coordinated" to match.

The committee which produced the *Miami Linguistic Readers* was guided by certain basic objectives. Its purpose was to produce stories and materials that had a basic interest to children; that would be phrased in "natural" speech patterns, yet with controlled vocabulary and controlled grammatical structure with hope that the difficulty of the materials would not increase faster than the acquired skills necessary for success in those materials. Their objectives were:

1. That the content of beginning reading materials must deal with those things which time has shown are truly interesting to children.
2. That the materials must reflect the natural language forms of children's speech.

3. That the child must have aural-oral control of the material he is expected to read.
4. That grammatical structure as well as vocabulary must be controlled.
5. That the child must learn to read by structures.
6. That sound-symbol correspondences should be in terms of spelling patterns.
7. That the focus must be on the process of reading.
8. That writing experiences reinforce listening, speaking and reading.
9. That the learning load in linguistically oriented materials must be determined in terms of the special nature of the materials.
10. That the learner achieve success as he progresses through the materials.

Throughout the program, there are activities which involve listening, speaking, writing, spelling, and reading as part of every lesson. The objective is to help the child "learn to understand, speak, read and write standard English."

"The focus of the language activities is on the acquisition of patterns; the techniques are those of drill." Much of the speaking and reading is dependent upon imitation of the teacher's exemplary model, with "whole-word" sight reading as the first step.

This is not an impossible task for the child, however, for the first booklet, *Biff and Tiff*, utilizes only seven different words: *Biff, Tiff, sit, is, dig, and, drink*. The verbs *sit, dig,* and *drink* are augmented with the *-ing* ending. Many teachers and reading specialists might be concerned that this feature is introduced so early, for it involves an abstract concept of grammar and, in addition, necessitates the doubling of the *g* to create the word, *digging*. This, alone, is a concept which is not only unexplainable but introduces the child almost immediately to one of the rules of the language which most linguistics scientists recommend be eliminated in the early stages of learning.

The stories in the little pre-primer and primer booklets are conveyed through the medium of the personification of animals in the first year. The first book, *Biff and Tiff*, contains episodes in which Biff, the big dog, teaches Tiff, the puppy, to sit, to dig, and to drink. The second pre-primer, *Kid Kit and the Catfish* provides an Aesop-style storyette on Kid Kit, the cat, who goes fishing for catfish. (Note the early introduction of a double-noun compound word.) Kid Kit slips into the water, rescues himself, drips, and thinks about catching a bird.

In *Nat the Rat*, the story has a fairy-tale characteristic of a pack rat who steals the king's diamond pin, ring, and wig while the king sleeps.

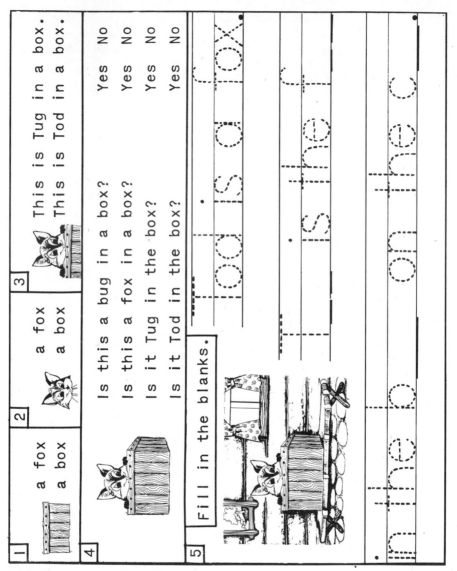

13

Fig. 5–10   Reproduced from the Miami Linguistic Readers *by permission
of D. C. Heath and Company.*

His majesty's court helpers, Cab Cat, Rab Rabbit, and Pap Pig, discover the thefts, search and find Nat the Rat burying the treasures, and, without any intervening script or pictures, the story ends with sad Nat the Rat in prison, "sitting . . . and thinking and thinking."

Tug Duck and Buzz Bug is another animal story in the fairytale tradition. All the characteristics are present: the bad guy (Tug Duck) who captures the good guy (Buzz Bug); puts Buzz in his burlap sack and then sits down by a tree and goes to sleep. Buzz then cuts his way out of the sack, steals the sack, and takes off with Tug pursuing him. Tug meets the fate of a villain by falling in the mud, whereupon the hero, Buzz, cuts up the sack to cover the outer walls of his new hut. Thus, good triumphs over evil.

The Sack Hut is a sequel to the preceding books, and brings Pap Pig, Rab Rabbit, Cab Cat, Nat the Rat, Tug Duck, and Buzz Bug together in a story of conflict, treachery, and turmoil which ends with Nat the Rat back in his jail cell. *The Sack Hut* is a so-called "plateau story" designed to consolidate some of the previous linguistics-phonemics learning before moving to new materials.

Although at least eight linguistics scholars served from time to time in an advisory capacity, how the *Miami Linguistic Readers* trace their ancestry to linguistics is not entirely clear. There is some hint that the "structural linguistics" area has been tapped, for the teacher's manual states that "The child must learn to read by structures if he is to master the skills involved in the act of reading".

It may be surmised that the committee had in mind the development of repetitious patterns which would be learned through a regularly recurring pattern of phrases. An example or two from the *Teacher's Manual* will illustrate the "patterning".

> Show the pupils Chart 1 and tell them that the name of the rat is Nat. Guide them in asking *Is that (Kid Kit)?* and in answering *No, it isn't, It's Nat the Rat,* and *Yes, it is, It's Nat the Rat.* Then guide them to ask *What is (Nat)?* and to answer *A (rat)*. Follow techniques in A, B, and C of the foldouts at the back of this manual.

(The foldouts show the large classroom charts and suggest first, that the teacher (a) point to the picture of Nat and say, "Nat is a rat," and children repeat. (b) Teacher points to Nat and/or to some other animal character. Children say "Nat is a rat", when she points to Nat's picture. (c) Children work in pairs. One asks, "What is Nat doing?" His paired pupil responds, "Nat is singing". The teacher demonstrates this procedure first for the children to imitate.)

The manual goes on to explain the procedure:

> *Teacher*: (pointing to Nat on chart 1)
>   Is that Kid Kit?
> *Group 1*: Is that Kid Kit? (repeat in unison)
> *Teacher*: No, it isn't. It's Nat the Rat.
> *Group 2*: (repeats in unison) No, it isn't.
>   It's Nat the Rat.
> *Pupil 1*: Is that Kid Kit?
> *Pupil 2*: No, it isn't. It's Nat the Rat.

In that manner it is assumed that the structure will be learned. Such structuring comes under the heading of "Language", which is designated as separate from "Reading", and rightly so. Much of the patterning is with prepositional phrases: "The king is sitting in the chair (on the floor)," etc. "Is Buzz Bug in the sack?" and others provide opportunities for the children to imitate the teacher in turning questions into statements.

It must be remembered that these language patterns are being taught to children who do not yet know English as their common language. Hence, it is necessary to establish phrases rather than to place emphasis on words and parts of words in isolation.

It is, perhaps, this last factor that lies at the base of the differences between this *Miami Linguistic* system and others which are also called "linguistic" but which ordinarily place emphasis on the parts of words and letter-sound relationship. Yet, the *Miami Linguistic Readers* do provide practice in somewhat similar elements, i.e.

> That is Cab.
> Cab is a cat.
> That is Cab Cat.
> Cab is the king's cat.

The emphasis is upon the *-at* and *-ab*, as well as upon the "hard" *c*, appearing in both lower and upper case forms. The "hard" *c* is simultaneously compared with the *k* sound in *king*, and in other words such as *Kid*, *Kit*, and *Kim*. Thus the "structure" of *cat* and *Cab* are compared for similarities and differences, together with the "structure" of other monosyllabic words that have the same initial phoneme.

From the very beginning, an effort has been made to present sound-symbol correspondences in terms of whole spellings rather than individual isolated letter-sounds.

Moreover, inasmuch as the children are learning the total language, rather than just reading, great emphasis is given to intonation, and enunciation. Exclamation, sadness, surprise, command, etc. are all a dramatic part of the reading, and children are expected to learn and use those features of everyday speech inflections in their reading. Consequently much reading is done aloud.

Research Findings

During the classroom-testing period, beginning with the opening of school in the Fall, 1964, centers in Arizona, California, Colorado, New Mexico, Texas, and Puerto Rico used books published on an experimental basis by the Dade County schools. The first ten books and accompanying teacher's guides, seatwork activities and two "big books" were used in those centers. At that time, D. C. Heath and Company accepted the option of publishing the additional eleven books and accompanying materials in experimental form.

Close contact was kept with the experimental centers as well as with the nearby Dade County project. On the basis of feed-back, some revisions were made in the materials, and the staff continued to work on a tight schedule in order to supply the centers with the second year materials. By October, 1966, a total of 21 pupils' books, with accompanying teacher's guides and seatwork booklets and the two "big books" had been produced.

During the two year tryout period, the *Miami Linguistic Readers* were tested not only with Spanish-speaking children but also with Miccosukee Indian children and with several groups of culturally-disadvantaged English-speaking children.

The Director of the Ford Foundation Project, Pauline M. Rojas, in her final report[29] stated:

> Experience with the Readers materials seems to indicate that the non-English mother tongue pupils, given reading materials which are linguistically structured and which provide for adequate oral interpretation before each reading step, can be brought to a satisfactory level of achievement without the retardation so characteristic of these pupils when they are taught with traditional materials.

Dr. Rojas also stated that

> The Readers materials also seem to indicate that pupils can learn English and learn to read in English simultaneously if the materials are so selected and organized that they reflect principles

---

29. Rojas, Pauline M., *Final Report—Ford Foundation Project in Bilingual Education*, Miami: Dade County Public Schools, August 31, 1966. Dittoed. 11.

specifically geared to the special needs of language-handicapped pupils.

It is, probably, too soon to expect any substantive or definitive results from the use of the *Miami Linguistic Readers*. It will, moreover, be many years before comparative studies can be designed to indicate whether or not the series has the merits hoped for, when compared with other available approaches.

THE PALO ALTO PROGRAM

Origins

The *Palo Alto Reading Program* is published by Harcourt, Brace, Jovanovich under the title "Sequential Steps in Reading." The program originated in the Palo Alto Unified School District during the years when its author, Dr. Theodore E. Glim, was Language Arts Consultant for that school system.

Although Dr. Glim has moved to the position of Assistant Superintendent for the Shoreline Schools of Seattle, the program retains the Palo Alto name.

According to the *Teacher's Guide*, "Its development sprang from a general feeling of dissatisfaction with existing reading programs." The *Guide* describes the limited success many children had with conventional materials and methods and states: "It was clear that *some* children did not succeed in learning to read, whereas others achieved only partial success. Those children, like their counterparts in other schools, developed feelings of frustration; they lost self-confidence and became disoriented in school. Too, it was noted that many children did not reach the stage of self-reliance, or independence, in reading soon enough."[30]

The Palo Alto staff worked cooperatively in developing the program with several principles of learning in mind. They hoped to build a program in which continued success would be a persistent motivating factor. By so doing, the child would be spared the discouragement of failure. Such an objective demands step-by-step structured sequences in which small increments of learning are assimilated. Moreover, as in

---

30. Glim, Theodore E., *Teacher's Guide: Palo Alto Reading Program*. New York: Harcourt Brace, Jovanovich, Inc. Introduction, vi.

programmed reading materials, the learner must be able to check the accuracy of his responses at each step in the program. Thus the name, "Sequential Steps in Reading" was devised.

Other features of approaches to reading were also adopted and built into the *Palo Alto Program*. Most important is the linguistics-phonemics facet of the beginning segments of the program. Although much of the beginning reading materials is structured according to linguistics-phonemics regularity, some words do not lend themselves to "decoding". They are, therefore, introduced as sight words. The program, consequently, achieves somewhat more interest than if it had limited itself to a "pure" linguistics-phonemics content.

Materials and Method

The *Palo Alto Program* consists of 20 paperbound pupil's books and 20 workpads. These are not given grade designations. The child moves from one book to the next at his own pace.

Unlike traditional workbooks, the "workpads" incorporate writing activities that precede the reading, rather than following it. The child's involvement in writing activities forms an essential part of the method which provides skills and understandings necessary to succeed with a specific reading booklet.

Since writing is involved, spelling also is involved. Aids for this include letter cards, individual spelling pockets of the type often made by classroom teachers, flannel board practice, and word cards.

The first step in the program is pre-book reading readiness. The sequence is:

1. listen to the teacher pronounce the beginning sound *a* as in *astronaut*.
2. repeat the sound.
3. note the visual symbol (letter *a*)
4. print letter *a*
5. recognize and write capital A.
6. listen to sound of *m*, and say it.
7. recognize and print letter *m*
8. then say *m* together with sound of *a*.
   ma and *am*
9. write the two letters together
10. listen to sound of *r*; say it.
11. recognize *r* and write it.
12. add *r* to *a*; say it, write it.

13. Introduce word *I*, and then *I am* and *Am I*
14. develop the word *ram*
15. introduce other combinations:
     rat, Tam, Tat.
16. Finally, sentences:

I am the ram.	I am Tam.
Am I the ram?	Am I Tam?

These short, structured sequences are largely in the linguistics-phonemics pattern.

Books 1 through 4 cover the single consonant–short vowel–final consonant pattern which is so common to the linguistics-phonemics approach: *pat, pot, pit, put, pet*, etc. This, of course, is little different from the Hay-Wingo *Reading With Phonics*, described in Chapter 2.

The sequence in which the various phonics elements are introduced is as follows:

1. Consonant clusters (*spot, must, went, plan*, etc.) in Book 5.
2. Long vowels and silent-*e* (*make, like, note*, etc.) in Books 6 to 8, as well as *o* and *u* (*some, move, rule*, etc.) and the *s*-spelling of the *z*-sound (*wise, rose, use*, etc.) also in those same books.
3. Consonant digraphs in Books 9 to 11.
4. Inflectional endings (*ed* and *ing* in Book 12; *ur, er, ir*, and *or* in Book 13, as well as the long-*i* sound represented by *i* and *y*).

It is not until Book 14 that irregular phonemic elements are handled, plus the suffixes *er* and *est*.

The program concludes with vowel digraphs and diphthongs and a few prefixes in Books 18 through 20.

Anticipated achievement through these non-graded workpads and little paperback readers has been set. It is expected that the average class in Grade One will cover the materials through Book 6. Books 7 through 12 will be covered in Grade Two, and the remainder of the program through Book 20 will be covered in Grade Three. Of course, because of individual differences in children and with the possible use of some of the materials in structured Kindergarten programs, a wide range of achievement will be found and deviations from the anticipated norms will be expected.

The *Teacher's Guide* to the program reveals a wide adaptation of many of the usual classroom techniques of good teachers of reading. The result is a linguistics-phonemics approach that is enriched with an eclectic methodology.

Fig. 5–11   *Reproduced from the* Palo Alto Reading Program *by permission of Harcourt Brace Jovanovich, Inc.*

Research Findings

Although the *Palo Alto Program* was developed by the staff working over a period of three years, not enough time has elapsed to provide for the accumulation of definitive statistics. Careful research should be designed, for the *Palo Alto Program* tends to be a self-contained program for the first two years. Unlike many others, it does not depend upon transfer of skills into a basal reader series or into independent reading until the Third Grade. At that time, it is anticipated that the children will be moved into individualized reading selection.

It seems, therefore, that research could be devised which would be free from much of the contamination that exists in attempts to research other systems which "accompany" basal readers.

In summary, it should be noted that the *Palo Alto Program* was devised by the staff of a public school system for use with normal, average learners. It utilizes methods which are well-known to classroom teachers, and provides carefully written Teacher's Guides to the various steps in the program. Much of the work is done individually in the workpads, making individual progress through the program a regular feature.

The objective of this linguistics-phonemics approach is to provide "sequential steps" during which the child will acquire the decoding skills necessary for successful reading achievement. This involves limitations that prevent this program, as well as others, from being exciting and stimulating in content. There is no published evidence that its "sequential steps" are significantly better than other approaches.

Other Linguistics-Phonemics Approaches

One that is somewhat different is the *First Steps in Reading English*, coauthored by Christine M. Gibson and Ivor A. Richards. The books are also known under the title: "The Language Through Pictures Series", and are published by Washington Square Press with a 1959 copyright. The feature that is different is the use of "stick men" as illustrations. They are very limited in the extent to which they provide an exposure beyond the basic regular phonemic aspects of our language.

The Gibson-Richards materials tend to follow some of the structure of linguistics-phonemics systems. Indeed, they are highly structured in a very simplified sequence. For example:

This is a man. (stick picture)

This is a hat. (picture)
This is his hat. (picture)
It is his hat. (picture).

It is apparent that the series is designed to encourage children to depend upon the picture sketches to provide cues to the words. The perceptual task is simplified. In fact, the first thirteen sentences contain only seven different letters: *a, h, i, m, n, s,* and *t.* Letters with similar configurations are introduced simultaneously for purposes of contrast. There are no plots to the story lines . . . just factual presentation accompanied with simple black-and-white stick drawings.

Richards has stated that ". . . the ordering of the student's progress into reading, his progress into language, and his growth of understanding in his 'subjects' are ideally one undertaking."[31]

Some research on the *First Steps in Reading English* was reported by MacKinnon.[32] He observed the reactions of children who were using the Gibson-Richards materials in small group sessions. His observations are, of course, subject to the limitations of that technique. He noted that in these small group situations, children were observed helping each other to success in reading the sentences.[33]

Flinton[34] studied the achievement of children in the Delmar, New York, schools who were using the Gibson-Richards linguistics-phonemics readers and compared their achievement with children using basal readers. Although she found no significant differences, her study failed to account for several important variables.

The Gibson-Richards materials cannot be considered as one of the major linguistics-phonemics approaches in use at this writing, nor are they representative of the usual linguistics-phonemics materials.

Sounds and Letters by Frances A. Hall is a much more traditional linguistics-phonemics system. The little books that comprise the series have been available for more than a decade, but lack of adequate distribution facilities has limited their use.

The linguistic-phonemics pattern emphasizes the consonant-vowel-consonant pattern of word building, utilizing the short vowel at the start. The lines in the readers are similar to all others where an effort is made

---

31. Richards, Ivor A., *Speculative Instruments.* London: Routledge and Kegan, Paul, Ltd. 1955. 99.
32. MacKinnon, A. R., *How Do Children Learn To Read?* Toronto: Copp Clark Pub. Co., 1959. Chapter 7.
33. MacKinnon, A. R., Comments at the 1964 Rhode Island College Reading Conference at which Dr. MacKinnon demonstrated the Gibson-Richards materials.
34. Flinton, Doris H., *Results of a Five-Year Program of Sequenced English Language in Primary Grades.* Delmar, New York: Bethlehem Central School District, Mimeo, 1963.

to limit the vocabulary exclusively to phonemically-regular monosyllabic elements. The result, consequently, is:

"A fat man had Dad's cab."

As in many other strictly pure linguistics-phonemics systems, there are no pictures, and the story has no plot. The most that can be said in favor of this series is that it holds true to its pattern of developing regular phonemic elements.

Lift-Off To Reading is the work of Myron Woolman, a psychologist who achieved considerable attention through his "progressive-choice" learning theory.

The materials were developed in their original form for Dr. Woolman's daughter. Later they were adapted for classroom use by R. H. Bloomer, and compared with traditional reading methods.[35]

The *Lift-Off To Reading* program is essentially a linguistics-phonemics approach, holding to a phonemically-consistent framework in a two-year program for beginning reading. The materials are structured into three "Cycles", and are contained in 20 workbooks.

The 11 workbooks for "Cycle I" present the capital letters of the alphabet (except Q). The first segment of the program holds to those words which can be built from three letters: M, O, and P. Two more letters: T and S, are introduced in workbooks 4 and 5. A and G are added in the workbook 6, and D and L in 7. The remainder of the alphabet is introduced in books 8, 9, and 10. Workbook 11 is a review and test.

Cycle II does the same with lower-case letters, and introduces long vowel words. It also includes most of the consonant digraphs and a few other consonant-vowel combinations.

Cycle III completes the program with a number of irregular phonemic elements. The advertising brochure published by Science Research Associates, publisher of the Woolman program, states that, "When a child passes the Cycle III Final Checkout Test without error . . . he will have . . . a knowledge of approximately six thousand words, and he will be skilled in the process of decoding."[36]

This is one of the few approaches which uses capital letters. Woolman calls this feature "maximum discrimination" because they require less discrimination than lowercase letters.

---

35. Bloomer, Richard H., "A Progressive-Choice Technique of Organizing Reading Materials," Elementary School Journal, 65 (December, 1964), 153–158.
36. *Lift-off To Reading*, Advertising brochure, Chicago: Science Research Associates, 1966. 15.

Woolman also identifies five levels through which the child progresses in his system:

1. Audial meaning level (what a word means when it is heard).
2. Discrimination level (learning to print a letter and select it from others).
3. Identification level (matching sound and letter shape).
4. Compounding level (combining letters with other letters).
5. Visual meaning level (what a word means when it is seen and read).

CONCLUSIONS

Twelve separate linguistics-phonemics approaches to beginning reading have been described in this chapter. They are all relatively new, and most of them have been written by individuals whose professional commitment to reading is also a recent development. A few of the major approaches carry the names of distinguished linguistic scientists: Leonard Bloomfield, Henry Lee Smith, Jr., and Charles C. Fries. Others who have brought their particular competencies to reading via the linguistics-phonemics approach are a world-famous lexicographer, Clarence Barnhart; a noted literary critic, Charles C. Walcutt; a professor of literature, M. W. Sullivan; a sociologist, Donald E. Rasmussen; psychologists, Donald E. P. Smith and Myron Woolman; and a multi-media specialist, Glenn Mc-Cracken. Classroom teachers, supervisors, and consultants also are listed as authors or contributors in this field.

A diverse authorship of this kind accounts for the variations in the structure, scope, sequence, layout, and nature of the twelve approaches. To compare them here would be to repeat the content of the entire chapter. However, not to compare them might leave the reader confused.

These approaches have some characteristics in common: they view reading as a code-breaking process; they provide a sequential step-by-step practice on the phonemically-regular elements of our language; and they have caused reading materials to be devised that utilize those phonemically-regular elements with a minimum of irregular words necessary for adequate sentence structure.

There are also aspects of some of the linguistics-phonemics approaches that are rejected by others: some use full-color basal-reader-type illustrations; one uses stick figures; two use animal characters; and three reject illustrations entirely. One of the approaches drills for months prior to application in outside reading materials; others introduce the beginning student immediately to whole-word reading. Some of the programs are almost exclusively dedicated to "breaking the code"; others present the "code" as a means to meaningful comprehension. Most of the approaches develop linguistic "patterns" similar, if not identical, to the phonograms that teachers used in the pre-linguistics era.

The two characteristics that all promoters of linguistics-phonemics approaches have in common is their belief that they have discovered something new and their zeal in promoting it as *the linguistics approach* to beginning reading. An historical survey of the development of materials and methods of teaching beginning reading in the United States reveals that the linguistics-phonemics approach is little, if any, different from a number of structured phonics approaches suggested during the past century. Word patterns, word families, phonograms, initial consonant substitution practice, controlled phonics reading, phonics consistencies, and numerous other labels have "had their day" in reading.

The recent arrival of *linguistics*, surrounded by an aura of scientific-sounding terms, renewed hope and brought promise to the distraught world of reading. The wide acceptance of the linguistics-phonemic approach by educators has apparently encouraged some opportunists to develop, publish, and market untried materials under the linguistics banner.

In spite of the fact that many "outsiders" have developed linguistics-phonemics approaches to reading and naïvely think that they have discovered something new; in spite of the fact that some of the approaches were marketed with no definitive research to verify their claims; and in spite of the fact that some of the linguistics-phonemics reading materials are outrageous nonsense, there is one positive feature that outweighs these negative aspects. It is the fact that the phonemic elements of reading are structured in a developmental step-by-step sequence.

This structure which the linguistics scientist provides assures the teacher and learner that the sequence of learning will proceed in regular patterns. It will progress with minimum phonics differences introduced in carefully-ordered sequence.

Linguistics provides the orderly structuring of phonics skill learning as one facet of beginning reading instruction.

BIBLIOGRAPHY

BLOOMFIELD, LEONARD, "Linguistics and Reading," *Elementary English Review*, 19 (April, 1942) 125–130 and (May, 1942) 183–186.
BLOOMFIELD, LEONARD, and BARNHART, CLARENCE, *Let's Read, A Linguistic Approach*. Detroit: Wayne State University Press, 1961.

A 4-page newsletter, "Let's Read," is published occasionally and carries reports from school systems and individuals who are using the Bloomfield-Barnhart linguistics-reading materials. Available free from Clarence L. Barnhart, Inc., Box 359, Bronxville, New York 10708.

BUCHANAN, CYNTHIA DEE, "Teacher's Guide," *Programmed Reading, Series One*, Manchester, Missouri: Webster Division, McGraw-Hill Book Co., 1964.

CLELAND, DONALD D., "The McCracken Procedure in Teaching Reading," *Controversial Issues in Reading*, I (April, 1961) Proceedings of the Annual Reading Conference, Lehigh University. Reprinted in *New Perspectives in Reading Instruction*. Albert J. Mazurkiewicz, editor. New York: Pitman Publishing Corp., 1964, 491–505.

This is a critique of the "New Castle Experiment" and the claims made by Dr. McCracken.

FRIES, CHARLES C., *Linguistics and Reading*. New York: Holt, Rinehart and Winston, 1963.

GENTILE, CHARLES A., "Burlington Township Reports on First Year of Program," *Journal of Programmed Reading*, No. 7:6–12.

GOODMAN, KENNETH S., "The Linguistics of Reading," *Elementary School Journal*, 64 (April, 1964) 355–361.

A critical review of Bloomfield, Fries, and Henry Lee Smith, Jr., which emphasizes the phonemic structure of their approaches.

GOODMAN, YETTA M., and GOODMAN, KENNETH S., *Linguistics and the Teaching of Reading*. Newark, Del.: International Reading Association, 1967.

This is IRA Annotated Bibliography No. 12, compiled by Mr. and Mrs. Goodman.

GOLDBERG, LENINA, and RASMUSSEN, DONALD, "Linguistics and Reading," *Elementary English Review*, 40 (March, 1963) 242–247.

The authors describe the materials and methods they devised from Bloomfield's work.

HALL, FRANCES ADKINS, *Sounds and Letters*. Ithaca, New York: Linguistica Press, 1964.

Journal of Programmed Reading, Arthur Welch, editor. Published by Webster Division of McGraw-Hill Book Company in the interests of publicizing the Sullivan-Buchanan materials through reports from schools which are using them.

LEFEVRE, CARL A., "Reading Instruction Related to Primary Language Learnings—A Linguistic View." Paper presented at the Fiftieth Annual Meeting of the National Council of Teachers of English, 1960.

——, "Language Patterns and Their Graphic Counterparts: a Linguistic View of Reading," *Changing Concepts of Reading Instruction*, International Reading Association Conference Proceedings. New York: Scholastic Magazines, 1961. VI, 245–49.

——, *Linguistics and the Teaching of Reading*. New York: McGraw-Hill Book Co., Inc., 1964.

LIDDLE, WILLIAM, "Project Corrective Reteaching of Reading," *Journal of Programmed Reading*, No. 7: 2–4.

McCRACKEN, GLENN, *The Right to Learn*, Chicago: Henry Regnery Co., 1959.

The New Castle Experiment is described in the second half of this book.

Rasmussen, Donald, and Goldberg, Lenina, *Teacher's Handbook for the SRA Reading Series.* Chicago: Science Research Associates, 1965.

Reading Teacher, vol 21, #5 (February, 1968).

Entire issue is devoted to "Linguistics" and Reading.

Robinett, Ralph F., "A 'Linguistic' Approach to Beginning Reading For Bilingual Children," Chapter 9 in *First Grade Reading Programs*, Perspectives in Reading No. 5. Newark, Delaware: International Reading Association, 1965. 132–149.

This article explains the rationale for the linguistics-phonemics program which has become known as the Miami Linguistic Readers.

——, *Miami Linguistic Readers.* Boston: D. C. Health and Co., 1971.

These materials are based somewhat on the Bloomfield approach.

Rojas, Pauline M., *Final Report—Ford Foundation Project in Bilingual Education*, Miami: Dade County Public Schools, August 31, 1966. Dittoed. 11.

Sabaroff, Rose, "Breaking the Code: What Method?" *Elementary School Journal*, 67 (November, 1966).

Another approach derived from Bloomfield, but phased into meaningful stories.

Sampson, William A., "Programmed Reading in a Level II EMH Class," *Journal of Programmed Reading*, No. 7: 7–8.

Schneyer, J. Wesley, "Reading Achievement of First Grade Children Taught by a Linguistic Approach and a Basal Reader Approach," *The Reading Teacher*, 19: (May, 1966) 647–652.

Compares the *Merrill Linguistic Readers* and the Scott-Foresman basal series in the achievement of First Graders.

Sheldon, William D., and Lashinger, Donald R., "The Effect of First Grade Instruction Using Basal Readers, Modified Linguistic Materials and Linguistic Readers," *The Reading Teacher*, 19: (May, 1966) 576–579.

Groups taught by means of the *Ginn Basic Readers*, the L. W. Singer *Structural Reading Series* and *Let's Read* (Bloomfield-Barnhart) were compared with findings that there were no significant differences.

Smith, Henry Lee, Jr., "Review of *Let's Read*," *Language*, 39 (January–March, 1963).

Contrasts his linguistic approach to Bloomfield's.

Spache, George D., *Reading in the Elementary School.* Boston: Allyn and Bacon, Inc., 1964. Chapter 5. 116–129.

Stern, Catherine and Gould, Toni S., *Children Discover Reading.* New York: Random House, 1965.

Storch, Phil H., "Linguistics Reading Helps Fast and Slow Readers," Allentown, Pa.: *The Morning Call*, Thursday, March 17, 1966, 56.

Tabachnick, Robert B., "Linguistics and Reading," *Reading and Language Arts*, H. Alan Robinson (Ed.), 25. Proceedings, Annual Conference on Reading. Chicago: University of Chicago Press. 98–105.

Terman, Sybil, and Walcutt, Charles C., *Reading: Chaos and Cure.* New York: McGraw-Hill, 1958.

Tyler, Priscilla, "Linguistics and Reading," A reprint from *Elementary English*, December, 1965.

This pamphlet of 52 pages contains nine articles on various aspects of linguistics and reading which were presented at the Second Symposium of the Joint Committee of the NCTE and IRA.

WALCUTT, CHARLES C., *Tomorrow's Illiterates*. Boston: Little, Brown and Co., 1961.

WHITE, EVELYN MAE, "Linguistic Learning Cycles," *The Reading Teacher*, 21 (February, 1968) 411–415.

This article attempts to delineate the four phases which the author calls "cycles": imitating words, imitating sounds, saying phonemes, and discovering word patterns.

WILSON, ROSEMARY G., "A Linguistic Approach to Beginning Reading Based on Fries' Principle," *Improvement of Reading Through Classroom Practice*. 9th Annual International Reading Association Conference Proceedings, 1964. 225–227.

QUESTIONS AND ACTIVITIES FOR DISCUSSION AND GROWTH

1. Compare the programmed materials developed by Buchanan-Sullivan with those of Donald E. P. Smith. What elements do they have in common?

2. Compare the story characters of the Harper & Row *Linguistic Readers* with those of the *Miami Linguistic Readers*. What do they have in common? What is the main difference in their characterization?

3. In what way is the *Let's Read* approach different from the other linguistics-phonemics approaches?

4. *Basic Reading* has become a very popular approach. Analyze the materials and method and make an educated guess to account for its popularity.

5. In what way is the *SRA Basic Reading Series* different from the others?

6. What is the chief characteristic of the Gibson-Richards materials that makes them different from all the others?

7. Check back through this chapter and list the linguistics-phonemics approaches that were developed through actual classroom prepublication tryouts. Does it appear that the materials, consequently, are better than the ones that were marketed without tryout in the classroom? Support your decision.

8. Contrast the linguistics-phonemics structure for teaching phonics skills with the phonics sequence in one basal reader manual. What differences do you observe?

9. Does the Palo Alto approach have any feature that is significantly different from other linguistics-phonemics approaches? Defend your opinion.

10. You are a reading specialist. Your superintendent asks you to discuss the linguistics approach to beginning reading with the First-Grade teachers in your system. How would you do this?

"TOTAL" LANGUAGE-ARTS APPROACHES

6

Many teachers and most psychologists are committed to the concept that reading is not merely the pronunciation of a number of phonemic sounds in assembled sequence. Indeed, they look upon the pure phonemics approach to reading as a mechanistic and incomplete method of dealing with a highly complex and multi-faceted skill. Pure phonemics or linguistics-phonemics, they contend, is not concerned with meaning, much less with reading as a thinking process.

As a consequence, a group of approaches to beginning reading have been developed to utilize the several aspects of language arts and, consequently, may be classified as "total" language-arts programs.

A definition of a "total" language-arts approach would reflect the common characteristics of such systems by disclosing that listening, speaking, seeing, writing, spelling, and reading are integrated into a simultaneous and/or sequential process when dealing with our language. A "total" language-arts program would qualify as such if it incorporates the following features:

1. The teacher must provide an exemplary model for pronunciation, with strict attention to enunciation of the sounds of the language. In some cases the role of the teacher may be assigned to a taped or recorded presentation of the phonemes. But in either case, correct enunciation of normal American speech sounds is essential for ear training, or "listening", as the first facet of the "total" program.

2. Speaking, the second in the close sequence of steps, consists of repeating the speech sound which has been presented by the teacher. Success in this aspect of the program is not only dependent upon careful listening and hearing of the sound, but upon the ability to reproduce it

accurately. In this part of the program the learner may encounter sounds and word pronunciations which are counter to his normal pronunciation. Colloquial and regional manners of pronunciation may tend to hinder accuracy of hearing as well as the reasonably accurate reproduction of the sound. In spite of this fact, "total" language-arts programs are built around commonly-accepted American pronunciation.

3. A third element in the "total" program is presented simultaneously with aforementioned parts 1 and 2. It is the simultaneous presentation of the sound-symbol—the letter or group of letters which graphically represent the sound. Thus, as the teacher pronounces the sound, the grapheme for that sound is presented so that the learner sees it. It is presumed that through the psychological process of conditioning, the learner will associate the sound and symbol, and that, eventually, the teacher's cue may be eliminated, leaving the association of the symbol and the sound firmly fixed in the child's mind.

It is clear that such a process relies upon the child's visual memory, and that children with faulty and impaired visual memory will be unable to retain the associations without extensive and intensive periods of special training. The normal learner, however, will learn most of the sound-letter associations without any undue trouble. The difficulty is not inherent in the psychological principle nor in the learner, but it is a result of the same factor which plagues the pure phonemics approach and the linguistics-phonemics approach, namely, the phonemic irregularity of a number of our words.

Nevertheless, any approach to reading must eventually deal somehow with phonemic irregularities. At the beginning, however, most approaches to reading capitalize on the 85% of our language that is said to be phonemically regular. The learner who hears the sound, reproduces it with a reasonable degree of fidelity, and sees the grapheme symbol at the same time is learning a system that can be relied upon to help him with the pronunciation of a good percentage of the components of our language.

4. Recognizing the fact that learning can be acquired through one or more of the senses, promoters of the "total" language-arts approach to reading utilize the kinesthetic and/or tactile sense for reinforcing the learning of sound-symbol relationships. At the same time that the child is repeating the sound which the teacher has presented and is looking at the grapheme which represents the sound, he is required to write the symbol. This may be done simultaneously, or the writing may follow the pronunciation. In some systems which may be classified as "total" language-arts approaches, the writing follows the first three steps. In other systems, the child hears the sound, repeats it, sees the symbol and

then prints or writes the symbol and pronounces the sound simultaneously again.

Writing is thought by some psychologists to "fix" the visual pattern in the memory of the child. Such a concept has considerable ancestry in the work of Maria Montessori in Italy and in the work of Americans such as Grace Fernald and Dr. Samuel Orton. More recently, a group of specialists have promoted the concept under the name of "visual tracking", while others have devised the term, "training in directionality". Regardless of previous work in this area of learning, writing the sound symbols simultaneously with hearing the sound, seeing the symbol, and pronouncing the sound appears to be a logical approach. Moreover, it puts into practice one of the fundamental principles of learning, namely, the reinforcement of learning through the utilization of several senses.

5. Without the fifth aspect of the process, a system of reading could not rightfully be considered as a "total" language-arts approach. Indeed, to many reading specialists, the fifth facet is the essence of reading, namely, the blending of sounds to produce words, followed with the application of word pronunciation skills to the reading and the comprehending of the sequence of ideas spread on the printed page. Those who promote programs which may be classified as "total" language-arts approaches are primarily interested in the end-product of the learning process. It is, of course, the application of the listening, speaking, and writing to the unlocking of meaning.

Reading within this framework of reference transcends the mere pronunciation of sounds, or even the blending of sounds which permit the isolated pronunciation of words. Reading—the fifth step—is a thinking and relating process, and, as such, must involve the learner in stories, poems, and factual materials that have relevancy to him.

Most "total" language-arts approaches not only include these five steps: listening, speaking, seeing, writing, and reading; but provide a body of materials which are thought to be self-sufficient. Those materials usually are sold as a package deal and, in some cases, indoctrination and instruction in a particular "method" is a prerequisite for obtaining the materials which accompany that method.

In one or two other cases, the "total" program is a combination of "method" involving the first four steps, with "application" under step 5 being transferred to the existing basal reader series or to specially-designated children's classics and/or enrichment materials.

Some approaches to reading might rightfully have been classified under the "total" language-arts category, but have arbitrarily been classified elsewhere because this author assesses their strengths as lying in other directions. The fact that a particular system is classified elsewhere does not necessarily mean that it is not also a "total" language-arts approach as well. The reader who finds such a system which meets the five characteristics used as guidelines in this chapter is encouraged to think of that particular system as rightfully belonging here, as well as elsewhere.

THE CARDEN METHOD

Origins

Miss Mae Carden, originator of the method which bears her name, holds a Vassar degree, augmented by five years in Europe perfecting her German, French, Italian, Latin, and music. This classical background, coupled with a compulsion for *perfection*, provided Miss Carden with the drive to defy "progressive" methods in teaching reading—especially the "look-say" method.

She completed a master's degree at Columbia University and in the late 1920's started work on a doctorate in education, but eventually parted company with the progressives who considered her ideas old-fashioned and reactionary. Miss Carden then set about to build her own school of thought with headquarters in her own private day school in New York City. There she organized her "total" language-arts system for teaching reading, and prepared the books which are an integral part of her method.

The Carden School on East 67th Street in Manhattan operated from 1934 to 1949 as a coeducational K–6 day school. In 1950 Miss Carden moved to a small "estate" in Glen Rock, New Jersey which has served as headquarters.

She contends that, through her method, children are given individual security in learning and that self-reliance can come only if the individual masters the good reading habits which come through diligent and accurate study of words and their phonemic elements.

Miss Carden's crusade against the "Progressives" started in the 1930's when Progressive Education was being corrupted by a number of ill-informed individuals who interpreted it as a laissez-faire method of education in which the child did whatever came into his mind, and the teacher responded to spur-of-the-moment brainstorms rather than well-developed lesson plans. This may have been the case with a number of teachers during that decade, but observers of classroom teaching today would find few cases of such disorganization.

The "look-say" whole-word method in beginning reading also had its greatest heyday in the 1930's, and, as a consequence, many individuals came to regard "Progressive" education and the "look-say" method as one-and-the-same method of teaching the child nothing. Indeed, thoughtful educators, themselves, became alarmed at the widespread misinterpretation of the aims and philosophy of progressive education, but not in time to prevent some prophets of doom from declaring that progressive schools employing look-say methods were turning our nation into what is termed an "Educational Wastelands,"[1] and producing "Tomorrow's Illiterates".[2]

Such reactionary books as those helped create a fertile environment for the *Carden Method* to thrive. Knowledgeable parents who were demanding the best education for their children in their public schools became frightened by statements in those books and by speeches by alarmists charging that over 50% of today's elementary school children are below average in reading, are frustrated, confused, bored, bewildered, and are headed for failure. Parents began to ask questions and to demand answers.

Simultaneously, Miss Carden set out from her New Jersey base to spread her ideas with the sincere hope of solving the problem of poor reading. Up until that time, her method had found acceptance almost exclusively in New York and New Jersey. In fact, in 1961 it was reported that 90% of the 125 school systems using the *Carden Method* were in those two states, with Bergen County schools heading the list. The Pequannock (N.J.) Township Schools, for example, have been using Miss Carden's method and materials for more than fifteen years.

Wherever Miss Carden went as the missionary for her method, she was met with outstretched arms from worried parents' groups and with bristling fortifications from classroom teachers and administrators. Her claims that, with the *Carden Method*, "there will never again be a nonreader (the slower child may take a little longer); there will be no retarded readers; and children with IQs as low as 75 (lowest ⅔ of the school population) are regularly taught to read"[3] elicit beaming approval from parents' groups and incredulity from classroom teachers. Miss Carden then asks for permission to demonstrate with children and to prove that her claims are valid.

1. Bestor, Arthur E., *Educational Wastelands*. Urbana: University of Illinios Press, 1953.
2. Walcutt, Charles C., (Ed.), *Tomorrow's Illiterates*. Boston: Little, Brown and Co., 1961.
3. Carden, Mae, Speech at the 9th Annual Conference on Reading, University of Rhode Island. July, 1963.

Materials and Method

"The teacher should pronounce her words correctly, enunciate carefully, and read fluently, for it may be that this will be the *only time* that children will hear the English language spoken correctly."[4]

The above statement by Miss Mae Carden was made at the 10th Annual Conference on Reading at the University of Rhode Island and, in a large measure, is the key to the total-language-arts program which is known as the *Carden Method*. Listening to the teacher is the foundation for learning to speak, to write, and to read. The teacher must be the paragon of excellence for the children to imitate.

"Learning to Listen" is the child's first workbook in the readiness program. Words are spoken *rhythmically* by the teacher. The child listens and says the word. The teacher then checks understanding by having the child give a mental image of the word and identify a picture of the object the word represents.

Materials are available only to teachers who have taken the *Carden Method* course. Two records are available to such *Carden Method* "graduates". They provide a recording of basic phonics and rhythmic reading as advocated by Miss Carden. A manual of "Fundamental Sounds" is also available. Miss Carden assumes that most children will start their readiness in Kindergarten. Consequently the Kindergarten program includes several small booklets: *Cutting and Pasting; I See; Joan;* and a pre-primary workbook. Another workbook, *Getting Ready for School,* also has an accompanying teacher's manual provided.

The Kindergarten pre-reading readiness program is a recent addition to the *Carden Method* and is in response to requests for such materials. Formerly, Miss Carden felt that reading readiness was unessential, delaying children who already were anxious to learn to read.

There are five components in this "total" language-arts approach:

1. *Phonemic.* in which children are taught their ABCs, and then work is begun with consonants, followed by work on consonant pairs, and then vowels.
2. *Rhythmic.* in which there is emphasis on oral expression, clear enunciation, and musical intonation.
3. *Word Groupings.* in which groups of words forming one idea are spoken together, and later are read together for meaningful units of thought.

---

4. *Ibid.*

4. *Analytical.* in which sentence structure is analyzed for key elements, main words, essentials, non-essentials, and the grammatical labels are attached to the parts of speech.
5. *Children's Classics,* which are considered to be the "real" literature for children.

The method used throughout the entire Carden program is *patience;* the goal is *perfection.* Such noble means and ends require that the teacher work with small groups; that there be an orderly progression step-by-step; and that the procedure be followed religiously. For high standards of quality there must be discipline for both teacher and student. Above all is the quality of patience, augmented with encouragement and success.

The First Grade program is designed to cover the entire year for the slow child, and it is claimed that the bright child will be able to cover the program in six months of one-hour lessons daily.

When the consonants are introduced, the contour is associated with a familiar object, person, or act. It is claimed that in this way the children will avoid the confusion of the letters. The sound and name of the consonant is learned. The children learn the letters which "are formed on the letter 'C'" (*c, a, d, g, q, o, e,* and *s*). There may be some objection to that group of letters, but, nevertheless, that is what is done. Next, the pairs *lh, nm, kf,* and *rt* are taught. One of the features of this part of the method is the "bent legs": *v, w, y, z, u,* and *x.* Special attention is given last to *h* and *p.* It should be obvious that visual discrimination is the main objective of this part of the program.

Vowels are taught next, and the students are given the game of finding them in words. Soon the "two-vowel" rule is learned. An entire reader and workbook based on the "two-vowel" rule is used.

The first work in phonemics is done with the words which the teacher selects from a short paragraph which she reads as a story. The words are placed on the chalkboard. The names and sounds of the letters are learned. Children are encouraged to tell their own mental image of the object which the word represents. For example, Miss Carden tells of a class in which the teacher read a story of children playing with a pail. The children were asked to describe the pail. One child claimed that hers was "little and pink and has a white puppy in it." Another child boasted, "Mine is big and heavy and has snakes in it." Another child revealed that "I don't have any pail. My big brother stole it." Through such mental imagery, the child can reveal his inner feelings and self image . . . his needs and thoughts.

It is for this reason that Miss Carden prefers that children, learning by her system, do not have pictures in their books to structure their imagination. Thus, she rejects pictures—not as aids to guessing as do many phonics advocates—but because they set the pattern for the child's mental image of the object or situation—and "rob him of the joy of exercising mental imagery. Make believe is fun," she says.

The first "writing" is done by the children when they learn to form the shapes of letters by making a series of dots. They then form the whole letters, then assemble them together for words.

Book I is *The Red Book*. The reading group sits at their table with their *Red Books* flat. They point to each letter in turn as the teacher directs them. They also say the letter name and its sound. This exercise is done in unison. The exercise progresses through sounding digraphs, and finally putting the letters together to form the word. The teacher then checks for comprehension. The children also read the same words that have been selected from the book by the teacher and placed on the chalkboard.

The First Grade program also contains a booklet which is used for "Developing Comprehension and Building a Speaking Vocabulary". It is used in conjunction with Book I (*The Red Book*). There are helpful suggestions to the teacher for selecting words from *The Red Book* and putting those words into question form. The child must understand the words at every step of the program.

The questions must be based upon the child's own experience and must elicit mental imagery. To aid in this mental task, the teacher asks the children to close their eyes and "see *inside* your heads the thing I am going to name". The teacher then checks comprehension by having the students repeat the word and then use it in a sentence. It is assumed that, if the child can use it correctly in a sentence of his own, he has learned the true meaning of the word. Understanding and the development of a speaking vocabulary are the objectives of this adjunct to Book I.

The *Blue Book* is Book II, and provides work with words containing consonant sounds, digraphs, and vowels. The words are a little more difficult and the stories consist of several sentences.

The object of hearing children read orally at this stage is to correct the habit of reading jerkily word-by-word. The teacher sets the pattern of rhythmic reading and supplements imitation of her reading with daily drill on nursery rhymes. At this stage, the teacher exaggerates the connecting of words to form phrases and sentences. The objective is to develop a sense of whole thoughts and complete units, rather than the fragmentary word pictures which need modification as modifiers are related to them.

Dick and the Fish

Dick likes to fish.

He takes his pole and goes

to the stream.

One day he came back

with six fish.

He met Jim.

Jim said, "Oh, Dick, please teach

me to fish."

Dick said, "I will teach you

to fish.

Come with me next week.

I will meet you here. Get a

pole and a string."

Jim said, "Thank you, Dick.

I will be here next week."

62

Fig. 6–1 Reproduced from the Reader, *revised and copyright, 1970, by permission of the author, Mae Carden.*

Once the child has finished the *Blue Book* in the Carden materials, the teacher may give him any primer of any of the basal reading series as "supplementary" reading.

Spelling books are used in conjunction with each of the readers, and each spelling book emphasizes the words which the child at each level should be able to spell and write.

Sentence analysis is also a phase of the total program which runs concurrently with the *Red Book, Blue Book,* and *Green Book.* In that part of the program, the words are taken from the stories and are used by the teacher and by the children in constructing new sentences of which those words are a part.

In sentence analysis, there is emphasis on nouns and their function in a sentence. The teacher asks individuals for words which are persons, places, and/or things. The words are placed upon the chalkboard. The teacher helps the children study those words and to use them—emphasizing the fact that they are nouns and have a function in a sentence.

Prior to the end of Book II (*The Blue Book*) the children are asked to attempt to write original stories in their spare time. This takes place sometime after the Christmas holidays, so it is usual that many of the compositions are about Christmas toys, winter weather and winter fun, Valentine's Day, etc.

According to the author, "In the early steps, the child has learned what thinking is. Up to this time, he has been considering his feelings, his thoughts. Now he has to learn what the sensation of thinking is—the awareness of muscular activity of the brain."[5]

It is probable that Miss Carden's emphasis on rhythmic pronunciation and speaking has been influenced by her special life-long interest in music. "Speaking Rhythmically" is one of the main distinctive features of her method. She emphasizes and demonstrates this in every speech she gives. It is, consequently, difficult on paper to describe this feature of her method. It is more adequately demonstrated through the recording which she has prepared.

In the Pre-Primary manual there is reference to "rhythmic speaking" with the following example:

"t" is pronounced "tuh"
"paint" is pronounced "puh-ā-n-t"
"goat" is pronounced "guh-O-th"

In that manner, the method attempts to distinguish between the two final consonant "t" sounds. Most phoneticians would disagree with such an attempt.

In the teaching of vowels, the child is taught that, if a word has two vowels, the second is crossed off, and the first keeps its name sound.

---

5. Carden, Mae, *The Carden Method, Manual* I. Glen Rock, N.J.: Mae Carden, Inc., 1940, p. 2.

Thus, "rain" becomes "r–ā–i–n" with an accent on the initial consonant "r". "Feet" becomes "feeh–e–th". Although the method stresses speaking rhythmically, it stresses breaking up the words—even monosyllable words—into parts rather than the blending of sounds. Only when one hears Miss Carden demonstrate what she considers to be "correct" pronunciation can one be aware of the reasons for this exaggeration on the pronunciation of each phoneme.

The method by which the Kindergartner is taught to write his letters is equally surprising to most elementary teachers. To make a letter "C", for example, the child goes through the following steps with the teacher as "coach":

1. Draw a line on your paper.
2. Put a dot on the line.
3. Make a dot over the first dot. (up at what would be 2 o'clock on a clock dial—*author's note*)
4. Start at the second dot and draw "Way out—*way out*, and around and down to the dot on the line."

The Grade One program consists of a manual of 130 lessons, three workbooks, and two story books. The graphemes "i+" and "e+" are introduced as novel ways of distinguishing the pronunciation of the consonant "y". The teacher's manuals for Grade One are well planned and provide good questions for the teacher to use in determining story comprehension.

Finally, in Grade One, the children are introduced to "real" literature; near the end of the year they read *Peter Rabbit* and Elsa Beskov's popular children's classic, *Pelle's New Suit*. Miss Carden has developed teacher's manuals for those two books.

The outcomes of the First Grade Program (plus the Kindergarten Reading Readiness work) are claimed to be as follows:

1. It gives the child the knowledge of sounds to enable him to *solve* words and to spell words–Phonics.
2. It equips the child with the ability to *group words* within the sentence so that he may comprehend what he is reading–*Rhythmic reading*.
3. It equips the child with the ability to group the ideas of the sentences so that he grasps the significance of what he reads–*Comprehension*.
4. It develops *good work habits* for each child.
5. It develops *self-reliance* and *stamina*.
6. It gives the child the opportunity to increase his *vocabulary*.
7. It teaches the child *writing skills*.
8. It enables the child to express himself in *original compositions*.

9. It develops a *taste for reading*.
10. It teaches the child to *think*.

It is claimed that "the average First Grader learns to read and say 2000 new words in the first year alone—which is what First Graders in Russia learn." A count of the words used in the *Carden Method* books reveals a considerably smaller number than the 2000 claimed. The difference is accounted for in the Carden Word Lists and in the additional vocabulary taught in the First Grade selected classics: *Peter Rabbit, Pelle's New Suit, Benjamin Bunny, Squirrel Nutkin,* and *The Tale of Mrs. Little Mouse*. The latter is a recent addition to Miss Carden's list.

It would only be fair in summary to state first that the *Carden Method* utilizes childrens' "classics" of the "old school", and that this is done purposely to acquaint today's children with what its originator, Miss Mae Carden, believes to be the rightful heritage of children in our culture. Second, the *Carden Method* provides a highly-structured, inflexible procedure which each teacher agrees to follow. The procedure is to be a replication of Miss Carden in action, with faithful reproduction of her pronunciation, enunciation, and "rhythmic phrasing". Third, although the *Carden Method* has "perfection" as its objective, it does not expect all children to arrive at that objective at the same time. Consequently, it is assumed that the teacher will make some adjustments to the individual differences of beginning readers. Fourth, the teacher using the *Carden Method* must be prepared to work individually with children, utilizing unlimited patience in the process.

Contrary to many partially-informed people's statements on the *Carden Method*, it is *not* a phonemics reading system. It is a total language-arts reading system in which phonemic analysis is utilized in spelling phonemically-regular words. The child learns to control the homonyms by control of the pitch of the voice. Words which follow the same pattern of deviation are grouped together. Listening, speaking, writing of original compositions, reading and analysis of main ideas and sentence structure, outlining of paragraphs, mental imagery, and finally the free choice of many children's books are all phases of the total language arts program.

Finally, encouragement and praise are utilized by the teacher to provide a feeling of accomplishment, success, satisfaction, and security.

Research Findings

Comparative research findings on the performance of children who have learned by the *Carden Method* are not easy to find. Few statistical results are available through the usual channels of professional journals. The USOE First Year Study did not include the *Carden Method* as one of its sub-factors. No graduate theses or dissertations dealing with the *Carden Method* have been discovered so far.

The first public school system to use the *Carden Method* is said to have been the Garwood, New Jersey public schools, which adopted the method in 1942. Mrs. May Crissey, recently retired Supervisor of Reading in the Garwood system has furnished comparative statistics based upon the *Metropolitan Tests* for Grade One, the *Stanford* for Grade Two, and the *Iowa Basic Skills* for Grades 3 through 8. The *Carden Method* had been used for all grades in that school for the twenty-year period. The results are based upon tests taken by a total of 468 children in June, 1963.

Test Results of the Garwood (N.J.) School Using the Carden Method

	No.	No. "Below Grade"	% "Below Grade"	No. Below 1 yr. or more
Reading	468	84	18%	24 (5%)
No. Started in Garwood	361	51	14%	12 (3%)
No. Transferred to Garwood	107	33	30%	12 (11%)
Spelling	468	76	16%	29 (6%)
Language	468	66	14%	27 (5%)

Medians: Grades 1 through 8	Reading	Spelling	Language
Grade 1	2.9	3.8	
Grade 2	4.6	4.5	
Grade 3	5.1	5.4	5.1
Grade 4	5.4	6.4	6.0
Grade 5	6.7	7.4	8.2
Grade 6	7.8	8.2	8.9
Grade 7	9.0	9.1	9.5
Grade 8	10.0	10.4	9.8

Comparison of Median Scores in Reading

Grade 2	1943	1963	Grade 8	1941	1963
Comp.	3.0	4.8	Comp.	6.4	9.7
Vocab.	2.9	4.4	Vocab.	6.9	10.1
Spelling	3.4	4.5	Spelling	6.5	10.4
			Language	7.2	9.8

Without any further information on the nature of change in school population or facilities, or other variables in the twenty years that elapsed from 1942 to 1963, these figures by themselves would seem to indicate that the *Carden Method* alone accounts for some impressive gains in performance on standardized tests of reading factors. The 1963 figures alone show medians significantly above national norms for all grades. Such significant differences are not the result of chance, but, without further information, may possibly be the result of dedication to the use of the *Carden Method*. In the words of Mrs. Crissey, "Garfield has been faithful to the *Carden Method* and has appreciated its contribution to the education of Garfield children."

Similarly-impressive results have been quoted on the performance of children who have learned the *Carden Method* in the public schools of Franklin Square, Long Island, New York. It is said that, in the four primary schools in that system, "there are no nonreaders and no retarded readers". On the *Stanford Achievement Test*, Grade One children ranged from a "low grade-level score of 1.9 (at end of first year) to top scores of 4.5, 5.3, and even 6.0. The median scores in these classes were always above 3.0". It is further claimed that "the spelling averages were a year or more higher than the reading averages."

The report on the Franklin Square reading scores becomes even more enthusiastic by reporting that "Beginning a full year ahead, some Second-Grade classes averaged two full years' reading progress by spring, with the highest children reading at Ninth-Grade levels!"

Some of the leading specialists in reading have violently opposed the *Carden Method*, contending that many crusading parents' groups turn to the *Carden Method* as the panacea for what they have been told is the "deplorable state of reading instruction in the public schools". Experts, in their opposition, cite instances where parents' meetings frequently have resulted in the formation of militant civic investigating committees which demand reforms in reading, usually in the nature of more structured phonemics and, more specifically, calling for the adoption of the *Carden Method*.

In other instances, reading specialists have gone on record opposing the method because they consider it to be a backward step in education to a method which long since has been discredited as inappropriate for the modern school curriculum.

Regardless of the motives for opposition to the *Carden Method* or to Miss Carden, personally, the most effective and, actually, most truthful criticism is to say that the *Carden Method* borders on being "outmoded", "reactionary", "old-fashioned", or even "obsolete". Indeed, it is on those very points that many of Miss Carden's critics base their attacks upon her and her method. In addition, critics charge her method with abnormal exaggeration of phonemic pronunciation.

Unfortunately, critics of her method fail to note that in the Second Grade, her manual for teachers emphasizes the more normal pronunciation of whole monosyllables, graphemes and morphemes. The explanation is that, with her method, more normal pronunciation is possible since, by then, the child has learned the necessity of careful enunciation and correct pronunciation in a musical and rhythmic manner.

Moreover, critics of her method seldom are aware of her extensive bibliography of supplementary reading which she recommends in three parts: 1. to be read to the children by the teacher; 2. to be read by the children, and 3. to be read by the parents. Her listing of hundreds of books for children in the various grades is a good cross sampling of the thousands of modern children's books by our best writers, including Milne, Wanda Gag, d'Aulaire, Marjorie Flack, Gates, McCloskey, just to mention a few.

It would be erroneous to conclude that the *Carden Method* is entirely old-fashioned. It would be equally untrue to assume that it embodies much that is "modern" or "contemporary" in its methods. Indeed, it was a reaction against "modern" methods that prompted Miss Carden to embark on her crusade for a return to a more pure approach to language arts. It was her compulsion for perfection that drove her to overemphasis on enunciation and pronunciation as a means of providing a base of imitation for correct speech patterns. It was her background of music and linguistics knowledge that furnished the ideas for speaking and reading "rhythmically". It was her own classical background that furnished her love of the classics and belief that all children are being robbed of the fundamentals of Western civilization if they are not exposed to those classics of past generations.

To see Miss Carden's *Method* reproduced on paper is to know only part of it. Her insistence that everyone who uses her materials must first take her course has much to recommend it. For, in truth, the *Carden Method* is Miss Carden, herself. And only those who can understudy with her can learn to imitate "the master". And only those who learn to imitate can make her method be successful.

After seeing her in operation and seeing the response of children to her one can realize that the *Carden Method* is not for everyone. It is only for those teachers who can identify with her to the point of reenacting her mannerisms and her enthusiasm. She is a master teacher of the old school. Her method has found success at her hands and in the hands of those who faithfully imitate her. One observer recently said, "Without Miss Carden, there would be no Carden Method."

THE WRITING ROAD TO READING

Origins

The *Spalding Method* is a system of reading based upon a total language-arts approach, and, consequently, is referred to by its originator as the "Unified Phonics Method". It is also known as *The Writing Road to Reading*, which is the title of the book written by Mrs. Romalda Bishop Spalding, who developed the method as an outgrowth of experiences as a teacher in the elementary grades for many years.

Mrs. Spalding tells of her search years ago for ways to help intelligent children in the primary grades who could not learn to read or to spell adequately by any of the methods then in use. She states that her search for "the" way to teach reading led her to college courses in diagnostic and remedial reading, to reading clinics, and to books by experts on reading. One might say, therefore, that the *Spalding Method* is probably a distillation of a number of truths which were picked up over the years in actual classroom practice and in her search for a better way.

One of the most determining factors was her work under the direction of the late Dr. Samuel T. Orton, noted New York neurologist and authority on brain function and its relationship to total language learning. In the late 1930's Mrs. Spalding, while a classroom teacher in the Bronxville (N.Y.) elementary school, tutored a few non-readers for almost three years under the precise direction of Dr. Orton. His phonogram cards and his structured approach to teaching reading through the listening, speaking, writing, and seeing of all phonemic elements in words enabled the non-readers to learn to read and spell, whereas other methods apparently had failed.

Dr. Orton's work was remedial. Mrs. Spalding added to his techniques until she evolved her method of classroom teaching, the aim of which is to *prevent* reading failure. In 1952–53, a controlled experiment utilizing the *Spalding Method* was devised and carried out in one of the parochial schools of Honolulu. The results of the experiment were so remarkable that the *Spalding Method* was (and still is) the method of teaching reading recommended by the supervisory office for the 24 Catholic elementary schools of Hawaii. Encouraged by the results of the method, Mrs. Spalding and her husband, Walter T. Spalding, decided that she should share her method with others who might also be searching for "a better way". They concluded that the best way to do this would be to write a book which would describe the method fully enough for any teacher or parent to follow.

Their objective was to share the *Spalding Method* by presenting it in an accurate and clear manner so that anyone could use it, even by borrowing their book from a free public library.

To make the method more widely accessible outside the classroom, Wm. Morrow and Co. have published the authors' "self-teaching" edition, which was introduced as a paperback in September, 1966. It streamlines the *Spalding Method* into ten lessons, complete with a phonograph record of the phonogram sounds, and is designed primarily to help anyone in his free time to improve his own reading, writing, spelling and speaking of English.

Materials and Method

The *Spalding Method* could have been classified under the category of "Basic Phonemics Methods" except for the fact that it goes beyond the mere listening to sounds and associating them with printed symbols. It is, in fact, a total language-arts system, in that it teaches "unified phonics", which is an approach to learning the phonemic base of the language through listening, seeing, speaking, writing, spelling, and reading. It it not the phonemics that is unified, but the "language-arts" that are simultaneously employed to teach the phonemics.

As with many systems for teaching reading, there is a "readiness" phase, although the authors do not call it that. It consists of a short period of drill in which children are taught the "phonograms" and their use in the written spelling of words directly from the teacher's dictation.

It is stated that there are "70 common phonograms in English" and that "They are the single letters or letter combinations which represent the 45 *basic* sounds used in the spoken language."[6] The phonograms, which are printed on phonogram cards, were the work of language teachers under the direction of Dr. Orton. The *Spalding Method* utilizes them as a basic tool in teaching the system to an individual or to a class.

The phonograms are, actually, more than just the graphemes printed in bold-face lower-case type on $6\frac{1}{2} \times 4\frac{1}{2}$ cards, for on the back of each card are printed words showing the key sounds for the teacher. Unlike many other systems, it does not use "keywords" for teaching the phonemes to children. In fact, the book warns against the use of keywords, stating that "The test of a child's knowledge of the sounds is shown by his ability to write the phonograms when only the sounds are given."

---

6. Spalding, Romalda B., and Spalding, Walter T., *The Writing Road to Reading.* New York: William Morrow & Co., 1969, p. 14.

Because the teacher is such an important element in the method, it is imperative that the teacher use correct pronunciation and careful enunciation. The "sounds" are indicated on the backs of the phonogram cards to assure that the teacher is producing the sounds correctly. Emphasis is placed upon pronouncing the phonemes in strict isolation. For example, the teacher is to say "l", not "el"; "b", not "buh"; and "k", not "kuh".

Each phonogram is taught in a prescribed manner. The teacher practices pronouncing the sound so that it accurately corresponds to that on the recording. Each phonogram card and all its common sounds is presented to the children and they repeat the sounds orally in unison and write them. Starting the second week of school, a number of phonogram cards are covered in each lesson until each child knows the first 54 phonograms. Thus, by seeing, hearing, saying, and writing, the children experience what the Spaldings call a "Unified Phonics" approach. The sequence is: (1) hear the sound spoken correctly, (2) say the phoneme, (3) write the grapheme in careful printing, (4) read the grapheme they have printed. At the same time, the child is gaining a basis for spelling a good percentage of English words and is practicing the formation of letters which will soon become his writing.

The book, *The Writing Road to Reading*, warns against using letter names, stating that "In English words, only five (ā, ē, ī, ō, and ū) of the 26 letters *ever* use the sound of their names. . . ."

Through whole-class group instruction the children work on the phonograms through the process of listening, saying, writing, and reading. This structured drill teaches the first 54 phonograms in about two weeks, and the class is then ready to apply this to spelling words. The teacher dictates a word, and the children say the phonograms that they hear in it just before they write each one. After they have printed the word, they read aloud the word they have written.

This spelling of words by phonemic analysis is said to provide the first grade class with enough knowledge of the most-used 150 words to enable them to begin reading well before Thanksgiving.

Mrs. Spalding utilizes the "Ayres' List of Words"[7] and its Buckingham extension. The 1500 most-frequently-used English words are taught in the order of their frequency of use.

Inasmuch as the children are required to do much printing, it is essential that from the start, they learn correct position and the exact best procedures for forming the letters in order that good transfer to

---

7. Ayres, Leonard P., *Measuring Scale for Ability in Spelling*. Princeton, N.J.: Educational Testing Service.

printed symbols may be achieved, and good writing may result as well. The child's posture, sitting position, position of the paper for right-handed and for left-handed children, the way of holding the pencil, and the correct method of forming the letters are all illustrated in the book, *The Writing Road to Reading,* pages 68 through 73.

The unique feature of the printing phase of her method is the use of the "clock" face as a frame of reference for the formation of those letters that are made from parts of circles. Directions are given by the teacher, with rules for placement of the letters on the base line, height of letters, and the orientation points on the face of the clock. (Such attention to perfection is just the exact opposite of some other phonics systems, notably *Words in Color,* where the children are asked to print any sized grapheme anywhere on the page.)

In the *Spalding Method,* the lower case manuscript letters which begin at 2 on the clock face are taught first. They are *a, d, f, g, o, s,* and *q.* All other letters begin with a line and are taught next. Detailed directions are given in an effort to ensure attention to details, ease of writing, and resultant skill in reading. The aim is to prevent the formation of bad writing habits, and to direct concentration and attention to the details of letter similarities and differences.

An example will illustrate the method: For writing the letter "c", the teacher instructs the children to "start at 2 and go up and around and stop at 4." Or, if the directions are for "e", they are: "Start at 9 with a straight line drawn over to 3 and, without lifting your pencil, continue up around the clock from 3 and stop at 4." Directions for capital letters are similar. They involve more straight lines. Numbers are also similar.

There is no repetitive drill in this method, except for a frequent very short review on the phonograms as a warmup period, and, often, a quick review of the new words learned the previous day. It is recommended that the program in the First Grade be divided into half-hour sessions totalling two to three hours per day, and including the phonogram drill, the printing of sounds and/or words in the spelling lesson, work at the chalkboard, and reading. This is the total language arts program.

It is suggested that Kindergarten children may even enjoy this sort of work. However, the program for the First Grade starts with the readiness work of learning to hear, and say, and write and read the first 54 of the 70 phonograms.

According to Mrs. Spalding, the children should be given the opportunity to read aloud as much as possible, for this provides the teacher with a check on whether or not they are skipping words, and/or substituting their own words for those of the story. "There is another good

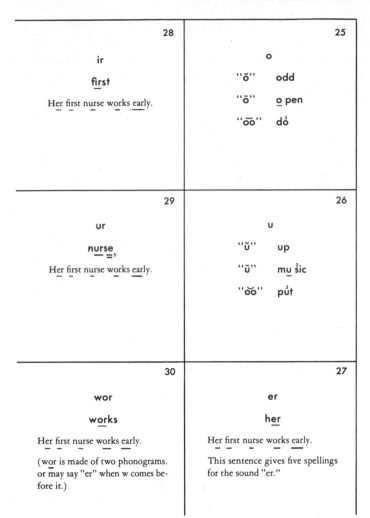

reason for reading aloud," she states. "It builds up good pronunciation and improves both vocabulary and grammar." In a sense, she sums up her theory when she states: "Correct meanings can only be learned from accurate reading. A knowledge of phonemics is usually a prerequisite to accurate reading."

The spelling practice, using the Ayres' List, is relied upon greatly to provide daily recurrent practice in figuring out the new words as they are dictated from the list.

One of the features of the *Spalding Method* is the use of notations in the spelling lesson only to indicate which sound of a phonogram is

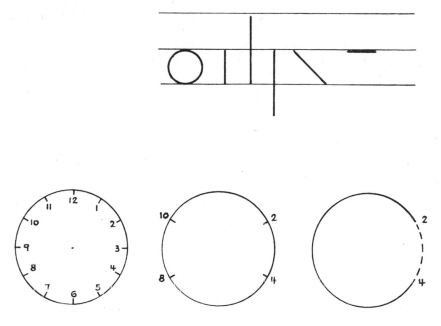

The Clock Face · These are the four points we use most often · This shows how we use the clock to write c (from 2 to 4)

Fig. 6–2   Reproduced from The Writing Road to Reading, copyright © 1957, 1962, 1969 by Romalda Bishop Spalding, by permission of William Morrow and Company.

used in a given word. Thus, a notation marking in the spelling lesson assures only one sound for each phonogram in the word. (This is, in effect, the main advantage claimed for some of the sound-symbol systems which have devised 44 or more symbols and are described later in this book.)

Page 3 in the Child's Notebook deals with the phonemically-irregular sounds of *ei* and *ie*. The learner has a "system" for knowing which spelling to use. The "system" includes a rule: "After *c* we use *ei*. If we say *ā*, we can use *ei*, but never *ie*. In the list of exceptions, we use *ei*. In all other words we use *ie*."

The "system" also involves the use of single and double underlining in both black and red in addition to numbering.

Page 4 deals with the various pronunciations represented by the digraphs *ti* (as in nation, patience, infectious); *si* (as in tension, transient, session, and explosion); *ci* (as in racial, gracious, associate); and *ce* (as in ocean).

Page 5 provides rules for occasions when final consonants are doubled when a suffix beginning with a vowel is added.

Page 6 is an explanation of rule 16, which deals with the instances when the final silent e is dropped when the base word is augmented with such endings as *ed, ous, ior, er, est, ing,* etc.

Page 7 provides the basis for teaching the additional 39 phonograms which were not presented on pages 1 and 2, and completes the 70 phonograms and the rules governing their use. Most of them are consonant digraphs which represent consonant blends, diphthongs, etc. As they are presented, the child learns their sounds and spellings. The *ough* spelling is presented with the six pronunciations which are the most difficult phonic irregularities in our language: (th*ough*, thr*ough*, r*ough*, c*ough*, th*ough*t, and b*ough*).

The authors of the *Writing Road to Reading* claim that, "In the whole Ayres List of a thousand words . . . less than fifty have any part which does not agree with the sounds of the phonograms or with these rules of spelling." The *Spalding Method* presents 28 spelling rules or patterns which have proven most helpful for spelling. Eighty-five pages of Chapter VI in the *Writing Road to Reading* provide the teacher with these spelling patterns and rules.

Although all dictation from the Ayres List is done with words in isolation, Chapter VI suggests that the children should use each word in a sentence immediately after writing it. Each child writes his own original sentence to show that he understands the word's meaning in context.

The rules, which at first appear to be the major element of the method that could be questioned, are actually not all taught as prerequisites to reading. In fact, they are phased in as the child progresses from the easy to the complex materials in his basal readers or individualized reading selections.

It is true that the child is held accountable for a knowledge of 28 rules which he should know, and is asked to state the rule which he is ignoring, if and when he makes a reading or spelling error.

In support of the use of rules, it is claimed that they give the child security and a frame of reference for attacking new words.

Research Findings

In addition to the many years of germination behind the system, use of the method by a number of teachers and school systems over the decade since *The Writing Road to Reading* was first published has resulted in a considerable body of testimonials and some statistical reports which focus attention on the positive results obtained.

The *Spalding Method* has been tried and is now used in a number of schools from coast to coast and in Hawaii, where the first experimental work was conducted through the cooperation of the parochial schools in Honolulu. The town of Lincoln, Massachusetts adopted the method and has used it for five years. Mrs. Adrienne L. Rubin, the Supervisor of Reading, states, "We in Lincoln chose this method when we were looking for an alphabetic, phonemic method because, of all those we examined, we felt this to be the most thorough and complete." She also states that another factor in the choice of the *Spalding Method* is its very minimal cost.

In two Sunday issues in July, 1964, the *Chicago Tribune*[8] published a lengthy special feature report by journalist Ruth Moss on the Lincoln (Mass.) Schools. The article tells of the problem which children with "specific language disability" have in learning such school tasks as reading. It states that the Lincoln schools used the Gillingham method (which was also developed in cooperation with Dr. Orton) until a visiting teaching Nun from a parochial school in Hawaii told them of the *Spalding Method* which she had used so successfully. The principal of one of the Lincoln schools is quoted as saying:

> "Since Spalding has been taught in the Lincoln schools, even the most optimistic of the enthusiasts have found themselves amazed at the reading record."

Children in the top reading group in Grade Three were reported to be reading *Treasure Island* with their older siblings in Grade Six just starting the same book. The school librarian is reported as stating that "Our top groups in First Grade are reading the *Betsy and Eddie* Series and Beverly Cleary's *Henry Huggins* (which former classes didn't get into until Third Grade)."

A rather significant and up-to-date body of data has been assembled showing the indisputable success that many schools are enjoying with the *Spalding Method*. For purposes of comparison, the data are reported here in tabular form. They cover scores on standardized achievement tests in reading, and are the results reported by the schools for almost 6,000 children of a wide range of backgrounds and intelligence. Moreover, they are from a representative sampling of small and large schools, public, parochial, and private. It should be noted, also, that the class sizes range all the way from a small class of only five students to the large classes

---

8. Moss, Ruth, "The Battle to Make Words Behave," Magazine Section *Chicago Tribune*. July 19, 1964 and July 26, 1964.

of fifty or more. In all, twenty-two schools of varied types and localities are represented, with 194 *different teachers.*

Median scores on the reading tests are reported in terms of grade equivalents and may be compared with national norms established for each of the standardized tests. Median scores on the *Morrison-McCall Spelling Scale* are also converted into grade equivalents. Variations in the national norms show slight differences which, of course, represent the differences in the month that the tests were given in the various schools.

The school systems are identified—with the exception of a large public school system in Texas which asked to remain unnamed. In some cases, the names of the teachers are given. Wherever possible, the top reading and top spelling scores made by individual students are shown as grade equivalents.

Critics, who have not had access to statistics as are presented here for the first time, have criticized the highly-structured systematic method of teaching. Certainly the *Spalding Method* is dependent upon repetition and stimulus-response learning for the 70 phonograms only. Any skill so structured is, to that extent, tied to some memorization. It is difficult, however, to conceive of the acquisition of any skill without intensive drill.

Some "phonics" advocates feel that the *Spalding Method* is too free in its interpretation of some of the more complicated phonemic elements.

The use of the phonogram cards and rules is attacked by some as a "step backward" into the past century.

Wherever and whenever possible, this writer visits and observes classes where various approaches to beginning reading are in progress. The *Spalding Method* was observed in two large classes in Star of the Sea School in Honolulu in January, 1967. In January, for example, in a First Grade class the children were reading at an almost unbelievable level of comprehension, voice inflection, knowledge of word attack through phonemics and pure delight.

The figures provided in the tables above indicate that the classes I observed were, perhaps, not isolated examples but were representative of the significant achievement of children taught by this method. When one finds reports of performance that is consistently and significantly above national norms, one looks for causes. Can it be that the children are specially selected? Or that it is one teacher who is better? The results from 194 different classes taught by 194 different teachers in 22 different and widely scattered small and large public, private, and parochial schools lead this writer to believe that it is the method that deserves the credit.

SCHOOL and DATE of Test	Name of Test	No. Pupils Tested	Reading Test (Total) Median Score	Spelling Test Median Score	National Norm	Top Reading	Top Spelling
			GRADE EQUIVALENTS				
Duxbury, Mass. Public School, Test Mar. '66	Metrop'n Ach't						
Grade 1	"	147	2.5	–	1.7	3.3	–
Grade 2	"	132	3.7	4.1	2.7	4.9	4.9
Grade 3	"	130	4.7	5.6	3.7	7.2	7.9
Grade 4	S. R. A.	136	5.8	6.1	4.7	11.1	11.1
Grade 5	"	132	7.2	7.4	5.7	11.1	11.1
Grade 6	"	138	8.4	7.8	6.7	12.1	12.1
Hale Keiki School, Aiea, Oahu, Hawaii, May 1966	Metrop'n						
Kindergarten	Ach't	–	1.9	–	–	–	–
Grade 1	"	21	2.8	3.8	1.8	4.1	4.7
Grade 2	"	22	4.2	4.9	2.8	4.9	4.8
Holy Family School at Pearl Harbor, Hawaii Sr. M. St. John, May '66	Stanford Ach't	39	2.6	3.3	1.8	4.7	4. +
Star of the Sea School Honolulu, Hawaii							
Sr. Denis Marie Gr. 1	"	50	2.5	3.0	1.8	4.0	4. +
Sr. M. St. Edward Gr. 2	"	52	3.6	4.6	2.6	6.2	6.6+
Sr. Rose Gr. 3	"	45	4.4	4.6	3.6	–	–
Sr. M. Joseph Gr. 3	"	41	4.7	5.6	3.6	7.0	6.6+
Maryknoll School Honolulu, Hawaii							
Sr. M. Cordes Gr. 1	"	45	2.7	3.4	1.8	4.2	4. +
Sr. Alma Vir. Gr. 2	"	47	3.4	4.7	2.7	–	–
Mrs. Mary L. Smith Gr. 3	"	48	4.3	5.2	3.6	–	–
Le Jardin d'Enfants Honolulu, Hawaii, June '66	Metrop'n	Not					
Kindergarten	Ach't	Reported	2.0	–	–	–	–
Grade 1	"		3.3	3.6	1.9	4.6	4.7
Grade 2	"		4.0	4.9	2.9	6.7	6.0
Epiphany School Honolulu, Hawaii Tested Oct. 1966	Stanford Ach't						
Grade 2	"	11	4.4	4.2	2.1	–	–
Grade 3	"	8	4.2	4.3	3.1	–	–
Grade 4	"	6	5.3	5.3	4.1	–	–
Grade 5	"	5	7.0	5.9	5.1	–	–

SCHOOL and DATE of Test	Name of Test	No. Pupils Tested	Reading Test (Total) Median Score	Spelling Test Median Score	National Norm	Top Reading	Top Spelling
			GRADE EQUIVALENTS				
Caledonia Public School, E. Cleveland, Ohio, Tested Feb. '66	Metropol'n Ach't						
Grade 2	"	30	4.3	4.4	2.5	–	–
St. Mary's School Rhinelander, Wisc. May '66	Stanford Ach't						
Grade 1	"	25	2.8	2.8	1.8	–	–
A large "Anonymous" Texas public school system, Tested March '66							
Grade 1	"	330	2.4	3.4	1.7	–	–
Grade 2	"	287	3.4	4.0	2.7	–	–
Grade 3	"	306	4.3	4.8	3.6	–	–
Grade 4	"	350	5.5	5.2	4.7	–	–
St. Michael School (Episcopal), Dallas, Tex. Tests May '65 and '66	Calif. Ach't						
Grade 1	"	48	3.2	3.4	1.9	4.0	4.0
Grade 2	"	52	4.1	4.3	2.9	4.7	5.0
Grade 3	"	47	4.5	4.5	3.9	5.0	5.0
The Advent School, 30 Brimmer St., Boston Test May '66	Stanford Ach't						
Grade 1	"	17	2.3	2.3	1.9	3.5	3.4
Grade 2	"	22	4.5	3.9	2.8	6.7	4.8
Grade 3	"	20	4.9	4.5	3.8	7.5	6.3
Grade 4	"	16	6.5	5.9	4.8	8.7	8.0
Grade 5	"	12	7.4	6.3	5.8	10.4	10.5
Grade 6	"	12	9.4	7.9	6.8	12.0	12.0
The Kinkaid School, Kinkaid Drive, Houston, Texas, Test April '66							
Grade 1	"	63	2.7	2.9	1.7	3.8	3.4
Grade 2	"	64	3.7	4.6	2.7	6.4	6.3
Grade 3	"	64	4.7	4.6	3.7	8.6	8.0
Grade 4	"	63	6.4	6.5	4.7	9.5	8.2
Grade 5	"	64	7.7	7.0	5.7	12.2	12.5

Nine schools of Galveston-Houston, Texas Diocese, 2975 pupils, tested Oct. 5 to 10, 1966; St. Augustine's, Qn. of Peace, St. Catherine's, St. Christopher's, St. Jerome's, St. Pius V, St. Pius X, St. Mary's Orange and Corpus Christi. Small variations of median scores between schools permit using the average medians, in each grade, of all nine schools.

	S. R. A. (Science Res. Assocs.)						
9 Grades 2 (Aver. Medians)	"	521	2.8	3.1	2.1	–	–
9 Grades 3 "	"	505	3.7	3.9	3.1	–	–
9 Grades 4 "	"	466	5.1	5.6	4.1	–	–
9 Grades 5 "	"	427	6.3	6.6	5.1	–	–
9 Grades 6 "	"	405	7.5	7.5	6.1	–	–
9 Grades 7 "	"	351	8.7	8.7	7.1	–	–
8 Grades 8 "	"	322	10.1	10.0	8.1	–	–

OPEN COURT BASIC READERS

Origins

The *Open Court Readers* were originated in 1962 when their publisher, M. B. Carus, asked Mrs. Priscilla Luetscher McQueen to write the first book in the series and Dr. Arthur Trace, Jr. to edit a beginning literary first reader for the series. In 1965, Mrs. McQueen left Open Court, taking her materials with her, establishing her own publishing firm, and developing her own phonemic language arts program described in the next section of this book.

The new "Foundation Program" was then written for the Open Court series by Mrs. Ann Hughes, who had been engaged in research on *Open Court* through the Hegeler Foundation. Mrs. Hughes states that she tried to incorporate what seemed to be the best features of a number of approaches to beginning reading through phonics.

The "Foundation Program," published in 1965 and modified in 1970, includes many aspects of a composition program developed by Mrs. Nellie Thomas, a teacher with experience from First Grade level through high school, and many aspects of the "workshop" (individual learning activities) of S. L. Bernier, Marymount College, Orange, California. Dr. Louise Gurren, Emerita Professor of Speech Education at New York University, was responsible for many of the phonemic insights. Mrs. Hughes did the major share of the writing of the program.

In September, 1966, an excellent 392 page "Teacher's Guide" was published to provide complete directions and supplementary suggestions for teaching and enriching the total "Foundation Program". It is probably the most complete teacher's guide available for any system outside of the traditional basal reader series.

The Trace book, *Reading Is Fun,* is retained as the second book in the First Grade program.

Materials and Method

The *Open Court* "Foundation Program" is designed as a complete correlated language arts program for the first half of Grade One.

There are two basic soft-cover reader-workbooks in the "Foundation Program"; in addition, each child needs a set of Anagrams and Response Cards.

The publisher recommends that each class should have an *Open Court Workshop Kit*. The kit contains teacher aids for all stages of the "Foundation Program": alphabet flash cards, wall sound cards, phonograph records, sound flash cards, movable alphabets in what is called the "printer's box", the word matching game, alphabet puzzle, plastic alphabet, tracing sandpaper, alphabet paper, and several copies of a *Word Line Book* which provides extra practice in blending for the slow group.

The "Foundation Program" is completed with 12 very small booklets which contain one story each and are read on an individualized basis.

The reading readiness program for the first two weeks of Grade One has some unique features in which materials from the "Workshop Kit" are utilized. Children are first introduced to stories and poems. They are taught to enjoy the skill of listening. Chalkboard demonstrations are carried out by the teacher in which the children are taught to print capital "A" and small "a", capital "B" and small "b", and so forth. The children go to the board to try to make a copy of the letters which the teacher has placed on the board.

Much of the activity is carried on as whole-class activity. However, to provide each child with the means for responding, a set of anagram squares is provided for each child. The anagram squares are for practicing responses to letter names. Later the so-called "response cards" (which are purchased as part of the same set) are to be used for responding to letter sounds.

In using the anagram squares, the child is able to fit them exactly over the same-sized letters printed on pages 104 and 105 at the end of the first reader-workbook, *Learning to Read and Write*. Practice in matching anagram letter squares with the letters on those pages goes on like a Bingo game for several days—even as much as two weeks—depending on the ability of the class.

Alphabet flash cards are used as part of the pre-reading readiness work. The cards have the capital letter on one side and the small letter on the back. They are for letter-name response, either as a total-class warm-up, or in the framework of a number of games that are suggested in the Teacher's Guide.

The "Alphabet Song", set to one of Mozart's tunes, is printed on page 15 of the *Teacher's Guide* and is recommended as a regular part of the daily class activity.

An "Alphabet Puzzle" consists of ten shapes which the child uses to form letters.

The plastic alphabet is made up of small plastic letters that fit exactly over the small letters on the alphabet flash cards. Children use the plastic alphabet letters for matching practice.

One of the features of the "Foundation Program" is the use of

"Alphabet Paper" on which have been printed capital letters and small letters of the alphabet in ghost printing. Children get practice in forming letter shapes by tracing over the faintly printed letters. The faint arrows provide guidance as to the direction in which the child should move his pencil in forming the letters.

When the children have practiced for two weeks on letters, the phonemic cards are posted around the room and the children start the task of learning the sounds which the cards represent. The *Open Court* phonograph record #1 gives a story which makes use of all the sounds on the wall cards in the order in which they are presented. The large colorful pictures on the wall cards act as cues to the sounds for they serve as key pictures. Phonograph record #2 describes each picture and gives each sound in the order in which the wall sound cards are posted. This order is suggested in the teacher's guide: the long vowels and single consonants are placed in alphabetical order; the short vowels are next; then come the vowel digraphs, consonant digraphs, etc.

With the use of the phonograph record and the wall cards the children are then ready to start to work on the same materials in their workbooks. There, in *Learning to Read and Write*, they find reproduced the key picture and the letters that appear on the wall cards, with letter practice provided with letters printed in ghost type on their workbook pages.

The first consumable reader-workbook of the program, *Learning to Read and Write*, usually referred to as the "Blue Book", contains twenty-four lessons. It is recommended that it be started after a pre-reading readiness program of two weeks at the beginning of Grade One. The sequence for introducing the phonics in the "Foundation Program" is:

Long $\bar{e}$, with drill using the consonant m (*me*)
The *ee* spelling for long $\bar{e}$, using the consonant s (*see*)
The *ea* spelling for long $\bar{e}$, using the consonant t (*meat*)
The consonant sounds $h\_$, $w\_$, f, th, l, d, r, z in connection with the long $\bar{e}$ sound (*heat, we, feet*, etc.)

It will be noted that the program often uses blanks to suggest that the spelling in question occurs at the beginning of a syllable or (in other instances) after a consonant, at the end of a root word, before a consonant, etc.

Several lessons on the sound of long i, represented by the spellings i, $-y$, $i\text{-}e$, and $-igh(t)$ (*my, side, right*).

The consonant sounds n, v, and sh (*need, vine, sheet*)
The long $\bar{a}$ sound taught in its different spellings: $\bar{a}$, $\_ay$, a_e, $ai\_$ (*say, ate, rain*)
The consonant b (*bite*)

The long ō sound in its various spellings: ō, _ōw, o_e, and oa_
(*no, low, home, boat*)

The consonant sounds g and y_ (*geese, year*)

The ōō sound and the long ū sound in their various spellings: ōō,
ū, u_e, and _ew (*too, Ruth, rule, blew; mule, few*)

The sound of _y at the end of *baby*

The three spellings of the combination of sounds at the end of
her: er, ir, ur (*her, bird, turn*)

Consonant *p* (*pay*)

Sound flash cards are used as a supplement to the workbook program.

One of the tasks that is undertaken early in the program is learning
to blend consonants with vowels. Practice is provided in the third large
soft-cover book in the "Foundation Program", the *Word Line Book*.
This is a re-usable exercise book, which is used concurrently with the
two basic reader-workbooks: *Learning to Read and Write* (Reader 1:1:1)
and *Reading and Writing* (Reader 1:1:2). In word line exercises, all
vowels are printed in red color as they appear in whole words. (The
McQueen phonics book which formerly served as the first book of the
Open Court Series uses red for vowels in word lists and in nonsense
syllables, and sometimes for a particular vowel or consonant in the reading
selections themselves.)

When the class is working with word lines, much work is done by
teacher and children at the chalkboard. Whole-class learning is an essential
element in the "Foundation Program" for it is claimed that total class
participation creates a feeling of accomplishment in all children. (Later
in the day, however, the children may read independently in the 12
Open Court story booklets.)

Learning to Read and Write, which is designated as the first reader
in the first half of First Grade consists of twenty-four lessons which an
average class is expected to complete in November. By Thanksgiving,
most classes are ready to move into the Reader 1:1:2, *Reading and
Writing*. Its reading selections consist of Aesop's fables, nursery rhymes,
and other poems, and the book provides practice in the following
sequence of phonetic elements:

Short i_ (*this*)

The consonant sound k with its spellings: k, c, and _ck (*beak,
crow, pick*)

The _ng sound at the end of a syllable (*sing*)

Short a_ (*man*)

Soft c followed by e, i, or y: ce, ci, cy (*place, racing, fancy*)

The j_ sound, with its spellings: j_, _dge, ge, gi, gy (*June, bridge,*

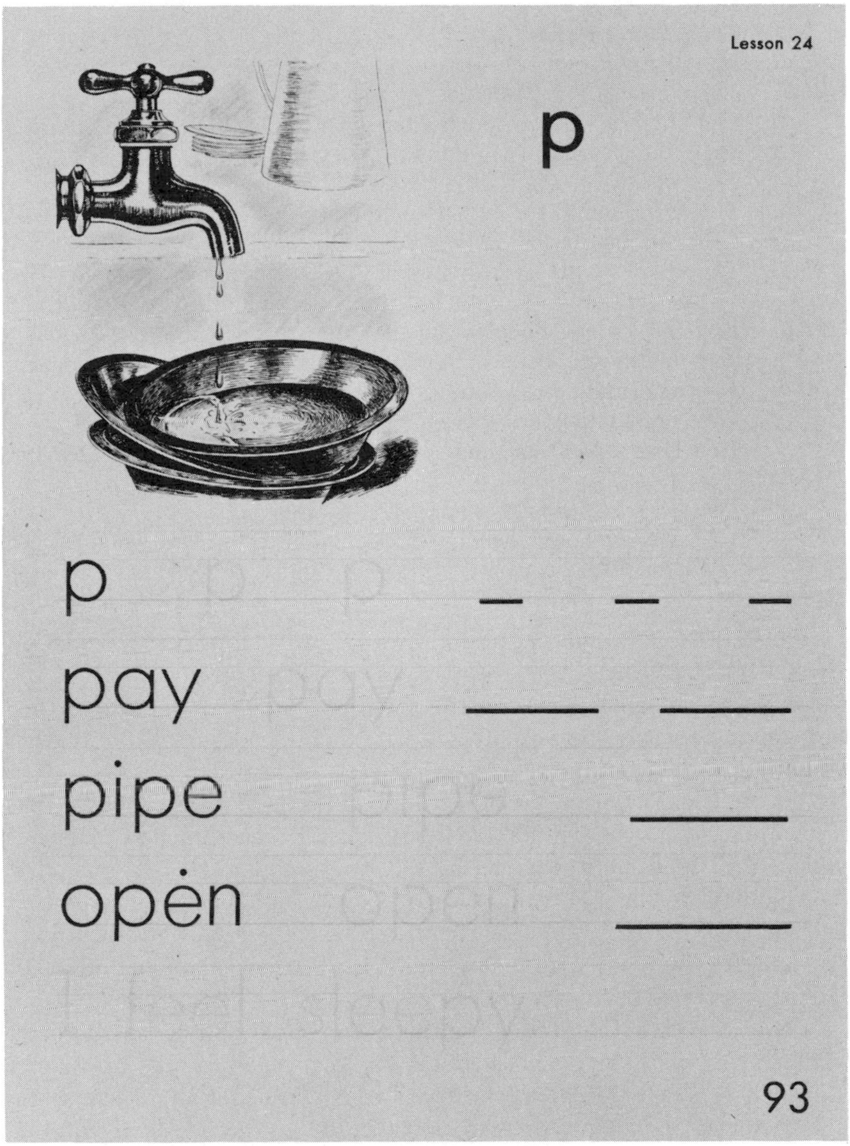

Lesson 24

p

p

pay

pipe

opėn

93

Fig. 6–3 Reproduced from the "Foundation Program" of the Open Court Readers *by permission of the publisher, M. B. Carus, and the Open Court Publishing Company.*

huge, giant, gym)
Short *o_* (*lock*)
Consonant *_x* (*fox*)
Short *e_*, with its two variations: *e_* and *_ĕa_* (*sent, instead*)
The consonant digraphs *ch*, *_tch*; *wh_* (*each, catch, why*)
The short *u_* sound represented by *u* or by other vowels topped
by a single dot (*cùt, whàt, anòther, opèn*)
The consonant sound *qu_* (*queen*)
The vowel sound *ow* with the alternate spelling *ou_* (*now, cloud*)
The combination *ar* (*dark*)
The vowel sound we hear in *jaw, haul, hall,* and *or*
The vowel sound *oi_* with the alternate spelling *_oy* (*toy, boil*)
The vowel sound *o͝o* with the alternate spelling *_u_* (*good, put*)
Four of the less-frequent spellings of common consonant sounds:
kn_, gn_, wr_, and *_mb* (*knot, gnat, wrong, thumb*)
The combination *wòr_* (*worm*)
Two less-frequent spellings of the *sh* sound: *_ti_, _ci_* (*patient,
special*)
The special consonant sound *_s_* (*pleasure*)
Two less-frequent spellings of common consonant sounds: *ph*;
ch = *k* (*phone, Christmas*)

All of the usual phonics drill routines are utilized in the "Foundation
Program" of the *Open Court Basic Readers*. The children write in the
air and at the chalkboard, trace letters and say sounds. In addition, they
write sounds, words, and sentences in their reader-workbooks from
dictation.

Unlike the McQueen program, the new "Foundation Program" has
the children learn the names of the letters; it recommends extensive
alphabet drill in exercises known as "Getting-Acquainted Sessions". At
the beginning of the phonemics lessons, daily alphabet drill is part of
the "warm-up". Much time is spent on reviewing previous learnings.
Each lesson is built upon prior learnings, with a new phonemic element
attached to previously-learned bases.

Once the class has worked through the "Foundation Program", it
is claimed that they then can read, and are then ready to take up Reader
1:2, which is Trace's *Reading Is Fun*. It is claimed that "there is no
longer any fear of meeting the extensive vocabulary because conventional
limitations of the 'look-say' method no longer exist, and the child ventures
into the well-chosen selections of *Reading Is Fun* with a spirit of challenge
because he has mastered the skill of unlocking words."

Reading Is Fun includes such children's literature as the Mother
Goose rhymes which the children had learned in Kindergarten, and

The Tiger and the Kid

A kid strayed away from the other goats to drink. As he drank, a tiger came to his drinking place and was going to eat him. "Wait!" said the kid. "I see that you have a fancy flute. Please play your flute first, and I'll dance for you."

The tiger liked music. He played his flute, and the kid pranced and danced.

The owner of the goats was able to hear the flute. He came with a big stick, and the tiger had to race away with no dinner.

"After this," said the tiger, "I shall eat first and play the flute later."

27

Fig. 6–4 Reproduced from the "Foundation Program" of the Open Court Readers *by permission of the publisher, M. B. Carus, and the* Open Court Publishing Company.

provides other poems which children seem to enjoy greatly. It also contains many fairy tales and folk tales.

One of the features of the *Reading Is Fun* book is the "Words to

Watch". These are essentially the non-phonemic words which are known as the "spelling demons". For First Graders, they furnish good practice in sight reading, spelling, and writing.

At the end of each selection are challenging thought questions. The questions do not just call for skimming to find an answer, but require intellectual involvement. This results not only in thinking but in creative writing, which can be just as good as the teacher expects it to be.

The new 176–page *Teacher's Guide* for Reader 1:2, published in 1970, provides day-by-day directions for teaching spelling, capitalization, punctuation, vocabulary study, composition, and oral activities in connection with the reading selections. This correlation of all the language arts is continued at higher levels, through sixth grade.

The only student materials needed for the *Open Court Correlated Language Arts Program* are the readers themselves. The other activities arise from the stories in the readers and are taught at the board from the teacher's guides and from the children's own compositions, according to explicit directions given in each lesson of the guide. The sequential development of reading skills, composition techniques, oral skills, vocabulary and spelling, dictionary and research skills, sentence structure (grammar), usage, style, capitalization, and punctuation is shown in the *Open Court* "Scope and Sequence" chart.

Research Findings

The Hegeler Foundation[9] which conducted research on the McQueen phonics system when it was part of the *Open Court* series has extended its reading study with the same schools in Columbus, Georgia; Newport News; Reno; Richmond, Virginia; and two Catholic schools in Chicago and New Orleans now experimenting with the "Foundation Program". Children in the control group used traditional basal reader materials.

First Graders from high socio-economic areas who were in the experimental group had a mean grade equivalent in word meaning of 2.3 compared with 1.8 for the control group. The tests were taken near the end of the First Grade in May, 1966. The same groups achieved a grade equivalent of 2.3 (experimental) compared with 1.9 (control) in paragraph meaning. In spelling, the experimental group mean grade equivalent was 2.8 compared to 2.0 for the control group.

The Hegeler Foundation reports that children who attended First

---

9. Hughes, Ann and Thomas, Nellie, *First-Year Report on the Hegeler Project Reading Study*. La Salle, Illinois: The Hegeler Foundation, 1966.

Grade and who came from lower socio-economic areas showed the following results on the *Stanford Achievement Tests* taken in May, 1966. The experimental group attained a grade equivalent of 1.8 in word meaning compared with 1.4 for the control group. The comparison in paragraph meaning was 1.7 for the experimental group and 1.5 for the control group. The difference appears to be greater in spelling with the experimental group at grade 2.5 and the control group at 1.6.

These figures are meaningless in themselves, since there is no indication of the significance of the differences (if any), nor is there an indication of the adequacy for matching the 278 children in the experimental group with the 267 in the control group.

The objective of the *Open Court Basic Readers* is said to be the reading of "good literature". To that end, our literary heritage is presented in traditional fables, folk tales, fairy tales, and poems. The greatness of our country and the people who made it great is presented in Second Grade readers through stories of the lives of famous Americans. Third Graders read of the exploits of world heroes and of the customs and traditions of peoples of the world. There is no control of vocabulary except to select articles that are judged to be within the average grasp of the average children in the grade in which they will be read.

In the McGuffey tradition, the *Open Court Basic Readers* attempt to instill industriousness through the story of "The Little Red Hen"; helpfulness through "David Teaches Beth," and other virtues such as perseverance, cooperation, kindness to animals, and self-sacrifice which were characteristic of the objective of the McGuffey series.

As worthy as those may be, it is impossible to evaluate the success of any reading series in terms of those objectives. We must be content, therefore, to attempt an evaluation of the *Open Court Basic Readers* exclusively on the basis of the question, "to what extent are they successful as an approach to beginning reading?" The answer to that question is at present found largely in testimonials[10] which have been offered by those who use the *Open Court* materials and who state their satisfaction with them. However, the introduction in 1970 of unconditionally guaranteed performance provides another dimension to the evaluation of the effectiveness of Open Court materials or, indeed, of any other materials and/or approaches to beginning reading.

Under the new contracts, Open Court Publishing Company guarantees to produce grade-level independent readers by the end of First Grade. Achievement is calculated on whole-class performance on pre-test

---

10. Annunciata, Sister Mary, "Report: Open Court Basic Readers, *Reading is Fun*," La Salle, Illinois: Open Court Publishing Co., (Mimeographed).

and post-test results on standardized tests of reading achievement. The cost to the school system is prorated according to the number of months increase in grade-level performance. For example, nine-months increase would equal the nine-month school year and would cost 100% of the materials; six-months increase would cost 70%; and a zero difference would cost 10%. In any case, the Open Court materials remain the property of the school where the "performance contract" is in operation.

The one provision is that *all* exercises in the student workbooks must be completed by all children.

Pretest and post-test scores are the only measure of performance and, as the guarantee of the effectiveness of any reading program, they leave much to be desired inasmuch as they do not allow for the several subfactors of learning nor for the several variables in the learner. It will be interesting to observe the adjustments that will be made in the decade of the 1970s as a result of the unconditional performance guarantee initiated by Open Court.

McQUEEN INTEGRATED PHONICS METHOD

Origins

The *McQueen Integrated Phonics Method* for beginning reading was developed by Priscilla Luetscher McQueen over a period of eighteen years from 1943 through 1962 while she was a teacher in the Central Institute for the Deaf and Director of a remedial reading clinic in Tiskilwa, Illinois. Mrs. McQueen was especially interested in the development of speech for the hard-of-hearing child, and for the aphasic child. Her interest in this field and her knowledge of the work of Professor Mildred McGinnis at the Washington University Institute for the Deaf in St. Louis were the bases for her program.

Although the method which is known as the *McQueen Integrated Phonics Method* is basically a phonemic approach to beginning reading, it has a number of characteristics (listening, seeing, pronouncing, and writing) which warrant its being classified as a "total language-arts" approach to reading.

The Book 1[1] in the new *McQueen Integrated Phonics Method* was, actually, the first book in the Open Court Publishing Company's *Open Court Readers* until the author formed the McQueen Publishing Co. in 1966. Since that time, Mrs. McQueen has been busy developing what eventually will become a Kindergarten through Sixth Grade program.

Materials and Method

At present the *McQueen Integrated Phonics Method* is confined to the materials in the workbook and the hard cover Book 1[1], both of which are titled *We Can Read*. The workbook provides the writing exercises which are part of the daily lessons which constitute at least 56 school days of work in reading. Essentially, the *McQueen Integrated Phonics Method* is what would be the equivalent of the first semester of concentrated work in listening, writing, and reading phonemic elements in the First Grade. Because of individual differences, it is possible that some children may not complete the program until well into the Spring. It is more normal, however, for First Grade classes to finish the *We Can Read* program in 4½ to 5 months. In fact, Mrs. McQueen cites over 200 classes which have all finished her program by the end of February.

Each daily lesson in the "integrated phonemic" approach follows the same pattern:

First, a "story" of a new sound is presented with the "key picture" which represents that sound. For example, the teacher introduces the consonant "b" sound through a story about Memorial Day and the sound a drummer makes with his big drum. The teacher is cautioned *not* to make the "buh" sound.

It is recommended that one new sound be introduced every day, with lessons proceeding a bit more slowly at first.

Second, the previous sounds which have been learned are reviewed and differentiated from the new sound that has been presented.

Third, the teacher utilizes the chalkboard to build new sounds by combining the sound-symbols of the day with previously learned sound-symbols. Drill at the board is done to concentrate on the development of new sounds by attaching old symbols to the new, as well as to accustom the children to left-to-right progression. It is claimed that children who watch the teacher perform this drill at the chalkboard will have fewer letter reversals.

Fourth, new words are presented, utilizing the sound-of-the-day.

Fifth, sentences are devised to use words having the new sound as part of their total sound.

Sixth, the teacher presents the new sound, writes it for the children to see, and then they write it as they say it. It is claimed that this procedure by the whole class makes it possible for the teacher to discover those pupils who are having difficulty.

Seventh, in the afternoon just before the children leave the classroom, they are given a review, with dictation of sounds, words, and even sentences which they are to write. It is claimed that "This review gives the children their last impression before they go home and is very helpful, since little academic learning takes place before it is reinforced with a drill the next day."

It is suggested that the morning phonemic drill will use up about 60 minutes of class time during which the entire class participates. In addition, a 20-minute period should be set aside for slow students. The afternoon review may take ten to fifteen minutes or more, depending upon the teacher's assessment of needs.

The author of the "Integrated" phonemic approach explains that "this procedure is a multi-modal approach: the children hear the sound, see or read the sound, say the sound and then write the sound." Mrs. McQueen emphasizes her strict methodological thinking by italicizing the statement:

> This method is not being used to its fullest advantage unless all of these approaches are followed meticulously.

An example using the first lesson in the book and accompanying workbook will describe the specific procedure:

The consonant *t* is to be learned.

1. The teacher shows a calendar and explains its use. She identifies the name of the day, name of month and date. This, perhaps, is the first exposure of many children to the concept of time reckoning.

In Book 1[1] the first page has on it a picture of a pocket watch. Using that picture, the teacher tells a little story of what we hear when we hold a watch to our ears. The sound *t t t t t t* is repeated by the children.

The letter-symbol *t* is placed on the consonant chart and the children anticipate that other sound-symbols will be added in future lessons.

The children then turn to their workbooks and go through a routine of learning the letter-symbol *t*. First the teacher writes the consonant *t* on the chalkboard. The teacher traces over it and then traces it in the air. The children imitate the motions by tracing *t* in the air.

The children then take turns writing *t* on the chalkboard. When they have demonstrated that they know the letter, they then start to trace it in their workbooks. The pages of the workbook are designed with the letters printed in dotted and ghost type so that the child can trace over them in making his own letters. The dotted lines and/or ghost type act as guides to the correct formation of the letters. As the child draws the letter *t* over and over as he goes across from left to right, he repeats the sound. He never learns the letter names in the beginning stages of the McQueen approach.

There is a separate page in the workbook for each graphemic representation of a sound. For example, Lesson 2 deals with the long o sound in the *oe, oa,* and *ow* spellings. The sound must be learned in the three ways it is presented and used graphically. The basic spellings are placed on the chalkboard in colored chalk. They also appear in the book printed in red. The consonant *t* is printed in black and, consequently, must be placed on the board in a contrasting color. The examples reproduced from *We Can Read* illustrate the method.

The uniqueness of the drill is illustrated by the following two directions:

"When the children are to say the sounds of the drill separately as in a pause between words, the pause will be indicated by a colon between the sounds. (The colons do not appear in the child's edition.)

"When this pause is wanted, the teacher will give the command *separate it.*"

"When the sounds are to be said as syllables, the teacher will give the command *smooth it.*"

The colon will appear only in the Teacher's Edition, and should not be used on the board to confuse the children.

"Smoothing the syllables" is unique to the *McQueen Integrated Phonics* approach, and has much to recommend it in contrast to the bumpy, halting performances which some children exhibit when attaching phonemes together.

A large amount of class time is utilized in having one group after another go to the chalkboard and write letters, to which another group is directed to add the letter *t.*

An adaptation of "sky writing" is employed in which the children trace the letter forms in the air. This is followed by chalkboard writing, first by the teacher and then by the entire class. This procedure is followed throughout the 57 lessons in the book and the 57 accompanying lessons in the workbook.

Actually, there are considerably more than the 57 basic lessons, for most lessons are divided into parts, depending upon the number of different spellings by which a sound is represented. Moreover, the afternoon review takes one page in most lessons.

The sequence in Book 1[1] and the 1[1] workbook, *We Can Read* is *t;* then *toe, toa,* and *tow* (in *tow* and *oat,* a line is placed over the long ō); then b:o-e, b:oa, b:ōw; followed by lesson five in which the two previous learnings are contrasted: bo-e, boa, bow, oat, ōwt, ote, and boat.

Later in the book when one grapheme or digraph stands for two different sounds, the McQueen approach utilizes factors of 1 and 2 to indicate the differences: the s^1 sound (teakettle steaming) and the s^2 sound of the bumblebee.

Although the *McQueen Integrated Phonics Method* utilizes listening, speaking, seeing, reading and writing letter sound-symbols, it makes use of those symbols chiefly in words out of context. Consequently, there is very little actual reading of story lines. Where a story paragraph does occur, it usually is a contrived paragraph in which as many words as possible are used to illustrate the sound being learned. The paragraph is set in black type, with the letters for the sound-of-the-day being printed in red.

As the sounds are learned, the teacher posts "story cards" which are colored reproductions of the drawings in the book. They serve as "key picture" reminders. Sound charts are developed as the sounds are taught, and are used as reference points when the picture cards are taken down. Great pains are taken to avoid "key words". Mrs. McQueen states that, "When a phonetic method is contaminated with distractions such as key words and alphabetism, it may mean more than double the time needed to acquire the basic associations". Consequently, additional cues such as key words and alphabet pronunciation are not included. This makes it unnecessary for the student to go through what psychologists call "cue reduction"[11] in the learning process. The McQueen approach is more direct associative learning.

The long vowels are taught first.

> . . . They are easier for the child to distinguish and remember than the short vowel sounds; they develop good breath control, voice production, and pronunciation; they are more easily distinguished auditorily; they train the eye to look to the end of the word to determine the vowel sound (final *e* rule); and they are convenient for building a useful vocabulary in a short time.

Mrs. McQueen further justifies the teaching of the long vowel sounds first by stating that, when the long vowels are taught first, "the three or four major spellings are introduced together so that the child is not faced with learning one exception after another."

Diacritical marks are used only when a sound is not obvious. This applies to the macron over a vowel to indicate a long vowel sound.

The *McQueen Integrated Phonics Method* lays major stress on symbol drill and upon writing and pronouncing the phonetic sound-sym-

---

11. When key words, key pictures, and/or alphabet names are introduced as aids to learning letter-sound relationships, the associations thus acquired must eventually be dropped out until the one association remains, namely, the letter symbol as a cue for the letter sound.

Fig. 6–5 *Reproduced from the* McQueen Integrated Phonics Program *by permission of the author and publisher, Priscilla McQueen.*

bols. Reading as such is relegated to a minor role during these first months of learning.

The order in which the graphemes are introduced has been worked out by the originator of the system and is arranged so that each new lesson is built from the learnings of the immediately preceding day. Some strange and unusual things are done in order to maintain consistency in the McQueen system. For example, the *ie* sound in *pie, tie,* and *by* is extended to include *igh,* in words such as *sigh* and *sight* and in syllables such as *pigh, bigh, tigh,* and in *bie, sie, py, ty* and *sy.* It is necessary to include all possible nonsense syllables in order to exploit the added value which nonsense syllables intrinsically have in allowing the greatest possible application of phonemic generalizations—a fact not possible with a "pure" phonetic system nor with a "pure" linguistics approach in which the text is confined to "meaningful" material.

A new book, called the "Individualized Reader" was introduced in 1967 and is intended for the second half of First Grade. It is predicated upon the assumption that the child has learned his basic phonemic skills through the *We Can Read* program.

The *McQueen Integrated Phonics Method* has been reworked into a paperback workbook for junior high school students who need remedial work or for functionally-illiterate adults. The workbook is called *Developing Potential Reading Ability.* It is essentially the same program as the *McQueen Basic Reader* program, but it has been enhanced with whole page illustrations of very interesting situations which vividly act as "key situations" in the place of key words to represent the sound being studied in each lesson. For example, the illustration of three boys blowing up balloons—with one bursting—illustrates the *p* sound. An additional feature is a silhouette showing voice mechanism in position to create the sound being studied. Thus, each new sound is introduced on a whole page which includes the interesting situation, the grapheme(s), and the silhouette of the voice mechanisms. The accompanying illustration is representative of this novel feature of the remedial reading workbook. It may, indeed, be the most valuable contribution of the McQueen system.

Research Findings

Research on the *McQueen Integrated Phonics Method* was done while Priscilla McQueen's book, *We Can Read,* was the first and basic phonemics book of the *Open Court Basic Readers.* The study was done

Paul taught August to play ball. They like to play on the lawn. Paul hit the ball to August. August caught the ball. August hit the ball, too. They had a good time. Then they walked home.

Lesson 36-E

Fig. 6–6 Reproduced from the McQueen Integrated Phonic Program *by permission of the author and publisher, Priscilla McQueen.*

by Miss Ann Hughes and Miss Nellie Thomas under sponsorship of the Hegeler Foundation of La Salle, Illinois.[12] The research was done as an extension of a study[13] previously done by Miss Hughes and reported in the *Journal of Educational Research*, April, 1965. In the latter study, known as the Gurren-Hughes review, a study was made of reports on investigations on the effect of an intensive-phonemics approach compared with a gradual phonemics approach. The Gurren-Hughes review turned up 22 comparative studies, 19 of which favored intensive phonemics and the remaining 3 were neutral.

According to the "First Year Report of the Hegeler Project Reading Study", 32 experimental classes and 32 control classes were involved during the year. Schools in Berkeley, California; Chicago; Georgia; Louisiana; Virginia; Texas; and Utah cooperated in the study with a parallel experiment conducted at Lincoln Park School of Rockford, Illinois.

Teachers in the experimental classes used the McQueen First Grade book, *We Can Read*, and taught the phonemics exactly as planned and in the sequence of routine set up by Priscilla McQueen. The control group teachers introduced phonemics "gradually" according to the instructions in the manuals for whatever basal series they were using.

At the end of the first year (1964–1965) the nine school systems involved in the study reported results as measured by the *Stanford Primary Reading Test*. On all five counts: Word Meaning, Paragraph Meaning, Vocabulary, Word Study Skills, and Spelling, the mean scores of the experimental groups exceeded those of the control groups with significances of difference beyond the .01 level. The more than 700 children in each group (control and experimental) were in schools serving low socio-economic neighborhoods.[14]

It appears that the *McQueen Integrated Phonics Method* is at present basically a phonemics foundation book, designed to provide the child with a background which he will be able to use in a basal reader, individualized reading selections or other possible reading materials. It does provide for writing of phonemic elements and words. It is, however, not a complete approach that covers all of the factors of beginning reading.

It is exactly what it claims to be: an *Integrated Phonics Method*, and in that sense it is an "approach to beginning reading." It is included in this chapter because it has most of the characteristics of a "total" language-arts approach.

---

12. Hughes and Thomas, *op. cit.*
13. Gurren, Louise and Hughes, Ann, "Intensive Phonics vs. Gradual Phonics in Beginning Reading: A Review," *Journal of Educational Research*, 58 (April, 1965) 339–347.
14. Hughes and Thomas, *op, cit.*

THE MOTT BASIC LANGUAGE SKILLS PROGRAM

Origins

The *Mott Basic Language Skills Program* was developed as a functional medium for the Mott Adult Reading Center in Flint, Michigan. The Mott Center is named for its donor, Charles Stewart Mott, who for many years was associated with the General Motors Corporation and the community life of the city of Flint. The Mott Center is one of the agencies indirectly related to the Mott Foundation of Flint, and also is a department of the Adult Education and Extended School Services Division of the Flint Public Schools.

The originators of the Language Skills Program are Byron E. Chapman, Director of the Mott Adult Reading Center, and Louis Schulz, Principal of the Adult High School and Continuing Education Program in the Flint Public Schools. Through their efforts, the advice of many specialists in reading, adult education, and education of the culturally disadvantaged has been pooled and used as the basis for the *Mott Basic Language Skills Program*.

Mr. Chapman has cited the need for an approach to beginning reading instruction especially designed for adults. He quotes figures to indicate the rapid decline in the number of unskilled jobs. The number in Michigan, for example, dropped in a five-year period from 1960 to 1965 from 7.3% to less than 2.5% of the total labor force. It has been estimated that 97% of all jobs require a high school education or its equivalent.

The significance of this is apparent. The literacy requirements for most jobs in America place an estimated 58,000,000 people below this requirement. Government figures show that 11,000,000 have not completed the Fifth Grade.

Programs for literacy are not new. Dr. Frank Laubach dedicated his long life to what he terms the "Silent Billions," and distinguished himself as the world-wide spokesman for literacy. His materials in reading for adult illiterates are presented elsewhere in this book. (Chapter VIII.)

One of the major problems in developing a reading program for American adults is the fact that, basically, they are a rather knowledgeable group of people, daily informed by radio and TV. The materials that are suitable for elementary school children, therefore, would be totally unsuitable and even insult adult intelligence.

The *Mott Basic Language Skills Program* was developed in an orderly and highly professional manner. It was not one of the "crash programs" developed by some "Johnny-come-Early" to skim off the cream of a new business. On the contrary, the Mott Program was developed only after twenty years of contact with many people around the country who were thinking and talking about the needs for basic adult education.

The program has many of the elements of any good elementary beginning reading sequence. At times, there are what appear to be gaps and short cuts. Some may think that the program moves too quickly; basing their opinion on the speed with which children are able to assimilate new learnings.

It appears to this writer that the *Mott Basic Language Program* is a decidedly worthwhile contribution to a specific area of need in the field of beginning reading.

Materials and Method

The *Mott Basic Language Skills Program* is divided into three basic "tracks":
"Reading—300"
"Reading—600"
"Reading—900"

The objectives of the program are specifically to teach beginning reading to adults and/or to teach adults who have developed only the most minimal reading skills. In either case, the series attempts to provide semi-programmed materials and a method for starting reading instruction from the base of sound-symbol recognition, keeping in mind at the same time that the method must be considerably different from that employed with children.

The first phase in the Mott approach is the learning of the alphabet. It is assumed that some or even all of the adults in the class may know enough of the letters to be able to print their own name and address on the registration card. In fact, it is suggested that the performance in filling out the registration card be closely observed in order to assess the alphabet knowledge of each individual.

The student's notebook contains twelve pages of squares and lines on which the learner is expected to practice *writing* the capital and small letters in cursive penmanship according to examples in the left-hand margins. Work on those pages is akin to the "Penmanship" practice of the lower grades. Heavy and light lines indicate the limits of height of the various letters. There is no expectation that the adult learner will achieve perfection. On the contrary, "cursive legibility" is the objective.

The second phase of the *Mott approach* is the learning of the consonants. This employs a unique presentation of the consonants (in heavy, large capital and relatively small lower-case type), together with a photographic reproduction of the "key word." The "key word" appears in the left-hand margin in both capital letters and in lower-case letters. Only four consonants appear on each page, thus making it possible to present them and their accompanying key words and pictures in large style. The photographs are of very common objects of the adult environment:

(B) book	(J) jacket	(Q) quilt	(X) box
(C) camera	(K) key	(R) ring	(Y) yarn
(D) door	(L) ladder	(S) saw	(Z) zipper
(F) fish	(M) milk	(T) telephone	
(G) gun	(N) nail	(V) valentine	
(H) hat	(P) porch	(W) windmill	

It is obvious that the "key words" are longer words than usually used in children's beginning reading materials. Yet, when the whole class calls off the key words which are associated with the letters, everyone is expected to feel success. With adults, success is the underlying motivational factor. As the class works together on the consonants, each student is asked to print the letter as the word is said.

The teacher pronounces the entire word—never the consonant alone, but emphasizes the consonant sound. It is suggested that groups within the class prepare themselves to present daily consonant lessons.

Unit 2 of the program is the first of the lessons on vowel sounds. The short $\breve{a}$ as found in the "picture-word" *hat*. The students are asked to read from their workbooks. Page 25, for example, provides practice within six "boxes". The students are asked to read the words within Box 1, then Box 2, and so on. All words are monosyllables containing two or three letters, such as *at, am, an, cat, tap, bag,* etc.

The program provides that the learners practice these for rote memorization of whole-words. It appears that some attempt has been made to control the vocabulary and to keep it to phonemically regular monosyllabic words. It is interesting to note, however, that in the consonant learning that preceded the work with short $\breve{a}$ on page 25, no written drill is given on the pronunciation of sound-symbol aspects of those consonants beyond imitation of the teacher in the pronunciation of the consonant in the "picture-words".

The teacher's manual emphasizes: "Do not attempt to *pronounce the consonant sound alone. Always say the whole word along with the initial consonant.*"

It is consequently assumed that the monosyllabic words on page 25, and the following pages covering the short vowel sounds, are going to be learned as whole-word learning.

The bottom half of the page is devoted to 25 sentences which closely resemble the linguistics pattern: "Ann, pass the ham." "Mag can tap a can." "A fat cat sat." "Nan can fan Dan." Included is the somewhat dubious observation: "The hag had a ragbag."

The objective of mixing the vowel sounds in the sentence is, of course, to provide practice in visual and auditory discrimination through the medium of similarities and contrast.

Following each lesson in which the new short vowel sound is introduced, there are three pages of practice materials. These utilize, first, the method of incomplete words. The word stems, however, are the opposite of those usually used with beginning readers. For example, in the lessons which provide practice on the short i sound, 25 such as stems hi-, pi-, si-, bi-, are provided to which the learner is supposed to attach consonant endings. Then, there are sentences in which words appear that need to be completed with initial consonants filled in on the spaces provided. Finally, the workbook provides sentences in which whole words must be written into the spaces provided. The words are suggested in a box above the exercise.

After the students have completed their work with short vowels, the *Program* presents practice on hard c and k as initial consonant sounds and then a sequence which involves four-letter words in which the final consonant sound of ck is learned. The ck verbs such as *pick, rack, rock,* etc. are then augmented with *ed* to form past tense, and with *ing.*

A section on capitalization is interspersed, followed with several more pages of final consonant sounds, and consonant digraphs. The s is presented without specifically separating it as a plural device or as a present tense indicator. This is followed with more final consonant sounds.

From page 65 through 94 in the student workbook, the *Program* presents work with consonant blends almost identical to that provided for learning the vowels. On those pages, the blends are presented with carefully-selected "picture-words" as cues.

(BL) blade, (FL) flag, (CL) clock, (GL) glasses,
(PL) plate, (SC) scale, (SK) skirt, (SL) slippers,
(SM) smoke, (SN) snow, (SP) spoon, (ST) stairs,
(SW) sweater, (TW) twelve
(BR) bread, (CR) crayons, (DR) dress, (FR) fruit,
(GR) grape, (PR) pretzels, (SCR) screw, (SPR) spring,
(STR) string, (SHR) shrub, (TR) tractor,
(QU) quilt, (TH) thumb,
(SQU) squash, (THR) three, (WH) wheel,
(CH) cherry and church, (TCH) patch.

CONSONANT SOUNDS

BOOK
book

B b

CAMERA
camera

C c

DOOR
door

D d

FISH
fish

F f

Fig. 6–7 *Reproduced from the* Mott Basic Language Skills Program *by permission of Byron E. Chapman, coordinator, the Mott Adult Education Program.*

This completes the *Mott Basic Language Skills Program* for Series 300 A. Series 300 B is an extension of the first workbook material and completes what ordinarily would be the basic reading, spelling and writing skills expected of a child through the Third Grade. It, too, is a highly-structured program of phonetic work which is to be followed specifically in the sequence printed. It is claimed that "To introduce materials out of sequence, to introduce other concepts at the same time, or to break sequence would destroy this simplicity".

Series 300 B starts with work on the long vowel sounds, with long ē providing the first learning activity, followed closely with long ē modified by *r*. Lesson II emphasizes the sounds of double "oo" as in *moon, soon, book,* and *good.* Practice with those sounds is given with materials and method similar to that which is familiar to primary teachers. For example, the teacher pronounces from a list of words. When a word having the "double oo" sound is heard, the students write the word or make a mark on the page or make some other designated response.

Other suggested activities are cued to adult interests. For example, an "object box" containing 100 or more "objects" is brought to class. As each object is selected from the box, the students attempt to write the object's name on a sheet numbered to 100. *Readers Digest* books are used as supplementary materials. Job-training pamphlets, job-application blanks, personal loan application forms, and other business forms are used for practice in finding words that contain certain phonic elements.

Other supplementary materials are to be found in travel folders, recipes, magazines, advertisements, etc.

The Series 300 A and 300 B of the *Mott Basic Language Skills* will be covered through 15 Units or lessons utilizing a maximum of 60 hours of classwork for each Series. Each Series may take 15 weeks of two 2-hour lessons each week. It would take an entire "academic year" to cover Series 300 A and Series 300 B. In effect, the learner would then have covered the equivalent of Grade One through Grade Three in reading, writing, and spelling.

Research Findings

The Mott Basic Language Skills Program was tested under controlled conditions by Greenleigh Associates of New York under a Federally-funded contract from the U.S. Office of Education. The test was carried on in New Jersey, New York, and California with 1800 adult students.

Test results showed the Mott materials to be equal, and in some cases superior, to the other three systems with which they were compared. In addition, the Mott program and materials showed a marked superiority over other systems when used by teachers having little or no training in the field of reading.

Basic Language Skills 300A   Page 29
Unit 3

LEARNING THE SHORT "E" SOUND

ĕ

PĔN pĕn ĕ

1	2	3	4	5	6
get	beg	hen	pep	leg	Les
bed	hem	let	bet	ten	men
web	sell	Ted	bell	Ken	peg
mess	Ben	led	jet	yet	den
led	Ned	net	well	Nell	yes
tell	wet	set	yell	fell	egg
less	fed	red	wed	pet	pen

1. Ned, get the net.

2. Ben is at the well.

3. The bell is red.

4. Ben led the men.

     5. The den is wet.

     6. Tell Ned to get Les.

     7. The web is wet.

     8. Ed, let Ned bet.

     9. Tell Ben the hen is wet.

     10. Ned, set the wet hen on the bed.

     11. The jet is red.

     12. The pen is a mess.

WORDS TO LEARN

it   to
  is
on   not

Parts of Words

Ed vet Les

Fig. 6–8 Reproduced from the Mott Basic Language Skills Program *by permission of Byron E. Chapman, coordinator, the Mott Adult Education Program.*

There were in 1967, 250,000 adult students using the *Mott Basic Language Skills Program* in all fifty states and in Canada, according to figures released by the publisher. The Mott materials were published in 1965 after two years experimental use and revision at the Center in Flint. The average improvement in reading proficiency according to the originators of the method is 1.5 grade levels for each 60 hours of class instruction. Among secondary school remedial students, the figures indicate an average gain of 2.5 grade levels for 180 hours of classroom instruction.

The need for effective materials in beginning reading for adult semi-illiterates and illiterates is very great. The Mott Program is a welcome leader in this field, and experience with it will undoubtedly lead to refinements and extensions of its best features.

The materials are now available in a semi-programmed format through the Allied Education Council of Galien, Michigan.

PRO-READING

Origins

Pro-Reading is a "total" language-arts approach to beginning reading, devised by Mrs. Gladys Sims Stump who for many years was a primary teacher and supervisor in California and Arizona. More recently, Mrs. Stump has taught graduate courses in reading at Arizona State University.

Mrs. Stump explains that it would be difficult to trace the origins of some of the features of her system. She admits that her methods are an outgrowth of many personal experiences in teaching and in studying, during which time she accepted and adapted ideas from many sources, especially to Dr. Anna D. Cordts and to the Montessorian influence during Normal School days.

While attending graduate courses at Arizona State University, Mrs. Stump presented some of her ideas in a seminar in curriculum taught by Dr. Donald O'Beirne. He was impressed with the materials and encouraged Mrs. Stump to put them in a form which could be used by others. It was Dr. O'Beirne who invented the name, *Pro-Reading*.

For several years Mrs. Stump worked in getting the materials structured into a program that could be published. Finally, in 1963, the first book, *Level One* of *Pro-Reading* was published and Mrs. Stump immediately found herself to be a demonstrator, a distributor, a salesman, and a workshop leader, as well as a teacher and author. Her materials first came to the attention of the world of reading on a nation-wide scale at the 1963 meeting of the International Reading Association. Lack of a national sales force still prevents *Pro-Reading* from becoming widely known by teachers and reading specialists.

Materials and Method

Pro-Reading is an approach to beginning reading which is designed for the First Grade, but early elements of which may also be used in the second half of the Kindergarten year. The materials are divided into three levels:

Level One—September and October of Grade One, or as readiness materials in the last half of the Kindergarten year.
Level Two—November, December, and January of Grade One.
Level Three—February, March, April and May of Grade One.

Each Level is a carefully-planned sequence of activities which are directed through a fine *Teachers' Guide*. This contains complete directions for the unique activities which are the main part of the classroom motivation and procedure. Each of the three Levels has a workbook, designated as *Application Time*.

At each Level, the *Teachers' Guide* and the *Application Time* workbook are bound in the same colors: Level One, red; Level Two, blue; and Level Three, yellow.

The *Teachers' Guide* presents the daily lessons in phonemics and complete suggestions for each daily lesson.

Pro-Reading recognizes two beginnings of a word: (1) The initial consonant which is never pronounced apart from the vowel sound which follows it; and (2) The initial consonant-vowel combination, blending as it does the consonant with the vowel sound. The author of *Pro-Reading* has designed all materials—pilot word cards, pilot picture cards, charts, etc.—to be used to develop skills deemed as those that every child must acquire if he is to become a proficient reader. He must be taught "how to look" and "how to listen." These skills must be so well developed that they become automatic.

1. The child must learn to look from left to right within a word as well as looking from left to right at a series of words. He must recognize that words have a "geographic" sequence.
2. The child must learn to listen across a word recognizing that a word has a temporal sequence.
3. The child must learn to respond orally to graphic representations of phonemes in the proper sequence.

4. The child must learn to respond graphically to the sequence of phonemes presented to him.

Large lesson charts are to be made by the teacher according to instructions given in the *Teachers' Guides*. The charts should be at least 24″ × 36″. It is suggested that they be covered with a large sheet of plastic film so that the charts may be protected and children can mark over them with water-washable felt pens. This procedure is called "Pro-Mark" (pronounce and mark). These charts are also available as transparencies for overhead projection.

One of the special features of the pre-reading materials is the collection of three-dimensional picture "Pilot" cards. "Pilot Words" are words used as cues in phonemic and structural analysis. The "Pilot Word Cards" are first used at Level Two. They are to be constructed by the teacher. The base is a heavy art board in various colors. The cards should be at least 14″ × 17″. Onto the cards are mounted with glue representations of "real" objects. All sorts of small objects can be purchased in the dime store. Most will be in plastic: bug, telephone, horn, magnet, truck, plum. Those objects should not exceed 3″ in size. The "Pilot Word" (key word which each represents) is carefully printed in manuscript below the mounted object. The cards are then mounted around the room on the corkboard which is located above the chalkboards. Those three-dimensional "Pilot Cards" are a vivid aid to mental imagery of the key words and initial sounds.

"Pilot Word Cards", consisting of the pilot words, only, are used as flash card drill. Pilot picture cards may be small cards which are also used for flash card drill.

A number of word games have been devised to aid in whole-word recognition practice. Phonemic word wheels or disks are suggested also as aids.

"Pilot Word" Cards which are introduced at Level Two

basket	bird	bug	fish
magnet	lock	dump truck	wigwam
Jet	ladder	glass	ticket
package	raccoon	bell	dolly
spoon	satellite	gun	telephone
fan	lollipop	jumprope	necktie
camera	plum	picture	web
hammer	jumping	dollar	shelf
cup	frog	brush	zig-zag
crutch	rocket	kitty	

A low kitchen stool is one of the "props" used by Mrs. Stump as a motivational device. It is called "The Ladder of Success", and is used

Fig. 6–9   Reproduced from the Pro-Reading *program by permission of the author, Gladys Sims Stump, and Language Arts Publishers.*

by a child who is working on a large chart which cannot be reached from the floor.

Mrs. Stump also uses a braided area rug to "frame in" the group of children who gather for story time or for small group instruction and activity. She states that such a rug is quite essential in providing a "togetherness" and a feeling of belonging to a group.

Perhaps the most unique of the many accoutrements of the *Pro-Reading* materials are the "Zip" and "Zippy" hand puppets and "Zip" and "Zippy" hats and children's costumes. When Zip pronounces a word or a sound correctly, Zippy claps for him. But when he makes a mistake, Zippy cries. When a girl is performing, it is Zippy who is "doing the acting" and it is Zip who either applauds or cries. Patterns for the puppets and for the hats are available from the publishers of the *Pro-Reading* materials.

The *Application Time* workbooks are designed to give the children independent work on the principles learned during class instruction. The lessons in the workbooks are planned to be do-it-yourself materials.

The children do a great amount of marking in the workbook. They cross out words, draw lines to connect words, underline words, cut-match-and-paste words, and do similarly with pictures of objects. Later in Level Two and Level Three, they write letters and finally words.

Simultaneous with the readiness work with words, the teacher may give the class lessons in auditory recognition of sounds such as sounds of drums, tops, horns, bells, and whistles, etc.

The children are then given a lesson on their "own sound maker", and learn something of the voice mechanism. They are given mirrors and can look inside their throats as they make certain sounds. From this exposure to the mechanics of throat, lips, tongue, teeth and breath control, the children are introduced to various phonemes such as the humming of the letters *m* and *n* and *ng*. This is followed with the "popping" sounds of *p* and *b* and *t* and *d*. The consonant *g* is next.

All of the phonemic work is introduced through clever poems and other sound rhymes and songs.

In the last half of Level One, the children work in their *Application Time* workbooks and in group work on visual and auditory discrimination of initial and final sounds, word families, phonogram substitution and a number of other of the usual aids in phoneme drill. Much marking is done on the large room charts and in the workbooks. Card strips and other games are also extensively utilized to maintain a high level of interest and activity. During the exercises and phonemic "games", tension is kept high as the class waits for the teacher to call "Zippy-Zip", whereupon the children all show their cards or respond in unison or in some other appropriate manner. In contrast to some other methods, *Pro-Reading* teaches the children letter *names*; not the phonemes.

Pro-Reading, Level Two provides interesting activities and practice with phonics in real reading situations. Initial consonant short vowel sounds and most-frequently-used endings are studied. The lesson plans are quite similar to those in Level One. Do-it-yourself *Application Time* workbooks are also an essential part of the program in Level Two.

Goals to be reached in *Pro-Reading* Level Two are:

1. Ability to identify the beginnings and endings of the 40 "Pilot" three-dimensional words.
2. Ability to identify those beginnings and endings in new words.
3. Ability to utilize those beginnings and endings in working out phonemically-regular words.
4. Ability to read those phonemically-regular words along with other whole-word sight vocabulary in sentences.
5. Extension of meaningful appreciation and interpretation of word usage.

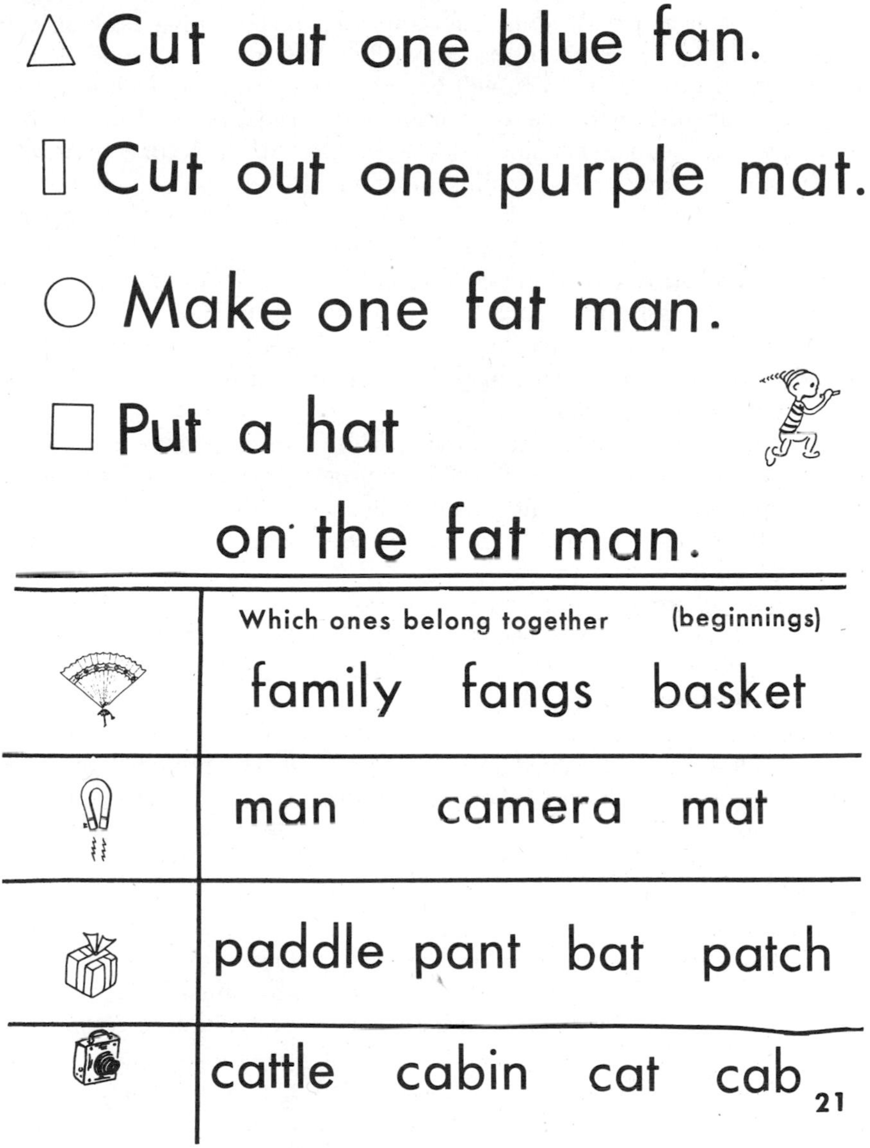

△ Cut out one blue fan.

▯ Cut out one purple mat.

○ Make one fat man.

☐ Put a hat

on the fat man.

	Which ones belong together (beginnings)
	family fangs basket
	man camera mat
	paddle pant bat patch
	cattle cabin cat cab 21

Fig. 6–10 Reproduced from the Pro-Reading *program by permission of the author, Gladys Sims Stump, and Language Arts Publishers.*

6. Ability to spell and write correctly the phonemic words comprising the beginnings and endings learned in Level Two.
7. Ability to work independently in the *Application Time* workbook and to work creatively alone and with others.

Inasmuch as *Pro-Reading* is an approach *to* beginning reading, the system devised by Mrs. Stump is compatible with any basal reader series. Its originator insists that "You will be able to carry on the work of Level Two simultaneously with the work of any basal reader series. *Pro-Reading* is designed to supplement and enrich reading with a natural approach to the phonic facet of the reading program."

The "Pilot Words" of Level Two are used in Level Three as the media for learning short vowel sounds. From lesson 10 through lesson 34, there are also many opportunities for children to find short vowel sounds in new words and to practice consonant substitution in creating new words. By the end of March, most children will begin practice with new sounds which constitute some of the irregularities of our language: *valentine, quilt, yellow,* and *buzz.*

By the end of Grade One, children who have completed Level Three will have been exposed to pilot words such as *star, turtle, bird* and *horn* as examples of the consonant *r* in combination with a preceding vowel. They will also have learned a number of consonant blends and digraphs in initial position.

Pro-Reading also has a few accessories, including the *Driveway Readers,* the small *Book About Me,* the *Book About My House,* a "Punch-out" game, and a "Match and String" game.

In conclusion, it may be well to review the fact that *Pro-Reading* is a pronunciation method based upon the child's natural speech patterns. It has been developed by Mrs. Stump on the principle that the phonemic elements of words should be studied within the natural setting of the word, and that those elements should be recognized and pronounced rather than "sounded". The children start the *Pro-Reading* approach to beginning reading the same way that they talk, using their own speaking vocabulary.

After a period of readiness, involving a profusion of auditory listening games and activities, children are phased into similar activities and games for visual development, speaking, word and sound consciousness, and writing. "Pilot" words are introduced and become the point of reference for all work in word recognition. Hence, they must be carefully selected to contain the elements of word beginnings and word endings that are a major part of *Pro-Reading.*

Basic to the entire program of materials and activities of *Pro-Reading* is Mrs. Stump's formula:

EFFORT $+$ SUCCESS $=$ LEARNING

This philosophy permeates the games, the activities and the materials. All seatwork is organized on the principle that the effort must be the child's own; that "power" goes to the child who does his *own* work; and to copy gives the "power" to the *other* child. One supervisor of reading in a large public school system remarked after a year of experimentation with *Pro-Reading*, ". . . it offers a set of values badly needed in an uncertain age such as ours."

Research Findings

Pro-Reading is a relatively new approach to beginning reading, being marketed without benefit of national advertising, promotional staff, or "big names". Several research studies by responsible masters and doctoral students have been uncovered. One, a doctoral study at Arizona State University, reports on a "Study of Two Methods of Teaching Phonics in the Second Grade Classrooms of South School, Casa Grande, Arizona". The subjects included all 72 children in the Second Grade during the 1963–64 school year.

The objectives of the study were "to statistically compare reading achievement, personality factors, and mental index growth of groups of children taught by the *Pro-Reading* method (experimental group) and by the *Phonetic Keys to Reading* method (control group)."

The findings reported by Dr. Abbott's study indicated that:

There was no statistical difference between the achievement of the study groups in total reading, vocabulary (word knowledge) and comprehension, as tested at the 5 per cent level of confidence.

There was no statistical difference between mental index growth of the study groups, as tested at the 5 per cent level of confidence.

There was no statistical difference between the personality development of the study groups, as tested at the 5 per cent level of confidence.[15]

It was also reported that it was observed that "complete teacher satisfaction was evident in the experimental method, whereas there were some teacher reservations with the control method." Moreover, the *Pro-Reading* group was reported to have had 100% participation compared with considerably less for the control group.

If anything significant is to be gathered from this study, it would

---

15. Abbott, Jan, *Study of Two Methods of Teaching Phonics in the Second Grade Classrooms of South School, Casa Grande, Arizona.* Tempe: Arizona State University, unpublished doctoral dissertation.

be that *Pro-Reading* method was as effective with those Second Graders as was another highly-publicized approach to beginning reading.

During the next school year, another study involving *Pro-Reading* was reported. This particular study involved two matched groups of remedial reading children. Each group consisted of 13 Spanish-Americans and 6 Anglos. The experimental group was taught daily with the *Pro-Reading* materials and method, five days per week for a total of eight weeks. The "control group" continued along in remedial reading with whatever materials and methods the teacher had been using. These were not identified.

At the end of the eight-week period the post tests showed gains of 5 percentiles for the control group and 12 percentiles gain for the *Pro-Reading* group in word recognition. No significant differences were found in gains in vocabulary or in rate. The most significant difference was found in performance on story comprehension. The control group gained only 2 percentiles while the experimental *Pro-Reading* group gained 10 percentiles.

The third study is a careful case study and day-by-day diary of work with a severely-retarded dyslexic girl who was at the bottom of a low-achieving Fourth Grade class. The child's I.Q. was measured at 61 verbal and 51 performance on the WISC. At the end of the first year of work, performance on the WISC had risen to 60. The Draw-a-Figure test scored an I.Q. of 60 in the first year of treatment. It rose to 75 in the second year.

Many gains were reported for this child who could handle Spanish and English orally. At first, she could not remember letters or words from one day to the next. After two years of one-to-one work in *Pro-Reading* she scored at a low Fourth Grade level and enjoyed reading in books of lower difficulty.

It would be tempting to criticize *Pro-Reading* as being a collection of gadgets and gimmicks—which it is—but to dissociate those accouterments of motivation, reward, and pure fun from the program would strip it of its essential features, namely, an *enjoyable* means for learning the sounds of our language and the identification of those sounds in words.

The little poems which embellish the program are reflections of Mrs. Stump's sensitivity to the world of childhood. The "Zippy-Zip" routine is motivation in the realm of the imaginative and fanciful. There is *much* activity in groups, in pairs, in and around the classroom. The teacher, too, is an actor, pretending in the fun-drama which surrounds the learning. Learning-by-doing is an obvious characteristic of the method.

Accordingly, *Pro-Reading* is the culmination of a lifetime of experiences with young children. As such, it reflects the magical world of child-hood; the unspoiled desire to find joy in listening and reading of stories; and the little rewards which children have a right to expect as they suc-ceed in dealing with the complexities of our language.

THE WENKART PHONIC READERS

Origins

The *Wenkart Phonic Readers* owe their name to their originator, Mrs. Heni Wenkart Epstein of Cambridge, Massachusetts. Mrs. Epstein, wife of an electronics engineer, and holder of a baccalaureate degree from Pembroke, master's degrees from Columbia and Radcliffe, and a doctoral candidate at Harvard, wrote the first of the little books in the series for her son, Jonny. At that time, Jonny was four years old and appeared to be ready to read.

She relates that Jonny knew all of his letters and letter sounds, but that, after purchasing some of the standard pre-primers, she discovered that Jonny couldn't read them. She ascribed this to the fact that the books of the basal series were based upon sight words, and not upon a regular introduction of words with letter sounds controlled.

"I couldn't stop and let him think he'd failed," she recalls. And consequently she set about the task of devising stories utilizing letter forms and letter sounds which Jonny knew. She also decided to illustrate the stories for fun rather than to provide "picture clues."

The theory upon which she operated was that children learn best when a very few, easily distinguishable units are presented at a time and drilled in varying contexts before any additional new units are added. This theory reflects her exposure at Harvard to the lectures of Professors Bruner and Miller.

At first she tried out such sentences as "O, I am so ill." She found that it was necessary to limit the number of vowels used at first, since vowels have many sounds. It was decided that the short ă and the "oo" sounds would be used first. She describes her first efforts: "I told Jonny that, when two big round o's get together, they look at each other and say 'oo!', and I taught him the short ă as in 'cat'. Then I figured out sentences—A kangaroo has a hoola hoop. A rat and a fat raccoon. Dad has a bamboo hat. Can I pat a baboon?"

Time magazine reported in its March 8, 1963 issue that, "When Jonny breezed through the 23-page *At a Zoo*, his delighted father paid for printing several hundred copies and launched Heni Wenkart as a publisher. Her 85¢ paperback sold out fast at the Harvard Co-op, which re-ordered and sold out again. Sensing a phonetic gold mine, Author Wenkart wrote *The Man in the Moon* . . . and three subsequent Wenkart primers."

At first the books sold rapidly to private schools and to parents who were interested in helping their children with beginning reading. It is reported that public schools are now using quantities of them, and that Head Start programs and other reading centers dealing with culturally-disadvantaged children are finding them helpful. It is reported that more than 200,000 copies have been sold in the brief time that they have been commercially available.

Materials and Method

The Wenkart approach to beginning reading begins with the workbook, *The Letters, One by One*. There are no pictures on the pages of the workbook. As each consonant is introduced, it is used in both initial and final positions. This is done, according to the originator of the system, "so that it is not blocked into any one position in the child's mind."

The consonants are practiced in conjunction with two main phonemes: short *a* and *oo*. It is explained that "These are selected because of their distinctness and simplicity—and because they make words that are FUN TO SAY."

The method of teaching *The Letters, One by One* is prescribed on the inside covers of the workbook:

1. When there is a new letter at the top of a page, teach its sound very carefully. Then have the child *read* you all words and phrases. DO NOT READ TO HIM from this workbook, or he will not come to realize that he could have read it on his own.
2. *Important* — "b" DOES NOT SAY "buh"! Tell the children: "Consonants, like *b*, do not make much of a sound of their own. The *b* will not say anything by itself, but when it meets an "oo" sound, it will say to it, "boo!"
3. Be sure that the children are gliding smoothly from one sound to the next. Be sure they do not make a stop between the *m* and the *o* in *mo*, for example.
4. *The vowels.* Tell the children that when a vowel stands alone, it always introduces itself and says its own name. Then teach the short sound of *a*, also—*a* as in *cat*. Tell them that an *a*, followed by a consonant, will make this sound. Tell them that when two round *o*'s get together, they look at each other and say, "oo!"

5. When a word is too long to be read comfortably, teach the children to begin by covering up all but the first syllable, and reading a syllable at a time until they are familiar with the word.

6. After a child has read you the line at the top of the page, have him copy it on the lines beneath, two or three times, PRONOUNCING EACH WORD AS HE WRITES. It makes the new learning stick better: to see it with your eyes, and say it with your mouth, hear it with your ears, and write it with your hand, all at the same time. BE SURE HE PRONOUNCES AS HE WRITES.

7. Be sure he leaves the bottom few lines blank, and begin each lesson by having him fill in one line on each page for review, pronouncing as he goes. Mix up the order of the review pages a bit, so as to be sure that he is not writing and pronouncing from rote memory—but is really reading each page.

8. Your faster groups will be able to attack several new pages in each lesson. Some groups will master only one new page a day. But no matter what the speed, progress will be steady if these simple directions are followed thoroughly.

The originator, who publishes under the name of Heni Wenkart, states that the workbooks must be taught to groups small enough for a teacher to be able to hear and observe the on-going work of each child.

When the children have learned the consonants and the first two vowel phonemes (ă and oo), they read the first little paperback, At a Zoo. The sentences in this first paperback are fanciful and are not the usual language of children. Neither are they the limited three-letter words of the linguistics-phonemics approach. On the other hand, they do represent an attempt to limit the vocabulary to words in which there are only two regular phonemes: the short ă and the oo. No attempt is made to control the number or regularity of consonants and consonant digraphs. The result is a vocabulary that includes such words as asks, Jack, black, pants, Frank's, cab, Dan's, raccoon, kangaroo, crabs, and others. A linguistics scientist would probably be shocked with the linguistics task which is involved in dealing with such a jumble of irregular consonant sounds. For example, the hard k sound is found in the word, raccoon, represented by "cc"; in Kangaroo, represented by "k"; in crabs, represented by "c", and in black, represented by "ck". Similarly, other phonemes having irregular grapheme representations are included with no apparent training accompanying their use.

This would disturb many teachers, reading specialists, and linguistics scientists. It is justified in the Wenkart approach on the theory that these are just readers, and are for practice primarily for establishing the short ă and oo sounds.

The next step is to introduce the short ĭ sound and the article, the.

The bat and Bill

will zoom at the moon.

Oops—it zooms in loops!

3

Fig. 6–11   Reproduced from the Wenkart Phonic Readers *by permission of Heni Wenkart, publisher.*

With these two new elements, it is claimed that the child can then read the next paperback, *The Man in the Moon.*

As soon as the child learns the short $\breve{u}$, he is given *Fun at Camp. Get Off the Desk* is the fourth booklet and adds the short *e* and short *o* sounds. *The Big Puppet Mix-Up* adds the long vowels which are controlled by the silent "final–*e*" rule.

As a response to requests from teachers, workbooks to accompany the little readers are now available. The author of the series is also working on new booklets which will utilize the *or*, *er*, and *ir* sound and the *aw*, *ow*, and *ew* sound.

Each booklet is a short 24-page pamphlet, and each is printed with cover and interior pages in a distinctive pastel color. The pictures, like the story lines, are imaginative and, consequently, they offer no clues to the meanings of the words.

Ask a Daffodil, the newest book in the series, is a 40-page poetry book by Adele Seronde, with full-color pictures by the author. It introduces most of the remaining regular vowel phonemes, repeating them in rhythmic poetic context.

The Wenkart Publishing Company also markets a 12-inch LP record which was designed to help parents know how to go about teaching their pre-school child. This amusing recording gives instructions, interspersed with a lesson utilizing Jonny's younger sister. The record is appropriately called *Teaching Jonny's Sister to Read*. In addition to being used as a parent-training device, the record also has been used as a teacher-training tool in private schools and Head Start programs where young women without adequate teacher training have been employed.

Research Findings

No controlled definitive research has been attempted on the *Wenkart Phonic Readers*. Moreover, it is doubtful if any would be appropriate, for too many other variables would be operating to permit factoring out the effect of the Wenkart method and materials upon total reading achievement.

Obviously, the purpose of the *Readers* is to aid parents in helping their pre-schoolers to become readers when and if the children display "readiness" for formal training. Whether it is the content, the method, or the one-to-one relationship of parent to child that causes the success would be difficult, if not impossible, to determine. Moreover, it is likely that success with pre-school children in such Readers depends upon another important and related characteristic, namely high intelligence. Child-centered intrinsic motivation and/or parent-centered extrinsic motivation may also be factors which defy statistical analysis.

One's first impression of the *Wenkart Phonics Readers* is that they represent a home-made, naive attempt to market a few little insignificant booklets which were devised by some mother for her son, Jonny.

Upon closer inspection, it is obvious that, although this may be partially true, the booklets do have some phonemic regularity in their content—especially in control of vocabulary within the pattern of short vowel sounds. The story lines are clever; so clever, in fact, that it appears to this reviewer than none but children with high intelligence and concerned parents would "get" the full benefit of such sophisticated lines.

Much of the "method" described in the pre-reading workbook leaves much to be filled in by knowledgeable teachers. It is, therefore, doubtful if parents could bridge the gaps in instruction entirely by use of the *Wenkart Readers* and the directions contained in the workbook. It is believed that those who do use the readers successfully must employ either previously-learned educational techniques or that they are dealing with children of superior ability who would be able to abstract many of the principles of pronunciation by themselves if given equal attention and materials.

LISTEN   LOOK   LEARN

Origins

The *Listen Look Learn* (LLL) approach to beginning reading is an extension of materials and equipment which have been marketed for twenty years by the Educational Developmental Laboratories of Huntington, Long Island. In turn, the original EDL materials and machines were an outgrowth of pioneer work in perception and learning done many years ago by Dr. Earl A. Taylor. In the 1930's Dr. Taylor attempted to develop some means of controlled reading through projection machines.

Later, his work was extended by Stanford E. Taylor, who formed the Educational Developmental Laboratories (EDL) to market the products. Controlled Reader films and projector constituted one of the main segments of EDL offerings. Tachistoscopic lessons were developed and marketed. The machine used for projecting the tachistoscopic work was called the Tach-X.

In 1965, EDL developed another dimension in what it called Aud-X which provided lessons combining visual presentation and the accompanying auditory narration and directions.

The capabilities of the three instruments were then combined and a program was written to integrate them into a listening, seeing, hearing approach to beginning reading. To this was added a writing phase, experience charts, and finally independent reading. The entire program is now known as LLL (*Listen Look Learn*).

During the two years, 1965–1967, when the LLL program was being researched and revised, the Educational Developmental Laboratories became a division of McGraw-Hill.

Materials and Method

The LLL program is referred to by its promoters as a multi-media approach, to be used as a total language arts approach to beginning reading.

Readiness lessons on colored filmstrips and accompanying workbooks provide whole-class, small-group, and/or individual instruction in beginning sounds and beginning letters. These are projected through the Aud-X for both sight and sound.

In the pre-reading period of three lessons, 24 words are taught as sight vocabulary. In the next eight lessons, the Aud-X provides sight and sound stories.

Skill building in word recognition and fluency of reading is provided through the Tach-X and the Controlled Reader films. The Flash-X trains most students to see words flashed at 1/100 second exposures. Individual work with hand tachistoscopes, called Flash-X, provides reinforcement and motivation.

The stories on the Controlled Reader are printed on film with four words per line. A workbook study guide is provided for each child. It supplies background for the story, vocabulary and questions for preview, and ten test questions for post viewing comprehension check. By means of the Controlled Reader, speed and fluency can be significantly increased.

The LLL program also provides for guided individualized reading opportunities starting with small paperbacks and progressing into larger paperbacks and finally into hard-cover books and anthologies, assembled into the "Carousel Library."

Individual growth in beginning reading is said to be possible through the flexibility of the machines and materials of the *Listen   Look   Learn* total language arts approach to beginning reading.

Research Findings

The Educational Developmental Laboratories conducted an extensive two-year research study during the formative and revision period, 1965–1967, in which the LLL materials and procedures were being revised. The study involved 1917 First Grade children in 82 classes in eleven states. High, medium and low socio-economic levels were represented. The experimental group was composed of 917 children in 40 classes and the control group contained 1000 children in 42 classes. Various tests indicated no significant differences between the control and experimental populations.

The results[16] of the research study are available through the Research Department of EDL. In 1966–67 twenty-one experimental and twenty-five control classes were tested on *Metropolitan Achievement Tests*, Primary 1 Battery. On the Word Knowledge sub test, LLL experimental groups had a mean score of 25.45 while the control group had 24.11. The t-test showed a significant difference at the 5 percent level.

On the Word Discrimination sub test, the mean scores were 25.92 for LLL and 24.70 for control; again significant at the 5 percent level.

In the Reading Test, the LLL mean was 27.27 and the control was 25.23, scores significant at the 1 percent level.

There was no significant difference between control or experimental groups containing children with low I.Q. and low readiness scores.

CONCLUSIONS

Eight approaches to beginning reading have been presented under the "total" language-arts category. The characteristic common to all of them is the emphasis on several or all of the components of the language arts.

Inasmuch as they are basically phonemic approaches, they could have been included in Chapter 4 as phonemics-reading approaches. They are more than that. They all place major emphasis on pronunciation and listening. Several specify writing as the prerequisite for reading.

No doubt some educators will reject the use of the term "total" language-arts, inasmuch as the emphasis on *each* of the language arts may not be of equal intensity. "Total" language arts implies that communication is more than decoding or encoding. It is in this total global concept that these approaches should be viewed. They all recognize that the total act of reading is more than memorizing grapheme-phoneme relationships, synthetic phonics, phonemic rules, or structured linguistics-phonemics.

The fact that these eight approaches are categorized under this chapter heading does not mean that they are alike. On the contrary, they have more differences than similarities. The Carden approach and *Pro-*

---

16. Heflin, Virginia B., and Scheier, Elaine, *The Formative Period of Listen Look Learn, a Multi-Media Communications Skills System*, Research and Information Bulletin No. 10, Huntington, N.Y.: Educational Developmental Laboratories, February, 1968.

Reading are related in method, but the materials are the antithesis of each other. *Open Court* materials and the *McQueen Integrated Phonics* reveal many similarities, making them the most closely related of all eight approaches. The *Writing Road to Reading* with its 70 phonograms and 28 encoding rules is unequalled by any of the others for rigidity and structure. The *Listen Look Learn* approach is a hybred resulting from previously-used materials and hardware marketed by EDL and, therefore, is an audiovisual machine-based approach. The *Mott* materials and method are directed toward illiterate adults. The *Wenkart Phonics Readers* were designed as one-to-one parent-child materials.

The *Open Court* and McQueen materials are visually attractive. The Carden books are purposely unattractive. The Mott workbooks are similar to programmed materials. The little *Pro-Reading* and Wenkart booklets cannot be classified as major works. Strangest of all is the fact that Spalding is marketing no student or classroom materials whatever: it merely provides a book that serves as a methods handbook for parents and/or teachers.

Until new research and demonstration convinces us to the contrary, statistics and personal observation indicate that the Spalding approach described in *The Writing Road to Reading* produces remarkable results. This seems illogical, since the method would appear to be boring and deadly. The intonation of rules and rules and rules, and the mass recitation of the 70 phonograms are contrary to accepted cognitive learning practices. The results, however, speak for themselves.

BIBLIOGRAPHY

ABBOTT, JAN *Study of Two Methods of Teaching Phonics in the Second Grade Classrooms of South School, Casa Grande, Arizona.* Tempe: Arizona State University, unpublished doctoral dissertation.

AYRES, LEONARD P., *Measuring Scale for Ability in Spelling.* Princeton, N.J.: Educational Testing Service, 19.

BESTOR, ARTHUR E., *Educational Wastelands.* Urbana: University of Illinois Press, 1953.

ANNUNCIATA, SISTER MARY, "Report: Open Court Basic Readers, *We Can Read*," La Salle, Illinois: Open Court Publishing Co., (Mimeographed).

This section of Sister Annunciata's report is a testimonial to the effectiveness of Mrs. McQueen's *We Can Read*, obviously done when *We Can Read* was the first book of the Open Court series.

CARDEN, MAE, *The Carden Method.* Glen Rock, New Jersey: Mae Carden, Inc., 1947.

CARROLL, JOHN B., A *Linguistic Evaluation of a Phonic Method For Teaching Elementary Reading.* Berkeley: Board of Education, (Mimeographed).

A report by Dr. Carroll of Harvard who was retained as a consultant to analyze the *Carden Method* from a "linguistic" point of view.

GURREN, LOUISE, and HUGHES, ANN, "Intensive Phonics vs. Gradual Phonics in Beginning Reading: A Review," *Journal of Educational Research*, 58 (April, 1965) 339–347.

HUGHES, ANN, and THOMAS, NELLIE, *First-Year Report on the Hegeler Project Reading Study*. La Salle, Illinois: The Hegeler Foundation, 1966.

MOSS, RUTH, "The Battle to Make Words Behave." Magazine Section, *Chicago Tribune*. July 19, 1964 and July 26, 1964.

SPALDING, ROMALDA B., and SPALDING, WALTER T., *The Writing Road to Reading*. New York: Whiteside, Inc., 1962.

WALCUTT, CHARLES C., (Ed.), *Tomorrow's Illiterates*. Boston: Little, Brown and Co., 1961.

A small volume sponsored by the Council for Basic Education, containing five chapters contributed by authors who reject the traditional basal reader approach, plus a beginning and a concluding chapter by Dr. Walcutt.

QUESTIONS AND ACTIVITIES FOR DISCUSSION AND GROWTH

1. Compare the 28 encoding rules in *The Writing Road to Reading* with the rules in *Breaking the Sound Barrier* (Chapter 3). What elements do they have in common? Are any contradictory?

2. Outline what would be a complete "total" language-arts approach to beginning reading.

3. Using the outline written for question two above, make a chart including all eight approaches described here and check off the elements that each has.

4. After a close analysis of Miss Carden's methods, try to determine why some educators are critical of her approach. Are they justified?

5. What elements of method are common to Miss Carden's approach and Mrs. Stump's approach (*Pro-Reading*)?

6. Examine the statistics presented on *The Writing Road to Reading* approach. Do they support or refute the frequent statement that "it isn't the method or materials that make the difference; it is the teacher"?

7. Why is it difficult to compare statistics presented as "grade equivalents" with mean scores and significant differences?

8. What elements in the Mott materials could be adapted for use with six-year-olds?

9. Practice one lesson for teaching some of the phonograms in the Spalding method and demonstrate it to the class. Note their reactions.

10. Practice one lesson based on Miss Carden's enunciation and "musical language" emphasis and present it to the class. Note their reactions.

LANGUAGE-EXPERIENCE
APPROACHES

7

It has been contended for many years that the language of the basal reader is far from the normal language of children. In spite of this apparent fact, new basal readers have tended to copy the format of the very ones which have for so long been criticized.

The reason, of course, is quite clear. The basal reader approach is, essentially, a whole word approach to beginning reading. As such, it is destined to rely upon the psychological principle of repeated exposure for memorization of the sight words. Moreover, sight words in any basal reader series must be limited in number in order to permit ten or fifteen repetitions of each new word.

The resultant story line from such limited sight vocabulary is the notorious

> Oh, Oh, look, look!
> See Tom run.
> Tom runs.
> See Tom run fast.

or something similar; just as unrealistic; and, perhaps, just as insulting to the child's intelligence.

As a result of dissatisfaction with such basal reader material, a few individuals have attempted to develop approaches to beginning reading which would utilize the realistic language of six-year-old and seven-year-old children.

There are at least two ways of doing this. One is to write a basal series in which the true speech of children is substituted for the stilted speech of the old basal readers. A second way would be to let the learners write the material themselves by dictating stories in their own speech patterns and with their own vocabulary.

In either case, the objective is to provide an approach to reading that is basically a whole word approach, at the same time utilizing the vocabulary and speech patterns of normal children.

The vocabulary and speech patterns of children vary, of course, according to regional and environmental differences. Although there would certainly be some common elements, any book or approach to beginning reading that undertook a language-experience approach would be faced with the task of discovering those commonalties. To do this would be a major research project, but it would have to be done if the essentials for such an approach were to be discovered.

A language-experience approach, therefore, is one in which the common language patterns and vocabulary would be the words and phrasing common to a cross-section of American children, or else it would have to be limited to a particular type of reader: the ghetto child, the suburbia child, the black, the Mexican-American, the Oriental-American, the Hawaiian, or any mixture or combination. The latter, of course, would be an ideal in terms of the philosophy of the language-experience approach, but it would probably be unacceptable even to the groups for which it might be designed. This needs to be researched.

Moreover, publishers would be reluctant to risk the costs for developing such specific and limited materials.

The middle-of-the-road language-experience approach would attempt to identify three factors: the common experiences of the "norm"; the common vocabulary of the "norm"; and the common language patterns of the "norm". Then, depending upon the intentions of author and publisher, any language-experience basal reader would either attempt to reach the broad middle group of children, or would specialize in the experiences and situations to a particular ethnic, geographic, cultural, and/or racial group.

A language-experience approach that would utilize the alternative of allowing the children to write or dictate their own actual or imaginative experiences would, of course, be faced with the necessity of being more individualized and more related to a particular ethnic, geographic, cultural, and racial group of children than any other approach to reading. It would, indeed, reach the children "where they are".

As with its counterpart, "individualized reading", (see Chapter 9) the demands of such an approach would be great. More of the teacher's time would be spent in a one-to-one relationship with each child. Masterful teaching would have to depend upon the creativity of both child and teacher, with tremendous resourcefulness called for in place of purchased pre-written materials.

The result, however, would certainly utilize many of the principles of learning so lacking in many other approaches to reading: individualized; related to individual self-concepts; significant to the real needs of each child; written in the experiential context of each child, thus utilizing his past experiences; highly meaningful; fewer repetitions needed, inasmuch as the language is his own language; unitary, or whole-learning, rather than fragmented bit-by-bit increments of vocabulary artificially strung together.

It is possible that a teacher could employ a combination of the two methods in a language-experience approach. The best of the language-experience basal reader could, thus, be supplemented by the individual dictated experience stories of the children. In no instances, however, should the latter be correlated to an ordinary basal reader, for to do so would be to violate the basic rationale of the language-experience approach by imposing a stilted and imaginary experience and language upon the children.

A language-experience basal reader would, however, have to utilize the principle of repetition through successive exposure to the same word to ensure learning. Experiments in learning, however, indicate that mere repeated exposure does not ensure learning. To rote repetition must be added the factor of concentration and the factor of meaningfulness. The latter accounts for the advantage claimed for the language-experience type of basal reader. Meaningfulness related to the actual experiences of children, and clothed in the realistic language of the child who is reading the material provides the optimum conditions for learning through a whole-word approach. Consequently the number of repetitions necessary for whole-word learning through the language-experience approach are significantly smaller, and the extent of vocabulary acquired through the language-experience approach is far greater than the limited vocabulary of the ordinary basal-reader approach to beginning reading.

Any language-experience approach to beginning reading would have to admit to the need for outside aid in teaching word-analysis techniques. Special instruction would have to be planned for phonemic training, structural analysis, and perceptual skills. Just as in the case of individualized reading (Chapter 9), part of the reading program would be planned for individual, small-group, and whole-class instruction.

Within the language-experience materials, themselves, are to be found the very best contextual clues. Hence, so-called "contextual analysis" becomes so integrated with the situations and with the language that it is caught rather than being taught.

The language-experience approach to beginning reading is just at its beginning, but it is intrinsically an effective means of providing a whole-word method in keeping with the experiential background, the language patterns, and the self image of each individual child.

LANGUAGE EXPERIENCES IN READING

Origins

Language Experiences in Reading is a series of pupil and teacher materials which are the outgrowth of the work of a number of educators over a period of years. The authors of the materials are Van and Claryce Allen. Dr. and Mrs. Allen have been engaged in developing the materials for a number of years, but only recently has the formalized approach to beginning reading been available in published form. The materials in the form of *Pupil Books* and looseleaf *Teacher's Resource Books* are published by Encyclopaedia Britannica, Inc.

The contribution of *Language Experiences in Reading* as an approach to beginning reading is that it implements a program of language development which does not separate reading from the development of other communication skills such as listening, speaking, writing, and spelling.

The need for materials became apparent to Dr. Allen as he moved from a position as classroom teacher in an elementary school in Canyon, Texas in the early 1940's to research in reading in the Austin Public Schools while working on the doctorate. Later he served as Director of Elementary Teacher Education at Southern Methodist University, and Director of Instruction at Harlingien, Texas. From there he was invited in 1955 to join the staff of the San Diego County Schools as Director of Curriculum Coordination, and for the next eight years he remained there. In 1963, he moved to his present position as Professor of Education at the University of Arizona.

All during those years, Dr. Allen was searching—as many do—for the "best" method of teaching reading. He refers to his efforts as "searching" rather than "researching". He explained his sequence of "searching" in an address to the Conference on Beginning Reading Instruction which was sponsored by the U. S. Office of Education in Washington in November, 1962. At that time, Dr. Allen stated, "We heard of methods and materials that were 'sure cures' . . . . some quick and easy remedies. . . We listened to proposals. . . But we were not satisfied with what we found and continued our search until we found, to our amazement, that the basic source of all reading is productive thinking which is most readily and easily communicated in the form of speech."[1]

The work with the large number of children in the schools of San Diego County gave Dr. Allen an opportunity to try out on a large scale some of the materials and the method which he and his teachers had been working with in Texas. His materials and method became known as the "language-experience" approach, and were tested along with the traditional basal reader approach and the "individualized reading" approach.

In October, 1960, the first report of the results of the San Diego County Reading Study Project appeared in a brief statement in *Elementary English*. From that time on, interests in the work of Dr. and Mrs. Allen has multiplied, and encouragement for having their materials published caused them to reassess their involvement at San Diego compared with the contributions that might be made nationally. Consequently, Dr. Allen moved to a professorship at University of Arizona, permitting him and his wife, Claryce, to devote much time to preparing the materials for publication. The materials carry 1966 and 1967 copyright dates.

Materials and Method

The language-experience approach uses the language and thinking of individual children as the basis for skill development. As each child matures, he thinks of reading in a rationale which has been outlined by Dr. Allen, the originator of the materials, as follows:

1. What I think about, I can talk about.
2. What I say, I can write (or someone can write for me).
3. What I can write, I can read (and others can read, too).
4. I can read what I have written, and I can also read what other people have written for me to read.[2]

The child uses the words he wants to say and to read, and then sees those words printed on paper for him to read and to copy and to read again. The words are *his* words. They are the words of his language and of his experiences; not the contrived vocabulary of a basal reader.

Inasmuch as children vary greatly in the fluency of their oral language—some recognizing as many as 20,000 spoken words in meaningful context—it is to be expected that any program utilizing the real

---

1. Allen, R. Van, Comments at the U.S. Office of Education "Conference on Beginning Reading Instruction," Washington, D.C., November, 1962.
2. Allen, R. Van and Halvorsen, Gladys C., "The Language Experience Approach to Reading Instruction," *Contributions in Reading*. Boston: Ginn and Co., 1961.

language of children would have to allow for extremes of individual differences. Similarly, the breadth and depth of children's experiential backgrounds would also necessitate a wide range of latitude in individual differences.

Moreover, some children speak a home and community language which is clear in meaning and interesting to other children and adults in their own environment, but which is not considered standard English in the schools. Since their speech is considered normal in their homes and communities, those children are oblivious to their language deficiencies and are happy and productive at school as long as they are accepted and wanted. Most of them are eager to paint pictures, play games, and dictate stories which the teacher can edit by comparing her own language with that of the children. A language-experience approach insists that those children *not* be branded as "problems" before they have had a chance to experience and explore a rich, meaningful language at school over an extended period of time.

The language and experiences of children from homes where English is a second language must also be provided for in any all-school language-experience approach.

The ways in which the materials and method devised by Dr. and Mrs. Allen accomplish these needs may best be understood through some of the description of materials and classroom organization and procedure.

Language Experiences in Reading is not just a reproduction of procedures of developing the familiar *experience charts* which have been used by Kindergarten and First-Grade teachers for many years. The emphasis is on helping each child to acquire English words for the things he is learning, and to record his language *individually*.

A wide variety of "experiences" is suggested in teacher materials:

field trips for simple observations;
demonstrations, showing how things work;
films on many topics of interest;
listening to stories and poems every day;
talking about real experiences;
listening to recordings;
painting pictures to represent what the individual child sees or imagines;
singing songs and playing singing games;
sensory experiences: feeling things, smelling, tasting and imagining a
    world that has never before existed for the child.

The experience charts are, however, only one part of a larger approach to beginning reading.

Language Experiences in Reading is a program divided into two major parts:

the "continuing program" in which children are surrounded with a multitude of opportunities to hear, see, read, write, and experience stories.

the "pupil activities program" which is chiefly centered in the *Pupil Books.*

Levels I and II are arranged in six Units; comprising three large (12″ × 18″) *Pupil Books* for Level I and two *Pupil Books* for Level II. Level III is built on a foundation of five units with one comprehensive *Pupil Book.* The Unit topics in Level I are:

1. "I Learn to Read and Write"
2. "Growing Up"
3. "Magic Plastics"
4. "Sounds Around Us"
5. "Animals Everywhere"
6. "From Roller Skates to Rockets"

The first Unit of Level I involves six daily activities:

1. reading selections from children's literature to the class
2. easel painting of a child's experiences and/or printing stories that children dictate
3. printing dictation (from at least one child or from the class) on the chalkboard
4. taking time to discuss interesting topics *as they arise*
5. exploratory work with manuscript printing
6. developing sight vocabulary

The program in the *Pupil Book* starts with the children making simple crayon drawings on newsprint (12″ × 18″) the same size as their *Pupil Books.* After two or three "tries", each child makes a drawing on his *Pupil Book* page which is entitled "I Can Make Reading from Talk". As children finish their pictures, the teacher sits with a small group, who observe as she prints the words of the story that each child tells about his picture. Of necessity, the stories must be short. Usually two important points are extracted from their stories and are printed on the page by the teacher.

The large pages are perforated and are removed from the *Pupil Books* and assembled into group "books", with a construction paper cover and a group-selected "title". On the following day, the "book" is "read" by the same children in the group. The teacher helps them recall the stories for each picture, and helps children pick out words that they may know.

The program then expands into telling stories about pictures furnished by the teacher or some of the more spectacular "story pictures" that are available commercially. This activity is called, "I Can Read Pictures". The next step is for them to read words. Charts are made of words common in the environment, and children make books of words that they know. The next step is the learning of letter forms through the practice of straight lines and circles in manuscript writing. With letters, children learn to write their own names and the names of the teacher, principal and custodian.

As the children progress through Unit 1, they print and color and draw pictures on the pages and the pages are removed and folded into "books", which they later "re-read" individually or in groups.

Self expression is the major emphasis of all of the Units in Level I. Yet, there is considerable planned and formalized instruction as the class covers Units 2 through 6. Children will learn sight vocabulary, not through formal drill, but through continued usage, with the service words of the Dolch list and the Madden-Carlson Basic Word list being learned by most children by the end of the first year.

The "continuing program" is essential to the development of a program in which there is a balance of listening, drawing, speaking, reading and writing. Without it, the program is likely to become too structured. All through the six Units of Level I, the teacher reads stories and poems to the class, tells stories to children, and encourages children to become story tellers, themselves. The children paint pictures and tell and write stories about them. The children read their own and other children's stories. Lists are made of high frequency words, and children will refer to them for aid in spelling as they write. Topics of interest will be discussed in order to encourage oral expression. To supplement the writing practice in the *Pupil Books*, each room has a "writing center" with charts of words, letters, and letter and word games. Schools with money to expend on supplementary materials will add such things as films, filmstrips, and listening stations to encourage additional "experiences" for children.

The essentials of two sample lessons may serve to illustrate the way in which the method operates. "I Look at Myself" and "Making Friends" are the first two lessons in Unit 2 of Level I.

On page 1 of their "Growing Up" *Pupil Book* (Unit 2) the First Graders draw "self-portraits" of themselves. The teacher prints the word "See" on the chalkboard. Each child traces it on the sheet with his portrait and adds his own name. Small groups of eight or ten children gather around the teacher at a table and tell about themselves and about their self-portraits. The teacher records a sentence or two from each child. For example: "I am Deborah. I am skinny and tall and have short hair".

Fig. 7–1 *Reprinted from* Language Experiences in Reading, Teacher's Resource Book, *level I, by permission of Encyclopaedia Britannica Educational Corporation.*

The children are then given directed practice in looking for letters that are used over and over. They discover that they are not always used in the same word. From this, they are supposed to abstract the concept that our written language is made from letters that are interchangeable. Subsequently, they are helped to discover that the beginning of each word is a sound—and that it can be identified. They also discover the fact that, even tomorrow, the teacher can read words that they have said today . . that written language lasts.

The teacher then gives the children a chance to draw another picture, "Something About Me" in the space provided on the other half of the *Pupil Book* page. She then reads stories and poems about "Me" and about "growing up". The children complete the lesson in four or five days by drawing more pictures and dictating more stories and facts about themselves.

A similar type lesson is followed on page 2. The suggested time for "Making Friends" is three days. The lesson starts with read-aloud poetry about dog friends, and discussion on friends, and school friends. The teacher prints all the names of the children on the chalkboard.

The children then draw pictures showing the things they would like to do with friends (or pets). Sentence completion work is provided with incomplete sentences such as, "_____ and I like to _____."

Again the teacher calls together eight or ten children to discuss their drawings and to write the names of their friends and a sentence about their activities shown in the pictures. On the back of the *Pupil Book* page the children are asked to write the names of other friends. They copy these from the names on the chalkboard.

The sheets are then bound together and a title "Friends" is put on the covers. Additional stories about friends are found among the suggested additional activities in the *Teacher's Resource Book.*

All through the program, the intention is to aid children in abstracting the common elements of language and language structure. They "discover" through usage that we use the same letters over and over; that many words sound alike but are not spelled alike; that some words that sound alike have the same letters at the beginning or at the end; that there are pairs of words with opposite meanings; that the words *a* and *an* mean the same; and that when we hear a word, we can hear the sounds in the word that help us know how to spell it.

Later in the program (Unit 4) practice is given in consonant sounds, blends, vowels, flexibility in making sounds. In Unit 5, attention is given to spelling and an introduction to handwriting, with the children being encouraged to read an increasing number of easy stories, utilizing their whole-word knowledge, and attempting to utilize some of their phonemic knowledge. This unit also stresses the use of colorful and more picturesque language. Imagery is fostered through imaginative stories and poems read by the teacher.

Finally, children are introduced to such ideas as prefixes and suffixes, plural endings and past tense. In "From Roller Skates to Rockets" they learn many new words about forms of travel in various parts of the world. They hear stories and poems about travel in other parts of the world and in other times.

The purpose of *Language Experiences in Reading* is to lead the child into reading through the media of listening to poems and stories; expressing himself in pictures and in words and sentences; perceiving the relationship of words to each other in our language; perceiving the construction

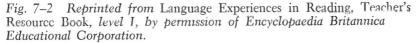

Fig. 7–2 Reprinted from Language Experiences in Reading, Teacher's Resource Book, *level I, by permission of Encyclopaedia Britannica Educational Corporation.*

of words by means of spelling and writing; and embellishing his spoken and written language by hearing and reading a wide variety of stories and poems by other authors. From the beginning the child becomes an author and illustrator of his own books, telling of his likes, needs, experiences, and interests. "As the children author their own books, they build interest and need to read many books from other authors". It is this last statement that best describes the objectives of this approach to beginning reading.

Research Findings

The authors of the Encyclopaedia Britannica LEIR program do not claim any definitive research statistics on their approach to beginning reading. In fact, Dr. Allen points out that the program is more the result of "search", rather than "research". The program has been in use rather extensively in certain schools in Texas, in San Diego County, and in other parts of California. A number of First Grade Studies in the USOE program of research in beginning reading attempted to "compare" the program with other approaches to beginning reading, but, unfortunately, the many variables and differences made adequate comparison impossible.

The language-experience approach was the subject of an extensive study conducted in the San Diego County schools during 1964–1965, the object of which was to determine whether or not it produced results that were significantly different than those obtained through the traditional basal reader approach. Teachers in the language-experience approach utilized daily blocks of 120 minutes. They were aided by Dr. R. Van Allen. Teachers in the traditional basal reader approach were aided by Dr. Mildred Dawson. There were 27 teachers in each group in 27 communities, with approximately 750 First Grade children in each group.

Among the various measures of achievement in the language arts were measures on the *Stanford Achievement Test*. Significant differences favoring the traditional method were found in scores made by boys in all socioeconomic groups on the paragraph meaning section, and by girls in the middle socioeconomic groups. There were no significant differences in word meaning, or in vocabulary. Boys from the low socioeconomic group showed significantly higher interest in reading after having been in the language-experience approach.[3]

Although the San Diego County staff has been developing the language-experience approach for a decade, this research study does not support the superiority of the language-experience approach to beginning reading.

There is no question that the *Language Experiences in Reading* program has elicited enthusiastic interest and a number of followers since its introduction commercially in 1966 and 1967. Even prior to that time, Dr. Allen was greatly in demand as a speaker explaining his new approach to beginning reading. A film[4] developed to explain the method has had wide circulation and has been viewed by thousands of teachers. Sound filmstrips explaining parts of the program have been produced by San Diego County.

It is too soon, however, to obtain reports of a statistical nature on the success of the commercial materials in First Grade classroom use. Indeed, it is doubtful if "pure" results could be obtained, for the program is designed specifically to be an approach to reading, utilizing many supplementary materials and a variety of stories from basal readers, as well.

Moreover, it would seem reasonable to expect that such a highly *unstructured* experiential approach would be subject to equally unpredictable improvisation by creative—and uncreative—teachers. Of all the ap-

---

3. Kendrick, William M. and Bennett, Clayton L., "A Comparative Study of Two First-Grade Language Arts Programs," *Reading Research Quarterly* II (Fall, 1966) 83–118.
4. Allen, R. Van, Lane, K. Boyd, and Halcomb, James F., *Reading—The Language-Experience Approach*. San Diego: La Mesa-Spring Valley School District, San Diego County Board of Education.

proaches to beginning reading, it is probable that this one will have the widest variations in its use and in the results. This may be one of its strong points, inasmuch as it permits great latitude for experienced and/or creative teachers. Moreover, and by the same token, it permits equally-wide ranges of individuality in pupil achievement.

It seems probable that the traditional basal-reader teacher will find *Language Experiences in Reading* an enigma. Where will she start with formal reading? How can one keep the class together? How does one group for instruction? How can one evaluate achievement? And a dozen more questions resist easy solution. Indeed, the *Teacher's Resource Books* are so different from the usual basal reader teacher's manuals that it is probable that many will need an orientation course to help them learn to use them effectively.

Many teachers prefer manuals that provide readily-found directions and sequences of standard classroom activities in reading. They will not find them in the huge *Resource Books* that are the core of the approach. Neither do the *Pupil Books* reflect the usual pattern of activities with which First Grade teachers are familiar. Somewhere in the program a teacher will have to find answers. This can only be done by reading the entire program or by seeing demonstrations and hearing the program explained.

Even after reading and/or demonstrations, the usual teacher may still be unconvinced that she could successfully teach beginning reading through such an unstructured program.

All this is one way of saying that *Language Experiences in Reading* is *not for the USUAL teacher*. If it be for anyone, it is for the unusual teacher; the teacher who, like the authors of the program, is "searching" for a means of capturing the real languages and experiences of children and utilizing them as the avenues to beginning reading.

THE CHANDLER READING PROGRAM*

Origins

Interest in the language and experience of children who live in urban settings has for more than a decade engaged the attention of a number of reading and child development specialists.[5] The Great Cities

---

* Formerly the *Chandler Language-Experience Readers*.

5. Edwards, Thomas, "The Language-Experience Attack on Cultural Deprivation," *The Reading Teacher*, 18 (April, 1964) 546–551.

Project[6] of the Ford Foundation and the Bank Street College of Education work[7] with urban children are counterparts of the series of books which are now published under the title, *The Chandler Reading Program.*

The series is based upon previous work by Dr. Lawrence Carrillo, Professor of Education at San Francisco State College. Working with him on the Chandler materials were two supervisors in the Ford Foundation's "Great Cities" project in San Francisco Mrs. Dolores M. Baugh and Mrs. Marjorie P. Pulsifer.

The objective of their separate and joint efforts has been to develop materials which would "reach" the culturally-different urban child. The assumption has been that the culturally-different urban child has a resultant pattern of different speech patterns and vocabulary, as well as certain specifically-different experiential backgrounds. This being true, it is apparent that most available reading materials are totally unrelated to those experiences and are, moreover, somewhat removed from the normal speech patterns of the individual child.

The starting point for the *Chandler Reading Program*, therefore, is "where the child is", and it can be easily claimed that this is one of the basic principles of learning.

To justify this position, the authors state:

> The textbook suburban Caucasian family has no analog in reality for millions of children. The drawings, while attractive, do not depict a life situation familiar to the urban child. The concepts presumed or developed are alien to many urban children, who do not have the middle-class background necessary for understanding them. The language is artificial and contrived, the conversations stilted and unnatural. Attaining the objective of meaning in reading is, therefore, difficult, if not impossible, with most of the materials currently available.

The beginning materials for the *Chandler Readers* were developed from tape recordings of the normal language patterns of the children for whom they are intended. The photographs, which replace the imaginative colored artwork of the usual basal readers, are photographs of actual children in actual urban situations.

To obtain such *Readers* was not as easy as instructing an artist

---

6. Wachner, Clarence W., "Detroit's Great Cities School Improvement Program in Language Arts," *Elementary English*, 41 (Nov. 1964) 734–742.
7. Bank Street College of Education, *The Bank Street Basal Reading Program*. New York: The Macmillan Co., 1965, 1966.

to compose a sketch to certain qualifications and including certain elements. Dr. Carrillo and his associates encountered many problems in addition to recording normal speech patterns. Hundreds of photographs had to be taken in order to obtain a very few that would satisfactorily illustrate a story sequence. The children selected had to be real inner-city children, and had to be typical of several ethnic groups. They had to be of an age equal to that of the children for whom each book is intended. Pre-primer and primer children had to be six-year-olds.

Once the children were selected, other problems arose in the development of the First-Grade program. Inasmuch as the children were usually from disadvantaged homes, it was necessary to purchase clothes for them to wear for the pictures. Indeed, two sets of clothing were purchased; one for picture taking day, and one for the washer. Play sequences had to be run through many times in order to obtain un-posed realistic photos. Story sequences had to be photographed before children went through "growth spurts" or lost teeth.

Dr. Carrillo relates that one of the stories in the book, *Let's See the Animals* ran into real trouble when the hippo, which was the main actor in the story, died suddenly. The shots all had to be done over with a "substitute" hippo.

Such attention to details was one of the requirements in developing the Chandler language-experience approach.

Unlike a number of other approaches to beginning reading, the Chandler books were carefully "field-tested" before going into final production. More than 1,500 experimental copies were printed and tried in regular classrooms in six major cities: Washington, D.C., Philadelphia, Pittsburgh, Cleveland, Milwaukee, and San Francisco. Comments and testimonials poured in, attesting to the effectiveness of the language-experience approach. Experienced teachers made suggesions for further extension and improvement, and changes were made.

The basic assumptions on which the program was developed were verified, namely, (1) that the stories do, in fact, depict the experiences that urban children have had, (2) that the pictures (in black and white) are of the multi-ethnic character to which city children can easily relate, and (3) the vocabulary and sentence patterns are appropriate for urban culturally-different children and do, in effect, provide realistic and factual conversation within the confines of their own recorded speech patterns.

The 1964 experimental edition was revised and published in its present form in 1965 and 1966, and is now marketed by Noble & Noble of New York.

Materials and Method

A carefully-structured reading readiness program has been developed as the first phase of the Chandler program. It begins with a teacher's manual developed by Dr. Carrillo, in which informal readiness activities are suggested. The book, *Informal Reading-Readiness Experiences* is actually a teacher's source book of good children's literature which may be read to pre-reading children, audio-visual aids for developing readiness, and diagrams and charts showing activities which the teacher (or parent) could use in aiding in the readiness period. The major focus is in informal and classroom readiness experiences tied to particular objectives.

Following the teacher's manual for readiness activities are three so-called "readiness" books. The first, *Pictures to Read*, is a portfolio of photographs for use with large groups or, indeed, with an entire class. The large, clear pictures are photographs of urban multi-ethnic children engaged in a number of city-activities, plus pictures of animals, city environments, etc., to provide stimuli for the oral and concept development of disadvantaged children.

Pictures to Read consists of 36 photographs 11½ × 15¼, and has a teacher's guide to accompany the portfolio.

Readiness Book 1, *Let's Look* is a usual-type workbook which hopefully will aid in developing readiness skills in discrimination of differences and likenesses, left-to-right progression, rhyming, and initial consonants. There are also a number of pads of worksheets in a set to accompany the workbook, *Let's Look*.

The teacher's guide provides detailed suggestions for introducing the work on the 32 pages of the workbook, as well as for additional related activities. Each day the children "read" the name on the cover of the book. They learn left-to-right progression by tracing through a maze (which, incidentally, goes not only left-to-right but in all directions as any good maze should). They look at a picture of a city scene and "read" the picture, identifying objects by name.

By page five, they are picking out pictures of objects, the names of which rhyme, i.e., *pan, can, house, bat, man.* Soon thereafter they are coloring with specific-colored crayons. At this point, one wonders whether or not the program might be used as a Kindergarten readiness program, which it appears to be, or that it could be a First Grade program predicated upon certain Kindergarten learnings.

Words to Read is the second book in the readiness program and is the first book that contains any words. It incorporates some of the features similar to those of the McKee-Harrison *Getting Ready to Read* program by having the teacher say a sentence, omitting the last word

which must be supplied by the children. In the *Words to Read* workbook, the children say the word and then select the picture that matches
that word. One such sentence is:

The boy said, "I will go for a ride on my (bicycle)." The children
look at the workbook page, select bicycle as the only word that can fit,
and circle the picture of the bike.

Gestalts, or word shapes, are presented for visual discrimination.
Thus, "I can look" is shown in large type, surrounded by dotted enclosures
which delineate the word-shapes. By this means, the child is encouraged
to associate word-shape as a visual clue in word identification. Experimentation with inner-city children showed that this was a feature which
aided many of them in word identification.

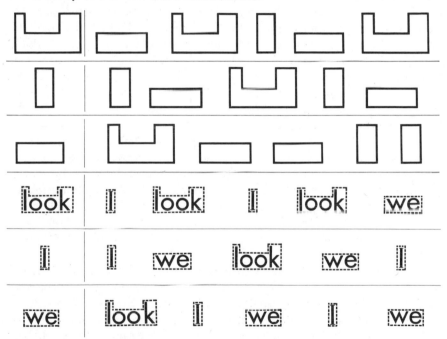

Fig. 7–3   Reprinted from the Chandler Reading Program, *copyright* © 1970
by Noble and Noble, Publishers Inc., and Materials for Today's Learning, Inc.

A great deal of cutting and pasting takes place within the workbook, after which the children finally arrive at words which are alike
and different, and words which appear printed in dotted-line print for
them to trace. Large printed word cards are also available to accompany
the workbook activities. Word "envelopes" are given to children, and
from their envelopes they select the words which match words in their

workbooks. The ten words taught in this book are found in any basal reader series.

The transition from the so-called "readiness workbooks" to the pre-primers brings the child into a direct relationship with what are called the "language-experience" features of the Chandler program. The paperbacks are titles: *Swings, Slides, Trucks and Cars to Ride, Bikes, Supermarket,* and *Let's Go!* Each of the 24-page paperbacks are printed offset with clear photographs and an increasing amount of reading materials as the series progresses.

The activities depicted in photograph and story lines in each booklet are suggested by the titles. It is assumed that these are the activities and "experiences" of urban children. Real inner-city children were selected by the authors of the series, and those children acted out the scenes which were photographed for the booklets. The authors refer to them as the "story children". The new clothes and new bikes which the Chandler team provided for their "story children" shine from the pages of the pre-primers in rather strong contrast to the everyday clothing and play equipment of the child in the "culturally-different" segments of most urban areas. This rather obvious incongruity apparently did not bother the authors.

The usual routine of teaching activities includes such things as chalkboard vocabulary development, pocket charts, word envelopes, listening activities with special emphasis on poems, phrase building by means of word cards, "framing" words, initial phonic elements, structural clues, and all of the other usual aspects of beginning reading in a basal series. The feature of the Chandler series that seems to be different from most others is the frequent use of the word-form gestalts in word identification practice.

Another exclusive feature which might escape the adult—but which is important to the child—is the use of a specially-prepared type-font identical to the manuscript printing used by most First Grade teachers.

The vocabulary is different from that of the usual basal series. It is this very point that is claimed to be one of its features. The vocabulary contains such words as *going, push, swing, bike, know, truck, watch, cart, store, milk, money, daddy,* and *hippopotamus.* It may be conceded that, if children can learn to identify words by the basal reader whole-word method, they may as well learn words such as mentioned above.

There is no linguistic control in the vocabulary and no pattern of phonemic regularity. Neither is there an effort made at providing the usual ten-or-more repetitions of words to "fix" them in the child's memory before proceeding to new words. This, too, is claimed as an advantage; for, it is pointed out by the authors, some children are able to

"Here is the milk.

Is this the milk you want?"

"I like this milk.

I'm going to get it.

Come on.

Let's go!"

12

Fig. 7–4 Reprinted from the Chandler Reading Program, *copyright © 1970 by Noble and Noble, Publishers Inc., and Materials for Today's Learning, Inc.*

learn a word upon one exposure because the word is in the child's own vocabulary and experience. Consequently, Dr. Carrillo has limited most repetitions to five to achieve the objective of his "language-experience" approach.

It should be observed that it is quite difficult to compare the spontaneous ideas of children as they are transcribed by a teacher onto experience charts with the contrived conversation of children which has been written to accompany the picture "experiences" in the *Readers*.

It is to be noted that, while the "story children" were being photographed, their conversation was being recorded on tapes. The ideas expressed by the story children were then edited into the story lines which appear in the Readers. A comparison of the language of the ordinary basal pre-primer and the *Language-Experience* pre-primers is interesting. A basal reader might read:

> Oh, look! Jump can ride.
> See Jump ride.
> Jump can ride fast.
> Ride fast, Jump.

The Chandler pre-primer reads:

> Push the swing.
> Push the swing high.
> Look how high we are!

Each contains about the same number of words. The Chandler lines are more natural, and an effort has been made to replace the usual basal reader's utilization of the activities of suburban children with the real-life activities of multiracial urban children on the playground, on the street, in the supermarket, and at the zoo.

Sets of word cards, alphabetical dividers, and five excellent technicolor films are available to complete the materials of the pre-primer phase of the series.

The primer is the hardback, *Let's See the Animals*, which really is a write-up of a field trip to the San Francisco Zoo. Similarly, *Let's Take a Trip* (the hard-back First Reader) is also organized around the theme of field trips around the neighborhood, to Marineland, to the library, and to road construction sites.

These books are excellent for use with *any* children who are in schools where field trips of this nature are a part of the curriculum. They provide the realism in reading which is necessary as preparation for such trips or as follow-up after such trips. Realism is the foremost objective of the *Chandler Reading Program*.

Accompanying those two hardbacks are more word cards; over twenty "concept" film loops; picture cards showing the "story-children" in their activities; worksheet pads, and teacher's guides. A poetry book and books for manuscript writing are recent additions to the first year program.

Research Findings

Nearly 2000 copies of the readiness materials, the pre-primers, and the primers were tried out in classrooms with inner-city children in cities across the country from Washington, D.C. and Philadelphia to San Francisco. The books and materials were furnished free to the school districts and no copies of these experimental editions were sold to anyone.

The reactions of the children, the problems of the teachers, the feelings of administrators, and the observations of supervisors were carefully compiled. On the basis of those extensive try-outs, many revisions were made. For example, the "Big Book of Pictures", which was spiral bound, did not survive classroom tests. It was found to be too cumbersome. The pictures now are packaged in "Picture Portfolios", which are more easily handled in the classroom and, also, are more flexible in their use.

Another mechanical change in production was made in the coverings of the books. It was supposed that smooth plastic covers would add life to the books and would permit easy wet-sponging of dirt marks. Although this was true, the slippery covers made the books too difficult to handle when stacked.

Citing the above examples is done to indicate the extent to which the author and publisher have responded to actual classroom tryouts of the books and materials. Naturally, many changes in content were made, and some of the stories and pictures had to be completely re-done.

The Chandler publishers indicate that many testimonials have been received from teachers who are using the Chandler approach to beginning reading. Dr. Carrillo has stated that teachers with whom he talks indicate that the black-and-white offset photographs engender much more identification by the children than can be achieved through a drawing.

Others who have reacted to the photographs have compared the posture, the clothes, and the situations of the "story children" as being highly artificial. Such critics point to the "new" clothes, "new" bikes, and uncluttered backgrounds of street, supermarket and homes as being utterly inconsistent with conditions known to the usual "culturally-different" urban child. In fact, one VISTA worker remarked that the children he knows in the urban slums "do not have bikes, let alone new ones", and "Who ever saw clean kids like that in a clean supermarket in the slums?" He quickly added, "In fact there aren't supermarkets like that in most slum areas."

Such criticisms may be significant and may eventually indicate further revisions of the Chandler materials. Moreover, it is difficult to accept the contrived story lines as being what is claimed to be the "real conversation of the children." Actually, the authors do not claim that it is the actual conversation which they taped. They merely claim that it reflects the ideas which the children expressed in their own cultural dialects and grammatical constructions. Obviously, it is not likely that publishers are ready to print the incorrect speech of slum children just to satisfy a desire for authenticity.

Photography, real-life story interest, and everyday vocabulary are features which, alone, may be enough to elicit the interest of culturally-different urban children and motivate them to the realm of reading. There are so many variables involved in working with culturally-different and culturally-disadvantaged children that it is extremely difficult to assess statistically the effect of one or two variables such as photographs and vocabulary without extremely limited and balanced research design.

Some so-called language-experience approaches utilize the "experience chart" medium for capturing the experiences and language of children. The experience chart which emerges from a field trip is a reflection of the ideas and suggestions of the children, subtly edited by the teacher. Many teachers do not feel adequate in handling such an approach. Others do not feel comfortable unless they have materials which are more nearly like the basal readers.

Except for the use of manuscript type-face, the encouraging of the language-experience approach, and the use of cultural and ethnic groups and situations in pictures, there is very little that could be called "culturally-different" in the basic reading skills as taught through the Chandler approach.

ORGANIC READING

Origins

Organic Reading is the name given to a most primitive method of teaching reading by Sylvia Ashton-Warner as found in her books *Spinster* and *Teacher*. Essentially, it is a method and an approach to beginning reading which Miss Ashton-Warner devised a number of years ago during her work with Maori children in her Infant Room in New Zealand. Her method and materials are most unassuming and unpretentious.

For twenty-four years Miss Ashton-Warner lived in the Infant Room with Maori children, and, after discovering the approach to their innermost needs and feelings, she then arranged to capture those needs and feelings as the heart of her *Organic Reading.*

Her novel *Spinster,* has been internationally hailed for its insights into teaching. The novel, *Teacher,* however, was written later and provides the diary entries of the day-to-day classroom experiences which are woven into the novel, *Spinster. Teacher,* therefore, is the un-retouched account of her work with her "Little Ones", as she calls her Maori children, and gives the reader an insight into the unique individualized approach to beginning reading which was so successful in forming the bridge between the actual language-experiences of Maori children and the middle-class books of the broader New Zealand culture.

Inasmuch as we are struggling with the same problems of bridging gaps between the disadvantaged and the norms of reading not only in America, but in other parts of the world, it seemed appropriate to include Sylvia Ashton-Warner's approach to beginning reading here even though she has nothing to sell except a lifetime of dedicated experiences and insight into an "Organic" approach to beginning reading.

Material and Method

The term "Organic Reading" is derived from the notion that it is related to the organism, itself. It is, to use psychological terms, "intrinsic" rather than "extrinsic". In this sense, then, "Organic" reading relies on the innermost thought-language of children contrasted with the awkward, unrealistic and stilted language of basal readers. For reading to be "organic", it must be related to *self,* to self needs, self concepts, and to self feelings.

The feelings of *fear* and *hate* proved to be the keys to the inner self of the Maori children. They live in a primitive culture in which fear and hate are still part of much of their experience, especially if, like those in Miss Ashton-Warner's Infant Room, they are of a disadvantaged and minority group. Rather than attempting to overlay the Maori culture with the veneer of middle-class British or American or New Zealand vocabulary and situations, the approach to reading should be through the feelings of love and fear and hate and the words which represent those feelings.

These are what Miss Ashton-Warner calls words with "intense meaning". And, because they have the intensity of being associated with internalized emotions, they are what she calls "one-look" words. They are, of course, deeply ingrained in the experiences and speech of each child who uses them. With such personalized attachment to the word and its meaning, the visual symbol for such a word is learned almost instantly.

Organic Reading utilizes words which Miss Ashton-Warner classifies as fear words and sex words. Under the fear words would be classified *frightened, cry, hit, ghost, mad, wild, fight, hate, growl, burn, die, drunk, hurt, sick, steal, lost*. The most important sex words would be *kiss, love, likes, me and you*, etc. The latter are the words which represent a good feeling about self and others.

The "Key Vocabulary" for each child is different and takes considerable time and patience in probing the depths of his inner being to discover it. By the same token, it is an intensely personal collection of words which need no "picture words" as cues. Indeed, each child carries his own mental imagery of the word. Moreover, many of the words are value judgments which under ordinary conditions would be adjectives and adverbs defying illustration on paper. But, from the experiences of each child springs the meaning to that child. The abstract nouns such as *love, hate, fear, fright, sick* also defy illustration on paper, but are representations of reality to the inner self.

Personalized vocabulary would also include those words which are a part of the everyday experiences of children; especially those words closely associated with TV programs with which they closely identify.

When an individual has acquired a "Key Vocabulary" he then can write his own stories in a true language-experience manner. The learning of the vocabulary is achieved through what Miss Ashton-Warner calls the "One-Look" cards. They are, actually, separate cards upon which the teacher has printed the "intense" "one-look" words. Each child tells what his word will be, after which the teacher prints it carefully on a card for him, and he may take it home as his own word when he has learned it.

It is reported in *Teacher* that children who spend four months on a set of words in the basal reader can learn an equally-large number of their *own* words in four minutes! Miss Ashton-Warner warns against the teaching of words which have no emotional significance as an introduction to reading; for, she writes, "They may teach him that words mean nothing and that reading is undesirable."

It would be correct to say that words which come from the usual basal reader are considered by Miss Ashton-Warner as being from the "outside", whereas words which come from the child's own language-experiences are from the "inside" . . . hence they are "organic".

Several other techniques are utilized in the learning of the "Key Vocabulary". The child watches the teacher print his own word. Together they say the word. He then traces it with his finger. They work in pairs, learning each other's words. The teacher mixes all their word-cards together in a pile and when they come in every morning there is a scramble to find their own words, thus utilizing visual memory and perceptual discrimination.

Each child has his own box in which he keeps his own word cards.

The originator of *Organic Reading* describes the individual child's words as "captions to the pictures in the mind." She admits that *Organic Reading* sounds difficult, but she claims that "it's the easiest way I have ever begun reading."

Vocabulary building is followed by writing. At first the children write their own words, but soon they want to write sentences. The sentences, like the "Key Vocabulary" are also "captions to the pictures in the mind". The sentences which the children write describe a situation which is very real to them. Invariably within each sentence is one of the key words already learned. The sentence describes the context in which the key word has meaning to the child. In this manner real experiences become labeled with sentences which are already a part of the child's language-experiences and thus become part of his reading.

The sentences are completely individualized just as were the one-look words. Each sentence represents a unitary language-experience. Several sentences together form a story which has intense meaning to the child. They are his words, his sentences, and his story. They are internalized . . . "organic".

At first the teacher helps them in writing their sentences, but soon they attain self-reliance and self-discipline and write their own stories with great creativity. Spelling and composition become an integral part of their writing, with reading as the outcome as well as the medium.

Sylvia Ashton-Warner says of their writing:

> The drama of these writings could never be captured in a bought book . . . no one book could ever hold the variety of subjects that appears collectively . . . each morning. Moreover, it is written in the language that they use themselves. These books they write are the most dramatic and pathetic and colorful things I've ever seen on pages. [8]

Research Findings

Sylvia Ashton-Warner has nothing to sell. Anyone who adopts her method must devise his own materials. And anyone who adopts her

---

8. Ashton-Warner, Sylvia, *Teacher*. New York: Simon and Schuster, 1963, p. 52.

method must adapt it and the materials to the particular situation and needs and experiences of the children with whom he is working.

Her book, *Teacher,* describes in detail how her method works and how the Maori children responded to it. It, moreover, carries the intrinsic possibility that here may be the discovery of a way to change the feelings of savage and primitive emotional responses into a homeostasis resulting in peace. Could this be done through *reading?*

Moreover, if Maori children in a school such as the Infant School of New Zealand can so earnestly capture vocabulary and learn to read through such a language-experience approach to beginning reading, is it not possible that the same principles, method and adapted materials would be successful with the children of our disadvantaged sub-cultures?

CONCLUSIONS

Many professional educators recognize the merits of a language-experience approach to beginning reading. Relatively few classroom teachers feel secure in such an unstructured one.

Although the three approaches described here are all language-experience approaches to beginning reading, the only factor shared by all three is their use of the experiences of children. Experiences, moreover, are never the same for any two children. The use of experiential background for reading is a worthy aim. However it may be achieved should be lauded.

The Chandler approach has structured the experiences in basal-reader style in an attempt to portray some of the normal experiences of inner-city children. The *Language Experiences in Reading* relies on the individual experiences of each child as a background for his writing and reading. The *Organic Reading* approach of Sylvia Ashton-Warner exploits the words that are expressive of feelings. All learning is based on past experience. This is the fundamental tenet of cognitive learning. The language-experience approach attempts to utilize that truth.

The three language-experience approaches attempt to capture the everyday language of children in totally different ways. The materials written by Dr. Carrillo contain story lines with language devised from conversation taped during the actual play of the "story children" with whom he worked. Similarly, the "organic" language used as the basis for Sylvia Ashton-Warner's approach is the vocabulary of words that represent the "intense" feelings of the Maori children whom she knew so well. The language that Dr. and Mrs. Allen rely on in their approach is the one dictated by the children in describing their own experiences. The dictated story lines are written by the teacher, later to be read by the children.

One should not expect an orderly progression of skill learning to be possible in a language-experience approach. The emphasis, on the contrary, is on meaningful involvement in the reading because of its relevance to the child who is reading it. The real experiences of children, expressed in their own words, constitute the core of the language-experience approach to beginning reading.

Questions and Activities for Discussion and Growth

1. Record the conversation of a group of children and list the vocabulary and expressions most common to their mode of expression. What do you observe?
2. Make a survey of the things that six-year-olds would *like to do* if their wishes could come true. How do those correspond with the children's activities in the usual basal reader stories?
3. How do the activities that children would prefer if they could have their wishes compare with those in the Chandler approach?
4. What activities in the Kindergarten readiness program could be considered as being language-experience reading activities?
5. Why are the usual "themes" assigned by teachers *not* language-experience-oriented?
6. If you were writing stories for a new basal reader series, what language-experience factors would you include? Be specific.
7. Make a list of the "organic" vocabulary that American children in disadvantaged areas would use. Compare this list with the words preferred by the Maori children as reported by Sylvia Ashton-Warner. What differences do you observe?
8. Is it possible to use Sylvia Ashton-Warner's approach with children from culturally advantaged homes in America? Give the reasons for your answer.
9. Why is insecurity the chief hinderance to the use of the language-experience approach to beginning reading?
10. How may a phonics program be used with the language-experience approach? Is one necessary?

BIBLIOGRAPHY

ALLEN, R. VAN, "Write Way to Reading: Language-Experience Approach," *Elementary English* 44: (May, 1967) 480–485.

ALLEN, R. VAN, and HALVORSEN, GLADYS C., "The Language Experience Approach to Reading Instruction," *Contributions in Reading.* Boston: Ginn and Co., 1961.

This has also been copied and paraphrased in a number of articles and speeches by and about Dr. Allen's language-experience approach.

ALLEN, R. VAN, LANE, K. BOYD, and HALCOMB, JAMES F., *Reading—The Language-Experience Approach*. San Diego: La Mesa-Spring Valley School District, San Diego County Board of Education.

This 16 mm. film provides a clear explanation of the techniques of the language-experience approach. It was photographed in unrehearsed classes in Kindergarten, First Grade, Second Grade, Third Grade and Sixth Grade.

ASHTON-WARNER, SYLVIA, *Teacher*. New York: Simon and Schuster, 1963.

Bank Street College of Education, *The Bank Street Basal Reading Program*. New York: The Macmillan Co., 1965, 1966.

EDWARDS, THOMAS, "The Language-Experience Attack on Cultural Deprivation," *The Reading Teacher*, 18 (April, 1964) 546–551.

HARRIS, ALBERT J., MORRISON, COLEMAN, SERWER, BLANCHE L., and GOLD, LAWRENCE, *A Continuation of the CRAFT Project Comparing Reading Approaches with Disadvantaged Urban Negro Children in Primary Grades, Final Report*. New York: Division of Teacher Education, the City University of New York, January, 1968.

HARRIS, ALBERT J., and SERWER, BLANCHE L., *Comparison of Reading Approaches in First-Grade Teaching with Disadvantaged Children*.

The Research Foundation of the City University of New York for the Division of Teacher Education, The City University of New York, 1966. The *CRAFT* Project is Cooperative Research Project No. 2677.

LEE, DORIS M., and ALLEN, R. VAN, *Learning to Read Through Experience*. New York: Appleton-Century-Crofts, 1963.

A 146-page paperback complete with visuals describing the language-experience approach.

KENDRICK, WILLIAM M., and BENNETT, CLAYTON L., "A Comparative Study of Two First-Grade Language Arts Programs," *Reading Research Quarterly* II (Fall, 1966) 83–118.

A comparison of the Language-Experience Approach vs. the traditional basal reader approach.

SPITZER, LILLIAN K., compiler, *Selected Materials on the Language-Experience Approach to Reading Instruction*. Newark, Del.: International Reading Association, 1967.

An annotated bibliography.

STAUFFER, RUSSELL G., "A Language Experience Approach," Chapter 7 in *First Grade Reading Programs*, Perspectives in Reading No. 5, Newark, Delaware: International Reading Association, 1965. 86–118.

This presents a good explanation of an experience chart type of Language-Experience approach.

——, *The Language-Experience Approach to the Teaching of Reading*. New York: Harper and Row, 1970.

——, *Teaching Reading as a Thinking Process*. New York: Harper and Row, 1969.

STRICKLAND, RUTH G., *The Language of Elementary School Children: Its Relationship to the Languages of Reading Textbooks and the Quality of Reading of Selected Children*. Bulletin, School of Education, Indiana University, 38: July, 1962.

VILSCEK, ELAINE C., "What Research Has Shown About the Language-Experience Program," A *Decade of Innovations: Approaches to Beginning Reading*, Newark, Delaware: International Reading Association, 1968, 9–23.

WACHNER, CLARENCE W., "Detroit's Great Cities School Improvement Program in Language Arts," *Elementary English*, 41 (Nov. 1964) 734–742.

ONE-TO-ONE SOUND-SYMBOL APPROACHES

8

A one-to-one sound-symbol approach to beginning reading is one in which one symbol has been devised to represent one and only one sound of our language.[1]

Inasmuch as there are reported to be some 40 to 45 basic sounds in our spoken language, systems that would be classified as "sound-symbol" approaches have invented additional symbols of some sort to augment our 26 letter alphabet. It is conceivable that certain letters could be altered slightly to represent their long and short sounds if they are vowels. Others could be altered to represent their whispered or voiced sounds if they are consonants. The letters of the alphabet might also be distorted to represent their use as silent letters. Additional letter-symbols could be invented to stand for blends and/or diphthongs.

Another approach to producing a one-to-one sound-symbol system is to devise a code of numbering that could be attached to parts of words or to letters and letter combinations. Such a code could indicate the consistent sounds which the numbered letters represent. The addition of numbers could take care of a majority of the irregularities of the language and could be used without altering the basic alphabet.

A third approach has been to add additional sensory clues in the form of color, texture, or shading. Such clues would be coded so that the phonemic irregularities of the language would be consistently represented by the elements of the code.

A less-acceptable, yet entirely possible, approach would be to adopt

---

1. See Chapter 3 "Artificial Orthographies," *Reading Instruction—Dimensions and Issues*, William K. Durr, editor, Boston: Houghton Mifln Co., 1967.

an entirely or partially new system of letters, thus constituting an entirely new alphabet.

Possibilities of solving the problem by using combinations of the four alternatives mentioned above also exist. It is predicted that the near future will bring an increasing number of proposals for codifying sound into written symbols. Moreover, the need for this becomes more critical daily as English becomes not only the world language of communication, but the encoding and decoding of the language becomes a part of the duties of many of our electronic devices for carrying on the business of the world and the technological research of the future. Indeed, the mere storage and retrieval of knowledge calls for a sound-symbol system that is consistent, phonemically reliable, and compatible.

i/t/a

Origins

The Initial Teaching Alphabet—popularly known as i/t/a—is the result of an amalgamation of earlier work done over the years by British advocates of the simplification of English spelling. The Initial Teaching Alphabet has essentially grown out of the efforts of Sir Isaac Pitman more than half a century ago in his efforts to apply a simplified short-hand method to the transcription of the sounds of English.

The Pitman method has enjoyed some considerable acceptance over the years. More recently, Sir James Pitman has promoted the concept of a simplified spelling of the English language . . . such simplification requiring the addition of eighteen new symbols which augment the alphabet from 26 letters to 44 letters. Thus, the early efforts at changing the orthography of English were known as the "Augmented Roman Alphabet."

It is not entirely clear whether the objective of Sir James was to change the entire printing of English by universal use of his "Augmented" alphabet or merely to provide a phonemically-regular sound-symbol system for translating the sounds of the language into printed and/or written symbols, with the possibility that those same symbols could regularly be translated back into the spoken sounds of English.

In any case, the Augmented Roman Alphabet was developed and publicized in England by the Pitman organization under the original title: "Initial Teaching Medium" (I.T.M.) beginning about 1960.

A long history of scholarship on sound-symbol relationships in the

English language lies behind the current interest in i/t/a. In the middle 1600s, a Southwark schoolmaster, Mr. Richard Hodges, published what he proclaimed as "The easiest and speediest way, both for the true spelling and reading of English, as also for the true writing thereof that ever was publically known to this day." His system utilized various pronunciation marks immediately above and below certain vowels and consonants, as shown on the reprint of the page from *The English Primrose*.

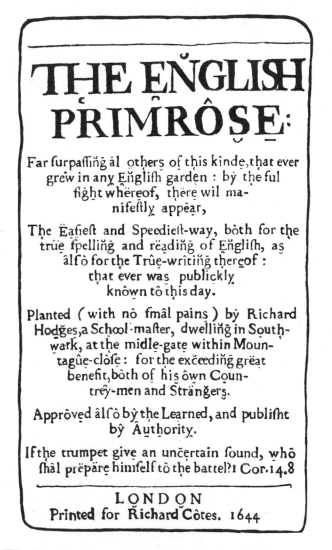

Fig. 8–1   "The English Primrose" by Richard Hodges 1644.

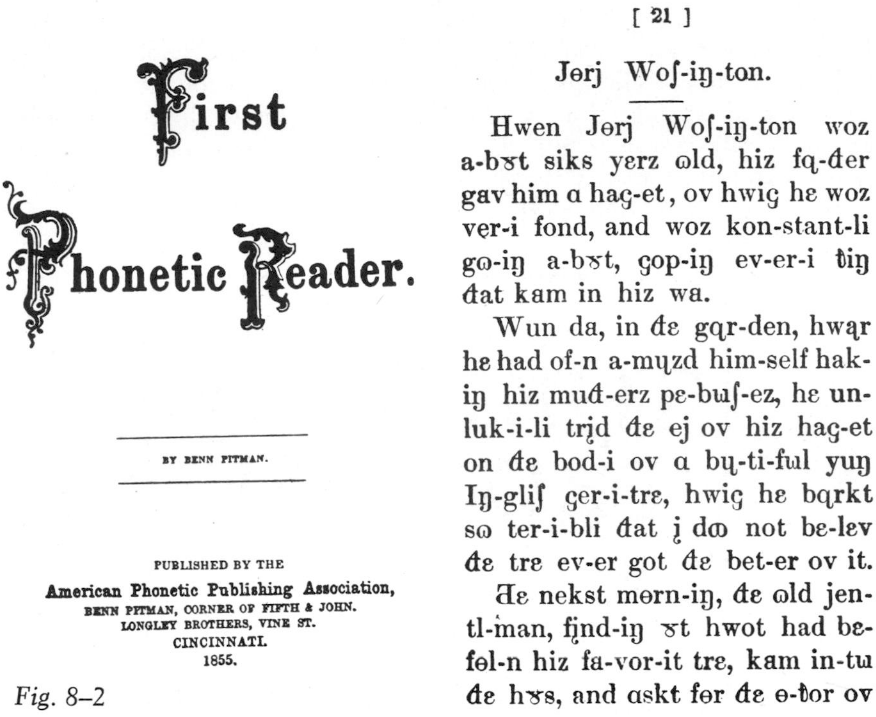

[21]

First Phonetic Reader.

BY BENN PITMAN.

PUBLISHED BY THE
American Phonetic Publishing Association,
BENN PITMAN, CORNER OF FIFTH & JOHN.
LONGLEY BROTHERS, VINE ST.
CINCINNATI.
1855.

Fig. 8–2

Jərj Woʃ-iŋ-ton.

Hwen Jərj Woʃ-iŋ-ton woz a-bʊt siks yɛrz ʊld, hiz fq-ɖer gav him ɑ haɕ-et, ov hwiɕ hɛ woz ver-i fond, and woz kon-stant-li gʊ-iŋ a-bʊt, ɕop-iŋ ev-er-i ƀiŋ ɖat kam in hiz wa.

Wun da, in ɖɛ gqr-den, hwɑr hɛ had of-n a-mʏzd him-self hak-iŋ hiz muɖ-erz pɛ-buʃ-ez, hɛ un-luk-i-li trjd ɖɛ ej ov hiz haɕ-et on ɖɛ bod-i ov ɑ bʏ-ti-fʉl yuŋ Iŋ-gliʃ ɕer-i-trɛ, hwiɕ hɛ bqrkt sʊ ter-i-bli ɖat j dɷ not bɛ-lɛv ɖɛ trɛ ev-er got ɖɛ bet-er ov it.

ɖɛ nekst mərn-iŋ, ɖe ʊld jen-tl-man, fjnd-iŋ ʊt hwot had bɛ-fəl-n hiz fa-vor-it trɛ, kam in-tʉ ɖɛ hʊs, and ɑskt fər ɖɛ ө-ƀor ov

A number of attempts at providing a phonemically-regular sound-symbol relationship always met with two possibilities: 1. a simplified spelling of English, or 2. an extension of symbols from the 26 letters of the alphabet to an alphabet of from 40 to 44 sound-symbols.

In the mid 1800s, a Benn Pitman of Cincinnati proposed a phonemic alphabet that combined simplified spelling and certain new symbolization, a reproduction of which is shown in the accompanying illustration. The utilization of a single grapheme to represent the *ng* sound in the *ing* syllable in a word is evident all through the Benn Pitman work.

At about the same time, Isaac Pitman, another schoolteacher and inventor of the Pitman system of shorthand, developed what he called "Fonotypy" which basically was a "rational" code for printing, writing, and reading the sounds of English. The example of *The Little Red Hen* set in Pitman's Fonotypy (1844) is shown. Note that it was all in capital letters with a number of strange symbols that bear little, if any, relationship to traditional orthography. When Pitman realized that the transition would be most difficult, he soon devised lower case letters. Never did Pitman concur with the spelling reformers of his day.

Fonotypy went through several stages of evolution in England and in the United States during the last half of the nineteenth century.

Fonotypy was tried with school children in Boston, and in Waltham, Massachusetts with very outstanding results but was dropped in Waltham five years later. A modification of Fonotypy was tried for twenty years in the St. Louis public schools during the superintendency of Dr. Harris. Superintendent Harris reported that one-and-one-half to two years could be saved by the use of the system.

Sir James Pitman's new Initial Teaching Medium (which is now known as "i/t/a") was developed from his grandfather's Fonotypy and

ᴧᴜ Lɪᴛɔʟ Rɛᴅ Hɛɴ

Wᴜɴs ᴜᴘᴏɴ ᴀ ᴛᴧᴍ ʟɪᴛɔʟ ʀɛᴅ Hɛɴ ʟɪᴠᴅ ɪɴ ᴀ ʙᴀʀɴ ᴡɪᴧ hᴜʀ fᴧᴠ ɛɪᴋs. ᴀ ᴘɪɢ, ᴀ ᴋᴧᴛ ᴧɴᴅ ᴀ ᴅᴜᴋ ᴍɛᴅ ᴧɛʀ hᴏᴍ ɪɴ ᴧᴜ sᴇᴍ ʙᴀʀɴ. fɛ ᴅᴇ ʟɪᴛɔʟ ʀɛᴅ Hɛɴ ʟɛᴅ hᴜʀ ɛɪᴋs ʊᴛ ᴛᴜ ʟᴜᴋ fᴏʀ fᴜᴅ. Bᴜᴛ ᴧᴜ ᴘɪɢ, ᴧᴜ ᴋᴧᴛ ᴧɴᴅ ᴧᴜ ᴅᴜᴋ ᴡᴜᴅ ɴᴏᴛ ʟᴜᴋ fᴏʀ fᴜᴅ.

Fig. 8–3

also makes use of some of the simplifications recommended for almost a century by the Simplified Spelling Society of Great Britain and by its American counterpart.

Pitman's basic objective, however, is not spelling reform but the provision of a consistent teaching medium for the initial learning of the language; a medium simple enough to permit easy transition over to the traditional orthography and spelling which is likely to persist for generations to come.

A large-scale experiment[2] was designed and started in 1960 in 75 schools in Great Britain. Its purpose was to investigate the effectiveness of the Pitman augmented alphabet as a medium for teaching beginning reading. More than 2,500 children in the experimental classes were matched with an equal number in traditional classes. Although a number of people were involved in the experiment, Dr. John Downing of the University of London's Institute of Education became its chief interpreter and spokesman. Through his writings[3] and talks to educational groups on both sides of the Atlantic the experiment soon became well known.

It attracted the attention of a number of reading specialists, one of whom was Dr. Albert Mazurkiewicz who went to England in January, 1964 under the sponsorship of a $2,000 grant from a local Pennsylvania newspaper foundation.

When Dr. Mazurkiewicz returned to his position as Professor of Education and Director of the Reading Clinic at Lehigh University, he set about the task of adopting and adapting the i/t/a alphabet to American-type reading materials for use in a research project. At first it was anticipated that the British materials of the *Jon and Janet* series would be used. It was found, however, that the philosophy behind the *Jon and Janet* was more of a basal reader approach and Dr. Mazurkiewicz was more oriented to a more experienced-centered approach. Consequently, Mazurkiewicz teamed up with Dr. Harold Tanyzer whom he had met in England for the first time. Tanyzer was also interested in i/t/a and had been sent by Pitman's of New York to see the British experiment in operation. A crash program of writing was undertaken by Mazurkiewicz and Tanyzer, resulting in the "Early-to-Read" i/t/a series being ready for use in the fall in the Bethlehem schools.

In May of that same year, 1964, the Ford Foundation's Fund for

---

2. Downing, John A., and others, *The i/t/a Symposium*. Slough, England: National Foundation for Educational Research in England and Wales, 1966. (Available in U.S.A. from A.S.U.C. Bookstore, Bancroft at Telegraph, Berkeley, California).
3. Downing, John A., "Recent Developments in i/t/a," *California English Journal*, 3; No. 3 (Fall, 1967) 64–74.

the Advancement of Education agreed to support the experiment through a center established at Lehigh University, and the public schools of Bethlehem, Pennsylvania were offered for the experiment[4] by Dr. Rebecca Stewart, who also had become interested in the potentialities of i/t/a.

Late in 1964 the University of London experiment enjoyed considerable impetus through a three-year grant from the international office of the Ford Foundation. Those monies for experiments in America and in Britain have made it possible for i/t/a to become the most widely researched approach in beginning reading in the history of our language.

As interest in i/t/a has swept across the land and school-after-school has accepted the challenge to try it, a number of publishers have produced materials printed in the Pitman i/t/a type.

"In itself, i/t/a is not a program; it is an alphabet", Dr. Mazurkiewicz stated in 1965 at the opening of the Second Annual International Conference on the Initial Teaching Alphabet.

It is i/t/a as an alphabet *and* i/t/a as a total language-arts program that will be described here.

Materials and Method

The i/t/a is a true sound-symbol approach to encoding the sounds of our English language and for decoding the graphemes back into the sounds which they represent. There may be some question as to whether or not there are actually 44 distinguishable sounds or only 40. The i/t/a provides two symbols for the one sound which is ordinarily represented by *c* and *k*. Furthermore the letter *y* sometimes represents a consonant sound and sometimes a vowel sound.

Such minor differences are relatively insignificant when one considers the many ambiguities of our language which are eliminated for the beginning reader who starts with i/t/a.

The traditional alphabet necessitates many inconsistencies. The i/t/a reduces those inconsistencies. At the same time, however, i/t/a reduces spelling and writing to a purely phonemic operation. The child who uses i/t/a can write anything he can say, and can pronounce anything that is written.

The symbols of i/t/a are obviously taught as sounds and not as letter names. Only lower case letters are used, based upon the theory that lower case letters provide for greatest differences. Capital letters

---

4. Mazurkiewicz, Albert, J., *The Initial Teaching Alphabet in Reading Instruction.* Bethlehem: Bethlehem Area Public Schools, 1967.

girls and bois lern

tω reed with i|t|a

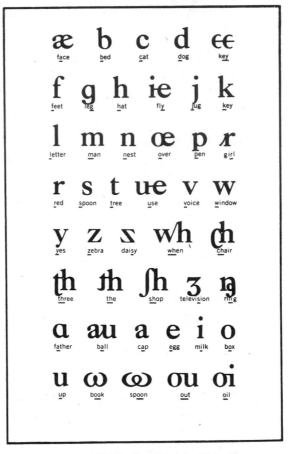

Pitman's Initial Teaching Alphabet, with its 44
symbols and words illustrating the sounds these
symbols represent.

*Fig. 8–4   Reproduced with the permission of Initial Teaching Alphabet
Publications, Inc., 20 East 46 Street, New York, N. Y.*

when necessary in i/t/a are obtained by merely increasing the size of
the symbol.

The consistency of the sound-symbol relationship is the greatest
advantage of i/t/a, for the symbol for the short vowel sound *a* is always

"a", whereas the symbol for the long *a* sound is always æ (æ) and the *a* in *father* is a slightly-different printed script *"a"*, and the *a* in *ball* is yet another digraph au, where the *au* is connected.

Originally, the child spells in i/t/a as he speaks, with each sound being represented by a phonemically-stable grapheme. In the transition stage, the child who has already achieved security in writing, speaking and reading then has to learn the "spelling demons" just as any other child who has learned by means of any other method. The difference is that the i/t/a child has been able through the use of i/t/a to far exceed the ordinary learner in the number of words he can use in his written work. Moreover, in i/t/a it may be said that there need be no words learned by rote as sight words. There need be no words that a child cannot pronounce.

Once the child has learned the symbols and has acquired the habit of transcribing the sounds which make up words into the i/t/a, he is able to write and to read. After the first year, the child begins to work toward a transition to traditional writing and traditional orthography in reading.

The i/t/a program in the United States as developed by Dr. Mazurkiewicz and Dr. Tanyzer includes three phases:

Phase I consists of a *Ready for Reading* workbook which, although similar to other readiness workbooks, appears to introduce graphemes much earlier. One of its features is its lack of conformity to the usual introduction of all the short vowel sounds. On the contrary, the short *ă* sound is reinforced by workbook materials that cover ten pages, followed by six pages of practice with workbook materials related to the consonant *n*, seven pages on *t*, four pages on short *ĕ*, and four pages on *b*. Most of the remainder of the book is devoted to grapheme identification and discrimination of likenesses and differences of actual i/t/a symbols. Finally, the *s* and *r* consonants are learned. Unlike many other readiness workbooks, the i/t/a *Ready for Reading* book provides unusually intensive work.

The readiness book is followed by the first pre-primer, *Rides*. The special feature of that little paperback is its use of sketches where a word would be too long for a beginning reader. For example, in the sentence on page 4, it reads, "You can ride in a . . . ." with a sketch of a car occupying the space where the word car might appear. The same scheme is followed throughout the book with pictures sketched in to illustrate such means of transportation on which one can ride as a camel, elephant, helicopter, submarine, etc.

The second pre-primer in the i/t/a program is the now-famous *Dinosaur Ben* which became immediately popular upon its introduction

lemonæd, lemonæd, fiev sents a glass!

wun dæ polly, molly and jack wer plæiŋ in the frunt yard.

up the street cæm a big truck. thær woz a sien on the truck that sed **"sircus."**

muesic cæm from the truck.

thær wer three clouns on the back ov the truck.

"the sircus iz in toun!" caulld the first cloun.

"wun week œnly!" caulld out the second cloun.

"cum wun, cum aull!" caulld out the third cloun.

49

Fig. 8–5   Reproduced with the permission of Initial Teaching Alphabet Publications, Inc., 20 East 46 Street, New York, N. Y.

as one of the first books written on this side of the Atlantic in i/t/a. There is also a workbook to accompany *Dinosaur Ben*.

Houses (and accompanying workbook) is the third pre-primer. Like the others, it is a 48-page paperback. It deals with children who live in all sorts of houses from igloos and grass shacks to apartments.

By the time the children have completed the three pre-primers and the workbooks, they can read a large number of small hard-covered books which are now available as small 24-page story books. There are twenty such trade-book type books specially written at the pre-primer and primer levels for independent reading during Phase I. Included are *The Rabbit and the Turtle* (Hare and Tortoise) and a book of poems. Through British publishers an additional large number of hardbacks are available printed in i/t/a at this level.

The primers of Phase I are *A Game of Ball* and *The Yo-Yo Contest*, both of which are 92-page hardback readers, and deal with *feelings* children have about themselves and others.

Special mention should be made concerning the artwork in the "Early-to-Read" books, for it is especially contrived to provide plenty of room for imagination by the reader. For example, the picture may be merely suggestive of a house, but without any special cultural setting. Children are always the main characters rather than grownups. They are depicted as white and shaded.

Another feature of the "Early-to-Read" books is their orientation toward real-life situations in which children must make decisions concerning their actions. For example, when a window is broken during a baseball game and the boys decide not to run, but to tell the owner of the house, the story ends with the question, "What will you do next?" Another story in Book 2 asks the question, "What shall we name your new baby brother?" This becomes a subject of discussion for the neighborhood children.

It is obvious and refreshing to find that the i/t/a "Early-to-Read" books have apparently been written by individuals who have had direct and recent contact with real children in real home and community situations. The stories are true characterizations of the feelings, real conversations, and real interests of children in real homes. Moreover, they include real words that are far beyond the ordinary reading level of children, yet are to be found in the children's conversation. Such difficult words as *policeman, surprised, storekeeper, giraffe, ventriloquist,* and *wonderful* are all part of Phase I, yet ordinarily would not be used until Third Grade. With i/t/a the children are freed from the traditional "word-control" necessary because of the irregular phonic elements of our language.

Phase II of the "Early-to-Read" i/t/a program is designed to reinforce the basic language skills of writing, spelling and reading which the child learned during Phase I. This is the period described by John

Downing as the "vocabulary extension period". His belief is that the beginning Phase I should not move as rapidly as provided for in the American "Early-to-Read" series. He claims that more careful control is necessary in order to fix the learning and insure that it is developmental step-by-step. Starting with a "look-say" approach, his "Downing Readers" move into a phonics stage, and then into a vocabulary-extension stage.

The sequence of the British i/t/a program and the American program is somewhat different. Dr. Mazurkiewicz explains those differences by pointing out that "Several programs using i/t/a exist, for i/t/a of itself does not demand that a particular structure be used for the reading program."

It is assumed that, when a child moves into Phase II, he will have learned the phonemic alphabet (i/t/a) and will have developed pronunciation skills which include emphasis and voice inflection which are usually indicators of comprehension. Books 4 and 5 are the hardbacks which provide a wide variety of interesting stories and poems. The stories deal with everything from fairy tales to space travel. It is claimed that Book 4 has a mean readability of 2.3 and Book 5 extends this up to a mean of 2.8.

The third phase of the first-year i/t/a beginning reading program takes the child to materials which are judged to approximate the Fourth-Grade level of difficulty. Thus, it is claimed, with i/t/a, the materials ordinarily covered in the first three primary grades of school are essentially covered in the First Grade. It is also claimed that the "Early-to-Read" i/t/a program developed by Mazurkiewicz and Tanyzer will "develop the major language arts skills by the end of the first school year when the majority of the children will already have made the transition to our traditional alphabet."

Transition to traditional orthography (t.o.) as the medium of reading is accomplished in Book 6 by a gradual movement from i/t/a phonemic spelling to the stories in Book 7 which are completely printed in t.o. The last eight stories, however, are "written down" to the Second-Grade level so that the child will be sure to have success with them even though his i/t/a reading previously has been at Third-Grade level or better.

Interest in i/t/a has been mounting rapidly, with the result that in Britain there are hundreds of books that have been transliterated into i/t/a. In fact, there are several basal reader series in Britain that are printed also in i/t/a and it was the Janet and Jon Series (known in Britain as the "*Janet and Jon Reading Scheme*") published by James Nisbet & Co., which was used originally in the University of London i/t/a experiment. *Through the Rainbow Reading Scheme, Beacon Reading*

Scheme (Ginn & Co. of London), *Old Lob Approach to Reading* (also Ginn), *The Downing Reading Scheme, The Oldham Readers* (known as the "Ken and Sue" series), and *The McKee Readers* (British version of "Tip and Mitten") are other basal series which have been transliterated into i/t/a.

In America, publishers are beginning to accept i/t/a with an attitude that it may be something to be reckoned with, rather than a fad to be avoided. After much investigation in England and in American schools where i/t/a experiments were being done, Dr. William Boutwell of Scholastic Publications became convinced that i/t/a was, indeed, a step forward in beginning reading. He, thereupon, committed Scholastic Publications to the production of 40 books printed in i/t/a. Some are originals, but many are old favorites with children. Scholastic also produced a classroom i/t/a wallchart similar to the *Phonovisual* wall charts and the *Words-in-Color* charts. Dr. Boutwell reports sales of *Scholastic* i/t/a publications all over the English-speaking world.

At this writing it appears that an ever-increasing number of American publishers are displaying positive interest in i/t/a. E. P. Dutton Co., for example, is one of the trade-book publishers producing in i/t/a such classics as Milne's, *Winnie, the Pooh* and others. The Henry Z. Walck Co. and the Follette Publishing Co. both are publishing enrichment materials in i/t/a. An i/t/a edition of Scott-Foresman's basal readers is now in publication. Some standardized reading tests in i/t/a are now available from the California Test Bureau and from Harcourt, Brace and World, Inc.

When publishers such as these become willing to support an approach to reading that is as different from the traditional as is i/t/a, it may be a good indication that the i/t/a approach has reached a level of acceptance and development which is more than just an educational fad.

In conclusion it may be repeated that i/t/a is a phonemically-based alphabet which enables a learner to reproduce the 40 or so basic sounds of English through the utilization of regular phonemic sound-symbols. Conversely, an English speaking child can reproduce his speech sounds in the written i/t/a script in exactly the order in which he makes the sounds. His speech, thus, may be written and then read by others who have learned the i/t/a.

The objective of i/t/a is not to promote a spelling reform, but to provide a somewhat regular sound-symbol system for teaching beginning reading. The i/t/a does not replace the traditional alphabet symbols of English, but augments them with about 20 consonant and vowel digraphs.

Teachers of children who are beginning reading are asked not to hold transition to traditional orthography as the immediate goal. The more immediate goal is the achievement of a strong and widely-used background in reading. Thus, it is claimed, children who learn through the use of the i/t/a generally achieve reading skill up to a mean beginning Fourth-Grade level by the time they have completed one year in i/t/a.

The greatest advantage in i/t/a is claimed to be in the area of creative writing, rather than in the unusual results reported in the area of reading. The i/t/a advocates claim superior creative writing is done by children who can use i/t/a to write any ideas and words that they use orally. Through i/t/a, the child is freed from the phonic irregularity of English.

The methods by which i/t/a materials are introduced and used differ considerably, ranging from a basal-reader step-by-step approach which is characteristic of some of the British experimentation to the more individualized reading type of approach which is advocated in America. In either case, however, basic skills of grapheme-phoneme representation are taught, and sentence length and vocabulary are limited through first small pre-primers. The differences become more apparent after the introduction of Phase II.

Regardless of differences in method, i/t/a in Britain, America, Canada, New Zealand, Australia, and other parts of the English-speaking world has created an impact upon education and upon reading in particular that far surpasses anything that has happened since the introduction of the first basal reader series.

Research Findings

The i/t/a experiments in Britain and in America have enjoyed money grants for research that have made an evaluation of i/t/a possible. Although much more needs to be done in carrying the research beyond its present stage, the results so far are impressive, to say the least.

Testimonials describing the success of children who have learned to read through i/t/a are almost endless. They have appeared with regularity in the *i/t/a bulletin*[5] in America and in the *i/t/a jurnal*[6] in Britain.

The Initial Teaching Alphabet Foundation was set up specifically to collect and disseminate information on i/t/a and i/t/a activities. The foundation *report*[7] contains bibliographies of all known research on i/t/a,

---

5. *i/t/a bulletin.* New York: i/t/a Publications, Inc., published periodically.
6. *i/t/a jurnal.* London: Initial Teaching Foundation, Ltd.
7. *report.* Hempstead: Initial Teaching Alphabet Association. The Association, housed at Hofstra University publishes its *i.t.a. report* periodically.

as well as descriptive information on all known available materials and supplementary devices for teaching i/t/a.

It would be beyond the limits of this review to attempt to quote all of the research statistics or even to attempt a summary of research reports on i/t/a. A few representative figures will suffice, with further reference suggested to the scores of research studies annotated in the publications cited above.

The University of London study[8] is of significance for it has been a longitudinal study started in the fall of 1961, although the matched groups did not actually begin full i/t/a instruction in comparison to regular orthographic instruction until the spring of 1963. 2,500 four- and five-year-olds were included from 75 Primary Schools. They were matched with an equal number of children using traditional materials. The British experiment has the advantage of using the *Janet and Jon* basal reading series printed in t.o. for the control group and in i/t/a for the experimental group. Such comparisons have not been possible in America until the recent publication of the Scott-Foresman series for the University of Chicago study. A new book, *The i/t/a Reading Experiment*, published by Scott-Foresman Co., Chicago, describes four years of the experiment.

John Downing has presented the British findings at various conferences in the United States, and his statistics show significant differences favoring i/t/a trained children in the speed with which they learned to read, their levels of comprehension, the percent at various levels of achievement, and their spelling ability—all after one and one half years of instruction in i/t/a compared with an equal time in t.o. In fact, i/t/a children did significantly better than their counterparts on tests that were printed in t.o.

Results in America have been pouring into the Reading Centers at Lehigh University and at Hofstra University, and have been widely circulated by Dr. Mazurkiewicz in articles in the College Reading Association's organ, *Journal of the Reading Specialist*, and in the proceedings of various reading conferences at which Dr. Mazurkiewicz and Dr. Tanyzer have reported.

Since much of the statistical evidence is reported on a variety of bases, comparisons are difficult to make. It is understood that attempts are now being made to obtain reports that provide compatible information. The promoters of i/t/a in America, Initial Teaching Alphabet Publications, Inc., were so sure of the results obtained through the use of their

---

8. Downing, John A., "The i/t/a (Initial Teaching Alphabet) Reading Experiments," *The Reading Teacher*, 18 (Nov., 1964) 105–110.

materials and method that in 1970 they were one of several publishers who initiated "guaranteed performance" contracts with school systems. Under i/t/a "Accountability Projects," the "Early-to-Read" materials and the i/t/a method must produce results after one year's use, or the materials can be returned and the school's investment will be refunded.[9]

Anyone who has observed classroom groups of children who have learned to read by i/t/a are confronted with sound empirical evidence that i/t/a works wonders in releasing beginning readers from the confines of a controlled vocabulary necessitated by the phonemic irregularities of our language. We still need proof of the statement that, "by the end of one year, the great majority of children can and do easily transfer to traditional orthography at a level of readability far beyond that possible with the traditional basal reader series."

The future holds the answer to the question, "Will i/t/a become a universal teaching medium not only for English but for all languages which have phonemically oriented patterns which can be represented by graphemic symbols?"

It seems safe to observe that i/t/a has been the most novel and most talked-about innovation in the teaching of reading in our day. Its impact, no doubt, will be felt for many decades in schools on both sides of the Atlantic where dynamic approaches to beginning reading are being considered.

UNIFON

Origins

UNIFON, a new 40-letter synthetic alphabet, may be said to have had its origin through the efforts of George Bernard Shaw, the great playwright and critic. It was Shaw who during his later years was one of the leading protagonists for a revised method of spelling, and particularly for the development of a new alphabet for the English language. In his will, he left a considerable portion of his estate to be used to sponsor research and experimentation with new alphabet schemes. In probating Shaw's will, the courts allowed a sum of $23,240 for prizes to contestants and the expense of cutting new type and producing 13,000 copies of "Androcles and the Lion" set in double pages of a new alphabet and traditional orthography.

---

9. Aukerman, Robert C., "Guaranteed Results—or Your Money Back!" *New England Reading Association Journal*, 6:1 (Fall, 1970) 1–3.

Among the finalists from among a total of almost 500 entrants from the English-speaking countries of the world was John R. Malone of Park Forest, a suburb of Chicago. His contribution in the contest is currently known as UNIFON, referring to a uniformly-phonemic representation of the sounds of the English language.[10]

The originator of the program, Mr. Malone, states that he began work on UNIFON in 1957 in an attempt to devise a simple orthography which would not only apply to English but would also fit the sounds of the other major European languages.[11] Although not a reading specialist, Mr. Malone was intrigued with the possibilities of finding a solution to the complexities of reading, chiefly because of his wide background as a newspaperman, economist, and inventor in the field of information handling and processing.

He states that the forerunner of UNIFON was developed as a rainy Sunday afternoon pastime for his young son back in 1959. On that day, he reports, his son seemed to master the sound-letter relationships almost without effort and immediately went off to teach a friend.

Small experiments with the UNIFON alphabet led to the establishment of what is known as "The Foundation for a Compatible and Consistent Alphabet", the purpose of which is to "test, demonstrate, and standardize the use of phonemic alphabets". It is hoped by its sponsors that its efforts will extend beyond the application of such alphabets to English, and eventually a universal alphabet will be discovered which will be "compatible and consistent",

In the spring of 1960, Dr. Margaret S. Ratz, then elementary education specialist in the public schools of Highland Park, Illinois, heard of UNIFON and began testing its use with pre-schoolers. Dr. Ratz was pleased with the results and became elementary education director of the Foundation in addition to her present position as Chairman of the Department of Education at Principia College, Elsah, Illinois.

The possibility of the use of such a consistent sound-symbol relationship as furnished by the UNIFON scheme has long been awaited. Even as it is being proposed by John R. Malone, there are many who refuse to entertain its possibilities. There are others, however, who are willing to experiment, knowing full well that modern technology and the explosion of knowledge signal the necessity for a compatible and consistently-reliable sound-symbol system.

---

10. Malone, John R., "The Larger Aspects of Spelling Reform," *Elementary English*, 39 (May, 1962) 435–445.
11. Malone, John R., "The Unifon System," *Wilson Library Bulletin*, 40 (Sept., 1965) 63–65.

Fig. 8–6 *Reproduced by permission of International Phoneme Corporation, copyright holder, U. S. Patents applied for. UNIFON™ property of International Phoneme Corporation.*

Method and Materials

There are eight principles which apply to UNIFON as a method of representing the sounds of English:

1. Each word will be spelled phonemically. The result will be such words as *alfubet, kat, kup, Jon,* etc.
2. All double letters in traditional spelling will appear as single letters in UNIFON, assuming that one of the pair of double letters is actually silent. By the same token, there will be no silent letters. Silent–e in such words as "come", "came", "house", etc. will cease to exist.
3. There is one symbol for each sound, and each sound will always be represented by the same symbol regardless of the variations of spelling that are current in traditional English spelling.
4. New UNIFON symbols have been devised to represent the diphthongs and so-called Latin consonant pairs. Thus, there are new symbols for the sound of "u" in "use" and the "u" in "due".
5. Short vowel sounds are represented by standard capital letters (all of UNIFON is in capital letters), but the long vowel sounds are represented in capital letters that have been augmented with horizontal bars, making them look somewhat like cattle-branding marks.
6. No digraphs nor symbols having *both* consonant *and* vowel sounds are used. Thus the final "y" that sounds like "e" and others are eliminated.
7. All words sounding the same are spelled the same. The reader must depend upon context clues for their meanings. This simplifies the problem which faces so many learners of selecting the correct spelling for "their" or "there"; "for", "four", "fore"; etc.
8. Separate symbols have been devised for diphthongs and other combination sounds such as "ai", "ch", "ng", "ou", "ow", "oi", (or "oy") "th" (in two usages); "yu"; and "zh".

The residual learning of UNIFON will have ultimate benefits for those working in data processing, and in the fields of business where the UNIFON will be used for dictatable typewriters. Such typewriters which are activated by spoken language require isomorphic (letter-for-sound on a one-to-one relationship) orthography in order to operate.

Research Findings

In the fall of 1962, the Mayor's Committee for Economic and Cultural Development of Chicago arranged for two classes for adult nonreaders, with UNIFON as the medium of instruction. Mr. Gordon Austin

Fig. 8–7 *Reproduced from* Chipper, *Copyright MCMXLIX by Western Publishing Company, Inc. Reprinted by permission.*

and Mrs. Mattie Hopkins taught the classes with what were described as "inadequate and makeshift materials".

One class was for English-speaking non-readers, and one was for non-English Speaking, Spanish-Reading-and-Spanish-Speaking adults who were non-readers of English. The classes met two nights per week, two hours per night throughout the school year. In May, 1963, the originator of the UNIFON medium arranged to teach an additional class four nights per week. He reports that those who continued through the program reached to about the Third-Grade level on the *Stanford Achievement Tests* after twenty additional hours of instruction.

The Mott Foundation of Flint, Michigan (described on pages 273–274) studied the UNIFON approach in 1963–64 and "concluded that there was a need for the UNIFON alphabet in the initial phases of reading instruction."

Mott materials with UNIFON are now being produced and tested in eight centers, six of them under the supervision and direction of the South Suburban Human Relations Council in South Cook County, Illinois, and two in Michigan. Materials include a basic teacher's manual, a UNIFON-traditional-spelling dictionary, large charts and a basic text in beginning reading. There also is a UNIFON *Language Builder*, and parallel text Readers in traditional orthography and in UNIFON. One interesting innovation is a bookmark which contains the new UNIFON words for the lesson in the Reader.

Teacher-training films and videotapes have also been developed.

No reports were available at the time this book went to press concerning the results of these layouts of UNIFON with adult non-readers.

In 1964–1965, twenty-two Kindergarten classes in a large metropolitan area were involved in a controlled UNIFON experiment. The eleven experimental classes contained a total of 251 students, while the eleven control classes contained 265 children. The classes were matched on the basis of age, race, social class and neighborhood. In many cases the two classes were in the same school.

Students in both experimental and control classes were tested initially on the *Metropolitan Readiness Test* and, at the end of the experiment, on the *Metropolitan Reading Test* in traditional orthography which, of course, would tend to favor the control group.

Teachers for both control and experimental classes were given special training in an attempt to reduce the "Hawthorne" effect.[12]

---

12. "Hawthorne Effect": In a statistical study involving testing. One variable that should be considered is the motivation for testing by reason of taking part in the research.

The test results indicated that the children in the control group were initially superior in readiness. On the post-test, however, the difference in favor of the experimental group is significant at the .01 level. A t-score of 3.17 was obtained, indicating that the children who were learning UNIFON not only overcome their initial deficiency in readiness, but emerged with significantly higher achievement on the reading test which included sub-tests on word knowledge, word discrimination, and sentences.

Inasmuch as the experiment was conducted with Kindergarten children, many reading specialists would question its validity and might find more substance in the 1965–1966 experiment carried out in the Indianapolis Public Schools. There, twelve First Grade classes were matched with twelve other First Grade classes to form the experimental and control groups. They were matched on age and reading readiness.

Metropolitan Achievement Tests in traditional orthography showed that the children in the twelve experimental classes achieved significantly higher than the control in World Knowledge and in Word Discrimination. There was no significant difference in reading comprehension.

Dr. Richard Wolf directed both research studies.

It is interesting to note that all over the world where English is becoming the international language, American tourists and businessmen are asked to use CAPITAL LETTERS in filling out forms of all sorts. This would seem to indicate that adults, who are experiencing their first contact with our language, feel more secure with the fewer differences in discrimination necessary when capital letters are used.

The first alphabets, themselves, were capital letters, and the Greek has maintained its capital letters, as have some of the others. Advertising on TV and in other visual media is almost exclusively capital letters. Street names throughout the world are almost universally in capital letters, as are most store front signs, theatre marquees, posterboards, and product packages.

Check-scanning devices and IBM equipment is all set up for capital letters, and the future seems to be foreordained in the direction of capital letters.

All of these barometers seem to indicate that UNIFON, or some of its features, may have a significant place in the evolution of English as the international language of business, commerce, and computerization. It is doubtful, however, if UNIFON is the answer to the need for a one-to-one sound-symbol approach to beginning reading instruction in the usual classroom.

THE LAUBACH METHOD[13]

Origins

It is probable that no one person in this century has dedicated his life more fully to the teaching of reading to the non-English-speaking peoples of the world than has the late Frank C. Laubach, Ph.D.

In 1915 he went with his wife to the Philippines as a Christian missionary. For the first seven years he gave himself to the building of evangelical church groups on the northern edge of the great southern island, Mindanao. It was there that he had first contact with the Mohammedan Moros of the island. They were a fierce, primitive people who looked upon the Filipino Christians as their traditional enemies. They were, however, completely unapproachable. To win their trust and friendship, Dr. Laubach well knew that it would take unbounded patience and resourcefulness.

It was not until 1930 that Dr. Laubach believed that he was in readiness to begin his work with the Moro people. He went alone to Dumaguetem, a mission station, to learn their language and to understand their way of life. It was not long before the Moros began to realize the nobility of spirit of this American who had come among them as their simple friend.

As he started to help them in various practical ways, their response grew until in an almost incredibly short time they came to regard him as their best friend. It was not long before he discerned that one of their greatest needs was to be able to read. They were almost entirely an illiterate people, wedded to the past and ill-prepared to take their place in the twentieth century.

Like the missionaries to Hawaii a century earlier, Dr. Laubach taught the Moros a modern method of planting, introduced better seeds, fostered health services, and taught them to read and write. During the process of teaching them to read, a remarkable thing happened. The chief of the Moros observed the wonders Dr. Laubach was effecting among his people. He requested that Dr. Laubach teach some of his leaders to read.

Inasmuch as the Moros had no written language, Dr. Laubach transliterated their speech sounds into English graphemes. The spelling

---

13. I have quoted freely from a "Foreword" by Dr. Alden H. Clark to *Letters by A Modern Mystic*—a collection of letters by Dr. Laubach written from Mindanao to his father in 1930. Conversations with Dr. Laubach also furnished background description of the origins of his method.

of the language, therefore, became completely phonemic, with one English letter representing one phoneme in the Moro language. In addition to constructing a written alphabet, it was necessary for Dr. Laubach to provide printed reading lessons and materials. This he did, and included a little local "newspaper" which proved to be one of the most successful motivational devices.

The most successful motivational device, however, was devised by the Moro chief, himself, when, on that day back in the early 1930's, he spoke these words: "Each one teach one." He ordered that, when any of his people had learned to read, they would be obligated under threat of severe punishment to teach another. Thus was born the movement which made Dr. Frank Laubach famous and successful in bringing literacy to the "silent billion of the world".

After his service to the Moros of Mindanao, Dr. Laubach carried his method and the slogan, "Each one teach one" to the peoples of Africa, the Middle East, the Orient and South America. Everywhere he went, he listened to the sounds of the language and to the common words and phrases which carried the mainstream of the culture. He then transliterated the spoken language into a sound-symbol phonemically-oriented spelling of the language. He always was faced with the necessity of printing stories and a "newspaper". And his method always worked.

As a result, the Laubach method has been credited with bringing literacy to more than 100,000,000 of the world's peoples. Originally, it was a one-to-one method. "Each one teach one". On his 46th birthday in 1930, Dr. Laubach wrote to his father:

> As I sit over in that old building day after day patiently toiling with one man or boy to teach him the alphabet, and so hold him to a larger world, I often wonder whether this work is becoming to a man of my age. But when that same man fondly runs his fingers through my hair [a Moro cultural symbol of thankfulness . . . editor's note] and looks his love while he says, "Mapia bapa" —good uncle—I know that a little love is created.[14]

During his lifetime Dr. Laubach personally conducted literacy campaigns in 65 countries and helped prepare lessons and teaching devices in 312 different languages! A record unequaled by anyone!

In 1930 he wrote from Mindanao: "Windows open outward as well as upward. Windows *especially* open downward where people need most!" Until his death in 1970 at age 86 Dr. Laubach actively campaigned on behalf of what he calls the "silent billion" . . . referring, of course, to

---

14. Laubach, Frank C., letter to his father, 1930.

the more than one billion people who cannot read or write—over half of the human race. He writes:

> In Asia and Africa, over a billion people are illiterate. This cold paper cannot tell you what that means. You think it is a pity they cannot read, but the real tragedy is they cannot speak. They are the silent victims, the forgotten men, driven like animals, mutely submitting. . . . I have not only seen these people across Asia and Africa, but I have sat beside many of them and taught them one by one.

The picture and word charts which he has developed for the 312 different languages have revolutionized literacy training throughout the world. "We can hardly believe what happens," Laubach said. "Many primitive peoples can actually learn to read and write their entire spoken vocabulary in one or two weeks."

After some twenty years of work in many other languages, Dr. Laubach tackled English, knowing well that, because of the irregularities of English spelling, the teaching of reading in English would take a matter of months rather than days. However, with the study of English spelling, he did develop keywords as he had done for other languages.

In English in the United States there are three series associated with the *Laubach Method: Learn English the New Way* (which is the main subject of this discussion); *Building Your Language Power*; and *Streamlined English*. There are also several centers in this country where teachers of the Laubach Method are being trained.

Materials and Method

Learn English the New Way basically consists of workbooks which provide sequential steps in learning to read and write, using the Laubach adaptation of our English alphabet.

Volume I contains twenty charts which are used to illustrate the twenty lessons. The main feature of the method is that it presents learning in purely phonemic spelling. In a recent letter to me, Dr. Laubach wrote: "It spellz the way I am rriting this letter. Thē effort iz tw make nō chanje that iz 'regūlar', and when a chanje is unavoidable, tw make it az nearly like ōld spelling az it can bē spelldd, ēven tw the number ov letterz."

Thus, the key to the system is a new English alphabet and a phonemic spelling. The "new" alphabet merely utilizes the 26 letters of the regular alphabet in ways that are somewhat different than the "traditional". At the Annual Reading Conference at the University of

Rhode Island, Dr. Laubach asked one of the teacher-participants to read one of his stories written in what he calls "Thu new Ingglish Fo/netic Alfubet". The teacher easily read through the material on the first reading. Dr. Laubach expressed surprise at her ability. She replied, "Oh that's nothing. I get letters from my grandson all the time that are spelled like this."

The alphabet is taught first. This is divided into groupings of six characters in each lesson. The six are presented, together with key words, in each of the charts. It should be noted that the Laubach method utilizes exactly the same psychological principles as the McKee-Harrison *Getting Ready to Read* segment of the Houghton Mifflin series. The psychological principle is that of "cue reduction" and "conditioned learning". The first stimulus is shown in the key picture in the first box. This is followed by a box in which the letter symbol is superimposed over a faded drawing of the original key picture. Finally the key picture is completely eliminated and the letter symbol then becomes the S^2 in the conditioning process. It is essentially the same process as demonstrated by Pavlov in his famous learning experiment with the meat, (S^1) and response of salivation (R^1). The bell (S^2) became the substitute stimulus, as the meat cue was reduced.

Some of the keywords in the Laubach method show clever relationships to the experience of today's children. Others may be subject to some question. The key pictures are a most essential part of the method for they serve as reference cues to the sounds which the letter symbols represent. Unlike many of the other purely phonemic methods, Laubach has devised sound-symbol key pictures for the many blends and diphthongs as well as the single words. There are 113 pictures and spellings used to differentiate the spellings and the sounds. They are used in two ways. First, semantic differences within our language are salvaged. For example: we have three spellings of "to", "two" and "too". The Laubach method spells them differently, also: "tw", "tww", and "too". The word, "their" is phonemically spelled "thair", and "there" is spelled "therr". Similarly, the past tense of "read" is spelled "redd", with the color "red" left unchanged.

All long vowel sounds are indicated with the long horizontal bar over the vowel symbol. This seems to be a logical move.

All double consonants are retained. Every final silent "e" is replaced with a double consonant.

Volume II of *English the New Way* builds bridges to the old spelling. The transition is made with only those rules that the originator of the system believes are really useful, and which "aar not too confūzing."

CHART-4

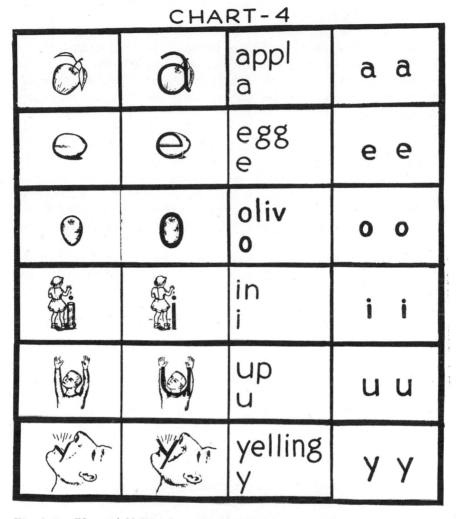

Fig. 8–8 *Chart of SkillBook I of* English, The New Way *reproduced by permission of the authors, Frank C. Laubach, Elizabeth Mooney Kirk, Robert S. Laubach, and the publisher, Laubach Literacy/ New Readers Press, Box 131, Syracuse, N.Y., 13210.*

In conclusion, it should be said that the life time work of Dr. Frank C. Laubach has finally found acceptance in his own country. His own adaptation of his work in providing a phonemic vehicle for the sounds of the language has resulted in an unconventional use of our alphabet with an attempt at regularized spelling of words and sounds.

Research Findings

It would be quite presumptuous for one to demand research studies to prove whether or not Dr. Frank Laubach has developed a successful method of teaching people to read. The estimated 100,000,000 people who have benefited from his methods and materials are more-than-adequate proof of that.

The lack of awareness of his methods in his own United States largely results from the fact that he labored long and hard with the emerging peoples of other continents. He died in 1970 at the age of 86, but his lifetime work of bringing an approach to reading for functional illiterates is being carried on by his son, Dr. Robert S. Laubach of Syracuse University. The Laubach method is now being marketed by the New Readers Press under the title, *The New Streamlined English Series*, copyright 1969.

It may be predicted with reasonable assurance, therefore, that the Laubach materials and method will be given careful consideration and that research studies with the material in normal classroom settings will be undertaken. The results of such controlled experiments will, no doubt, verify the fact that the Laubach method is a dynamic approach to beginning reading.

WORDS IN COLOR

Origins

Words in Color is a unique approach to reading which makes an attempt to code each of the various vowel sounds to a specific color, and, to a somewhat lesser degree, to do similarly with the consonant sounds. In addition, vowel digraphs and consonant digraphs also have their special colors for the beginning reader to learn.

The color-coding system known as *Words in Color* apparently evolved from some tryouts of the idea with non-readers and with illiterate adults. *Words in Color* was devised in 1957 by Dr. Caleb Gattegno, who also attained recognition for revived interest in the mathematical sticks, called "Cuisinarie Rods". The originator of *Words in Color* credits a number of people for encouraging his first efforts to relate what actually is "letters-in-color" to phonemics.

His early efforts were presented to teachers in California, Canada and later in Great Britain, with considerable interest ensuing therefrom. His first arrangement of "letters-in-color" was duplicated by Dr. Dorothea Hinman, who later joined Dr. Gattegno in the several revisions and more recently as the chief promotional agent for the system.

Early experimentation was done at Christ The King School in Dallas in the spring of 1959. Later in London, the system was tried with five-year-olds. In 1961, the author of the system showed teachers in a California school how his system works, and, later that summer, ran a four-week workshop on his method.

Apparently the interest of teachers and administrators in his approach was sufficient to motivate Dr. Gattegno to start producing the system for widespread sale. His claims that this is a "better" system, "because it reduces the learning time needed to master the skills of reading and writing English" need to be fully substantiated although there is considerable truth to his statement that "The slowness of the present process of teaching these skills may be a source of boredom for many children."

Words in Color was originally copyright in 1962 by Caleb Gattegno. In 1963, Learning Materials, Inc. of Chicago received a copyright and publication was started by Encyclopaedia Britannica Press, Inc. For several years it was published by the Xerox Educational Division. Dr. Gattegno and Dr. Hinman are now operating through a New York city organization entitled, "Educational Solutions, Inc.", and are marketing *Words in Color* privately.

Words in Color was introduced as "A new approach to teaching reading and writing." Although the system may be "new" in some respects, the idea of matching letter sounds and colored graphemes was suggested at least before the turn of the century by a Miss Nellie Dale. Although her system was not as well developed nor as widely publicized as the Gattegno method, it was, indeed, quite similar. It is unlikely, however, that Gattegno was aware of the work of Miss Dale, for he states: "Rather than spend time looking into the vast literature in the field already available, I attacked the problem from scratch with actual learners."

In disregarding the research in reading, he was speaking of his approach to illiterate adults in Ethiopia. He reports that, through the method he devised, he "found that from six to ten hours were sufficient to master reading of words [in the Amharic language].

Gattegno called his system the "morphologic-algebraic" method of teaching reading and writing. What, apparently, is a "new system" for teaching reading and writing actually is, of necessity, a phonemic approach to reading with color cues added.

Materials and Method

The author of the system known as *Words in Color* has developed the system on the theory that students may be taught to read by emphasizing written symbols as the recording of speech sounds. As a consequence, reading is merely the process of decoding the printed symbols and translating them into speech sounds. He concludes from this logic that reading and writing may be learned simultaneously. The use of color is introduced as part of the first phase of the written-symbol, decoding of symbol, and then writing process. The symbols are written or printed in colors. The child looks at the colored charts of words, writes the same letters or words in black-and-white, and then reads what he has written.

To fully understand the extent of the system, one needs to realize that there are 21 charts of letter sounds, letters in combination (digraphs), and word families which constitute the backbone of the *Words in Color* system. All together, the 21 colored classroom charts present what Dr. Gattegno claims are the 47 sounds of American English in 280 different instances of single letters and letter combinations. Moreover, to differentiate the 47 sounds of the language requires the utilization of 47 shades of colors. In this manner, the author deals with the irregularities of the phonemic elements of the language *without altering the orthography or spelling.* Thus he escapes the criticism which has surrounded i/t/a, UNIFON, Laubach, and others. By retaining traditional orthography and traditional spelling, *Words in Color* provides a sound-symbol relationship based completely upon color.

The method for using the colored word charts is based upon the strict rule that neither the teacher nor the child ever refers to a letter name. On the other hand, each letter sound is coded to a color, and any letters in combination with other letters which produce the *same* sound are, consequently, printed in the *same* color. Letters in combination that produce a quite *similar* sound are printed in a *shade* of the original color. Thus, "sound-shading" (which similar sounds might be called) is represented by "color-shading".

Conversely, when one vowel, for example, is a short sound in one word and the same vowel is a long sound in another word, two different colors are used to indicate the difference.

In the first instance, when, for example, the vowel *a* in the word *all* is pronounced with the same sound as the vowel *o* in *ostrich*, the two vowels, *a* and *o* are printed in the same color which is coded to the short *o* sound.

In the second instance, when the vowel *a* is used as short sound as in *hat*, it is colored differently from the *a* in *all* and differently from the long *a* in *hate*. If the word *eight* were to be used, the *eigh* would be colored the same as the long *a*, since the sound is the same. Similarly, the word *wait* would contain exactly the same coloring for its vowel digraph *ai* as in the two instances just mentioned.

The vowels are learned first in a novel way. They are introduced as sound-symbol *shapes*. The child learns that all vowels are related by *shape* to the written symbol,

The shapes of the written vowel symbols are presented to the children with emphasis on related elements. Page 11 of the *Background and Principles* booklet provides the commentary for the teacher:

". . . once *a* has been introduced, we take off its hat, obtaining *u*. We then cut *u* in half (adding the dot to indicate the cutting). Now *e* is obtained from *i* by dropping and extending the dot until it meets the trunk of the *i*. Finally, returning to *a*, we lift its leg and make an arm of it, thus obtaining *o*.

The first step in learning to distinguish what are claimed to be the 270 discriminable and distinctive symbols in English, *Words in Color* insists on the following routine:

The written symbol   is presented in white on the chalkboard by the teacher. She does not refer to it as the letter name, but indicates the color and sound to the children. The class is notified that, each time the teacher points to the white symbol, the teacher will expect the whole class to respond with the sound (short vowel sound of "a"). The teacher writes the grapheme   in several sizes in various places on the chalkboard, and points to each and calls for the whole-class response.

The same procedure is followed with the symbol   written in

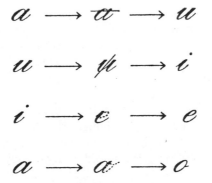

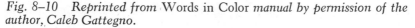

Fig. 8–10 Reprinted from Words in Color *manual by permission of the author, Caleb Gattegno.*

yellow chalk. After the children have been conditioned to respond with the short vowel sound whenever the teacher points to the written "e" symbol, drill is given in responding to both "a" in white chalk and "u" in yellow chalk. Similarly, pink chalk is used for the short "i" sound; light blue chalk for the short "e" sound; and orange chalk for the short "o" sound.

Any time the teacher points to a symbol on the chalkboard that is written in any of those colors, the class responds with the sound associated with that color. Thus, color cues are relied upon as the key stimuli in the conditioning process whereby the child learns the sounds which the symbols represent in our language.

The *Words in Color* system introduces the concept which Dr. Gattegno calls "temporal sequence". It is essentially the idea that our language is coded into a series of sounds which, when uttered in sequence, produce wholes which we call words. The timing of the sounds in sequence is an essential learning for correct pronunciation and, consequently, for correct recognition of a word.

Initial practice in sequencing is introduced very early in the program through what is called "Visual Dictation". This is, essentially, silent "dictation" by the teacher using the pointer and chalkboard and/or charts. As soon as the class has learned to respond with the short vowel sound of "ă" (as in "at") when the teacher points to the written "a" on the chalkboard, temporal sequencing can begin. If the teacher points to "a" twice in succession, *silently*, then the class responds with the same sound twice in succession. The teacher may then write "aa" in sequence and then point to them in sequence. The response, again, will be the same sound in sequence. If "aaa" is written and the teacher points to each symbol in quick succession, the children respond with three identical short-a sounds in quick succession. On the chalkboard may be written the following: "aa a aaa aa aaaa a aaa". The teacher points to each cluster of sound-symbols and taps the number of symbols that appear. The children respond with an identical number of sounds. The spacing shows where the pauses are to be made. The number of signs indicates the number of utterances that are to be clustered together for each "word".[15]

The children are asked to write the symbols in script as the teacher has done on the chalkboard. Although the teacher writes in colored chalk in written script, the child copies in pencil on paper, without the aid of color. Moreover, the child is allowed to reproduce his written symbols

---

15. Demonstration by Dr. Hinman at University of Rhode Island Annual Conference on Reading.

in whatever size and position he pleases. It is explained that this allows the child to concentrate on the main task—that of learning the reading—rather than concentrating on the mechanics of perfect printing or manuscript. Any copy that a child makes and can identify as a particular sound-symbol is to be acceptable to the teacher.

This, of course, is diametrically opposed to such systems as those promoted by Miss Mae Carden and by Mrs. Romalda Spalding, in which perfection of printing and writing are essential parts of the total language approach to learning to read. Dr. Gattegno, originator of *Words in Color*, states that later on a child may be given instruction in improving his writing, preferably after he has developed small muscle coordination.

Another element of the method is the fact that basic instruction in symbols in color—as well as the copies made by children—is usually in cursive script, whereas the print in all of the 21 charts are in plain non-serif type in color on black backgrounds. Promotors of the system claim that this difference in stimuli is of no consequence. Indeed, it is claimed that children are not aware of it as a difference.

When the teacher joins two vowel symbols together, the children learn that they must make the two sounds as close together as possible. They first practice on "a" written in white chalk; then "u"; then "au".

Consonant sounds are also designated by colors. Brown chalk is used for "p", the first consonant sound introduced. It is then combined with the white vowel symbol "a". The digraph is, then, a white "a" and a brown "p" making "op". The brown "p" is then combined with the other vowel graphs: "up", "ip", "ep", and "op", all in their special colors. The digraphs are then reversed for similar drill on "pa", "pu", "pi", "pe", and "po".

After the class has learned these combinations by rote visual and auditory memorization, the teacher asks the children to shut their eyes and listen. The teacher sounds one of the digraphs mentioned above, and the children are asked to name the colors which represent the sounds they have heard. For example, if the word were "up", the answer would be "yellow and brown".

Once the class has demonstrated sufficient visual and auditory memory, the children are given dictation, first by seeing the symbols written on the chalkboard in colored chalk as the teacher sounds them. The next step is for the teacher to trace over the chalk symbols, giving the sounds, followed by the children repeating the sounds. Many variations are possible, for "pap", "pep", "pop", "paap", etc. When the consonants "t" and "s" are added, the number of combinations are greatly augmented, and it is possible to construct sentences such as "it is pat"; "is pat up?"; "pat is up". The apostrophe is then added with an accompanying specially-colored "s".

The small 16-page paperbook *Book 1* is used by the child for his first practice with the five vowels and the three consonants. Worksheets, providing daily exercises help in directing children in the construction of new words from the phonetic symbols which they know and are learning.

A game called "transformations" has been devised and is described in detail on page 25 of the *Teacher's Guide*. Essentially it consists of four operations: (1) reversals, in which "tap" is reversed to "pat", etc.; (2) substitutions, in which initial and final consonants are kept and different vowels are substituted in the middle; (3) insertion, in which a letter is inserted, making "pat" become "pant"; and (4) addition, in which a letter is added to make "ten" become "tent".

At this stage, each child is expected to proceed in inventing his own words. The teacher stands ready to help but the responsibility for progress is the child's. Book 2 is a small 24-page paperback providing additional practice in certain words containing the consonants "m" and double-m; "n" and double-n; "f" and double-f; "d" and double-d; and more than fifty other consonants. Consonant digraphs and consonant-vowel digraphs, diphthongs, etc.

Book 3 of the *Words in Color* method provides fifteen pages of additional consonants, digraphs, and the words which are representative of their use in ordinary English. Opposite each of the 15 pages is a page of one-line sentences which the learner can read. It is noteworthy that no capital letters and no sentence punctuation (except possessive apostrophes) is used until the very end of the *Words in Color* method. Capitals are first introduced on page 39 of Book 3 and long vowel sounds are first introduced in the book. Almost all of Book 3 deals with the irregularities of our language.

Questions are often asked concerning the provision which *Words in Color* makes for individual differences. In a sense, this may be one of its strengths, although it is obscured by whole-group or whole-class responses to teacher-directed drill. By the time the class gets to Book 3, the authors of *Words in Color* suggest that "ability groups" be set up, for it is obvious that many children will be slower in remembering the great variety of symbolization and heavy amount of abstract learning necessary to master Charts 11 through 21.

A *Book of Stories*, consisting of 40 stories, is available and is to be phased into the program when the class has mastered the first ten charts and Books 1 and 2. Word cards and worksheets are all part of the reinforcement media which accompany the program. The worksheets contain a good variety of exercises and games for the children. In fact, some of the innovations in the worksheets are quite clever.

Although *Words in Color* makes every attempt to control the introduction and use of sounds in much the same way that linguistics-phonemics systems do, it makes no claim to being a linguistics-phonemics method. It does not emphasize "families" of sounds as do some other systems which depend upon phonemics. On the other hand, it is unique in its presentation of all possible spellings of a particular sound. Moreover, those spellings are all presented in the charts in the same consistent color. It retains the alphabet and our peculiarities of irregular spellings without change; providing color cues to aid the child in dealing with regular sounds which are represented by irregular spellings.

Research Findings

Words in Color was introduced chiefly on the empirical evidence gained from a UNESCO project in Ethiopia in which color was used in teaching Amharic. It is reported that pupils were taught to read and write in ten hours of instruction, whereas it ordinarily required as many as eighteen months. In the UNESCO project, the 231 characters of the Semitic-type Amharic were introduced and practiced in the first five lessons.

The *Words in Color* method was then tried in Spanish. Illiterate adults in South America were reportedly reading after only three hours of instruction in which the essential features of the method were used. The method also was used in India in an adaptation of the method to Hindi.

As teachers heard of the success of the method in other countries, they began to consider its possible application to English. Pilot projects were tried in Christ The King school in Dallas in 1959; with some five-year-olds in London in 1960; and in Pine Crest school in Sebastopol, California in 1961. Although those tryouts were not scientifically-planned experiments, they did serve to demonstrate that *Words in Color* provided a dimension to beginning reading that had heretofore been neglected.

An "instant literacy" experiment was conducted by Dr. Gattegno in Washington in 1964. Twenty-six illiterate adults voluntered for a course in which *Words in Color* was demonstrated. It is reported that, after three sessions, they could read words in a newspaper. The demonstration was done as part of a conference on literacy sponsored by the U. S. Office of Education.

Probably the most extensive project involving *Words in Color* so

far has been the "Right to Learn" pilot program in adult literacy sponsored by the PACE Association in Cleveland.[16] The project was undertaken during the 1964–65 school year. Five demonstrations in teaching
Words in Color were given by Dr. Hinman. Twenty-one instructors
observed the demonstrations and then did "practice teaching" for three
weeks with adult volunteers.

By February, 1965, almost 1000 illiterate adults enrolled as a response
to clever TV public service spot announcements. More than 100 citizen
volunteers aided in the program.

The program was set up and run as a 30-hour course. The final
report from the director of the project states that this was far too short
a time. "The fact is that those students who were totally illiterate when
instruction began were not independent readers when it ended." This
was, of course, to be expected and is in sharp contrast to Dr. Gattegno's
unbelievable implication that illiterates (even adults) can learn in a
very few hours.

An attempt was made to "measure" achievement by means of pre-
and post-tests, but this had to be abandoned.

In July 1965, Gretchen Jones filed a master's degree research report at Stetson University (Florida) on a Fourth- and Fifth-Grade
experiment with *Words in Color*. The project had been done with
twenty-four disabled readers at Coronado Beach Elementary School during the 1964–65 school year. Scores on the *Iowa Silent Reading Test* in
May, 1965 showed that "*Words in Color* instruction improved the
experimental group's reading ability by a grade-placement value of 1.6
over that which had been anticipated."

A rather extensive study[17] comparing *Words in Color* with traditional basal reader techniques was undertaken in the suburbs of Cleveland by Dr. Mary Austin. Twenty-four First Grade teachers in the
Willoughby-Eastlake schools were involved, as were a total of 560 pupils.
The reading time allotted to the study amounted to 110 minutes daily
for a period of 9 months. This study ran through the 1965–1966 school
year.

The study was prompted by a pilot study in 1965–1965 in which the
results indicated a significant difference beyond the 1% level of confidence
between *Words in Color* and the Scott-Foresman basal series. The
difference was in favor of *Words in Color*.

---

16. *Right to Learn.* PACE Project, Cleveland: Cleveland Public Schools, 1965.
17. Dodds, William G., "A Longitudinal Study of Two Beginning Reading Programs:
    Words in Color and a Traditional Reader," Cleveland: Western Reserve University,
    unpublished doctoral dissertation, 1966. See also the *Ohio Reading Teacher* III, 1
    (October, 1968), 8–11.

A number of less-extensive studies have been reported and all indicate good gains for children who have concentrated on the *Words in Color* approach. For example, Sister Mary Carol reported on nine children who attended sessions of a 6-weeks' summer program at Holy Trinity Reading Clinic in Donaldson, Louisiana. The children were Third- and Fourth-Graders. Gains made in the six weeks ranged from .9 to 3.3 grades.

Sister Carol also reported the achievement of First Grade children in a one-year tryout with *Words in Color*. The median achievement at the end of the First Grade was 2.3 with the range extending from 1.1 to 3.0.

Words in Color was tried in the Steger (Illinois) Junior High School for 9 weeks during the 1964–65 school year sessions with Seventh- and Eighth-Graders. The Eighth-Grade class of 20 pupils had I.Q. scores at the low edge of "average" and below. They were also an average of three grade-levels below average in reading. After the 9-week sessions, the scores all showed some improvement, ranging from .3 to six who scored +1.1. In the same school with a mixed Seventh- and Eighth-Grade group, five scored increases of 1.1 or better, out of the 19 who were in the group.

In the spring semester of 1966, Second-Graders in Lincoln School of Elgin, Illinois were given special instruction in *Words in Color*. Twenty-three children completed the 4-month program. Their teacher, Mrs. von Behrun reports "average reading" gains in *Stanford Achievement* scores (word meaning, paragraph meaning, and word study) of from —4 to +1.9. The mean gain was a +.8.

Reports from England indicate that schools there using *Words in Color* have experienced gains. The British usually report gains in "reading age" rather than in grade levels. From the Grange Infant's School of West Hartlepool, the head teacher states: ". . . We began in February, 1963 with a backward [below grade-level in reading—ed.] class of 7-year-olds who had a reading age of 5 to 5.2 years. By July of the same year, these children had a reading age of up to 7.6 years." She continues, "We now use your scheme with all our 452 children and have found that they progress very well . . ."

Wherever Dr. Gattegno has gone to demonstrate *Words in Color*, his novel system has caught the fancy of columnists and feature writers. Consequently, newspapers in England, America, Australia, and elsewhere have publicized his claims. Quotes from Dr. Gattegno usually make headlines such as the following: "I am sure that quite average children could reach gce standard by 11 and take a university degree at 16" (*Daily Herald*, May 13, 1964); "Briton Says Illiterates Can Read in 3

Days" (Washington D.C. *Evening Star*, April 2, 1964); "Ten Weeks to Write and Read" (London *Observer*, Dec. 9, 1962); "Illiterates Taught to Read After Six Hours" (*Courier*—Australia); "Reading Taught in Few Hours" (Austin, Texas *American-Statesman*, July 19, 1964); "Children Learn to Read in Week" (Dallas *News*, April 9, 1964). These claims may be true.

To justify them and to add dignity, rather than sensationalism, to the *Words in Color* approach, it will be necessary for its founder to apply the research techniques in which he was trained before he joined the field of reading.

Demonstrations of *Words in Color* might also be more convincing if performed by actual classroom teachers acquainted with the children who are performing. When, for example, Dr. Gattegno tried to demonstrate his system with culturally-disadvantaged children in New York City's P.S. 113, he was undertaking an almost impossible task, and the result was far from satisfactory. The one-month experiment should have been carried on by master teachers who were well acquainted with the severe and complex learning disabilities of those children.

It is certain that, in the hands of exceptional teachers, *Words in Color* could be magic. In Euclid, Ohio, for example, Dr. William Jordan, assistant superintendent in charge of elementary schools was quoted by *Time* as saying, "We have never seen such progress. Our color readers are far ahead of any comparable groups."

Another encouraging report is available from an obviously gifted teacher in Australia. She is Sister Mary Leonore Murphy, R.S.C., who reports her own day-to-day success with *Words in Color* in her recent book, *Creative Writing*.[18] The book, copyright in 1966, provides a complete description of the system in use with Sister Leonore's children in St. Mary's Cathedral School, Sydney. It is, essentially, a day-by-day log and describes the growth in creative writing of the six- and seven-year olds in her classes. The book is enriched by full-page color-plates of the children's paintings with which they illustrated some of their writing.

A few quotes from Sister Leonore's account of her work will readily indicate her enthusiasm for the *Words in Color* approach to writing:

> We notice that the children's spontaneous writing at this stage is replete with the naturalness of spoken speech.
>   At a certain stage (it varies with each group of children) the class suddenly experiences a "break-through." It seems that

---

18. Murphy, Sister Mary Leonore, *Creative Writing*. Reading, Berkshire, England: Lamport Gilbert and Co., Ltd. 1966.

light dawns in the child's mind and the workings of the scheme
become crystal clear. . . . In our third-year of experiment with
Words in Colour, this 'break-through' occurred with one group in
only the second week of work.

Sentences are invented with ease and fluency.

Connected sentences with a plot began to appear . . . to
us, this was one of the most thrilling stages of our adventure.

Now, after daily contact with *Words in Colour* for nearly
three years, I respect it as a refined instrument which requires professional handling with precision, perception and detachment . . .

There may be some, therefore, to whom *Words in Color* will be
a novel idea. To others, *Words in Color* may look like our old friend,
"Phonics", with a new colored dress and some linguistics decorations
on her hat.

In any event, *Words in Color* is classified here, not as a phonemics
system, but as one of the "new" *sound-symbol* approaches to beginning
reading. It deserves that classification for, actually, that is its main
objective and its true claim to "newness".

Words in Color is an interesting and promising approach to beginning reading. It, probably, promises too much too soon, but has within
its structure some worthwhile elements which comply with good principles of learning.

Use of color as an added cue to knowing the sounds which printed
symbols represent is a most logical approach. It would also seem logical
that, if there are 47 distinct sounds in our language, 47 different colors
and shades could be cued to those sounds. This, essentially, is what
Words in Color does for the child. Experimenters with the method
report that, actually, the number of colors can be reduced without any
apparent loss of effectiveness.

The organizational pattern of *Words in Color* is apt to be completely overlooked by those who see color as its most novel feature.
When its founder, Dr. Caleb Gattegna, referred to his system as "alge-
braic", he was referring to the similarity with algebra . . . in which there
is progression, substitution, and values (sounds) which are the same
regardless of spellings.

Another feature of *Words in Color* which should not be discounted
is the fact that it retains our spelling patterns (inconsistent as they may
be) and provides the learner with a regular color code which can be
relied upon to provide the cue to the sound.

There are, therefore, some features of *Words in Color* which, undoubtedly, account for its success as an approach to beginning reading.

PSYCHOLINGUISTIC COLOR SYSTEM

The *Psycholinguistic Color System* was devised by Dr. Alex Bannatyne, a specialist in the problems of children with learning disabilities. He received his Ph.D. at the Institute of Psychiatry, University of London; was a member of the faculty of the University of Illinois Institute for Research on Exceptional Children for several years; and is presently the director of the Bannatyne Children's Learning Center in Miami.

The system of using color in phonics evolved out of an interest in the so-called "Letter Case" which had been devised by the late Edith Norrie, founder of the Ordblinds Institut in Copenhagen.

Dr. Bannatyne has developed his color coding from the Norrie Composing Letter Case as a start. He states that ". . . too many people of the 'whole-word' school seem to disregard the fact that English *is* a sound-symbol associated language; that the letters *do* actually stand for sounds and *not* for the object, itself."[19]

His system was developed primarily for dyslexic children, but it is possible that some of the elements of the system may be of more than just passing interest to teachers of normal children who are beginning to read, and certainly to teachers of remedial reading.

Method and Materials

The *Psycholinguistic Color System* is based upon eleven criteria:

1. That there must be a phonemic base, inasmuch as the logical structure of English is phonemic, and there must be arbitrary sound-symbol relationships.
2. The individual letters of the alphabet must be printed on separate cards so that the learner may see them as discrete and separate.
3. There must be logical cues to help the learner over the irregularities of the language.
4. There must be "overlearning" of the sound-symbol relationships.
5. There must be a two-way relationship between printed word and spoken word, and between spoken word and printed word.
6. Any system for teaching reading must utilize traditional orthography.
7. The learner must become active in pupil-centered learning activities.

---

19. Bannatyne, Alex, "The Colour Phonics System," *The Disabled Reader, Education of the Dyslexic Child.* John Money and Gilbert Schiffman, compilers, Baltimore: The Johns Hopkins Press, 1966. Ch. 12.

8. The method must provide attainable goals, in which the learner must feel the success of completing a learning task.
9. There must be attainable intermediate goals.
10. All of the steps of any system must apply to beginning readers, children, dyslexics, or university students.
11. There must be enjoyment in the learning-by-doing. To this end there must be a variety of interesting approaches.

The original materials developed by Dr. Bannatyne were based upon the "Norrie Letter Case" which was similar to an old-fashioned typesetter's composing case. It contained plastic tabs in various colors. Although the colored tab system was an ingenious scheme of color coding, it proved to be cumbersome and expensive.

The new materials consist of twenty-four medium-sized wall charts in color. There is also a box of flash cards, also in color, and kits of colored pencils for each child to use in the six workbooks.

The essence of the color coding is contained in the seventeen vowel color-coded phonemes. The children learn the seventeen color names as their cues to the sounds which those seventeen colors represent.

The *Teacher's Handbook* gives detailed directions on the manner in which the teacher demonstrates with colored crayons on 12 × 18 in. demonstration paper, later using the flashcards for practice through overlearning.

The term "psycholinguistic" has been adopted because the method employs sensory input through auditory, visual, and kinesthetic senses, followed by visual, articulatory, and motor output through the reading, writing, and speaking processes. The linguistic aspects of the system include sequencing of phonemes, graphemes, visual and auditory discrimination of differences such as *tea* and *eat*, and the sequence of words in meaningful context.

The stories in the pupil workbooks are not the usual dull linguistics-reading, but are enjoyable. The object of the entire *Psycholinguistic Color System*, according to its originator, is to provide a "highly motivational program which is worthwhile, totally absorbing, and fun."

The material is to be taught in four "Stages":

Stage I.

Learn shapes of letters of alphabet as phonemes.

Stage II.

Gradually learn sounds of consonants and vowels. At this stage the child overlearns the color coding. The child learns that there are several ways of spelling some sounds. At first the work should be restricted to the phonetically-regular words. Also in Stage II the child is required to begin cursive writing.

Stage III.

Extend the range of color-sound associations and have the child use color coding to build his own stories. Start syllabication. Build rhymes using color to represent rhyming sounds. Blend complex phonemes.

Stage IV.

Start to learn twenty or so spelling rules which will help him in reading and spelling, Introduce the black-on-white vowels, assuming that by now, the learner will have mastered the sounds represented by color.

At the end of Stage IV, the learner discards color and writes and reads in black-on-white.

It is recommended that, once an individual has mastered the color code, he should be introduced to interesting reading materials at his own level of interest and maturation.

Research Findings

The original color system devised by Bannatyne drew upon previously tested materials developed in Copenhagen and in London. Those materials, as well as the experience of the originator of the system, have been largely related to the learning problems of the word-blind or dyslexic child.

The new Psycholinguistic Color System appears to be worthy of attention over the next few years as it is tried out in classrooms of normal children as well as with children who exhibit learning disabilities. The simplified color-coding, using only seventeen colors, should prove very helpful in the establishing of the multiple clues which many children need as guides through our phonemic jungle.

PEABODY REBUS READING PROGRAM

Origins

For centuries and even eons before civilized man learned to communicate through a structured alphabetical language, records of his ancestors' accomplishments were preserved in the form of picture stories. Some were scrawled on the walls of caves; others were carefully engraved on the facades of temples. As picture writing evolved into alphabetical writing, traces of the picture-symbols remained in the resultant stories.

In the nineteenth century, pictures again were interspersed with words and parts of words in little story puzzles designed for the entertain-

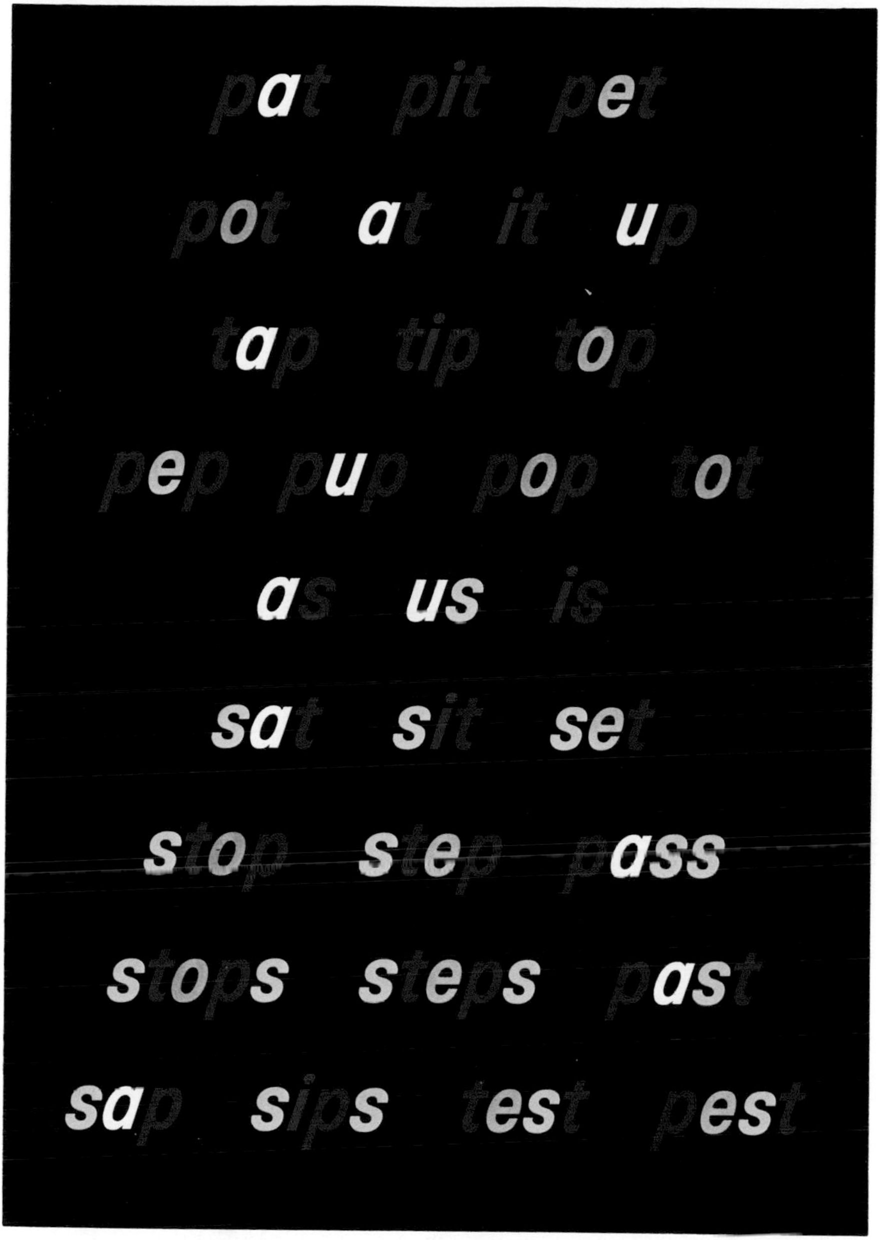

Fig. 8–9 Reprinted by permission of the author, Caleb Gattegno, from the Phonic Code Chart Words in Color. Copyright © 1962 C. Gattegno.

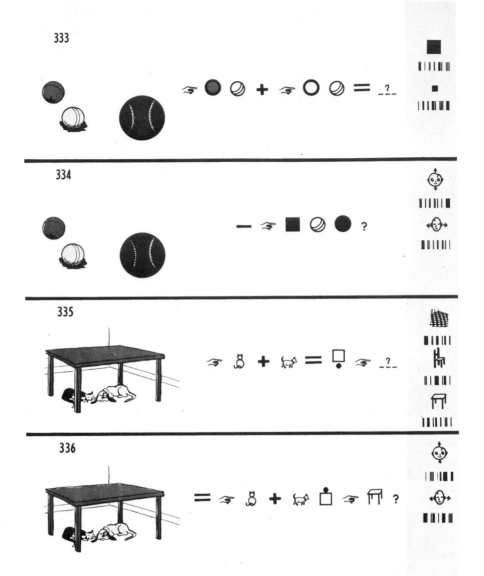

ment of children. For example, in the Mother Goose rhyme "Little Jack Horner", a sketch of a horn was inserted with *er* added. Likewise, a sketch of an ear of corn plus *er* represented the word *corner*. A sketch of the human eye usually represented the letter *I*, etc.

These devices are called *rebuses* (Latin: *with things*), inasmuch as pictures of things are substituted for the graphemes which constitute a word or part of a word.

In a sense, the language of mathematics utilizes rebuses extensively. The symbols are universally understood to stand for words, actions, and meanings. The rebus has become a useful device of communication in international airports throughout the world. The symbols for luggage, phone, restrooms, etc. have become international language symbols. Similarly, international traffic and highway signs utilize universally accepted rebuses.

Now and then the reading profession has been chided with the suggestion that we may as well use rebuses, inasmuch as we already employ pictures in our basal readers to convey the meaning of the story. In contrast to this, it has been pointed out that the child would be forced to learn the words if all picture aids were eliminated.

In 1964, Dr. Richard W. Woodcock and L. M. Dunn conducted extensive research at Peabody College for Teachers, Nashville, Tennessee, in an attempt to develop a rebus approach to beginning reading for mentally-retarded children. That experimental program was the nucleus for the Peabody-Chicago-Detroit Reading Project which compared six different approaches to teaching young mentally-retarded children to read. One of the approaches was the rebus approach. The children in the project were in 120 classes in the public schools of Detroit and Chicago.

Inasmuch as rebus materials were not available for the project, Woodcock devised an experimental series known as the *Rebus Reading Series*, published in experimental form in 1965 by the Institute on Mental Retardation and Intellectual Development of the George Peabody College for Teachers.

Materials and Method

The *Rebus Reading Series* is a set of eight readers, each consisting of from 60 to 80 pages of text. After experimental use, the series was revised in 1968 with the help of C. R. Clark and C. O. Davies of Peabody College and is now published and available through American Guidance Service of Circle Pines, Minnesota as *The Peabody Rebus Reading Program*.

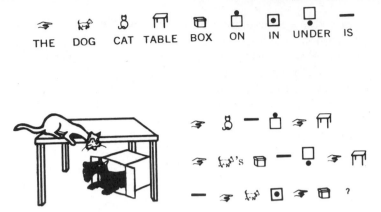

THE   DOG   CAT TABLE   BOX   ON   IN   UNDER   IS

Fig. 8–11A   *Peabody Rebus Reading Program* © *American Guidance Service, Inc. Circle Pines, Minnesota 55014. Copyright 1969.*

The materials of the *Peabody Rebus Reading Program* consist of three programmed texts, two readers of 80 and 72 pages respectively, and some supplementary instructional materials.

The program has the same instructional goals as the traditional basal reader approach. Books One and Two are the readiness level. The Rebus Readers are the preprimer level. In the first session the teacher tells the children, "I am going to show you some pictures. I will tell you what they say; then I want you to tell me what they say."

At the top of the page are four rebuses: cowboy, horse, dog, +. The last represents the word *and.* The child then "reads" the rebus vocabulary and then the phrases "cowboy and horse" and "dog and horse" appearing in rebuses.

With the use of rebuses, the child is able to read the following by the time he gets to page 8 of his preprimer:

> The little cowboy can see the big dog sitt/ing.
> The cowboy is rid/ing the black and white horse.
> The horse is walk/ing.

Note that the *ing* ending is printed out in traditional orthography and is attached to a rebus which represents an action.

The originators of the rebus approach recommend 15 to 20 minute sessions of instruction with their materials.

Research Findings

A very limited research project, funded by the National Institute of Child Health and Human Development, was carried out in May, 1968 in

Nashville. Ten subjects were selected from the Kindergarten program for culturally-disadvantaged children at the Centenary Community Center.

Two identical sets of materials were prepared; one in traditional orthography and one in rebuses. The cumulated accuracy scores of the five children in the rebus group and the five in the T.O. group were analyzed by means of analysis of variance. The results indicated a significant difference in favor of the rebus group, with the differences becoming greater with increase in complexity of tasks. It is reported that the number of words learned by means of rebuses in one 15-to-20-minute lesson exceeded the number of words learned in an entire pre-primer of the usual traditional basal reading program.

Woodcock, in his discussion of the significance of his research, indicates that the problem is the symbol system which is the medium of instruction in reading, and not understanding or comprehension. He suggests that "more use of rebuses in beginning reading, to represent either a part or the entire text of beginning reading materials, should be given serious consideration by educators, authors, and publishers."[20]

As in i/t/a and other non-traditional orthographies, the problem of transfer to traditional orthography is inherent in a rebuses approach. Woodcock claims that, at the end of the *Peabody Rebus Reading Program*, the child will have gone through the readiness and preprimer levels covered in traditional programs. "At the end of the program," he writes, "the children have a T.O. vocabulary of one hundred twenty words as well as certain skills."[21]

The original Peabody-Detroit-Chicago Reading Project reported that after two years of classroom instruction there were no significant differences among the six approaches with respect to reading achievement. It was also stated that, at the completion of that experiment, "the children had a vocabulary of approximately 150 rebuses, of which 100 had been transliterated into T.O."[22]

The most obvious problem with rebuses is that inherent in any whole-word approach. It is the problem of the phonemic and graphemic elements within the words. Eventually this must be faced. Rebuses cannot solve this problem. Indeed the utilization of rebuses beyond the most elementary steps in reading poses the same problem that has plagued

20. Woodcock, Richard W., "Rebuses as a Medium in Beginning Reading Instruction," *IMRID*, V, No. 4, 1968, 10. Nashville: Peabody College.
21. Woodcock, Richard W., "Forty-Five Ways to Teach Reading: A Model for Classifying Reading Approaches," *IMRID*, V, No. 5, 14, Nashville: George Peabody College, 1968.
22. Woodcock, V, No. 4 *op. cit.* 4–5.

oriental cultures which have depended upon the memorization of tens of thousands of whole symbols in learning Chinese, Japanese, and Korean characters.

The research reported by Dr. Woodcock is just a beginning. Perhaps further investigation may reveal some critical areas where the utilization of rebuses is just what is needed to bridge the gap caused by the irregularity of our language.

The rebus approach as a one-to-one sound-symbol system of learning to read may have significance beyond that of being a novelty for the *divertissement* of children.

Other One-to-One Sound-Symbol Approaches

Fōnetic English is included in this discussion of approaches to beginning reading because it is illustrative of the attempts which are being made to devise a one-to-one letter-sound relationship.

The *Fōnetic English* system is, essentially, an outgrowth of the efforts of such famous critics of our language as Benjamin Franklin, Noah Webster, and George Bernard Shaw.

In 1966, a compilation of phonemic elements of the language was arranged to provide for a regularized one-to-one relationship and was published in a 50-page booklet entitled, Fonetic English Spelling. The initial compilation was done by Traugott Rohner, and was published by the newly-formed Fonetic English Spelling Association whose headquarters are in Evanston, Illinois.

It was reasoned that, "If everyone in the world could read and write one world language, everyone could communicate with everyone else." It was also observed that "English is already the most widely-used international language. It would seem, therefore, that English is more desirable for a world language than any other, including the fabrications. Esperanto, Interlingua, etc."

The objective, therefore, is to eliminate the inconsistencies of English so it will be more acceptable as the international language.

The aim of the non-profit Fōnetic English Spelling Association is threefold: to eliminate adult illiteracy by providing a simplified means of learning to read and write; to provide a superior method for teaching children to read—it being suggested that the child who learns through the *Fōnetic English* first can easily make the transition to conventional

THE
29-LETTER
FE ALPHABET

Letter	Its Name	Word Example
ā	ā	āt (ate)
a	a(t)	at
b	bē	best
c	cē (hard c)	cat
d	dē	dog
ē	ē	ēt (eat)
e	e(t)	eg (egg)
f	ef	fat
g	gā (hard g)	get
h	hā	had
ī	ī	īs (ice)
i	i(t)	it
j	jā	jet
k *	kā	Karl
l	el	let
m	em	man
n	en	not
ō	ō	ōld
o	o(t)	hot or father
p	pē	pen
q *	cyū	Quebec
r	or (är)	rat
s	es	sat
t	tē	top
ū **	ū (also yū)	fūd (food)
u	u(t)	up
v	vē	veri (very)
w	wā	wish
x	ecs	fix
y	yā	yes
z	zē	zērō

* Used only in proper nouns.

** Within a word, *ū* is pronounced without the y (as in *food*); for starting a word and for the pronoun *you* it is pronounced *yū*. See p. 13.

Fig. 8–12   Reproduced by permission of the Fonetic English Spelling Association, 1418 Lake Street, Evanston, Illinois 60204.

English; to eventually replace conventional English spelling all over the world with their suggested version of *Fōnetic English.*

At present, there are no reading materials being marketed in *Fōnetic English,* but the method is available to any and all who would use it, without charge from its originators and promoters.

Although there are no reading materials, as such, in the *Fōnetic English* system at present, it is worthwhile to note some of the features of the system and to observe its similarities and differences compared with i/t/a and UNIFON.

A 29-letter alphabet is devised by eliminating the *k* and *q*, except as capital letters in proper nouns such as *Karl* and *Quebec,* and adding the five long vowel sounds. The latter are inserted as "new" letters with the macron (long vowel mark) over them.

The spellings which are suggested are based upon a rather extensive compilation of the many inconsistencies of our language. They based their report on the spellings in the *American College Dictionary.* They report 50 different ways of spelling the five vowel sounds; with 28 spellings of the short vowel sounds, alone. In conventional English spellings, they found 91 ways of spelling the 19 consonant sounds. It was also pointed out that there are 39 spellings for 7 digraphs (two letters pronounced as one), 5 spellings for 2 diphthongs, 7 spellings for the *ir* sound, and 6 spellings for the *ar* sound. In addition to this irregularity, they have reminded the reader of the problems created by double letters and by silent letters. Finally, they point to the fact that the same spelling may call for different pronunciations, examples of which are numerous.

The basic principle in *Fōnetic English* is, consequently, the one-to-one relationship: each consonant, vowel, and letter-combination is given one basic pronunciation or sound.

Another phonemic-spelling approach that has attracted some attention is the hobby of a retired teacher, Leo G. Davis. His approach is based upon a 31-letter "fonetik alfabet". Among other adjustments of the alphabet, Davis suggests a ten vowel arrangement in which the long vowels are represented by small-sized capital letters, to be used within words which contain the long vowel sounds.

The Davis program is set forth in detail in two small books: *the davis speller* and *k-a-t spelz cat.* Both are published by Carlton Press, New York. The *speller* delineates the method, and the *k-a-t* book is to be used with children as a teaching medium. Although both books are hard cover, they both are apparently photo-lithographed from typewriter copy.

THE TURTL   AND THE RABIT

turtl   rabit

.wuns upan ʌ tɪm thʌr waz ʌ rabit hu waz alwʌyz braging abaut hau fast hє kood run. .hє that it was funy tu strut up-and-daun the path asking ?hu wants tu run mє ʌ rʌs?

.altho al thє uther animalz wur sik and tɪrd av hєring him bost so much, nun had ever afєrd tu run him ʌ rʌs. .but wun dʌy thє mopy old turtl sed "ı wil run yu ʌ rʌs, mister rabit.".and al thє uther animalz shur wur serprɪzd,- bєkaz thʌy al nu that thє turtl waz never in ʌ hury, and koodnt hury єven if hє wanted tu.

.but thє funy buny shur did think it was funy, and laft til hiz sɪdz wur sor. .when hє fɪnally finisht lafing hє sed, ";wɪ ı kan bєt yu withaut haf trɪing!" ".nau , just wʌt til yu hav wun, mister rabit, bєfor yu laf. .rʌsez ar wun only at thє finish,- nat bєfor thʌy start." sed thє turtl in hɪz slo texas dral.

.so thє rʌs trak waz al stʌkt aut,- starting fram thє єst end av thє big brij,- daun thє єst sɪd av thє valy ,- araund thє north end av thє lʌk,- bak up thє west sɪd av thє va-ly, and akras thє brij. .thє brij rʌlingz mʌd good grandstand

43

Fig. 8–13   Reproduced by permission of the author, Leo G. Davis, from The Turtl and the Rabit, and the publishers, Carlton Press, Inc.

CONCLUSIONS

Of the eight approaches described in this chapter, only one, i/t/a, is a major approach to beginning reading. It has undergone several years of intensive tryouts in numerous school systems throughout the country. Many supplementary reading materials have been written especially for the i/t/a program, and many more have been transliterated from T.O. into i/t/a. Moreover, one major basal series has been printed experimentally in i/t/a, and Scholastic Publications has printed scores of books in the new type medium.

Words in Color also has had wide promotion but has lacked the research necessary to verify the claims of its originator. It is limited by the specialized nature of its charts and by its method of presenting the teaching sequence. Although its raison d'etre is logical enough, the method is strange to most First-Grade teachers. There are inadequate materials for a complete approach to reading. In short, it is still too esoteric to be classed as a major approach to beginning reading.

The *Psycholinguistic Color System* also uses color as a cue to pronunciation, but it limits itself to seventeen color-coded vowel phonemes. In addition to being an approach to pronunciation, a set of six little reading workbooks provide an interesting introduction to reading.

The other approaches categorized as one-to-one sound-symbol approaches are little more than encoding systems. As such, they may be considered as spelling approaches to reading. UNIFON uses a 40-symbol synthetic alphabet, part of which reminds one of cattle brands. Laubach, Fonetic English, and Davis' *fonetik-alfabet* are systems for spelling phonemically.

The Peabody Rebus system is a symbol-substitution scheme for capturing the imagination of youngsters. It has the inherent limitations of any picture or hieroglyphic symbolism.

The dream of the ages for a perfect language continues to remain a dream. But there is hope for the future. Modern technology has finally cracked the resistance to the universal adoptation of the metric system of weights, measures, and money. The closing decades of this century witness the entire world's uniting on the metric system. A uniform symbol system for encoding the sounds of English is inevitable as the world adopts English as the universal language of commerce, communication, science, and computor printout.

An educated guess leads to the prediction that some slight adjustments in our alphabet and the modernization of the spelling of some of our "spelling demons" is a probability before the end of this century. Such a simple move toward providing an acceptable one-to-one sound-symbol approach to beginning reading will do wonders in removing some of the major problems in beginning reading.

The i/t/a approach has broken much of the resistance of generations of educators to changes of this kind. This, alone, may be its greatest contribution in the long run.

BIBLIOGRAPHY

AMES, WILBUR S., "Research Findings Regarding the Use of i.t.a.," *A Decade of Innovations: Approaches to Beginning Reading*, Elaine C. Vilscek, Editor. Vol. 12, Part 3, Proceedings of the Twelfth Annual Convention, IRA. Newark, Delaware: International Reading Association, 1968, 126–137.

Reactions to Dr. Ames' paper were given by Dr. Robert Emans of Temple University and by Phillip G. Hilaire of Oakland (Michigan) County Schools. Their discussions follow Dr. Ames' presentation in the reference given above.

BANNATYNE, ALEX, "The Colour Phonics System," *The Disabled Reader, Education of the Dyslexic Child*. John Money and Gilbert Schiffman, compilers, Baltimore: The Johns Hopkins Press, 1966. Ch. 12.

BENTLEY, HARRIET, "Words in Color—A Reading Program?" *Issues and Innovations in the Teaching of Reading*. Joe L. Frost, compiler. Glenview, Illinois: Scott, Foresman and Co., 1967. 184–191.

BOWYER, H., "Experiments in Phonemic Spelling," *Education* 83: (November, 1962) 182–186.

CRAYMER, H. S., "Color-Keyed Reading: Words in Color," *Instructor* 76: (November, 1966) 147.

DAVIS, LEO G., *k-a-t spelz cat*. New York: Carlton Press, 1963.

——, *the davis speller*. New York: Carlton Press, 1965.

DODDS, WILLIAM G., "A Longitudinal Study of Two Beginning Reading Programs: Words in Color and a Traditional Reader," Cleveland: Western Reserve University, unpublished doctoral dissertation, 1966.

——, "Words in Color and Basal Readers: A Follow-up Study of Two Beginning Reading Programs," *Ohio Reading Teacher*, III, 1 (October, 1968) 8–11.

DOWNING, JOHN, *Evaluating the Initial Teaching Alphabet*, London: Cassell and Co., 1968.

This book is a "must" for all who wish to probe deeply into the research on i/t/a. Dr. Downing describes both the first and second i/t/a experiments in Britain.

——, "The i/t/a (Initial Teaching Alphabet) Reading Experiments," *The Reading Teacher*, 18 (Nov., 1964) 105–110.

——, and others, *The i/t/a Symposium*. Slough, England: National Foundation for Educational Research in England and Wales, 1966. (Available in U.S.A. from A.S.U.C. Bookstore, Bancroft at Telegraph, Berkeley, California).

——, "Recent Developments in i/t/a," mimeograph from author. Publication forthcoming.

In this article, Mr. Downing reviews much of the recent writings concerning i/t/a. His article is an excellent annotated bibliography.

DURR, WILLIAM K., *Reading Instruction: Dimensions and Issues.* Boston: Houghton Mifflin Co., 1967.
Chapter 3. "Artificial Orthographies" 58–98.

GATTEGNO, CALEB, "Words in Color," *The Disabled Reader, Education of the Dyslexic Child.* John Money and Gilbert Schiffman, compilers, Baltimore: The Johns Hopkins Press, 1966.

HARDMAN, HELEN W., "Using a Simplified Phonetic Alphabet," Indiana Reading Quarterly, II, 2 (January, 1970), 9–11 ff.
Reports experience with the use of a simplified alphabet in the First Grade in the Manchester, Indiana, Community Schools.

HINDS, LILLIAN R., "Studies in the Use of Color," A *Decade of Innovations: Approaches to Beginning Reading,* Elaine C. Vilscek, Editor. Vol. 12, Part 3, Proceedings of the Twelfth Annual Convention, IRA. Newark, Delaware: International Reading Association, 1968, 66–75.

Hinds reports on several projects in which *Words in Color* was used in Cleveland area schools.

i/t/a bulletin, New York: Initial Teaching Alphabet Publications, Inc., 20 East 46th St.

i/t/a journal, London: Pitman's i/t/a Foundation, Ltd., 9 Southampton Place, London, W. C. 1, commencing in 1962.

i/t/a report, Hempstead: Initial Teaching Alphabet Association. The Association housed at Hofstra University, publishes its *i/t/a report* periodically.

LAUBACH, FRANK, *Letters By a Modern Mystic.* New York: Student Volunteer Movement, 1937.

MALONE, JOHN R., "The Larger Aspects of Spelling Reform," *Elementary English,* 39 (May, 1962) 435–445.

——, "The Unifon System," *Wilson Library Bulletin,* 40 (Sept., 1965) 63–65.

MAZURKIEWICZ, ALBERT J., *The Initial Teaching Alphabet in Reading Instruction.* Bethlehem: Bethlehem Area Public Schools, 1967.

This 81-page booklet is the comprehensive final report on the Lehigh University–Bethlehem, Pa. Area Schools Evaluation-Demonstration Project on the use of i/t/a.

MARSH, R. W., "Some Cautionary Notes on the Results of the London i/t/a Experiment," *Reading Research Quarterly,* II, No. 1 (Fall, 1966), 119–126.

Marsh points out some discrepancies in statistical methods employed in reporting. See also the response to Marsh in the *Reading Research Quarterly,* III, No. 1 (Fall, 1967) 85–99.

McHUGH, WALTER, J., "Reactions to Using Color in Early Reading Instruction," A *Decade of Innovations: Approaches to Beginning Reading,* Elaine C. Vilscek, Editor. Vol. 12, Part 3, Proceedings of the Twelfth Annual Convention, IRA. Newark, Delaware: International Reading Association, 1968, 82–88.

Dr. McHugh criticizes the validity of three studies of *Words in Color* and presents eleven theses in which he cautions and suggests need for more definitive research on this method of beginning reading.

MORRIS, J. L., "The Teaching of Reading Using a Phonetic Alphabet," *California Journal of Educational Research* 18: (January, 1967) 5–22.

MURPHY, SISTER MARY LEONORE, *Creative Writing*. Reading, Berkshire, England: Lamport Gilbert and Co., Ltd., 1966.

NORRIE, EDITH, "Word-blindness in Denmark—Its Neurological and Educational Aspects," *The Independent School Bulletin*. April, 1960.

RAPHAEL, SISTER MARY, "Color, A New Dimension in Teaching Reading," *Catholic School Journal* 66: (October, 1966) 56–57.

RATZ, MARGARET S., "Unifon: A Sound Way to Read," *A Decade of Innovations: Approaches to Beginning Reading*, Elaine C. Vilscek, Editor. Vol. 12, Part 3, Proceedings of the Twelfth Annual Convention, IRA. Newark, Delaware: International Reading Association, 1968, 92–99.
Professor Ratz of Principia College is an enthusiast for UNIFON.

Right to Learn. PACE Project, Cleveland: Cleveland Public Schools, 1965.

ROHNER, TRAUGOTT, *Fonetic English Spelling*, Evanston: Fonetic English Spelling Association, 1966.

SERLIN, JANET, "Peabody Rebus Reading," *Reading Newsreport*, IV, 2 (November–December, 1969), 46–47.

SEYMOUR, DOROTHY Z., "Three Linguistic Problems in Using i/t/a." *The Reading Teacher* 21 (February, 1968) 422–426.

TANYZER, HAROLD J., "The Nature and Functions of i.t.a. in Beginning Reading," *A Decade of Innovations: Approaches to Beginning Reading*, Elaine C. Vilscek, Editor. Vol. 12, Part 3, Proceedings of the Twelfth Annual Convention, IRA. Newark, Delaware: International Reading Association, 1968, 116–125.

THOBURN, TINA, "i/t/a in Color," *The Initial Teaching Alphabet and the World of English*. Hempstead, N. Y.: The Initial Teaching Alphabet Foundation of Hofstra University, 1966, 230–232.
An interesting suggestion, documented by classroom experience, that i/t/a could utilize color cues as an additional aid to learning.

WOODCOCK, RICHARD W., "Rebuses as a Medium in Beginning Reading Instruction," *IMRID*, V, No. 4. Nashville: George Peabody College, 1968.

QUESTIONS AND ACTIVITIES FOR DISCUSSION AND GROWTH

1. Obtain an old phonics textbook written at the "turn-of-the-century" and examine the scheme used to obtain a one-to-one sound-symbol relationship. How does it differ from i/t/a?

2. Study the symbols used in German, Danish, French, and Turkish to designate special pronunciations of certain vowels and consonants. Which of these symbols easily could be adopted in English?

3. Study the International Phonetic System diacritical marks and select some

that would be helpful if they were incorporated as part of our grapheme system.

4. Using the information collected in questions two and three above, write some stories using the various symbols you have adopted. Which seem to be most useful?

5. Using the experience you have gained in working on questions three, four, and five above, make an alphabet chart that is a practical one-to-one sound-symbol approach to our language.

6. What elements of the *Words in Color* approach could be adapted and adopted in a simplified color-coding approach to reading?

7. Compare the Laubach simplified spelling system with that of *Fonetic English* and Davis' *fonetik alfabet*. What common elements, if any, can you detect? What do your findings imply?

8. Practice printing in i/t/a and then write several simple stories in i/t/a manuscript. Have some six-year-olds who have just begun to read in T.O. try to read the i/t/a stories. What problems do you observe? What does this imply for children who move from one part of the country and find themselves in a First Grade where i/t/a is the learning medium in beginning reading?

9. Obtain some of the Scholastic Magazine books that have been printed in i/t/a. Analyze them in contrast to the same stories in T.O. Is it any more difficult to *begin to learn to read* in i/t/a than in T.O.?

10. Try to replicate Dr. Frank Laubach's task of devising a written language for a spoken language by listening to the sounds of a foreign language spoken by someone and attempting to isolate the sounds of that language. What do you discover?

THE INDIVIDUALIZED READING
APPROACH

9

Individualized reading is an approach which utilizes the interests of children and permits them to select their own reading materials in keeping with those interests rather than confining them to the devised and restrictive materials of basal readers or any of the other more traditional sequenced materials in reading.

The philosophy behind individualized reading is one which is directed toward optimum growth of self. It rejects the concept that norms of reading such as are found in series of basal readers or in various systems of language arts materials are adequate for any but a very few individuals. Moreover, the supporters of individualized reading contend that self-selection of reading materials should be part of the privilege of all children; that the opportunity for self-selection forces self-evaluation and stimulates plans for self-growth.

Advocates of individualized reading would supplant the common text used by all children with a classroom filled with a variety of reading materials at many levels of difficulty and in many areas of interest, always available to the children. Through the individualized reading approach to beginning reading, the child learns to read because he wants to do so, and he learns through materials which he wants to read, and he learns at a pace which is consistent with his needs and motivation.

Every aspect of individualized reading is a concomitant to the individual, himself. Consequently, individualized reading conforms to the basic principle of learning which insists that learning is the function of the learner and that teaching is merely the arranging of the optimum conditions for learning.

383

Origins

There always has been an individualized approach to beginning reading. Children who apparently are self-taught in reading have learned through their own individualized approach. Long before reading became a structured discipline, replete with batteries of tests, clinics, systems, methods, series, workbooks, machines, and specialists, children were learning to read by the simple process of reading. No doubt these were the above-average children of their day, and they utilized their superior intelligence to abstract the regularities of grapheme-phoneme relationships and developed their own sub-conscious generalizations about word attack.

In BBR days (Before Basal Reader days), children read and were read to. They practiced reading for the sake of learning to read, for the sake of finding out facts, and for sheer fun. They listened and watched while parents read to them. They asked the pronunciation of unknown words on a page and demanded the meaning of unknown spoken words. Much of their day was spent in reading over and over the limited books available to them. In pre-TV days, reading and radio listening were just about the only means children had of finding out about the world around them. Many of us were fortunate enough to have had parents who spent extremely-hard-to-get money for encyclopedias which we literally "ate up" in our thirst for knowledge. Reading was no problem for such children. Reading was an individual operation in which self-selection and self-pacing were intrinsic elements.

As the publishing business became deeply involved in producing reading series and in a complex of many supplementary materials, systems, workbooks, and associated aids, reading became more structured into a pattern of routines closely correlated with basal readers and sequenced from the simple to the complex in such a way that the "average" child would be led through the materials at a standard pace "with the class". Obviously, the reality of individual differences eventually had to be reckoned with. Those who were slower were allowed to go slower. Those who were faster were put into a group who "covered the material" faster. When they were through with their prescribed basals, they were conscripted to help the slow ones, or "permitted" to do "free-time" activities. In some unusual classrooms, they were given the opportunity of going to the "library corner" and snatching bits from some book that happened to be there. The latter was appropriately termed "recreational reading".

"Individualized reading" is something quite different and naturally grew out of dissatisfaction with the so-called "reading establishment" which had developed into a basal reader cult comprising more than 80% of the primary classrooms of America.

Dr. May Lazar,[1] formerly of the Bureau of Educational Research of the New York City Public Schools may be considered as the spokesman for individualized reading when the concept was in its infancy. Inasmuch as New York City seems to have been the center of concern for an individualized reading approach, several were prominent in promoting the idea. Dr. Gertrude Hildreth[2] and Dr. Sam Duker[3] of Brooklyn College; Dr. Leland Jacobs[4] of Teachers College; and Dr. Alvina Treut Burrows[5] of New York University were all supporters of individualized reading in the 1940's and early 1950's. Their ideas spread as their protégés moved out from New York to positions of leadership in reading in other parts of the country.

Today, the leading proponent of individualized reading is Dr. Jeanette Veatch, whose articles and books constitute the most important resource on individualized reading methods and practices.[6] After receiving her doctorate at New York University, Dr. Veatch taught at NYU, Goucher College, University of Illinois, the Pennsylvania State University, Jersey City State College, and presently is on leave to work in a project for the culturally-disadvantaged in the Watts section of Los Angeles.

Materials and Method

Individualized reading is not a commercially pre-packaged kit of materials nor a series of books. It is a concept and a way of learning.

Individualized reading is the application of the best we know concerning individual differences and self.

Individualized reading provides for the utilization of the thousands of children's books that come from the presses yearly, freeing the in-

---

1. Lazar, May, "Individualized Reading: A Dynamic Approach," *The Reading Teacher*, 11 (Dec., 1957) 75–83.
2. Hildreth, Gertrude, *Teaching Reading*. New York: Henry Holt and Co., 1958.
3. Duker, Sam, "Needed Research on Individualized Reading," *Elementary English*, 43 (March, 1966) 220–225.
4. Jacobs, Leland B., "Reading on Their Own Means Reading at the Growing Edges," *The Reading Teacher*, 6 (March, 1953) 27–30.
5. Burrows, Alvina Treut, *Teaching Children in the Middle Grades*. Boston: D. C. Heath Co., 1952. See Chapter 10, "Individualizing The Teaching of Reading."
6. Veatch, Jeanette, *Individualizing Your Reading Program*. New York: G. P. Putnam's Sons, 1959.
    ———— "In Defense of Individualized Reading," *Elementary English*, 36 (April, 1960) 227–234.
    ———— *How to Teach Reading With Children's Books*. New York: Bureau of Publications, Teachers College, Columbia University, 1964.

dividual child from the lock-step of the basal reader series or the phonemic-reading program or the workbook-oriented plan or from the structure of the programmed reading sequence.

The materials for individualized reading are the thousands of books on the adventures of people and animals, real and imaginary; on the world of places and things; on poetry, biography, fiction and fantasy. It is limited only by the energy and resourcefulness of teachers and students.

The approach to beginning reading through individualized reading may be directly through books, or indirect through the medium of experience charts such as described in Chapter 7, "Language-Experience". If the latter, the child is first brought to reading through the acquisition of a large whole-word vocabulary. This, then, provides him with the means for constructing his own stories which he later reads back to himself and to others.

If the approach is directly through books which the child selects for himself, he most easily will "read" those books which the teacher or parent reads first to him. Frequently in the Kindergarten the teacher reads a simple story and places the book on the library table for children to look at later. Occasionally a child may be interested enough in the story to take the book and attempt to read it. With such motivation, that child may easily be started on the road to reading through the individualized reading approach. He needs only the encouragement and guidance of the teacher.

When books are used as the direct approach to individualized reading, the task of the teacher is to obtain a large collection of easy-to-read beginning books on a variety of subjects that are of interest to the type of children in her class. Each day the teacher should read aloud from one of those books. Each day all children in the class should be expected to spend "reading" time with books. It is understood that reading time is exploratory time with beginners. Some will look only at pictures, while others will actually be attempting to identify certain words on the page.

In order for the teacher to develop this reading program to its fullest potential, she must be constantly alert and sensitive to the individual needs of all children in her class.

A third possible approach to individualized reading is through the readiness and pre-primer materials of a basal reader series. Such an approach provides the teacher with a whole-class vehicle and also provides a unity of beginning which could be substituted for the experience chart phase described earlier. After work in the pre-primers, the teacher would then move over into individualized reading as the various children indicate a readiness to deal with words and simple sentences.

Whichever the approach, directly through individual books, through experience charts, or through the pre-primer work, the individualized reading program calls for the individual selection of books and the separate reading of those books by each child at his own rate. This requires that the teacher use a means for recording progress and for noting special instructional needs. This is accomplished through the so-called "individual conference."

The conference is a short five to ten minute period spent with each child, hearing him read and talking with him about the book he is reading. It provides a means for checking on errors and on comprehension. It also is a time for guidance and evaluation. It is a time for listening and noting the child's reactions, his likes, dislikes, fears and joys, and his concept of self. It is a one-to-one relationship over a book which is of the child's own choice. In the best practice, the conference is also scheduled at the request of the child although, of course, there may be times when the teacher "arranges" for a conference when it is obvious that one is overdue.

Dr. Veatch describes in detail the elements of the individual conference in *Reading in the Elementary School*,[7] pages 120–165.

The individual conference provides the teacher with a variety of facts concerning each child's needs and interests. As a result of conferences, the teacher can group children for special instruction in specific reading skills. Children may also be grouped for discussion on common interests or for purposes of sharing their reading experiences.

CONCLUSIONS

As an approach to beginning reading, individualized reading methods have much to be recommended, and have some restrictive features which must not be discounted.

Individualized reading does utilize many of the most effective principles of learning, interest, motivation, and past experiences. It treats individuals as individuals and allows them to learn to read through the process of reading.

The fact that more than 80% of elementary teachers are basal reader oriented is an indication of the problem of initiating an individualized reading program into any school system. Teachers would have to be

---

7. Veatch, Jeanette, *Reading in the Elementary School*. New York: The Ronald Press, 1966.

convinced that individualized reading approach is, indeed, better, and then would have to make a commitment to learn how to make it succeed. Reaction to change of such a radical nature often precludes even a modest try at individualized reading.

Moreover, many basal-oriented teachers are insecure or unsure of the success they might have with such an unstructured program. Others feel unwilling to undertake such an expenditure of time and energy which individualized reading necessitates.

The negative factors which seem to attend the suggestion of individualized reading as an approach to beginning reading probably account for the possibility that individualized reading may never become a widely-accepted approach to beginning reading even though it provides a means for surrounding reading with many of the optimum conditions for learning.

BIBLIOGRAPHY

BURROWS, ALVINA TREUT, *Teaching Children in the Middle Grades.* Boston: D. C. Heath Co., 1952. See Chapter 10, "Individualizing the Teaching of Reading."

DARROW, HELEN F., and HOWES, VIRGIL M., *Approaches to Individualized Reading.* New York: Appleton-Century-Crofts, 1960.

DOLCH, E. W., "Individualized Reading vs. Group Reading," *Elementary English,* 37 (Dec., 1961) 566–575.

DUKER, SAM, "Needed Research on Individualized Reading," *Elementary English,* 43 (March, 1966) 220–225.

——, *Individualized Reading: Readings.* Metuchen, N. J.: Scarecrow Press, Inc., 1969.
This is an anthology of 60 articles and theses on individualized reading. It was selected as one of the outstanding reference works of 1968.

FOX, GUDELIA A., and FOX, RAYMOND B., "The Individualized Reading Controversy," *National Elementary Principal,* 44 (Sept., 1964) 46–49.

GROFF, PATRICK, "Individualized Reading in First Grade," Chapter 2 in *First Grade Reading Programs,* Perspectives in Reading No. 5, Newark, Delaware; International Reading Association, 1965. 7–27.
This review of the past, present, and future of Individualized Reading contains an extensive bibliography. Dr. Groff's review of the research led him to question the claims made by the proponents of this approach.

HILDRETH, GERTRUDE, *Teaching Reading.* New York: Henry Holt and Co., 1958.

JACOBS, LELAND B., "Reading on Their Own Means Reading at the Growing Edges," *The Reading Teacher,* 6 (March, 1953) 27–30.

LAZAR, MAY, "Individualized Reading: A Dynamic Approach," *The Reading Teacher,* 11 (Dec., 1957) 75–83.
Dr. Lazar also developed extensive bibliographies on individualized reading while with the N.Y.C. Bureau of Educational Research. Also

see: *Individualized Reading Interim Report Survey in Selected Schools,* 1956–1957. (Mimeographed)

MIEL, ALICE, compiler, *Individualized Reading Practices.* New York: Bureau of Publications, Teachers College, Columbia University, 1958.

SAFFORD, ALTON L., "Evaluation of an Individualized Reading Program," *The Reading Teacher,* 12 (April, 1960) 266–270.

SARTAIN, HARRY W., "A Bibliography on Individualized Reading," *The Reading Teacher,* 13 (April, 1960). 262–270.

STAUFFER, RUSSELL G., "Individualized and Group-Type Directed Reading Instruction," *Elementary English,* 37 (Oct., 1960) 375–382.

VEATCH, JEANETTE, *Individualizing Your Reading Program.* New York: G. P. Putnam's Sons, 1959.

—— "In Defense of Individualized Reading," *Elementary English,* 36 (April, 1960) 227–234.

—— *How to Teach Reading With Children's Books.* New York: Bureau of Publications, Teachers College, Columbia University, 1964.

A delightful 32-page illustrated booklet.

——, *Reading in the Elementary School.* New York: The Ronald Press, 1966.

This is Dr. Veatch's major publication on Individualized Reading.

WITTY, PAUL A., and others, "Individualized Reading—A Summary and Evaluation," *Elementary English,* 36 (Oct., 1959) 401–412.

QUESTIONS AND ACTIVITIES FOR DISCUSSION AND GROWTH

1. How does one group for individualized reading?
2. How does one conduct the individual conference as a day-to-day activity?
3. Visit a school where individualized reading is the approach being used. What do you observe?
4. Many people confuse individualized reading and the language-experience approach. In what ways are these two approaches similar?
5. How are they different?
6. Make plans for obtaining the materials for an individualized reading approach with 27 First Grade children. What is your conclusion?
7. How do you know that you are covering a complete phonics program within an individualized reading approach?
8. List some of the major bookkeeping problems in the individualized reading approach. How can they be solved?
9. Obtain a copy of Dr. Veatch's text. Find out how she suggests starting beginning reading via the individualized approach.
10. Is an individualized reading approach possible for a beginning teacher? Give good reasons for your answer.

EARLY-READING APPROACHES

10

Interest in the learning capabilities of very young children has encouraged a growing number of research studies, learning materials, and debates. Many of these have concentrated upon reading as the medium of learning, often placing the characteristics of the learner in secondary position.

It would appear logical that concern for the learning of very young children should be identified with the maturational abilities of the learners. Such is not always the case. Yet there are obvious differences in learning abilities in any randomly-selected group of four-year-olds or five-year-olds. The multi-faceted individual differences which characterize the range of observable and/or measurable factors affecting learning are only part of the pluralistic nature of the individual learner. Any accounting of learning abilities must also recognize the unmeasurable and imponderable factors which constitute "self". To attempt to measure reading achievement of very young children engendered by any particular approach to beginning reading without reference to the individual differences of those young children is to rest claims upon highly-questionable and extremely-inadequate bases.

It is appropriate that certain questions be raised and specific opinions be expressed. Some questions emerge from an evaluation of some of our current practices and/or time-honored concepts: 1. "When should a child begin formal learning activities?" 2. "How can a child be aided in becoming ready to read?" 3. "How is readiness to read measured?" 4. "Should Kindergarten children be taught to read?" 5. "Should four-year-olds be taught formal reading readiness learnings?" 6. "What

391

should four-year-olds and five-year-old be taught in the area of reading?"
7. "What approach to reading should be used with very young children?"

A four-year longitudinal research project on some 7,000 Kindergarten children in 56 schools in New York City's disadvantaged areas was undertaken to provide additional pertinent information on the efficacy of early reading instruction. The study was supported by funds from the Center for Urban Education and was directed by Professor Miriam Goldberg of the Department of Psychology of Teachers College, Columbia University.

The plan called for the continuous evaluation of the children, with a final evaluation of their reading abilities at the end of the Third Grade in June, 1970. The main objective was to answer several questions, one of which is whether or not early formal reading instruction (in Kindergarten) has significant effect on achievement in the later grades of school. To answer this question, some of the 7,000 children were taught to read as Kindergartners, some as First Graders, and others did not begin until the end of the First Grade.

Some of the children in the study received varying amounts of pre-reading instruction, and some received no readiness work. Some experienced instruction in a synthetic alphabet; others learned to read in traditional orthography; and some used materials in phonemic spelling patterns.

At present, most Kindergartens stress only reading-readiness activities, relegating formal reading instruction to the First Grade. Wherever an individual Kindergarten child exhibits a readiness for reading, opportunity is given in the Kindergarten for incidental unstructured teacher help with pre-primer type booklets.

This may not remain the situation in the very near future, for there is now and will undoubtedly continue to be increased pressure to institute more formalized instruction in reading with five-year-olds and, perhaps, even four-year-olds.

Supporters of such a move base their arguments upon instances in which very young children apparently have learned to read before the traditional First-Grade experience. Some question the necessity of spending an extended period of time on so-called reading-readiness activities. Others, apparently, do not recognize the difference between reading readiness and readiness for reading, assuming that the former automatically metamorphoses into the latter.

Aukerman[1] has described in detail the reading readiness activities of a good Kindergarten year. She identified six segments of the Kindergarten

---

1. Aukerman, Louise R., "Reading in the Kindergarten," *New England Reading Association Journal*, 5:3, (Spring, 1970), 19–24.

program that are specifically planned to generate reading readiness. They are the following.

1. Learning to identify names.
2. Language-experience reading activities.
3. Learning the sounds of letters and whole words.
4. Communications skills.
5. Experiences with books.
6. Listening to poetry.

Readiness for reading is quite another aspect of the larger concept of readiness. Readiness for reading is a point on the maturation growth curve when all physical, emotional, psychological, and perceptual systems are optimum for "GO". How early this optimum condition occurs depends on individual differences.

Perceptual readiness has been cited by Bruner[2] as a significant factor when considering the differences in children's utilization of learning situations. Interest in developing perceptual readiness has recently been spurred by the sudden focus on the problem of dyslexia and the problems of the perceptually-disoriented child. Some Kindergartens and Nursery Schools have purchased "perceptual training" materials for use with all of their children regardless of whether or not there be any proof that they need them. Now that the term, "dyslexia" is popular, more and more incidence of dyslexia is being reported.

Ilg and Ames[3] describe the readiness tests which have been developed at the Gesell Institute of Child Development. Their concept of readiness for school learning is the result of the distillation of thousands of case studies at the Yale University Clinic and at the Gesell Institute. They state that "Fifty years of experience in the use of a battery of developmental tests has shown that the child's developmental level can be determined through the use of such behavior tests."

In their book, Ilg and Ames do anticipate that parents will be playing games with pre-school children and that some of those "games" will have the characteristics of pre-reading materials. Indeed, some may have the elements of reading readiness activities and others may even contain subtle training in listening to phonemics.

Although Ilg and Ames support the age norm of six years for entrance into First Grade and five years for entrance into Kindergarten,

---

2. Bruner, Jerome, "On Perceptual Readiness," *Psychological Review*, 64: (1957) 123–152.
3. Ilg, Frances L., and Ames, Louise B., *School Readiness*. New York: Harper and Row, 1964.

they emphasize their own point of view as being one in which age is expressed in normative behavior rather than in chronological terms. Consequently, a child who displays a behavior which approximates the norm for five-year-olds will be ready for Kindergarten and one who exhibits a six-year normative behavior would be ready for First Grade.

A mental age of six years and six months has been a rule-of-thumb measure for readiness for formal reading instruction. Anderson[4] reported on the success of children below that age in identifying phonemes and graphemes. It certainly is not new to discover that there are some children who can and do differentiate phonemes and graphemes at an early age. Moreover, many instances have been reported over the years of children who have learned to read at an early age and yet who have not been considered as being "child prodigies."

In some cases, early readers have been taught by parents or by older brothers and sisters who "played school" with them. In other cases, no apparent instruction was given; but, in its place, was a persistence and a compulsion to learn to read.

Organized attention to reading has been directed toward very young children in a number of instances. Montessori schools, specifically-designed research studies, and "Operation Head Start" have from time to time incorporated early reading activities for four-year-olds. Whipple reported on some of the Head Start programs to the World Congress on Reading, summarizing by stating that "Our emerging [American] concept of reading readiness provides for prereading curriculums for four- and five-years-olds . . . and introduces reading in kindergarten for most capable children."[5]

In view of these and other pronouncements on the capabilities of some very young children to learn to read, it is not surprising to find a number of approaches to beginning reading designed for the very young child. It is not the purpose here to debate the question of whether or not Kindergartners or Nursery School children should be given formal reading instruction; but, rather, to describe some of the approaches that are available for use in school and in the home. Comments indicating where further research is needed may point to a need for restraint in attempting value judgments.

Some of the approaches are intriguing, some are expensive, some

---

4. Anderson, Dorothy, "A Study to determine if children need a mental age of six years and six months to learn to identify strange printed forms when they are taught to use oral context and the initial sound of the word," unpublished doctoral dissertation, Greely: Colorado State College, 1960.
5. Whipple, Gertrude, "The Concept of Reading Readiness in The United States of America," *Reading Instruction: An International Forum*, Marion D. Jenkinson, editor, Newark, Delaware, International Reading Association, 1967.

are minimal, but most are predicated upon a one-to-one ratio of learner and teacher. Within these approaches to early reading may be indications of what may be one future trend in reading.

THE MONTESSORI METHOD

Origins

It is not at all surprising that the Montessori Method should have had a strong revival in the United States in recent years. Indeed, the similarities between the problems of "slum" children with whom Dr. Maria Montessori worked in Rome at the beginning of this century and those which surround the targets of inner-city concern today are so striking that it would have been a miraculous oversight if her method had not been "rediscovered".

The fact, however, is that her method was rediscovered some years before concern for the disadvantaged and before Martin Deutsch and Jerome Bruner became popular prophets of the "new" approach to learning. The fact that many of their recent "discoveries" support or parallel prior "discoveries" by Montessori half a century ago derives more from the commonalty of their *approach* to the investigation of how children learn, rather than any common features of the slums of the San Lorenzo quarter in 1900 and the slums of Harlem.

To Mrs. Nancy McCormick Rambusch should go a good measure of credit for promoting the revival of the Montessori Method in America.[6] While studying languages at the University of Paris, she became acquainted with the method and became a devoted convert to Montessori. She took instruction in the method and became "certified" as a Montessori teacher. Upon returning to America, she started a Montessori nursery school in her own Manhattan apartment. Moving to Connecticut a few years later, Mrs. Rambusch found that her fellow Catholic neighbors were eager to work with her in founding a Montessori school for their children.

The school was started in a renovated stable in 1958 and was christened "The Whitby School"[7] after Whitby Abbey in Yorkshire. Mrs.

---

6. Rambusch, Nancy McCormick, *Learning How to Learn—An American Approach to to Montessori.* Baltimore: Helicon Press, Inc. 1962.
7. "Joy of Learning: The Whitby School," *Time* 77 (May 12, 1961) page 63.
   "Intellectual Leap: Montessori Revival at Whitby School," *Newsweek:* 61 (June 24, 1963) 106.

Rambusch was so successful with her Montessori method that in two years her neighbors decided that a new Whitby School should be built and set about to raise the funds necessary. It was opened in January, 1961 on a 37 acre estate with 150 children (aged 3 through 12), many of them non-Catholic. Montessori-trained teachers were recruited from France, England and Ireland to form a staff of fifteen. The Whitby School, subsequently became the "headquarters" for the revival of the Montessori Method, as well as the "motherhouse" for the training of "approved" Montessori teachers. Thus it was inevitable that the American Montessori Society be formed by followers of Nancy Rambusch and that she be elected as its first and very dynamic president.

The movement is essentially non-denominational now, although its beginnings in both Italy and in America were strongly Catholic. A survey of 38 Montessori schools in 1963 found that only 13 were Catholic and 1 was Presbyterian. The rest were non-denominational and almost all were private schools.

It is interesting to note that at the Henry Barnard Training School of Rhode Island (State) College, Montessori methods have persisted as a very essential part of the curriculum for the training of early elementary teachers for more than half a century. Consequently, through the years since 1913, many Montessori-type activities have been carried into the public schools of Rhode Island by teachers trained in Montessori techniques. The same may be true in other sections where shades of Montessori have lurked.

The revival of Montessori in America, oddly enough, was not directed toward the economically disadvantaged children, as was the case in Montessori's Rome, but toward what Nancy Rambusch fondly calls "pushy parents" in the upper income brackets.[8] Children from these advantaged homes in suburbia not only are enrolled in parent-financed Montessori schools as a "status symbol" but because parents are convinced that their children deserve the special benefits of "early" learning that the Montessori school provides.

To fill the need for "approved" Montessori teachers who are entitled to start schools and who are exclusively permitted to purchase genuine Montessori equipment, the American Montessori Society has developed special training courses, and cooperates with the Association Montessori Internationale and the Italian Montessori Society. There are close to 200 Montessori schools now in operation in America and many more which have some aspects of Montessori Method as part of their curricula.

---

8. Rambusch, Nancy McCormick, Speech at 9th Annual Conference on Reading, University of Rhode Island, 1963.

The original Montessori Method grew out of a lifetime of work directly with children by Dr. Maria Montessori who, in the closing years of the 1800s observed mentally retarded children's learning in her role as Directress of a school for the mentally deficient. During those years, Dr. Montessori related her medical training to the needs and growth patterns of children and began to develop a theory of teaching which was so successful that year after year her "non-learners" passed public examinations for primary certificates. Heretofore, such children had been relegated to what was then common terminology, "Idiot."

Her triumph with new methods convinced her to move from her medical profession to the new challenge of education. Her first work was undertaken in "Childrens Houses" established as islands of culture in hopelessly-degrading slums in Rome. Within weeks, frightened, inarticulate, disadvantaged children were transformed into eager learners.

When Maria Montessori passed away in the Netherlands in 1952, she left her methods as a legacy to the education world.[9] Her method in reading depends to a large extent upon maturational activities of infancy and very early childhood. The sequences which she described and which are known as the "Montessori Method in Reading" will alone be investigated and evaluated here.

Materials and Method[10]

Many times in the writings of Maria Montessori, reference is made to "the prepared environment", or to "preparing the child" for certain learnings. This is also true in the case of reading.

"Preparation" for reading is achieved through writing.

Dr. Montessori describes how she discovered that retarded children could learn complicated tasks if they were first "prepared" through mastery of simple tasks. She concluded that "we should really find the way to teach the child *how*, before *making him execute* a task." She continued: "I saw especially that preparatory movements could be carried on, and reduced to a mechanism, by means of repeated exercises not in the work itself but in that which prepares for it. Pupils could then come to the real work, able to perform it without ever having directly set their hands to it before."

The significance of this to reading and writing is this: (1) reading

---

9. Montessori, Maria, *The Advanced Montessori Method*. Vol. II. *The Montessori Elementary Material*. Cambridge, Massachusetts: Robert Bentley, Inc., 1964.
10. The description of the Montessori approach to beginning reading is derived directly from the writings of Dr. Montessori.

is preceded by writing; (2) writing is preceded by a series of "preparatory movements" which become habits; (3) then, without ever having written before, the child applies the "prepared habits" and he writes; (4) if he can write, he can read.

Dr. Montessori stated that the idea was so simple that she admitted being annoyed that she had not thought of it long before.

She first had an expensive alphabet manufactured. The letters were in flowing script. The consonants were painted with blue enamel and the vowels in red. The letter forms were strengthened with backs cut of bronze. When it was necessary to duplicate the letter forms, a less expensive means had to be invented. It was thus that the now-famous sandpaper letters were devised. With their first use, it was discovered that they were not only much less expensive, but that the rough surfaces greatly aided in the learning process for, when a child traced over the letter he could feel its surface and, when he slid off the rough sandpaper surface, he would be warned immediately that he needed to correct his error. Thus were born what are now known as "self-correcting" materials.

The sandpaper script letters were mounted on smooth cards, thus providing a raised surface for the letter and a smooth background which would warn the learner that he was "off the track".

The sequence of tracing first involves the index or pointer finger, then the index and middle finger. This is to be done first as the child looks at the letter, and then with his eyes closed. In this manner, the child is creating sensory pathways through both sight and touch, and then is dropping out one of the cues (sight) in preparation to the time when the touch cue must also be dropped out and he must then rely on mental imagery to provide the cue for him to recreate the letter by writing. This is, certainly, in keeping with one of the basic principles of learning: "cue reduction".

Another step was referred to by Montessori when she described the use of a stick as a third step in tracing. The stick was used in preparation for holding a pencil, chalk, or pen.

A reinforcing exercise for visual memory of letter forms is provided with cards on which have been printed the letter forms and the child is to place his cut-out letter forms superimposed upon the printed symbols. The child's cut-out letter forms are not the same as the sandpaper letters, but are more like large cut-out lower case letters. They are made available to the child in a partitioned box in which the letters are separated by partitions.

The children also use their alphabet letters for the construction of words. Actually, they should be referred to as *phonograms* rather than alphabet letters, for nowhere is the alphabet taught. On the contrary, the letters are always taught as sounds. This, of course, was much more simple in Italian than in our English where, according to a recent study there were 311 regular long vowel sounds and 262 irregular long vowel sounds; 567 regular short vowel sounds and 107 irregular short vowel sounds; 103 regular short *u* sounds and 188 irregular *u* sounds. These irregularities in English tend to complicate the system in ways which Dr. Montessori did not encounter in Italy.

A large board is made available for children to use in arranging the vowels. On the board (or card) the vowels are arranged in what Dr. Montessori called "analogy of form". In other words, the vowels which are related to the circle are arranged across the top and those related to a straight line across the bottom. The arrangement is:

o   *e*   *a*

i   *u*

The above-named letters are printed on the card or board in exactly the same size as the child's phonograms. The child then is given the task of placing his letters upon the same letters on the card. This is for visual discrimination, and for reinforcing the idea that some letters are formed by curves that are similar and some by strokes that are similar.

The materials so far described are referred to by Montessori as "Didactic Materials". Using the didactic materials, the child is given exercises to work upon first using the vowels (by sound) and then the consonants (by sound). In tracing over the sandpaper letters and saying the sound at the same time, the child is adding another element to his learning, and it involves two more senses: the sense of muscular tension in his voice mechanism (sometimes referred to as kinesthetic) and the sense of sound. Thus, in the process of learning to trace the sandpaper letters, the child uses four senses. Moreover, he is "without fear of the mistakes of which a child writing with a pencil for the first time is so conscious".

This first stage of tracing fixes the mental image of the letter with the auditory sound of the letter. In the second stage, the teacher (referred to by Montessori as "directress") asks the child to select certain letters from the child's compartmentalized box of phonograms. The teacher says: "Give me *ĭ*" (pronouncing the short vowel sound); "Give me *ŭ*". She never calls the letters by name.

In the third stage, the teacher holds up a phonogram and asks, "What is this?" The child responds with the letter sound. In teaching consonants, the Montessori Method insists that, after the consonant sound has been stressed, it must be followed by a vowel sound. When the child repeats it, he must pronounce the consonant sound and add a vowel sound to it.

Dr. Montessori wrote: "If he has exercised himself sufficiently in these exercises, he will be *potentially* ready to write all the letters of the alphabet and all of the simple syllables, without ever having taken chalk or pencil in his hand."

The relationship of this "preparation for writing" to the act of reading is easy to understand if one applies the psychological principle of contiguity to Dr. Montessori's scheme. She suggested that the teaching of reading should be begun at the same time as the teaching of writing. She reasoned that, in the process of writing, the child hears the sound of the letter and sees its shape and also writes its shape, thus utilizing several senses. In essence, then, the child is reading the letter when he is learning to write it. In the Italian language where there is a somewhat closer relationship between the graphemes and phonemes, the process is considerably less subject to irregularities than in English. Thus, the only difference that Montessori could see was that, when a child sees the letter and recognizes it, he is reading; and, when he traces the shape of the letter, he is writing. She concluded that, if the two processes are contiguous, the child will achieve both simultaneously.

According to Montessori, "preparation" is necessary in three areas: (1) muscular composition of the letter; (2) pronouncing the letter sound (3) manipulation of the writing instrument.

Once the child is prepared, the child *writes,* as if by magic. Montessori described such a moment when she was holding a class on the roof terrace. The children had been "prepared". She handed a piece of chalk to a child and asked him to draw a picture of the chimney which was adjacent to their play area. The child drew the picture on the terrace floor, and then carefully began writing words, whereupon he jumped up with joy shouting, "I can write, I can write!" He had never written before. He made the discovery and believed that it had come through the magic of having grown up. Others then took the chalk and "discovered" that they, too, could write.

Montessori concluded that, after the "preparation", "language develops, not gradually, but in an explosive way; that is, the child can write any word." This may have been true in Italian, but in the irregular framework of English, it may be true only after more extended "preparation" in the many sounds of some letters and letter combinations. Apparently, Montessori experienced this sudden discovery and ecstasy over the child's first writing many times, for she referred to it and described many such happy moments.

The didactic material for reading consists of slips of paper on which the teacher has written names of objects. The various reading games which the class plays involve selection of the slips, reading of the name of a toy and then being permitted to play with that toy. This had tremendous motivational implications for slum children in Rome in the year 1900. It might also have similar attraction to "children without" in today's American slums. Montessori soon discovered that the joy of learning to read superseded the fun of having a toy, and that children played with the word slips in preference to doing many other fun activities.

After the word game comes phrases and then sentences. The sentences are in the form of "directions" such as: "Go to the window and close the blinds". "Get all the girls in a line and walk past me and back to your seats". The directions are long and involve a sequence of tasks which demand that the reader understand and then remember the directions. Children of age four were able to perform this type of reading in Montessori's school.

One of the most effective phases of Dr. Montessori's Method is what she called "Graphic Language". In "Graphic Language", the teacher writes a question on the chalkboard. If the children really can read it, they spontaneously answer the question in excited unison. For example, she wrote, "Do you love me?" "Yes, Yes" was the excited response. Whereupon, she started to write in careful and clear script, directions, asking them to be very quiet. "Watch me." She then wrote, and the children answered her questions which she asked through "Graphic language".

The Montessori Method decries the system of reading aloud. Dr. Montessori felt that it was almost as difficult as preparing a speech and giving it. Silent reading must be isolated from the articulate. Language transmits thoughts over distances by means of printed pages. Sounds of spoken words are not necessary for reading, according to Montessori, after a child has been prepared through writing.

In the Montessori school, each child usually works alone unless invited to work together by another child. Each child is responsible for his own discipline, and for his own materials. He is also responsible for completing his own tasks. This has been a criticism by some educators, who feel that this violates the advantages of group work, and places a premium on silent isolated existence. In Montessori schools in America, there is generally more freedom of movement and sharing than implied in the older application of Montessori principles in the 1920s.

Those who work with Montessori Methods feel that the desire to learn is stressed and, inasmuch as children are working only with those things that interest them, discipline is naturally obtained. The ground rules are: (1) a child must not touch another child who is working; (2) a child may not touch another child's work while it is being worked upon, (3) a child is free to invite others to share in work, and also is free to refuse help from another child.

There is no time limit on activity. Work may be left until tomorrow. In this context, the Montessori "timetable" for learning to read differs greatly from the usual school. There is no structuring of the curriculum into formal "First Grade" or "Second Grade," nor into specific course areas. When the child in the Montessori school learns to read, he is then master of his own learning activities, and can work at his own pace on anything related to reading.

Reading actually begins when the child composes words by using his movable phonograms (alphabets). Since Montessori felt that over-emphasis on pronunciation of parts of words and words in isolation was detrimental to reading, the objective is to promote the reading of phrases and sentences just as early as possible.

In *Learning How to Learn* Nancy Rambusch describes the American Adaptation of the Montessori Method. Several suggestions are made for helping children practice in the area of phonemics. For example, it is suggested that the vowels should be of blue cut-out cards and the consonants of red cardboard. The teacher (or parent) should pronounce a phonemically-regular word, and the child assembles letters from his Phonogram Box (called the Movable Alphabet Box). Most children like to work on the floor, according to observations of Montessorians.

Puzzle envelopes contain words which are phonemically irregular, e.g., cough, laugh, etc. The children are to work with these words, reconstructing them with their phonogram letters. The teacher needs to help.

In vocabulary development, it is suggested that pictures dealing with objects in the classroom and in the environment be collected and used in enlarging a child's vocabulary. Phonemically regular three-letter words of objects should be used first. Such words as *pan, bed, lid, pig*, etc., are easy for the child to reconstruct and pronounce.

A number of exercises dealing with the "Function of Words" are suggested. They consist of boxes of small objects such as nails, buttons, pencils, clips, etc. The child practices using the article, *a* and *the*, with the word *one* sometimes used.

The "function" of adjectives, prepositions, conjunctions, verbs, and adverbs are also learned through similar games involving pictures of situations, action, etc. Symbols are used: arrows to designate action; arrows with question marks to designate where a subject and an object

Fig. 10–1 Reprinted through the courtesy of Educational Teaching Aids Division, A. Daigger and Co., Inc., Chicago.

are to be placed; circles for subject and object. Such a game leads to sentence analysis and diagramming in later grades. It is claimed that children aged five and six can do this sort of sentence analysis, using the little cut-out symbols to represent the nouns, verbs and adverbs.

The Montessori Method is based upon what Dr. Montessori believed to be the freeing of the child in an environment in which he learns self-discipline and in which he can create order out of the many chaotic things around him. By learning to become "civilized", the child can then utilize his time in developing his intellectual facilities.

Many educators believe that the Montessori school is a structured school environment. To some extent this is so. In other ways, the child is completely free to choose from the many materials that surround him. A good Montessori school is organized around the principle that learning succeeds best when the instruction is kept as nearly as possible to a one-to-one basis. To this end the teaching load of students per teacher is kept small. There is only a limited amount of "group" learning.

Dr. Montessori believed that the joy of learning was directly related to the self-involvement of the child. Self motivation and self-direction demands that the Montessori materials be self-correcting. Up until recently, Montessori (Materials) Apparatus was available only through the American Montessori Society and only then to "approved" Montessori-trained teachers. Federal monies have elicited a collection of so-called Montessori-type materials which are available from *Teaching Aids,* a division of A. Daigger and Co. of Chicago, and prepared by Dr. Urban H. Fleege of the Department of Education at DePaul University. The Montessori aids are, in reality, true Montessori Apparatus. Those specifically related to reading and writing are the sets of small alphabets cut from laminated cardboard and available in four colors, a similar set of larger lower case alphabets, and a set of sandpaper alphabet cards. The latter are mounted on Masonite boards. All of the alphabets and sandpaper cards are in manuscript letters. The individual letters come packed in partitioned boxes as described by Montessori.

The catalog from Teaching Aids emphasizes that the "Montessori-Type" materials will be effective *"if properly used"*.

There is no shortage of information on how Montessori materials should be used. Nancy Rambusch's book *Learning How to Learn* has previously been referred to as a source of ideas on the Montessori revival in the United States. Robert Bentley, Inc., publishers in Cambridge,

Fig. 10–2 Reprinted through the courtesy of Educational Teaching Aids Division, A. Daigger and Co., Inc., Chicago.

Massachusetts, have just recently made available a fine collection of the complete writings of Dr. Montessori in a new and more accurate translation. In the same collection are the books written by Dorothy Canfield Fisher, who spent considerable time in Italy visiting Dr. Montessori and studying her method and her schools. Mrs. Fisher wrote these books on return to America in 1912 and 1913. They are *Montessori for Parents*, and *The Montessori Manual for Teachers and Parents*. The books by Dr. Montessori, herself, are considerably more detailed but, in the new translation, make interesting reading. The closing words from Martin Mayer's "Introduction" to the new 1965 edition are most significant:

> "Nobody who reads Montessori ever looks at education in quite the same way again, and the change is always for the better."[11]

Research Findings

Apparently there has been little actual research performed on the Montessori Method of teaching reading in comparison to other methods. There is a wealth of descriptive articles and speeches, pamphlets and books, but nothing of a definitive research nature. We can, therefore, only estimate the effectiveness of the Montessori Method by attempting to assess results in terms of the variables that surround the learning.

One report from London, England indicates that a group of Montessori children were transferred to a regular school and it was found that all were advanced by at least one grade.

Many articles were written, praising the work of the Whitby School and its energetic founder, Mrs. Rambusch. Articles appeared in *Saturday Review*,[12] *Time*,[13] and *Saturday Evening Post*,[14] all praising the remarkable achievement of the children. It is reported that children at the Whitby School know the alphabet, and its sounds at age four. At five many are reading, and at six and seven, they are said to be able to write original compositions and to analyze sentences using colored cut-out symbols described previously.

There is some criticism of Montessori as well. Evelyn Beyer, a Nursery School specialist visited Montessori schools and concluded that

11. Montessori, Maria, *The Advanced Montessori Method*. Vol. II. Cambridge, Mass: Robert Bentley, Inc., 1964. (Introduction by Martin Mayer).
12. Wakin, E. "Return of Montessori," *Saturday Review* 47 (November 21, 1964), 61–63.
13. "Joy of Learning," *Time*, 77 (May 12, 1961), 63.
14. Morris, J. A., "Can Our Children Learn Faster?" *Saturday Evening Post* 234 (September 23, 1961) 17–25.

they were highly structured and unimaginative . . . dedicated to ritual, with no dramatic play. She felt that there was little, if anything, creative in the Montessori environment.

Another study having some relevance is that reported by Karnes[15] in which five different programs for four-year-old disadvantaged children were described. Although it did not initially deal with reading *per se*, the focus of the study was to determine the effect of each of the approaches on the intellectual and language development of the children. One of the five approaches was a true Montessori program. It was concluded that the Montessori program did little to alter the intellectual functioning of the disadvantaged child.

In the area of language development, some significant differences were noted. After one school year of instruction, four of the approaches resulted in gains greater than the test interval, whereas the Montessori group barely held its own. In fact, the gains were quite notable: 14 months greater than the test interval, 13 months greater than the test interval, 11 months greater than the test interval, and 10 months greater than the test interval, respectively. The Montessori group failed to make gains equal to the test interval.

The failure of the Montessori group to register psycholinguistic gains is not surprising in view of the fact that there is very little discussion of verbal sharing in the program. This, naturally, raises the question of the extent to which verbalizing of experiences is a prerequisite to early reading.

A teaching nun in a Boston area Montessori school recently reported on learning in her school. She revealed that Montessori methods had to be adjusted to the realities of American life. She also observed that not only are Montessori materials (apparatus) expensive but that the method, if truly adhered to, would also be prohibitive in most situations inasmuch as it involves a one-to-one relationship between learner and teacher. This, of course, is the case in most successful "early" learning situations.

The sister made two other pertinent observations that have grown out of her involvement with the Montessori Method. "The child is supposed to explode into formal reading," she said, but wryly observed, "I've never seen such an explosion." She also noted that brighter children do not need to undergo extensive "preparation" with the sandpaper letters, but may easily bypass such pre-reading activities.

In a dissertation comparing the Montessori Method with those used

---

15. Karnes, Merle B., "A Research Program to Determine the Effects of Various Preschool Intervention Programs on the Development of Disadvantaged Children and the Strategic Age for Such Intervention," paper presented at the annual convention of the American Educational Research Association, Chicago, February, 1968.

in ordinary American public schools, Dr. Joyce DiVillareal states "... the innovations of Montessori served a two-fold purpose: they inspired adoption and emulation in considerable circles in American education. Later, indirectly, they led to independent developments of procedure and in technical aids that excelled the Montessori procedures, rendering most of them obsolete."[16]

The DiVillareal dissertation was done prior to the revival of Montessori in America. Obsolete or not, the Montessori Method is definitely in the ascendency. How far it will rise is a matter of conjecture. Certainly with the "release" of Montessori materials, many teachers will begin to use them and, unfortunately, many will be used NOT "in the proper way". The release of the materials may also serve as a deterrent to those who otherwise would enroll in courses leading to a Montessori certificate as an "approved" Montessori teacher. Such outcomes are mere guesses on the future.

Three things are certain; (1) that the American Montessori Society continues to grow in membership and influence; (2) that concern for the culturally disadvantaged child will again direct the focus of attention onto the magnificent work of Dr. Maria Montessori more than half century ago in the slums of Rome; (3) concern for the "early" reading experience of children demands a fresh look at the Montessori Method, with subsequent carefully-designed projects to test its effectiveness with American children compared with other approaches to early reading.

Until such time as we can have adequate research findings to direct us, we may well live with the words of Montessori, herself, who wrote:

"It is through such pleasures as these that the ideal man grows, and only such pleasures are worthy of a place in the education of the infancy of humanity."

GETTING READY TO READ

Origins

Anyone who has attempted to set up rigid categories into which all possible items may be classified is quite aware of the difficulty which one has with those which could just as easily be placed in one as in another. The cause of this spillover is usually attributable to the dual

---

16. DiVillareal, Joyce Costa-Minneci, "The Montessori Elementary Curriculum and The Corresponding American Curriculum Content," doctoral dissertation, Washington, D.C., American University, 1958.

characteristics of the system, itself. This certainly, is the case with the Houghton-Mifflin basal reading series, originated by Dr. Paul McKee, M. Lucile Harrison, Dr. Annie McCowen, and Elizabeth Lehr, as an outgrowth of their many years as colleagues at Colorado State College at Greeley. It is the *Getting Ready to Read* initial segment of the basal series to which special attention is directed.

During the 1940's, Dr. McKee and Miss Harrison developed a pre-reading program that taught pupils: (1) to recognize by name all the letters of the alphabet, (2) to recognize when printed letters or words are identical and when they are not, (3) to recognize, for eight beginning consonant sounds, when spoken words begin with the same consonant sound and when they do not, (4) to recognize when a spoken word makes sense in a specific spoken context and when it does not, and (5) to use spoken context and a given beginning consonant sound to determine the identity of a word omitted from that context. The teaching of the actual grapheme-phoneme associations for any one of the consonants was not undertaken until pupils had met *two* words in their reading matter that began with that consonant. Later, in the early 50's, further experimentation led these authors to develop the specific grapheme-phoneme associations as seen as a *single* word beginning with a particular consonant had appeared in the reading matter.

Following their retirement at Greeley, Dr. McKee and Miss Harrison accepted positions as consultants to the Denver Public Schools in a longitudinal research project in teaching Kindergartners the basic skills necessary for beginning reading. Through their efforts and involvement in the Denver program, they also became instrumental in inaugurating a television series for parents. The programs in the series were designed to elicit parental involvement as a significant part of the Kindergarten pre-reading program.

Getting Ready to Read is the direct outgrowth of the work done by Dr. McKee and Miss Harrison in the Denver early reading experiment. It is for that reason that it is classified here as an "Early Reading Approach". In 1970 the entire Houghton-Mifflin basal reading series was revised and was introduced with a 1971 copyright date. Dr. William K. Durr of Michigan State University joined Miss Harrison in the revision of the *Getting Ready to Read* segment.

Materials and Method

The 1971 *Reading For Meaning* series is divided into twelve levels, the first one being *Getting a Head Start in Reading. Getting Ready to Read* is Level 2.

As the title of the series implies, *meaning* is an important and basic ingredient in the process of reading, even in the very beginning pre-reading work.

"Using Spoken Context" is the first step after a series of informal readiness activities. The objective is to increase the awareness of children to the flow of language, thus providing the children with the habit of dependence upon the context for meaning. Consequently, all work with words is done in context, never in isolation. Context thinking comes first, wherein the teacher reads a sentence which is complete except for the final word. The entire class is asked to think what word could be supplied to complete the meaning of the sentence:

"I went wading in the _____."

Children from various cultural, experiential, and environmental backgrounds would give any one or several words such as *water, ocean, lake, pool, pond,* etc. Obviously all are correct.

The beautiful, strong illustrations in full color in the *Getting Ready to Read* workbook provide pre-reading exercises in which the kindergartner or first grader may select the picture which represents the word that "makes sense". In many sentences there will be several possible words that "make sense". The pictures help the child decide during the earliest stages of pre-reading work. Later the beginning sounds and/or letters of the word serve as the clue to the correct word, and those beginning sounds and letters are, in fact the *essence* of the approach.

Since beginning sounds of words are used as keys, the children very early must learn the letters which represent those sounds. The fourth lesson in the *Getting Ready to Read* workbook provides practice on the six capital letters which initiate the alphabet learning. They are: D, F, G, I, M, U. Children have letter cards that are duplicates of the teacher's set. Immediately following the development of recognition of these letters in both capital and small-letter form, the children are given extensive practice in listening for the beginning sounds of words which begin with those same letters. One of the most clever and effective elements of the phonemics work is provided by the practice children get in categorizing small objects according to the beginning sounds of their names. Small toy articles, approximately the size of a large charm, are available in plastic. They represent such things as a fish, mop, dog, gun, bell, goat, girl, boy, dish, mouse, ball, bat, moon, seal.

Cardboard cartons, about pint size, are available, imprinted with the drawings of the pictures which represent the key words. The teacher starts with two cartons, let us say D and F. The D carton has the symbol of lower-case *d* superimposed upon its key-word picture of a *dog*.

The *F* carton has the small *f* superimposed upon the *fish* which is its key word. Children select the small plastic objects whose names begin with the *f* sound and the *d* sound and sort them into the proper boxes. The teacher and the children are encouraged to augment their collection of objects by bringing additional small "prizes" from Cracker Jack, etc. which will give them additional objects to sort and to classify by their initial sounds. Children are fascinated with this game, and soon can handle three boxes, four boxes, and eventually the entire set of boxes which represent the beginning consonant sounds.

Any teacher using any approach to reading could purchase the small plastic objects from Houghton Mifflin Co. and use them as introductory to the phonemics learning which inevitably is a part of any system of reading.

The principle of learning involved in introducing the initial consonant sounds through the letter-picture cards is a clever one. It is the use of associative learning—in which the child first associates the initial sound of the name of the picture (for example, baseball bat). A second identical card has the picture plus the lower case letter (in this case *b*) superimprinted on the picture. Again the child *associates* the picture, the initial sound, and the grapheme *b*. The third card has only the letter *b*.

The 1971 edition of *Getting Ready to Read* is almost identical to its predecessor for the first 82 pages providing, as it does, hundreds of opportunities for identification of key pictures and other pictures having initial consonant sounds. The children place lines under the pictures which start with the sound being practiced each particular day. The key pictures over which the graphemes are printed are called the "magic pictures", and are used as reference cues for association of sounds with graphemes.

The total sequence[17] of learning during the Kindergarten program, using the *Getting Ready to Read* workbook is:
1. Using Spoken Context—Students supply the missing word in a sentence that is spoken by the teacher. They choose a word or words that would make good sense in that sentence. In that manner, they learn the first essentials of contextual clues.
2. Recognizing Letter Forms—Kindergartners learn the names and letter forms for all capital and small letters in the alphabet, but not necessarily in alphabetical sequence.
3. Listening for Beginning Sounds—Students first decide whether or

---

17. Durr, William K., and Harrison, Lucile *Teachers Manual*, Boston: Houghton Mifflin Co., 1971.

not certain spoken words, which the teacher provides, begin with the same sound. They then supply words from their own vocabulary which they think begin with the same sound as the word given by the teacher.

4. Associating a Letter Form with the Sound It Stands For—Students use the clever, full-color cards that show the letter forms superimposed upon the key pictures. By the process of associative learning and cue reduction they are able to learn the letter sounds which are associated with the letter forms.

5. Using Spoken Context and Letter-Sound Association—As the teacher reads a sentence, the students use the oral contextual clues together with the initial consonant, which the teacher indicates is the beginning grapheme, to supply the missing word in the sentence.

6. Using Spoken Context and the First Letter in a Printed Word—Finally, Kindergartners use oral context, together with the initial consonant of a printed word to identify that word.

7. Although most of the work is with initial consonant sounds, two lessons in the new 1971 edition teach final consonants: *n*, *d*, *t*, and *l*. The child is taught that these are sounds in "end" position.

8. The 1971 *Getting Ready to Read* introduces the fifteen words of highest frequency as determined by a computer study of 105,000 running words in children's reading. They are:

a	in	the
and	is	to
go	it	we
he	not	will
I	on	you

In those words that begin with vowels, the children are told the sound of that vowel in initial position in that particular word. They then may decode each of the fifteen words, using letter-sound associations and contextual clues.

Reading specialists generally agree that the child who has experienced reading, as Froebel stated: "at the mother's knee", is the child who more easily learns to read. The beginning stages of *Getting Ready to Read* utilize that fact with the requirement that the teacher *and* the parents read, read, read to the child.

It has been indicated that this will be the work of Kindergartners, although the authors believe that parents can do some of this work with children who are particularly bright even in the pre-school years. Also, it is effective for First Graders to follow the sequence if they have not been in a Kindergarten which provides this type of pre-reading instruction. In any event, children who have practiced through the six types of pre-reading phonemics exercises will acquire the basic understanding they must have for identifying unfamiliar words in context—words which, of course, are in their spoken vocabulary. The authors of the program further claim that the completion of this program will make pupils not only ready, but also anxious to learn to read.

Work in the First Grade is dependent upon the completion of the 18 consonants and 4 so-called "speech consonants" (consonant digraphs) in *Getting Ready to Read*. In addition to that phonemics-reading work, the children will have learned the letter names of the capital and small letters of the alphabet. It is recommended by the authors that the *Getting Ready to Read* program be a part of the second half of the Kindergarten year. Such a suggestion is strongly opposed by child-centered Kindergarten specialists, and is mildly rejected by some middle-of-the-road Kindergarten teachers who, ordinarily, give a rather full program of readiness activities, but who would not wish to structure learning with five-year-olds too much.

The child has learned through the *Getting Ready to Read* program that the letter *b* stands for the sound heard at the beginning of the words *bat* and *ball*. He also has learned that the letter *g* stands for the sound heard at the beginning of *gun* and at the end of *rug*.

The teacher then places on the chalkboard the letter *b* and a dash, followed by the letter *g*. The child is then told that the teacher is purposely not letting him see the vowel that comes between *b* and *g*. The child is then asked to listen to a sentence and to supply the correct word at the end of the sentence without seeing the vowel in the word. Here could be the sentence:

We brought the groceries home in a paper ——.

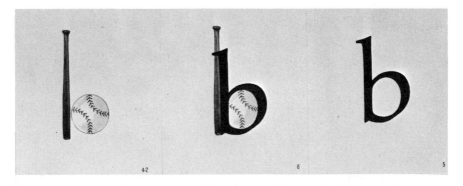

Fig. 10–3, 4, 5   Reproduced from Getting Ready to Read, 1971 *edition, by Lucile Harrison and Paul McKee. Permission granted by Houghton Mifflin Company, publishers.*

The child then would immediately supply the word *bag*. He would not be making an educated guess, for there would essentially be no choice and no need to guess. If the word begins with *b* and ends with *g*, it couldn't be *sack* or *poke*.

As the children move through Levels 2 and 3, they begin to utilize consonant sounds as clues to pronunciation wherever they are found in the words; not just as beginning consonants. Throughout the remainder of the First Grade program, children are constantly required to check their word choices in terms of their knowledge of consonant sounds wherever these occur in the word. By the end of the First Grade, pupils whose teachers have followed the recommended program closely will have been introduced to, and will have used in unlocking new words, grapheme-phoneme relationships for all the consonants except *q*, for all the consonant digraphs, and for most of the common consonant blends, including final blends as well as initial blends.

Fig. 10–6 Reproduced from Getting Ready to Read, *1971 edition, by Lucile Harrison and Paul McKee. Permission granted by Houghton Mifflin Company, Publishers.*

Although *Getting Ready to Read* is an integral part of the total Houghton Mifflin basal reader series, it has been included here because it seems to have a rather new and dynamic approach to beginning reading.

It is possible that its strengths lie in its unique visual and auditory aids which augment the basic workbook. For example, the Picture and Key Word Cards have already been described as providing vivid visual associative learning practice with 18 single consonants and 4 consonant digraphs.

A similar set of smaller, but more expensive cards are the very clever "Animated" Key Cards. Those little plastic cards are designed so that by tilting the card slightly to one side and then to the other the key pictures and the printed letter symbols can alternately be brought into view or made to disappear. These are highly-movitational devices.

A set of ten numbered cards to be used in "Letto," a game like "Bingo," is available and is appropriate for use after Lesson 62 of the *Getting Ready to Read* approach.

In addition to the materials described as basic to the program, there is an auxiliary program of sixteen 10″ 33⅓ r.p.m. records. On each side of each of these records, except for three orientation lessons and seven cumulative review lessons, is a fifteen-minute lesson that provides additional teaching and practice on one of the grapheme-phoneme associations taught in *Getting Ready to Read*. To accompany the records, there is a set of duplicating masters that makes it possible for the teacher to duplicate worksheets for pupils to use as they listen to the thirty-two lessons on these records. This is known as the *Listen and Do* program.

A battery of twenty-two full-color filmstrips, entitled *Learning Letter Sounds Filmstrips,* is also available to reinforce the learning provided by *Getting Ready to Read* and the Picture and Key Cards.

Research Findings

The 1971 *Getting Ready to Read* approach is the product of the combined thinking of a crew[18] of elementary education specialists who have pooled their lifetimes of experience and interest in learning in the primary grades. No doubt many techniques which have become "second nature" to the authors have been incorporated.

The fact that the approach "seems to be effective" is not enough, yet it is difficult to point to a great variety of definitive research. The most famous experiments with the system have been made in Denver. Indeed, it is often referred to as the "Denver Plan"—especially that adjunct to the program which involved parents through the television sequels.

---

18. Dr. Paul McKee remains as the editorial consultant.

The Denver research has been described in publications[19] by Joseph Brzeinski, Supervisor of the Reading Research Office and Director of the Project. The project was funded by money from the USOE Cooperative Research Branch. It was a five-year study extending from 1960 through 1965. Its objective was to attempt to test the effectiveness of teaching beginning reading to Kindergartners.

One hundred twenty-two Kindergarten classes in Denver were selected at random and divided into two groups . . . 61 classes to be the control group and 61 to be the experimental group. The children were not equated or matched in any way. It was assumed that the 4000 children so selected would match reasonably well. The experimental Kindergartners received beginning reading instruction for 20 minutes per day.

When children in the study entered First Grade, they were divided into four groups. Group I were those children who had a regular Kindergarten program, and who started reading instruction in the normal way in Grade One. Group II included some children who had had the regular Kindergarten program, but in First Grade some adjustments were made in their reading program (the nature of those adjustments is not indicated). Group III included children who had the beginning reading instruction in Kindergarten, followed with the usual First and Second Grade reading program. (This seems contradictory, for, it would not be possible to give the "usual" First and Second Grade program to children who had already been taught the *Getting Ready to Read* program in Kindergarten.) Group IV were those who had the reading program in Kindergarten and who went on with First and Second Grade reading adjusted to their head start in reading.

Testing of Kindergartners who had learned the phonemics-reading showed that they did not forget the beginning reading skills throughout the summer vacation. Tests at the end of First Grade showed that those children who had been given the Kindergarten reading program scored significantly better on the *Gates Primary Reading Test* and on the *Gates Advanced Primary Reading Test* than did those children who did not receive instruction in reading in the Kindergarten. Group IV—those children who had Kindergarten instruction in reading and whose First and Second Grade programs were consequently adjusted for their head start in reading scored best, and the results were reported to be beyond the .001 level of confidence. No ill side-effects were discovered when the children were tested for vision, hearing, or social and academic adjustment.

---

19. Brzeinski, Joseph E., *Summary Report of the Effectiveness of Teaching Reading in Kindergarten.* Denver: The Denver Public Schools 1967.

An additional grant of money was obtained (from the Carnegie Corporation of New York) for a parallel study of the effectiveness of enlisting parents' aid in teaching beginning reading skills to preschool children. A guidebook was developed for parents: *Preparing Your Child for Reading*. Eighty-five percent of the parents involved in the project reported favorable opinions toward it. Its distinctive feature was the TV program in which parents were guided step-by-step in the use of the types of materials found in the *Getting Ready to Read* workbook.

Obviously, the now-famous "Denver Study" is not a study of the effectiveness of the *Getting Ready to Read* approach compared with other approaches to teaching reading. It is almost exclusively a study of pre-school and Kindergarten instruction in reading. What would have happened had the same, or matched groups of children used *Phonovisual*, Bloomfield's linguistics, or McCracken's film is still entirely unknown.

The 1971 revision of *Getting Ready to Read*, which appears to be so attractive, still awaits a definitive and longitudinal study to assess its merits compared with the dozens of other approaches to reading.[20]

A, B, C, DICTATION SKILLS PROGRAM

Origins

The *A, B, C, Dictation Skills Program* was developed by Dr. William C. McMahon, a member of the faculty of Western Connecticut State College, as an outgrowth of a number of years of work with children who needed remedial instruction in reading. The program was revised and refined during the early years of the 1960's and was published by Educators Publishing Service of Cambridge, Massachusetts with a 1968 copyright.

Dr. McMahon states that he developed the skills program originally for the slow learner and the dyslexic. The program as it is published, however, is directed toward the Kindergarten child, with the intent to *prevent* reading failure by structuring a learning sequence which teaches one skill at a time through the process of overlearning.

Because the *A, B, C, Dictation Skills Program* is designed for the Kindergarten child, it is included under "Early Reading Approaches". On the other hand, the originator of the program also claims that it is to be used with the dyslexic child, and, consequently, much of the rationale for the program is based upon its use with the dyslexic child.

The program is largely the result of work by Dr. McMahon and selected graduate students in his graduate courses in reading at Western Connecticut State College. Miss Ruthann Wein, a Kindergarten teacher in Thornwood, New York is credited as being the co-author with Dr. McMahon.

Materials and Method

The "Alphabet Book" is the first step in the A, B, C, Dictation Skills Program. Like all of the books in the program, the "Alphabet Book" is a paperback 8½" × 11" workbook. It was written because the authors of the program were convinced that a knowledge of the alphabet and of letter names is essential to beginning reading success. To support their claim, they refer to Dr. Donald Durrell's study, "Success in First Grade Reading," published as the entire February (1958) issue of the Boston University School of Education Journal of Education. In fact they recommend that "Every primary teacher in America should read Durrell's report."

The rationale for teaching the alphabet first is four-fold:

1. The names of the letters provide the child with the actual names of the "tools" with which he works in reading and spelling. It is stated that, if he does not know the names of the letters, he cannot refer to the letters, and that learning of the letters greatly facilitates his learning grapheme-phoneme relationships.

2. The work in the "Alphabet Book" provides the child with motor development exercises in keeping with his potential. The authors reject the concept that the five-year-old is not able to develop fine muscle control. Instead, they state, the five-year-old does have the potential, but lacks the experience. Consequently, it is claimed that the A, B, C, Dictation Skills Program sets about immediately to develop that control. The child progresses in the "Alphabet Book" from large five-inch letters to two-inch letters and then to one-inch letters.

3. The child traces the letter forms rather than tracing a maze or differentiating likenesses and differences in the usual "readiness" workbooks. It is proposed that the child who is started directly on letter tracing will utilize one of the basic principles of learning, namely that transfer of learning is best when identical elements are present. In the case of the "Alphabet Book" the trans-

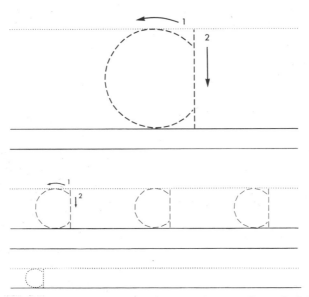

Fig. 10–7   Reprinted by permission of the author, William C. McMahon.

fer is specific through the learning of the actual letters that will
later be used in reading.

4. The large letters in the "Alphabet Book" provide a means
   whereby the far-sighted young children can perceive the letter
   forms with a minimum of discomfort and/or distortion.

The main objective in teaching the "Alphabet Book" is to provide
practice leading to "mastery". The authors define this term as "the
ability to identify the letters by name and to write the forms of the
letters from dictation".

To accomplish this in the Kindergarten requires a carefully structured sequence. The first step in the sequence is correct pencil position.
Anyone who has worked with Kindergarten children knows that many
have never held a pencil or even crayons before entering Kindergarten.

Perfection is one of the objectives of the program. To ensure perfection, two things are insisted upon: the child must erase all errors and
substitute the correct letter formation, and the child must religiously
follow the correct sequence of strokes in forming the letter. It should

be noted that insistence upon correct letter formation is also one of the essentials of the *Writing Road to Reading*, described in Chapter 6.

The method required for learning the letter is basically one of tracing "until the letter image is firmly impressed on his mind". The "Teacher's Manual" then warns that the child should never be allowed to copy the letter. Instead, he is to place a mask over all the letters on the page and attempt to reproduce the letter at the bottom of the page from memory without looking above at the sample.

The pupil's workbook indicates the direction of the strokes by means of arrows and the sequence by means of numbering. Page 5 of the "Teacher's Manual" suggests that the teacher should do likewise on the chalkboard, demonstrating the method to the student and saying the letter name each time. The entire class repeats the letter name and joins in skywriting, using the strokes and sequence demonstrated by the teacher.

The Manual indicates that "The working time needed to teach a letter should be from fifteen to twenty minutes."

Dr. McMahon has devised a list of 300 "high utility words" which he recommends be used to reinforce the retention of the letter names. He states that the spelling of those words immediately following the learning of the letter names and shapes will also prevent reversals.

It is interesting to note that the first letter to be learned in the "Alphabet Book" is E. The authors explain that it is given first because it is the most frequently occurring letter in the "McMahon List of High Frequency Words". Moreover, they indicate that very young children "will not know what is meant by 'top', 'middle' or 'bottom' of a space. The capital 'E' provides your best opportunity to teach these concepts".

The "Teacher's Manual" shows evidence that at least one of the authors has had direct experience with very young children:

> You may find some with the book upside down, some will be writing several inches away from the dotted lines, some will trace one line over and over again, some will connect the ends of the horizontal lines to make nice squares, some will have to go to the lavatory, and one may just sit and cry."

Throughout the Manual for the "Alphabet Book" there are numerous suggestions for procedure and warnings and admonitions for the Kindergarten teacher. It is obvious that the "Teacher's Manual" is the outgrowth of real tryouts in the Kindergarten.

A dictation test is to be given after the children have learned their alphabet letter names and graphemes. The Manual states: "If you have followed the advice of this manual to the last letter (i.e., not to teach new material to any child who has failed to master previously taught letters), all your children will write all the letters correctly from dictation."

After work on the chalkboard has been completed, the Kindergartners are given their "First Consonant Books" and are ready for dictation by the teacher. The words are dictated with stress on the initial consonants. Care is to be taken not to distort the initial consonant sounds. The children are to write the letter which represents the sound. As this procedure continues, the teacher circulates around the room watching for errors, "correcting errors as they happen". The usual lesson is designed to last about fifteen minutes.

In his methods class at Western Connecticut State College, Dr. McMahon has his students use the "First Consonant Book" as soon as the Kindergarten children have learned the letter forms of E, H, T, and S—in capital and small—and the letter names. The "First Consonant Book" is a 96 page workbook, each page of which contains ten incomplete words printed in manuscript. The task of the child is to insert the beginning consonant which completes the word.

The Manual for the "First Consonant Book" recommends "that this program be initiated in Kindergarten at the beginning of November or later at the teacher's discretion." It further states that "Sound-symbol association has been taught to three-year-old children with complete success with this program".

The purpose of the "First Consonant Book" is to provide Kindergarten children with phonemic practice in actual words rather than in isolation.

The first word is *said*. It is printed on the chalkboard in lower case letters. In fact, *all* work with words in the entire program is in lower case letters. The children listen for the initial consonant sound and, since they have had introductory practice on the "s" sound, they will be able to identify the "s" sound and to indicate which letter represents that sound.

After the sounds of *h, s,* and *t* have been mastered through page 22 of the "First Consonant Book", the teacher is expected to initiate instruction in the first "High Utility Words" *he, see, she, the,* etc.

The words dictated for page 52 in the "First Consonant Book" are:

1. some	6. soon
2. today	7. no
3. water	8. too
4. report	9. start
5. himself	10. rolling

The "Second Consonant Book" is also a 96 page workbook for dictation. With it, the Kindergarten program is normally completed.

The "Vowel Program" workbook for dictation is designed to be used in conjunction with whatever basal reader series is used in the First Grade. It is extensive enough to be used in the Second Grade, as well.

Schools which do not have Kindergartens will have to telescope the

40

Score:_____

Items failed:_____

Fig. 10–8   *Reprinted from the* Second Consonant Book *by permission of the Author,* William C. McMahon.

Kindergarten program described above into the first weeks of September in the First Grade in order to prepare the child for work in which the dictation skills are phased into the basal reader whole-word approach.

The words to be dictated for page 40 in the "Second Consonant Book" are:

1. read	6. good
2. bring	7. cut
3. start	8. work
4. life	9. you're
5. try	10. done

The authors of the A, B, C, Dictation program make numerous references to the fact that there are no picture clues in the program; no guessing from context; no use of configuration gestalts; and no other crutches or mnemonic devices commonly found in basal reader programs or other approaches to beginning reading. They indicate pride in the fact that learning through their method is "direct" association and "embodies a pure teaching method".

The authors insist on 100% mastery before a child is permitted to move on to each new step. The experienced teacher could well ask how this could be done and still provide for individual differences and, at the same time, keep the class all together for total class work and for dictation. Teachers will immediately expect the answer to be "grouping". This, however, is not the case. In fact, grouping is to be avoided. The authors state that "There is absolutely no justification for designating a group of children as losers before you have given them an opportunity to learn". Their solution to individual differences is to "Try to get some volunteer parents to work with your slow learners under your direction . . . Upper grade students can also be very helpful in this capacity."

Research Findings

In addition to original experimentation done by Ruthann Wein in her Kindergarten at Thornwood, New York, the A, B, C, Dictation Skills Program has been tried in schools in Patterson, New York; Mohegan Lake, New York; Cortland, New York; Ridgefield, Connecticut; New Fairfield, Connecticut; Danbury, Connecticut, and Weston, Connecticut.

Reports from teachers who have tried the program indicate that the careful slow structure of the program actually does permit very young children to learn letter shapes, letter names and letter sounds.

Although it may be several years before widespread research reports are available, the originators of the A, B, C, Dictation Skills Program are optimistic about its future. They recognize the fact that their program is not reading, *per se*. As an approach to beginning reading, however, they state: "The philosophy of this program includes the tenet that the most valuable readiness program which can be used with Kindergarten children is direct, crutchless teaching of the letters and their most common sounds. *A, B, C, Dictation* is not a traditional readiness program (at least it is not of the 'Cross out the bunny that is different' variety), it is the most fundamental instruction for beginning readers."

THE "RESPONSIVE ENVIRONMENTS" APPROACH

Origins

The "Responsive Environments" approach to beginning reading has evolved from work of Dr. Omar Khayyam Moore, Professor of Social Psychology and his colleague at the University of Pittsburgh, Dr. Alan Ross Anderson, Professor of Psychology.[21]

In the mid 1950s Dr. Moore and Dr. Anderson came to the conclusion that work in the behavioral sciences was being hampered by a lack of sophisticated equipment of the sort available in the exact sciences. In a search for a means of simulating human responses and of studying humans in an ideally-responsive environment, it became obvious that a machine would have to be invented to replace the totally unideal environment of true life. Moreover, a learner responding to a machine could be studied with other factors controlled.

The original objective of Dr. Moore's research effort, whose present formal title is "The Responsive Environments Project", was to develop a theory of human problem solving and social interaction which would be grounded in observable experimental research. In the process of following this objective, it soon became apparent that new "machines" would have to be devised for simulating environments and behaviors.

The first such instrument was invented by Dr. Moore with the help of Richard Kobler during 1958 and 1959. It is called "ERE", the "Edison Responsive Environment". This machine is popularly known as the "Talking Typewriter", and in one form or another has been used in research with children from 1959 to the present. The automated type-

---

21. Moore, Omar K., and Anderson, Alan Ross, "The Responsive Environments Project," Ch. XIII in *The Challenge of Early Education*, R. Hess and R. M. Bear, Compilers, 1967.

writer thus became the first piece of responding equipment in the "Responsive Environments Laboratory" which Dr. Moore set up at Yale University and then on a much larger scale at Hamden Hall Country Day School on the outskirts of New Haven, Connecticut.

From its inception, the "Responsive Environments Project" has had the support of the Office of Naval Research, Group Psychology Branch. Soon additional funds were made available from the Carnegie Corporation of New York. In recent years, many foundations and government agencies have helped with funds. The largest of these recent grants has been the funding of a $2,000,000 program through the Office of Economic Opportunity, part of which has been carried out in Greeley, part in Chicago, and part in New York City.

Experiments carried on with children from the Hamden School gained widespread publicity in national publications because of the novel learning environment which involved a typewriter electronically programmed to teach them to read, and spell, and write. More amazing to the general public and to educators as well was the fact that little children of age three and four were learning under automated laboratory conditions.

The imagination of many people was sparked by this news. The concern of other individuals mounted when it was learned that small children were being placed in learning cubicles with non-human machines as teachers. All sorts of dire consequences were predicted. Early films showing very young children who had learned to read under automated laboratory conditions aroused educators who thought they detected in the behavior of the children shown in the films evidences of frustration, nail biting, stuttering, and other malfunctions as concomitants of being pressured into early learning.

The urge to see first-hand motivated me to seek permission to visit Dr. Moore and to observe his Hamden School Laboratory in operation. This was done in the spring of 1962. The description of the Responsive Environment Laboratory and the method and procedure which follows results from that observation, supplemented by the many scholarly articles written by Dr. Moore and by Dr. Anderson.

Materials and Method

Dr. Moore describes a "responsive environment" as one which meets the following conditions:

1. It permits the learner to explore freely.

2. It informs the learner immediately about the consequences of his actions.
3. It is self-pacing, i.e., events happen within the environment at a rate determined by the learner.
4. It permits the learner to make full use of his capacity for discovering relations of various kinds.
5. Its structure is such that the learner is likely to make a series of interconnected discoveries about the physical, cultural and social world.

In 1959, Anderson and Moore devised the term "autotelic" to represent any activity which is engaged in for its intrinsic value, as contrasted with any activity that is engaged in for extrinsic regard. The intrinsic reward of engaging in an "autotelic" activity is described as being desirable, especially for experimental purposes, for, it is pointed out by Dr. Moore, extrinsic reward and/or punishment complicates any learning experiment.

The Responsive Environments Laboratory was built with one major objective, that of making it a place where so-called "autotelic" activities could be carried on. It was designed with three conditions in mind: (1.) it had to be a simple structure, devoid of all irrelevant gimmicks and gadgets that might detract from the major aspects of the learning environment; (2.) it had to be distinct from the Hamden School on whose grounds it is located; and (3.) it had to be separate, whereby the learner would be separated from any observer.

One could easily envision a jail cell as meeting those three criteria, and essentially that assumption would be true. In setting up the laboratory, Dr. Moore has made every effort to exclude outside "significant others", such as parents and friends, from entering into the "environment". They are definitely excluded.

Knowing all of these criteria, I went to the Responsive Environment Laboratory with some pre-conceived notions of what I would see and the type of reading I would observe.

Instead of seeing frustrated children locked into learning cubicles, children were observed arriving from their regular classes across the lawn at Hamden School. They arrived on scheduled appointments, and individually met a "teacher" whom I felt more like calling a "responder". The staff of "responders" had been recruited largely from among wives of graduate students at Yale University in New Haven. They had been trained in a number of essential routines of observation and some standards of response which had been set up for the experiment.

The child and the "responder" entered a soundproof 7' × 7' × 7' booth which was built with one-way observation windows and equipped with microphone and outside listening posts that enabled outside observers to see and hear the conversation between learner and responder. Other objects in the cubicle were an electric typewriter, a dictaphone, table, and two chairs.

One larger learning room was set up with a much larger "talking typewriter", with wholly automated environment, and was used by a child when he had progressed to a point of independence from his teacher-responder. In other cases, the talking typewriter was used with three-year-olds to observe their very first reactions to a typewriter that talks and to an automated responding environment.

The staff and children understand the rules of operation: (1.) the child does not need to come to the learning laboratory unless he wants to; (2.) the child may leave whenever he wants to even though his entire appointment time has not been used up; (3.) he must leave when his 30-minute period is ended; (4.) he does not have to explain to anyone his coming and going; (5.) he must go to the booth to which he is assigned for that day. Assignments are made to booths and to "booth assistants" (whom I have called "responders") at random each day; (6.) if he leaves before his time is up, he may come back the next day, but not again on the same day that he leaves early.

One of the features of the operating staff of "responders" is that they are trained to "respond" and are cautioned not to "teach" a child. This is essentially the distinguishing feature of the method. The child initiates all activity. The environment responds. This is an exact opposite of the stimulus-response learning which Pavlov demonstrated. In S-R learning, the environment produces the stimulus and the learner responds. In the Moore experiment, the learner produces the stimulus and the environment responds.

The method is divided into four parts: Phase 1, Free Exploration; Phase 2, Search and Match; Phase 3, Word Construction; and Phase 4, Reading, Writing and Handwriting.

During the sessions in Phase 1, Free Exploration, the child may work either in the fully-automated booth or at the semi-automated typewriter with his booth assistant. Let us assume that he has entered the fully-automated responding booth. He is told that he should enjoy himself and raise his hand if he wants anything. The door is closed, the booth assistant steps outside, turns on the switch on the control panel and watches the child through the one-way window.

The child sits in front of the typewriter and other associated apparatus. His fingernails have been painted with non-toxic water colors

Fig. 10–9 Photo of SLATE "Talking Typewriter" courtesy of Research and Development Center, Westinghouse Electric Corporation.

to match vertical banks of keys that are similarly tinted. He is not told this fact, but in time may discover it through the process of exploration.

The typewriter in front of him is programmed so that it will "say" the name of the letter or figure or symbol which the child strikes. It is also programmed on a time sequence, so that 1/10th of a second must elapse before the keyboard unlocks to permit the child to depress another key. Thus, it is set so that the keyboard cannot be jammed, nor can he strike keys too fast and garble the responses. As he explores the possibilities of the new machine which is totally at his control, he learns in a few sessions that he can do things and that the machine will respond not only by printing letters but also by naming the letters and later on by providing him with programmed directions and with concluding assurances that what he has done is correct. The machine, also, can prevent him from making errors in a programmed sequence in a story, wherein the machine is set so that it will print only the correct letter characters, and will not operate until the child hits the correct key. At the end of the line, the carriage automatically returns. The "sheet" of paper is actually an endless multiple fold roll.

Some children explore in a systematic way, depressing a key, waiting and listening for the response, repeating it, and then proceeding to the next try. Others pound and hit the machine with random motions and no understanding at first of their relationship to its responses. All children are fascinated with the new "toy" and want to return to it tomorrow.

Exploration goes on until the staff decides that interest is beginning to wane and that it is time to shift the learner to Phase 2.

Phase 2, Search and Match, is a machine adaptation of matching letter symbols on the margin of a readiness workbook page with a correct symbol chosen from five possible symbols on the line. This is a well-known exercise, but on the machine it takes on quite a different nature. In the "window" immediately above the carriage is displayed a letter or several or a word, and a red arrow moves to a letter which the child must find on the keyboard and press before the machine will respond with the letter name and the arrow will move to the next letter. This in a sense is associated learning of the S-R type, but, if one considers the entire process, the child is actually doing and the machine is responding and moving to the next "ready" position. In this manner, children learn letter names and learn their position on the keyboard. It is possible to program the machine to "say" phonemes rather than letter names, but this is not done in the Moore laboratory.

Phase 3 is Word Construction. When a child has "learned" the keyboard so that his search time is cut to a minimum, he is moved to Phase 3. One form of "Word Construction" leads to writing and the other form leads to reading. The child learns both by alternating daily his booth sessions between the two programs.

The reading "track" consists of a word displayed in the "window" above the carriage. The word may be *house*. The child follows the arrow and types h o u s e, with the machine naming each letter as he types. Then at the end of the sequence, the machine again spells the entire word and pronounces it. To reinforce learning, the machine can also flip on an illuminated picture of a house, but it has been found that many words cannot be pictured adequately and, therefore, pictures are used sparingly, and generally only on nouns.

A basic vocabulary is developed in Phase 3. The words are learned in spelling sequence. The words chosen for the Moore experiment were those that were constituents of interesting stories which the children later would read.

In the writing "track" of Phase 3, the child dictates his own stories into a dictating machine and then plays his own words back and types from his dictation. In this sequence, the machine does not provide the words in the window nor does it pronounce the completed word for the child, unless, of course, the booth assistant takes the child's dictation and programs the machine from it. This could be done, but rarely has it been tried.

Phase 4 is Reading and Writing, and, according to Dr. Moore, comes easily and naturally. The Responsive Environment machine reads a sentence, and the child types it. It then can be programmed to read it again with the child reading along. The Responsive Environment can ask questions. The questions call for responses by the child. The child can either type the answer or respond verbally. Responses may be expected at differing levels of sophistication.

In the non-automated form of instruction in Phase 1 through Phase 4, the booth assistant takes the place of the machine as a "responder". The role of the responder is supposed to approximate as nearly as possible the non-personal aspects of the machine as much as is "humanly" possible.

Dr. Moore states, "The task of designing optimal environments for learning is in its infancy, and the theoretical problems of understanding what is going on in the laboratory are staggering."

Certainly anyone who has struggled with the problems of designing materials and an environment for the learning of reading will appreciate the task of attempting to control the imponderables and the variables that surround and, indeed, are a part of the learner.

Research Findings

Hundreds of children have passed through the Phases of the Responsive Environment approach to beginning reading and writing. Exhaustive records have been kept in the form of elaborate case studies and follow-up on each child. Dr. Edith S. Lisansky, who has been in charge of the Project's work in clinical psychology has administered tests and has kept educational and psychological records on the children. Dr. Lisansky permitted me to check the reading of one of the children in the program and to assess the comprehension of the child and to compare my judgment with the figures taken from her performance on the *Metropolitan Achievement Test*. The performance of this child, even when her high intelligence was taken into consideration, was nothing short of amazing. Indeed, Dr. Moore claims that his figures show that, "At the end of the First Grade, . . . children who have been in the E.R.E. (Edison Responsive Environment) program at least two years (including Kindergarten) read, on the average, at the beginning Sixth-Grade level on the *Metropolitan Achievement Test*."

In recent years, Dr. Moore has been on the staff of the University of Pittsburgh; thus, he has had an opportunity to work more closely with the Research and Development Center at Westinghouse Electric Corporation where data on the first Westinghouse automated typewriter were being developed by Dr. J. G. Castle, Jr., B. R. McAvoy, and Paul R. Malmberg. Their automated typewriter was christened SLATE (Simulated Learning by Automated Typewriter Environment).

READ ALONG WITH ME

Origins

The *Read Along With Me* materials, published by the Bureau of Publications, Teachers College, Columbia University, were originally designed to be used by an individual child with his parent or teacher. In fact, it was out of the personal experiences in using the experimental materials with their own son that the authors, Dr. Robert L. Allen and his wife, Dr. Virginia F. Allen, produced the *Read Along With Me* workbooks, Rhyming Cards, and manual that are the basic elements of the program.

The Allens are both on the English faculty of Teachers College, Columbia University. Dr. Robert Allen serves as Chairman of the Department of Languages and Literature. While on a Fulbright assignment in Burma, he designed a system for teaching literacy to the members of the Burmese army which is still being used. Both of the Allens have been specially interested in teaching English as a second language to foreign students and to non-English-speaking children and youth in other countries.

Mrs. Allen is a member of the Board of Directors for the newly-formed organization of Teachers of English to Speakers of Other Languages.

Together they have collaborated on a number of books. Their *Read Along With Me* is their first effort in the application of linguistics to beginning reading to be used directly by the learner. They are frank to point out that most of the directions in the manual are a result of their experience with their own son and with foreign students with whom they have used the materials. The materials carry copyright dates of 1964 and 1965.

Materials and Method

Because of a prior interest in linguistics,[22] the Allens have designed their approach to reading readiness as a linguistically based one.[23] The system employs a large number of phonemically-regular words, together with a few essential irregularly-spelled words like *a, the,* and *was.* The child then progresses to simple sentences and then to stories which employ a kind of antiphonal response device in the reading . . . with the teacher (or parent) doing much of the reading and the child supplying certain words at the proper time. Parts of the story are read aloud by the parent or teacher, and the child then reads those parts which are phonemically regular, hence, the name *Read Along With Me* was devised to describe the system. It also reveals the fact that this method is a one-to-one method in which there is one teacher for each child. This was the original intent. However, the system is being tried with whole classes in regular school situations with very young children.

The 25-page manual provides very clear directions, along with the underlying philosophy for each step in the method. The purpose of the *Read Along With Me* is primarily to provide a background for reading for the child *before* he enters First Grade.

"Picture Alphabet" cards are the first part of the program. There are two $8\frac{1}{2}'' \times 11''$ cards, one of which contains the capital letters printed in black superimposed upon sketches of "key word" pictures printed in red. For example, the key picture for the letter "T" is a

22. Allen, Robert L., "Descriptive Linguistics: Implications for the Teaching of Reading and Writing," a chapter in *New Frontiers in Education*, Guggenheim, Fred., and Guggenheim, Corrine, compilers New York: Grune and Stratton, Inc., 1966.
23. Allen, Robert L., "Better Reading Through the Recognition of Grammatical Relations," *The Reading Teacher*, (December, 1964) 194–198.

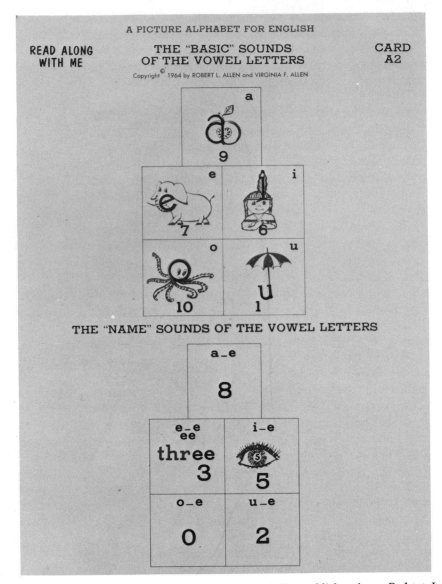

Fig. 10–10 *Reprinted with the permission of the publisher from Robert L. and Virginia F. Allen's* Read Along With Me (*New York: Teachers College Press*), © *1964.*

telephone pole. The letter "S" is superimposed upon a snake. The lower case letters are similarly arranged over red sketches of their key pictures. Some of the other letters may not have such close congruency.

The manual recommends that the capital letters be learned first. The authors suggest that the following four steps should be followed:

1. The child "names" the pictures on the picture alphabet cards.
2. The child says the first sound of each picture's name.
3. With the picture-alphabet card in front of the child, skip around and then on a separate sheet of paper, draw only the letter and he should be able to say the word. (The explanation to the child is that you cannot draw as well as the artists, so you will draw only part of the picture—which happens to be the letter.)
4. Draw the letter and ask the child to say the first sound instead of the picture's name.

Each of the four steps is a "game", and is not to be thought of as a reading lesson. It is necessary to repeat each step over and over as a daily game until the child knows that step before proceeding to the next step.

After the child has learned to pronounce the sounds of the capital letters, the parent teacher should explain that most letters have several forms and that now we can learn the small shapes. The "games" follow the same four steps with the small letter alphabet card.

The next part of the *Read Along With Me* approach is to introduce the booklet, "Rhyming Words and Simple Sentences". This 24-page manual of rhyming words contains extensive lists, first in capital letters, and then the majority of the pages are in lower-case letters.

The rhyming words are essentially word families of three letter monosyllable words, *e.g.*

-ET

BET

GET

JET

and all of the other endings to which are prefixed the regularly-phonemic consonants. Consonant digraphs are also used very early in the booklet, as are also double consonants. The short vowel sounds are used throughout the first major part of the booklet. The long vowel sounds are introduced through the device of the "final e".

The authors suggest that the parent-teacher should print the rhyming words on separate 3 × 5 cards. As the cards in a stack are turned over, the child pronounces the word.

One of the features of the *Read Along With Me* approach to reading is the use of numbers to indicate the basic sounds of the vowels. Short *a* is numbered 9, short *e* is 7, short *i* is 6, short *o* is 10, and short *u* is number 1. The authors explain their choice of numbering thus: ". . . the 7, 6, and 1 sounds are also the vowel sounds in the (accented) syllables of the words *seven*, *six*, and *one*, respectively. The numbers 9 and 10 have been assigned to the sounds of *a* and *o* arbitrarily."

The child then practices a game in which the teacher calls off the numbers 9, 7, 6, 10, and 1 and the child responds with the short sounds of the vowels. After the child learns this thoroughly, the teacher calls off the sounds and the child responds with the numbers. This is followed with practice in which the teacher pronounces a consonant followed with a short vowel sound and the child responds with the number for that sound.

Number 1 is utilized to indicate the short *u* sound in the words: a, an, and the.

a, an, and the.
1 1   1

a, an, and the. The manual states that the child should always pronounce those three words with the short *u* sound as in *umbrella*. The only objection might be to the use of the short *u* sound in the word *an*.

More practice in the pronunciation of regularly-spelled words is obtained when the child plays with the anagram cards. The vowel letters are printed in red and the consonants in black. The child builds mono-syllable words by starting with a red vowel and placing a black consonant or consonant digraph card after it. He pronounces the two sounds together. Then he places a consonant in front of his two anagram cards and pronounces the syllable or word he has formed. It is suggested that the teacher "guide him at first in his choice of letters so that the words he forms will be actual English words." Later he is permitted to construct nonsense syllables.

Antiphonal reading is provided in the little 40-page paperback reader. The first story is "Tess". The parent-teacher reads the light typewriter-type print in the story. The child reads the bold-face larger print. Short vowel sounds in irregularly-spelled words are indicated by numbers placed under the letters. Long vowel sounds are indicated with the number 3 for long e, 5 for long i, 8 is for long a, 0 (pronounced number Owe) is for long o and 2 is for long u. Practice with the numbering system for long vowels is the same as for the short vowel sounds.

Vowel digraphs are then constructed with the anagram cards, and the child is told to pronounce the *first* letter with its name. A great deal of practice is necessary with vowel digraphs and with single vowels in isolation to establish the contrast between the short sound in isolation and the long sound in combination. Practice with double long vowels and with vowels in combination with consonants follows.

The *Read Along With Me* materials are boxed and sold in a package for use in individual parent-child or teacher-child learning sessions. The print and paper is of higher quality than the usual paperback workbook. In fact, the materials should not be considered as workbooks in the usual sense of the word, for they are not expendable, but serve as manuals, pre-primer readers, and the anagram cards are used in word-building games. The flash cards ("Rhyming Cards") and large picture-alphabet cards are printed on heavy stock for long use and repetitious drill.

Although the method is essentially limited to the phonemically-regular words, it cannot be said that the *Read Along With Me* materials are as severely limited nor as unnatural as some of the other systems that are linguistics-phonemics in nature.

Research Findings

The *Read Along With Me* method is primarily a linguistically-based approach to reading readiness. It was evolved from the personal experience of its originators with their own son's early success in learning to read.

It has been found to be effective when used in a one-to-one situation with a number of children. Parents have responded to advertising and have purchased the materials and have reported considerable satisfaction.

Recently, the materials have been used experimentally with twelve classroom groups in four New York City schools. The coordinator of the project is Mrs. Marion Kershner of the staff of the Center for Urban Education. Many of the children in the classes are non-English-speaking children. Mrs. Kershner reports tremendous enthusiasm for the *Read Along With Me* materials that are being used with these children in whole-class-response situations. A few films have been developed for use with the printed materials, but the method as used in the New York experiment seems to be limited to the picture cards and the flash cards. The non-English-speaking children enjoyed learning the names of the pictures from the cards and later as projected from the film.

Inasmuch as the *Read Along With Me* materials are rather new, it is too early to assess their relative effectiveness when compared with other linguistics-phonemics systems and/or with other methods of approaching beginning reading.

They do have the advantage of providing a personal one-to-one method which any parent can follow in providing a basis of readiness in phonics for pre-school children. To be effective, the materials would

have to be used by adults who are dedicated to careful and patient work
with their own children. Further experimentation may indicate how
the manuals may be used in a total class of pre-school children in nursery
or kindergarten. It is probable that such a situation may call for some
revision in the materials and method so that it may be logistically feasible.

PLAY 'N TALK PHONICS

Origins

Play 'N Talk Phonics is a system for teaching beginning reading to
very young children. It consists primarily of several recordings and
workbooks with sound, patter, and cartoon-like sketches pitched not
only to the interests of four-year-olds, but equally acceptable to primary
youngsters.

The originator of the *Play 'N Talk* phonics course is Mrs. Marie
Le Doux, who, at the age of 35 was singled out by the *Miami Herald*
as "the youngest female 'tycoon' in America." She was, in fact, president
of 26 privately-owned corporations, and had not only achieved financial
independence but was famous as "Marie of Hollywood", a well-known
designer.

When it came time to educate her own two sons, Mrs. Le Doux
enrolled them in the Isabelle P. Buckley School of Beverly Hills. It is
reported that the older son was soon reading "everything he could get
his hands on." Amazed at his success, Mrs. Le Doux discovered that
the Buckley Schools had devised a system of training in which they had
extracted some of the best features of a number of other phonemic
methods. She also reports that "all the very young children at the Isabelle
Buckley School could read well."

Mrs. Evelyn M. Toboco, Principal of the Isabelle Buckley School
in Beverly Hills, worked with Mrs. Le Doux in preparing the material
for the course. Margaret M. Redding, a First Grade teacher agreed to
act as the "teacher-narrator" on the recordings.

The recorded music which accompanies the readings on the records
was written by William Marx, son of the late Harpo Marx, and the
illustrations for the reader-workbooks were done by a Walt Disney artist.

International headquarters for *Play 'N Talk* Records has been
moved from Hollywood to Oklahoma City. The organization set up
by Mrs. Le Doux is a non-profit corporation, the proceeds from the sale
of the recordings going to Technical Assistance Plan which also is a non-

profit organization established to provide technical assistance for the culturally-deprived. Mrs. Le Doux explains that she and her husband, Victor, have directed their efforts to helping others since February, 1960, when they feel certain that a "miracle healing" took place for Victor who, up to that time was severely disabled from injuries suffered in World War II. Their gratitude is now being demonstrated under the motto: "It is more blessed to give than to receive," says Mrs. Le Doux.

Mrs. Le Doux has traveled widely across America, appearing on more than 500 radio and television programs discussing the *Play 'N Talk* phonemic program, and encouraging parents to help their children with a phonemic background for reading and spelling. She was selected as the 1967 winner of the Col. Augustine G. Rudd Fund Award, which is made annually to persons who have made an outstanding contribution to American education.

Materials and Method

Play 'N Talk is a course in phonemics, the basic course consisting primarily of five 12-inch LP recordings in albums, plus two paperback manuals that are interestingly illustrated in cartoon style. The manuals contain the words that are taught on the recordings and the phonemic rules that are given in rhyme, then structured into meaningful sentences to insure comprehension.

Series I consists of two 12-inch recordings, the first of which is a explanation of phonemics and consonants; and the second is an explanation of long and short vowels and "vowel families".

Series II contains three 12-inch LP recordings which expand the course in phonemics by giving practice in digraphs, long vowels—with the so-called "Magic 'E' " rule, consonant blends, etc.

The five recordings present over 700 words, all of which are produced in print in the small paperback manuals.

The manual for *Series I* provides instructions to the parents for introducting the "course" and for proceeding through the first two LP recordings. It is stressed that the parent should "FIRST teach your child the ALPHABET; then proceed with the record". The manual also emphasizes the importance of a systematic approach in order to "insure the greatest progress".

It may be helpful to see the instructions for use of recordings and manual for *Series I* in order to understand the extent and nature of the materials and method. The following suggestions were prepared for parents by Evelyn M. Toboco, Principal of the Isabelle Buckley School of Beverly Hills:

1. Set aside 15 minutes each day (minimum time) for listening; make it exciting and enjoy the rewarding results.
2. Sit with your child while he or she *listens*, and *sounds*, and *reads*; which will show to them your approval and interest: the family that studies together stays together.
3. Concentrate their attention on one portion of the record until it is fully mastered; some children require 2 to 3 weeks concentrated attention for one side. Only after this has been accomplished should you proceed to a new portion thereof.
4. Learn and fully master the CONSONANTS *first!*
5. Make certain your child follows the book along with the record. *Audio-visual-vocal* aid insures quicker learning. Your child must listen, sound, and read with the record to insure maximum results.
6. Use the same procedure for the VOWELS, after the consonants have been *fully mastered*. Remember, it is with a CONSONANT that you "unlock" the door and sound out the word.
7. When the CONSONANTS and the VOWELS have been learned, review the words in the book with your child.
8. Cover the objects and point to certain words on a page, until your child is capable of sounding and reading the word independent of the recording.
9. Repetition and review are the secret to firmly entrench each phase of the phonetic training.

The practice given in consonant sounds proceeds from "b" through "z". The pronunciation used for "b" is "buh". Similarly the "uh" sound is attached to the phonemes represented by "c", "d", "g", "h", "k", "p" and "y". Capital letters and small letters are presented together. Each page in the handbook provides the consonant grapheme (both capital and small), the suggested sound, the key picture, the key word, and four of five pictures and words that have the same initial consonant sound.

The fourth consonant, "f" may be used as an illustration of the manner in which the "teacher" on the recording helps the child listen, think, and respond. After some clever narration, the "teacher" gives instructions on how to form the letter "f", and carefully enunciates its sound. She then asks the listener to think of a word which rhymes with *dish* and begins with "ff", etc. The "f" page from the handbook illustrates the words which the child learns.

Several schemes are simultaneously employed for presenting the vowels, both on Recording #2 and in the second half of the Handbook for Series I. The vowels are all presented together on one page. Large capital letters with the long-vowel bar over them dominate the page.

F - f (ff)

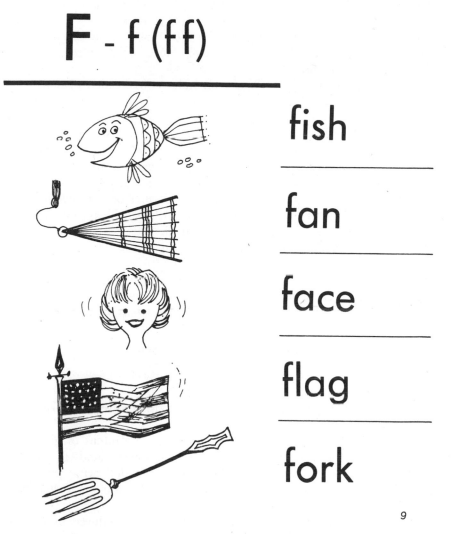

fish
_____

fan
_____

face
_____

flag
_____

fork

9

Fig. 10–11 Reproduced from Play'n Talk *by permission of the author and publisher, Marie A. LeDoux.*

Illustrations of *apple, elephant, indian, ox,* and *umbrella* are superimposed as key pictures. Key words are also included in small letters, with a short-vowel sign over the first letter of each of the five words.

Families of sounds are phased into the program as the child begins to utilize the vowel sounds. At the same time, of course, he must begin to make use of the consonant sounds he learned from the Recording #1.

The "at" family, for example, is the usual development of three-letter words using the initial-consonant-substitution technique.

Other "families" presented on the recording and in the handbook are "-ad", "-ag", "-an", "-en", "-ell", "-ed", "-in", "-ig", "-ip", "-ill", "-ot", "-ob", "-ug", "-un", and "-ut".

The recording and handbook conclude with practice with the "Y" grapheme pronounced as a long "i", and the "Y" grapheme pronounced as a long "e".

Series II of *Play 'N Talk* consists of three 12-inch LP records. It starts with a review of vowels and vowel sounds, but soon provides considerable practice with initial consonant digraphs, and the trigraph, "thr" in "three", "thrill", "thrash", "throb" and "thrush".

Phonemic rules are one of the special features of *Play 'N Talk* and are presented in clever rhymes. The rule for "Magic 'e' " appeals to young children. "Magic 'e' " is presented as a magic fairy with a magic wand. In fact, the handbook contains a magic wand in the form of a 4″ little colored stick with a gold star attached. The child can detach the magic wand (which is fastened by Scotchtape) and can use it as his "own magic wand" for changing vowel sounds by utilizing the final-e rule. The rule as devised by the *Play 'N Talk* course is, in part, as follows:

> A magic "e" is strange as can be—
> It comes at the end of words you see,
> -
> But usually makes the first vowel—
> -;

The rule for vowel digraphs is placed in rhyme similar to the usual "When two vowels go walking. . . ."

Several other little rules are included with the intent of giving the child a number of aids for remembering which vowel sounds to use.

The remaining records give extensive practice with consonant digraphs not previously learned. A few trigraphs also are included to complete the program.

A novel and fascinating typing program was introduced by *Play 'N Talk* in 1968. It is called *Ring 'N Key*, consisting of a recording, a typing booklet, alphabetical word lists, and color-coded tabs for the typewriter keys with matching color-coded plastic rings to fit the child's fingers.

Ring 'N Key is, essentially, an encoding scheme, glamourized with the colored finger rings and the interesting recording. It could well be named, "The Typing Road to Reading."

The materials are structured in sequence: short vowel families, consonants, digraphs, long vowels, and blends. One fringe benefit is that the child also learns to type.

Color-coding for typing is not new, and its application on the electric typewriter was described earlier in the discussion of Omar K. Moore's *Responsive Environments* approach.

Research Findings

There is no statistical research available on *Play 'N Talk*, nor is it likely that there will be, for it must be remembered that these recordings are directed almost exclusively to parents who are interested in helping in the pre-school training of their children. Such parents have voluntarily provided an impressive body of testimonials concerning the value of the program.

The records definitely have the Hollywood touch, and, consequently, are more professionally finished, more exacting in speech enunciation, and are more glamorized than other phonemic recordings. Teachers certainly would object to the pronunciation of initial consonants in isolation with the addition of the "uh" sound ("cuh", "buh", "duh", etc.). Others would object to the process being almost entirely a listening one, with limited utilization of other senses. True, the handbooks demand "looking", but little else. Inasmuch as the usual approach to reading by means of phonemics is accomplished by teachers doing just about what is done by the recordings, it might well be that the recordings will provide a more interesting approach than the usual deadening phonemics lesson in First Grade.

HOW TO TEACH YOUR BABY TO READ

Origins

In 1938, Glenn Doman and about seven others formed a team to cope with the problem of the brain-injured child. The activities of World War II interrupted their study, but after the war, the team was expanded and in 1955, the Rehabilitation Center in Philadelphia was formed as a non-profit corporation. When a brain-injured child was unable to move correctly, he was taken through a routine which had been abstracted from observing the movements in the development of normal children. To abstract those generalities about normal development, hundreds of normal children were studied. Eventually, the objectives of Doman's center were expanded to include the development of normal as well as brain-injured children. The name, consequently, was changed to "The Institute for the Achievement of Human Potential".

In their search for answers, the group of researchers discovered that brain injured children could be taught to perform at average and above-average levels. They also report finding that brain-injured children could be taught to read at very early ages. The resultant and logical question was then, "Why can't normal children learn to read at very early ages, too?"

Glenn Doman is a certified R. T. (Rehabilitational Therapist) from the University of Pennsylvania. One of the members of his group is Carl Delacato (Ph.D. in Education from Temple University). The latter achieved considerable notice in the field of reading with the publication in 1959 of some untraditional views on reading in his book, *The Treatment and Prevention of Reading Problem*. Together, Messrs. Doman and Delacato originated their method in about the year 1961 as a method for teaching reading to the brain-injured children at the Institutes for the Achievement of Human Potential.

The authors, who are basically therapists, found that, in the rehabilitation of brain-injured children in particular, it was helpful to teach those children to read. The reasons for this were said to be neurological and to involve some subtleties and complexities of brain development. But, basically, it was claimed that all language (spoken and read) stems from the same area of the brain—which in most people is the left temporal cortex. Consequently, they reasoned that a child learning to speak may, at the same time and through the same neural pathways, learn to read, with speech, in particular, reinforced.

In developing their reading program, they tried to pattern it after what they believe to be the way the child learns to hear and speak oral language. Inasmuch as they feel that the neurological aspects of reading are exactly the same or comparable to the neurological aspects of hearing the spoken language, they reasoned that anyone who could learn to hear and speak a language could also learn to read it. Moreover, if the child— the very young child—can begin to differentiate speech sounds and to imitate them at the age of 1½ or 2 years, why shouldn't he also be able to do the same with printed language, assuming, of course, that the neurological process is identical?

That, essentially, is the rationale behind the materials and method described in *How to Teach Your Baby to Read*.

In justification of attacking the problem of reading at an early age, the originators of the system refer to Professor Benjamin Bloom's book,

Stability and Change in Human Characteristics[24] in which he reported that he had found that "the child attains half of his general intelligence by about age four, and half of the general school learning which will serve him through high school and college by about the age of nine."

Doman and Delacato reason that, if an infant can figure out the complicated similarities and differences of our complicated language in the remarkably short span of two years from birth, he is also able to do likewise with printed language symbols. At their Institute, they found that they could actually do this with brain-injured children and, they reasoned, normal children should be able to do likewise if the conditions and procedure were structured correctly.

How to Teach Your Baby to Read is, simply, a treatise on how to create the same kind of conditions that exist when a child is learning to hear a language.

Materials and Method

Parents who wish to teach very young children to read will find not only the rationale to support their ambitions, but also will find full directions in Glenn Doman's very controversial little book by the same name: *How to Teach Your Baby to Read*.[25] When the book was published by Random House in 1964, it was not entirely unexpected in the world of reading, for the Doman method and claims of success had received nationwide publicity in a lead article in *Ladies Home Journal*[26] the previous spring. Following publication of the book, *Life* devoted three pages of pictures and description of mothers, fathers, and children working with Doman's materials and method.

In the book and in the articles Doman's reasoning is consistently explained. His four tenets are:

"Tiny children *want* to read."
"Tiny children *can* learn to read."
"Tiny children *should* learn to read."
"Tiny children *are* learning to read."

24. Bloom, Benjamin, *Stability and Change in Human Characteristics*, New York: Wiley, 1964.
25. Doman, Glenn J., *How to Teach Your Baby to Read*. New York: Random House, 1964.
26. Doman, Glenn J., "You Can Teach Your Baby to Read," *Ladies Home Journal*, May, 1963.

In the book, parents are informed that, beyond two years, reading gets harder every year. "Two years of age is the best time to begin if you want to expend the least amount of time and energy." "Should you be willing to go to a little more trouble," Doman states, "you can begin at eighteen months." And, "If you are *very* clever," he writes, "you can begin at ten months of age."[27]

Such claims, of course, caused quite a stir in the field of reading. Reading centers, reading experts, and classroom teachers were almost immediately swamped with calls from parents who read the article and/or the book and wanted to be assured that they should start "teaching their babies to read." Thousands purchased the book and set themselves to the business of following its formula for success.

The "key" to early reading, according to the founder of the system, is *exposure*. "Just as the mother speaks instinctively in loud, clear tones to a baby, so must the reading stimulus be large, clear, and repeated for very young children." Working for just two or three minutes at a time with small groups of children (or the mother working with her own child alone), the teacher *"exposes"* them to large word cards with words in large print.

"After only two or three exposures, some children begin reading words. Others take a little longer."

The first cards which the child sees are 6″ wide and 24″ long. The letters of the word printed on each card are to be 4″ high, with ½″ spaces between. The first words in the program are printed in red and represent what may be called "anatomy" words: *toes, head, nose, ear, belly,* etc. These words are used first because it is common knowledge that the infant explores his anatomy first and enjoys identifying his toes, head, nose, etc. by names.

At this point it should be stated that the materials in *How to Teach Your Baby to Read* have been adapted to a packaged program which is published by Systems for Education of Chicago. This program was designed by Messrs. Doman and Delacato for use by Nursery School or Head Start teachers and is quite similar in nature to the do-it-yourself materials and method originally designed for parents. Consequently, when the materials and method are described herein, the reader will imagine the mother in the home with infant and/or the teacher with a small group of young children. The program for teachers was copyrighted in 1965 and consists of a kit of materials marketed under the title, *Reading A.*

---

27. See Krippner, Stanley, "The Boy Who Read at 18 Months," *Exceptional Children*, 30:3 (November, 1963).

The kit of materials in the *Reading A* program contains the "Giant Word Cards"—330 of them, "carefully selected to be familiar to children from both normal and culturally disadvantaged environments." Each phase of the program "exposes" the child to words printed on progressively smaller cards and in smaller type. The child works down through eight sizes to words printed in black in 1" type, "thus training their visual pathways" in keeping with the neurological theory of Dr. Delacato.

The method of "exposure" involves seeing the card at eyelevel at a distance of 3 feet or more. The mother then points to her own foot and informs the child, "This is my foot". She then points to the word *foot* and points to the child's foot and says, 'This is your foot." Then, again pointing to the card, says, "This says 'foot'." Then again with the child she says, "Where is your foot?" After a short period of "exposure" to this one word, the mother puts the card away and the "game" is over until later in the day.

In the home, it is suggested that mother "play the game" several times during the day. In school, it is suggested that "exposure" be at least two sessions. After a few exposures, the teacher holds a card and asks a child in the group, "Joe, what does this say?"

All the group is "exposed" to the word and, if the child responds correctly, the teacher exhibits "a major demonstration of pleasure and joy", according to directions in the *Teacher's Manual* for *Reading A*. In the parent's book, one of the major essentials underlying the system is for the parent to be "joyous" and to reward each success with an almost overwhelming show of joy and affection.

The vocabulary of "self" is followed by words which identify members of his family: *mommy, daddy, boy, girl, brother,* etc., including blank cards for the proper names of family members.

At this point in the program, the teacher may enlist the help of the mother to reinforce the school training through supplementary periods of "exposure" to the same words at home.

Words which describe objects and parts of the child's room at home (or, in the case of the school, those features of the schoolroom) are next, followed by words identifying objects and parts of the entire house and/or school. Next in order are "neighborhood" words, followed by what might be called "environment" words: *fork, dress, milk, vegetables, cookies,* etc.

The *Teacher's Manual* calls the next set of words, "Nature Study Materials", for they are *dog, cat, tree, bird, sun, moon,* etc. When the child has mastered that list, he will have learned 92 sight words. According to the *Manual*, "They are now reading more than most beginning first grade children read."

Other vocabulary cards should be categorized as "quantitative" "comparative", "motion or movement", and 18 additional words that are articles and prepositions and other "helpers".

When the child at home or in Nursery School has mastered this so-called "Basic Reading Vocabulary", he is then ready to construct the *Make-It-Yourself* book. The Make-It-Yourself project is the happy, culminating creative adventure in this particular approach to beginning reading.

The title of the book is *"my magic words"*. The 8″ × 13″ loose-leaf pages contain imaginative sketches of family members, things, and situations, all reproduced in strong full color. Sheets of words and phrases, perforated and "gummed", are used by the child in constructing the story lines of his book. A few examples are: "came in the door"; "on the floor"; "The cat"; "Daddy smiled at me," etc. The teacher presents the correct words for each page; the child reads them and pastes them into his book.

To aid the children in constructing the book, the teacher uses large easel cards which duplicate the pages of the *Make-It-Yourself* book. The children read the words on an easel card, then paste similar words on the matching page of their *Make-It-Yourself* book.

When completed, the lines of the "reading"—which were written by James Ertel, Editor-in-Chief of Systems for Education, Inc.,—form little rhymes, one of which will serve as an illustration:

> I will read CAT
> and the cat will stop.
> I will read MOUSE
> and the mouse will hop.

The *Reading* A kit of materials for school use contains a "Giant Teaching Book" of 32 (24″ × 18″) cards, which are enlargements of the exact pages of the child's *my magic words* book. For additional reinforcement, a 32 frame full-color slide film with the same pictures is optional. With it, and the sound recording that accompanies it, a review of all of the words can be had without any additional outside effort on the part of teacher or parent.

The authors of the *How to Teach Your Baby to Read* (and *Reading* A) assure parents and/or teacher that "From now on there are really only two questions: How much will they read, and what will they read?" In the Epilogue in the *Teacher's Manual* a few suggestions are given for strengthening a child's experiential background and for providing a variety of reading materials. There are also a few "dont's" included.

Praise is lauded as the best motivator for encouraging the very young child in reading.

Fig. 10–11A   Reproduced from the Make-It-Yourself Book of the READING
A *program by permission of Systems For Education Inc.*

Research Findings

Systems for Education, Inc., publisher of the Doman approach to
beginning reading, reports that some research studies have been made by
school systems using the materials, but that those schools have not yet

made the data available. The only evidence that those schools have been "satisfied" is the fact that they have reordered the program, *Reading A*, in larger quantities.

At this writing, it appears probable that a good number of parents have purchased the book, *How to Teach Your Baby to Read* and/or the materials available in kit form. Obviously there is little feedback of information on the success those parents have had. As far as can be ascertained, there are no reports available from schools where children who have used the Doman-Delacato approach have been compared with children who have learned to read by more traditional methods.

There are a number of features of *How to Teach Your Baby to Read* that are controversial. For example, a good discussion could easily be started over two statements that appear in the book: "Only good children should be given the opportunity to play the reading game" and "Badly behaved children should be denied the opportunity to learn to read."

Teaching two- and three-year-old children to read through such a structure of "exposure" as suggested in the program is, in itself, a highly questionable procedure. Reading specialists and child development specialists, both, are not convinced that the effort at an early age would justify the results, much less be beneficial.

Until there is more definite proof that it is neurologically expedient to teach very young children to read at the same time they are learning to speak—as claimed by Doman—*How to Teach Your Baby to Read* (and its school counterpart, *Reading A*) will continue to be controversial.

DISTAR

Origins

Distar is an acronym for "Direct Instruction Systems for Teaching Arithmetic and Reading". The *Distar* reading materials evolved during several years of research in one of the programs being conducted at the Institute for Research on Exceptional Children at the University of Illinois. The study concentrated on children who were socio-economically disadvantaged and, thus, qualified as "exceptional".

This project was originated in 1964 by Dr. Carl Bereiter, a psychologist, and Mr. Siegfried Engelmann, a former advertising and promotion man. Dr. Bereiter subsequently joined the staff of the Ontario Institute for Studies in Education in Toronto, and Dr. Wesley Becker took his place on the Illinois project.

The Bereiter-Engelmann approach to learning was the basis of the original project, and, although some major adjustments and revisions in materials have recently been made, it is not possible for *Distar* to disinherit its ancestors. Because of the unconventional and challenging nature of their methods, Bereiter and Engelmann have received nationwide publicity in the press[29] and on television.[30] Moreover, the Bereiter-Engelmann book has been the subject of at least two recent critical reviews. In the first, psychologist Bernard Z. Friedlander observed that "It challenges a host of entrenched values and assumptions in education and child development, and it does so with a self-confidence and an absence of scholarly humility that are bound to irritate more cautious practitioners in the scholastic community.[31]

The so-called entrenched ideas are such things as traditional readiness programs, middle-class family activities in the basal readers, whole-word approach, teacher enrichment through a total-language-arts method, and acceptance of any and all answers and comments from the children. Engelmann states: "Our motto in trying to work out a successful reading approach was simply, keep the baloney out of the program".[32]

Although until recently the subjects in the University of Illinois experiment have been disadvantaged preschool children, Engelmann spent at least three years working out specific curricula for preschool children of all socio-economic levels and writing the book, *Give Your Child a Superior Mind*.[33] The method used with preschool children has, in fact, drawn criticism from the child development professionals. Some of their criticism is reflected by Sarah T. Moskovitz when she states that "the learner in the Bereiter situation is treated as if he is without any interests, desires to know, feel, experience, compare, relate, and describe". She concludes with the statement that "Bereiter has taken an obvious, simplistic approach to a complex problem".[34]

Such criticism reflects a child-centered point of view, whereas the Bereiter-Engelmann approach is a teacher-centered method. Engelmann is unequivocal in stating that their approach is "an attempt to develop curricula, methods, and diagnostic instruments that are consistent with

29. "Unlocking Early Learnings' Secrets," *Life*, 62:13 (March 31, 1967) 40–47.
30. "Twenty-First Century" television program, spring, 1968.
31. Friedlander, Bernard Z., "The Bereiter-Engelmann Approach," *The Educational Forum*, 32:3 (March, 1968) 359–362.
32. Engelmann, Siegfried, "Teaching Reading to Children With Low Mental Ages," *Education of the Mentally Retarded*. In preparation.
33. Engelmann, Siegfried and Engelmann, Therese, *Give Your Child a Superior Mind*. New York: Simon and Schuster, 1966.
34. Moskovitz, Sarah T., "Some Assumptions Underlying the Bereiter Approach," *Young Children*, 24:1 (October, 1968) 24–31.

the condition imposed by the teaching situation".[35] Elsewhere he states: "Since objectives must be absolute, they cannot possibly be derived from a study of the child. . . . We cannot have one objective for some children and another objective for others. . . . Objectives that cannot be translated into specific tasks cannot be allowed in program construction. The objectives of teaching the whole child, stimulating self-realization, and providing readiness can be accepted as objectives only if they can be translated into specific tasks".[36]

Further in the same article, Engelmann reiterates his teacher-centered philosophy by stating: "The major difficulty with developmental explanations is that they are based on the assumption that children learn. The teaching assumption is that children are taught. . . . Education is not designed to satisfy the individual needs of the child . . . the aim of the process is conformity . . . and there is no way to have education without conformity".

The Bereiter-Engelmann approach, therefore, consists of a unitary concept of learning, centered upon the basic premise that children will learn those concepts and skills which they should know only if those concepts and/or skills are taught. Moreover, it is necessary that the teacher attend to the business of teaching, and not be tempted to digress and, by so doing, confuse the unity of instruction. Once it is determined exactly what skills, facts, or behaviors are to be learned, it follows that direct instruction in those skills, facts, or behaviors must be given. The assumption is that, if direct instruction is properly carried out, learning will take place, and specific testing will reveal that the children have, indeed, learned that which is taught.

To most educators, such a teacher-centered concept of learning may appear to be a retrogression to methods of past centuries. To Engelmann, it is an imperative, especially in dealing with disadvantaged preschoolers whose learning deficit is so great that time must be utilized to its utmost. The teacher must structure every moment with concentrated and structured teaching. The objective is to "teach disadvantaged Negro children the same set of skills we require for middle class white children".[37]

The originators of the approach have coined several terms which highlight their thinking: the *criterion task* is a term used in place of "objective"; *presentational economy* represents the highly-structured teach-

35. Engelmann, Siegfried, "Relationship Between Psychological Theories and the Act of Teaching," *Journal of School Psychology*, Vol. V (Winter, 1967) 93–101
36. Engelmann, Siegfried, "Teaching Communication Skills to Disadvantaged Children," *Education for the Culturally Disadvantaged*, Chapter 4. South Central Educational Laboratory. In preparation.
37. *Ibid.*

ing method in which the teacher uses a "presentation book" containing absolute directions for the teacher, absolute acceptable answers by the learner, and absolute responses and feed-back by the teacher; and *specific tasks* are those sequenced step-by-step skills which must be taught in producing the learning which can be tested and measured according to the criterion set up as the objective. In Engelmann's words: "In summary, the teacher must be a highly trained technician, not a combination of educational philosopher and social worker".

It is out of this rationale that the *Distar* materials were developed. Much of the credit for their development should be given to Mrs. Elaine C. Bruner, the specialist in education working in the Bereiter-Engelmann program at the Institute. With more than ten years teaching experience in elementary and secondary schools, Mrs. Bruner undertook the task of testing the reading materials which she and Engelmann produced. As a result of several years of tryout and revision, the *Distar* materials are now published by Science Research Associates of Chicago with a 1969 copyright.

Materials and Method

The method and the *Distar* materials are so closely interrelated that it is not possible to consider them separately. Moreover, the assumptions of the Bereiter-Engelmann approach to learning are the nuclei. Briefly stated, they are:

1. Disadvantaged black children are faced with a serious learning deficit which must be corrected before they enter the competition of the middle-class, white-oriented school situation.

Time is running out for them; and, at age four, a concentrated, structured, no-nonsense program is an absolute necessity to bring them up to a performance level that will permit them to succeed when they enter the formal school program.

2. Culturally-disadvantaged preschool children are generally non-verbal and non-committal when spoken to in a normal classroom manner. The particular cognitive style of their family environment must be overcome so that the children will develop habits of listening and responding. This requires strenuous intervention and direct instruction.

3. Current psychological theories of learning allow too many imponderables, centered as they are upon the satisfaction of individuals' needs, development of self, and individual differences. Such generalized and all-inclusive objectives result in generalized and

non-effective learning. The solution to this is to determine the specific educational deficits and to structure the teaching of skills sequenced to overcome those deficits. The objectives are not to be discovered in an assessment of each individual, but are to be determined by what needs to be learned. Objectives must be stated in terms of desired facts, skills, or behaviors.

4. The learning process must be teacher-dominated. The responsibility for learning the desired facts, skills and/or behaviors is upon the teacher. The teacher, therefore, must use a clean, structured, step-by-step, fast, specific, absolute, and direct instructional method, together with relevant materials.

5. Direct instruction toward specific learnings will result in specific learnings which can be tested. Thus, it can be demonstrated that learning has taken place because it has been taught.

It is claimed that disadvantaged preschool children can make significant increases in performance if they are given direct instruction soon enough. A corollary to this is the observation that they will continue to slip farther behind if they are allowed to remain in the usual school pattern.

The authors identify their approach as "an intensive, fast-paced, highly-structured program of instruction. . ." . The program is, indeed, all of those things. Intensive drill sessions, as demonstrated by Engelmann, generate the excitement of cheering sections, with the children enjoying the rhythmic, whole-group response. It is fast-paced by means of the oft-repeated direction, "Say it fast". Insistence on immediate and fast responses is one of the features of the program. It is highly structured, with word-by-word instructions provided in the spiral-bound teacher presentation booklets. Creative teachers are admonished not to resort to a language-arts approach. Direct instruction does not provide for pleasantries or side trips that might embellish the lesson; for, by so doing, the sequential steps in instruction would be broken.

"Sequencing" is the essential feature of the method. Mrs. Bruner explains it this way:

1. There is a correct sequence. The teacher performs two actions, such as clapping her hands and slapping her lap with one hand. She says, "I'm doing it the right way. Do it with me."

2. When the children can perform the sequence, the teacher presents two incorrect actions and asks, "Is this the right way?"

3. The teacher also presents the correct actions in an incorrect sequence, such as slapping her lap first, and asks, "Is this the right way?"

4. After the children can do many similar tasks, they start

to learn terminology of "first this; then this" when the teacher performs the first part of a sequence and asks the children, "Then what did I do?"[38]

The objective of such patterning in sequence is to train the child to pay attention and observe sequence so that he will be ready to handle the sequence of letter sounds in the formation of words. The sequencing is then transferred to a series of tasks on paper. These are in a fixed order from left to right, with arrows inserted to aid the child.

The intensive use of *time* is, probably, the focus of much reaction to the Bereiter-Engelmann approach. The four-year-old is continually pressured by the teacher. Sitting in groups of five or six, the child learns that he must "shape up or ship out". The instruction is terse: "Sit up!" "Look at me!" "Turn around!" "Pay attention here!" "This is school: school is work!" "Do it!" "Right! You did it right!"

The "21st Century" television program showed an unretouched version of the *Distar* program at the Institute and has produced a lingering concern especially among educators and child development specialists. In order to double-check on the various aspects of the approach, I spent a day at the Institute in Champaign and observed both Mr. Engelmann and Mrs. Bruner and the children in action. Subsequently, they have both been very generous in providing materials and personal explanations of the *Distar* approach.

After a warm-up of sequencing with motions accompanied by the statement, "I'm doing it the right way; now you do it with me," direct instruction in the *Distar* reading program began.

Nine basic sounds are taught. The first is *m*. After getting attention, the teacher says, "Listen to me: mmmmmmmm. [pause] Say it slow: mmmmmmmmm". The nine basic sounds are: *m*, *a* (as in *and*), *s*, *ē* (as in *eat*), *f*, *d*, *r*, *i* (as in *in*), and *th* (as in *this*). The sounds are represented by lower-case letters, and some practice is given in visual perception through the presentation of constrasting symbols in pairs, such as *u – n*, *f – t*, *b – d*. Similarly, *th* is contrasted with *sh*, *ch*, and *wh*.

The *Distar* alphabet (like i/t/a) joins several letters and distorts several as a temporary initial teaching measure. "Silent letters" appear in half-size print at first, reaching full size by the end of Phase I (180 school days). All letters (representing sounds) are lower case (with the exception of the personal pronoun, *I*) throughout the first year of instruction.

---

38. Bruner, Elaine C., "The DISTAR Reading Program," *Proceedings*, College Reading Association, Vol. IX, Fall, 1968.

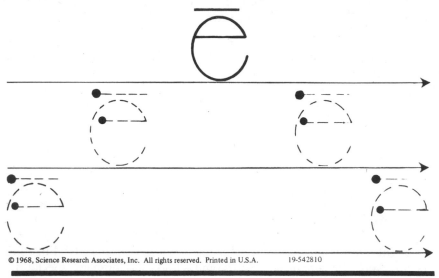

Fig. 10–12   Reprint of Take-home sound #5 (the e sound) from DISTAR by Siegfried Engelmann and Elaine Bruner. © 1968 Science Research Associates, Inc. Reprinted by permission of the publisher.

Rhyming is another feature of the program. The objective is to focus on parts of words. On the day that I visited the Institute, the children were rhyming *ham burger* (slow and fast), *ram burger,* and *Sam burger.* This may be explained psychologically as practice in auditory constancy and/or auditory memory. The authors explain it by indicating that words have parts that look the same and sound the same.

The sequence of "reading sounds" in the *Distar* program includes what might be called "sound families" in much the same manner as the phonograms and word families of traditional phonemic programs. Non-sense syllables are included where necessary to construct a sound family, e.g.: *in, fin, sin, rin.*

Irregular words are taught, but not until midyear. Spelling by sounds is an important part of the program for the first sixty days. Each sound is held for several seconds until the next sound is reached. Then, children responding to the direction, "Say it fast!" could then make a real word out of the sounding-out. They are then asked, "What are you spelling?" They respond by saying the word fast.

Rewards are also part of the program. As the teacher uses her presentation booklet with her small group of four-year-olds, she sometimes rewards one or more with the privilege of placing a mark in an appropriate place on the plastic-coated page. At other times, after she has read a very short "fast story", she rewards them by showing them a picture.

One of the rewards which seems to be an integral part of the early weeks of the program is a payoff of a small handfull of raisins for good work. Small take-home books are also rewards which the student "earns" and may keep.

Praise is part of the program, but it is, surprisingly, structured as to what the teacher is to say and when she is to say it. The presentation book prescribes such statements as, "That was good remembering". "You are smart; I can't fool you today". "That was hard work, but you did a good job".

Several devices for patterning in directionality are utilized. A dot is used along with broken line letters to indicate the starting point and the direction which the pencil should take in forming the letter. Arrows from left to right and the return sweep to the next line are aids for the eye to follow. Macrons indicate long vowel sounds. Black squares, called blocks, separate the words from each other.

The *Distar* program of direct early reading instruction differs greatly from the enrichment program of the usual nursery school or Kindergarten. It is a high-pressure, hurry-up program, structured in method and materials, the objective of which is the training of the child so that he will not be a failure when he joins his more privileged classmates in Kindergarten or First Grade. The program appeals to teachers who feel the need for structured statements and a rigid step-by-step approach to teaching facts and skills.

Research Findings

Data on the *Distar* materials and method are being collected, but, at this writing, very few published results are available. Nevertheless, Mr. Engelmann states that, "Conservatively speaking, I would say that there was a hundred times more research—hard data—behind the Bereiter-Engelmann approach than is behind any new approach that has ever been introduced".[39]

Thirty teachers in schools, chiefly in the Chicago area, have been engaged in using *Distar* materials and method in beginning reading instruction with approximately 1200 middle-class and disadvantaged children in nursery schools, Kindergartens, and First Grades. Results from those experiments are not available at this writing.

---

39. Note to the author.

The *Distar* program was matched against a conventional Head Start program in the Canton (Ohio) public schools during the summer, 1967. It is reported that phenomenal gains were registered by the *Distar* group on the *Pre-School Inventory Test*, the expermental group gaining 126 points, cómpared with a gain of 69.7 points by the Head Start Group. On the *Concept Inventory Test*, the experimental groups made a gain of 158 points, while the control group gained 75.8 points.[40]

Dr. Merle B. Karnes, director of the over-all research projects on culturally disadvantaged preschool children at the Institute for Exceptional Children at the University of Illinois, reported[41] on the effectiveness of five programs, one of which was the Bereiter-Engelmann direct instruction approach. The others were a traditional nursery school program; the Karnes approach, a psychologically-based, yet highly structured, program of games and multi-sensory manipulation; a true Montessori program; and a community pre-school program.

Results were reported as measured by Binet means, ITPA scores, *Metropolitan Readiness Test* scores, and *California Achievement Tests*. Among a number of comparative findings reported by Karnes is the startling fact that the direct verbal group *(Distar)* at the end of the second year had progressed from a mean Binet IQ of 97 to the superior range (IQ 120). Fifteen months progress was also made by the *Distar* group in language as measured in the *Illinois Test of Psycholinguistic Ability*. The purpose of the Bereiter-Engelmann approach is to provide disadvantaged children with the means for performing normally in a traditional classroom. How well this was achieved is evidenced by the results obtained by the *Distar* group on the *California Achievement Tests* in the spring of First Grade. The *Distar* group (and the Karnes group) exceeded the expectancy norms in both reading and arithmetic.

The above results are for very small numbers of children. Significance of differences is derived through *t*-score statistics, yet it appears that more adequate statistical treatment would have to be applied to several variables before the results could be accepted by statisticians.

A study conducted in the Stockton, California, school system reports that the 98 First Grade children in the *Distar* program achieved a mean raw score of 39.05 on the *Stanford Achievement Test* in reading compared

---

40. Young, Biloine W., "A New Approach to Head Start," *Phi Delta Kappan*, XLX, No. 7, (March, 1968) 386–388.
41. Karnes, Merle B., "A Research Program to Determine the Effects of Various Pre-school Intervention Programs on the Development of Disadvantaged Children and the Strategic Age for Such Intervention," Paper presented at the Convention of the American Educational Research Association, Chicago, February 10, 1968.

with 28.38 for the 112 children in the basal text program. The difference in the means was 10.67, which is significant at the .01 level.

Engelmann has appeared before rather large audiences of teachers and administrators in major cities, describing his program and citing success in reading and large gains in IQ scores. Nonetheless, the *Distar* program will undoubtedly encounter some difficulty. Its intense structure calls for a psychological and physical commitment which few teachers could stand for any extended period of time. It is designed for small groups and calls for the undivided attention of one teacher for twenty to thirty minutes. Additional help, therefore, would have to be hired to handle the remaining segment of children in any nursery school or Kindergarten where *Distar* materials and method were being used.

Because of the untraditional method, an entire new team of teachers would have to be trained. It is most likely that this would have to be accomplished outside the usual nursery school or elementary education training programs of our colleges and universities.

The program most certainly will continue to draw static from child development specialists. One well-known spokesman for the child-centered, experience-permeated nursery school has recently warned of the pressure which is being exerted upon four-year-olds to "get ready for first grade". He cited *Teaching Disadvantaged Children in Preschool* by Bereiter and Engelmann as " . . . the best book to read to appreciate how devastating a program for young children of the poor can be, once first grade time-panic sets in".[42]

CONCLUSIONS

A motley collection of approaches to beginning reading qualify for inclusion as early-reading approaches because of their claims as systems for teaching very young children to read. The approaches range from phonograph records to sophisticated electronically-programmed type-writers—from basal readers to babies. They have nothing in common except their insistence that preschoolers have learned to read via their materials and/or method.

Getting Ready to Read has had the greatest exposure to tryout in the classroom and enjoys the widest acceptance by teachers. This is natural because of its place as part of a well-known basal reader series.

---

42. Hymes, James L. Jr., *Teaching the Child Under Six*, Columbus: Charles E. Merrill Co., 1968, 14.

Moreover, it is designed for use with class-size groups. All other approaches described here are designed for a one-to-one teacher-learner situation or for, at most, very low teacher-learner ratios.

Many of the approaches are controversial and will continue to generate static whenever they are presented to regular classroom teachers. Moreover, some of the approaches outrage the child development point of view and affront basic psychological foundations of learning. Probably the *one* factor that "turns off"the professional educator is the manner in which the promoters of some of these approaches ignore or pervert research on their materials and methods.

One does not have to look far to discover that there are hidden variables operating within the methods which, if applied to other approaches to beginning reading, would make them appear to be successful, too. I am referring to the fact that *any* approach that sets up *one* teacher (or dedicated parent) and *one* learner is almost sure to produce results above "national norms," which are obtained in large-class situations. Another factor that should appear obvious is the fact that, when an approach is directed toward parents who are dedicated to the task of teaching their preschooler to read and those pushy parents pay out money for the materials and method handbooks, that approach is a sure bet for superior performance when compared with large-scale educational classroom techniques. Even the statistics reported on the Denver study are not as pure and uncontaminated as they appear to be. The involvement of parents and television inserted two massive variables that make the conclusions from the raw statistics quite invalid.

This considerable concern for the manner in which the "success" of some of these approaches is presented is to emphasize the fact that we have no definitive statistical evidence that, in usual classroom situations with equal time and equal effort, shows us whether any of these approaches is superior to the other approaches described elsewhere in this book.

In spite of lack of satisfactory research, there are some interesting and adoptable features in some of these approaches. What is interesting is not always adoptable. What is adoptable depends largely on whether or not it is needed to fill a void in an eclectic system.

BIBLIOGRAPHY

Allen, Robert L., "Better Reading Through the Recognition of Grammatical Relations," *The Reading Teacher*, (December, 1964) 194–198.
———, "Descriptive Linguistics: Implications for the Teaching of Reading and

Writing," a chapter in *New Frontiers in Education*, Guggenheim, Fred, and Guggenheim, Corrine, compilers, New York: Grune and Stratton, Inc., 1966.

AMES, LOUISE B., "The Sense of Self of Nursery School Children as Manifest in Their Verbal Behavior," *Journal of Genetic Psychology* 81 (1952) 193–232.

ANDERSON, DOROTHY, "A Study to determine if children need a mental age of six years and six months to learn to identify strange printed forms when they are taught to use oral context and the initial sound of the word," unpublished doctoral dissertation, Greely: Colorado State College, 1960.

ANDERSON, VERNA DIECKMAN, *Reading and Young Children*, New York: The Macmillan Co., 1968.

Chapters 4 and 5 on reading readiness and Chapter 6 on "the Beginnings of the Reading Act" are especially pertinent in a consideration of early reading approaches.

AUKERMAN, LOUISE R., "Reading in the Kindergarten," *New England Reading Association Journal*, 5:3 (Spring, 1970), 19–24.

She describes the specific activities of a good Kindergarten reading readiness program.

BEREITER, CARL and ENGELMANN, SIEGFRIED, *Teaching Disadvantaged Children in the Preschool*. Englewood Cliffs, N. J.: Prentice-Hall, 1966.

BLOOM, BENJAMIN, *Stability and Change in Human Characteristics*, New York: Wiley, 1964.

BRUNER, ELAINE C., "The DISTAR Reading Program," *Proceedings* College Reading Association, Vol. IX (Fall, 1968).

BRUNER, JEROME, "On Perceptual Readiness," *Psychological Review*, 64: (1957) 123–152.

BRZEINSKI, JOSEPH E., *Summary Report of the Effectiveness of Teaching Reading in Kindergarten*. Denver: The Denver Public Schools, 1967. Preliminary reports also appeared in *The Reading Teacher*, 18 (October, 1964), 16–21.

CANDLE, F., "Pre-Reading Skills Through The Talking Typewriter," *Instructor*, 75 (1965), 39.

CHURCH, JOSEPH, *Language and the Discovery of Reality*. New York: Random House, 1961.

See especially the discussion on "The Acquisition of Language," Ch. 3, 56–91.

CRAIN, ROY, "A Home-Centered Reading Readiness Program," *The National Elementary Principal*, 35 (September, 1955).

CUTTS, WARREN G., (Editor) *Teaching the Young Child to Read*, Washington: U.S. Office of Education, HEW, 1964.

Proceedings of the 1962 Conference on Beginning Reading Instruction.

DI VILLAREAL, JOYCE COSTA-MINNECI, "The Montessori Elementary Curriculum and The Corresponding American Curriculum Content," doctoral dissertation, Washington, D.C., American University, 1958.

DOMAN, GLENN J., *How to Teach Your Baby to Read*. New York: Random House, 1964.

——, "You Can Teach Your Baby to Read," *Ladies Home Journal*, May, 1963.

DOUGLASS, MALCOLM P., and SIMMONS, G. MILDRED, "Early Reading and

Writing," 27th Yearbook, Claremont Reading Conference, Claremont (California) Graduate School and University Center, 1963, 61–67.
Surveys some of the interest in early reading programs for very young children.

DURKIN, DOLORES, "Children Who Read Before Grade I," *The Reading Teacher*, 14 (1961) 163–166.

——, "An Earlier Start in Reading," *Elementary School Journal*. 63: (December, 1962) 147–151.

——, "Children Who Read Before Grade I: A Second Study," *Elementary School Journal* 64: (December, 1963) 143–148.

——, "A Fifth-Year Report on the Achievement of Early Readers," *Elementary School Journal* 65: (November, 1964) 76–80.

——, *Children Who Read Early*. New York: Bureau of Publications, Teachers College, Columbia University, 1966.

——, "When Should Children Begin to Read?" Chapter II in *Innovation and Change in Reading Instruction*. The Sixty-Seventh Yearbook of the National Society For the Study of Education, Part II, Chicago: University of Chicago Press, 1968. 30–71.
This is an excellent resume of past, present and future trends in the movement toward early reading instruction. It is well-documented with more than 100 footnotes, indicating the extent of the literature on the subject.

ELLIOTT, LEE, "Montessori's Reading Principles Involving Sensitive Period Method Compared to Reading Principles of Contemporary Reading Specialists," *The Reading Teacher*, 21 (November, 1967) 163–168. also Reprinted in the *American Montessori Society Bulletin*, 5:4, 1967.

ENGELMANN, SIEGFRIED, "Teaching Communication Skills to Disadvantaged Children," Chapter 4 in *Education for the Culturally Disadvantaged*, in preparation. South Central Educational Laboratory.

——, "Relationship Between Psychological Theories and the Act of Learning," *Journal of School Psychology*, Vol. V, (Winter, 1967) 93–101.

——, "Teaching Reading to Children with Low Mental Ages," *Education of the Mentally Retarded*, in preparation.

ENGELMANN, SIEGFRIED and ENGELMANN, THERESE, *Give Your Child a Superior Mind*. New York: Simon and Schuster, 1966.

FOWLER, W., "Structural Dimensions of the Learning Process in Early Reading," *Child Development*, 35 (December, 1964) 1093–1104.

FRIEDLANDER, BERNARD Z., "The Bereiter-Engelmann Approach," *The Educational Forum*, 32:3 (March, 1968) 359–362.

GOINS, JEAN, *Visual Perceptual Abilities and Early Reading Process*. Supplementary Educational Monograph No. 87, Chicago: University of Chicago Press, 1958.

GOULD, LAWRENCE, *DETECT*, Chicago: Science Research Associates, 1968.

HILLERICH, ROBERT L., "Pre-Reading Skills in Kindergarten: A Second Report," *Elementary School Journal*, 65 (March, 1965) 312–317.

——, "Kindergartners Are Ready! Are We?" *Elementary English* 42 (May, 1965), 569–573.
Dr. Hillerich reports on the experience in Glenview, Illinois.

HYMES, JAMES L., JR., *Teaching the Child Under Six*, Columbus: Charles E. Merrill Co., 1968.

ILG, FRANCES L., and AMES, LOUISE B., *School Readiness*. New York: Harper and Row, 1964.

"Intellectual Leap: Montessori Revival at Whitby School," *Newsweek:* 61 (June 24, 1963) 106.

"Joy of Learning: The Whitby School," *Time* 77 (May 12, 1961) 63.

KARNES, MERLE B., "A Research Program to Determine the Effects of Various Preschool Intervention Programs on the Development of Disadvantaged Children and the Strategic Age for Such Intervention," Paper presented at the annual convention of the American Educational Research Association, Chicago, February 10, 1968.

KARNES, MERLE B., *et. al.* "An Evaluation of Two Preschool Programs for Disadvantaged Children: A Traditional and a Highly Structured Experimental Preschool," *Exceptional Children*, Vol. 34, (May, 1968) 667–676.

KASDON, LAURENA, "Early Reading Background of Some Superior Readers Among College Freshmen," *Journal of Educational Research*, 52 (December, 1958) 151–153.

KELLEY, M. L. and CHEN, M. K., "An Experimental Study of Formal Reading Instruction at the Kindergarten Level," *Journal of Educational Research* 60: (January, 1967) 224–229.

MARTIN, JOHN H., *Freeport Public Schools Experiment in Early Reading Using The Edison Responsive Environment Instrument*. Englewood Cliffs, N.J., The Responsive Environments Corp., 1964.

———, "Using the Computerized Typewriter for Early Reading Instruction: Edison Responsive Environment Instrument," *Audiovisual Instruction*, 10 (April, 1965) 309–310.

McCRACKEN, ROBERT A., "A Two-Year Study of the Reading Achievement of Children Who Were Reading When They Entered First Grade," *Journal of Educational Research*, 59 (January, 1966) 207–210.

McKEE, PAUL and HARRISON, M. LUCILE, *Getting Ready to Read; Teacher's Manual*. Boston: Houghton Mifflin Co., 1966.

McMANUS, ANASTASIA, "The Denver Pre-Reading Project Conducted by WENH-TV," *The Reading Teacher*, 18: (October, 1964) 22–26.

A report of the New Hampshire experience with the TV program which accompanies the Denver experiment and the materials: "Preparing Your Child for Reading."

MILLER, ARNOLD, *Symbol Accentuation*, International Communications Films, 1371 Reynolds Avenue, Santa Ana, California, 92705.

MOFFITT, M., "Is It True That Children Can Be and Should Be Taught to Read at a Younger Age Than Before?" New York: Elementary Division, Board of Education, 1962. Pamphlet.

MONTESSORI, MARIA, *The Advanced Montessori Method*, Vol. 1, *Spontaneous Activity in Education*. Cambridge, Mass.: Robert Bentley Inc., 1964.

———, *The Advanced Montessori Method*. Vol. II, *The Montessori Elementary Material*. Cambridge, Mass.: Robert Bentley, Inc., 1965.

The description of the Montessori approach to beginning reading is derived directly from the writings of Dr. Montessori.

"Montessori Melee," *Wall Street Journal*. June 27, 1967. *The Montessori*

Method A Revolution in Education. Fresno, California: Academy Literary Guild, 1962.

MOOD, D. W., "Reading in Kindergarten? A Critique of the Denver Study," *Educational Leadership.* 24: (February, 1967) 399–403.

MOORE, OMAR KHAYYAM, "Autotelic Responsive Environments and Exceptional Children," in *The Special Child in Century 21,* J. Helmuth, compiler, Seattle: Special Child Publications, 1963 and abridged in *The Revolution in the Schools,* Ronald Gross and Judith Murphy, compilers, New York: Harcourt, Brace, and World, Inc., 1964, 184–219.

——, and ANDERSON, ALAN ROSS, "The Responsive Environments Project," Ch. XIII in *The Challenge of Early Education,* R. Hess and R. M. Bear, compilers. Chicago: Aldine Publishing Co., 1967.

This chapter contains an extensive bibliography relating to Dr. Moore's work.

——, Three Motion Pictures on *Early Reading and Writing. Part 1: Skills; Part 2: Teaching Methods; Part 3: Development.* Available from Basic Education, Inc., Washington Plaza Apartments, Pittsburgh, 1960.

MORRIS, J. A., "Can Our Children Learn Faster?" *Saturday Evening Post* 234 (September 23, 1961) 17–25.

MOSKOVITZ, SARAH T., "Some Assumptions Underlying the Bereiter Approach," *Young Children,* 24:1 (October, 1968) 24–31.

MUEHL, SIEGMAR, "The Effects of Visual Discrimination Pre-Training With Word and Letter Stimuli in Learning to Read a Word List in Kindergarten Children," *Journal of Educational Psychology,* 52 (December, 1961) 215–221.

"Operation Head Start," *The Reading Teacher,* 19, No. 5 Entire February, 1966 issue.

PIAGET, JEAN, *Language and the Thought of the Child.* New York: Meridian Press, 1955.

PINCUS, MORRIS, and MORGENSTERN, FRANCES, "Should Children Be Taught to Read Earlier?" *The Reading Teacher* 18 (October, 1964). 37–42

PINES, MAYA, *Revolution in Learning,* New York: Harper and Row, 1966.

PLESSAS, GUS and OAKES, CLIFTON, "Pre-Reading Experiences of Early Selected Readers," *The Reading Teacher* 17 (January, 1964) 241–245.

RAMBUSCH, NANCY MCCORMICK, *Learning How to Learn—An American Approach to Montessori.* Baltimore: Helicon Press, Inc. 1962.

ROWAN, HELEN, " 'Tis Time He Should Begin to Read," *Carnegie Corporation Quarterly,* 9: No. 2. (1961) 1–3.

SHELDON, WILLIAM D., "Should The Very Young Be Taught to Read?" *NEA Journal,* 52 (November, 1963) 20.

SKINNER, B. F., *Verbal Behavior.* New York: Appleton-Century-Crofts, 1957. See Chapters 1 and 2.

SMITH, NILA BANTON, "Early Reading: Viewpoints," *Childhood Education,* 42 (December, 1965) 229–232.

STEVENS, GEORGE L., and OREM, REGINALD C., *The Case For Early Reading.* St. Louis: Warren H. Green, Inc., 1968.

The main thesis of this defense is that the earliest years of a child's life are most critical. The book supports the claim that language learning is developed in the first four or five years of life and that reading should also be attained during those same years.

Both authors have previously expressed support of early reading and Montessori methods in articles in the *National Catholic Kindergarten Review*.

SUTTON, MARJORIE HUNT, "Readiness for Reading at the Kindergarten Level," *The Reading Teacher*, 17 (January, 1964).

This is a digest of her master's degree thesis. Its chief contribution is an excellent list of questions yet to be answered.

——, "First Grade Children Who Learned to Read in Kindergarten," *The Reading Teacher*, 19 (December, 1965) 192–196.

"The Big Box That Teaches," *The Reading Newsreport*, II, No. 5, March, 1968, 22–31.

This article reports on recent experiments using the "talking typewriter" with very young children in New York City, Philadelphia, Chicago, and Chester, Pennsylvania.

"Unlocking Early Learnings' Secrets," *Life* magazine, 62, No. 13, (March 31, 1967), 40–47.

This interesting popular account of some recent research in early learning contains a reference to the work of Siegfried Engelmann at the University of Illinois.

WAKIN, E. "Return of Montessori," *Saturday Review* 47 (November 21, 1964), 61–63.

WHEELER, ARVILLE, *Readiness For Reading*. New London, Conn.: Arthur C. Croft, 1959.

WHIPPLE, GERTRUDE, "The Concept of Reading Readiness in The United States of America," *Reading Instruction: An International Forum*, Marion D. Jenkinson, editor, Newark, Delaware, International Reading Association, 1967.

Dr. Whipple was one of the speakers at the First World Congress on Reading, Paris, August 8–9, 1966.

YOUNG, BILOINE W., "A New Approach to Head Start," *Phi Delta Kappan*, XLX, No. 7 (March, 1968) 386–388.

QUESTIONS AND ACTIVITIES FOR DISCUSSION AND GROWTH

1. Visit a Montessori school. Observe the strategy under which the children must operate.

2. At the Montessori school, what do you find in the way of equipment that is exclusively "Montessori"?

3. Research the success that the Responsive Environments Corporation is having. Ask your broker to find out about their operation and the amount of success that is anticipated.

4. If possible, visit or talk to someone who teaches the *Getting Ready to Read* approach. What aspects of all of the McKee-Harrison materials are being used? Why is not the entire program being used (including the involvement of parents and television, etc.)?

5. Try the *ABC Dictation* materials on a First Grade class. What reactions can you report?

6. Try the *Read Along With Me* materials on a First Grade class. What did you discover?

7. Play the *Play 'N Talk* phonics recordings for a First Grade group, using the individual pupil materials. What did you discover?

8. Interview several mothers of two-year-olds. Describe the *Teach Your Baby to Read* approach. What are their reactions?

9. Try some of the first *Teach Your Baby to Read* techniques on some two-year-old you know well. What did you discover?

10. If possible, obtain the video-tape or film (there may be a cost involved) of the *Distar* program. Study it carefully and prepare lesson plans for three *Distar* lessons with four-year-olds. What limitations must you place on yourself in preparing to teach this approach?

PERCEPTUAL-DISCRIMINATION APPROACHES

11

What may accurately be distinguished as a "perceptual-discrimination" approach to beginning reading is one which emphasizes auditory and visual perceptual factors of learning.

Such an approach is predicated upon the fact that reading is, essentially, the decoding of visual stimuli representative of auditory language, and that such decoding entails visual perception and discrimination preceded by auditory perception and discrimination. From a basic analysis of the physiological and psychological processes involved in reading, advocates of a "perceptual-discrimination" approach to beginning reading have developed a theory that they believe explains the reading process.

Basically, the theory consists of two parts: First, that an individual must be able to hear and to differentiate between spoken words and between parts of spoken words and then must be able to see and to differentiate between visual word symbols and between visual letter symbols which represent those spoken sounds; Second, that auditory and visual perceptual-discrimination is a learned skill. Consequently, a number of systems of auditory and visual perceptual-discrimination training have been devised as approaches to beginning reading. Indeed, they are generally considered by their sponsors to be prerequisites to reading.

It would appear logical that, inasmuch as reading is an auditory and visual perceptual-discrimination process which is learned, training in a developmental sequence of auditory and visual perceptual-discrimination learning tasks is basic to beginning reading. Ideally, the sequence of learning tasks would include exercises in listening to speech sounds, identifying likenesses and differences of speech sounds, and recalling speech sounds. Similarly, a developmental sequence of visual learning

465

exercises would include visual perception, identification, and recall of basic shapes, gestalts, letters, and words. In addition, it would be incumbent upon any perceptual-discrimination approach to beginning reading to include patterning in left-to-right directionality.

Being psychologically-oriented, a complete perceptual-discrimination approach would utilize several sensory modalities, thus making it possible for the learner to receive reinforcement from tactile and kinesthetic stimuli as well as from auditory and visual stimuli.

Finally, such an approach logically demands a sequence of structured learning tasks which progress from the simple to the complex—from the gross to the fine—culminating in the discrimination skills directly involved in reading words in isolation and words in context.

Origins

Although it is probable that concern for the perceptual-discrimination abilities of a child who is beginning to learn to read pre-dates the turn of the century, organized scientific investigation of the problem was first noted in the 1920's along with the popular "scientific movement" in education. The 1930's were a plateau during which relatively few people maintained an interest in this aspect of beginning reading. It was not until the 1950's and the mid-century explosion of knowledge that perceptual-discrimination became a major concern of researchers, followed by the proliferation of published materials in the 1960's.

Most of the interest in perceptual-discrimination as it applies to beginning reading was, originally, an outgrowth of the gestalt school of psychology. Gestaltists emphasized figure-ground relationships, perceptual patterns, forms and shapes, and sensory discrimination of likenesses and differences. They also pointed out that the successful learner selects certain specific stimuli from the great milieu of stimuli which environmentally surround him.

Educators who have adopted some of the gestalt principles theorize that the reading process is dependent upon the learner's ability to factor out appropriate sounds and shapes. This school of thought also dates from the 1920's and 1930's.

Interest in having the beginning reader acquire facility in visual discrimination of gestalts resulted in the 1930's and 1940's in a number of dittoed sheets and workbooks containing discrimination tasks, most of which had little, if any, direct relationship to the discrimination of letter shapes or word gestalts.

It would appear that the originators of those materials were either unaware of or chose to ignore the work of a rather distinguished group of pioneers working on the problem of the relationship of perceptual-discrimination and reading. Or it may be that, since the research tended to concentrate upon children with severe learning disabilities, classroom practitioners and workbook writers felt compelled to originate materials which they considered more appropriate for the "normal" child.

In any event, it was not until the 1960's that the reading profession seemed to become fully aware of the forty years or more of research on perception-discrimination, the perceptually-handicapped child, and reading disability resulting from perceptual dysfunction. The word "dyslexia" appears to be the "flux" which has brought clinical research and the reading profession together. Although the many definitions of "dyslexia" tend to confuse the novice, it is generally accepted as the term covering the condition in which an individual of apparently normal intelligence just cannot learn to read by means of ordinary classroom techniques and materials. A corollary would state that such an individual tests out as subnormal on measures of perceptual discrimination and cognitive factors related to reading.

Previous to the popularization of the term "dyslexia", researchers in visual perception and visual memory were using the term "word blindness", and later, Orton and his followers preferred the terms "strephosymbolia" and "specific language disability."

In 1917, Bronner[1] described case studies of children who apparently had poor perceptual-discrimination abilities. Fildes' study[2] of visual discrimination indicated a definite relationship between perceptual abilities and reading. Orton's studies, probably, were most influential in focusing attention on the contributions that the neurologist and psychiatrist might make in this field. In his 1925 report,[3] he used the "word-blindness" term, and, later, introduced the "strephosymbolia" (twisted symbols) term at the 1928 American Medical Association meeting. At that time, he hypothesized upon the concept of three levels of perceptual-discrimination: (1) basic visual awareness of objects; (2) auditory and visual memory of objects, with ability to remember their names and identify them by name; (3) visual elaborative level in which association and cognition are

1. Bronner, Augusta F., *The Psychology of Special Abilities and Disabilities*. Boston: Little, Brown, 1917.
2. Fildes, Lucy G., " A Psychological Inquiry Into The Nature of the Condition Known as Congenital Word-blindness," *Brain* 44: (1921) 286–307.
3. Orton, Samuel T. " 'Word-Blindness' in School Children," *Archives of Neurology and Psychiatry* 14: (November, 1925), 581–615.

most important. "At the third or associative level, however, destruction in one hemisphere (of the brain) may result in complete loss of the associative function, resulting in inability to read. . . ."[4]

Monroe was one of the first reading specialists to investigate the causative factors of reading disability and to include inability in the perceptual-discrimination of forms and complex visual patterns as well as directionality.[5]

Following the death of Dr. Orton, his followers founded the Orton Society in 1949. The *Bulletins of the Orton Society* have carried a succession of significant contributions by researchers who have distinguished themselves in their investigations of the perceptual-discrimination factor in learning to read.

The pioneer work of the Orton Society has been eclipsed by the formation in 1963 of the International Association For Children With Learning Disabilities. This group has now grown to huge proportions and has succeeded in holding an annual major "International Conference" attended by thousands from most sections of North America, and with expectations of enjoying a world-wide membership.

The purpose of the ACLD is "To advance the education and general well-being of children with normal and potentially normal or above average intelligence who have learning disabilities arising from perceptual, conceptual, or subtle coordinative problems, sometimes accompanied by behavior difficulties."[6]

When one reviews the work of the past half-century in this field of perceptual discrimination, it becomes apparent that the area of *reading* is most usually involved. This is not at all surprising, for reading is the common-denominator of most academic learning, and a sensory impairment of one of the basic factors in reading would, logically, result in an impairment of reading skill. Conversely, it could be supposed that the improvement on one of the basic sensory factors in learning would result in an improvement in reading skill. Efforts to identify the sensory factors involved in the psychology of reading have led almost invariably to the perceptual-discrimination approach to beginning reading.

It is not surprising, therefore, that the contributions of psychologists, neurologists, and practitioners in special education have considerable

---

4. Orton, Samuel T., "Specific Reading Disability, Strephosymbolia," *Journal of American Medical Association*, 90; (April 7, 1928) 1095–1099.
5. Monroe, Marion, "Methods For Diagnosis and Treatment of Cases of Reading Disability," *Genetic Psychology Monographs*, 14: 4 and 5 (October-November, 1928.) and Monroe, Marion, *Children Who Cannot Read*, Chicago: University of Chicago Press, 1932.
6. See the new publication of ACLD: *The Journal of Learning Disabilities*, 5 North Wabash Avenue, Chicago, Vol 1, 1968.

relevancy to normal children who are learning to read. In fact, if one were to compare the concepts which the gestalt psychologist uses to explain perceptual discrimination in normal children who are beginning reading with the concepts which are used to explain failure to read (dyslexia) among children with learning disabilities, it is probable that they would appear identical. It is only recently, however, that the findings of those working with children with learning disabilities have had any major impact upon an approach to beginning reading for normal learners.

Materials and Method

The use of forms and shapes has for many years been standard practice in reading-readiness training. Montessori used the square, circle, and triangle as "preparation" (see Chapter 10), and various "Copy Forms" exercises and tests have long been used with pre-readers. Gesell's original Copy Forms were arranged in a sequence of increasing difficulty: circle, cross, square, triangle, divided rectangle, and diamond. Data reported from the Gesell Institute of Child Development indicate that, at first, the young child perceives a square as being closer to a circle and not until about age four can the learner copy a square shape. At five he is just beginning to copy a triangle. "Note how often the child who has trouble in the early school years and who has trouble in grasping reading, may also have trouble in mastering the use of the oblique stroke [in the triangle] earlier."[7]

Among the many so-called "reading readiness" materials which have been widely used in Kindergartens and First Grade classrooms are the worksheets produced by the Continental Press.[8] Their use has been based upon the expectation that the child will benefit from a sequence of perceptual-discrimination tasks.

Also for a number of years, reading-readiness activities have included many variations of matching, comparing, positioning, and copying tasks. The wide range of activities includes dominoes, cut pictures, insert picture puzzles, parquetry cards and boards, maze tracing, copy forms, sandpaper shapes, and stencils. Observation of shapes and the procedure known as the Fernald technique[9] has been widely copied and adapted.

Monroe and Rogers[10] reflect the wide interest in perceptual-discrimi-

7. Ilg. Frances L., and Ames, Louise B., *School Readiness*, New York: Harper & Row, 1965, 65. See all of Chapter 8, "Copy Forms".
8. "Visual Motor Skills, Level 1 and Level 2", and "Visual Discrimination, Level 1 and Level 2", Elizabethtown, Pennsylvania: Continental Press, 1958.
9. Fernald, Grace M. *Remedial Techniques in Basic School Subjects*, New York: McGraw-Hill, 1943.

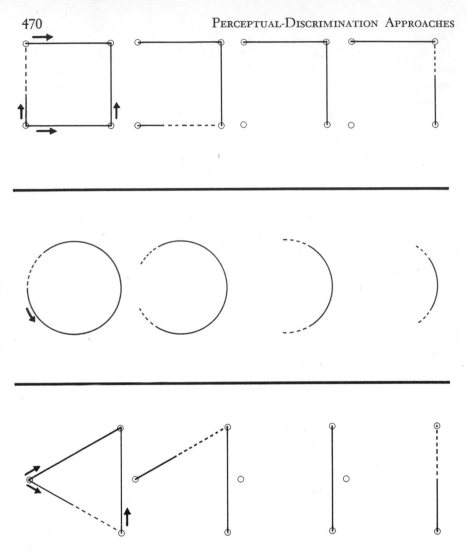

Fig. 11–1   Reprinted from Readiness For Reading *by permission of*
J. B. Lippincott Company.

nation activities as an approach to beginning reading by devoting a considerable part of their discussion of informal pre-reading procedures to
perceptual discrimination and perceptual training.

An ever-increasing number of perceptual-discrimination materials

10. Monroe, Marion and Rogers, Bernice, *Foundations For Reading*, Chicago: Scott,
Foresman and Company, 1964. Chapter Five and Chapter Seven.

are being produced as a result of the suddenly-increased concern for children with learning disabilities. The Frostig materials,[11] the Slingerland Kit,[12] the Strauss materials,[13] Kephart technique,[14] the Winter Haven Program,[15] the Barsch Perceptual-Motor Sequences,[16] KELP,[17] the ITPA,[18] the Erie County Program,[19] the Pathway School Eye-Hand Coordination Exercises,[20] Ruth Cheves' materials,[21] the Dubnoff School Program,[22] the Fairbanks-Robinson exercises,[23] Getman's visual-motor-tactile skills readiness program,[24] and Long Island optometrist Lawrence Gould's DETECT materials[25] are an indication of the widespread production of materials and methods of perceptual-discrimination training now available.

Most, if not all, of these materials and techniques concentrate upon activities which purport to structure and enhance perception. Many of the publishers of these materials are promoting them as approaches to beginning reading. They are offered for this purpose on the deduction that, if they are used to remediate the child who is diagnosed as having a learning disability, they, therefore, should be effective for aiding normal children who are learning to read and who do not have such dysfunction.

The materials, essentially, may be divided into four categories:

11. Frostig, Marianne, Miller, Ann-Marie, and Horne, David, *Developmental Program in Visual Perception,* Chicago: Follett Publishing Co., 1966.
12. Slingerland, Beth H., *Training in Some Prerequisites For Beginning Reading.* Cambridge, Massachusetts: Educators Publishing Service, 1967.
13. Rogan, Laura Lechtinen, Larson, Charlotte L., Lukens, Jean, and Clements, Sam D., *Developmental Learning Materials,* Chicago: Developmental Learning Materials, 1967.
14. Kephart, Newell C., *The Slow Learner in the Classroom.* Columbus: Charles E. Merrill Co., 1960.
15. Winter Haven Lions Club, *Perceptual-Development Program,* Winter Haven, Florida, 1966.
16. Barsch, Ray H., "A Perceptual Motor Curriculum": Vol. 3, *Perceptual-Motor Sequences.* Seattle: Special Child Publications (71 Columbia Street). 1968.
17. Wilson, John A. R., and Robeck, Mildred C., KELP (Kindergarten Evaluation of Learning Potential) New York: McGraw-Hill Book Co., 1967.
18. Bateman, Barbara, *Manual on Profiles of the Illinois Test of Psycholinguistic Abilities.* Seattle: Special Child Publications(71 Columbia Street), 1968.
19. Hatton, Daniel A., Pizzat, Frank J., and Pelkowski, Jerome M., *Erie Program of Perceptual-Motor Teaching Materials.* Boston: Teaching Resources, 1967.
20. Getman, G. N., *Pathway School Program of Eye-Hand Coordination Exercises.* Boston: Teaching Resources. 1967.
21. Cheves, Ruth, *Visual-Motor Perception Teaching Materials,* Boston: Teaching Resources, 1968.
22. Dubnoff, Belle, and Chambers, Irene, *Dubnoff School Program of Sequential Perceptual-Motor Exercises,* Boston: Teaching Resources, 1967.
23. Fairbanks, Jean and Robinson, Janet, *Fairbanks-Robinson Program of Perceptual-Motor Development.* Boston: Teaching Resources, 1967.
24. Getman, G. N. and others, *Developing Learning Readiness: A Visual-Motor-Tactile Skills Program.* Manchester, Missouri: Webster Division, McGraw-Hill, 1967.
25. Gould, Lawrence, DETECT, Chicago: Science Research Associates, 1968.

auditory perceptual-discrimination; visual perceptual-discrimination; kinesthetic and tactile perceptual-discrimination; and spatial and directional orientation.

Training in auditory perceptual-discrimination skills usually is in the form of recordings on phonograph discs or on tapes. Developmental training in visual skills includes a wide spectrum of materials in black and white and color. All of the following are parts of programs now being used: inlay puzzles, inlay parquetry boards, shapes, mazes printed on paper, shapes printed on paper for comparison of similarities and differences, three-dimensional designs printed in two dimensions on paper. alphabet cards, word gestalts, letters and words printed in dotted lines, partial words and letters printed to necessitate the "close" technique of completing the designs, and perhaps others. Kinesthetic and tactile materials include sandpaper letters, guided learning sheets which require special pencils and which have a built-in error-recording quality, parquetry blocks and puzzles in three dimensions for manual manipulation, form boards, tracing forms, flocked designs and letters, silhouettes, and stencils. Spatial and directional orientation not only includes mazes printed on paper, letters with directionality indicated by numbers and arrows,

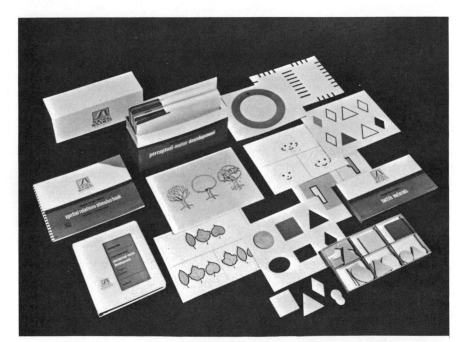

Fig. 11–2 *Layout of the* Fairbanks-Robinson Program/1 *materials, reprinted by permission of the publishers, Teaching Resources, Boston.*

practice in drawing straight vertical and horizontal lines, circular lines, intersecting lines, and diagonals.

Symbol Accentuation is another and quite different variation of the perceptual-discrimination approach to beginning reading; and, like most of the other programs discussed under this heading, *Symbol Accentuation* was devised for individuals with perceptual learning disabilities.

The materials and method are an outgrowth of work done by Dr. Arnold Miller at the Language Development Laboratory of the Wrentham (Massachusetts) State School For the Mentally Deficient. Dr. Miller's original experiments were conducted with ten severely retarded people (mean age, 15; mean I Q 45). Flash cards were used. One side of a flash card contained a word which was carefully distorted to look like the object which the word represents. The opposite side of the flashcard contained the word in normal print. Some of the words were presented in both their distorted (accented) form and their normal form. Other words were presented only in normal form. The "accented" words were learned in fewer trials than the conventionally presented words.

In a second study with a larger group of retarded people the "accented" words were presented alternately with the normally printed words by means of two projectors. The stroboscopic action of the projection resulted in the illusion of motion in which the distorted word straightened out into the normal word.

A third study utilized motion picture techniques for phasing the "accented" words into normal configurations. A fourth study using letters instead of words was conducted with normal five- and six-year-olds.

Miller indicates that "three- and four-year-old normal children as well as retarded children did significantly better on 'accentuated' . . . presentations . . . [and] five- and six-year-old normal children no longer required Symbol Accentuation".[26]

The main contribution of the Miller studies[27] is to provide a rationale for investing distorted printed words with meaningful forms which can be fused by means of motion picture animation into the abstract word-form symbols. This adds an entirely new dimension to the visual perceptual-discrimination approach to beginning reading.

Miller's *Symbol Accentuation* approach is available through International Communication Films, which is a division of Doubleday and Co.

26. Miller, Arnold, "Symbol Accentuation: Outgrowth of Theory and Experiment," *Proceedings,* First International Congress for the Scientific Study of Mental Deficiency, 1968.
27. Miller, Arnold and Miller, Eileen E., "Symbol Accentuation: The Perceptual Transfer of Meaning from Spoken to Printed Words," *American Journal of Mental Deficiency,* 1968.

The program includes 30 films in 8 mm cartridges, two workbooks, flash-cards assembled in spiral booklets to accompany the films, and a teacher's manual. The materials and method are being promoted for use with normal pre-school and Kindergarten children.

As can readily be seen from this array of perceptual-discrimination training materials, the intent is to convince practitioners in reading that readiness for reading consists of developmental exercises and that such exercises are, indeed, an essential element in the sequential development of the learner. Consequently, because of several factors, not the least of which are the very number of different programs and the vigor with which they are being promoted, these perceptual-discrimination materials are being seriously considered by some as another possible approach to beginning reading.

One reading specialist has, in fact, produced an elaborate program of visual perceptual discrimination exercises which are specifically directed toward readiness for reading. The program, known as *Readiness for Learning*,[28] is by Pierce H. McLeod, director of reading in the Macomb County (Michigan) schools.

Readiness for Learning is a 78-page consumable pupil workbook. The teacher's edition contains additional pages describing the training activities. The program is designed to provide a "foundation for successful learning, particularly in reading."

The instructional program is divided into three sequential levels: physical motor activities such as crawling, walking a balancing beam, jumping, push-ups, puzzles, visual tracking, and other perception games; more elaborate motor training activities designed to pattern directionality; and, finally, tracing geometric forms which gradually merge into work with upper-case letter forms, followed by lower-case letter forms.

The *Readiness for Learning* program is designed for Kindergarten or First Grade. The bilateral perceptual-motor activities of Level One cover a six to ten week period, with a minimum of twenty minutes daily. Level Two is planned for an additional six to ten weeks. The activities in the workbook for Level Three engage the Kindergartner through the remainder of the year until April or May when he is to be given a readiness test.

The program incorporates a number of features found here and there in other perceptual-discrimination programs. In addition, it has minimal but adequate directions for a number of physical coordination exercises and games which heretofore have been claimed as the prerogative of highly trained psychologists, neurologists, optometrists, and physio-

---

28. McLeod, Pierce H., *Readiness for Learning*, Philadelphia: J. B. Lippincott Co., 1965.

therapists. It is a highly structured, sequential, and developmental program which moves very rapidly from simple to quite complex visual patterns. It is obviously predicated upon the psychological theory of transfer of identical elements. It stops short of reading by ending the program with mastery of letter forms and the ability to perceive words correctly when they are exposed on a hand tachistoscope.

CONCLUSION

The advocates of perceptual-discrimination approaches to beginning reading base their strategies on the theory that the reading process is a visual tracking skill. Their materials and methods are designed to provide sequential practice in visual-motor skills. Many, indeed most, of the "originators" of materials are engaged in special programs for children with special learning disabilities.

The routines that the perceptual-discrimination specialists prescribe as approaches to beginning reading, consequently, are identical to the ones they use with neurologically and/or visually impaired learners. The schema are highly structured and call for the attention of a practitioner or proctor on a one-to-one basis or, at most, in very small groups of learners.

The only validity that can reasonably be admitted for most of the perceptual-discrimination approaches to beginning reading is that they contain many elements of perceptual readiness. This, obviously, is nothing new, since Kindergartens for years have employed most of the materials that the new cult of perceptual specialists is now promoting and using in rigid sequence.

Child development specialists, on the other hand, have not supported the theory of structured readiness for learning. Hymes, for example, a decade ago wrote: "When we spend time and energy trying to 'build' readiness to read, we move in the wrong direction."[29] He, of course, emphasized the range of individual differences found in Kindergarten classes, and suggested that a very few children may be ready to read, given a little help. He also suggested that workbooks be delayed until the First Grade. Almost as though he were predicting the sudden deluge of perceptual-training materials, he wrote: "Neither five-year-olds nor six-year-olds need workbooks—special added drills or made-up exercises—to 'build' their readiness or to jog it along."[30]

---

29. Hymes, James L., Jr., *Before the Child Reads.* Evanston: Row, Peterson, 1958. 41
30. *Ibid.* 75.

Fig. 11–3 Photographed for Eli Lilly and Company by Phoebe Dunn.
Reproduced by courtesy of Eli Lilly and Company, Indianapolis.

Ilg and Ames are even more firm in revealing their concern for the natural growth in readiness as opposed to structured patterning:

> Let's consider for a minute the child we wish to know, on the threshold of coming into the world on his own as a kindergartner. What a lovely image this word stimulates—a child's garden. Is it still the same garden it once was or was meant to be? We need to ask ourselves this question when we see the vultures of experimental education poaching on this tender territory, forcing advanced curricula in learning into the young child's receptive but unknowing mind. When and if this happens, the sympathetic flow between adult and child may cease. There is the danger of setting up an unnecessary hierarchy of learning steps through which the child may have to endure.[31]

In spite of many warnings, there is little doubt about the future of the perceptual-discrimination approach to beginning reading. Head Start programs have invested heavily in many of the materials described here. Montessori-type Kindergartens have used certain facets of the approach for many years. As the Kindergarten program becomes increasingly structured, more of these exercises will be introduced for all children in place of the self-selection of puzzles, parquetry blocks, and shapes which has

---

31. Ilg and Ames, *op. cit.* 32.

been the practice in child-centered programs. The next step which the reading profession cannot avoid is for alert publishers to replace present-day readiness books with a structured program of the perceptual-discrimination materials described here.

In spite of the fact that there is little, if any, documented evidence that such an approach is valid for all or even a large portion of children, it appears that the reading profession will be forced into acceptance. It is a *fait accompli,* and proof of the efficacy of this perceptual-discrimination approach to beginning reading must wait till another day.

BIBLIOGRAPHY

AMBLE, B. R., and MUEHL, S., "Perceptual Span Training and Reading Achievement of School Children," *Journal of Educational Psychology.* 57: (August, 1966) 192–206.

Association for Children With Learning Disabilities, *The Journal of Learning Disabilities,* 5 North Wabash Avenue, Chicago. Vol. 1: January, 1968.

BARRETT, THOMAS C., "The Relationship Between Measures of Pre-Reading Visual Discrimination and First Grade Reading Achievement: A Review of the Literature," *Reading Research Quarterly,* I (Fall, 1965) 51–76.

This is a major contribution through a review of 21 studies of various types of visual discrimination tests and their relationship to measures of First Grade reading achievement.

BARSCH, RAY H., "A Perceptual Motor Curriculum": Vol. 3, *Perceptual-Motor Sequences.* Seattle: Special Child Publications (71 Columbia Street), 1968.

BATEMAN, BARBARA, *Manual* on "Profiles of the Illinois Test of Psycholinguistic Abilities." Seattle: Special Child Publications, (71 Columbia Street), 1968.

BRONNER, AUGUSTA F., *The Psychology of Special Abilities and Disabilities.* Boston: Little, Brown, 1917.

CHEVES, RUTH, *Visual-Motor Perception Teaching Materials,* Boston: Teaching Resources, 1968.

Among the perceptual training materials available are several designed to be used as an approach to beginning reading: form puzzles, geometric shapes, association cards, and phonics game.

Continental Press, "Visual Motor Skills, Levels 1 and 2," and "Visual Discrimination, Level 1 and Level 2", Elizabethtown, Pa.: Continental Press, 1958.

These are portfolios of pre-printed masters for liquid duplicators. They provide lessons in tracing, completing designs, spatial relationships, visualization, discrimination of differences of shape, size, position, reversal, and inversion.

CONNELL, DONNA, "Auditory and Visual Discrimination in Kindergarten," *Elementary English,* XLV (January, 1968) 51–54.

A good description of some discrimination exercises used in a Napa, California project based upon the theory that children do not automatically acquire discrimination skills as a result of maturation alone.

CROSBY, R. M. N., and LISTON, ROBERT A., *The Waysiders—A New Approach to Reading and the Dyslexic Reader*, New York: Delacorte Press, 1968.

This excellent volume is by a pediatric neurologist and neurosurgeon. It is a distinct contribution to our understanding of perceptual-discrimination processes related to reading.

DELACATO, CARL H., *Neurological Organization and Reading*, Springfield, Illinois, Charles C Thomas, 1966.

DOUGLAS, MALCOLM P., Editor, *28th Yearbook, Claremont Reading Conference*. Claremont, California: Claremont Graduate School, 1964.

Of special interest is the symposium: "Delacato in Review". The yearbook presents three critiques of the Delacato theory.

PERKINS, THEODORE F., "Problems Arising From Assertions or Assumptions of Delacato," 119–122.

OETTIGER, LEON JR., "The Theory From the Standpoint of Pediatrics," 123–125.

HUDSPETH, WILLIAM J., "The Neurobehavioral Implausibility of the Delacato Theory," 126–131.

DUBNOFF, BELLE, and CHAMBERS, IRENE, *Dubnoff School Program of Sequential Perceptual-Motor Exercises*, Boston: Teaching Resources, 1967.

This program consists primarily of four sets of worksheets, designed to provide practice in patterning of straight lines (vertical, horizontal and squares), circular lines, diagonals, and intersecting lines. An Instructor's Guide provides an explanation of the purposes and procedures of the Dubnoff Program.

FAIRBANKS, JEAN, and ROBINSON, JANET, *Fairbanks-Robinson Program of Perceptual-Motor Development*. Boston: Teaching Resources, 1967.

This is a boxed kit of materials and individual worksheets. Included is a set of tactile stimulus forms and exercises in patterning, discrimination of form, size, figure-ground, and spatial relations.

FERNALD, GRACE M., *Remedial Techniques in Basic School Subjects*, New York: McGraw-Hill, 1943.

FILDES, LUCY G., "A Psychological Inquiry Into The Nature of the Condition Known as Congenital Word-blindness," *Brain* 44: (1921) 286–307.

FRIERSON, EDWARD C., and BARBE, WALTER B., compilers, *Educating Children with Learning Disabilities*. New York: Appleton-Century-Crofts, 1967.

This 500-page hardback book of readings contains some of the best from Bateman, Clements, Bender, Barsch, Kirk, de Hirsch, Wepman, Strauss, Kephart, Frostig, and many others.

FROSTIG, MARIANNE, MILLER, ANN-MARIE, and HORNE, DAVID, *Developmental Program in Visual Perception*, Chicago: Follett Publishing Co., 1966.

The workbooks and Teachers' Guides provide the paper-and-pencil components of the Frostig program. Dr. Frostig also uses what she terms "movement education" exercises which are both free expression movements and highly structured exercises as warm-up for the visual-perceptual training that follows.

GETMAN, G. N., and others, *Developing Learning Readiness: A Visual-Motor-Tactile Skills Program*. Manchester, Missouri: Webster Division, McGraw-Hill, 1967.

This program provides targets, charts, templates, walking beam, tach work, and other materials designed for "practice in general coordination, balance, eye-movement, eye-hand coordination, form recognition, and visual memory," according to promotional flyers.

———, *Pathway School Program of Eye-Hand Coordination Exercises.* Boston: Teaching Reseources. 1967.

The prospectus indicates that the Pathway Program "is designed to help in preparing the child for more advanced perceptual-motor skills necessary for reading and writing."

GLASS, GENE V., and ROBBINS, MELVIN P., "A Critique of Experiments on the Role of Neurological Organization in Reading Performance," *Reading Research Quarterly*, III, No. 1, (Fall, 1967) 5–51.

This is a major critical review of fifteen studies which purport to support the Delacato neurological approach to reading. The authors analyze the statistical treatment used in the studies and conclude by expressing serious doubts concerning the validity of the studies.

GOULD, LAWRENCE, DETECT, Chicago: Science Research Associates, 1968.

HATTON, DANIEL A., PIZZAT, FRANK J., and PELKOWSKI, JEROME M., *Erie Program of Perceptual-Motor Teaching Materials.* Boston: Teaching Resources, 1967.

These materials include exercises in form discrimination, using triangles, discs, and squares "providing one of the bases for later discriminating between letters of the alphabet. . . . This is an effective reading 'readiness' series."

HYMES, JAMES L. JR., *Before the Child Reads.* Evanston: Row, Peterson, 1958.

ILG, FRANCES L., and AMES, LOUISE B., *School Readiness*, New York: Harper & Row, 1965, 65.

See all of Chapter 8, "Copy Forms".
This excellent book describes the philosophy of the Gesell Institute and emphasizes developmental and behavioral age norms rather than C.A. or I.Q. It also is a manual describing the behavior tests used at the Gesell Institute in New Haven.

KEPHART, NEWELL C., *The Slow Learner in the Classroom.* Columbus: Charles E. Merrill Co., 1960.

This is a well-known guide describing techniques which are now being suggested as appropriate as an approach to beginning reading.

MILLER, ARNOLD, *Symbol Accentuation,* International Communications Films, 1371 Reynolds Avenue, Santa Ana, California 92705.

MONROE, MARION, "Methods For Diagnosis and Treatment of Cases of Reading Disability," *Genetic Psychology Monographs*, 14: 4 and 5 (October–November, 1928.)

———, *Children Who Cannot Read*, Chicago: University of Chicago Press, 1932.

———, and ROGERS, BERNICE, *Foundations For Reading*, Chicago: Scott, Foresman and Company, 1964.

Chapter Five and Chapter Seven provide a good discussion of techniques designed to develop perceptual-discrimination skills as an approach to reading.

MOSKOVITZ, SARAH T., "Some Assumptions Underlying the Bereiter Approach," *Young Children*, 24, 1 (October, 1968) 24–31.

ORTON, SAMUEL T., " 'Word-Blindness' in School Children," *Archives of Neurology and Psychiatry* 14: (November, 1925) 581–615.

——, "Specific Reading Disability—Strephosymbolia," *Journal of the American Medical Association*, 90: (April 7, 1928) 1095–1099.

ROGAN, LAURA LECHTINEN, LARSON, CHARLOTTE L., LUKENS, JEAN, and CLEMENTS, SAM D., *Developmental Learning Materials*, Chicago: Developmental Learning Materials, 1967.

These are the materials developed at the Cove Schools which the late Dr. A. A. Strauss and Dr. Laura Lichtinen founded in 1947. They consist of boxed shapes puzzles, stencils, alphabet cards, cubes, cube designs and parquetry designs.

SHEA, CAROL ANN, "Visual Discrimination of Words and Reading Readiness," *The Reading Teacher* 21: (January, 1968) 361–367.

Reports an investigation in Hamden, Connecticut of tests of visual discrimination as predictors of reading readiness.

SLINGERLAND, BETH H., *Training in Some Prerequisites For Beginning Reading*. Cambridge, Massachusetts: Educators Publishing Service, 1967.

This is a revised edition of what is known as the "Slingerland Kit". It consists of a portfolio of photographs and a Teacher's Manual which describes the games and exercises.

SLOBODIAN, J., and CAMPBELL, P., "Do Children's Perceptions Influence Beginning Reading Achievement?" *Elementary School Journal* 67: (May, 1967) 423–427.

TINKER, MILES A., "How Children and Adults Perceive Words in Reading," *Invitational Addresses of the Tenth Annual Convention, IRA*. Newark, Delaware; International Reading Association, 1965, 75–91.

Dr. Tinker has consolidated some of the material from Chapter 2 and Chapter 3 of his book: *Bases For Effective Reading*, Minneapolis: University of Minnesota Press, 1965. His main theme is that children generally employ very ineffective methods of word perception in beginning reading.

VERNON, M. D., "Ten More Important Sources of Information on Visual Perception in Relation to Reading," *The Reading Teacher*. 20 (November, 1966), 134–135.

WHEELOCK, WARREN H., and SILVAROLI, NICHOLAS J., "Visual Discrimination Training for Beginning Readers," *The Reading Teacher*, 21 (November, 1967) 115–120.

The authors found that it was possible to effect significant differences in favor of children who had been given specific tach training in letter-form discrimination.

WILLIAMS, J. P., and LEVIN, H., "Word Perception: Psychological Bases," *Education*, 87: (May, 1967) 515–518.

WILSON, JOHN A. R., and ROBECK, MILDRED C., KELP (Kindergarten Evaluation of Learning Potential) New York: McGraw-Hill Book Co., 1967.

KELP learning materials were developed for use in Kindergartens for developing association, conceptualization, perception and discrimination. A 260-page Teacher's Book provides guidelines.

Winter Haven Lions Club, *Perceptual-Development Program*, Winter Haven, Florida, 1966.

YONAS, ALBERT and GIBSON, ELEANOR J., "A Developmental Study of Feature-Processing Strategies in Letter Discrimination," *Project Literacy Reports* No. 8. Ithaca: Cornell University, 1967. Mimeo. 11–20.

This is a report of a research project in which the authors found that it was possible to effect significant differences in the perceptual-discrimination ability of children in responding to letter stimuli. The project was very limited, and needs to be replicated on a much larger scale to obtain definitive conclusions.

QUESTIONS AND ACTIVITIES FOR DISCUSSION AND GROWTH

1. Look through the catalog of a major school supply house and list the games and equipment that are available for use in the Kindergarten that are similar to those being sold by perceptual-discrimination specialists.
2. Compare the Slingerland materials with those of Frostig and with those that have been available for many years on purple masters from Continental Press.
3. In what ways does the Fernald approach act as the foundation for many recent perceptual-discrimination approaches?
4. Examine the Cheves materials and compare them with materials that are already in use in many Kindergartens. What do you discover?
5. Compare the Fairbanks-Robinson materials and the Cheves materials. What similarities do you detect?
6. Compare the Dubnoff program and the Getman approach. What similarities do you find?
7. Why are the materials in the perceptual discrimination approach so similar? What does that similarity mean?
8. Look over the *Readiness for Learning* workbook. Does it provide for the same learnings as the three-dimensional materials in the kits?
9. Go to a center where they are specializing on working with children who have perceptual problems. Observe the children's activities. What forces do you think you see in operation?
10. How do you react to the child development point of view in contrast to the perceptual development movement?

POSTSCRIPT

This book could go on and on; for, even as its final pages are put on the press, new approaches to beginning reading will be appearing and others will mushroom into being with the dawning of another day.

An attempt has been made here to provide the student, the teacher, the administrator, the supervisor, and the researcher with a summarization of approaches to beginning reading apart from the "traditional" basal reader approach.

The great diversity of approaches stems from the different philosophies of the originators, and from their concepts of and definitions of the nature and process of reading. It has been shown that some originators drew greatly upon their own classroom experiences as empirical evidence that their own systems work. In some cases this seems to have been sufficient motivation to encourage them to publish their materials and methods to be shared with others.

One group of originators has relied upon the logic of its own academia, assuming that the orderliness of knowledge is synonymous with the learning sequences which it provides for beginning readers and, therefore, the child will learn to read by mere exposure to the sequence. The resultant regularity of materials and method suggested by this group reveals a definition of reading probably quite different from that held by most classroom teachers.

Another group of originators has factored out of the total reading process one or another single element for concentrated attention. In several cases, the focus is upon an expanded alphabetical graphemic-phonemic correspondence. In other cases, it may be such specifics as rules, or key picture-words.

Yet another group has devised its method on the concept that beginning reading should be equated with the vocabulary and conversation of the learners, themselves; or, as in the case of individualized reading, with the undulating interests of young children.

Finally, some beginning reading advocates have developed materials, methods, and/or machines which will aid children to begin to learn to "read" at an earlier age than the customarily-accepted six-year-old norm.

The fact that the many approaches to beginning reading presented here have been "effective" should be of great concern to all who are interested in beginning reading. The claims made for these systems can, in most cases, reasonably be accepted, for personal acquaintance with most of the originators of the approaches convinces this writer that these are, indeed, reasonable and sincere people.

However, once we have accepted the thesis that 100 different approaches to beginning reading can all be effective, we immediately are faced with a dilemma. On the one hand we have the obvious fact that children *can and do learn to read by most any materials and method.* On the other hand we have the obvious fact that many of these methods and materials are incompatible, incomplete, inadequate, or naïve, and that they all cannot be equally effective—even in the hands of superior teachers.

It is this last point that should increase our concern; for, if the conclusion[1] suggested by the USOE First-Grade Studies is undisputed, it leaves us with the highly-improbable and equally-illogical conclusion that it is the teacher and not the materials or method that makes the difference. The possibility that such might be the case cannot be denied, but a careful analysis of the USOE First-Grade Studies reveals absolutely no evidence that teacher characteristics and/or performance were sufficiently controlled or assessed to warrant such a conclusion.

The thoughtful student of approaches to beginning reading must reject the idea that it is the superior teacher which accounts for the success of one method or another—at the same time admitting that superior teachers do exist. With such rejection, however, comes the necessity of determining which thesis to explore.

The one that seems most logical is that the diversity of approaches seems to lead to the possibility that some may be more effective than others. If that be the case, then it impinges upon us to apply adequate research techniques to prove this.

---

1. See *The Reading Teacher*, 19 (May, 1966) and 20 (October, 1966). Also: Bond, Guy L., and Dykstra, Robert, *Coordinating Center for First-Grade Reading Instruction Programs*, Minneapolis, University of Minnesota Press, 1967. This is the Final Report on the USOE Project No. OE-5-10-263, No. X-001.

This has not been done; and, considering the multi-faceted nature of reading and the pluralistic nature of the learners, it would appear *next to impossible to do it.* Indeed, if we would but examine the huge body of knowledge concerning the nature of the learning process, the conditions of learning, and the characteristics of individual differences in learners, it would be apparent that a study of approaches to reading would yield quite unsatisfactory results if attempted independently of the psychology of learning, itself.

Until such time as we can assess the true nature of the learning process and learn to program input in keeping with the process, we must be satisfied with lesser goals and primitive means. In reading, we must accept the fact that this means that whatever we discover concerning materials and methods will be but fragmentary, at best.

Such a long-term view should not deter us from doing the best we can. In fact, the one note of optimism should be that we certainly can do better than we are doing at present. For one thing, we should design more discreet research studies which recognize the fact that we cannot concentrate on one factor alone when reading is a multi-faceted process. Time and again in the discussion of the research findings on the various approaches to beginning reading it has been noted here that a study of the effect of one factor, such as learning vowels before consonants, would have on reading achievement could not be studied with the inadequate research designs ordinarily used.

It has been pointed out repeatedly here that the inability to control such important variables as past experiences, environment, motivation, intelligence, vitality, and expectancy, as well as the permissive loose sampling techniques make much of our research in reading a mockery.

The picture, however, is not entirely bad. We do have a variety of interesting and enjoyable materials. Some of the approaches utilize a number of the senses, thus employing several pathways to the brain. Some of the materials provide the learner with concrete and specific regularized sequences in learning which are so necessary as prerequisites to the more advanced processes involved in synthesizing the parts into wholes or attempting to analyze wholes for purposes of generalizing.

Most of the originators of materials and methods recognize that their approaches are adjuncts to a larger constellation of factors affecting reading. This is a mark of good judgment. It is, moreover, a fact which should not continue to be ignored when one is considering a study of the effectiveness of a particular approach to beginning reading.

The decade of the 1970s has been designated for major emphasis on the processes of reading, with an expressed hope that a massive Federally funded effort will result in the discovery of the optimum materials, method, and conditions for universal success in beginning reading. A major step was taken in August 1970 when President Nixon appointed a fifty-member National Reading Council, consisting mainly of the chief executives of large national organizations and associations plus a few congressional leaders. A National Reading Center also was established and a concerted effort was thus begun. One of the major tasks that confronts the National Reading Council is the investigation of the materials and methods available in the field of beginning reading. It is for this same purpose that this book was written.

Under each sub-section of each chapter, comments have been made on each approach to beginning reading. Several conclusions now seem to be appropriate as one terminates this study of reading approaches:

1. An approach to beginning reading is one which has within it the possibility of changing our stance in reading instruction. There are almost one hundred such approaches in addition to the fifteen basal reader approaches.

2. The originators are sincere people who believe that they have found better ways to beginning reading instruction.

3. The diversity of approaches leads to the conclusion that some, of necessity, must be more effective than others.

4. The reports of research that are available tend to favor some materials and methods, yet it is apparent that there is little or no research on a considerable number of systems.

5. Few, if any, comparative studies provide adequate and definitive statistical information that would prove one approach to be superior to others.

6. Statistical reports do indicate that two or three methods and materials do, indeed, result in reading performance that is far enough above national norms to be significant and beyond mere chance. Moreover, the fact that those statistical reports have come from a wide distribution of schools and teachers seems to rule out the possibility that the superior performance of the children is due to superior teachers alone.

7. A surprising number of "others" have entered the field of reading from such areas as: business, linguistics, speech, hearing, sociology, technology, languages, homemaking, television, psychology, physical-therapy, audio-visual materials, programming, statistics, medicine, and optometry.

If we assume that few of those people are opportunists, we would have to conclude that it is well to heed what each is trying to tell us about his own approach which he, obviously, believes is superior to the established methods.

8. The proliferation of new approaches to beginning reading necessitates not only a complete knowledge of each, but a restraint from un-

founded criticism and/or from unsupported acceptance. Each new approach deserves a chance to prove itself under reasonable research conditions and in normal classroom environments.

9. The fact that children have "learned to read" by means of all of these many approaches to beginning reading should be a sobering fact, leading to the question of how adequate are our measures of achievement?

10. Lack of even an elementary basic understanding of the various approaches to beginning reading is so widespread that it has severely limited dialog between teachers using different methods.

"Which is the *best* method of teaching beginning reading?" is a question many would like to have answered. To say that there is no one-best method might possibly be true, yet it would be begging the question. The answer lies within neither the materials nor the methods, but in the commitment which a practitioner is willing to make. Some teachers may be willing to "give their all" to the task of extracting the best from several methods and synthesizing those elements into their teaching. Others are satisfied with the "easiest" method. For an administrator or a committee to select one method to the exclusion of the good elements of others would be ignoring the individual differences of the teachers who would use the methods.

Most teachers, of course, are willing to "go along" with the decisions of administrators and/or committees. For them, a philosophy of education and an approach to learning is adjustable to that which seems expedient. Many of the older teachers have lived with change and innovation long enough to take a rather detached view of some of the newer approaches to beginning reading. Many slyly admit that, regardless of the "new" approach that is under experimentation in their school, they still teach the children to read.

Teachers who are willing to make a "total commitment" to beginning reading will find that many of the approaches to beginning reading contain elements which are based upon sound psychological principles of learning.

First, and probably most important, is the inescapable fact that our language is based upon phoneme-grapheme relationships. To attempt to learn to read our language without learning the phonemically-regular relationships is to place an unnecessary burden on the learner. Previous reference has been made to Hanna's monumental study[2] of phoneme-

---

2. Hanna, Paul R., and Project Staff, *Phoneme-Grapheme Correspondences as Cues to Spelling Improvement*, Washington: USOE, Bureau of Research publication 32008, 1966. 120–121.

grapheme relationships in our language. The study seems to suggest that, if the options of pronunciation for the vowels and consonants are learned and adequate rules are provided for a framework of reference, the phonemic regularity of our language is between 80% and 90%. In fact, the study reports that "The eight phonemes which have individual predictability of less than 78 percent are: A_2 (as in *air* or *vary*); E_2(as in *hear* or *weird*); O_6 (as in *lose* or *soup*); O_7 (as in *could*); U_2 (as in *burn* or *urge*); SWA; N_1 (as in *shorten*); and Z".[2] Consequently, the study of phonemics seems to be most important. Although Dr. Jeanne Chall investigated research on only a limited number of approaches to beginning reading, her three-year study financed by the Carnegie Corporation has relevance on this point. One of her conclusions is that better results in beginning reading are achieved through a code-emphasis method.[3]

The fully committed teacher of beginning reading will seek out those elements of approaches to phonemics which she feels most comfortable in using. There are many good materials available: charts, recordings, tapes, workbooks, picturecards, etc.

Second, to expect a child to generalize our rather complicated system of relationships of phonemes and graphemes is asking too much except for the very few at the top of the intelligence scale. Pyschologists have repeatedly indicated that learning proceeds from the concrete to the abstract. The child who is attempting beginning reading needs some concrete rules as his frame of reference. The Hanna study just referred to was possible only because the computer was programmed according to specific rules for pronunciation and spelling. Several of the approaches to beginning reading provide rules which help the child decide on his pronunciation and/or provide the feedback necessary for him to be self-corrective.

Third, the teacher who likes additionally-structured regularity of materials and method in teaching the phoneme-grapheme relationships will find plenty of material in the various linguistics-phonemics approaches. In addition, some of the linguistics-phonemics approaches have story-type reading materials phased into the program for direct application of the phonemic learnings. Immediate practice thus provided utilizes the principles of "use" and "reinforcement", and does not depend upon the questionable "transfer" claimed in some basal reader approaches.

---

3. Chall, Jeanne, *Learning to Read: The Great Debate*, New York: McGraw-Hill Book Co., 1967, 307–310.

Fourth, the approaches categorized as phonemics-reading also provide for immediate transfer of learning to story-type materials.

Fifth, a number of approaches include listening, writing, spelling, and speaking activities as part of a "total" language arts approach to reading. By so doing, they utilize the psychological principle of reinforcement of learning through the several sensory pathways to the brain.

Sixth, inasmuch as the objective of beginning reading is to provide the means by which a child can begin to get meaning from printed pages, any fully-committed teacher will most certainly seek out materials that are meaningful. The language-experience materials claim to be oriented in this direction. Materials that are meaningful are learned easier and retained longer than rote materials. That psychological principle cannot be ignored.

Seventh, in selecting meaningful materials, the fully-committed teacher will be guided by the fundamental principle of individual differences, and will provide a wide variety of stories that are meaningful to children who have a wide variety of abilities, interests and needs.

Eighth, some type of one-to-one sound-symbol scheme will be useful as a frame of reference for dealing with the several options of pronunciation of the vowels and some of the consonants.

Ninth, attention will continue to focus on the probability that much of present-day readiness for reading can effectively be supplanted with more pertinent work at the Kindergarten level. The school that is fully-committed to reading will explore the efficacy of an earlier start in beginning reading, and will find some useful materials in the various "early-reading" approaches.

Finally, the lesson to be learned from this investigation into these approaches to beginning reading is that, together, they incorporate the best that many thinkers from many academic backgrounds have to offer. The contributions of these many people have enriched our store of materials and have provided many elements of method which need to be explored further.

In time, decisions must finally be made; materials and method have to be selected. So that those decisions may be made with some certainty that they will lead to better instruction in beginning reading, we must make every effort to explore the good in each approach and to give each approach a chance to prove itself.

Responsible caution should lead to responsible choice.

> Be not the first
> by whom the new is tried;
> Nor yet the last
> to lay the old aside.

BIBLIOGRAPHY

AUKERMAN, ROBERT C., "Implications for Further Research on Beginning Reading Instruction," *Reading and Realism*. Newark, Delaware: International Reading Association, 1969. Proceedings of the Thirteenth Annual Convention, Part 1, 596–599.

BOND, GUY L., and DYKSTRA, ROBERT, *Coordinating Center for First-Grade Reading Instruction Programs*, Minneapolis, University of Minnesota Press, 1967.

This is the Final Report on the USOE Project No. OE-5-10-263, No. X-001. It is a 227 page summary of the twenty-seven First Grade Reading Studies.

"The Cooperative Research Program in First-Grade Reading Instruction," *Reading Research Quarterly* II, 4: (Summer, 1967) entire issue.

For summaries of the First-Grade Reading Studies, see *The Reading Teacher* 19: (May, 1966) and 20: (October, 1966.

CHALL, JEANNE, *Learning to Read: The Great Debate*, New York: McGraw-Hill Book Co. 1967

ELLER, WILLIAM, "Contributions of the First and Second Grade Studies," *Reading and Realism*. Newark, Delaware: International Reading Association, 1969. Proceedings of the Thirteenth Annual Convention, Part 1, 585–588.

HANNA, PAUL R., and Project Staff, *Phoneme-Grapheme Correspondences as Cues to Spelling Improvement*, Washington: USOE, Bureau of Research publication 32008, 1966.

SIPAY, EDWARD R., "An Evaluative Look at the Cooperative Studies of Reading in First and Second Grade: Limitations," *Reading and Realism*. Newark, Delaware: International Reading Association, 1969. Proceedings of the Thirteenth Annual Convention, Part 1, 588–596.

SPACHE, GEORGE D., "Contributions of Allied Fields to the Teaching of Reading," Chapter VII in *Innovation and Change in Reading Instruction*. The Sixty-seventh Yearbook of the National Society for the Study of Education, Part II, Chicago: University of Chicago Press, 1968: 237–290.

APPENDIX

This is an alphabetical listing of the approaches to beginning reading, giving the publishers and their addresses.

A.B.C. Dictation Skills Program
Educators Publishing Service
301 Vassar Street
Cambridge, Massachusetts, 02139

A V Electronics
240 South Teilman Avenue
Fresno, California, 93706

Alpha One: Breaking the Code
New Dimensions in Education, Inc.
Long Island House
Jericho, New York, 11753

Bank Street Readers
The Macmillan Company
866 Third Avenue
New York, New York, 10022

Bannatyne Color Phonics
See Psycholinguistic Color System.

Barsch Perceptual-Motor Sequences
Special Child Publications
71 Columbia Street
Seattle, Washington, 98104

Basic Reading
J. B. Lippincott Co., Educational Publishing Division
East Washington Square
Philadelphia, Pennsylvania, 19105

Basic Reading Series
    See SRA.
Bateman Materials
    See ITPA.
Bereiter-Engelmann
    See DISTAR.
Bloomfield-Barnhart
    See *Let's Read.*
Bourn Sound Method
    820 Bradley Road
    Joppa, Maryland, 21085
Breaking the Sound Barrier
    The Macmillan Company
    866 Third Avenue
    New York, New York, 10022
Building Reading Skills
    McCormick-Mathers Publishing Co.
    P.O. Box 2212
    Wichita, Kansas, 67201
The Carden Method
    Mae Carden, Inc.
    619 South Maple Avenue
    Glen Rock, New Jersey, 07452
Chandler Language Experience Readers
    See *Chandler Reading Program*
Chandler Reading Program
    Noble and Noble
    750 Third Avenue
    New York, New York, 10017
Christian Child Reading Program
    Reardon, Baer and Co.
    21079 Westwood Drive
    Cleveland, Ohio, 44136
Cove Schools Program
    See Developmental Learning Materials.
Davis "fonetic alfabet" Materials
    Carlton Press
    84 Fifth Avenue
    New York, New York, 10010
Decoding Games
    Multimedia Education, Inc.
    11 West 42nd Street
    New York, New York, 10036

DETECT
> Science Research Associates
> Division of IBM
> 259 East Erie Street
> Chicago, Illinois, 60611

Developmental Learning Materials
> Developmental Learning Materials, Inc.
> 3505 North Ashland Avenue
> Chicago, Illinois, 60657

DISTAR
> Science Research Associates
> Division of IBM
> 259 East Erie Street
> Chicago, Illinois, 60611

Dolch Word Games and Phonic Cards
> Garrard Publishing Company
> 1607 North Market Street
> Champaign, Illinois, 61820

Dubnoff School Program
> Teaching Resources
> Educational Service of the New York Times
> 100 Boylston Street
> Boston, Massachusetts, 02116

Edison Responsive Environments
> See *Responsive Environments.*

efi Patterns in Phonics
> Electronic Futures
> 57 Dodge Avenue
> North Haven, Connecticut, 06473

Erie Program
> Teaching Resources
> Educational Service of the New York Times
> 100 Boylston Street
> Boston, Massachusetts, 02116

Fairbanks-Robinson Program
> Teaching Resources
> Educational Service of the New York Times
> 100 Boylston Street
> Boston, Massachusetts, 02116

Fernald Technique
> found in *Remedial Techniques in Basic School Subjects*
> McGraw-Hill Book Co.
> 330 West 42nd Street
> New York, New York, 10036

Filmstrip House
    432 Park Avenue South
    New York, New York, 10016
First Experiences With Vowels and Consonants
    The Instructo Corporation
    180 Cedar Hollow Road
    Paoli, Pennsylvania, 19301
First Steps in Reading English
    Washington Square Press (Simon & Schuster, Inc.)
    630 Fifth Avenue
    New York, New York, 10020
Fonetic English Spelling
    Fonetic English Spelling Association
    1418 Lake Street
    Evanston, Illinois, 60204
Fries-Wilson
    See *Merrill Linguistic Readers*
The Frostig Program for the Development of Visual Perception
    Follett Publishing Co.
    1010 West Washington Blvd.
    Chicago, Illinois, 60607
Functional Phonetics
    Benefic Press
    10300 Roosevelt Road
    Westchester, Illinois, 60153
Getman Materials
    See *Pathway School Program.*
Getting a Head Start
    Houghton Mifflin Company
    110 Tremont Street
    Boston, Massachusetts, 02107
Gibson-Richards
    See *First Steps in Reading English.*
Hay-Wingo Phonics
    See *Reading With Phonics.*
Illinois Test of Psycholinguistic Abilities (ITPA)
    Institute for Research on Exceptional Children
    University of Illinois
    Champaign, Illinois, 61820
Imperial International Learning
    Box 548
    Kankakee, Illinois, 60901

Individualized Phonics
    Teachers Publishing Corporation
    Collier-Macmillan Services
    866 Third Avenue
    New York, New York, 10022
i/t/a
    Initial Teaching Alphabet Publications
    20 East 46th Street
    New York, New York, 10017
i Med Phonics
    See *Selma Herr Phonics.*
Journal of Learning Disabilities
    5 North Wabash Avenue
    Chicago, Illinois, 60602
KELP Components
    McGraw-Hill Book Company
    330 West 42nd Street
    New York, New York, 10036
The Landon Phonics Program
    Chandler Publishing Company
    124 Spear Street
    San Francisco, California, 94105
Language Experiences in Reading
    Encyclopaedia Britannica Educational Corporation
    425 North Michigan Avenue
    Chicago, Illinois, 60610
Language Master
    Bell and Howell
    7100 McCormick Road
    Chicago, Illinois, 60645
Language Through Pictures Series
    See *First Steps in Reading English.*
The Laubach Method
    New Readers Press
    Box 131
    Syracuse, New York, 13210
Let's Read: A Linguistic Approach
    Clarence L. Barnhart, Inc.
    Box 250
    Bronxville, New York, 10708
Letters in Words
    Curriculum Associates
    572 Washington Street
    Wellesley, Massachusetts, 02181

LIFT-OFF to READING
Science Research Associates
Division of IBM
259 East Erie Street
Chicago, Illinois, 60611

The Linguistic Readers
Benziger, Inc.,
Subsidiary of Crowell, Collier, and Macmillan, Inc.
8701 Wilshire Boulevard
Beverly Hills, California, 90211

Listen   Look   Learn
Educational Developmental Laboratories, Inc.
Division of McGraw-Hill
Huntington, Long Island, New York, 11743

McQueen Integrated Phonics
See *We Can Read.*

Merrill Linguistic Readers
Charles E. Merrill Books, Inc.
a Bell & Howell Company
1300 Alum Creek Drive
Columbus, Ohio, 43216

Miami Linguistic Readers
D.C. Heath and Company, a division of Raytheon Education Company
Lexington, Massachusetts, 02173

Michigan Language Program
L. R. I.
1501 Broadway
New York, New York, 10036

Montessori
American Montessori Society
175 Fifth Avenue
New York, New York, 10010

Montessori Materials
Teaching Aids
Division of A. Daigger and Company
159 West Kinzie Street
Chicago, Illinois, 60610

Mott Basic Language Skills Program
Allied Education, Inc.
Galien, Michigan, 49113

Open Court Basic Readers
Open Court Publishing Company
Box 399
LaSalle, Illinois, 61301

Organic Reading
    Teacher (Sylvia Ashton-Warner)
    Simon and Schuster, Inc.
    Rockefeller Center
    630 Fifth Avenue
    New York, New York, 10020
Orton Phonics Program
    Orton Reading Center
    106 North Hawthorne Road
    Winston-Salem, North Carolina
Overhead Projector Transparency Program
    International Education and Training, Inc.
    1776 New Highway
    Farmingdale, N.Y., 11735
Palo Alto Reading Program
    Harcourt Brace Jovanovich, Inc.
    757 Third Avenue
    New York, New York, 10017
Pathway School Program
    Teaching Resources
    Educational Service of the New York Times
    100 Boylston Street
    Boston, Massachusetts, 02116
Patterns in Phonics
    See *efi Patterns in Phonics.*
Peabody Rebus Reading Program
    American Guidance Service, Inc.
    Circle Pines, Minnesota, 55014
Phonetic Keys To Reading
    The Economy Company Schoolbook Publishers
    P.O. Box 25308
    Oklahoma City, Oklahoma, 73125
Phonics and Word Power
    American Education Publications
    Division of Xerox Corporation
    Education Center
    Columbus, Ohio, 43216
Phonics in Rhyme
    Teaching Technology Corporation
    5520 Cleon Avenue
    North Hollywood, California, 91601
Phonics is Fun
    Modern Curriculum Press
    21079 Westwood Drive
    Cleveland, Ohio, 44136

Phonics We Use
  Lyons & Carnahan
  407 East 25th Street
  Chicago, Illinois, 60616
Phonics Workbook
  Modern Curriculum Press
  21079 Westwood Drive
  Cleveland, Ohio, 44136
The Phonovisual Method
  Phonovisual Products, Inc.
  4708 Wisconsin Avenue, N. W.
  Washington, D. C., 20016
Play 'N Talk Reading Program
  Play 'N Talk—Phonics in Action
  P.O. Box 18804
  Oklahoma City, Oklahoma, 73118
Professor Phonics Gives Sound Advice
  The St. Ursula Academy, Phonics Department
  1339 East McMillan Street
  Cincinnati, Ohio, 45206
Programmed Reading
  McGraw-Hill Book Company
  Manchester Road
  Manchester, Missouri, 63011
Progressive Choice Reading Program
  See *LIFT-OFF to Reading.*
Project Read
  See Sullivan.
Pro-Reading
  Language Arts Publishers
  P.O. Box 14705
  Phoenix, Arizona, 85033
Psycholinguistic Color System
  Learning Systems Press
  P.O. Box 64
  Urbana, Illinois, 61801
Read Along With Me
  Teachers College Press
  Teachers College, Columbia University
  New York, New York
Readiness for Learning
  J. B. Lippincott Co.
  East Washington Square
  Philadelphia, Pennsylvania, 19105

Reading A
  Systems For Education, Inc.
  612 North Michigan Avenue
  Chicago, Illinois, 60611
Reading Reform Foundation
  36 West 44th Street
  New York, New York, 10036
Read to Learn
  Hoffman Information Systems
  5623 Peck Road
  Arcadia, California
Reading With Phonics
  J. B. Lippincott Company
  East Washington Square
  Philadelphia, Pennsylvania, 19105
Rebus
  See Peabody Rebus Reading Program.
Responsive Environments
  Responsive Environments Foundation, Inc.
  20 Augur Street
  Hamden, Connecticut, 06517
Ring 'N Key
  Play 'n Talk
  P.O. Box 18804
  Oklahoma City, Oklahoma, 73118
The Royal Road Readers
  Chatto and Windus
  40162 William IV Street
  London, W.C.1., England
  Available in USA from
  Educators Publishing Service, Inc.
  75 Moulton Street
  Cambridge, Massachusetts, 02138
Ruth Cheves Program
  See *Visual-Motor Perception Teaching Materials.*
Selma Herr Phonics
  Instructional Materials and Equipment Distributors
  1415 Westwood Blvd.
  Los Angeles, California, 90024
Sequential Steps in Reading
  See Palo Alto Reading Program.
Sight and Sound Phonics Program
  Weber, Costello Co.
  1900 North Narragansett Avenue
  Chicago, Illinois, 60639

Slingerland Kit
    Educators Publishing Service
    75 Moulton Street
    Cambridge, Massachusetts, 02138
Sounds and Letters
    Linguistica
    Box 723
    Ithaca, New York, 14850
The Sound Way to Easy Reading
    Bremner-Davis Phonics, Inc.
    161 Green Bay Road
    Wilmette, Illinois, 60091
Spalding Method
    See *Writing Road to Reading.*
Speech-To-Print Phonics
    Harcourt Brace Jovanovich, Inc.
    757 Third Avenue
    New York, New York, 10017
SRA Reading Program—Linguistics
    Science Research Associates
    Division of IBM
    259 East Erie Street
    Chicago, Illinois, 60611
Strauss Perceptual Materials
    See Developmental Learning Materials.
Streamlined English Series
    The Macmillan Company
    866 Third Avenue
    New York, New York, 10022
Structural Reading Series
    L. W. Singer Company, a Division of Random House, Inc.
    501 Madison Avenue
    New York, New York, 10022
Sullivan-Buchanan Materials
    See *Programmed Reading.*
Sullivan Decoding Kit
    Behavioral Research Laboratories
    Ladera Professional Center
    Box 577
    Palo Alto, California, 94302
Sylvia Ashton-Warner
    See *Organic Reading.*

Symbol Accentuation
    International Communication Films
    Division of Doubleday & Company
    1371 Reynolds Avenue
    Santa Ana, California, 92705
Talking Typewriter
    See *Responsive Environments.*
Teacher
    See *Organic Reading.*
Teaching Your Baby to Read
    See *Reading A.*
The Road to Reading
    Spoken Arts, Inc.
    59 Locust Avenue
    New Rochelle, New York, 10801
Time For Phonics
    McGraw-Hill Book Company
    Manchester Road
    Manchester, Missouri, 63011
The READ Series
    American Book Company
    300 Pike Street
    Cincinnati, Ohio, 45202
TRY: Experiences for Young Children
    Noble and Noble
    750 Third Avenue
    New York, New York, 10017
20 Keys to Unlock the Meaning of Words
    R. V. Weatherford Co.
    Glendale, California
UNIFON Reading Program
    Western Publishing Educational Services
    1220 Mound Avenue
    Racine, Wisconsin, 53404
Visual-Motor Perception Teaching Materials
    Teaching Resources
    Educational Service of the New York Times
    100 Boylston Street
    Boston, Massachusetts, 02116
We Can Read
    McQueen Publishing Co.
    Box 198, Rte. 1
    Tiskilwa, Illinois, 61368

Wenkart Phonic Readers
    Wenkart Publishing Company
    4 Shady Hill Square
    Cambridge, Massachusetts, 02138
Winter Haven Perceptual Training Program
    Winter Haven Lions Club
    Winter Haven, Florida, 33880
Woolman Program
    See *LIFT-OFF to Reading.*
Words-in-Color
    Schools for the Future
    P.O. Box 349 Cooper Station
    New York, New York, 10003
Write and See Phonics
    Appleton-Century Crofts
    440 Park Avenue South
    New York, New York, 10010
The Writing Road to Reading
    William Morrow and Company
    105 Madison Avenue
    New York, New York, 10016
Your Child Can Learn to Read
    Kenworthy Educational Services, Inc.
    138 Allen Street (P.O. Box 3031)
    Buffalo, New York, 14205

INDEX